I N T R O D U C T I O N   T O

WORK AND ORGANIZATIONAL PSYCHOLOGY

WITHDRAWN

To Rees Janek Russell Arthur-Chmiel, born during the editing of this book, and my delight.

The Master said, 'Ssu, do you think that I am the kind of man who learns widely and retains what he has learned in his mind?'
'Yes I do. Is it not so?'
'No. I have a single thread binding it all together.'

Confucius, *The Analects*, XV:3

INTRODUCTION TO

WORK AND ORGANIZATIONAL PSYCHOLOGY

A EUROPEAN PERSPECTIVE

EDITED BY NIK CHMIEL

Blackwell
Publishing

© 2000 by Blackwell Publishers Ltd
a Blackwell Publishing company

350 Main Street, Malden, MA 02148-5018, USA
108 Cowley Road, Oxford OX4 1JF, UK
550 Swanston Street, Carlton South, Melbourne, Victoria 3053, Australia
Kurfürstendamm 57, 10707 Berlin, Germany

First published 2000 by Blackwell Publishers Ltd
Reprinted 2001, 2002

Library of Congress Cataloging-in-Publication Data

Introduction to work and organizational psychology : a European perspective / edited by Nik Chmiel.
    p. cm.
Includes bibliographical references and index.
ISBN 0-631-20675-2 (alk. paper). – ISBN 0-631-20676-0 (pbk. : alk. paper)
1. Psychology, Industrial – Europe. 2. Organizational behavior – Europe.
I. Chmiel, Nik.
HF5548.8.1576   1999   99-32109
158'.7 – dc21   CIP

A catalogue record for this title is available from the British Library.

Set in 10.5 on 13 pt Galliard
by Best-set Typesetter Ltd., Hong Kong
Printed and bound in the United Kingdom
by T. J. International Ltd, Padstow, Cornwall

For further information on
Blackwell Publishing, visit our website:
http://www.blackwellpublishing.com

CONTENTS

CONTRIBUTORS

Professor Neil Anderson, Goldsmith's College, University of London, New Cross, London SE14 6NW, UK

Mr Tom Carruthers, 115 Dowanhill Street, Glasgow G12 9EQ, UK

Dr Nik Chmiel, Institute of Work Psychology, University of Sheffield, Sheffield S10 2TN, UK

Professor John Cordery, Department of Organisational and Labour Studies, University of Western Australia, Nedlands, Perth, Western Australia 6907, Australia

Ms Nicole Cunningham-Snell, PSRC, Shared People Services, Shell Services International, London SE1 7NA, UK

Dr Jan de Jonge, University of Nijmegen, Department of Work and Organisational Psychology, PO Box 9104, 6500 HE Nijmegen, The Netherlands

Professor Clive Fletcher, Goldsmith's College, University of London, New Cross, London SE14 6NW, UK

Dr Jeremy Foster, Department of Psychology and Speech Pathology, Manchester Metropolitan University, Elizabeth Gaskell Campus, Hathersage Road, Manchester M13 OJA, UK

Professor Dr Michael Frese, Department of Psychology, University of Giessen, Otto-Behaghel-Str. 10F, D-35394 Giessen, Germany

Professor G. Robert J. Hockey, Department of Psychology, Hull University, Hull HU6 7RX, UK

Ms Rebecca Lawthom, Department of Psychology and Speech Pathology, Manchester Metropolitan University, Elizabeth Gaskell Campus, Hathersage Road, Manchester M13 OJA, UK

Dr Pascale Le Blanc, Department of Social and Organisational Psychology, PO Box 80.140, 3508 TC Utrecht, The Netherlands

Dr Catherine Lees, Department of Organisational and Labour Studies, University of Western Australia, Nedlands, Perth, Western Australia 6907, Australia

Dr John Patrick, Department of Psychology, University of Wales College of Cardiff, PO Box 901, Cardiff CF1 3YG, UK

Prof. Dr Wilmar B Schaufeli, Utrecht University, Department of Social and Organisational Psychology, PO Box 80.140, 3508 TC Utrecht, The Netherlands

Barbara Senior, Faculty of Management and Business, University College Northampton, Park Campus, Northampton NN2 7AL, UK

Dr Vivian Shackleton, Organisation Studies Group, Aston Business School, Aston University, Aston Triangle, Birmingham B4 7ET, UK

Professor Andrew Tattersall, Centre for Applied Psychology, Liverpool John Moores University, 15–21 Webster Street, Liverpool L3 2ET, UK

Ms Kerrie Unsworth, Institute of Work Psychology, University of Sheffield, Mushroom Lane, Sheffield S10 2TN, UK

Dr Peter Wale, Organisation Studies Group, Aston Business School, Aston University, Aston Triangle, Birmingham B4 7ET, UK

Professor Peter Warr, Institute of Work Psychology, University of Sheffield, Sheffield S10 2TN, UK

Dr Patrick Waterson, Institute of Work Psychology, University of Sheffield, Sheffield S10 2TN, UK

Professor Michael West, Organisation Studies Group, Aston Business School, Aston University, Aston Triangle, Birmingham B4 7ET, UK

PART I

INTRODUCTION

Old type of labour. (J. Allan Cash)

CHAPTER ONE

HISTORY AND CONTEXT FOR WORK AND ORGANIZATIONAL PSYCHOLOGY

Nik Chmiel

Contents

This chapter aims to provide a context for reading about the areas of work and organizational psychology which follow. Two questions arise: what purpose does a context serve; and what kind of context should be provided? The book is an introduction; that is, it assumes no previous knowledge in any of the areas discussed. Thus, a possible contextual approach would be to outline simply the current scope of the field of work and organizational psychology, and comment on the methods used to gain knowledge in the field. However, this book has other ambitions, in that it aims not only to introduce the reader to the subject, but also to provide a thorough grounding in the topics discussed, enough to allow the reader to form a critical overview of the field. Thus the background to the field should be more than a simple description.

The purpose of the context here is to provide a richer appreciation of the knowledge and theories in the area. The context may therefore give a sense of why certain perspectives related in the body of the book are held to be important, why there are obvious gaps in knowledge, how the nature of research and knowledge is to be weighed and how the practice of work and organizational psychologists relates to research.

The kind of context provided is: first, to explore historical perspectives to account for why certain concerns lie within the field of work and organizational psychology; second, briefly to detail the ways in which knowledge is gained, and thereby what kind of knowledge is obtained; and, third, to provide an overview of what the field of work and organizational psychology consists of. Finally, a guide to using the book is given, which consists of brief introductions to the sections.

A Historical Perspective

An obvious starting place for anyone new to a field of inquiry is to ask what has already been done, by whom and why. In short, to explore the history of the subject. Of course, each chapter contains historical information, because each chapter draws on work done before, and summarizes current ideas in the light of past studies. Each chapter could therefore be viewed as a history of ideas relating to the particular topic area covered. Thus the historical perspective in this introductory chapter is of a different order. It is concerned more with the broad sweep of events.

A less often asked question is: what is the purpose of investigating history, what does it tell us that is useful? There are at least three possibilities in answer to this question. First, a study of history may point the way forward, to the development of the subject, to the next 'big thing'. Second, history will account for where we have been, and thus may not need to go again. Third, a history can provide a sense of orientation in a subject; that is, allow oneself to locate and position oneself in relation to past events.

The first possibility, that of pointing the way forward, seems the most exciting, from both a research and a practical point of view. If, by an investigation of past events, the future of the discipline can be discerned, then funding for research can be spent wisely by targeting appropriately to maximum effect. Astute practitioners can gain a competitive edge by moving into what will become most important. Attractive as this possibility is, however, there are severe limits to what can be predicted in the future by the study of history.

The philosopher Karl Popper has detailed an argument which proposes that, in principle, it is not possible to know the future through a study of the past. His argument is that 'the course of human history is strongly influenced by the growth of human knowledge. . . . We cannot predict rationally or scientifically, the future growth of our scientific knowledge. We cannot, therefore, predict the future course of human history. This means that we must reject the possibility of a theoretical history. . . . There can be no scientific theory of historical development serving as a basis for historical prediction' (Popper, 1991, pp. vi–vii).

Of course, future developments are not totally unconstrained. What happens in the future is a function of the present, and in turn the present is a function of the past. In most cases there is a statistical connection between the present and the future; that is, certain developments are more likely than others. This is particularly true over short timescales. However, what Popper was implying is that the precise direction of future events is uncertain, and that discoveries themselves have an impact on the political and social context within which research and hence a discipline proceeds, influencing its development. This is nowhere more evident than in those periods in a discipline marked by changes in the mindset or 'world view' surrounding knowledge, discussed by Kuhn (1962). Kuhn argued that science proceeds through periodic paradigm shifts, which have the effect of changing the way we think about events, and what we consider important to observe and theorize about. The change, which took place in the 1950s, in the dominant paradigm from behaviourism to information processing in psychology is an example. A shift to new ways of working could bring about a similar paradigmatic reorientation in work and organizational psychology.

In these circumstances, it seems to me, the most important contribution an introductory chapter can make is to provide a sense of orientation with respect to past events, an opportunity to locate and position oneself to some degree, rather than a historical critique or evaluation of past ideas, or a detailed reconstruction of the political, social and economic conditions leading to particular pieces of research. The latter two approaches would consume a book in themselves, and as matter of course some of the history behind currently held ideas is discussed in the chapters in this book. The question then is what should be discussed in a general historical overview, and why.

Several ways of organizing past ideas and studies present themselves, and one general approach is to list the ways, and provide an account from different perspectives. Furnham (1998) has done just this, and his classes include the 'models of man' perspective, the 'great thinker' perspective, the 'time-based' perspective, the 'school of thought' perspective, the 'seminal study' approach, the 'textbook content-analysis' approach and a topic-based historical approach. Each perspective is, of course, problematic in terms of what to include, how the material is to be organized and why. Brock (1998) laments the lack of proper historical research into psychology. One telling point he makes is that there is little reflection on the subjective nature of historical accounts, which frequently simply pass on received wisdom. Taking an 'inclusive list' stance does have its uses, however. At a minimum it gives a sense of what can be done with historical observations. Set against the benefits is the possibility that being inclusive may delude readers into thinking that they have a complete overview of the historical background. In terms of the old Hindu proverb about the blind men and the elephant, the reader could end up with a nose, a leg, a tail and a skin, but no animal. An inclusive account may be so all-encompassing that it does not give a strong sense of place and orientation.

Popper (1991, p. 150) argues there can be no history without a selective point of view, unless 'it is to be choked by a flood of poor and unrelated material'. Furthermore, he proposes that the selective point of view be preconceived; 'that is to write that history which interests us'.

Hollway (1991), for example, provides a historical and thought provoking critique of dominant ways of viewing the person at work. Her historical perspective is motivated by considering how work and organizational psychologists intervene in the workplace. Broadly, interventions focused on the individual level at the beginning of the twentieth century, the social level around the middle of the century and now the organizational level. Hollway characterizes the first two phases by titling the parts of her book that refer to them as 'Factory hands' and 'The sentimental worker' respectively. The essence behind this structure is to emphasize the critical touchstone she uses throughout her book, that knowledge is not produced in a vacuum, but is a product of power and practice, and that much of work and organizational psychology has been developed from the perspective of managers. She bases her analysis on the understanding of the relationship between power, knowledge and practice developed by Michel Foucault.

It is, none the less, a matter of empirical observation that interventions at all levels take place today, but the way of thinking about the person at work has been marked by a progressive acceptance that psychology and behaviour at work cannot be understood only in terms of the individual, but must refer to the work and organizational context. The present book is produced with this in mind, and case studies are used to provide contextual richness.

Another way of providing a historical account is to refer to documents and personal recollections, filtered through the experience of the author or authors. Shimmin and Wallis (1994) have produced an account of work and organizational psychology from their own involvement in post-war British practice, relying on their own experiences, documentary research and personal knowledge of many of the figures involved. The book provides a rich source of information for the reader, as well as an engaging account of the times.

My point of view, for the purposes of this introduction, is to outline briefly the effects of the industrial revolution as they impacted on work, to give a sense of location by placing in time some events at the start of work and organizational psychology, and then to discuss those historical *zeitgeists* which continue to be referred to today.

The industrial revolution

The industrial revolution started in Great Britain in the eighteenth century. Its effects can be summed up under two headings: the social and economic reordering of society; and technological invention using harnessed power. Before the industrial revolution there were no big manufacturing towns, the social unit was still the village and most families owned some means to make a living: land, or the right of common pasture, or simple wooden machines. Coal, where available, was for domestic use, and aside from a primitive steam pump, the only sources of power were wind and water (Halliday, 1995).

The late eighteenth century saw huge improvements in agriculture through the application of scientific farming, producing vast increases in food production. The improvements were a result of land enclosures for arable farming, with the effect of wealthy landowners buying out small holdings, and depriving cottagers of their rights to common pasture. A landless labourer class was created. Cotton and wool production was transformed. In 1769, Arkwright patented the spinning machine, which could do the work of 12 women, and was driven by water power. The power loom was invented by Cartwright in 1785, and perfected some 30 years later. Weavers became factory employees (Halliday, 1995).

The industrial revolution brought about dramatic changes in the way society and work were organized in the UK. Halliday (1995, p. 158) reports that after 1780 large-scale production of food and manufactured goods 'began rapidly to supersede inefficient small-scale farming and the domestic system, dislocating the old way of life'. At a global, and necessarily simplified, level, the industrial revolution brought about a society ordered by work imperatives. The change to an economy dominated by factory production and urbanization neccesitated constant effort in pursuit of production, and the development of large manufacturing towns such as Manchester (Messinger, 1985).

The history of technology at work since the industrial revolution can be divided into three phases: power provision; automation of function; and information and control of process.

Traditional manufacturing technology most often was an aid to work, especially physical work. Thus steam was harnessed for power and used to drive weaving machinery for example. The machines were still controlled by people. Second, machinery became sufficiently sophisticated to automate some functions performed previously by people. Third, the change from traditional to computerized technologies in the recent past has involved the extensive use of computers to control technology.

McLoughlin and Clark (1994) outline a slightly different set of three phases in manufacturing automation: primary mechanization, which was the use of water or steam power to replace human physical and manual labour in the transformation of raw materials into products; secondary mechanization, which used electricity, and facilitated continuous flow assembly lines and processes; and tertiary mechanisation, which used electronics-based computing and information technologies to coordinate and control production tasks. McLoughlin and Clark report that primary mechanisation was predominant up to the end of the nineteenth century, and that since 1945 tertiary mechanization has assumed increasing importance.

Britain led the way to industrialisation, and for most of the nineteenth century reaped the economic benefits of being first. By the turn of the century, however, both the USA and Germany began to overhaul the UK.

Dates, topics and institutions

Landy (1997, p. 467) suggests that 'Industrial and Organizational Psychology was peculiarly American in its inception', and its early history concentrated on individual differences. A key book, *Psychology and Industrial Efficiency*, was published in an English edition in 1913 by Munsterberg, one of the pioneers in American industrial and organizational psychology. The American Psychological Association (APA) was formed in 1892, but it was not until 1945 that it created a division for industrial and business psychology.

Katzell and Austin (1992) detail the development and use of psychological testing by the US Army. In 1919 one of those involved in the army work, Walter Dill Scott, formed an consultancy called The Scott Company, whose psychological techniques included a group test of mental ability, job standards for career progression and personnel planning, a performance rating system, oral trade tests and apprentice training materials, and a programme of personnel administration. Another US consulting organization founded after the First World War was The Psychological Corporation, organized in 1921.

By the 1930s in the USA there were several universities and colleges offering training in industrial and organizational psychology, and during 1937–8 the American Association for Applied Psychology (AAAP) came into being, and included an industrial and business psychology section. By 1943, 79 people had joined the section. The APA merged with the AAAP after the Second World War, creating a division of business and industrial psychology (division 14). In 1960, it was estimated that 756 psychologists were members of division 14, approximately 25 per cent of whom were academics. In 1970, division 14 was renamed the Division of Industrial and Organizational Psychology, and by 1980 had 2005 members. Divison 14 was incorporated as the Society for Industrial and Organizational Psychology (SIOP) in 1983, and boasted approximately 2500 members in the early 1990s.

In terms of the topics studied, Katzell and Austin (1992) organize their review in time periods. The First World War and the 1920s saw army selection techniques develop, a unit charged with facilitating the adjustment of soldiers to army life, work sample tests, person and job analysis concepts emerge, the measurement of vocational interests and the measurement of work performance. In the 1930s to the Second Word War the study of employee attitudes and morale developed, and leadership and group dynamics was investigated. During and after the Second World War to the 1960s, selection, assessment, performance appraisal and training were major areas, and organizational factors began to be investigated with increasing vigour, notably in relation to the satisfaction and well-being of workers. Some investigation of labour relations was carried out in this period, including conditions associated with cooperation and conflict between unions and management. Katzell and Austin (1992) note the emergence of a separate discipline of applied experimental and engineering psychology (division 21 of the APA), embracing biology, engineering, systems analysis and computer science, as well as psychology. From the mid-1960s to the mid-1980s job analysis and selection tests received considerable attention in terms of validity and fairness. Work motivation and job attitudes also attracted interest, as did the scope or challenge of the job. Behaviourist and cognitive approaches were also seen to gain ground in this period. The shift to organizational issues continued, with communication, conflict management and organizational socialization forming some of the topics investigated. Katzell and Austin (1992) summarize the period from the mid-1980s to the early 1990s as characterized by the methodological and conceptual refinement of previous work, while noting the developing interest in mood and affective states on work attitudes, the interest in organizational culture and the burgeoning of the cognitive movement in industrial and organizational psychology, mentioning, for example, the merging of psychometric and cognitive conceptions of ability.

In Britain the First World War had produced studies, begun in 1915 under the auspices of the Health of Munitions Workers Committee, investigating industrial fatigue and factors affecting the personal health and efficiency of workers in munitions factories. The Industrial Fatigue Research Board, later renamed the Industrial Health Research Board (IHRB), was set up in 1918 to continue the work. Subsequently, responsibility for the IHRB was assumed by the Medical Research Council. In 1921 the National Institute of Industrial Psychology (NIIP) was established to 'promote and encourage the practical application of the sciences of psychology and physiology to commerce and industry by any means that may be found practicable' (Shimmin and Wallis, 1994). Shimmin and Wallis report that by 1922, when Morris Viteles, and American industrial and organizational psychologist, visited Europe he noted that industrial psychology in both England and Germany was expanding at a rapid rate and was more extensive in its scope than in the USA.

In the 1930s the Industrial Health Research Board reports included topics under headings such as hours of work, rest pauses, dexterity, industrial accidents, atmospheric conditions, vision and lighting, vocational guidance and selection, time and movement study, methods of work and posture and physique, plus miscellaneous topics such as the psychological effects of noise and toxicity of organic solvents. The National Institute of Industrial Psychology had become the focus for work on job analysis, psychological testing, interviewing, vocational guidance and personnel selection.

During the war years, 1939 to 1945, military selection procedures were considerably revamped, and War Office Selection Boards set up. These boards were considered a great success, and became the basis for subsequent Civil Service Selection Boards. The Cambridge Psychological Laboratory, with backing from the Medical Research Council (MRC), began investigating aspects of human performance related to 'gun-laying, radar surveillance and piloting aircraft' (Shimmin and Wallis, 1994). Key concerns included the effects of fatigue on pilot skill, and the effects on vigilance of a number of factors including 'time on watch'. The MRC Applied Psychology Unit was set up in Cambridge in 1944, under the directorship of Kenneth Craik.

After the war a Committee on Industrial Productivity was set up by the UK government. There were four panels; the Human Factors panel was most important for occupational psychology, and acted as a facilitator of research. The panel noted the lack of good scientific knowledge and trained researchers (Shimmin and Wallis, 1994). Topics the panel had an interest in included: the human side of technological change, and communications in industry, examined by the Tavistock Institute, itself established in 1946; the effects of age on human skill; company morale; and employee–management relations.

In 1950 a new 'Psychologist Class' was established in the Civil Service, attracting about 40 graduates. Topics investigated included assessment methods for selection, training and human factors generally. During the 1960s and 1970s occupational guidance was developed for school-leavers and adults. A postgraduate diploma in occupational psychology was begun in 1951, and the first department of occupational psychology in Britain was set up in 1961. In 1968 the MRC established the Social and Applied Psychology Unit in Sheffield, with work motivation and job satisfaction as early investigations. Shimmin and Wallis (1994) summarize the 1960s as containing work in the areas of personnel selection, vocational guidance, ergonomics, vocational training and, importantly, the newly emerging organizational psychology.

Shimmin and Wallis (1994) pick out several areas for comment as indicative of dominant activity between the 1970s and the 1990s: personnel selection; job satisfaction; design of work; the quality of working life; occupational stress; stress management; unemployment; absence and accidents; unfair discrimination; training; and occupational guidance and counselling. They note that the British Psychological Society formed a Division of Occupational Psychology in 1971 (of which more below) with 131 members. The membership was 241 in 1980, and 661 in 1993.

Zeitgeist studies

One of the most dominant approaches to the way jobs should be viewed was the philosophy of 'scientific management' espoused by Frederick W. Taylor around the beginning of the twentieth century (1911). Taylor was first a labourer, working up to become maintenance chief engineer at the Midvale Steel Company, USA (van de Water, 1997). He was not a psychologist by training (not many people were then), having gained a mechanical engineering degree. His first published paper was on a piece-rate system, and appeared in 1895. His views were founded on the premise that people are motivated primarily by economic factors, and hence hard work should be linked to pay. He argued that work should be standardized on the most efficient way of doing it, and 'time and motion' studies of metal cutting were carried out to establish this. Thereafter workers were paid on a piecework basis. In other words, so much pay for so much work. The approach of scientific management demanded that the knowledge and skills needed to carry out production processes became vested in management. Shopfloor workers were then told how, when and in how much time they should carry out tasks assigned to them. Supervisors became very important in the system.

A second major influence on how work should be seen came from studies done at the Hawthorne plant of the Western Electrical Company in the USA, from about 1924 to 1932. The researchers demonstrated that social relations at work, and not just economic self-interest, were important for productivity. In one set of observations a small number of women workers were transferred from their usual work area to a separate test area. There the workers experienced a series of controlled changes to their conditions of work, such as hours of work, rest pauses and provision of refreshments. During the changes the observer maintained a friendly manner, consulting with the workers, listening to their complaints and keeping them informed of the experiment. Following all but one of the changes there was a continuous increase in production. The researchers formed the conclusion that the interest shown in the workers, and the additional attention given to them, was the principal reason for the higher productivity. Another set of observations involved a group of men. It was noted that the men developed their own informal pattern of social relations and 'norms' for working behaviour. Despite a financial incentive scheme which offered more money for more productivity, the group chose a level of output well below what they were capable of producing.

Despite the dominance of the two approaches above, Taylorism and human relations, there are those who feel that the British contribution to the early development of work and organizational psychology, what could be called 'human factors', is considerable, and potentially more valuable than either (Rose, 1975).

Research in Occupational Psychology

Although much of the work of work and organizational psychologists is practical in nature, the strength of their advice is based on knowledge acquired systematically, through scientific means where possible. Thus research into behaviour at work plays an extremely important part in informing professional practice, as well as in developing more fundamental theories of the psychology of people at work, and how this is influenced by the context of work organizations.

There are two traditional types of ways to gather knowledge about work: the experiment and the correlational study, explained below. Recently, other ways, such as case studies, have also become more accepted (see Robson, 1993, for a detailed discussion). Within these three main approaches a variety of information gathering techniques and analyses can be deployed, ranging from interviews and questionnaires on the one hand, to behavioural observation on the other. Some techniques fit better within some approaches than others, though. Thus, the case study approach often goes with interviews, whereas there are difficulties in using interview data in an experimental analysis.

Experiments, whether in the laboratory or the field, allow inferences to be made about causality between the variables studied, whereas correlational studies only observe whether factors change alongside others, but causality cannot be inferred. Case studies provide a very rich picture of a particular work setting, but the picture may not generalize to other settings. Occupational psychologists are often limited to observing natural variation and change within organizations and work settings, and hence experimentation is difficult. Many studies tend to be correlational in nature. However, despite the constraints of the work environment, some field experimentation is possible and fruitful.

Field experimentation has the same procedures as laboratory-based methods, and tries to follow them as closely as possible. Thus, the experiment involves forming a hypothesis, selecting experimental and control groups, introducing an experimental manipulation, measuring the change and making inferences as to causality. However, it may not always be possible to achieve the ideal experimental constraints in the field. Thus control and experimental groups may not be randomly determined, and other factors may alter along with the experimental manipulation.

   The advantage of the field experiment over a laboratory-based one is that the real-life conditions of the work setting can be preserved, in contrast to the artificial environment of the laboratory. For some investigations this is crucial, for others it is not, and the laboratory is the best place to produce the knowledge required. In addition to deliberately changing workplace factors to investigate their effect, experimenters can take advantage of naturally occurring change, especially when there is no control over the workplace, or it is undesirable. Here quasi-experimental methods are used to set up comparison groups, measure them before any change, measure them after the natural change and analyse the results and draw causal inferences as appropriate. Often other factors also change in addition to the factor(s) of interest, and the effects of these need to be taken into account.

   The experimental approach has the advantage of allowing causal inferences between variables to be drawn. However, it is often the case that such experimentation is difficult to achieve in the field, and the artificial environment of the laboratory is an impediment to finding satisfactory connections between work-related variables. Under these circumstances the correlational study comes into its own.

   Correlational studies concentrate on examining what factors change together, without making any inferences as to the causal nature of the relationships. Thus manipulation and control of variables are not as important, and natural variation in the workplace is central. What matters is the degree of relationship (the correlation) between factors, and its direction; that is, whether both factors increase together (a positive correlation) or whether one factor decreases as the other increases (a negative correlation). A fictitious example would be whether people who work longer hours feel less alert, but more satisfied with their work. In this case the length of the working day would correlate negatively with alertness (as the length increases, alertness decreases) but positively with satisfaction (as length increases satisfaction also increases).

   Finally, case studies look at individuals or small groups of people at work. Focusing on a small number of people, or a small company, provides an opportunity to look at the group in depth, and over a period of time. Case studies are most useful in an exploratory context. The case study provides for studying a situation in depth, and from a variety of angles, through interviews, observations and the analysis of documentation. However, a case study does not allow statistical generalisation.

   The usefulness of any of these approaches to understanding psychology at work can be greatly enhanced if the results from one work situation can be generalized to others. In order to generalize successfully certain conditions need to be met. The key factor is representativeness. First, if a particular finding is to generalize beyond the people involved in a study, the people studied must be representative of the larger population to which generalizations are to be made. Second, the context of a study should not constrain generalizability by findings being specific to it, or to the people studied. A fictitious example of a non-generalizable context might be workgroups studied on the shopfloor. A study of such groups could suggest that certain personality aspects are important to successful team-working. However, a group of office managers might work well together, but exhibit completely different personality profiles. Successful team-working attributes do not generalize across workgroups in this hypothetical example.

Contexts for research knowledge

Work and organizational psychology is an applied discipline. Thus the issues which commonly arise are connected with how and why workers behave as they do. Companies, on the whole, want to know the answers to these questions in order to improve productivity, although they may have an interest in how satisfied their employees are. Academics, while possibly being concerned with productivity, are concerned to understand the fundamental aspects of human nature at work. Consultants are asked to give advice to companies and industry, usually on a case by case basis.

The relationship between academics, consultants and work organizations influences the type of questions, and thus the type of research that is done. Psychologists with an interest in work-related issues can adopt different roles in relation to the organizations and work culture they study. A broad division is whether the psychologist works within, and is employed by, the organization, or whether he or she is an outsider. The psychologist could be motivated by an academic concern with theory, or by a desire to give consultancy on best practice. In most situations, though, the ability to do research or provide consultancy is heavily dependent on the cooperation of work organizations.

Some critiques of the development of knowledge in work and organizational psychology therefore argue that the relationship between power, knowledge and practice should be made explicit. Hollway (1991, p. 7) laments: 'There is virtually no debate about the status of the knowledge which makes up work psychology and this state of affairs is the result of the uncritical identification of work psychology with behavioural science, which in turn identifies with natural science.' Her view is that science 'prescibes that the knowledge gained through scientific methods is unproblematically true and that scientists are potentially neutral agents in the process', and further that science assumes 'such knowledge would necessarily be progressive'.

She argues that knowledge in work and organizational psychology cannot be separated from its effects, and should be understood, in contrast to a 'scientific' view, from the perspective of the social and political conditions producing that knowledge. She gives the example of the concept of job satisfaction, arguing that '[it] would have been an unthinkable concept in a feudal regime, where tied workers had few means of opposing the power of landowners and monarch. Neither was it produced in the context of pre-industrial, self-employed craft workers whose control over work was a condition of their existence' (p. 8). Hollway uses ideas on the production of knowledge advanced by Michel Foucault to give a historical reading of the development of work and organizational psychology.

However, the position Hollway advances concerning science, while providing a starting point for a thought-provoking analysis, is something of a straw man. It is doubtful that many scientists would hold that scientific knowledge is anything more than provisional since the work of the highly regarded and influential philospher of science, Karl Popper (for example, *Conjectures and Refutations*, published in 1963). Popper presented compelling logical arguments that theories should be testable in principle to be counted as scientific. This implies that all scientific theories could be found to be false at some point, if not now.

None the less Kuhn (1962, p. 4) recognized that:

> Observation and experience can and must drastically restrict the range of admissable scientific belief, else there would be no science. But they cannot alone determine a particular body of such belief. An apparently arbitary element, compounded of personal and historical accident, is always a formative ingredient of the beliefs espoused by a given scientific community at a given time.

Further in relation to the 'neutrality' of scientific knowledge, Popper also published a critique of science, and in particular the social sciences, arguing that science itself was a social institution, and therefore knowledge produced by its practice was necessarily influenced by politics, social considerations, economics and the particular interests and experiences of the scientists involved (Popper, 1991).

However, the points made by Kuhn and Popper do not imply that science is simply another way of 'reading' or interpreting a set of observations, in the way 'historicism' is. The touchstone for scientific theories is testability, not fecundity. Medawar (1969, p. 59) summed it up eloquently:

> The purpose of scientific enquiry is not to compile an inventory of factual information, nor to build a totalitarian world picture of natural Laws in which every event that is not compulsory is forbidden. We should think of it rather as a logically articulated structure of justifiable beliefs about nature. It begins as a story about a Possible World – a story which we invent and criticize and modify as we go along, so that it ends by being, as nearly as we can make it, a story about real life.

Psychological research in the workplace

The kinds of psychological topics researched in the workplace are influenced to some degree by at least two large concerns: the needs of the workplace; and the person(s) giving permission for research access to the workplace.

Work organizations have purposes different from those of psychologists, although their interests may overlap. Work organizations exist to fulfil their aims and objectives. In the manufacturing industry sector these objectives could include the production of a quality product at minimum cost. In the public sector the aim could be the provision of a diversity of services within existing resources. Organizations are usually under pressure, commercial and/or political, to achieve their aims. Psychologists, on the other hand, are trying to understand people at work, and base advice on this understanding. However, psychologists research, and advise, dynamic, changing organizations subject to the pressures just outlined. It is, therefore, difficult for psychologists not to be influenced by the pressures organizations are under. Such influence can, and often does, determine the kinds of research psychologists do, and the sort of advice it is possible to give.

The persons giving permission to do research in the workplace are often at managerial level within the work organization. Indeed, Hollway (1991) asserts that managers are the largest group who use work and organizational psychology, a conclusion supported by an assessment of the impact of industrial-organizational psychology in the USA (Katzell and Austin, 1992).

The issues management may be concerned about could differ markedly from the concerns on the 'shopfloor' or lower down the organizational hierarchy. An example of the foregoing is that often it is the managers who want to know the best way to select a person for a particular job, or who want to know the best way of organizing work teams in order to get maximum work efficiency. Stress at work, or job dissatisfaction, may only be important in so far as it stops workers carrying out their jobs efficiently, rather than as an end in itself. Performance at work is a very prominent theme in work psychology.

An Overview of Work and Organizational Psychology

A European perspective

The European Network of Organizational and Work Psychologists (ENOP) has produced a reference model for a European curriculum in work and organizational psychology, designed to serve as a common frame of reference for the training of work and organizational psychologists. The curriculum was produced through discussion with interested parties, including the European Association of Work and Organizational Psychology (EAWOP). Its starting point incorporated the view that work and organizational psychology was both a discipline and a professional speciality.

ENOP itself was founded in 1980, and comprises a network of university professors in work and organizational psychology from around 20 European countries. Their expectation is that the reference model will be used for evaluating existing educational curricula and modifying them to include a common core of work and organizational topics, and thereafter experience gained by ENOP will be important in a number of related developments, including the accreditation of European work and organizational psychologists.

In terms of content, the ENOP reference model includes three areas: personnel psychology, work psychology and organizational psychology. Personnel psychology concerns the relationship between persons and the organization, in particular the establishment, development and termination of the relationship. Important topics include recruitment, training and performance appraisal. Work psychology concerns the work processes and tasks people have to perform at work. Important topics include workload, the work environment, error and equipment design. Finally, organizational psychology concerns how people behave collectively. Important topics include leadership, working in groups and organizational structure.

Occupational psychology in Britain

Since 1971, the British Psychological Society has had a division of occupational psychology which has three main aims. These are: to develop the practice of occupational psychology; to promote high standards of professional competence and behaviour among occupational psychologists; to increase public awareness of occupational psychology for the advantage of individuals and organizations. The division oversees professional development and sets the standards for becoming a Chartered Occupational Psychologist. Chartered Occupational Psychologists are concerned with the performance of people at work and in training, with developing an understanding of how organizations function and how individuals and groups behave at work. Their aim is to increase effectiveness, efficiency and satisfaction at work.

The main areas in which occupational psychologists have skills are: personnel selection and assessment; identification of training needs; organizational change and development; interviewing techniques; performance appraisal systems; vocational guidance and counselling; job and task design; group and inter-group process and skills; design of and adaptation to new technology; career and management development; industrial relations; ergonomics and equipment design; attitude and opinion surveys; occupational safety; design and evaluation training; equal employment opportunity; and stress management.

The Division of Occupational Psychology delineates eight main knowledge areas for occupational psychology which members of the division should demonstrate knowledge in. These are:

- human–machine interaction;
- design of environments and work, health and safety;
- personnel selection and assessment, including test and exercise design;
- performance appraisal and career development;

- counselling and personal development;
- training (identification of needs, training design and evaluation);
- employee relations and motivation;
- organizational development.

Applicants for membership of the division will generally have in-depth experience of at least one of the four main practice areas of occupational psychology, which are: work and the work environment (including health and safety); the individual (including assessment, selection, guidance and counselling); organizational development and change; and training.

Using This Book

Each author or authors was/were asked to write 8000 words approximately, and to address final-year undegraduate and MSc level students. They were to assume a knowledge of basic psychology, start with work-based issues and analyse them using basic and applied empirical research where possible. Each chapter was to use a mini case study or practical example as a theme or work-related reference point, offer solutions to issues and evaluate them, include all main approaches to the topic and provide an integrated, comprehensive and evaluative account. Authors were asked to emphasize a European perspective where possible. The chapters differ in the way they fulfil the brief just outlined, partly because different authors have different views about how to realize the objectives set for each chapter, and partly because different areas of work and organizational psychology shape what can be said about them. The strength of the text is in the freshness and vigour with which the authors have approached their task, and the fact that they are actively engaged with the topics they discuss. I hope this has led to an invigorating introduction to a diverse and complex field.

An Introduction to Work and Organizational Psychology can be read in many different ways. If you have turned to this section first you will have missed the broad introduction to the history and context surrounding the field. This introductory chapter has been written to put the reader in a critical, but interested, frame of mind. Chapter 2 is aimed at giving the interested reader a flavour of the practice of occupational psychology. Thereafter, parts II, III and IV provide the building blocks for an appreciation of the field, and closely parallel the content of European Network of Organizational and Work Psychologists reference model for knowledge in work and organizational psychology.

Part II concerns the person at work. The area comes first because it is how most people think about work when first confronted with a job: what job do I have to do, how will I be selected for it, what will be the nature of the training I receive in order to do it, how will I be appraised in doing it and what consequences will the job have for me in terms of the pressures I feel in it?

This part is concerned largely with the differences between people and jobs, and much of the research relies on a social/psychometric approach.

Part III considers the detail of the workplace. The area follows the job level because it is about aspects of jobs and the work environment, probably the next set of concerns to be noticed at work: what is the workload involved in what I do, what is the impact of my working environment on my performance, how and why have the technologies I work with paid heed to my capabilities and what are the consequences of my capabilities and attitudes to working safely? This part covers a considerable part of what has been called 'human factors', and the approach has been largely to consider people from a cognitive point of view.

Part IV discusses working with other people, and general organizational effects at work: what effect does leadership have, how does the design of the job and organization influence motivation, and hence my satisfaction and performance, what are the factors involved in my working in a team and what does it mean to consider organizational development and change? This part covers what is often termed organizational psychology, and is frequently concerned with analyses at the group or organisational level of behaviour.

Clearly there is a progression evident in parts II, III and IV. However, in terms of a particular area of inquiry the reader could cherry pick any chapter in order to find out more, and read an up-to-date critique of where we are in that part of work and organizational psychology. Reading a whole part will provide a comprehensive introduction to a major aspect of the discipline. The parts need not be read in the order they are presented to make sense. Each of the chapters in these three parts includes discussion points and key studies to help the student to explore the subject matter.

Part V is concerned with issues which transcend the previous parts. Whatever your job, work environment, group membership or organization, it is clearly important to consider issues of diversity in gender, race and age. The last chapter in the book discusses the very nature of work itself, and how this might change in the future. The chapter presents possible scenarios for all of us at work, and implies new and exciting challenges for understanding behaviour related to working.

CHAPTER TWO

ROLES AND METHODS

T. E. Carruthers

Contents

This chapter is concerned with the ideas which underlie the work of psychologists who are concerned with people and work – whether we call ourselves 'work and organizational' or 'occupational' psychologists.

The chapter is composed of three parts. We will look at the activities involved in the consultancy process, at the processes of assessing individuals and environments, then at forms of intervention, and we will touch on evaluation of outcomes – the last an essential activity if professional standards are to be maintained and improved. Next, we will distinguish the roles of expert and of enabler/facilitator (if this is a new one to you, see the end-of-chapter glossary), and the need for their integration in practice. Finally, we will look at methods of gathering data for assessment, and methods of intervention.

I hope that this will give you an outline frame within which to nest the material of the other chapters. Later, you may find it helpful, once you have extended your knowledge and understanding with more detailed material on specific topics, to cast your eye over this chapter once again, as a way of working on your own overview of our integrated but diverse field.

I will, throughout, follow a naming convention: where 'psychologist' is used in this chapter, the word refers to 'occupational' or 'work and organizational' psychologists. If we need to refer to the work of clinical, counselling or educational psychologists, they will be so specified.

This chapter starts with some detailed accounts of work done by psychologists, of various specialisms within our field. The first account starts with what may be, for some, a glossary word, 'ergonomics'. As a topic, it appears here; then like other topics, it is dealt with in greater detail in subsequent chapters.

Psychologists at Work

Ergonomics

The psychologists A group of engineers and ergonomists, some them psychologists (usually calling themselves 'work' or 'engineering' psychologists), worked in a national road research laboratory to design a nation's motorway system.

The problem The particular problem facing the psychologists' group was how to design direction signs to be easily read by drivers approaching them at around 70 m.p.h. – and in time to make well paced decisions. The specific question to which they sought an answer was: what, on a motorway sign, will be the most easily read symbols, shape and size of letters, and against what contrasting background?

The investigation   Using a laboratory setting to allow tight control of variables, the psychologists presented subjects with displays (suitably to scale) of town names and other messages, varying the type of letters, their size, their colour and their background colour; and with combinations of words and symbols. Their outcome measure was a complex one of speed of response with accuracy of perception. Existing road signs in use on ordinary roads were of upper case (capital) black letters on a white ground.

The outcome   On the basis of their findings the psychologists recommended the use of white symbols and lower case white letters, with initial capitals, on a mid-blue ground. The finding was used, and a design of signs, of appropriate size, using these colours and typeface, was adopted for use throughout the system. This, for most drivers in the UK, is what they have grown up with. Such signs are a regular part of the motorway environment.

Underpinning psychological knowledge/concepts   That research was done some forty years ago in the UK's Road Research Laboratory; and we, today, live with its findings as we drive on a motorway. Human perceptual and cognitive processes will not have changed substantially in that time span; nor, in consequence, need a built environment be changed for users' benefit, if its design is based on sound research findings about the characteristics of these prospective users. An existing skill – the competence to read normal printed text – was capitalized on. Motorway users were not required to develop a new skill for occasional use. The environment was shaped to suit the users' capabilities: a basic aim in ergonomics.

Career guidance

The psychologist   A psychologist offers career guidance services to the general public. He is a Chartered Psychologist, is listed in the directory published by the British Psychological Society (BPS) as offering such a service and advertises in the phone company's Yellow Pages, in a panel organized through the Society.

The problem (facing the client, not the psychologist)   Today he receives a client who has phoned to arrange to consult him, having seen both entries. She is aged 24, is a graduate in biological science, has wearied of 'looking down a microscope' and wonders if she should change direction – and if so, to what.

The investigation (and aspects of work with individual clients)   He meets the client in a consulting room, welcomes her and, when she indicates interest, describes how he works:

- By acting as her counsellor throughout – listening, questioning, summariz-ing and reflecting back what seem to be her thoughts, offering interpre-tations and suggestions when appropriate. He will extend her assessment and understanding of herself and help her to explore possibilities for change.
- By drawing on his understanding of how people relate psychologically to work situations, before they take them up and when they are doing the actual job.
- By offering the use of a computer-based process which relates a person to possible jobs by a matching process. This gives a systematic, well informed review of the likely world of work for the client, and will be a base from which she will be able to proceed.

Since thinking and reflecting about such an informed review needs time, he further suggests that the consultation process should be spread over two ses-sions, each of about an hour and a half to two hours. The client will have the annotated list at the end of the first session; and they will arrange to meet again in a week or so's time to review the client's work on the list and subse-quent thoughts about future direction.

This introduction and a review of the client's career to date (good degree followed by work as a research assistant) takes about 20 minutes. From that they move on to data gathering for the computer matching process. This is done by having the client complete a standard interest questionnaire (one question at a time, presented on a computer screen), then answer a set of ques-tions (also via the screen) on past work experience and on preferences for job conditions. These data are then used by the program to match the client with each of a large number of job descriptions which it contains. The 20 best matches (from some 300 searched) are then printed out by title, each with a brief job description, for the client to examine. Ability and aptitude are not directly assessed; but the search is set to the level of a person's actual or likely educational attainment.

The client's interest profile (from the Occupational Interest Guide, the stan-dard interest questionnaire used) showed a high point (a strong interest) in work activities where the client could write or speak, presenting information to others, a moderate interest in biological and chemical matters, and also in physics or technology, a slight dislike of helping people in some situation of need or difficulty, a dislike of activities involving artistic/aesthetic matters and a strong dislike of economic and managerial activities. The review of the job list brought out the client's strong personal interest in always having a com-prehensive grasp of any field she worked in, and her enjoyment in presenting ideas and information to people.

Outcome After a week's reflection and a second meeting the client decided to explore possibilities of working in the information side of science. Together they then made plans for how she would find out about information work (in science libraries) and about the possibilities of scientific journalism.

Underpinning psychological knowledge   In working with the client, the psychologist drew on his knowledge and understanding of developmental psychology. A particular aspect was the way in which, for a person in a position to choose her career path, long-term satisfaction lay in the direction of some activity which fitted with her whole idea of herself – her self-concept. In addition, he relied on a well established research finding that long-term job satisfaction could reasonably be predicted from a person's answers to a systematic and extensive list of questions about likings and dislikings for work activities. He knew that the Occupational Interest Guide used in the computer matching process was such a list. Throughout, his contributions to the discussion were based on his skills as a counsellor, attending to the client, respecting her points of view and being ready to offer suggestions to be considered.

Personnel selection

The psychologists   A group of ten people, a mix of psychologists and senior staff from a client organization, all experienced as assessors in assessment centres, have the task of maintaining, improving and developing techniques used in these centres. Two psychologists and a staff member have been working on a project, and the group hears the results.

An 'assessment centre'? Let us clarify the term before we go on. The words 'assessment centre' do not primarily refer to a location but to a special, complex process used to reach selection decisions for complex jobs. In the course of it each candidate is interviewed, usually more than once, works, over one or two days, at a range of tests and engages in tasks as an individual and in groups with other candidates, while being observed by assessors who grade the performances they observe, using rating scales. The basic procedure was invented in the 1930s and 1940s and is widely used. Feltham (1991) reviews the procedure.

The problem   Analysis of the use of rating scales in the organization's assessment centres showed that the results were unreliable. Using rating scales required raters to grade candidates for particular characteristics – initiative, leadership, inventiveness – on scales from 1 (no evidence) to 5 (consistently shown). Ratings from different assessors of the same individuals did not match. Investigation showed that raters each had different underlying ideas of what was meant by such words as 'leadership' or 'initiative', and that raters varied in the range of grades on a scale they habitually used; hence the unreliability of results.

The investigation   Three assessors on the technical group (two psychologists and a staff member from the organization) were assigned the task of developing an improved rating system. The psychologists recommended, from their knowledge of techniques, that they develop and try out a set of BARS – the acronym for behaviourally anchored rating scales.

BARS are built on the finding that a person seeking to match what he or she observes with the best fitting description, in a selected set of such descriptions, will be more likely to be in agreement with other observers than if he or she attempted to rate an observed characteristic on an unillustrated numerical scale (of, say, 1 to 5). (See chapter 6, this volume.)

The three researchers developed a scale for grading descriptions (or 'illustrations', technically termed 'descriptors') of a presentation exercise (where candidates made a prepared six-minute presentation to the whole group). They gathered from assessors working in assessment centres a sizeable number of brief descriptors of performances that had been observed, and then used a set of assessors, working individually, outside any involvement in a centre procedure, to grade each of the descriptors on a scale from A ('ideal') to E ('unacceptable'). From this material the researchers retained those descriptors about which there was substantial agreement, and compiled a grading scale. Descriptors retained ranged from grade A – 'An effective communication which strikes home and remains in the memory' – to grade E – 'Fails to engage listener's interest and attention. Unlikely to be asked back.'

Assessors were then trained in the use of this scale, and a set was used in centres for six months alongside the usual system. Selection decisions were made using only the data from the usual system. The results from the BARS were not taken into account but were simply set aside. At the end of six months the reliability of the usual scales was compared with that of the BARS results, and each set of results was correlated with the overall results to discover which had a higher correlation.

Outcome The BARS developed for the presentation task showed markedly higher reliability than the simple rating scheme, and more agreement with the overall result. The sub-group of three presented a report of their work and their findings. The technical group recommended the adoption of the new procedure, and authorized further work to develop BARS for use with other group tasks in the assessment centre.

Underpinning knowledge Central were the cognitive and other processes involved in how an observer rates an observed performance; and the researchers applied principles of data gathering and analysis in constructing the BARS.

Organizational development

The psychologist This organizational psychologist is a member of a team of consultants brought in by the directors to help an organization work on problems. The team comes from a large consultancy firm and is a mix of psychologists, as well as accountancy, marketing, information technology, personnel, engineering and other specialists. Our concern is with one day's particular activities.

The problem   Our consultant is concerned with one department in the organization. Comments from various people suggest that it is below standard in its delivery of service. Her task is to find out what happens and help its members to make any necessary improvements.

How the psychologist investigated the problem   As she sees it, her project will consist of a number of cycles of activity, characterized by the alternating, cyclic process of gathering information from individuals and groups and prompting their review of their situation by feeding that information back to them in a systematic way.

Her interviews with individual members of this department revealed some contradictory ideas about the performance of the department, and a general wish to get a better overview of how they stand. Her aim is to help members of this department to develop a clearer understanding of their actual performance, as each of them sees it, and as it is seen by those they give service to (their 'customers') and by their 'suppliers' (who supply information and resources to them for their work). She has already gained the trust of members of the department, by talking with them individually and in groups. They know what she plans and, disturbing though it may seem, they are willing to take part.

Today's work involves a meeting attended by the ten members of the department and by some ten of their 'customers' and 'suppliers' (all fellow employees). The consultant has already gathered information from these customers and suppliers about their satisfactory and unsatisfactory experiences in dealing with the department. She has recorded events as described and tried to avoid expressing approval or disapproval or saying what she thinks was meant. She opens the meeting by recalling how the idea for it came about; and goes on to present, in list form, the information she has gathered on the events described to her. Then the outsiders (who have produced this feedback) go inside a 'fishbowl' (see below) to discuss and interpret the data which have been presented, while the members of the department listen, without commenting.

'Fishbowl' is a convenient jargon term for a technique in which one group sits in a circle to talk with each other, within the 'fishbowl' of the other group, who can listen but must remain silent throughout. Then the others may go into the inner circle, while those who were inside now form the fishbowl around them and listen to the discussion of what has been heard. The discussion may lead into a listing of points needing clarification, and the fishbowl process can be repeated; or the meeting can move to an open plenary (a full meeting of all members of both groups) to identify problems and to move to joint problem-solving and action planning. Throughout, the psychologist acts as enabler/facilitator, ready to remind participants of the structured process they are engaging in, and ensuring that each can feel personally safe in what can be experienced as a threatening situation, while all develop a clear, common understanding of the actual state of affairs.

Outcome Throughout this process of fishbowling followed by plenary group discussion and possible planning, the facilitator guides the two groups. The outcome will be determined not by the consultant but by the efforts of all participating. Her contribution will have added to the likelihood of a constructive outcome, devised by the participants.

Underpinning knowledge The psychologist is working with the basis of a body of knowledge, principles and techniques which have their origin in the work in the 1940s and 1950s by Kurt Lewin and his successors on group dynamics and communication within and between groups. It has become the underpinning for much subsequent work in organizational development and change.

Activities

The stages of consultancy

To those seeking to qualify professionally, the British Psychological Society (BPS) offers guidance on the stages in the consultancy process. On this model a practitioner could expect, in working with a client, to work through the following stages – or perhaps to be involved only in some of them, while colleagues were involved in others, as long as the whole sequence was covered. The stages are:

1 Identification of needs/problems.
2 Analysing needs/problems.
3 Formulating solutions.
4 Implementing solutions.
5 Evaluating outcomes.

According to the detail of this model, any qualified psychologist should be capable of exercising what are thought of as the generic skills of the first stage, i.e. identifying a problem in the realm of occupational or work and organizational psychology. Beyond that, the psychologist should be able to exercise proper professional caution, recognize whether the necessary analysis and development of solutions is within his or her specialist competences and, if they are not, to point to which specialists should be called on – in ergonomics, in selection, in training or organizational development, or whatever. Professional psychologists are required to show responsibility by knowing the limits of their own competences; and to be knowledgeable enough about the whole scene to know when work should be handed on, and to which specialist.

Recall the illustrations.

• The ergonomists contributed to stage 3 (formulating solutions) of the larger project by producing evidence-based recommendations.
• The career counsellor/psychologist worked through stages 1 to 3. He identified needs and problems (stage 1) in the initial discussion. With the job list he helped the client to discern ('analyse') what her deeper goals were (stage 2), and to begin to plan what she might seek to do (stage 3). Stage 4 depended on the client, and stage 5 could come only in the course of time, when he might write to the client, in months' or some years' time, to ask for information on how the plans had worked out.
• The sub-group of the assessment centre technical group received the analysis of the problem and carried out stage 3, the devising and testing of a solution. Further monitoring of results from its use would lead (stage 5) to evaluation of this solution in action; and so to possible further investigation.
• The psychologist/consultant contributed to stages 2 and 3 (analysing the needs/problems and formulating solutions) in the total project which was being delivered by the whole team of consultants.

Assessing, intervening, evaluating

Back in the late 1950s and early 1960s, two American psychologists, Cronbach and Gleser (1965), wrote about the use of psychological information in making what they called 'personnel decisions'. For them these decisions were not just those made in industry by managers; the terms applied to any decisions about people. They distinguished between two basic types of decisions and adopted a medical terminology, characterizing the two distinct decision activities as 'diagnose' and 'treat'. Any process or procedure which enabled a practitioner to establish the state of the person examined was a 'diagnosis'. Any process or procedure which then brought about a necessary change in the person examined was 'treatment'. It was a curious formulation, but it did serve to raise awareness to the idea that psychological information about a person was put to particular uses.

Now, over forty years later, and applying the concept to our area of psychological practice, the terms 'assess' and 'intervene' would more suitably represent these two basic procedures; and these are the terms we use here to refer to two of the sets of activities engaged in by all practitioners. 'Evaluation', the third core activity, is the foundation of professionalism, in that is completes any consultancy cycle and leads to a refocusing of effort as the cycle is repeated and the work progresses.

Assessing This is a process of producing a comprehensive account of an individual or of a situation by using whichever of the following methods of obtaining data are appropriate:

1 Observation (perhaps guided by a category or classification system).
2 Description of particular behaviour.
3 Ratings of observed behaviour and reports on the individual's performance.
4 Questions and other enquiries producing qualitative data.
5 Standard questionnaires, giving profiles of personal style, interests, attitudes.
6 Standard tests of cognitive functioning, attainment, motor coordination and perception.
7 Gathering data on perceptual and cognitive performance in specific laboratory or site conditions.

Again, recalling the four illustrations, the ergonomists asked the research data, 'Which combination of font and colour is most readily read?' Assessment involved a scrutiny of the comparative results (from 7 above) to establish the relative merits of each possible perceived environment. Assessment of the client by the career counsellor, communicated to the client, became self-assessment, and was based on the measured interest profile (5, above), the job list and the joint review generated by these. Assessment centres produce a job relevant account of each candidate on the basis of the pattern of grades (3) and test scores (6), in combination with the verbal reports and descriptions produced by the assessors who interviewed (4) and observed (1). Assessment (using 4 above) of the department's possible slowness would, throughout, become self-assessment by individuals and the group.

Intervening Intervention is whatever a psychologist does to promote some immediate or ultimate response from a person or a group.

Intervention can take surprising forms. The motorway junction warning and direction board, large enough and legible enough to allow time for a driver's decisions, stands static in all weathers; but it is an intervention from the built environment, shaped by psychologists, for every driver who attends to it; and it contributes to the action he or she decides to take. So also is the colour of a waiting room, chosen for its mixture of 'warmth' and the response of relaxation which it evokes; or other features of the environment whose design has been shaped by research on user responses and characteristics.

In the career illustration, all the psychologist's behaviour as he welcomed the client and went on to hear her problem (part of his assessment work) was also the early stages of intervention. The client's trust and readiness to work with him depended on his conduct of these initial stages when he was primarily assessing. Intervention was dominant in the second interview, as he promoted the client's self-review and possible plans for action.

The psychologists developing the BARS were not intervening with candidates, since only assessors would see the BARS. When, however, psychologists act as assessors, meeting candidates in assessment centres, they do intervene – in the working of the organization, by helping to formulate the final assessment and recommendation, and, directly, with candidates by interviewing and, at times, offering feedback.

The organizational psychologist's prominent intervention with the groups was in the meeting, when she presented to the assembled groups the information she had gathered; and in then facilitating the fishbowl process. If, however, we look more closely at the events, we can possibly recognize interventions she made before the meeting. She gathered information in interviews – and thereby she promoted trust in her by the way she conducted each interview with individuals or with groups. Her data gathering for assessment was thus, inevitably, also an intervention, of whose effect and potential she needed to be aware as a practitioner.

A conventional, everyday idea about assessment and intervention is of a complete separation of the two, i.e. a psychologist assesses, so reviewing the situation, then intervenes. In actuality, it is not like that. As indicated above, the two are often part of the same process. Data collection can itself be intervention and does affect behaviour. We see this both in the career counselling process and in the organizational development situation.

Evaluating   A report to a client at the end of a project is usual; and professional activity, based on continual learning, requires the outcome of evaluation.

Evaluation is the process of gathering information on the output or the outcome of a project, and comparing that with the aims and goals which were specified as part of stages 2 and 3 of the work that constituted the consultancy cycle. The information can come from many of the same kinds of sources used for the assessment work; or the net may be cast more widely to pick up whatever serves as an indicator of an outcome of a process or of a particular condition. In studies of built environments it might be level of vandalism, ratings of aesthetic quality, number of passengers passing through per minute before any queuing develops; for a selection programme for military pilots it might be accident rate on the training courses which followed selection. Evaluation establishes the level of validity of a procedure

The purpose of evaluation is to answer the questions:

- What was the outcome?
- What outcome did I or we expect?
- Do these coincide?
- If not, why not?

The Roles and Activities of Practitioners

Roles

In terms of conventional, analytic thinking, the activities of practitioners involve two roles:

- acting as expert in the matter of knowledge about relevant human behaviour;
- acting as enabler/facilitator of the activities of a client.

In practice, in the delivery of a service, these roles are integrated and not separate.

The expert

The consultant as expert: for many people, that is what psychologists and other consultants are, experts. They are called in when a situation seems to be beyond (local) conventional, accepted understanding, and are expected to be able to come up with solutions, because they have access to specialist knowledge *and* possess understanding of the significance of what they know, so that they can effectively apply their knowledge to the task of solving problems.

An expert in knowledge, and in understanding that knowledge. What knowledge?

1 *Knowledge of general and social psychology and research methodology*, in common with those aspiring to other psychological specialisms, such as counselling, educational, clinical, health, criminological or sport. It is the outcome of basic, university level study, and the same coverage of topics is found in the curricula of most university psychology courses in Europe – as in the first year of the doctorandus in the Netherlands, in the Vordiplom in Germany, the license or maitrise in France or the bachelor's degree in the UK.

2 *Specialist knowledge of occupational or work and organizational psychology*, as studies, for instance, in the later years of the doctorandus in the Netherlands, in the Hauptdiplom in Germany, in the diplome (of higher studies) in France and in the master's degree or individual postgraduate study in the U.K. The various areas of study involved in work and organizational psychology have already been presented in chapter 1, and I invite you to refer to it as background information on the topics on which psychologists should be knowledgeable.

As experts we have the opportunity and the responsibility of drawing on information and ideas in our field. Knowledge of some ideas may be common in the community; other areas may be specialised and esoteric. Only we, however, have been brought to the awareness of all of them as a more or less integrated body of knowledge and ideas. In that lies our advantage – and our responsibility. We are expected to be knowledgeable, and to use the knowledge responsibly.

The enabler/facilitator

A person who is enabling or facilitating contributes on the basis of a respect for the personal autonomy of a client. This is in contrast to the contribution from the expert, who contributes on the basis of specialist knowledge. The expert is, however, always open to the error of assuming ignorance and lack of comprehension on the part of another person, without checking just where he or she does stand. An expert who, as a facilitator, is sensitive to the possibility of such a situation would check with the person he or she was working with.

The terms enabler and facilitator are almost interchangeable. The first emphasizes the enabling function, i.e. the active work with a client (individual or group) which enables him or her to maintain control over the situation. The enabler will also intervene in ways which ensure that each person in a group feels personally safe in the situation. The aim is to intervene in such a way that the client does *not* develop a dependent relationship and is enabled to maintain, extend and develop 'ownership' of the work of a project and its outcome, or of his or her own self-management. The client's autonomy is respected.

'Facilitator' (from Latin *facilis*, easy) has perhaps a slightly more general sense. The origin of the word points up how the facilitator 'eases the processes' of individual thinking and of interpersonal communication by intervening – with statements, with summaries of what seems to have been said and with questions about how people seem to be working together and how they are experiencing the process. Facilitators may propose procedures to enable decisions to be made; but they, themselves, will not propose conclusions or decisions.

This approach has evolved from the recognition that the best and longest lasting help that can be offered to people is that which enables them to help themselves and to manage their own affairs. The exception is in an emergency, when strong, directive advice or plain direction can be vital to ensure a person's or organization's survival. In the long term, however, people as individuals and people in organizations seek to manage their own affairs, and they actively select from what is offered. This fact – of the human draw towards autonomy and self-management – is a fact of (human) nature. Consultants/psychologists can deliver results effectively only if they, as expert psychologists, recognize and understand this constraint and work within it.

The integrated role

The last point brings us to the matter of the integration of the two roles. The knowledgeable expert who, as a person, does not enable the activities of clients may be listened to; excuses and jokes may be made about his or her brusque or otherwise disturbing style; but the relationship will not be of equals, and the effect of any changes will usually not be lasting. If a client does not implement a recommended solution, even if it is very well grounded in expert psychological knowledge, then the expert might as well not have started work.

Only if the expert also works with clients as a skilled enabler is there a real chance of the expertise having an effect – of solutions being 'taken on board' and implemented. Hence there is a need for the integration of the two roles, so that we think of the psychologist at work as both knowledgeable – and so an expert – *and* effective as an enabler.

Methods of Data Acquisition and Intervention

Data acquisition (for assessment and for some aspects of evaluation)

Data are gathered from observation, interviews, questionnaires, rating scales, simulation and laboratory investigation.

Observation   Various approaches are possible:

- open-ended, where the observer deliberately goes into observing 'with no preconceived ideas';
- with a question in mind to focus the process;
- using some form of mapping or behaviour classification scheme.

The first of these sounds very praiseworthy – the disinterested observer sees more of the game etc. In practice, it is a simplistic approach. We all approach all situations with our own frame of ideas, assumptions and expectations. As professionals we need to bring such preconceptions into our own awareness. If that is done, the observation is likely to be more fruitful than when it is ostensibly, but unself-critically, 'open-ended'.

Given that self-awareness, the second approach will be more fruitful. The observation is directed and is likely to bring out useful data. The focused observer uses the focus given by the question, to observe – but can, of course, also stand back and be open to noticing other aspects and to detecting patterns in behaviour or in the flow of events which may be relevant.

The third approach would come after such an initial process. Once the area of difficulty has been clearly identified, then specific, even quantitative, data can be gathered from observation, using the frame of a category system or based even on the physical mapping of behaviour on a site, so that movements, communications or inferred preferences can be recorded.

Interviewing   A three-part categorization of interview structure is used:

- open-ended, following wherever the points raised seem to take it;
- semi-structured, with headings for topics to be explored within the flow of the interview;
- structured, using a set series of questions.

The first is open to the same comments as were made about open-ended observation. The definition of an interview as a 'purposive conversation' reinforces the point. A purpose gives focus. The actual process can, however, be complex. The career counsellor in the illustration managed the flow and sequence of his interview in the light of the client's responses to his initial exposition (a mutual focusing process) and his invitation to the client to describe where she is now at and what she is seeking. In as much as he followed the trend of her ideas, his structure was open-ended.

In an organizational development project, at an early stage, a series of interviews in which each interviewee was invited to talk about his or her work, and then simply listened to, might produce useful statements, produced from the respondent's point of view and not from a direction by the interviewer; and these freely generated points might give a researcher fruitful insights. The only focus is 'your work.' There is, however, one context in which interviewing is used constantly – the process of selection – and all the research evidence indicates a low reliability and validity for the unstructured interview. If, however, the topics of a semi-structured interview are chosen in the light of previous job analyses and information indicating which personal and other characteristics are relevant to effective job performance, the correlations with effectiveness go up. Further, the more such interviews are structured to ensure that they cover the relevant details in specified areas, the higher the correlations with reliability and predictive validity. (See chapter 4, this volume.)

Questionnaires   Questionnaires are means of gathering data as a basis for some kind of quantified measure of certain characteristics. They may be a paper and pencil medium or computer presented and scored, and may be tailor made (i.e. specific to a client organization) or produced by publishers for general use.

Attitude questionnaires assess feelings and potential behaviour towards 'objects' in the environment, whether physical (attitude to a building or type of building) or more abstract (attitude to work, to new systems of reward in the organization etc.).

Interest questionnaires produce a quantified profile of an individual's relative preferences for different kinds of activities in the world of work. The

Interest Guide used by the career counsellor in the illustration is part of a pro-cedure (JIIC-CAL, Job Information and Ideas Generator–Computer Assisted Learning; see Closs, 1993) widely used since the early 1980s in UK career guidance services. The Guide is the product of a long process of develop-ment and revision by a research team led by a psychologist in Edinburgh, and is based on careful and extensive research with senior school pupils and adults.

Personality questionnaires produce profiles describing an individual's per-sonal style or type. Sixty years of development seem now to have produced a partial consensus on the five basic dimensions (the 'big five') of extro-vert/introvert, neurotic/emotionally stable, agreeable/abrasive, open to expe-rience/closed to it, conscientious/undirected. Some researchers would argue for a 'big nine', subdividing parts of the above. In turn, these major dimen-sions seem to allow the discernment, by test researchers and developers, of many sub-dimensions, from to 15 or 16 to 30 or even more, according to the outcomes of their analyses.

Personality questionnaires are particularly widely used, often under the label of 'psychometric testing'. The aura of precision conferred by that title is not given strong support by the actual evidence on reliability and validity. The fewer and more basic the dimensions, and the more items per dimension in a 'test' or questionnaire, the more likely the coefficients are to be reassuring. They can be useful devices in research work and in generating profiles and per-sonality descriptions which can then be used as a basis for extending the self-awareness and self-assessment of an individual. Their use in selection is more questionable, since results can be affected by the beliefs held by a respondent about the kinds of answers which are appropriate from applicants for a par-ticular post, i.e. 'faking' does affect and may distort results.

There is a persisting debate about the value of personality questionnaires, largely because different researchers produce a wide range of results, from con-firmatory to those casting strong doubts. The basic reason seems to lie in the nature of the original data. They do not involve actual behaviour (the ground of a psychologist's work). They depend on self-report – on people reporting their behaviour, as they remember it, as they make generalizations about it and about their feelings and preferences. Does what people say they do map exactly on to what they actually do? The use of standard questionnaires does, more or less, assume such a congruence. If we observe the world of people and the frequency of self-deception, we might have grounds for doubting that assumption.

In addition, the probable lack of complete congruence is compounded by the fact that people are reporting on aspects of themselves which are not con-stants. People behave differently in different social or other contexts, accord-ing to their roles and how they construe themselves in relation to a particular situation. An assessor working with an individual can respect the uniqueness of personality which underlies this variation: a set questionnaire, with its set format, has to be accommodated to by the respondent, with a consequent loss of actual information.

Rating scales   Rating scales were described in the personnel selection illustration, and the faults of simple rating scales were indicated there. Check back if you need to.

For a rating procedure to work, raters need to be considering the same characteristic or behaviour on the same scale. Hence the value of the BARS, as described. A behaviourally anchored rating scale presents an observer with a clear task – and one which is essentially a recognition task, not one involving individual mental models of scales. The observer, seeking to grade the behaviour exhibited, scans the descriptors offered, recognizes the one which best describes what was seen and grades accordingly, producing results shown to be of significant reliability and validity.

Tests   Tests of ability, aptitude, special abilities, scholastic aptitude, various forms of cognitive and perceptual functioning (although, surprisingly, the extensive work in cognitive psychology of the past thirty years seems to have had little impact on the processes of test development): really, all are tests of some form or other of attainment, in that the the data come from the performance of tasks. These involve sensory acuity, perceptual processes, cognitive functioning (verbal, numerical, spatial, mechanical etc.) and motor performance, or combinations of any of these (an example might be a visual tracking test with responses via a hand control). 'Spatial' refers to the ability 'mentally to manipulate shapes'; and 'mechanical' refers to the ability to think in terms of relationships and forces in the physical world.

When a test is thought of as a means of measuring a particular mental capacity, the ideas of 'pass' and 'fail' are conceptually inappropriate. However, the data on which a measure is based do involve the person who is taking the test in the process of getting an answer correct, or of hitting a target – or of getting it wrong or missing it. 'Success' and 'failure', even if only at the subjective level, are actually implicit in the process for the person taking a test.

A score on a test can be set against the range of performance obtained from a suitable, sizeable group of others who took the test under the same conditions. That allows us to locate an individual on a scale measuring an ability or aptitude for a particular kind of task in a work or study/learning situation.

For convenience of administration, tests are usually administered to a number of subjects at a time, but increasingly they can now be presented by computer on a touch screen monitor, with immediate scoring and the possibility of obtaining complex additional data on the length of time taken to complete each item. In the form of attainment tests, versions can be used at the start and end of a training procedure to assess outcomes, but their major use is in selection procedures, as predictors of future performance.

Simulations   These are of three kinds and serve different purposes.

- Models or full-scale replicas of physical environments. Data on user or occupant response leads to design development and modification. A full-scale simulation might be the driver's seat, displays and controls of a car or other operator setting; or it could be a proposed room or set of rooms in a building. People would use the environment. Their responses and behaviour would be observed, their task performance recorded and their own personal reactions obtained from self-report. Decorative colours of rooms, type and arrangement of furniture could all be varied and further data collected. Computer simulations of rooms and whole buildings now enable people to 'walk' through them, using virtual reality.
- Simple simulation of a work task, as in operating a piece of equipment. This might be used as a form of job sample in a particular selection procedure – as in establishing an applicant's level of keyboard skills – or it might be a stage in a training process – operating a model excavator from a full-size cab, to master the techniques of gripping and lifting with a grab, before moving on to work on site.
- Social simulations, where a group of people form the relevant environment of each of those involved and where a task of some sort has to carried out, involving interaction, whether interviewing to gather information or group cooperation to solve problems posed. This kind of simulation could form one or more of the exercises in an assessment centre. Some simulations might involve physical tasks, others the work of a supposed committee. Groups tackling such tasks might be set up as leaderless groups, or as ones where each member of a group was designated leader for a time. In the assessment centre illustration, the exercise of making a six-minute presentation to an audience was a simulation exercise.

Alternatively, social simulation can be a training technique. The Benefits Agency regularly uses professional actors to play the parts of worried or aggrieved claimants in simulations, in order to train staff in how to handle situations constructively, without their own worry or fear spoiling the process.

Laboratory investigation   This is the investigation of sensory, perceptual and cognitive processes and responses relevant to a particular work situation. Of most use to the ergonomist, this situation depends on much work that has gone before in establishing which variables are involved in a particular work situation, the analysis of problems and the generation of ever more specific questions which can then – and then only – be answered with the kind of data obtainable in the controlled setting of the laboratory experiment or trial. It gives the most focused and precise answers, but all the preparatory work, using other, less precise methods, is essential to ensure that the questions finally being asked of the laboratory process are the relevant ones for the problem being faced.

Forms and methods of intervention

This section concludes with a scheme for categorizing 'interventions' made in face-to-face dealings, but it needs some introductory comments before we look at it.

Central is the question of why we now use 'intervention', when Cronbach and Gleser (1965) suggested 'treatment' in the 1950s. The answer is that times, views, assumptions and approaches have changed since then. Then and earlier, most practitioners had a particular set of assumptions about their work and their clients. A client, to them, was relatively passive, compliant and ready to take advice and direction. In that scenario, experts prescribed treatment (changed equipment, made changes in selection procedures or changes in organization) and clients complied by adopting them. People received 'treatment' directly, or through a shaped environment. They were assumed to be absorbers of what was given to them.

Nowadays we use 'intervention' because we have a different mental model of the individual. (This was touched on in the section on activities.) We now think in terms of a more active, attending, selective, autonomous being, on whom decisions are not imposed, who is not 'given' training, but who develops most fully when involved as a participant in the process, as a party in any negotiation and as an 'owner' or stakeholder in the particular project.

'Intervention' (as defined in the *Shorter Oxford English Dictionary*, 1993) is a 'coming between, an interfering, especially so as to modify or prevent a result or outcome'. We talk of intervention because we, as professionals, recognize that we can be thought of as intruding on another and on his or her their life-space when we act to help, and even when we have been given permission to do so. Our intentions are benevolent, but the psychological reality is that we are inevitably an intrusion on the active living process of the other person or persons. In consequence, we, as psychologists, work best if we see ourselves as working *in collaboration with* those we serve as professionals.

Central, in turn, to this change in the approach of psychologists is the awareness of the importance of a sense of self underlying each person's responses to all that happens to him or her; and what each of us construes as relating to that. Much resistance (to even the most well intentioned advice, guidance and direction) is a response to perceived assault upon the self, i.e. perceived neglect or non-recognition of the self of the other, of self-regard and of a person's understanding of the world, as he or she experiences it.

Some interventions are intrusions which are not recognized as such by the person involved. The motorway sign, specially designed to be optimally legible, is, as we saw earlier, an intervention; but, except to a seriously mentally disturbed user, it presents no threat to self-respect. In contrast, a selection assessment and decision process does carry a threat to self-regard, and the effective professional, running a selection process, recognizes this aspect of the intervention ('the intrusion') and works to minimize its effect.

It is because of these underlying psychological processes which affect all participants (including the psychologists) that psychologists must, if they are to be effective, play two roles in an integrated way – the roles of technical expert and of enabler/facilitator. And that is why the forms and methods of intervention, whenever these involve direct communication (face-to-face, or any other form) with a client, must be fundamentally the methods of facilitative (or 'collaborative') intervention.

Forms of facilitative ('collaborative') intervention   Specific forms and instances of interventions are described in a number of the chapters in this book. At this general overview stage, it will be helpful to finish by briefly examining a scheme which classifies interventions made to help individuals. Training courses can be built upon its frame and it is a model for all forms of collaborative intervention.

Some thirty years ago two American consultants, Blake and Mouton (1972), developed a scheme of five categories of intervention which, they claimed 'characterized what applied behavioural scientists do as they work with people in organizations'. Working from that, John Heron (1990) of the University of Surrey developed a six category scheme. He saw the Blake and Mouton scheme as focusing primarily on interventions made in organizational life by organizational development consultants. His development and extension of it presents a scheme which applies to all one-to-one interventions.

The scheme of practitioner-to-client interventions (which he entitled the 'six category intervention analysis') deals with the basic process of the work of a consultant with one person, in an interview. From that interview come plans for the individual's future; or, when the person is a member of an organization, then such an interview, repeated with others, will be the basis for work with groups and arrays of groups in the organization. (Heron (1989) also developed a related scheme for work in the facilitation of groups.)

Six category intervention analysis   There are two groups of interventions. Each contains three categories:

Authoritative
- Prescriptive: offering suggestions and direction, but checking for acceptability.
- Informative: offering information, but checking for relevance.
- Confronting: highlighting inconsistencies in a client (as these are perceived by the facilitator).

Facilitative
- Cathartic: accepting emotional discharge (tears, fear, anger, joy).

- Catalytic: questioning, listening, summarizing (and checking, as the person intervening, that the other has really been understood).
- Supportive: welcoming the other as a person, promoting psychological safety.

Each category contains a vast range of phrases, statements, questions, comments and actions. Each intervention derives from a particular intention on the part of the user, e.g. to intervene with the intention of making a suggestion (prescriptive category) or of supporting emotional release (cathartic category).

This applies to a wide range of practitioners: doctors, lawyers, trainers, tutors, advisers, consultants, counsellors, therapists, teachers, as well as psychologists. It applies to anyone whose work requires intervention to help to promote others' effective self-management, whether the others go by the name of client, patient, student or whatever.

Authoritative interventions are so called because they come from the authority of the practitioner as an expert, as experienced and knowledgeable about good practice. He or she offers information, points out inappropriate behaviour, raises levels of awareness about actions, beliefs etc. and suggests possible actions.

Facilitative interventions, on the other hand, are enabling interventions. They help clients to get into their own self-exploration, their own self-disclosing and their own problem-solving and discovery learning.

Conclusion

There, you have it: the ideas that underlie the work of psychologists concerned with people and work. We have looked at the ideas of assessing individuals and environments, of intervening to bring about change in what may have been established behaviour; at the idea of the integrated role of knowledgeable expert who needs also to be an effective facilitator; and, in a constructively critical way, at methods of assessment and intervention. I wish you well in the future.

D i s c u s s i o n   P o i n t s

1   One early idea of what industrial psychology (as it was then termed in UK) was about was in terms of changing the person and changing the work environment. How well does that frame fit the four illustrations of psychologists at work?

2   The management cycle for managing projects is often examined in textbooks on management. Four stages are specified:

- planning a project, starting with aims and objectives;
- developing the organization and procedures for the project;
- implementing the project;
- monitoring the outcome, in terms of objectives achieved.

How well does this apply to the stages of consultancy?

3 What will a practitioner have to do to become an effective enabler/facilitator?

4 What forms of intervention have you experienced? Which were effective in the long run?

PART II

PEOPLE AT WORK

Seminar. (Ace Photo Library)

CHAPTER
THREE

JOB ANALYSIS AND DESIGN

**Catherine D. Lees
and John L. Cordery**

Contents

Following major technological change in its operator services section, designed to make the delivery of directory assistance, fault rectification and call connection services more efficient and effective, a large telecommunications organization is faced with increasing performance problems. Customer call waiting times, rather than declining, have actually increased by 20 per cent, with a commensurate increase in customer complaints. Staff morale is very low. Absenteeism in some centers is running as high as 25 per cent and turnover in the organization as a whole was 140 per cent over the past year. How do you begin to deal with these performance and quality issues? There are many possible causes and many possible solutions. First, you have to work out where the source of the problem lies. Do the employees have the right knowledge, skills and abilities for their work? Is the work do-able; that is, is it possible for the employees to prevent the productivity and quality problems, and to produce work of the required standard at all times? Do they get the necessary information to enable them to control problems as they arise, or is it too late by the time they have an opportunity to act? Do you need to retrain the employees, redesign their jobs, re-engineer the production process, reform the performance appraisal and compensation systems or simply terminate the 'dead wood' and get in some 'new blood'? How will you know what is the right action to take? The short answer is that you will have to begin by collecting, recording, and integrating information about the job(s). This process, 'the systematic collection of data describing the tasks that comprise a job and the knowledge, skills, abilities, and other characteristics that enable a person to carry out those tasks' (Landy, 1993, pp. 75–6), is called *job analysis*.

Why Carry out a Job Analysis?

Job analysis is a necessary precondition for a number of human resource management activities, which are:

- human resource planning;
- efficient utilization of human resources;
- performance management;
- training and development;
- knowledge management;
- job design and redesign;
- safety and health management;
- classifying and grouping similar jobs;
- job evaluation and compensation;
- legal/quasi-legal requirements.

In human resource planning, for example, business objectives are translated into human resource objectives. To implement human resource strategic plans effectively, we need to know the flows of human resources in the organization. Human resources are people carrying knowledge, skills, abilities (KSA), personality, attitudes and values around with them. As people move into, out of and through the organization, these valuable tools and assets move with them. There is no point in determining the flows of human resources in the organization if those resources are described only as names and staff identification numbers; we need to describe them in terms of their knowledge, skills, abilities, competencies and record of performance achievements.

The efficient utilization of human resources requires accurately specifying the person requirements for particular work or a job (job requirements specification), and accurate placement of a person having those assets into that work (person classification), as well as an efficient work process that enhances rather than damages the employee. The job specifications can only be based on job analysis, and the appropriate selection and accurate placement of the person depends on knowing which of the individual's many assets are applicable to this job, in what form and to what level; that is, knowing what to look for in an applicant and how to measure it. As we shall see, these also depend on job analysis.

To create a performance appraisal and feedback system it is necessary to establish criteria or standards of performance on some dimensions, whether in output terms, process terms or competence terms. Understanding what constitutes good or poor performance on a job entails knowledge of the desired outputs, the appropriate process behaviours and the attendant competencies that distinguish the superior performer – this information is the product of job analysis.

One of the main uses of job analysis data is in proactive training needs analysis and determining detailed training content. Here the breadth of the concept of job analysis can be extended even further. Training needs analysis itself is not job analysis. It can be carried out by interview or questionnaire, with generic questions, relying on the incumbent, supervisor or subject matter expert to provide job specific information. Yet, in answering the questions, the respondent is drawing on an implicit analysis of the job and its knowledge and skill requirements, without which, training needs cannot be determined. When a training programme is designed and training content is determined, detail becomes very explicit. Training objectives are specified in terms of desired levels, or improvement in those aspects of job behaviours, skills and competencies that are to be trained. Their appropriateness depends on the adequacy of the implicit job analysis on which they are based.

More commonly, a formal job analysis provides the basis for the content of a training effort. For the purposes of training system development, job analysis must provide detailed information about the work process; this is obtained through task analysis. Apart from providing specific training content, the information from task analysis can be used to track training. For example, Kirwan and Ainsworth (1992) describe the use of hierarchical task analysis to develop a system for recording and tracking the training of apprentice fitters. The task analysis provided information on the nature and type of various skills, and the maintenance actions and locations in the plant where each skill was required. Through maintaining records of the provision of training to apprentices on each of these skills, and providing each trainee with a record too, it was possible to ensure that all training opportunities were maximized and progress was made on all skill areas. In some of these areas apprentices had typically not been given training because the plant involved was critical, and when maintenance work was needed it was given only to the most skilled fitters so that the plant would be operational again as quickly as possible.

The training database can be a partner to a skills inventory. Effective knowledge management requires accurate inventories of both the physical and documented knowledge stock, such as procedures, processes, software and patents, and the less tangible knowledge embodied in the skills of the employees. To understand the relevance of skills, their application potential and their value to the organization requires an understanding of the role of the employee in accomplishing the activities and tasks comprising the work. That understanding is achieved through job analysis. We would argue here that job analysis is an integral component in modern knowledge management.

Across the full spectrum of occupational safety and health, from the micro level of repetitive movements to sudden accidents or the long-term effects of shiftwork schedules, the management of safety and health outcomes can only be achieved through an explicit consideration of what it is that the employees are asked to do, how they go about doing it and under what environmental conditions. Again we see the breadth of the job analysis construct, going far beyond the definition in terms of 'describing the tasks that comprise a job and the knowledge, skills, abilities, and other characteristics that enable a person to carry out those tasks', to embrace the effects that carrying out these tasks has on the employee. Here, describing the job is not just creating a collection of task descriptions, it is describing the job *as designed*, in accordance with Campion's (1994) suggestion that job analysis should include measurement of aspects of the design of the job. The role of job analysis in job design and redesign will become apparent when we address that topic below.

Job analysis is the major activity involved in the classification of jobs into similar groups. For example, the Australian Standard Classification of Occupations (ASCO) is primarily a statistical classification that classifies jobs according to skill level and skill specialization into five hierarchical categories, major group, sub-major group and minor group, unit level and, at the finest level, occupations. There are nine major groups, separated largely by skill level. Within these are 35 sub-major groups, 81 minor groups distinguished on skill specialization, 340 unit groups distinguished again further on skill specialization and 986 occupations based on both skill level and specialization. ASCO has somewhat more categories than the International Standard Classification of Occupations (ISCO) developed by the International Labour Organization in Geneva. In the USA, the Dictionary of Occupational Titles (DOT) serves a similar role.

Job evaluation, the construction of grades and ranges of pay and the structure of progression through these grades depends on job analysis information. Even a system that simply pegs pay to the relevant labour market requires that the content of the job is known, so that the relevant comparison to similar jobs in other organizations can be made. Any attempt to assess the value contributed to the organization by each job grouping requires even more: an analysis of the importance and criticality of performance levels in that job. This again goes beyond the boundaries of the simple definition of job analysis to consider the relationship between performance in the job in question, and performance of the work unit or even of the wider organization.

Finally, in many countries there is some form of legislation concerning equality of opportunity. In the European Union, for example, equal pay for men and women is enshrined in the Treaty of Rome. Other specific forms of equal treatment, such as equal access to employment, depend on the legislation enacted in member states. In Australia, at national level, the Sex Discrimination, Race Discrimination and Disability Discrimination Acts all use a definition of employment discrimination that specifically does not include as discrimination 'any distinction, exclusion or preference in respect of a particular job based on the inherent requirements of the job'. These acts do not specifically state that any form of job analysis is required, and courts and tribunals decide for themselves in each case whether the selection process, criteria and tests used constitute employee selection that is based on 'the inherent requirements of the job'. However, a minimum defence against claims of discrimination in employment is to establish a link between the selection criteria or treatment of the employee and the requirements of the job. Evidence for such a link would normally be based on information gathered under some activity that would fit our definition of job analysis. In the United States a requirement to conduct job analysis is specified directly through the Uniform Guidelines on Employee Selection Procedures (1978), which were created to assist organizations to comply with Equal Employment Opportunity Commission expectations of practice, and thus to help to buffer them against discrimination claims.

In summary, job analysis can serve many purposes, and, appropriate to each of those purposes, the outputs or results of job analysis activity will differ. This chapter outlines the process of conducting a job analysis, including the kinds of data that are collected, the steps in the job analysis project and descriptions of a number of formal, structured job analysis methods. The implications of job analysis for the validity of activities such as selection are discussed, and the important relationship between job analysis and job design is explained. Finally, the role of job analysis in the future world of the 'boundaryless job' is considered.

We have said that job analysis is gathering information about the job. What kind of information or data should we gather to solve the problems described at the outset of this chapter, or for each of the purposes described above?

Major Categories of Job Analysis Data

McCormick (1976) classified job analysis methods into those that gather information about the job (or task) and those that gather information about the worker. The job-oriented approach collects information about the tasks and duties carried out on the job, in terms of descriptions of the outcomes accomplished by the tasks. The worker-oriented approach is centred on the person and collects information in the form of descriptions of behaviour required and actions carried out, rather than the outcomes of execution of the task components. Table 3.1 shows the main types of information gathered under the worker-oriented and job-oriented approaches.

We need a hybrid of both task and worker approaches for most job analysis purposes. For example, in the diagnostic task that confronts us in the presenting performance problem, the performance criterion or criteria will be an important starting point. One of the purposes of job analysis is criterion development for validating selection processes, for example, or for developing a performance appraisal system. In diagnosis of performance problems, it is possible to start with the criteria, and to examine the way in which those criteria can be satisfied, or met, through task execution, breaking down the component tasks to a progressively more molecular level until the source of the performance difficulties or obstacles is identified. At each grain of analysis both the task-oriented and the worker- or behaviour-oriented analysis is necessary, because we do not know where the answer lies. Perhaps there are components of the task that cannot be carried out as specified in standard operating procedures, because materials or components are not always correctly sized or do not arrive on time, or flow is hindered by other participants. Or perhaps the employee is unsure of procedure in some configurations of work, is too inexperienced or uninterested and unmotivated.

Harvey (1991) has created a further taxonomy of job analysis methods. Harvey's taxonomy categorizes methods using two dimensions. The first of these dimensions, the behavioural or technical specificity of job analysis items, refers to the grain of analysis. How detailed or molecular is the breakdown of actions required by the job analysis technique? The more fine-grained an analysis is, the less useful it is for comparing across jobs because, at the finest level of analysis, every job is unique. Thus, this dimension tells us something about whether the job analysis technique is useful for between-job comparisons, such

Table 3.1 Two main types of job analysis data

Tasks and duties	(Job-oriented)
Required *behaviours* and implied knowledge, skills and abilities	(Worker-oriented)
A hybrid of task and worker approaches is needed for most purposes	

Information gathered from both types of data
Tasks
    Frequency performed?
    Importance of performance?
Skills/knowledge needed for performance of task or behaviour
    When are they learned?
    Importance for tasks or behaviours?
Abilities
    Necessary for task performance?
    For new skill/knowledge acquisition?

as those used for job evaluation and compensation setting purposes, and for classifying jobs into similar groups; for example, to help to determine which jobs could be grouped together for multi-skilling. Harvey's second dimension is the degree to which the rating system used is applicable across jobs. He observes that many of the frequency and importance ratings commonly obtained for job analysis provide only 'ipsative' information, which is relative in magnitude to other ratings for the same job, but is not comparable across jobs. Harvey gives the example of 'negotiating with others' being given the same high importance rating by a chief executive officer and a head janitor in describing their jobs. Those ratings may well be appropriate relative to other components of each job, but they do not mean that the absolute importance of that item is the same for both jobs, that the difficulty, intricacy and criticality of negotiations is the same for both jobs or that marginal returns for increasing levels of negotiating skills will be the same in both jobs.

Steps in a Job Analysis Project

Determining the scope of the job analysis project

As we have indicated that there are many purposes for job analysis, and that the type of approach taken will depend on the purpose, it follows that one of the initial steps in a job analysis project is to take some decisions concerning the explicit purposes and the breadth and depth of the analysis effort. It is very important that these decisions are made explicit and written down as part of the planning stage of job analysis. The scope of the analysis tells us in advance at what point we will stop gathering and analysing data about the job.

For example, if the job analysis project only involves a detailed study of one particular job in one area of an organization – for example, in association with work redesign – then more detail can be collected about the job than if the project was for the purposes of updating descriptions of all jobs in a very large organization. If there are a number of positions in the organization doing the same job, only a sample of those positions need be analysed. In this way the scope can be responsive to cost constraints.

Deciding the methods to be used in collecting information

Many of the formal job analysis methods that have been developed, some of which are described below, involve strict procedures for data collection, and so once the choice of a formal method has been made, data types and sources are also fixed by that method.

Preliminary data from existing records   In any job analysis the preliminary source of data is the existing documentation concerning the job. Previous job analyses may have been carried out and should be consulted. Even if the full records of previous analyses are not available, there may be a report, or at least there will be job descriptions. Job descriptions are a central starting point, but if you can obtain it, other documented information about the jobs, such as performance records, absenteeism and sickness/injury records, turnover and complaints and grievances, may also be useful.

Collecting job analysis data   If the existing information is not adequate and a new job analysis project is required, there are various kinds of data that can be gathered and various ways of collecting them. Some methods covered in Gael's (1988) collection, for example, include interviews, questionnaires and checklists, content analysis of job documentation such as operating procedures, observing the work directly, holding interviews or meetings with subject matter experts (SMEs), having workers complete work diaries, time and motion studies and work sampling. As well as the job-oriented and worker-oriented data, there are a number of other types of data, such as the equipment used and regulations and policies the worker should know.

Examples of specific job analysis techniques

There are a number of job analysis methods that have been developed by practitioners and researchers over the years, to the point where they are clearly defined and distinct procedures. The examples given here are only some of the many such methods.

Position analysis questionnaire   The position analysis questionnaire (PAQ) is a job analysis instrument developed by Ernest McCormick and colleagues

(McCormick, Mecham and Jeanneret, 1989). It was designed to be a structured questionnaire that could be applied to any job. The questionnaire instrument requires careful completion, so the respondent should have some training in the use of the questionnaire. For this reason the PAQ is not used as a mail-out questionnaire, but is completed by a job analyst, or occasionally the supervisor or SME after training in the use of the questionnaire. It may take one or two hours to complete a single PAQ for a job. This, combined with the requirement that the respondent should be trained, if not an experienced job analyst, means that only relatively small numbers of questionnaires can be completed for a given job. It has been suggested that independent job analyses by three respondents will provide adequate reliability traded off against cost for most purposes (PAQ Services Inc., 1997).

The PAQ itself has 195 items. The first 187 items are questions concerning job elements and are grouped into six divisions dealing with: (a) information input, (b) mental processes, (c) work output, (d) relationships with other persons, (e) job context and (f) other job characteristics. The remaining eight items ask about aspects of pay, compensation and employment status, such as full-time or part-time. Each item is rated by the respondent on one rating scale assigned to that item as indicated in the questionnaire. For illustration, figure 3.1 is a reproduction of page 9 of the PAQ – it lists the questions for the job element B3, 'use of learned information', containing items 44 to 49. The 'importance to this job' scale is used for items 44 and 45, while each of the other items has its own specific rating scale.

The raw ratings on the 187 items do not provide the important output of the PAQ analysis. Factor analysis of ratings for a sample of 2200 jobs has been used to derive job dimensions. There are 45 dimensions, 13 from an overall analysis of PAQ items and the remainder from separate analyses of each of the six divisions of the PAQ. Some examples from among the 13 overall dimensions are (McCormick et al., 1989):

- decision/communication/general responsibilities;
- public/customer/related contact activities;
- unpleasant/hazardous/demanding environment.

Score profiles on the dimensions can be used for designing selection, for matching jobs, for designing career paths and sequence flows between jobs and particularly for job evaluation, job grading and compensation setting. The PAQ is quantitative and it produces a detailed profile of the job. Pay data are also collected about the job, so with a sufficient job database it is possible to use statistical techniques such as multiple regression to relate the multiple job dimensions to pay, either in the organization itself or in the relevant labour market.

The PAQ has a number of advantages as a job analysis technique. It can be used for purposes such as selection program design, because it provides

B3. Use of Learned Information

Importance to This Job

0 Does not apply
1 Very minor
2 Low
3 Intermediate
4 High
5 Extreme

44. Use of job-related knowledge
The importance to job performance of specific job-related knowledge or information gained through education, experience, or training, as contrasted with any related physical skills.

45. Short-term memory
Learning and retraining job-related information and recalling that information after a brief time, e.g., food server or telephone operator.

46. Education
Using the response scale below, indicate the level of knowledge typically acquired through formal education that is *required* to perform this job. (Do *not* consider technical or vocational school training-see item 48.)

Education (acquired through formal education or equivalent)

0	Does not apply (little or no formal education required)	2	Completion of high school	5	Completion of advanced degree (e.g., graduate school, law school, or medical school)
		3	Some college work		
1	Less than that required for completion of high school	4	Completion of 4-year college program		

47. Job-related experience
Using the response scale below, indicate the amount of all previous job-related experience in other related or lower-level jobs generally needed as background to learn this job.

Job-related Experience

0	Does not apply (no experience required)	2	1 month to 12 months	4	3 years to 5 years
1	Less than 1 month	3	1 year to 3 years	5	Over 5 years

48. Training
Using the response scale below, indicate the training generally needed for persons with no prior job training to learn this job; consider all types of required job-related training except for education described in item 46; include training at technical, vocational, or business schools, apprenticeships, on-the-job training, and orientation training.

Training

0	Does not apply or very limited (no more than one day's training)	1	Up through 30 days	3	Up through 1 year
		2	Up through 6 months	4	Up through 3 years
				5	Over 3 years

49. Using mathematics
Using the response scale below, indicate the highest level of mathematics needed to perform the job.

Level of Mathematics

0	Does not apply	3	Intermediate (e.g., fractions, decimals, and percentages)	5	Very advanced (advanced mathematical and statistical theory, e.g., calculus, topology, vector analysis, factor analysis, or probability theory)
1	Simple basic (addition and subtraction of 2-digit numbers)	4	Advanced (e.g., algebra, geometry, trigonometry, and statistics)		
2	Basic (addition and subtraction of 3-digit numbers, multiplication, and division)				

Figure 3.1 Page 9 of the Position Analysis Questionnaire.

Source: PAQ Services, Inc., 1625 North 1000 East, North Logan, UT 84341, USA. Copyright © 1989 by Purdue Research Foundation. Reprinted with permission.

extensive information about the characteristics required for the job. It can be used for job evaluation and classification, because it is perhaps the best example of a generic job analysis instrument which enables direct comparisons between many jobs (one of Harvey's taxonomic dimensions). On the negative side, the

PAQ may be too generic for some requirements. It does not provide detailed job-specific competencies such as those produced by criterion sampling in the competency approach. For example, the completion of a particular type of weld to a standard using specified equipment, the construction of a particular type of electrical relay and the preparation of a real estate contract of sale are highly specific criterion behaviours.

Functional job analysis   Another technique based on a particular structure of job dimensions is functional job analysis. Functional job analysis (FJA) arose through a development process aimed at developing a job classification scheme for the *Dictionary of Occupational Titles (DOT)* in the USA. Through extensive empirical work, several dimensions emerged as representative of most of the descriptions commonly used by respondents to describe aspects of tasks for quite different jobs. As might be expected in the development of a classification system for the *DOT*, a concern with building a language of words and definitions for accurate and reliable description of jobs and tasks is a theme that runs through writings on the FJA technique (Fine and Getkate, 1995). Fine (1988) reports that it was observed that many of the verbs describing the work performed could be put into one of three categories, to do with things, data and people. These became the worker function scales of FJA, each independent of the others and scaled internally with a hierarchy of degrees of complexity in bands of low, medium and high complexity. Figure 3.2 shows the things, data, and people dimensions.

In addition to the three worker function scales, there are three scales describing the extent to which the job requires reasoning, mathematics and language skills. Fine and Getkate (1995) provide descriptions and benchmark tasks that illustrate each of the levels of the scales. There is also an 'instruction' scale to indicate the extent to which the worker operates under supervisory instructions.

Another feature of the FJA technique is the specific nature of task descriptions. Task descriptions are narrative but must contain highly specific information on the behaviour or action carried out, the objective of the action, the source of information used for the task, the nature and source of instruction received, the machines, tools or equipment used for the task and the result or outcome of the task. FJA is centred on the collection of job task descriptions, and the description of jobs in terms of the tasks they comprise. Thus the FJA technique is very much a job-task-oriented technique of job analysis. Like the PAQ, however, it is based on a predetermined set of dimensions of work and work requirements.

Task inventories   A task inventory is a list of tasks that are relevant to a particular job or type of work. The list itself is not a description of the job, it is a tool used in the process of analysing the job. The task inventory technique is a job-oriented method in terms of McCormick's taxonomy, and job-specific in terms of Harvey's taxonomy.

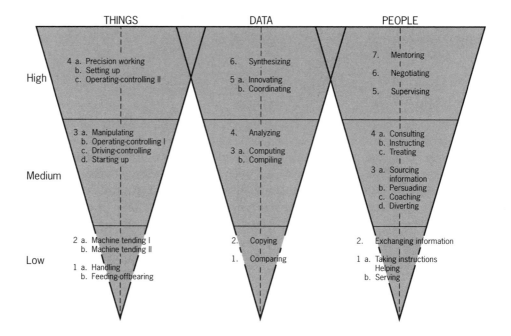

THINGS   DATA   PEOPLE

High

4 a. Precision working
  b. Setting up
  c. Operating-controlling II

6. Synthesizing
5 a. Innovating
  b. Coordinating

7. Mentoring
6. Negotiating
5. Supervising

Medium

3 a. Manipulating
  b. Operating-controlling I
  c. Driving-controlling
  d. Starting up

4. Analyzing
3 a. Computing
  b. Compiling

4 a. Consulting
  b. Instructing
  c. Treating
3 a. Sourcing
    information
  b. Persuading
  c. Coaching
  d. Diverting

Low

2 a. Machine tending I
  b. Machine tending II
1 a. Handling
  b. Feeding-offbearing

2. Copying
1. Comparing

2. Exchanging information
1 a. Taking instructions
    Helping
  b. Serving

Notes

1. Each hierarchy is independent of the other. It would be incorrect to read the functions across the three hierarchies as related because they appear to be on the same level. The definitive relationship among functions is within each hierarchy, not across hierarchies. Some broad exceptions are made in the next note.

2. Data is central since a worker can be assigned even higher data functions although Things and People functions remain at the lowest level of their respective scales. This is not so for Things and People functions. When a Things function is at the third level (e.g., Precision Working), the Data function is likely to be at least Compiling or Computing. When a people function is at the fourth level (e.g., Consulting, the Data function is likely to be at least Analyzing and possibly Innovating or Coordinating. Similarly for Supervising and Negotiating. Mentoring in some instances can call for Synthesizing.

3. Each function in its hierarchy is defined to include the lower numbered functions. This is more or less the way it was found to occur in reality. It was most clear-cut for Things and Data and only a rough approximation in the case of People.

4. The letterhead functions are separate functions on the same level, separately defined. The empirical evidence did not support a hierarchical distinction.

5. The hyphenated functions, Taking Instructions-Helping, Operating-Controlling, and so on, are single functions.

6. The Things hierarchy consists of two intertwined scales: Handling, Manipulating, Precision working is a scale for tasks involving hands and hand tools; the remainder of the functions apply to tasks involving machines, equipment, vehicles.

Figure 3.2 Summary chart of Worker Function Scales and associated notes. It is most important to understand the definitions of these scales and levels, which can be found in appendix A of Fine and Getkate (1995).

Source: S. A. Fine and M. Getkate (1995) *Benchmark Tasks for Job Analysis: a Guide for Functional Job Analysis (FJA) Scales*. Mahwah, NJ: Lawrence Erlbaum Associates, p. 4. Copyright © 1995 by Lawrence Erlbaum Associates, Inc. Reprinted with permission of Lawrence Erlbaum Associates, Inc., and the authors.

    The task inventory method was initially developed by the US military (Christal and Weissmuller, 1988). As might be expected from its origins, the task inventory technique is appropriate when a large number of jobs in an occupational category are to be analysed, especially if they are geographically spread out and incumbents cannot be interviewed individually; for example, mine foremen in a multinational mining company, or flight attendants in a global airline. Unlike the PAQ, the task inventory is a mail-out questionnaire which is completed by the incumbent without special training or assistance. Combined with computer analysis of the results, this makes it relatively inexpensive to obtain a large sample of incumbent responses. The questionnaire itself, however, requires intensive development and, therefore, the technique overall is not necessarily inexpensive.

A number of tools for human resource management have arisen out of the task inventory approach to job analysis. For example, a matrix of job knowledge or KSA requirements by job title can be created, and from this a matrix of training requirements by job title. This enables users to see easily what training is required to allow movement from one position to another.

Unlike a generic questionnaire such as the PAQ, no two task inventories are the same, and jobs from different occupational fields cannot be compared using this method.

Job element method   The job element method was developed by Ernest Primoff and colleagues for use by the US Office of Personnel Management. A job element is a combination of behaviour and the type of evidence used to indicate the occurrence of the behaviour. Primoff and Eyde (1988) give the example of a job element termed 'reliability', comprising the behaviour of acting in a dependable fashion, evidenced by punctuality, commendations for dependability and doing exactly what is required in the job. The element is reliability, and its components are sub-elements.

The special features of the job element method are the rating dimensions used and the formulae used to combine ratings. The job analyst asks a panel of SMEs to produce an initial set of job elements and sub-elements in terms of knowledges, skills, abilities and work habits that are significant for the job. The SMEs rate each element and sub-element on the following four scales: its importance for the work to be barely acceptable; its importance for selecting superior workers; the trouble likely if the element or sub-element is not used in selection; and how practical it is to expect applicants to have the element or sub-element (Primoff and Eyde, 1988). It can be seen from these scales that the job element method is primarily concerned with selection and worker characteristics.

Specified formulae are used to combine the ratings on the four scales into three measures, an 'item index', the 'total value' of the element and a 'training index'. The item index suggests the extent to which the element is of value in the content of a selection program, and the total value indicates the usefulness of the element or sub-element for differentiating the abilities of applicants. The training index indicates the value of ensuring that the element or sub-element is included and assessed in on-the-job training. Established cut-off scores on these dimensions are used to indicate various roles for the element or sub-element; for example, whether it is significant for ranking applicants, for training content, as a minimum requirement for screening out applicants or both as a significant ranking element and as a screen-out element.

The job element method of job analysis provides a good example of the characteristic data gathering technique traditionally used in job analysis; that is, the conscious opinions and introspections of subject matter experts. While SMEs do know more about the job than any job analyst could, there is cause for concern in the nature of opinion as a data source. Taylor, Gilbreth, and others who sought to conduct work study in a scientific manner would not have been satisfied with opinion as a source of data. In the job element method, opinion as a source of data is taken to the extreme. For example, SMEs provide ratings on whether it is practical to require applicants for all job openings to have a particular job element, or just for some job openings, or not to require it for any job openings (Primoff and Eyde, 1988). If very few applicants are likely to have the element it is not practical to require it in filling all job openings, but it may be practical to require it for some job openings. To make this judgement the SME must form an opinion regarding how likely it is that an applicant for the job would satisfy the job element concerned. That is, the SME is being used as a source of opinion-based data on the extent to which an element would be present in the job applicant population.

Critical incidents technique   The critical incidents technique (CIT) was originally developed by John Flanagan and others in studies for the US Army Air Forces towards the end of the Second World War. The method was reported by Flanagan (1954) as being used mainly for the purposes of job requirements specification, training needs assessment and performance appraisal, as well as providing useful information for the design of instruments and controls and their arrangement; for example, in the aircraft cockpit. The strength of the CIT is the production of very specific behavioural descriptions, sometimes thousands of them, which can then be categorized into types of related behaviours. The five steps of the CIT procedure are described below.

1   Determination of the general aim of the activity (job being studied).
2   Development of plans and specification for collecting factual incidents regarding the activity. (a) Decide who will be the *sources* of incidents. The sources should have substantial recent experience of observing incumbents in their work. (b) Decide how the data will be collected. Several options include individual interviews, workshop groups or distributed questionnaires. A further option is to provide respondents with a form on which to record incidents, one incident per form. The form can begin with a simple instruction such as the following, adapted from Flanagan (1954): 'Think of a time when you witnessed a subordinate (supervisor, fellow-worker, team member etc.) do something that was very helpful (effective) or very unhelpful (inef-

fective) in meeting the aim of the work.' This can be followed by a set of questions, with sufficient space to write a short answer to each question:

- What were the general circumstances leading up to the event?
- What did the person actually do?
- Why was this helpful (unhelpful)?
- What was the outcome of this action?
- What was the person's job title?
- How long had the person done this job?
- When did the incident happen?

If dimensions of performance or competence have been hypothesized before the incidents are collected, the respondents should be made familiar with the set of dimensions. An additional question on the form can ask the respondent to assign the incident to just one of the dimensions – for example, customer service – and to rate its effectiveness on that dimension on a numbered rating scale with ends labelled 'poor' and 'good'.

3   Collection of the data (the incident descriptions). (a) Ensure that the respondents share the job analyst's understanding of the general aim of the work activity being reported, and what the incident descriptions will be used for, and that the people described in the incidents remain strictly anonymous. (b) Ensure that the respondents understand what constitutes a well written incident description:

- It should be simple, describing a single incident.
- It should be written in active voice, describing what the incumbent did. (The incumbent is the subject of the sentence, and the verb is a behaviour by the incumbent.)
- The incident should make a significant contribution, either positively or negatively, to the general aim of the activity (this is what makes it critical).
- It should begin with a brief statement of the context of the incident.
- It should end with a brief statement of consequences of the behaviour.
- It is not judgemental. That is, there is no mention of underlying motives, attitudes or competencies.

To illustrate these principles, an example of a well written critical incident description adapted from Bownas and Bernardin (1988, p. 1121) is: 'The firefighter left the pumper in a low gear after stopping at the edge of a lake to draft water. When the firefighter engaged the pump and revved up the engine, the truck drove off the bank into 5 metres of water.' A poorly written version of this description might be: 'Because of the firefighter's careless actions, a pumper rolled off a lake bank into 5 metres of water'. (c) Keep a periodic running check on the number of new types of incidents appearing in reports. Stop collecting incidents when there have been no, or very few, new kinds of incidents among a substantial number of the most recently collected incidents.

4   Analysis of the data (categorization of incidents). The analysis of the data depends on whether dimensions of performance or competence are to be derived from the data themselves, or whether such dimensions have already been hypothesized and the incidents are simply to be used to provide behavioural anchors for points on these rating scales; for example, customer service. If the dimensions are to be derived from the data a content analysis is required. If the incident descriptions have been collected in computerized form – for example, on forms on an organizational intranet – or if they have been scanned in, it is possible to use statistical content analysis software to facilitate the analysis. The established manual method with written incident descriptions is to carry out initial sorting of the incidents into groups of apparently related incidents. The common theme identified in a group of incidents is then given a dimension name, and incidents representing points of differing effectiveness along the dimension are chosen as behavioural anchors.

5   Interpreting and reporting the requirements of the activity. In the taxonomy of job analysis methods, the CIT is behaviour-oriented, but very fine-grained. In Harvey's taxonomy, it is a very job-specific technique and does not allow comparison between jobs, as would be necessary, for example, for job evaluation and determination of pay levels. This is because the behavioural incident descriptions are so job-specific. Even if the emerging dimensions are relevant in more than one job (for example, 'courtesy to customers'), the behavioural descriptions that anchor the points on the scale are derived in a particular situational context under particular constraints, and do not generalize to other contexts.

Competency profiling   The competency approach to job analysis attempts to overcome a number of perceived problems associated with the measurement of performance predictors in organizational settings (McClelland, 1973; Boyatzis, 1982; Spencer, 1983). First, it attempts to get away from the notion of one underlying general intelligence factor predicting performance in all jobs, the level of which is relatively fixed from early adulthood. Second, it seeks to recognize cultural influences on selection by acknowledging that competence can arise from many different sources, can be developed and does not depend on cultural or group membership. Third, the method tries to overcome bias in criterion measurement by creating performance dimensions using performance analysis. Typically, the competency approach to job analysis involves the following stages (Spencer, 1983; Hooghiemstra, 1992):

1   Establishing the criteria of performance effectiveness.
2   Selecting a criterion sample.
3   Task/function analysis.

Table 3.2 Summary of management competency model from Boyatzis

Cluster	Competency	Threshold competency
Goal and action management cluster	Concern with impact (skill, motive) Diagnostic use of concepts (skill, social role) Efficiency orientation (skill, motive, social role) Proactivity (skill, social role)	
Leadership cluster	Conceptualization[a] (skill) Self-confidence (skill, social role) Use of oral presentations (skill, social role)	Logical thought (skill, social role)
Human resource management cluster	Managing group process[a] (skill) Use of socialized power (skill, social role)	Accurate self-assessment (skill) Positive regard[b] (skill)
Directing subordinates cluster		Developing others (skill, social role) Spontaneity (skill) Use of unilateral power (skill, social role)
Focus on others cluster	Perceptual objectivity (skill) Self-control[c] (trait) Stamina and adaptability (trait)	
Specialized Knowledge		Specialized knowledge (social role)

Items in parentheses indicate levels of competency for which empirical support was found.
[a] Supported as a competency at middle and executive level management jobs only.
[b] Supported as a competency at middle level management jobs only.
[c] Supported as a competency at entry level management jobs only.

4 Performance characteristics analysis.
5 Behavioural event interviews.
6 Data analysis and creation of the 'competency model'.
7 Validation.

Boyatzis's original work on managerial competencies provides an example of a competency model and is shown in summary in table 3.2 (Boyatzis, 1982). The model identifies 21 basic competencies in managerial work, and these are grouped together into clusters of related competencies. The first three clusters, 'goal and action management', 'leadership' and 'human resource management', are the most important for the management role in Boyatzis's model.

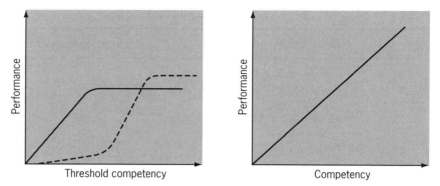

Figure 3.3 Schematic representation of the relationship between the level of a competency and performance. The left-hand panel is for a threshold competency, the right-hand panel for those competencies that are predictive of superior performance.

Some of the competencies are designated as 'threshold' competencies. A person must have a certain level of a threshold competency to perform the job at all at an acceptable standard, but beyond that certain level, having more of the competency does not help performance. Figure 3.3 is a schematic representation of the relationship between the level of a threshold competency and performance, as compared to the relationship for those competencies that are predictive of superior performance. The threshold competencies are those for which Boyatzis was not able to find a causal relationship to superior performance.

We have not yet provided a formal definition of the word 'competency', the central construct of this method. Defining this construct is fraught with difficulties, as the competency movement has been developing along several fronts. In a report of their 1993 survey of business in Britain, Human Resources Business Consultants and Industrial Relations Services (1993) noted that there seemed to be a 'UK model' and an 'American model'.

Rutherford (1995, p. 6), in Australia, has defined competency as 'job-related performance in its widest sense'. Boyatzis (1982, p. 21) gave the following definition: 'A job competency is an underlying characteristic of a person that results in effective and/or superior performance in a job.' This distinction between competence as performance itself and competence as an underlying characteristic that enables performance to occur is at the heart of the apparent emergence of dual approaches. It appears that for technical and trade types of vocational training, and the extensive educational applications of competency methods, the performance view is taken, with strict criterion sampling and assessment of objectively observable behaviours representing competent performance. For managerial and professional level applications of competency methods, following Boyatzis (the American model), underlying characteristics are sought, perhaps because the managerial role is seen as inherently flexible and unpredictable, and it is much more difficult to develop an adequately representative sample of criterion behaviours for managerial work.

In the 'underlying characteristic' approach the competency does not have to be an innate characteristic like a personality trait; it can be learned, such as a body of knowledge or skills, or a particular social role. Because of this generic nature the competency is not observable directly, it 'underlies' the observable behaviours, which may be quite different in different situations. Because the competencies cannot be observed directly in this approach, we have to develop test items or simulations to assess the level of the competency indirectly, through the performance of situation-specific behaviours that we infer would follow from the competency.

McClelland (1973, p. 2) noted the psychologist's 'in' joke that intelligence is what intelligence tests measure. This is a joke partly because it takes operationalism (as a way of defining constructs) to absurdity, and partly because it shows up just how difficult it is to define psychological constructs such as intelligence. At the risk of being flippant, Boyatzis's definition also lends itself to parody: 'Competency is that which leads to superior performance.' This brings home to us very clearly the advance due to the competency movement, for superior performance *is* the criterion, while performance on an intelligence test is not. It also heralds a warning that the competency approach will maintain this advantage only while performance itself remains the criterion. When measures of the possession of competencies stand in place of the criterion – for example, when 'underlying' competencies are the basis of 'person measures' in performance appraisal – there is substantial danger of drift into the realms of the underlying characteristic, such as accurate empathy or political sensitivity.

The competency approach has been very widely adopted in countries such as Australia, especially where job analysis intersects with organized education and training systems. For example, in Australia it is the method adopted by the National Training Board when determining competency standards for technical and professional qualifications. In the UK the competency approach has been used in both the National Vocational Qualifications and the Management Charter Initiative standards programmes.

The competency approach is very much a worker-oriented job analysis method, directed particularly towards selection, training and development, and performance appraisal (measured through person characteristics) system development. At the initial stage of criterion sampling this method describes the job, but at the final stage of derived competencies it does not describe the job at all. The method specializes in the derivation of KSAs as competencies, the job specification component of job analysis. As such, it is not particularly suitable for job design purposes, except in so far as it assists in analysing the skill variety provided in a job, and provides information that can be used in aspects of job redesign such as multi-skilling.

Job Analysis and Job Design

Consider the problem we raised at the outset. Conventional job analysis techniques, such as those listed above, would tell you the nature of the tasks performed by the telephone operators and/or the KSAs needed to perform those tasks, but one is left to make inferences about the relationship between those job and worker attributes and the performance problems being experienced. Is the poor performance due to a lack of appropriate training on the tasks, or is it in fact because operators find the nature of the job highly repetitive and stressful? If the latter, how might we reconfigure the tasks and responsibilities within the operator jobs to improve overall performance? Most of the techniques described above, such as the CIT, are procedures without an underlying theory of what causes performance. Job analysis methods generally are devoid of theory (unless we consider that the whole structure of characteristics rated and checked off in methods such as the PAQ and functional job analysis form a theory of the types of dimensions that contribute to work). However, there are methods which are derived from specific theories of work motivation and performance. An example of one of these is the job diagnostic survey (JDS) (Hackman and Oldham, 1975).

The JDS does not tackle the description of tasks, or the derivation of knowledge, skills and abilities; it is concerned with what Schneider and Schmitt (1986) have referred to as the reward aspects of tasks rather than with the job requirements. The JDS is designed to be used as a diagnostic tool for studying jobs that are being considered for work redesign (Hackman and Oldham, 1975; Kulik and Oldham, 1988). Thus it gathers information regarding aspects of the design of work. The JDS is based on the job characteristics model of work motivation (Hackman and Oldham, 1976), and the information it collects describes the job in terms of five 'core' job characteristics:

- *Skill variety*: the degree to which the job requires use of a number of different skills.
- *Task identity*: the degree to which the job entails completing a complete and identifiable piece of work.
- *Task significance*: the extent to which the job makes an impact, either internal or external to the organization.
- *Autonomy*: the degree to which the job provides the freedom to exercise choice and discretion.
- *Feedback*: the degree to which the job itself generates performance feedback.

The job characteristics model proposes a relationship between these core job characteristics and outcomes, namely work motivation, job satisfaction and work effectiveness, moderated by the individual characteristics of job knowledge and skill, growth need strength and satisfaction with the job context, including aspects such as supervision and pay and conditions. The JDS has been the subject of extensive research and some revision over more than two decades (Idaszak and Drasgow, 1987; Kulik, Oldham and Langer, 1988; Oldham, 1996; see also chapter 13, this volume).

In the case of the telephone operators, the application of the JDS indicated very low levels of autonomy and skill variety relative to occupational norms. Work redesign, which combined sets of tasks into the one job (multi-skilling), which reduced the degree of external supervision and pacing and which organized these jobs into self-managing teams, was successful in reducing absenteeism and turnover, increasing job satisfaction and bringing system performance up to acceptable levels.

Another job analysis technique which has been developed for use for job redesign purposes is sociotechnical systems (STS) analysis (Pasmore, 1988). The primary aim of STS theory is to achieve an optimal balance between the inherent requirements of social and technical sub-systems in an organization (Parker and Wall, 1998). STS analysts analyse the technical system (tasks and technology) in terms of 'key variances': elements of the operating system that have a significant impact on overall performance if not effectively controlled. Social system requirements are analysed in terms of a set of criteria (Cherns, 1976) which parallel those assessed within the job characteristics model.

Finally, Wall and his colleagues at Sheffield University have argued that the range of job characteristics assessed by both job characteristics and STS approaches does not adequately encapsulate psychologically salient aspects of contemporary manufacturing jobs (Jackson, Wall, Martin and Davids, 1993; Wall, Jackson and Mullarkey, 1995). They have developed a set of new measures to assess, additional aspects of job content, such as attentional demands (the requirement for passive monitoring), problem-solving demands (the requirement to solve complex operating problems) and production responsibility (the financial impact of an error).

Campion (1994) has argued that job analysis should always include measurement of aspects of the design of the job. He and his researchers have developed a multidisciplinary approach to analysing job design that considers motivational, mechanistic, biological and perceptual/motor determinants of human performance, and an accompanying job analysis instrument, the multi-method job design questionnaire (MJDQ) (Campion and Thayer, 1985; Campion, 1988, 1989; Campion and McClelland, 1991, 1993). According to this approach, different aspects of the design of jobs measured by the MJDQ will predict different outcomes, such as employee satisfaction, efficiency and comfort (Oldham, 1996).

Validity and Job Analysis

Strictly speaking, it is not appropriate to speak of the 'validity' of job analysis. Rather, job analysis plays an important, perhaps central, role in establishing the validity of inferences made concerning practices such as the use of selection tests, or performance appraisal instruments that are designed on the basis of job analysis. Job analysis itself is descriptive, while validity concerns the degree to which available evidence supports inferences made. Typically, this definition of validity refers to inferences made on the basis of a selection measure (Gatewood and Feild, 1994), but it applies equally well to the making of inferences about other practices in human resource management.

Morgeson and Campion (1997) reviewed the sources of inaccuracy in job analysis, and Landy (1989, 1993) has categorized factors that can affect the results of a job analysis as demographic, process and individual differences.

Demographic factors should be considered with regard to sources of job information; for example, when composing a sample of SMEs. Among the demographic factors, race, gender and work experience have been shown to have some small effects in research studies (Schmitt and Cohen, 1989; Landy and Vasey, 1991). This highlights the need to use representative stratified samples of SMEs, and to consider the work groups at whom the job analysis is aimed. For example, in a typical job analysis using any of the techniques we have described, a small sample of highly experienced SMEs is often called for. In the police context studied by Landy and Vasey, such a panel reporting on their own jobs would be likely to under-represent the mundane activities typically assigned to less experienced police officers.

The process factors identified by Landy (1993) largely concerned influences on, and of, the motivation of SMEs to provide information that is reliable, and either biased or not biased. SME information could be biased for at least two reasons. First, most job incumbents probably tend towards an enhanced view of the importance of their jobs, relative to the views of others such as supervisors and managers. This helps to support self-esteem, and if they did not view their jobs as important they would probably have low job satisfaction. Second, job analyses are often carried out because job classifications are being re-examined or reviewed in an organization. SMEs who are incumbents may have a vested interest in making the jobs appear more important and more complex than they really are. Nevertheless, if SMEs' information is going to be doubted, the grounds for suspicion must be very well founded indeed. Motivation to produce quality job information can also depend on involvement in the job analysis process. To maintain the credibility of the job analysis and the positive cooperation of SMEs, Landy (1993) has suggested a number of essential features of the job analysis process, which are:

- instrument development should be thorough and complete;
- pilot test at least once, or with several waves of SMEs;
- make it user-friendly;
- motivate SMEs by giving them 'ownership' of the job analysis outcome;
- give them clear training and instructions, examples and some practice;
- let them be anonymous;

• gather ratings in small groups on company time, but mutually convenient for them.

Finally, individual differences may affect the results of a job analysis, especially in methods where very small numbers of SMEs are used, such as the PAQ. People do have different preferences in their work – they like different things about it, they do it slightly differently, and so they may describe it differently too. For example, Sanchez, Zamora and Viswesvaran (1997) have shown that the difference in JDS ratings between incumbents and non-incumbents was affected by the complexity of the job being rated and also by the job satisfaction of the incumbents.

The Future for Job Analysis Research and Practice

Changes to the world of work brought about by the rapid influx of information technologies, competitive pressures and globalization have caused some commentators to question the need for job analysis in the future. Critics such as Risher (1997) argue that the notion of 'the job' encourages an inflexible and static view of work that is incompatible with the need for flexibility in the utilization of human resources and the rate of task and technological change within contemporary work organizations. Others have argued that, while there is a need for job analysis techniques to become more strategically focused and adaptable (Schneider and Konz, 1989), the need to back up human resource decisions with valid and reliable information is paramount. In our view, the latter view seems sensible and likely to prevail in the long run. The telephone operators' case with which we began this chapter is an example of change without consideration of job design leading to performance problems: problems that could only be solved by job analysis and job design.

Chapter Summary

In this chapter we have considered job analysis as the foundation stone of human resource activities, from human resource planning to selection, performance management, training and compensation. The theme throughout has been that the efficient utilization of human resources requires jobs to be designed to maximize performance, while at the same time enhancing rather than damaging the employee. If this design and ongoing redesign of jobs is to place them at the ever-advancing frontier of performance, it must be based on informed decision-making, not fashion, fad or guesswork. The source of the information used in all these decisions is job analysis.

Discussion Points

1   Is job analysis really necessary?

2   How can a job analysis project contribute when an organization is undergoing change and is expected to change even more in the future?

3   Jobs have been broad-banded in many areas and work roles for individuals are now seen as flexible and dynamic. How can job analysis be applied in this situation?

4   What is the difference between job-oriented and worker-oriented methods of job analysis, and why does this matter?

5   If jobs have disappeared and in many organizations the team is now seen as the basic unit that carries out work, is job design important any more?

6   What symptoms would suggest that the structure of tasks, skills and resources available to individuals (or teams) does not allow them to meet their objectives (e.g. resolve customers' complaints, or meet quality and delivery specifications)? What action would you take if presented with these symptoms?

Key Studies

Harvey, R. J. (1991) Job analysis. In M. D. Dunnette and L. M. Hough (eds), *Handbook of Industrial and Organizational Psychology, volume 2*, 2nd edn. Palo Alto, CA: Consulting Psychologists Press, pp. 71–163.

Wall, T. D. and Jackson, P. R. (1995) New manufacturing initiatives and shopfloor job design. In A. Howard (ed.), *The Changing Nature of Work*. San Francisco: Jossey Bass, pp. 139–74.

Further Reading

Gael, S. (ed.) (1988) *The Job Analysis Handbook for Business, Industry, and Government, volumes 1 and 2*. New York: John Wiley & Sons.

Fine, S. A. and Getkate, M. (1995) *Benchmark Tasks for Job Analysis: a Guide for Functional Job Analysis (FJA) Scales*. Mahwah, NJ: Lawrence Erlbaum Associates.

Kirwan, B. and Ainsworth, L. K. (1992) *A Guide to Task Analysis*. London: Taylor & Francis.

CHAPTER FOUR

PERSONNEL SELECTION

Neil Anderson and Nicole Cunningham-Snell

Contents

Few topics in European or North American work and organizational (W/O) psychology have received such a substantial volume of pure and applied research, while simultaneously representing such a mature industry of consultancy and professional practice, as employee *recruitment* and *selection*. Indeed, staff selection is the cornerstone of many in-house W/O psychology sections, and it is nowadays rare to find an independent consultancy firm that does not offer selection expertise as a core competence to potential clients. Underpinning the consultancy industry, there lies a highly developed and sophisticated body of research which has expanded rapidly over several decades. Indeed, the published literature is now vast, spanning a range of topics from personnel resource planning, to the accuracy of alternative selection procedures, to selection systems design, to the psychological and behavioural impact of recruitment procedures upon candidates.

The sheer scale of this research base means that any introductory chapter can realistically provide only a selective overview of the major research findings and the crucial trends in the professional practice of employee selection. Nevertheless, the synergy between robust research and effective practice in selection is emphasized throughout this chapter. To illustrate the dynamics of the selection process as experienced by both organizational recruiters and applicants, we have used a 'rolling' case study which develops over the chapter in line with our coverage of different aspects of the recruitment and selection process.

The structure of this chapter is as follows. In the first section we explore two different perspectives emphasized in the selection literature, the 'predictivist perspective', which exclusively examines organizational decision-making, and the 'constructivist perspective', which highlights the involvement of both the applicant and the organization in a bilateral decision-making process. Next, we discuss the 'systems view' of recruitment and selection to highlight the involvement of several stages in the process. The selection system commences with a recognition of the need for new staff and is completed by an estimation of decision-making accuracy which forms a feedback loop for improvements to be made to the system. Then we discuss a range of different selection methods and techniques (e.g. interviews, psychometric tests) and provide a review of research pertaining to the popularity and validity of each method. Finally, we explore the candidate's perspective in selection and present a theoretical model which highlights the impact of candidates' perceptions of selection fairness on candidates' attitudes, behaviours and self-perceptions.

Perspectives on Selection

While North American industrial/organizational (I/O) psychology has tended to emphasize almost exclusively the organizational perspective in selection decision-making, European W/O psychology has been more eclectic in its concerns over both organizational and candidate decisions which emerge from the selection process (e.g. Ostroff and Rothausen, 1996; Herriot and Anderson, 1997; Borman, Hanson and Hedge, 1997). The North American *predictivist perspective* has dominated this area for many years (see, for instance, Schmitt, 1976; Smith and Robertson, 1993), with thousands of published studies having adopted this perspective. More recently, acknowledgement has been given to the importance of the European approach, perhaps best termed the *constructivist perspective* (e.g. Herriot, 1989; Schuler, 1993; Iles and Robertson, 1997). We are not of course suggesting that each perspective is mutually exclusive and wholly attributable to either continent; indeed, there are overlaps between the two, as evidenced by authors researching on either continent adopting a more pronounced predicitivist or constructivist approach (e.g. Gilliland, 1993; Rynes, 1993; Salgado, 1997). But, before we turn our attention to the processes and methods of selection, it is important to consider these perspectives, especially in the light of changing work design and job role requirements.

The predictivist perspective

In essence the predictivist perspective views the job as a given and stable entity into which the most suitable candidate needs to be recruited *Person-job fit* is therefore of primary importance (e.g. Cook, 1993). In this viewpoint the recruiter is responsible for a series of actions put forward in most traditional predictivist selection textbooks:

1 *Job analysis*: conduct a detailed and comprehensive job analysis in order to establish the task and activities which comprise it.
2 *Person specification*: translate the findings of the analysis into a schedule of the skills, knowledge, abilities and other factors (SKAOs) needed by the person to perform the job effectively.
3 *Selection criteria*: from the job analysis and person specification establish discrete criteria for the selection process against which to screen applicants.
4 *Recruitment*: advertise in appropriate media and pre-screen applicants to reduce numbers down to manageable proportions.
5 *Selection*: choose between candidates by use of assessment methods such as psychometric tests, interviews, assessment centres.

From the predictivist perspective, since the number of applicants usually exceeds the number of job vacancies (and sometimes far exceeds, depending on the labour market conditions), it is the recruiting organization which is seen as making the vital decisions of whom to shortlist, and eventually whom to appoint (e.g. Smith and Robertson, 1993). Selection methods are therefore referred to as 'predictors', with the more accurate methods accounting for future job performance more fully than less accurate predictors. The applicant is seen as 'subject' to selection methods for which control is vested squarely in the hands of the organization (e.g. Anderson, 1992). Recently, however, doubts have been expressed over the ongoing viability of this perspective given widespread changes towards flexible forms of working and team-based work roles. These changes in job design have swept away many stable, specialized jobs, the specialization of which was the *sine qua non* of person–job fit in the predictivist perspective (Cascio, 1995; Herriot and Anderson, 1997).

The constructivist perspective

As job roles become more flexible and as organisations become increasingly aware of the need to compete for the best candidates (Murphy, 1986), selection research from the constructivist perspective has gained momentum. This perspective emphasizes that candidates, as well as organizations, make decisions in selection. Several European authors have highlighted how, during selection, expectations of the organization and the potential employee build up and both sides use their meetings during the process to construct a 'viable psychological contract' (Herriot, 1989) which underpins their future working relationship (Anderson and Shackleton, 1993; Dachler, 1994). The psychological contract has been defined by Kotter (1973, p. 92) as 'an implicit contract between an individual and his [or her] organization which specifies what each expect to give and receive from each other in their relationship' The constructivist perspective views selection as a series of social episodes providing an opportunity for both parties to explore whether a future working relationship would be viable. Selection therefore serves as an opportunity for information exchange and the development of mutual expectations and obligations (Herriot, 1989). Hence, from this perspective, selection aims to ensure not only person–job fit but also *person–organization fit* (that is, the fit between the applicant's values and organizational culture) and *person–team fit* (that is, the fit between the applicant's skills and attitudes and the climate of the immediate working group).

The constructivist perspective also acknowledges that selection is not an isolated activity, but the first of possibly several encounters between the individual and the organization. For applicants who accept an offer of employment, interactions with the organization during selection will be the starting phase of their working relationship. In particular, selection methods may influence the socialization process, which concerns the period during which new employees adjust to and become integrated into the organization. For example, interactions between the applicant and organization during selection

Table 4.1 Key elements of the predictivist and constructivist perspectives

	Predictivist perspective	*Constructivist perspective*
Primary focus	Organizational decision-making between numerous candidates Person–job fit	Organizational and candidate decision-making Construction of a viable psychological contract Person–team and person–organization fit
Selection methods	As 'predictors' of future job performance As information elicitation techniques applied to applicants As representative samples of behaviour	As social episodes As opportunities for information exchange As 'socialization impact' upon applicants
Selection decision	Unilateral, made by the organization upon candidates Primarily as (numeric) predictors of subsequent job performance	Socially negotiated, each party deciding whether to continue the relationship further The 'tip of the iceberg' concealing complex social and psychological processes 'under the surface'.
Seminal references	Schmitt et al. (1984) Schmidt et al. (1992) Guion (1997)	Herriot (1989) Rynes (1993) Anderson and Ostroff (1997)

may affect the applicants' initial expectations and attitudes about the organization. The extent to which these expectations are confirmed will influence the adjustment of the new employee during socialization. This has been termed the *socialization impact* of selection (Anderson and Ostroff, 1997).

To summarize both the predictivist and constructivist perspectives, table 4.1 provides a comparison of the key elements of each perspective.

The Recruitment and Selection Process

An important characteristic of most recruitment and selection procedures is that they involve several stages that occur over time. The process usually includes an initial recognition of the need for new staff, then recruitment advertising, followed by pre-screening applicants, then final selection decisions and induction of new employees into the organization. This systems view is generally based on the traditional predictivist perspective on selection. Figure

Pre-recruitment

The organization's perspective

David Henderson, Personnel Manager for Speedlink Stationery International, an office and stationery supplies company, is pleased with the outcome of the most recent personnel strategy and resourcing committee meeting. The company has agreed to his projected graduate recruitment targets for next year of a total intake of 50 graduates spread across the company's four main manufacturing and distribution sites in Europe – London, Rotterdam, Helsinki and Verona. It is planned that graduates will be recruited from all European countries, but that the selection process will be managed and conducted from the company's head office in London. David realizes from past experience that the company has tended to recruit mostly from the UK, but he is keen to ensure that the intake for this year meets the diversity targets of the company. The international language of the business is English, so all graduates will need to be fluent in English, plus one other relevant language. Beyond these initial rather hazy criteria, however, David Henderson has yet to finalize and agree precisely the qualities in graduate recruits that the company is looking for. Moreover, he has yet to agree a Europe-wide advertising strategy, a list of target university courses from which to recruit, and exact details of how the selection process will be carried out over the coming months.

Issues to consider

1 How can David Henderson establish the skills, qualities and abilities needed by his company in graduate recruits?

2 What problems might the company face in recruiting across several countries in Europe?

4.1 illustrates the whole process by subdividing it into four phases of 'critical objectives', with 'key activities' within each phase.

Figure 4.1 is reasonably self-explanatory in terms of the critical objectives and key activities at each phase. The advantage of taking such a 'systems view' of selection is that it provides a holistic overview of the entire process (see Anderson and Shackleton, 1993; Smith and Robertson, 1993, for a more detailed discussion). The day-to-day mechanics of the process are not our principal concern here. More important is to note two pertinent issues: bilateral decision-making and *validation feedback loops*. First, decisions are made by both the recruiter and the candidate at several points in the process (see decision-making stages in figure 4.1), supporting the constructivist perspective that both parties make decisions over whether to accept a working relationship with each other. At the initial stage of any recruitment process, both the organization and the candidate will be considering possible employment options for the future. The first part of our 'rolling' case study introduces these choices and the main characters, to whom we return below.

Second, the systems view highlights the importance of the validation feedback loop. In larger-scale selection processes, where numerous recruitment

The applicant's perspective

Neeha Shahma, a final-year undergraduate on the honours degree course in Management and Modern Languages at Birmingham University in the UK, is pondering her future career options. Neeha has worked diligently over the four years of her degree, and she expects to obtain strong grades in her final examinations. Her course included a placement year of work experience to develop her spoken and written Italian language skills. She worked as an administrative assistant for a high-quality office furniture manufacturer in Rome and she gained wide-ranging experience of different aspects of the business as well as improving her

Italian to become completely fluent by the end of her placement. Neeha realizes that she now needs to firm up her career plans and has already booked an interview with the university careers officer to discuss her options. Fluent in English, Hindi and Italian, she feels that her language abilities may well be attractive to potential employers.

Issues to consider

1 How can Neeha Shahma establish which types of job would be most suitable for her as a first step on the career ladder?
2 Who could Neeha turn to for advise and guidance?

decisions are reached over a period of time, the crucial question from the organization's perspective is: 'How accurate are these decisions in selecting individuals who subsequently turn out to be effective job performers?' This question has driven much of the research from the psychometric perspective. Validation feedback loops recycle information on the effectiveness of selection decisions into the selection process at different stages in order to modify and improve the procedure. Selection accuracy can be determined by a *contingency table* and the *correlation coefficient* between selection ratings and subsequent job performance ratings. Having overviewed the main phases of the recruitment process, we now move on to describe the use of contingency tables and correlations in determining selection accuracy.

Contingency tables

Figure 4.2 illustrates the contingency table for a fairly typical selection scenario. The distribution of data points (marked by X's in the table) represents the cross-tabulation between individuals' selection rating and the evaluation of their subsequent job performance. Note that:

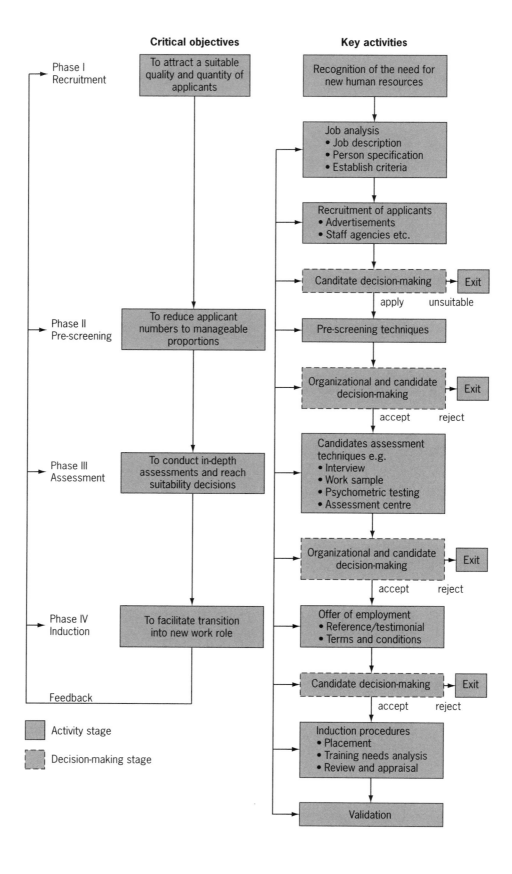

Critical objectives

Key activities

Phase I
Recruitment

To attract a suitable quality and quantity of applicants

Recognition of the need for new human resources

Job analysis
- Job description
- Person specification
- Establish criteria

Recruitment of applicants
- Advertisements
- Staff agencies etc.

Canditate decision-making → Exit

apply   unsuitable

Phase II
Pre-screening

To reduce applicant numbers to manageable proportions

Pre-screening techniques

Organizational and candidate decision-making → Exit

accept   reject

Phase III
Assessment

To conduct in-depth assessments and reach suitability decisions

Candidates assessment techniques e.g.
- Interview
- Work sample
- Psychometric testing
- Assessment centre

Organizational and candidate decision-making → Exit

accept   reject

Phase IV
Induction

To facilitate transition into new work role

Offer of employment
- Reference/testimonial
- Terms and conditions

Candidate decision-making → Exit

accept   reject

Feedback

Induction procedures
- Placement
- Training needs analysis
- Review and appraisal

Validation

Activity stage

Decision-making stage

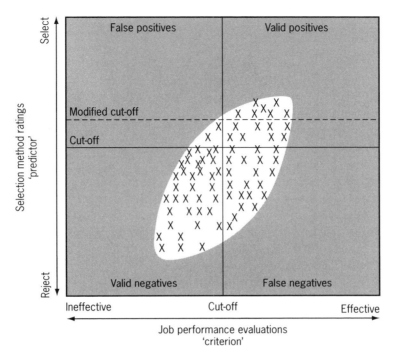

Figure 4.2 A typical contingency table.

- *valid positives* are individuals rated above the cut-off in selection who, it transpires subsequently, are rated as effective job performers (i.e. above cut-off);
- *valid negatives* are individuals rated below the cut-off in selection who, if they had been taken on, would have subsequently been rated as ineffective job performers (i.e. below cut-off);
- *false positives* are individuals rated above the cut-off in selection who, it transpires subsequently, are rated as ineffective job performers (i.e. below cut-off);
- *false negatives* are individuals rated below the cut-off in selection who, if they had been taken on, would have subsequently been rated as effective job performers (i.e. above cut-off).

Clearly, any organization seeks to minimize both false negatives and false positives while also maximizing valid positives and valid negatives. In reality,

◀

Figure 4.1 The recruitment and selection process.

Source: adapted from Anderson and Shackleton (1993).

it is the false positives who may be seen by recruiters to be most costly, as an organization actually employs these individuals, who, it transpires, do not perform the job to satisfactory standards. For false positives, then, the 'selection failure' is highly visible, whereas individuals in the false negative category have been rejected without having had the chance to prove that they could have been effective job performers. Theoretically, an organization could increase the selection method cut-off to the modified level shown in figure 4.2 in an attempt to eliminate all false positives. Unfortunately, as can be seen, this would have two deleterious effects: (a) rejecting a considerable number of valid positives, and (b) rendering only a very few individuals as acceptable ($n = 7$ individuals above the modified cut-off), hence risking not meeting recruitment targets. In practice it is rarely possible to eliminate all false negatives and false positives. It can be said, then, that selection is not an exact science but is more about maximizing correct outcome decisions (Cook, 1993).

Correlation coefficients

A more fine-tuned way of determining selection accuracy is by using the correlation coefficient. This is a statistical measure which assesses the association between two variables (symbolized as r) and ranges from $r = -1.00$ (perfect negative relationship) through $r = 0.00$ (no relationship) to $r = +1.00$ (perfect positive relationship). *Criterion-related validity* studies assess the magnitude of the correlation coefficient between the *predictor* in selection (e.g. psychological test score, interview rating) and the *criterion* (usually a rating of job or training performance) to determine decision-making accuracy. In the example from figure 4.2, the correlation coefficient between the selection method and subsequent job performance would be approximately $r = +0.3–0.4$. That is, applicants who obtain higher predictor ratings tend to obtain higher criterion scores, and, conversely, applicants with lower predictor ratings tend to have lower criterion scores. Of course, in principle, the closer the correlation coefficient to $r = +1.0$, the more accurate the selection method, but in reality it is unlikely to exceed $r = +0.5$ (see for instance, Smith and Robertson, 1993).

Criterion-related validity

The contingency table and correlation coefficient provide methods for determining the criterion-related validity of selection. Hence, criterion-related validity is concerned with the extent to which future performance on the job is predicted accurately at selection. Two main types of criterion-related validity can be distinguished: *concurrent validity* and *predictive validity* (see table 4.3). First, concurrent validation provides criterion-related validity results within a short timeframe by obtaining selection and criterion ratings from job incumbents already working for the organization. However, there are a number of disadvantages with this design: first, unlike job applicants, existing employees may be less motivated to give their best performance (Cronbach, 1970); second, existing employees represent a pre-selected group and are unlikely to represent accurately the potential applicants; third, unlike a group of applicants, job incumbents may obtain similar ratings on the predictor and criterion scores, since weak applicants would have been rejected and poor job performers would be unlikely to remain in the organization for any length of time. It is therefore likely that the scores from job incumbents will have a *restriction of range*; in other words, they will not represent the full spread of scores that might have been generated from candidates. The restriction of range lowers the magnitude of the correlation coefficient between predictor and criterion scores, but this can be corrected for by statistical procedures (see, for instance, Guion, 1997).

The second approach to criterion-related validity is predictive validation. This approach uses a longitudinal (over time) design by obtaining criterion ratings from successful candidates after a period of employment with the organization. However, in order to identify the true relationship between selection and job performance, measures are required from applicants with the full range of predictor scores. Clearly, though, few organizations are prepared to hire applicants with low predictor scores, so information is usually only available on a narrow band of candidates who score above the selection cut-off. Again, this results in a *restriction of range* in the distribution of predictor variables, which lowers the magnitude of the correlation coefficient. As with concurrent studies, this restriction of range can be corrected for by statistical procedures (see, for instance, Guion, 1997).

Meta-analysis and validity generalizations

A major methodological advance in criterion-related validity over the past two decades has been the refinement of *meta-analysis* and *validity generalization* techniques by American selection psychologists. Meta-analysis allows many individual validation studies reporting the correlation coefficient between selection method predictors and criterion ratings of work performance to be combined and summarized into a single overarching mean coefficient for the method (e.g. Hunter and Hunter, 1984; Schmitt, Gooding, Noe and Kirsch, 1984). This has permitted definitive evaluations of the predictive accuracy of different selection methods, in contemporary managerial terminology, 'to benchmark' methods against one another and a single organization's procedures against the mean coefficients reported in meta-analytic investigations (see also Murphy, 1997; Schmidt and Hunter, 1998). Below we explore and discuss the meta-analytic results for different selection methods.

The criterion problem

A final word of caution on criterion-related validity is required. Often it is problematic to obtain an unbiased rating of performance. A supervisor may, for example, be prone to various errors, such as personal-liking bias, or over-estimating performance when he or she was personally involved in the selection decision (known as *criterion contamination*). Moreover, for some types of job, objective and independent measures of performance are virtually impossible to obtain. This is especially the case for service-related jobs where no physical output is involved (e.g. social workers, police officers, university lecturers). Collectively, these difficulties are known as the 'criterion problem'. The crucial point to note is that 'measures' of performance will almost always be imperfect or biased in some way (e.g. Flatter, 1997b).

Choosing selection methods

When one is choosing between different selection methods, it is necessary to consider not only criterion-related validity, but also alternative forms of validity, *reliability* and potential *adverse impact*. Three additional types of validity should be examined: construct validity, content validity and face validity, as illustrated in table 4.2. First, an examination of construct validity is necessary, since many selection constructs are abstract (e.g. 'analytical ability') and can only be inferred indirectly from behaviour during selection techniques. Second, consideration should be given to content validity to ensure that the selection method adequately samples all the competencies required in the job. However, the flexibility and instability surrounding many contemporary job roles makes this requirement increasingly difficult to fulfil (Herriot and Anderson, 1997). Finally, face validity should also be examined; if applicants do not perceive the selection method to be relevant to the job then they may not perform at their optimum level. We return to the candidates' perspective below.

Another important requirement is that a selection method is reliable. *Reliability* is the extent to which the selection technique is consistent and free from random variation. Three approaches to measuring the reliability of a selection test are illustrated in table 4.2. In practice, though, there are difficulties associated with estimating reliability. Nevertheless, it is axiomatic that reliability is highly desirable and that an organization should be attempting to use selection methods which possess the highest level of reliability practicable.

Consideration must also be given to the potential *adverse impact* of selection techniques on minority groups protected by law. The negative consequences of adverse impact involve not only possible legal action, but also the failure to offer employment to candidates who will prove to be the more successful job performers. Across Europe, countries have different legal approaches to dealing with discrimination. For example, discrimination is

Table 4.2 Types of validity and reliability

1 *Predictive validity*: the extent to which selection scores predict future job performance. Successful applicants are tracked through the selection process and after a period of employment with the organisation, a subsequent measure of performance is obtained. The selection and criterion ratings are correlated.

2 *Concurrent validity*: the extent to which selection scores predict current performance. Selection techniques are administered to existing job incumbents and correlated with ratings of job performance taken over the same time period.

3 *Construct validity*: the extent to which selection accurately measures the constructs or dimensions it was designed to assess. The selection method is correlated with another method which is known to accurately reflect the construct.

4 *Content validity*: the extent to which the selection process adequately samples all the important dimensions of the job. This requires a thorough examination of the job description and job specification.

5 *Face validity*: the extent to which the applicant perceives the selection method to be relevant to the job.

6 *Parallel reliability*: the measurement consistency. Each candidate completes two equivalent selection methods and the two scores are correlated.

7 *Test–retest reliability*: the measurement consistency. Candidates complete the same selection method at two time points. The two scores are then correlated.

8 *Split-half reliability*: the measurement consistency. Items from a measure are divided into two halves (e.g. odd-numbered versus even-numbered items) and the scores from each half are correlated.

unlawful in the UK under the Sex Discrimination Act (1975), Race Relations Act (1976) and Disability Discrimination Act (1995), while the Netherlands does not have formal anti-discrimination legislation, but constitutional rights for the equal treatment of all persons on Dutch territory (Pearn, 1993).

Unfair discrimination may occur either directly or indirectly. *Direct discrimination* involves the conscious decision to reject certain applicants on the basis of irrelevant criteria, such as race or sex. *Indirect discrimination* is usually unintentional, arising when the selection method turns out to be favourable to one particular group, despite similar treatment for all groups. Anti-discrimination research has tended to define selection fairness within the predictivist framework, with fairness being measured statistically, as pertaining only to minority groups, purely in terms of the selection outcome and not the process (Arvey, 1992). Below we explore an alternative conceptualization of selection fairness, which considers the perceptions of all candidates and places greater emphasis on the candidate's perceptions of selection process fairness.

We have highlighted that a number of vitally important factors or contingencies should influence an organization's choice between different selection methods. Figure 4.3 summarizes the main contingencies, but also represents the trade-off that is so often observed between the more valid, reliable and

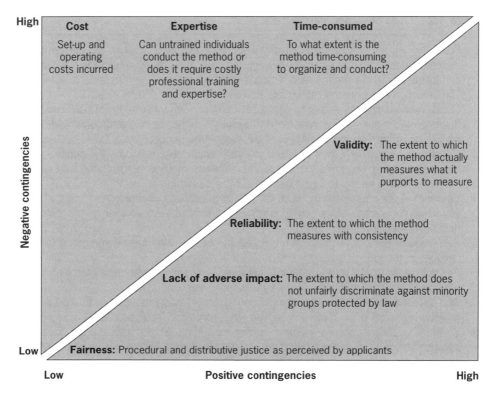

Figure 4.3   Contingency factors in selection method choice.

fair methods and their immediate cost, need for expertise and time-consuming administration. Before we turn our attention to different selection techniques, it is important to note that no method is 100 per cent accurate all the time. Choices therefore have to be made between efficacy and administration costs. However, the results from *utility analyses*, which estimate the financial payback of more accurate selection to an organization (Cronbach and Gleser, 1965), demonstrate that substantial financial gains accrue from the use of more valid and reliable methods (see Cook, 1993; Guion, 1997).

Figure 4.4   A comparison of predictive validity and popularity ratings for selection methods.

Predicitive accuracy figures use a correlation scale ranging from 0 (chance prediction) to 1.0 (perfect prediction). Results are based upon meta-analyses conducted by Reilly and Chao (1982), Hunter and Hunter (1984), Gaugler et al. (1987), Ones et al. (1993), McDaniel et al. (1994) and Schmitt et al. (1994).

Popularity figures are derived from Keenan (1995) for interviews, cognitive ability tests and personality tests, and from Shackleton and Newell (1991) for all other methods. Both surveys relate to British graduate and managerial selection practices among larger employers.

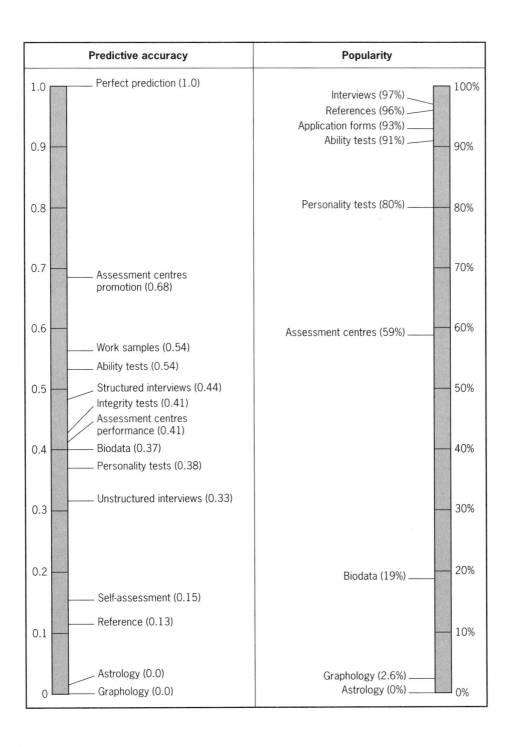

Predictive accuracy	Popularity
Perfect prediction (1.0) — 1.0	100%
	Interviews (97%)
	References (96%)
0.9	Application forms (93%)
	Ability tests (91%) — 90%
	Personality tests (80%) — 80%
0.8	
0.7	70%
Assessment centres promotion (0.68)	
0.6	Assessment centres (59%) — 60%
Work samples (0.54)	
Ability tests (0.54)	
0.5 — Structured interviews (0.44)	50%
Integrity tests (0.41)	
Assessment centres performance (0.41)	
0.4 — Biodata (0.37)	40%
Personality tests (0.38)	
Unstructured interviews (0.33)	
0.3	30%
0.2	Biodata (19%) — 20%
Self-assessment (0.15)	
Reference (0.13)	
0.1	10%
Astrology (0.0)	Graphology (2.6%)
0 — Graphology (0.0)	Astrology (0%) — 0%

Selection Methods and Techniques

Larger-scale surveys have shown that some selection methods are more popular than others in terms of their frequency of use by organizations (e.g. Shackleton and Newell, 1991, 1997; Keenan, 1995). The most widespread methods are interviews, references and the traditional application form. It is interesting to compare selection method popularity against predictive validity as indicated by meta-analytic studies. Figure 4.4 compares the findings of these two streams of research.

For some selection methods there is clearly a reasonable concordance between predictive validity and popularity (e.g. graphology and assessment centres). However, other methods would appear to be more popular than the predictive validity merits (e.g. unstructured interviews and references). Notably, references are used by 96 per cent of organizations in the UK, but their predictive validity is weak at $r = 0.13$. We now turn our attention more specifically towards exploring these different selection methods in turn.

Application forms, curricula vitae and biodata

Although application forms are very popular in the UK, there are cultural differences across Europe with standard application documents being more popular in Germany and curricula vitae being more prevalent in Denmark (Shackleton and Newell, 1997). Both these methods can be used to pre-screen applicants in order to generate a shortlist to be invited to the next stage. To facilitate effective pre-screening decision-making, an application form should ideally be designed according to the selection criteria and a systematic screening process adhered to. However, research into graduate recruitment suggests that the typical process is far from systematic (Wingrove, Glendinning and Herriot, 1984; Knights and Raffo, 1990), and this can clearly impact negatively on the selection process in the longer term (Keenan, 1997).

An alternative method for pre-screening is to use *biodata*. Biographical data include information about a person's past life and work experience and can be obtained from either the application form or a tailor-made biographical questionnaire. Identification of valid biodata predictors usually involves establishing significant correlations between biographical data and criterion measures for a group of job incumbents. The significant items are then used as criteria for future selection decisions. Confirmatory validation studies are required to ensure that valid biodata items for job incumbents are also valid for actual job applicants (Stokes, Hogan and Snell, 1993; Keenan, 1997), but the evidence suggests that biodata have a good level of criterion-related validity (Reilly and Chao, 1982; Hunter and Hunter, 1984; Schmitt et al., 1984). For example, in one meta-analysis which included 23 studies of biodata validity for different criterion measures (total $N = 10\,800$), Hunter and Hunter (1984) found that the average mean validity coefficient was 0.37. Despite their strong validity, biodata are rarely used. This is probably owing to the poor face validity of biodata, as items may have no obvious connection with the job. Indeed, a number of studies have noted that candidates react negatively to the use of biodata for selection purposes, as they doubt their accuracy and usefulness (Robertson, Iles, Gratton and Sharpley, 1991; Smither Reilly, Millsap, Pearlman and Stoffey, 1993; Stone and Jones, 1997). In addition, practitioners may have some concerns when using biodata as the extent to which applicants falsify biographical details remains unclear (Owens, 1976).

Realistic job previews

Realistic job previews (RJPs) provide applicants with literally a realistic preview of the job and sometimes the organization, so as to give a 'warts and all' picture of the vacancy being applied for (Wanous, Poland, Premack and Davies, 1992). RJPs therefore assist self-selection out of the process if applicants feel the job is unsuitable for them (Anderson and Ostroff, 1997). Traditional RJPs focus on the requirements and nature of the job and the company, but Schneider, Kristof-Brown, Goldstein and Smith (1997) recommend that future RJPs should also incorporate the firm's values to provide information on likely person–organization fit. The results from a meta-analysis which included 21 studies of RJP validity for eight different criterion measures (total $N = 6088$) found that the average mean validity coefficients ranged from 0.02 to 0.34 (Premack and Wanous, 1985). These findings indicated that RJPs tended to lower initial job expectations while increasing self-selection and job survival. However, research indicates that RJPs do not necessarily reduce absolute levels of labour turnover, but rather the rate at which turnover occurs (Dean and Wanous, 1984).

Interviews

The interview, in all its guises, remains the most popular method of candidate assessment across Europe (see figure 4.4 and Shackleton and Newell, 1997). Applicants also tend to rate the interview highly (e.g. Smither, Reilly, Millsap, Pearlman and Stoffey, 1993; Steiner and Gilliland, 1996). Recent meta-analyses have found that interviews, especially structured interviews, are considerably more valid and reliable than earlier discursive reviews had suggested (e.g. Huffcutt and Arthur, 1994; McDaniel, Whetzel, Schmidt and Maurer, 1994; Conway, Jako and Goodman, 1995). Indeed, it has become an unfortunate part of human resource management folklore that the interview is fundamentally flawed, but has to remain a component of any selection process simply because it provides the best opportunity for a face-to-face meeting

Case Study 4.2   The interview

The organization's perspective

David Henderson was tiring. Having sat on Speedlink Stationery's interview panel conducting graduate 'milk round' interviews over the past five days at the company's London offices, he had become so accustomed to the structured format that he could totally recite the standardized questions asked of all candidates in reverse order if so required. More to the point, his two line management colleagues on the interview panel had needed strict chairing throughout the interviewing process, as both had pronounced tendencies to stray away from the structured format. One in particular, Bill Ruff, the Director of Stationery Production, could not on occasions resist the temptation of asking candidates questions on their personal and family circumstances. This was especially unfortunate, David Henderson felt, given that the company had paid a firm of consultant chartered occupational psychologists a considerable sum to introduce a highly struc-

tured interview format. Still, he mused to himself, only one more candidate to see today and they would be finished. He glanced at the clock – 5.00 p.m. – settled back into his chair, composed himself and enquired of his fellow panel members whether they were ready for the last interviewee, a Neeha Shahma from Birmingham.

Issues to consider

1   Was David Henderson correct to commission a firm of occupational psychologists to develop a highly structured interview format?

2   If structure is a 'good thing' in terms of improving interview validity and reliability, can there be situations where structure is disadvantageous?

3   How should the chair of an interview panel deal with maverick interviewers who either:
(a) deviate from the standardized format;
(b) ask personal or intrusive questions?

between the organization and the applicant. This received wisdom is widely believed among personnel practitioners, but the unambiguous results of all the recent meta-analyses indicate that interviews can be as valid and reliable as other more costly selection methods (for a recent review see Anderson, 1997). In one meta-analysis which included 160 studies of interview validity (total N = 25 244), McDaniel et al. (1994) found that the average mean validity was 0.37 for all types of interview combined. But for structured interviews the average validity was 0.44, whereas for unstructured interviews this coefficient dropped to 0.33. Clearly, as is supported by numerous other studies and meta-analyses, structured interviews are more valid and reliable than unstructured interviews.

What exactly is meant by 'structure' in the selection interview? Structured interview designs usually incorporate several of the following elements:

- in-depth job analyses, commonly using critical incident techniques (see chapter 3);

The applicant's perspective

Neeha Shahma had tolerated the worst imaginable journey down from Birmingham to London: cancelled trains, delays on the underground and a map of the company's location so unintelligible that it may as well have shown the whereabouts of Speedlink Stationery's Verona offices! An interview at 5.00 p.m. in the midst of her end-of-first term examinations was an inconvenience she could really do without. Still, she resolved, the company had seemed impressive from their graduate recruitment brochure and Speedlink Stationery was one of her more preferred companies from the six others whom she had already been interviewed by.

The interview started off well – the usual polite introductions and then down to business. Obviously fairly well organized, she remembered thinking, in fact moderately impressive compared with other employers'

efforts. And then in stepped the Director of Production with all manner of intrusive questions about her willingness to travel (she had lived in Italy for a year after all), her family ties and, most intriguing, his comment that she spoke English with an 'unusually clear accent, considering'. The saving grace, she reassured herself, was the Personnel Manager's comment at the close of the interview that 'her personal circumstances would of course not be a factor in the selection decision'.

Issues to consider

1 If you were Neeha Shahma how would you interpret Bill Ruff's off-the-cuff questions?
2 Would you perceive any of Bill Ruff's questions as being discriminatory? If so, which of the following categories might his questions fall foul of equal opportunities legislation in: (a) racial discrimination; (b) sex discrimination?

- standardized questions asked in the same order of all candidates;
- candidates' replies rated on behaviourally anchored rating scales (BARS; see chapter 2);
- interviewer training to ensure that all interviewers understand and adhere to the standardized format;
- computation of the outcome evaluation via arithmetic combination of ratings on job-relevant dimensions.

Although structured interviews appear under a variety of names in industry (e.g. patterned behaviour description interviews, situational interviews, behavioural event interviews, multimodel interviews, all these formats contain several of the key elements listed above.

Paradoxically, one of the reasons why the interview remains so popular is that it offers a flexible and unstructured opportunity for recruiters and candidates to exchange information (Herriot, 1989; Dipboye, 1997b). Excessively structured designs, which allow absolutely no deviation from scripted questions or any *ad hoc* communication between the parties, have been criticized as being 'oral administrations of biodata items' (Herriot, 1989). It can also be difficult in practice to ensure that all interviewers stick to the 'script', as it were. The dilemma then is between maximizing predictive validity and simultaneously retaining sufficient flexibility. This has resulted in many organizations developing semi-structured formats which include elements of the highly structured approach but leave some free time for more open discussion (Anderson and Shackleton, 1993; Dipboye, 1997b). This format also helps to ensure that the candidate, as well as the interviewer, feels that he or she has gained useful information from the interview meeting.

To capture some of these issues, the second part of our 'rolling' case study explores the use of structured and semi-structured interviews as part of the selection process from both the organization's and the candidate's perspectives.

Cognitive ability tests

Psychometric tests are standardized measures designed to assess a specific construct, and can be divided into two main categories: cognitive ability tests and personality tests (e.g. Toplis, Dulewicz and Fletcher, 1997). Cognitive ability tests measure specific aptitudes or abilities, such as numerical, verbal or spatial ability, while personality tests measure personality dimensions such as conscientiousness or extroversion. For both categories, test administration is governed by fixed procedures and test results are typically interpreted by comparing an individual's score to data collected on previous samples who have taken the same test. There is variation across Europe in relation to the use of psychometrics, with Britain, Belgium and Portugal making more substantial use of both types than Germany or Italy (Shackleton and Newell, 1997). Candidates respond moderately well to cognitive tests (Steiner and Gilliland, 1996), but tend to rate tests with concrete items as more job-related than abstract tests (Smither et al., 1993). In a recent study involving undergraduates, the face validity of cognitive ability tests was found to affect test performance positively, but this effect was mediated by test-taking motivation (Chan, Schmitt, DeShon, Clause and Delbridge, 1997). Hence, organizations may generate higher performance from candidates by selection ability tests which have high face validity. In the UK, the British Psychological Society has published a series of independent authoritative reviews of tests in print which can assist recruiters in choosing between the ever-increasing number of tests on the market (Bartram, Anderson, Kellet, Lindley and Robertson, 1995; Bartram, Burke, Kandola, Lindley, Marshall and Rasch, 1997).

Cognitive ability tests are generally based around general mental ability, or 'g', and the results of meta-analyses have demonstrated good predictive validity for these tests (e.g. Hunter and Hunter, 1984; Levine, Spector, Menon, Narayanon and Canon-Bowers, 1996). For instance, Hunter and Hunter

(1984) found the average validity was $r = 0.54$ (see figure 4.4). In addition, cognitive ability tests are likely to predict success across a range of job types and in different organizational settings, providing evidence of validity generalization (Guion, 1997). However, progress in this area has been impeded by a lack of research in the development of cognitive ability tests which move beyond the classic model of intelligence (Landy, Shankster and Kohler, 1994).

Personality tests

The use of personality tests for selection has become increasingly popular in Britain (Keenan, 1995), although applicants tend to react somewhat less favourably to these tests than cognitive ability tests (e.g. Smither et al., 1993; Steiner and Gilliland, 1996). Research into the structure of personality has converged upon the *five factor model* (FFM) or 'big five' model of personality, incorporating the following factors (e.g. Tupes and Christal, 1992; Goldberg, 1993):

1   Neuroticism (insecure, anxious, depressed versus emotionally stable).
2   Extroversion (sociable, assertive versus timid and reserved).
3   Openness to experience (creative, curious, versus practical with narrow interests).
4   Agreeableness (likeable, cooperative versus antagonistic).
5   Conscientiousness (hard-working, dependable, versus lazy, disorganized).

Over the years numerous models of personality have been proposed by psychologists, and the question of how many dimensions are necessary for a model comprehensively and parsimoniously to represent personality across the entire range of individual differences has promoted near continuous research attention. Recent favouring of the FFM has been supported by compelling research findings, although there is an ongoing debate over its comprehensiveness (e.g. Hough, 1992; Cellar, Miller, Doverspike and Klawsky, 1996).

Early meta-analyses of personality tests reported relatively disappointing results. Schmitt et al. (1984) for example, examined validation studies from a variety of occupational groups and found the mean overall validity to be $r = 0.15$. More recent meta-analytic studies have provided more optimistic results by identifying the theoretical link between personality dimensions and effective job performance (e.g. Tett, Jackson and Rothstein, 1991; Robertson, 1993; Robertson and Kinder, 1993). For example, in a carefully conducted meta-analysis of 20 studies, Robertson and Kinder (1993) generated *a priori* hypotheses by asking practitioners to rate the predictive value of 30 personality scales for 12 criterion areas. By combining the personality scales hypothesized to correlate with each criterion, Robertson and Kinder (1993) produced better results than previous meta-analyses that averaged all scales. They found that uncorrected validity coefficients for half the criterion areas exceeded $r = 0.20$ and some exceeded $r = 0.33$. The highest values were for criteria such as creativity, analysis and judgement.

Nevertheless, these meta-analytic studies may underestimate the potential value of personality tests, since this research examines each selection method in isolation. Studies of *incremental validity*, however, examine the combination of methods in order to assess the unique or overlapping validity accounted for. More recent research suggests that personality tests may provide significant incremental validity above that provided by cognitive ability tests (e.g. McHenry, Hough, Toquam, Hanson and Ashworth, 1990; Robertson and Kinder, 1993). For example, in Robertson and Kinder's (1993) meta-analysis, they found only limited overlap between the criterion-related validity of cognitive ability tests and the validity associated with personality tests. That is, the personality test accounted for significant improvements in the criterion-related validity on several dimensions, beyond that provided by ability tests. In addition, other evidence suggests that personality tests can add incremental validity over assessment centres (see Goffin, Rothstein and Johnston, 1996). It would therefore appear that personality tests measure characteristics which are not replicated by other selection methods.

Integrity and honesty tests

Integrity and honesty tests are used to predict the likelihood that the individual will engage in counterproductive behaviour such as theft, violence, excessive absenteeism and dishonesty (Hogan and Brinkmeyer, 1997). Integrity tests are more popular in the USA than in most European countries (Iles and Robertson, 1997), although both US and French applicants have been found to react somewhat negatively to these tests (Steiner and Gilliland, 1996). Sackett, Burris and Callahan (1989) distinguish between overt integrity tests and personality-oriented tests; the former directly assess attitudes regarding dishonest behaviour, while the latter are personality-based and include questions on various dimensions, such as dependability, conscientiousness and social conformity. Meta-analytic studies provide quite positive results for integrity tests of both types. Ones, Viswesvaran and Schmidt (1993) conducted a meta-analysis and located 180 studies containing 665 coefficients. For studies involving a predictive validity strategy, an applicant sample and an external non-theft criterion (i.e. non-self ratings of all forms of counterproductive behaviour except theft, e.g. disciplinary action, absenteeism), Ones et al. found a mean corrected coefficient of 0.39 for overt tests (based on ten coefficients) and 0.29 for personality based tests (based on 62 coefficients). Sackett and Wanek (1996) suggest caution in using these figures to indicate that overt tests are a superior predictor of counterproductive behaviour. The two test types may relate differentially to different criteria; for example, the absenteeism criterion has been shown to have higher validity for personality tests. The representation of various types of non-theft criteria may therefore have influenced the meta-analytic results. Interestingly, the underlying personality dimensions measured by integrity tests appear to be linked not only to counterproductive behaviour but also to productive work behaviours (e.g. work performance: Sackett and Wanek, 1996). In their meta-analysis, Ones et al. (1993) examined 222 validity coefficients using overall performance as the criterion measure. The mean validity obtained was $r = 0.41$, with comparable results for overt tests and personality-based tests. However, there remains some scepticism about the validity of integrity testing owing to low correlations between different overt tests and concerns over the impact of publisher sponsorship of research upon published results (Sackett and Wanek, 1996).

Work samples

Work samples involve identifying tasks representative of the job and using these for pre-employment testing. For example, a typing test may be used as part of the selection process for a secretarial position. Not surprisingly, therefore, applicants rate work sample tests positively, perceiving them as fair, valid and job-related (e.g. Robertson and Kandola, 1982; Smither et al., 1993; Steiner and Gilliland, 1996). Work sample tests also have highly acceptable predictive validity. A meta-analysis by Hunter and Hunter (1984) identified the average mean validity coefficient as 0.54. Again, perhaps not surprisingly, rating the applicant actually performing key tasks is an accurate means of evaluating his or her subsequent performance in jobs which require little further training before proficiency can be achieved by the individual.

Assessment centres

Assessment centres (ACs) involve a combination of the selection methods already discussed, e.g. work samples, ability tests and interviews. These are given to a group of candidates over the course of a day, or several days. ACs usually involve a number of trained assessors who rate candidates' performance along identified selection dimensions. Organizations may use ACs for selection, promotion and development purposes (see chapter 6, this volume). Across Europe, there are wide differences in the use of ACs for selection; they are more common, particularly in large organizations, in the UK, Belgium, Denmark and Germany, and less common in France, Switzerland, Spain and Italy (Shackleton and Newell, 1997). Overall, applicants tend to favour ACs, probably because of their use of work sample tests and the opportunity that they provide to meet assessors and to perform job-related exercises alongside other candidates (Iles and Robertson, 1997).

The criterion-related validity of the AC is strong, although higher validities are observed when predicting potential rather than actual performance

(Hunter and Hunter, 1984; Gaugler, Rosenthal, Thornton and Bentson, 1987). In a meta-analysis by Gaugler et al. (1987), which included 12 validation studies of selection ACs (total $N = 3198$), the mean validity coefficients for selection was 0.41. When assessment centres are used for promotion purposes, the validity is somewhat higher (Gaugler et al., 1987: see figure 4.4).

None the less, it is not entirely clear why ACs have good criterion-related validity, since their *construct validity* is typically weak (e.g. Bycio, Alvares and Hahn, 1987; Robertson, Gratton and Sharpley, 1987; Schneider and Schmitt, 1992). Construct validity can be assessed by examining the *multitrait-multimethod matrix* (Campbell and Fiske, 1959). Figure 4.5 provides an example of a multitrait-multimethod matrix which displays the correlation coefficients for part of an AC involving two selection methods (work sample and group exercise) and three traits or dimensions (communication, analysis and achievement). Two critical aspects of construct validity are *convergent validity* and *discriminant validity*. Convergent validity is apparent if a measure of one construct correlates highly with other measures of the same construct (e.g. if high correlations are observed between measures of communication in the work sample and communication in the group exercise). Discriminant validity is apparent if measures of one construct do not correlate highly with measures of another construct (e.g. if the measure of communication in the work sample does not correlate highly with measures of analysis in the work sample or group exercise). As demonstrated in figure 4.5, research has consistently found that ACs have low convergent and discriminant validity; in fact, the correlations between dimensions within exercises are usually higher than the correlations for each single construct across exercises (e.g. Sackett and Dreher, 1982; Bycio et al., 1987; Robertson et al., 1987; Schneider and Schmitt, 1992).

This suggests that the dimensions being measured are not stable across exercises, or that assessors' ratings are influenced by a halo effect, whereby general evaluations, rather than distinct dimension evaluations, are made of candidates for each exercise. This poor construct validity is referred to as the *exercise effect*, since ACs appear to measure situationally determined behaviour and not the set of job-relevant constructs that they are designed to assess. Although research suggests that use of behavioural checklists or behaviourally anchored rating scales (see chapter 2) may improve AC construct validity, the improvement appears to be only moderate, leaving unanswered concerns over the real value of ACs in selection as they are a comparatively costly and time-consuming method (Woodruffe, 1997).

To illustrate some of the dynamics that may be present in a multi-day AC, our rolling case study highlights vividly that regardless of how sophisticated the organization's recruitment procedures are, at the end of the process, it is the successful candidate who actually makes the final decision of whether or not to accept or reject the offer of employment.

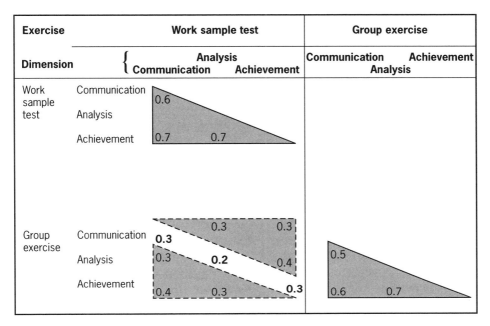

Figure 4.5 Part of a multitrait–multimethod matrix for an assessment centre with poor construct validity.

Bold values: the same dimension in different exercises. Continuous line triangle: different dimensions in the same exercise. Broken line triangle: different dimensions in different exercises.

References

References involve the assessment of an individual by a third party; for example, the applicant's previous employer. The use of references is more common in the UK, Ireland and Belgium than in France, Sweden, the Netherlands and Portugal (Shackleton and Newell, 1997). References may involve either an open-ended format or a structured format with questions developed from selection criteria. References may serve at least two purposes: first, to confirm the accuracy of information provided by the applicant; second, to obtain information on the applicant's previous work experience and performance (Smith and Robertson, 1993). However, the criterion-related validity evidence for references is poor (see figure 4.4), suggesting that not too much reliance should be placed upon their content. Indeed, research suggests that references suffer from leniency errors, with few applicants given negative evaluations (Browning, 1968). References are therefore rarely used in the decision-making process, but are more likely to be used merely as a final check before any job offer is made.

Case Study 4.3   The assessment centre (AC)

The organization's perspective

Another day, another international graduate assessment centre 'wash up' discussion, David Henderson thought to himself ruefully. As Personnel Manager he had been responsible for the smooth running of the AC, but fortunately the previous three days had progressed well and the assessors were now meeting to agree overall assessment ratings (OARs) on all ten candidates. David reflected to himself that the occupational psychology consultancy firm that had designed the AC had done a thorough job; his challenge now was to chair the discussion vigorously to keep the assessors to the rating pro forma developed by the consultancy to reach OAR by actuarial methods, and not to allow the discussion to degenerate into an opinionated free for all.

The problem, and David knew this only too well, was that certain assessors found the pro forma 'inhibiting', and they preferred instead to judge candidates 'holistically'. Moreover, as many assessors were line managers of graduate trainees, they could be influenced by feelings of personal preference for particular candidates. As one assessor had put it, 'I need to feel comfortable that I could have this person working for me.' On the upside, David was well aware that the company was perceived as an attentive employer by graduates – this year they had invited over 150 candidates to AC for the allotted 50 graduate vacancies.

Fortunately, the wash up session went according to Henderson's plan. Assessors used the rating proforma and its OARs calculation metric for all candidates. Of the ten seen that day, three could be made offers – one from Germany, one from the Netherlands, but their top-rated choice was a graduate in Management and Italian from Birmingham University, Neeha Shahma.

Issues to consider

1 Is the company correct to rely upon the rating pro forma using actuarial (i.e. statistical) calculation of the OAR rather than an open discussion (i.e. clinical judgement) among assessors?

2 Are the line managers who acted as assessors justified in being influenced by whether they would get on with graduate applicants?

3 If you were commissioned to validate the predictive validity of this AC, might there be some form of contamination between the AC ratings and subsequent performance ratings of line mangers and assessors? If so, how would you overcome such contamination?

4 How much has it cost the company to lose the top choice candidate, Neeha Shahma to their prime competitors?

Self-assessment

Self-assessment (SA) is an introspective self-evaluation made by a candidate of his or her own strengths and weaknesses in relation to a given job role. SA is rarely used in selection and perhaps rightly so, as SA in validation studies has provided inconsistent results (e.g. Byham, 1971; Schmitt, Ford and Stults, 1986). In a meta-analysis of three studies ($N = 545$) incorporating validity coefficients with overall performance criteria, Reilly and Chao (1982) found

The applicant's perspective

Neeha Shahma had already lost ten days of examination revision through attending ACs with potential employers. It was now early May and she was in two minds over whether even to attend the AC at Speedlink Stationery. She remembered the interview with them vividly, but persuaded herself that it was important to attend even at this late stage, despite knowing that she had already secured a formal job offer and was still awaiting the outcome of the other AC.

At the end of the Speedlink AC Neeha reflected that she had made the right decision to go along after all. It had been a useful experience and, luckily, the only assessor she recognized from her previous interview debacle was the Personnel Manager, David Henderson. Yet, despite a well run AC which appeared to be job-relevant, Neeha had persistent doubts over accepting a job offer, especially if she would be working for Bill Ruff, the Director of Production, who had asked such odd personal questions in the interview.

Some days later, Neeha received Speedlink Stationery's offer of employment as a graduate trainee based in their London office, but with some travel to the Verona plant involved. She now had three job offers, all from highly reputable multinational organizations, all looking for graduates who had work experience and language skills. Each job had its attractive points, but in the end Neeha decided to accept the offer by Office Solutions plc, Speedlink Stationery's principal competitor and arch rival in Europe. Although both companies' selection procedures were similar, Office Solutions offered a better training scheme and had treated her well throughout the entire selection process. Having reached her decision, Neeha began to write a courteous but firm letter of rejection to Speedlink Stationery.

Issues to consider

1 If you were in the same fortuitous position as Neeha Shahma in having three job offers, how would you decide which to accept?

2 Was Neeha correct to be so negatively influenced by Bill Ruff's questions at the earlier interview?

3 Is it common for graduates to experience notably similar selection procedures having applied to several organizations?

4 What sort of impressions of Speedlink Stationery do you feel Neeha will have formed as a result of her experience of the selection procedure?

the average weighted validity was 0.15. Problems associated with SA include leniency effect and poor reliability of ratings (see Smith and Robertson, 1993). However, more recently it has been shown that in comparison to assessor ratings, there are differences between the accuracy of SAs for successful and unsuccessful candidates, with the latter misjudging the effectiveness of their performance (Fletcher and Kerslake, 1992). This has led to the suggestion that the variability in SA accuracy between candidates can be used as an assessment dimension to predict subsequent job performance (Fletcher and Kerslake, 1992; Fletcher, 1997b).

Alternative methods: graphology and astrology

Graphology involves the interpretation of a sample of handwriting as a means of generating personality descriptions or behavioural predictions. This method is most common in French-speaking cultures (Shackleton and Newell, 1997). However, even French candidates tend to rate this method negatively (Steiner and Gilliland, 1996), and the predictive validity evidence is extremely weak (see figure 4.4). Astrology is another 'alternative' selection method, although it is very rarely used. Neither graphology nor astrology deserves to be part of any professionally respectable organization's selection procedures.

Theory versus practice in selection

It would be remiss of us in this review of selection methods not to draw attention to the gulf that still exists between research findings on the one side, and the practice of less informed organizations on the other. Having overviewed the key research findings, it is important to note that these have not necessarily been translated into common practice by organizations in their day-to-day selection procedures. Indeed, in some recalcitrant companies even the basic principles of effective selection systems remain conspicuous by their absence (Cook, 1993). Although surveys suggest that some elements of organizational selection procedures have improved (for instance, the use of psychometric testing is more widespread), other evidence is far less optimistic. Many organizations fail to conduct proper job analyses, rely solely upon totally unstructured interviews (Anderson and Shackleton, 1993), use inappropriate, or even misuse, psychometric tests (Toplis et al., 1997) or, perhaps most common of all, do not validate their selection procedures in order to verify effectiveness (Smith and Robertson, 1993; Anderson and Herriot, 1997).

The Candidate's Perspective in Selection

A recurrent theme in this chapter has been the acknowledgement of the increasing importance of the candidate's perspective in selection. Indeed, our rolling case study has highlighted that it is imperative to view the selection procedure as a two-sided decision-making process. Several studies have examined candidates' preferences for different selection methods, and these suggest that candidates prefer methods which appear to be more job-relevant (Robertson et al., 1991; Rynes, 1993), are non-intrusive (Ryan and Sackett, 1987), do not invade personal privacy and in general seem to be fair and objective (Rynes and Connerley, 1991).

More recently, a number of frameworks for examining the social issues involved in selection have emerged, providing more detailed insight into the aetiology of the applicant's perspective (e.g. Arvey and Sackett, 1993; Gilliland, 1993; Schuler, 1993). Gilliland's (1993) model is notable in moving beyond a list of the likely determinants of fairness perceptions, towards developing a framework that is rooted in organizational justice theory. Organizational justice theory distinguishes between *procedural justice* and *distributive justice.* Procedural justice refers to the fairness of the selection process and distributive justice refers to the fairness of the hiring decision (Gilliland, 1993). Gilliland suggests that it is the combined satisfaction or violation of specific rules which produces overall evaluations of procedural and distributive fairness. Procedural rules include the job-relatedness and consistency of selection methods, opportunity to perform, honesty in communication with the candidate, the interpersonal effectiveness of the recruiter, two-way communication and propriety of questions. Research indicates that candidates' reactions to selection justice can have an impact on three important outcomes (Gilliland, 1993). First, perceptions of justice influence applicants' reactions and decisions during hiring; for example, the extent to which the candidate will recommend the organization to others (Smither et al., 1993; Gilliland, 1994) and the decision on whether to pursue discrimination cases (Gilliland, 1993). Second, perceptions of fairness impinge upon candidates' attitudes and behaviours after hiring; for example, organizational commitment, intention to leave and work performance (Konovsky and Cropanzano, 1991; Robertson et al., 1991; Gilliland and Honig, 1994; Anderson and Ostroff, 1997). Third, perceived fairness influences applicants' self-perceptions, such as self-esteem and self-efficacy (Robertson and Smith, 1989; Gilliland, 1994).

While organizations may undermine the importance of the candidate's perspective, the evidence suggests that candidates' perceptions of selection not only affect their decision-making but also influence motivational factors and their attitude to the job and the organization (Cunningham-Snell, Fletcher, Anderson and Gibb, 1997). And, of course, if an organization goes through the whole selection process only to have its offers of employment turned down by its top choice candidates, this is far from a desirable outcome (Murphy, 1986). It is axiomatic, then, that applicants' reactions to selection should remain just as important a concern as validity, reliability or adverse impact (Iles and Robertson, 1997).

Chapter Summary

In this chapter, we have overviewed some of the critical theoretical approaches, design principles, research findings and practical ramifications of personnel selection. Although it is something of a 'whistle-stop tour', our intention throughout has been to provide an introduction to the fast-moving field of research and day-to-day applied practice which today constitutes recruitment and selection. We have explicitly emphasized a 'European' constructivist perspective by arguing that candidates, as well as organizations, reach decisions as a result of their experiences during selection. Ironically, by the time this introductory review is published it will be somewhat out-of-date; such is the pace and volume of current research and development in this area. Yet, despite this academic and consultancy-based research activity, some organizations remain blissfully unaware of the huge paybacks that can be gained from the application of modern, sophisticated selection system techniques. It is our hope that this chapter may stimulate readers to reconsider personnel selection in the light of these key research findings, and eventually to apply some of the principles of a systems approach to real life organizational selection procedures.

Key Studies

Personnel Psychology (1990) 43(2), Special issue. Project A, The US Army Selection and Classification Project.

Borman, W., Hanson, M. and Hedge, J. (1997) Personnel selection. *Annual Review of Psychology*, 48, 299–337.

Further Reading

General

Anderson, N. R. and Herriot, P. (eds) (1997) *International Handbook of Selection and Assessment*. Chichester: Wiley.

Cook, M. (1993) *Personnel Selection and Productivity*, 2nd edn. Chichester: Wiley.

Smith, M. and Robertson, I. T. (1993) *The Theory and Practice of Systematic Personnel Selection*, 2nd edn. London: Macmillan.

Specialized

Anderson, N. R. and Shackleton, V. J. (1993) *Successful Selection Interviewing*. Oxford: Blackwell.

Toplis, J., Dulewicz, V. and Fletcher, C. (1997) *Psychological Testing: a Manager's Guide*, 3rd edn. London: Institute of Personnel and Development.

Woodruffe, C. (1997) *Assessment Centres: Identifying and Developing Competence*. London: Institute of Personnel Management.

Key journals

International Journal of Selection and Assessment

Journal of Applied Psychology

Journal of Occupational and Organizational Psychology

Journal of Organizational Behavior

Personnel Psychology

CHAPTER FIVE

TRAINING

John Patrick

Contents

- Chapter Outline
- Definitions and Contexts of Training
- Rational Stages of Training Development
- Identifying Training Needs and Content
- Designing the Training
- Evaluating Training
- A Case Study of Training in the Steel Industry
- Chapter Summary
- Discussion Points
- Further Reading

Chapter Outline

This chapter outlines the development of training in a manner that generalizable beyond the context in which such training takes place. First, the rational stages of training development that are discernible from Instructional Systems Development models are described. Each of these stages – identifying training needs and content, designing the training and evaluating the training – is then discussed. A case study of training in the steel industry follows.

Training is an important part of the process of enabling individuals to perform the tasks and jobs created by society. The principles of good training practice are diffuse and derive from both cognitive (formerly experimental) psychology and occupational and organizational psychology. These two rather separate literatures complement each other and both are important to our understanding of how to develop training or instructional programmes. For example, a cognitive perspective emphasizes variables that determine learning and skill development, such as the role of practice with feedback, and principles that determine whether trainees transfer skills between tasks. However, a training programme that is well designed in terms of learning and transfer may fail if the training developer has not taken account of the wider organizational context within which training normally takes place. New training or professional development programmes involve organizational change that has to be managed carefully. Organizational issues often interact with, and influence, variables relating to a trainee's cognitive and motivational state with respect to future training. This chapter therefore attempts to integrate both perspectives in the discussion of training. The chapter is necessarily selective, and for a more extensive treatment the reader is referred to Goldstein (1993) and Patrick (1992).

Definitions and Contexts of Training

A simple definition of training, adapted from the Department of Employment's *Glossary of Training Terms* (1971, p. 29), is: 'The systematic development of the knowledge/skill/attitudes required by a person in order to perform effectively a given task or job.' Training is mostly concerned with improving the performance of personnel in job situations, although outside of work it might involve the development of skill for leisure pursuits, music, sport, information technology etc.

Training is a pervasive activity in society. It takes place within industry and commerce, government agencies and departments, health care organizations and all branches of the armed services. Within each organization, training embraces all levels of personnel, including operators, supervisors, administrative staff, sales personnel, researchers and management. Trainees may vary in terms of age, work experience, disability, educational background, ethnic origin and abilities. Therefore, training, as a set of principles concerning how to design and effect learning, has to embrace diverse training contexts, heterogeneous trainees and various skills.

The changing nature of work over the past fifty years has affected the type of task for which training is needed. In manufacturing industry there has been a shift away from perceptual motor tasks involving manual intervention, to more cognitive, supervisory tasks often requiring teamwork. This is partly due to the automation of many routine tasks; for example, sorting letters in the post office, heating and transporting materials in process control and, even, the landing of an aircraft. As Bainbridge (1987) points out, this is not without various ironies because eliminating the human from the performance of some tasks means that not only are those remaining more difficult, but their execution, often in emergency situations, is problematic because the human has to update his or her mental model of the situation before appropriate action can be taken. While increasingly complex technologies have forced workers to develop new skills, they have also offered the training developer the opportunity to employ these technologies in the design and delivery of better instruction; for example, interactive video and intelligent tutoring systems. With the widespread availability of computers, trainees no longer have to be trained at their place of work. Another trend is an increase in jobs in the service sector of industry, which means increased training in supervisory and customer relation skills (Thayer, 1997). Companies are becoming leaner as they enter more global markets and, with rapidly changing technology, many of them are using external consultants and training agencies to meet their training needs (Bassi et al., 1997).

Traditionally, training and education have been viewed as distinct. Glaser (1962) attempted to clarify this distinction by suggesting that training had more specific objectives and tried to minimize individual differences, in contrast to education, where objectives were more general and the aim was to maximize individual differences. However, the changing nature of jobs and advances in technology have made this distinction blurred today. On the one hand, educational curricula involve increasingly specific objectives in the attempt to standardize the scope of education and make it vocationally more relevant. On the other hand, training for complex tasks, such as nuclear power operation and air traffic control, may take many years and involve wide-ranging instruction. The term 'instruction' is a compromise term that is acceptable to both the training community and those involved in education. While the contexts of these two areas of instruction may differ, there are no fundamental differences in the theoretical principles underpinning instructional development.

Training is, or should be, a continuous process, for both individuals and organizations. In the armed services this is particularly necessary, given the constant changes in technology and personnel. In other organizations, while employees are given formal training, particularly at the onset of a new or changed job, engagement in other training or professional development activities is sometimes on a voluntary basis. In these situations, a trainee's values, perceptions and motivation will determine participation in voluntary learning or development activities. Maurer and Taruli (1994) found that aspects of the trainee's perceptions of the organizational environment and of the outcomes of the development activity affected voluntary participation. The former included whether the organization's policies and values were perceived as facilitating participation, and whether the company emphasized employee learning and development. In addition, if the trainee is involved in a mentoring relationship within an organization, this is likely to have a direct and indirect effect not only on the nature of any training undertaken but also on how the person perceives it. A mentor is defined as an experienced and more senior individual who can provide various forms of advice and support in order to advance his or her protégé's career and job performance (Kram, 1985). Therefore, a mentor can not only influence what further training and professional development a protégé undertakes but also provide some limited informal instruction.

Training can take place either on or off the job. Coaching on-the-job was originally termed 'Sitting by Nellie'. Its main drawback concerns timing and organizing the instruction during job performance in an effective manner. There may be limited opportunities, while carrying out a job, for adequate practice that is accompanied by good instructional support from the trainer. Training off-the-job provides the trainer with a better opportunity for organizing an effective instructional environment. How this might be achieved is discussed further in the section concerned with designing the training (pages 114–15).

Rational Stages of Training Development

A couple of decades ago, a great deal of effort was directed at specifying the *process* of training development in terms of the nature and sequence of stages that are involved. This was accomplished by adopting what is known as a systems perspective, in which training development is viewed as a system that performs a function and attempts to achieve a particular goal. This system can be broken down into constituent subsystems, their interrelationships and the different function each performs. Models of training development that adopt this perspective are known as Instructional Systems Development (ISD) models. Many different ISD models exist. Andrews and Goodson (1980) identified over sixty such models. One of the most well known is the IPISD model: Interservices Procedures for Instructional Systems Development (Branson et al., 1975). This was adopted by the different US armed services, since the process of training development was viewed as a common activity. The IPISD model divides training development into five main phases/subsystems, concerned with analysis of training needs, design, development, implementation

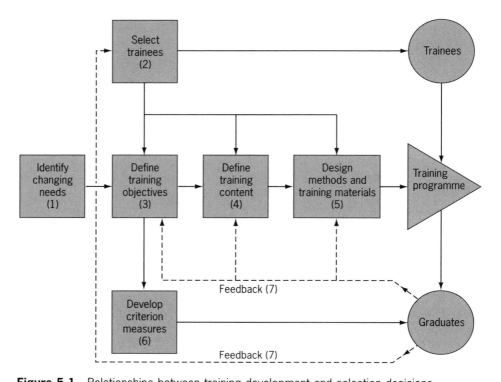

Figure 5.1   Relationships between training development and selection decisions.

Source: J. Patrick (1980) Job analysis, training and transferability: some theoretical and practical issues. In K. D. Duncan, M. M. Gruneberg and D. Wallis (eds), *Changes in Working Life*. New York: John Wiley and Sons, p. 59. Adapted from G. A. Eckstrand (1964) Current status of the technology of training. Technical report AMRL-TDR-64-86, Wright Patterson Aerospace.

of training and evaluation. Each of these is further subdivided, so that, in effect, the sequence and nature of the tasks involved in training development are made explicit.

One ISD model that is simpler than the IPISD model is represented in figure 5.1. This model also shows how the selection function can interact with different phases of training development. There is often a need to select for retraining, and the trade-off between selection and training is important. If trainees are to be selected for training, then it is necessary to estimate their 'transferability' to the new job. This involves considering trainees' existing knowledge, skills and motivation, together with the nature of the training that would be required to train them successfully, including both the content and design of training. Those who can be trained most easily or economically can then be selected. The ISD model (figure 5.1), as others, begins with the function of identifying some changing needs within an organization that require a training solution (1). This may be due to the introduction of new technology or work procedures, personnel changes or a failure to achieve business targets in terms of quality and/or quantity. Some analysis of the new or revised job is required so that training objectives can be defined (3) and appropriate training content can be derived (4). Accurate specification of training objectives is important to ensure that the content of training is relevant to training needs. These training objectives have to be translated into what are known as 'criterion measures' (6), which can be used to evaluate whether, after training, trainees have achieved the necessary objectives. The final stage before carrying out the training involves the design of the instructional materials (5). It is here, in particular, that a variety of psychological principles can be brought to bear in order to produce effective training. Finally, in any ISD model there are feedback loops so that the system of training development is capable of modifying and improving itself on the basis of various evaluations that can be performed.

The advantages and disadvantages of ISD models in general have been discussed by Patrick (1992). Their main advantage is that they specify the different tasks in training development and their interrelationships in a context-free manner. In other words, the training development process is generalizable across different types of training content. This feature is helpful not only to those unfamiliar with training development but also to large organizations that have to coordinate the activities of many personnel involved in different aspects of training development. An ISD model provides a framework which can be used for allocating training personnel to specific instructional development activities and coordinating the inputs and outputs from each. Sometimes such models are referred to as the 'training development cycle'. They are used throughout the military establishment and in some large educational and business organizations. A second advantage is that such models can be used to evaluate the *process* of training development within an organization in addition to the more conventional evaluation that focuses on whether training has achieved the correct *products* (i.e. trainees' reactions, learning, job performance etc.). Evaluative questions include:

- How were the training needs identified?
- What were the training objectives and how were they derived?
- What techniques were used to identify training content?
- What principles were used to design the training programme?
- What forms of evaluation were carried out before and after training?
- What revisions have taken place to the training programme, and for what reasons?

Answers to such questions will begin to reveal the extent to which the development of a training programme has been carried out systematically.

The main disadvantage of the ISD approach is that these models specify *what* instructional development tasks exist but not *how* they should be accomplished. In other words, prescriptions or guidelines concerning how each training development function should be performed are largely missing. Exceptions are the

Briggs and Wager (1981) model and the Patrick et al. (1986) Learning Systems Development (LSD) model. The Briggs and Wager model defines fifteen training development functions within the context of classroom teaching, whereas the LSD model describes twelve functions that are organized into three phases of training development, corresponding to analysis, design/development and implementation/control. Briggs and Wager (1981) provide instructions on how each function should be performed within each chapter of their handbook. In the LSD model the four training development functions associated with designing and developing a training programme are subdivided into fourteen subfunctions, including structuring the learning material, using various assessment tests and optimizing presentation of the training material. Each of these development tasks has some guidelines concerning how it should be completed. To a lesser degree, some guidelines have been developed for performing the nineteen instructional development tasks in the IPISD model, although training developers have criticized them for being insufficiently specific.

Given that, on balance, there is some overall benefit accruing from use of an ISD approach, it is intriguing why this approach is not more prevalent in organizations. Hays (1992) argues that training development is still too fragmented, even within large-scale military organizations. There is a lack of information transfer and communication between: training analysts and personnel responsible for procuring training equipment; curriculum designers and end users; and, generally, different departments involved in training development. ISD models represent a rational and idealized approach to training development that is often not followed by individual and organizational practice, even when such an approach is well known. Training activities are often opportunistic and idiosyncratic (Bunderson, 1977), and fall short of complete rationality as prescribed by the nature and sequence of training development tasks in ISD models. This is often due to a lack of knowledge and information among those involved in developing and implementing training (Dipboye, 1997a). There are various organizational barriers to implementation of an ISD approach, which are discussed by Dipboye (1997a). These include: the tendency for training practice to be overly influenced by simple fads and fashions; negative perceptions that the approach is costly and too impersonal, and may understate organizational contexts; and a lack of power by those involved in training to effect the necessary organizational change.

The remainder of this chapter focuses on the three main phases of training development suggested by the ISD approach, namely: identification of training needs and content through various types of analysis; design of training programmes; and evaluation of training.

Identifying Training Needs and Content

There is unanimous agreement that the first steps in training development involve some form of analysis. Goldstein (1993) differentiates between four types of analysis in what he terms the 'needs assessment phase'. The first two types are an organizational analysis and a requirements analysis. These forms of analysis are relatively informal and include: identifying organizational goals and legal issues that may constrain training development; identifying resources required; determining personnel involved in the needs assessment process; specifying contact points in the organization; and mapping out the practical stages involved. The next two forms of analysis concern analysing the task and the skills required to perform the job, and a person analysis to identify on an individual basis the skills to be learned by each trainee. There is less consensus concerning which techniques should be used to accomplish this, as there are many forms of job or task analysis, summarized in Fleishman and Quaintance (1984), Gael (1988) and Patrick (1991). Some forms of task analysis, such as Hierarchical Task Analysis (Annett et al., 1971), which is discussed below, include in their analysis of the task some consideration of the individual trainee's needs. A disadvantage of traditional job or task analyses is that they are not oriented to analysing cooperative team work, which is increasingly prevalent in both industrial and military situations (Bowers et al., 1994; see also chapter 3, this volume). Recently, Van der Veer et al. (1996) reported on the development of Groupware Task Analysis, which is a rapprochement of various analytical techniques that collects information about people, work and the situation in order to identify design issues in complex situations where teams cooperate with technology.

Hierarchical Task Analysis (HTA)

Hierarchical Task Analysis, developed by Annett and Duncan (1967) and described by Annett et al. (1971), is a technique that adopts a systems perspective in breaking down a job or task into subtasks. More recently it has been described by Shepherd (1985) and Patrick (1992). It has been used to facilitate the design of complex systems (e.g. Shepherd, 1993), although it is particularly suited to breaking down an area of work and providing a framework for the development of training content. There are various reasons why HTA is frequently used for training purposes. First, it specifies tasks, subtasks and so on in terms of their objectives. (To understand how to specify objectives, see the next section.) Formally, Annett et al. (1971, p. 3) described tasks as operations which are 'any unit of behaviour, no matter how long or short its duration and no matter how simple or complex its structure which can be defined in terms of its objective'. Analysis of work in terms of objectives means that the output of HTA can be translated easily into training objectives which have a pivotal role in the development of training, as discussed below. A second advantage of HTA is that the level of analysis can be geared to the competence of trainees. In other words, it does not have a fixed level of analysis but will attempt to specify tasks at a level of breakdown at which training can be developed for either one trainee or a population of trainees. This is achieved through the application of a series of questions that determine when further analysis is unnecessary. Finally, HTA, unlike some other forms of job analysis, such as the Critical Incident Technique (Flanagan, 1954), should enable a task or job to be broken down in a comprehensive and exhaustive manner. I use the word 'should', as whether this criterion is achieved will depend upon the skill of the analyst. Anecdotal evidence and a recent study by Patrick et al. (1999) suggests that HTA is a difficult technique to master, and performing HTA is itself a complex task.

HTA breaks down an area of work into a series of subtasks which logically comprise and exhaust it. There are three main features of this type of analysis. First, HTA provides a hierarchical breakdown of tasks and subtasks using the rule of logical decomposition. This is illustrated in part of an analysis of an industrial task concerned with warming up a furnace, adapted from Shepherd (1985) and represented in figure 5.2. Work concerning warming up the furnace is broken down into four subordinate tasks (1.1–1.4) and tasks 1.1 and 1.4 are broken down into a further three and four tasks respectively. The reader might notice that tasks 1.1–1.4 are not logically equivalent to the superordinate task of warming up a furnace unless the sequence and conditions for carrying out these four tasks are specified. This leads us to the second feature of HTA, which is the concept of a 'plan'. A plan is a necessary complement to an 'operation' or task, and specifies under what conditions and in which sequence the tasks or subtasks should be performed. Plans are therefore necessary at every level of analysis in HTA, such that a hierarchy of plans exists alongside a hierarchy of operations/tasks. In the example of warming up the furnace (figure 5.2), the plan for tasks 1.1–1.4 is a fixed sequence, specifying that 1.1 should be performed first and then 1.2, 1.3 and 1.4 in that order. There are many work procedures, some involving equipment, that constitute fixed procedures, and it is quite straightforward for the plans governing them to be mastered, assuming that they need to be and they are not automated. Other plans may be more complex and decisions involving the work situation will dictate the sequence of operations to be followed. This is evident, in the example, for plan 1.4, which represents a flow chart that specifies the sequence and conditions under which tasks 1.4.1–1.4.4 should be completed. This plan ensures that the temperature of the furnace has reached 800 °C before the furnace is switched to automatic mode. The extent to which plans present a training problem in contrast to their complementary operations will vary between different types of work. In work that involves distributing items or materials in a dynamic environment, plans can be more important to train than the operations themselves. This might apply to an air traffic controller, a general deploying military forces and a power grid controller. Shepherd and Duncan (1980) describe the work of a controller of a chlorine plant who has to 'balance' the production of gas from various units with consumption. The main difficulty in analysing this task using HTA was to identify the plans and subplans that could not be verbalized by the expert controllers.

The final feature of HTA is its stopping rule, which guides the level of detail of the analysis. While one is carrying out an analysis, two questions should be

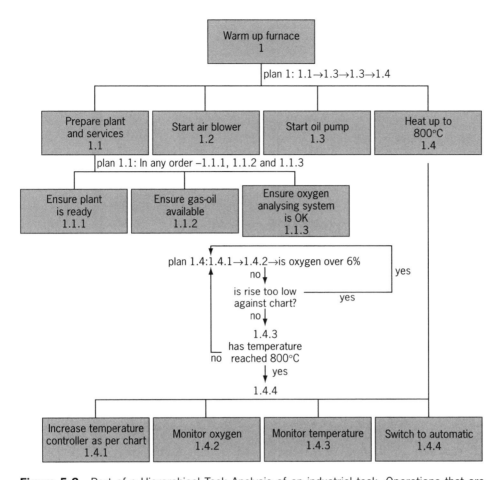

Figure 5.2 Part of a Hierarchical Task Analysis of an industrial task. Operations that are underlined do not require further redescription. Either *p* and *c* are acceptable or a training programme can be devised at this level of task specification. (See text for explanation.)

Source: J. Patrick (1991) Types of analysis for training. In J. E. Morrison (ed.), *Training for Performance: Principles of Applied Human Learning.* Chichester: John Wiley and Sons, p. 143. Adapted from A. Shepherd (1985) Hierarchical task analysis and training decisions. *Programmed Learning and Educational Technology,* 22(3), 162–76.

asked of each operation and the person who has to be trained to perform it: (a) what is the probability (p) without training of inadequate performance; and (b) what would be the cost (c) to the system of inadequate performance? If either of these estimates is unacceptable and a training solution cannot be identified, then the task is analysed in greater detail. Thus, task 1.4 of warming up the furnace is broken down into four subtasks, 1.4.1–1.4.4, because the analyst judged that the probability that the operator could do this without training was unacceptable, the cost of inadequate performance was too high or it was not evident how to develop a training programme at this level of task specification. Therefore, while estimates of p and c are unacceptable for task 1.4, they are satisfactory for subtasks 1.4.1–1.4.4 and no further analysis is necessary. Estimating whether p and c are acceptable as the analysis progresses enables the level of task analysis to be geared to the level of competence of each trainee. The mathematical formulation of the stopping rule by Annett and Duncan (1967) suggests that it should or can be quantified precisely. However, it is acknowledged that in practice this is not feasible and the stopping rule is a rough guide only (Shepherd, 1985; Johnson, 1992). Generally, values of p and c are only judged subjectively by the analyst as satisfactory or unsatisfactory.

Specifying training objectives

The objectives of training are vital ingredients in the development of training, and influence or determine the content, design and evaluation of training. This is evident in our discussion of their role in ISD models, where they can be viewed as providing cohesion and consistency between various instructional development activities. This perspective is emphasized by the Instructional Quality Profile (Merrill et al., 1979), which questions, in any specific training situation, whether training objectives are consistent with both the purpose of training (i.e. the training needs) and the tests used to evaluate the effectiveness of training. In addition, one can ask whether all aspects of the training material map on to, and are consistent with, the objectives of training. Unfortunately, in many organizations the linkages between the training objectives and other training development activities are not sufficiently precise to ensure a high level of consistency. In some cases there is a failure to specify objectives and consequently training content may be inappropriate for the needs being tackled.

It is difficult to appreciate how an apparently small change in a training objective can have a dramatic effect on training content. For example, it is frequently said that a person should be trained to 'know' or 'understand' something. But what does this mean precisely? There is much ambiguity inherent in both of these verbs. The meaning of 'to know' might range from reciting a series of facts to repairing a malfunctioning piece of equipment. As Mager (1962) argued in his classic account of how to specify training objectives, such ambiguities can be resolved by specifying what evidence is necessary to demonstrate that the trainee has indeed mastered the objective. Mager (1962, p. 12) states that the following three elements are necessary in the specification of an objective:

> *First*, identify the terminal behaviour by name; you can specify the kind of behaviour that will be accepted as evidence that the learner has achieved the objective.
>
> *Second*, try to define the desired behaviour further by describing the important conditions under which the behaviour will be expected to occur.

Third, specify the criteria of acceptable performance by describing how well the learner must perform to be considered acceptable.

Mager's suggestion means that the type of activity, the conditions in which it is performed and the level of performance are three aspects of a training objective, all of which require careful specification. Changes in any of them will lead to changes in the skill being taught and consequently the nature of the training programme. Specification of an objective not only enables instructional intent to be communicated, which Mager viewed as important, but also details precisely what the trainee should be able to do after training. This is important in the design, implementation and evaluation phases of training.

There are further reasons why the careful specification of objectives is important in the development of training. An old proposition in the literature, emanating from the work of Gagné (e.g. 1985), is that *what* has to be learned has ramifications for the design of training courses and educational curricula. Thereafter, researchers became intrigued with identifying different types of learning, which they linked to different objectives and also attempted to relate to varying training designs. An example of this is Component Display Theory (CDT), developed by Merrill (1983), which aims to provide help to those designing instruction. It identifies ten types of learning by distinguishing three performance verbs (remember, use and find) which can be applied to four types of content (fact, concept, procedure and principle). This results in ten permissible combinations rather than twelve, as Merrill argues that 'use-fact' and 'find-fact' do not exist because of the nature of a fact.

Below are some examples of the possible performance–content combinations, each of which is illustrated by a performance situation:

- *Remember-fact*, e.g. recall the features of the ISD approach.
- *Use-procedure*, e.g. use Mager's three prescriptions to specify fully a behavioural objective, such as making a cup of tea.
- *Find-principle*, e.g. carry out some research to determine under what circumstances training parts of a task separately is superior to training the whole task.

Each of the ten performance–content combinations in CDT can be linked to a different generic form of training objective, with each objective stating the behaviour, conditions and level of performance, as recommended by Mager. The important point is that these different training objectives imply differences not only in training content but also in design of training. For example, if a technician is taught to *remember* a concept, this does not mean that he or she will be able to *use* the concept by applying it to previously unseen examples. Remembering and using a concept constitute different skills that require differences in both training content and design. Remembering a concept may involve some mnemonic embellishment with recitation, while using a concept requires practice, with feedback, in applying the concept to a full range of instances.

Training objectives are therefore of major importance in training development.

Designing the Training

The second major phase of training development concerns designing the training programme so that trainees can learn as easily as possible. This phase therefore involves engineering an optimal learning environment, such that appropriate knowledge and skills are not only developed in training but can also be translated into appropriate job performance. There are various theories and principles which can be used to guide the design of training, although the reader will disappointed if she or he expects these to prescribe systematically and comprehensively *all* aspects of training design. Much ingenuity and common sense is still needed by the training designer. Theories can be divided into two types: psychological theories that describe how skills are acquired and transferred (e.g. Fitts, 1962; Anderson, 1993, Gick and Hollyoak, 1987); and theories of instructional design that specify the conditions that are necessary to effect learning (e.g. Reigeluth, 1983; Gagné et al., 1992; Tennyson et al., 1997). Psychological theories of skill acquisition emphasize the qualitative changes in behaviour as a novice progresses to an expert. Initially, performance at any new task is ragged and characterized by many errors, in contrast to the smooth and automatic performance of an expert, which is largely error-free. Theories of transfer began with Thorndike and Woodworth's (1901) theory of identical elements, which stated that transfer of skills between two tasks will take place only to the extent that they share common elements. Subsequent cognitive theorists (e.g. Anderson, 1987) interpreted what an element constitutes in different ways, although the notion that similarity between task situations determines transfer of skill is still a contemporary one.

Factors that affect training design can be divided into three areas (figure 5.3). First, as discussed previously, different types of training content may involve different categories of learning that require different training designs. This notion has been championed by Gagné in many publications (e.g. Gagné et al., 1992). The second set of issues affecting training design might be loosely termed the training methods and strategies that organize, sequence and supplement the training content into an effective learning programme. This is what is conventionally referred to as training design, and it includes a very mixed bag of principles. According to Patrick (1992), these include: providing pre-training; using practice coupled with different types of knowledge of results; providing the trainee with guidance in the form of demonstrations and verbal advice; breaking the task into parts for training; adapting the training to the individual trainee as learning progresses; spacing the training and determining the duration of training sessions; providing overtraining so that performance is not brittle and the skill learned during training is resilient to stress

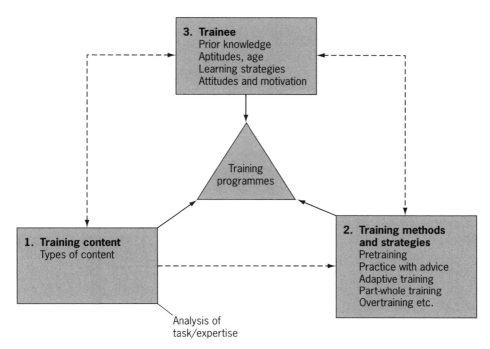

Figure 5.3   Three components in the design of training.
Source: J. Patrick (1992) *Training, Research and Practice.* London: Academic Press, p. 272.

and other factors when performed in the actual job. Finally, the third set of issues concerning training design relates to characteristics of the trainee, as indicated in figure 5.3. Some individual difference variables, such as age, intelligence and learning strategy, have been found to interact with the design of a training programme. For example, a training programme covering the same content may require a different design for a very intelligent person in comparison to one less intelligent. Many studies of this sort were carried out in the 1960s and 1970s under the banner of 'Aptitude Treatment Interaction' (ATI) research. However, a comprehensive review by Cronbach and Snow (1977) concluded that no ATI effects 'are so well confirmed that they can be used directly as guides to instruction'.

Motivating trainees

One characteristic of the trainee that is a prerequisite for the success of any training is motivation. Motivational aspects of training have been a neglected research area except during approximately the past decade. This is surprising, given that there are well established theories of work motivation, summarized by Campbell and Pritchard (1976). Only relatively recently have these theoretical notions been placed in a training context. Traditionally, it has been assumed that a well designed training programme from a cognitive perspective would necessarily be motivating to trainees. This is not so. However, there is a complex interplay between cognitive and motivational factors relating to training that are difficult to disentangle. For example, providing trainees with goals prior to training will have both cognitive and motivational benefits (e.g. Hesketh, 1997). Knowing what you are trying to master enables attention and other cognitive resources to be directed more efficiently and also has an energizing effect, assuming that these goals fit in with the trainee's career path, job expectations etc. The attitudes and perceptions of trainees concerning not only the training programme but also the wider organizational context have been increasingly recognized as determinants of training success (Tannenbaum and Yukl, 1992).

Two notable attempts have been made by Keller (1983) and Noe (1986) to synthesize the literature concerning work motivation and put it into a training context. Keller (1983) identifies seventeen strategies for improving the motivational design of instruction, which he subsumed under four categories:

- Maintaining the trainee's *interest* by, for example, arousing curiosity through the introduction of novel and incongruous events.
- Establishing the *relevance* of the training situation for satisfying the trainee's needs or values by, for example, providing opportunities for no-risk cooperative interaction in order to satisfy the need for affiliation.
- Increasing personal *expectancy* for success by, for example, increasing experience with success.
- Establishing good *outcomes* from training for the trainee by, for example, using rewards that normally follow from the task to maintain intrinsic satisfaction.

Subsequently, Keller and Kopp (1987) developed the ARCS (Attention, Relevance, Confidence and Satisfaction) theory of motivational design in which the original seventeen strategies were revised and reduced to twelve. This theory covers some of the same theoretical issues, although the strategies are described under the four category headings of ARCS, three of which differ from Keller's (1983) original formulation. The strategies cover getting the trainee's *attention*, establishing the *relevance* of the training material to the trainee's goals, encouraging the trainee's *confidence* to engage in training and increasing the trainee's *satisfaction* by rewarding appropriate performance.

Noe (1986) published a model of the motivational influences on training effectiveness (represented in figure 5.4) that has stimulated considerable interest and subsequent research. Noe argues that locus of control is important because those trainees who make internal attributions (i.e. ascribe their performance as being under their own control) are more likely to accept and benefit from feedback concerning their performance during training. Locus of

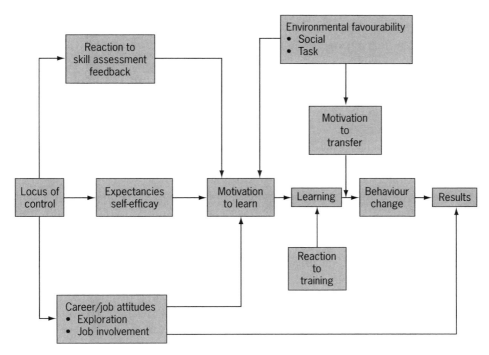

Figure 5.4　Motivational influences on training effectiveness.

Source: R. A. Noe (1986) Trainees' attributes and attitudes: neglected influences on training effectiveness. *Academy of Management Review*, 11(4), 738.

control will, in turn, affect both a trainee's reaction to any skill assessment that is received before training and a trainee's career and job attitudes. Both of these factors are hypothesized to determine a person's motivation to learn from a training programme. While Noe and Schmitt (1986) found some evidence that trainees who were active in career planning and more involved in their jobs benefited from training, Matthieu et al. (1992) failed to find any effect of either career planning or job involvement on training motivation. More recently, Quiñones (1995), in a study of students tackling a naval simulation task, found support for the proposition that how training programmes are labelled can provide trainees with feedback concerning past performance, which, in turn, affects their motivation levels prior to training. 'Remedial' training implies poor past performance and this may have a detrimental effect on motivation, in contrast to 'advanced' training. Quiñones found that the effect of these types of training assignment on motivation was affected by trainees' perceptions of past performance relative to their expected assignment and locus of control.

A further component in Noe's (1986) model is derived from Vroom's (1964) work motivation theory in relation to a trainee's self-efficacy; that is, a person's belief in his or her ability to perform competently before, during and after training. Trainees will develop expectancies concerning whether, if they expend effort trying to learn, they will develop the necessary skills, and these will be associated with desirable outcomes, such as a better job or improved pay. It has been found that self-efficacy is not only enhanced by training but also determines the effectiveness of training (Tannenbaum et al., 1991). Saks (1995) examined the adjustment of accountants during their first year of employment. He found that training was particularly beneficial in terms of ability to cope, job performance and intention to quit for those newcomers with low levels of self-efficacy.

A final remark concerning motivation relates to our previous discussion of ISD models and training objectives. Keller and Kopp (1987) suggested that one can view motivational design as mirroring the stages involved in training development. Thus, to start with, one should carry out needs analysis to identify in what areas trainees may be lacking in motivation. When motivational needs have been identified, motivational objectives can be specified. The next stage involves selecting some strategies for meeting these objectives and improving the motivational level of trainees in the training programme. Finally, some evaluation is carried out that aims to ascertain whether the motivational objectives have been met, and, if not, how the motivational design can be improved.

Designing practice

The most potent and ubiquitous training variable is practice accompanied by appropriate instructional support from a trainer, a teacher or even a computer. The notion that it is only by 'doing' the task that a person is able to learn the necessary knowledge and skills is a strong one, grounded in various psychological theories (e.g. Anderson, 1993). Various qualitative and quantitative changes occur during practice as trainees progress from novices to experts. By definition, speed and accuracy of task performance improve. In addition, theorists have described the qualitative changes that occur in the structure of knowledge during skill acquisition. Initially, trainees develop factual or what is termed 'declarative' knowledge about the task. Fitts (1962) refers to this as the cognitive phase of skill acquisition, where the trainee tries to understand any instructions and other requirements concerning the nature of the task to be learned. In this initial stage of training, performance is uncoordinated and error-prone. Subsequently, with practice, 'procedural' knowledge is gradually compiled concerning *how* to carry out the task, and rules are developed that specify this (Anderson, 1993). These rules are refined with practice, becoming more efficient and hierarchically organized (Miller et al., 1960; Anderson, 1993). These rules can be thought of as 'action units' and gradually, through training, those at the lower levels are executed automatically without the need for much attention. This is why a person who has attained a high level of skill has spare capacity to either concentrate on more refined aspects of task performance or perform another task at the same time.

Practice is important for the development not only of perceptual motor skills, as, for example, in gymnastics, but also of social and cognitive skills, If the trainee has to develop covert reasoning skills in problem-solving situations, it is necessary for training to provide opportunities for such skills to be practised. Even interpersonal skills trained through behaviour modelling, a form of observational learning, are developed with the trainee engaging in some practice. Various questions arise concerning how practice should be designed and organized in order to maximize learning (see chapters 8 and 9, this volume).

What information should be given prior to practice? Providing the trainee with advance information concerning the nature and scope of the training programme has both cognitive and motivational benefits. A long time ago, Ausubel (1960) suggested that a trainee should be provided with an advance organizer, a sort of overview of the material to be learned. A similar proposition was put forward by Reigeluth and Stein (1983), who suggested that training should begin with what they termed an 'epitome' (or advance organizer), which was then progressively elaborated in increasing detail during the training. Methodologically it is difficult to test the effect of advance organizers, and the evidence concerning their value is equivocal (e.g. Hartley and Davies, 1976). However, Mayer (1979) concludes that advance organizers are particularly helpful when conceptual material has to be mastered that is unfamiliar to the trainee.

What instructional support should accompany practice? It is not true that practice makes perfect, not only because perfection is rarely associated with human performance but because practice *per se* is of little use unless it is accompanied by instructional support from the trainer, teacher or computer during the learning period. This instructional support needs to provide the trainee with advice or feedback concerning how his or her performance is deficient and how this might be remedied. Formally, this type of information is termed 'extrinsic feedback' because it is in addition to the 'intrinsic' feedback normally available during task performance. Feedback concerning task performance comes from the performer's different sense organs, and which type is most important will depend upon the task in question. Generally, visual feedback is an important part of intrinsic feedback, although this may be supplemented by extrinsic feedback of a visual and auditory nature, from, for example, a supervisor debriefing a trainee from a video recording of task performance. Extrinsic feedback can take many forms, including a written appraisal at the end of a trainee's induction period, and results from a computer administered test. Extrinsic feedback will be of benefit to the extent that it is unambiguous, can be related by the trainee to the discrepancy between current and desired performance, does not distract the trainee from using cues inherent in the task and is provided before the trainee's next attempt at task performance. It is important that this extra information provided during training does not become a crutch to performance, so that when it disappears after training, performance returns to pertraining level. This has led to the suggestion that, as training progresses, the degree of instructional support should be gradually reduced, thus avoiding the sudden withdrawal that a trainee otherwise would experience after training. Karlsson and Chase (1996) found that college students made twice as many errors after training to use a computer-based spreadsheet when they were training with continuous prompting of the correct key as they did when these prompts were progressively delayed. They argued that because most commercial training involves a continuous prompting method, considerable savings could accrue if prompt-fading methods were introduced into training. Another solution is to ensure that any prompting or extrinsic feedback to the trainee is provided only on alternate practice sessions.

Should the practice sessions be spaced?   The answer to this question is an unequivocal 'yes'. A considerable psychological literature, from the review by Woodworth and Schlosberg (1954) onwards, has found that avoiding massed practice is of benefit, although the theoretical basis of such an effect is less certain. A recent review by Dempster (1996) emphasizes the importance of spacing both the learning and remembering sessions in classroom learning. He bemoans the fact that there is little application of distributed practice, in the form of reviews and tests, in conventional instructional situations.

Baddeley and Longman (1978) investigated the training of Post Office workers in keyboard skills, pointing out that research into the effect of spaced practice had largely ignored the issue of how long each training session should be. They found that while spacing had an effect, the duration of each practice session was more influential. A training group that received one hour training per day was superior after sixty hours of training to groups that had a two-hour session either once or twice a day. This finding may only apply to training of the sort of perceptual motor skills involved in this study. A practical problem is that training for the group having one hour's practice per day takes four times as long as that for the group receiving four hours a day. One solution that may be feasible in some organizations is to fill the gaps with training in other tasks, because the spacing effect still occurs even when the interval between practice sessions is filled with other activities. This led Goettl et al. (1996) to compare the training of three relatively complex tasks using an alternating practice regime in contrast to a massed one. It was found that learning and retention were superior for two of the tasks, and not reduced for the third, when practice sessions alternated between them. However, the authors speculate that this effect may depend on the similarity between the tasks to be trained. In their study the tasks were relatively dissimilar.

What should be practised?   This question is deceptive in its apparent simplicity. Two important issues will be discussed that relate to what is practised:

whether it is the actual job/task or a simulated version of it, and whether components of the job are practised separately or together.

First, there are many reasons why it is often desirable for training to take place off-the-job with some form of simulation, as opposed to on-the-job. Training in the work situation may not be desirable because of the costs, in the widest sense, of trainees' errors, the stress and difficulty of performing the task and the problem of developing a good instructional situation. The principle guiding the design of simulated task situations for instructional purposes is that they should faithfully represent the psychological demands made by the actual task on the performer. Technically this is known as high psychological fidelity. This principle has been used successfully not only to design aircraft simulators for training pilots but also to identify what behaviours should be demonstrated to the trainee in interpersonal and supervisory skills training. In behaviour role modelling (Sorcher and Goldstein, 1972), a model demonstrates or enacts the behaviour required in a simulated role play and the trainee rehearses and practises this behaviour, with feedback provided by the trainer or possibly other trainees. Baldwin (1992) found that including positive and negative model displays during assertive communication training had a beneficial effect when this behaviour had to be generalized outside the training situation. However, when the behaviour had to be reproduced in a situation that was very similar to the one in training, using only a positive model was more beneficial.

The second issue concerns whether the whole or part of the task should be practised. Some tasks are so complex that they inevitably have to be broken up in some manner and practised separately. A complex task may be divided into parts according to the principles of either partitioning, in which the nature of the parts is preserved, or simplification, where part-task difficulty is reduced in order to help the trainee to learn. Part-task training has been found to be particularly effective when the part that is practised involves an important sub-skill (Fredericksen and White, 1989; Goettl and Shute, 1996). However, care has to be taken that the part selected for practice represents a meaningful sub-skill that does not interact substantially with other parts of the task. For example, learning to fly an aircraft involves part-task training on procedures, stick control, navigation etc., each of which is practised separately before being integrated into whole-task training.

Evaluating Training

Evaluation of training is a major phase of training development, yet it is often neglected by organizations. The reasons for this range from insufficient technical competence to a lack of political will on the part of those developing the training. There are many different methods and criteria advocated by by different enthusiasts in the literature that make evaluation potentially a confusing topic. Patrick (1992) suggested that the evaluation literature concerning training can best be understood by differentiating the aims of evaluation, which in turn can often be associated with different criteria and methods. Four main approaches to evaluation of training can then be distinguished, each of which is discussed briefly below.

The conventional approach of evaluation concerns determining whether the programme 'works' in the sense that trainees react positively to the training, master what they should and translate their learning into improved job performance. Trainees' reactions, learning and job behaviour constitute the criteria for evaluation, to which can be added the criterion of whether changes in job behaviour improve various indices of organizational performance; for example, production and turnover. These four evaluation criteria were specified originally by Kirkpatrick (1959, 1960). Different evaluation methods may be associated with the four criteria. In order to evaluate changes in learning from pre- to post-training, a research design is necessary, either involving a training group and a control group that does not receive training, or using some form of quasi-experimental design (Campbell and Stanley, 1966). This can be used to assess not only quantitative gains in performance attributable to training but also qualitative changes in, for example, knowledge organization (Kraiger and Cannon-Bowers, 1995). Trainees' reactions can be divided into enjoyment, perceived usefulness and difficulty of training (Warr and Bunce, 1995), all of which can be assessed through either questionnaire or interview methods.

The aim of this traditional approach to evaluation is to ascertain the effectiveness of training and to make improvements where necessary. Evaluation therefore functions as a means of *controlling* and regulating the objectives, content and design of training as specified in the ISD approach, discussed previously. However, while evaluation in this role acts as a feedback mechanism, planning for the evaluation of training should be carried out early in the training development cycle. It has already been mentioned that training objectives specify the criteria for assessing whether the necessary knowledge and skills have been acquired. Further, what Scriven (1967) termed 'formative evaluation' involves pilot testing the training materials to assess their practicability and effectiveness, so that revisions can take place prior to implementation of the actual training.

A second approach to evaluation operates at the level of an individual trainee. Here the goal is to advise the trainee or to make decisions about his or her career path, further training etc. Therefore, in contrast to the previous approach, individual rather than group training records are used for evaluation.

A third, administrative, approach to evaluation involves making value judgements about whether the throughput and pass levels of trainees justify the resources put into training. This boils down to estimating the costs and effectiveness of training. Costs include not only those involved in implementing, evaluating and revising training but also those in the planning and development stages. However, the difficulty in developing cost-effectiveness formulations lies in determining the effectiveness of training in terms of its financial impact on an organization. Various suggestions have been made concerning how this should be estimated (e.g. Schmidt et al., 1982), although they remain speculative and difficult to validate.

Finally, the aim of evaluation may be to investigate the effectiveness of training variables or manipulations; for example, the amount of practice or the design of a simulated training scenario. Typically this research-oriented approach to evaluation involves using the scientific method and developing a hypothesis, designing and carrying out an experimental study and then analysing the data in order to determine whether there is sufficient support for the hypothesis. The design of the research study has to be internally valid, so that the inferences drawn concerning the results are justifiable. Further, for a training study, it is important that it has ecological validity, so that the effects of the training variables can be generalized to their appropriate work contexts.

A Case Study of Training in the Steel Industry

Training development can be divided into three main phases: identifying training needs and content; designing training; and evaluating training. These phases are consistent with the ISD approach, discussed previously, and correspond to three of the main heading of this chapter. Principles concerning how each of these three phases might be accomplished have been discussed separately in this chapter. In order to illustrate how some of these principles may come to together in one training situation, a field study by Patrick et al. (1996) will be described. The aim of the study was to develop and implement training to improve fault-finding in a hot strip steel mill. The steel mill was fully automated and controlled by a network of computers. Operators monitored and supervised the process of steel production from three control rooms.

The first phase of this work entailed identifying training needs and content. Management reported that, in one area of the mill, fault-finding was problematic even for experienced technicians/engineers. Failure to fault-find effectively and efficiently could result in poor quality steel, damage to equipment and/or personnel and, ultimately, shutdown of the mill. Steel production was worth at least £10,000 per hour in the late 1980s. Examination of plant records and discussions with personnel responsible for fault-finding confirmed that there was indeed a training need in this area. In order to analyse the nature of this need in greater detail and to develop training content, three forms of analysis took place. First, errors and problems that arose in connection with fault-finding were collected. Various data sources and methods were used, including retrospective analyses of reported faults, observation of technical personnel during shifts and 'talking through' proposed actions, intentions and decisions while locating hypothetical faults. This revealed various inefficiencies during fault-finding. Surprisingly, personnel frequently failed to utilize all the initial symptoms that were available in the fault scenario. This tendency was compounded by a failure to set and tackle systematic subgoals in the search for the source of the problem. This was not surprising given the overwhelming complexity and size of the technical domain. Further, personnel tended to adopt a rather risky hypothesis-driven search for the fault rather than a more painstaking and systematic one, and considerable time could be lost by searching in an area of the plant which did not contain the fault. The second form of analysis was to use Hierarchical Task Analysis (HTA) in order to break down the task of fault-finding into a series of goals and subgoals that *should* be followed. In this sense, HTA provided a prescriptive goal-oriented model of the behaviour that should take place from a logical perspective. These goals were pieced together from some of the goals, often implicit, of experienced personnel, although 'complete' experts did not exist. The aim of the HTA was to identify systematic and tractable goals and subgoals that could be pursued by the fault-finder, thus avoiding risky and inefficient hypothesis driven searching. The three main goals, in sequence, were:

1   Determine initial symptoms of the fault.
2   Determine faulty plant subsystem.
3   Identify the fault within the faulty plant subsystem.

The third form of analysis involved identifying all the knowledge and skills required to perform these goals and all their associated subgoals. The goals and subgoals, together with the knowledge and skills that were involved in each, demarcated the training content.

The second phase of training development concerned design of the training programme. One constrain was that relevant training had to be available for both experienced personnel and apprentices. It was decided to develop an intelligent computer-based training system that enabled differing individual training requirements to be met. The training material was divided into tutorials that taught the knowledge and skills associated with each subgoal, and simulated faults which provided the opportunity for personnel to practise setting and pursuing appropriate subgoals and using the associated knowledge in finding the fault effectively. Trainees were able to select material for study, with the caveat that competence at the first subgoal of 'determining the initial symptoms' had to be demonstrated before the second subgoal of 'determining the faulty plant subsystem' could be studied. This chapter has emphasized the importance of designing practice so that it not only targets the exact skills required in the job but is also accompanied by advice or feedback that the trainee can use to improve subsequent performance. The training system advised trainees on the basis of past performance and selected relevant tutorials and particular faults for personnel to practise that corresponded to their training needs. It also provided feedback to the trainee, both during tutorials and after each simulated fault had been tackled. A part-task training regime was used as trainees learned and practised, separately, the different goals and subgoals associated with fault-finding before attempting the whole task. Further details concerning the training design can be found in Patrick et al. (1996).

The third and final phase of training development concerned evaluating the computer-based training system. The aim of this evaluation was to assess the effectiveness of training and to improve it as necessary. Some informal and what is known as 'formative' evaluation took place before formal training began. This involved personnel working through instructions, individual tutorials and some of the simulated faults to identify where the training material and instructions were unclear, long-winded etc. Subsequently, training materials were revised and two major training studies took place, one of which is described by Patrick et al. (1996). Unfortunately, these training studies could not evaluate the effects of training on actual job behaviour, partly owing to the scarcity of major faults and partly owing to the lack of control over the many factors that affect job performance. Consequently, pre-training and post-training tests were designed using simulated faults on the computer-based system in order to evaluate the effectiveness of specified tutorials and practice that were given to all participants. Evidence showed an improvement between pre- and post-training that reflected a more systematic approach to fault-finding. Trainees were better at collecting and reasoning about the initial symptoms of a fault and were also able to narrow down the area containing the fault to a plant subsystem in a more efficient and effective manner. A questionnaire also evaluated participants' reactions to various aspects of the training material, which were generally positive, particularly for inexperienced personnel.

Chapter Summary

This chapter has discussed the development of training or instruction in a generalizable manner that cuts across the varying contexts in which it takes place. From a rational perspective, training development involves a series of stages or tasks that are described by Instructional Systems Development models. Three major stages in training development form the basis for the discussion of training principles and techniques in this chapter. These are: identifying training needs and content; designing training; and evaluating training. In order to accomplish the first stage it is necessary to carry out some form of job or task analysis and to prescribe precisely the nature of training objectives. The latter activity is critical, as it ensures that the subsequent training is relevant and that it is clear *what*

Continued

skills should be evaluated after training. There are many important factors in the second stage: designing the training. Two that are highlighted in this chapter are: the provision of practice opportunities so that the trainee can develop automated and error-free skills; and the development of good motivational levels in trainees tackling the training programme, and issue which is often neglected. While practice is probably the most potent training variable, it is important that relevant skills are practised in spaced sessions and that this is accompanied by guidance and feedback from the trainer that specifies clearly to the trainee *how* to improve. A prerequisite for any practice is that the trainee is suitably motivated during training. These factors include not only the interest and stimulation provoked by the training programme itself but also the trainee's views concerning whether training will facilitate his or her future career or pay prospects, and his or her ability to master the new or upgraded skills. The final stage of training involves evaluating trainees to ensure that the necessary skills have been acquired and, if not, to make appropriate revisions to the content or design of the training programme. The fact that jobs and tasks in society are changing more rapidly nowadays means more than ever that training, both formal and informal, should be viewed as a continuous lifelong activity.

Discussion Points

1   What are the main stages in the development of training?

2   Why are training objectives important in training development?

3   How might you evaluate a training course for car mechanics?

4   Discuss how to design practice sessions to improve your typing and keyboard skills.

5   What are ISD models and what are their advantages and disadvantages?

6   Try to analyse a simple familiar task, such as making an omelette, using hierarchical task analysis.

Further Reading

Goldstein, I. L. (1993) *Training in Organizations: Needs Assessment, Development and Evaluation*, 3rd edn. Monterey, CA: Brooks Cole.

Patrick, J. (1992) *Training: Research and Practice*. London: Academic Press.

CHAPTER SIX

PERFORMANCE APPRAISAL: ASSESSING AND DEVELOPING PERFORMANCE AND POTENTIAL

Clive Fletcher

Contents

C h a p t e r   O u t l i n e

This chapter begins by outlining the purposes of performance appraisal – which include assessing ongoing work performance, giving feedback, trying to increase work motivation and to enhance quality and quantity of output and developing potential. It goes on to examine the various approaches taken to assessing the individual's effectiveness at work, including the use of rating scales, competencies and achievement against objectives. The shift in emphasis of research from assessment issues to studying the social and motivational context of appraisal is outlined, and issues such as reactions to feedback and the personal and political agenda of the participants are discussed. Moving from present performance to potential, methods such as assessment centres, development centres and multi-source feedback systems are outlined and evaluated. Finally, the impact of organizational change on performance appraisal systems and the emergence of broader performance management strategies are considered.

What Is Performance Appraisal?

Just for a few moments, put yourself in the position of a senior manager in a major company. You have five managers reporting directly to you, and another twenty managerial and professional staff reporting to them. How are you going to assess the performance of the people working for you? What criteria will you use to judge whether anyone is not performing well enough, or to decide whether any of them are ready to take on greater responsibilities and perhaps achieve a promotion? How will you seek to drive up performance in your division, and how will you try to motivate and develop your staff to bring this about? These are the questions that managers face every day; they are central to the manager's role. The answers to them are often expressed, in a formal way, through the performance appraisal system that the organization puts in place. Not surprisingly, organizations vary in the kind of answers they come up with, and so the approach taken to appraisal varies widely too. In this chapter, we will look at performance appraisal in its many guises and evaluate it from the viewpoint of theory and research in occupational psychology. First, however, it is necessary to understand what performance appraisal systems look like, how they work and what they are trying to do.

Essentially, performance appraisal is a generic term used to describe a range of processes whereby a manager and a subordinate meet on a periodic basis (usually annually) to review the work of the latter and to seek to raise performance levels. Box 6.1 presents a fairly traditional example of how the whole process can work, but, as we will see below, more progressive organizations at the present time often go some way beyond this in what they do under the banner of performance appraisal.

Steps in the annual appraisal process in a telecommunications company

1 The period for doing appraisals is April to May, so at the end of March the personnel department sends out the appraisal forms and guidance documents (for both those doing the appraisal and those being appraised) to all managers who have staff to appraise.
2 The appraisers then pass on to their appraisees a preparation form, which invites them to make a self-assessment against various competency headings, and also against the objectives they set last year. Meanwhile, the appraiser from his or her own point of view is making those same assessments for each person to be appraised.
3 The appraisal interview takes place, and can last anything between one and two hours. The appraiser will invite the appraisee to comment on his or her performance over the past year, to identify any problems that have arisen and to review progress against objectives set. Discrepancies between the two of them in how they see the appraisee's performance may arise, and will be discussed. Finally, objectives for the year ahead are agreed, as is any development activity needed to help the appraisee.
4 An appraisal report form is now completed – it may have been partly written by the appraiser before the interview, but now it becomes the formal record and is signed by both parties. It includes a set of ratings of the individual on the key competencies associated with the role, a statement of the objectives for next year, an overall performance rating and a list of action points relating to the appraisee's development needs. They each keep a copy of it, and another copy is sent to the personnel department.
5 Various kinds of follow-up activity will take place. The personnel office scans all the appraisal forms for development recommendations that may require their input (to advise on relevant training courses, or to assist in possible job changes). At three-monthly intervals, the progress against objectives set is monitored and discussed by the appraiser and appraisee.

One of the key issues in understanding appraisal – and for research perspectives on it – is establishing the aims of the exercise: what are we trying to achieve? Perhaps one of the most frequently cited purposes of appraisal is to enable some kind of assessment to be made of the appraisee. But assessment, while constituting a core element of appraisal, is not in itself one of its purposes – assessment done for its own sake is of little value. What it provides is a basis for several central purposes of appraisal, in particular:

1 *Improving performance.* One of the basic psychological principles of learning is that to improve performance, individuals need to have some knowledge of the results they are already achieving. Forming an assessment and conveying it should meet this requirement and help to enhance performance.

2   *Making reward decisions.* If the organization is to seek to distribute rewards in a fair and equitable manner – be they pay, promotion or whatever – then some method of comparing people is necessary. If an assessment of performance is made annually, it can be used to direct rewards to those most deserving of them.

3   *Motivating staff.* There are three ways in which appraisal seeks to motivate employees. Even since the earliest appraisal schemes, it has been an article of faith that giving feedback, quite apart from assisting in task performance, is something that motivates people. And there is some justification for this, as employees in all types of organization frequently express the view that they want to know where they stand, i.e. they desire feedback. The assessment made in appraisal provides the basis for the feedback, and thus contributes to motivation. Second, assessment also increases motivation through its role in facilitating the fair distribution of rewards. Third, setting targets that improve on previous performance is also a motivating device.

4   *Developing subordinates.* People need training, on and off the job, to help them develop, and it is part of the appraisal's role to facilitate this. Identifying what short- and medium-term development needs the individual has, and planning how to meet them, is a key aim for appraisal.

5   *Identifying potential.* By identifying good and poor performers, the appraisal enables the organization to focus succession planning and resources on the individuals who are most likely to respond positively and effectively to it.

6   *Formal recording of unsatisfactory performance.* In its most negative garb, appraisal can be part of the process whereby unsatisfactory performance is documented and used in evidence in disciplinary or dismissal proceedings.

These are some of the purposes that, in theory at least, can be served by an appraisal scheme that includes an element of assessment. On the face of it, they seem very reasonable and entirely justifiable. And each one in itself is indeed sensible enough. But together they form a formidable agenda – can we really assess, motivate, reward and develop people all in one annual process that largely consists of a single interview and a report form? To answer this question, we can turn to the psychological research relating to appraisal. Much of the research that has been done splits into two broad themes: how to assess performance effectively, and the social and motivational context of appraisal.

The Assessment of Work Performance

The rating of performance dimensions

If one is to assess ongoing work performance, the decision has to be made as to how this is to be done: what is to be assessed, and the method used. In the early years of appraisal systems (and they have been around since before the First World War), the tendency was to assess the individual on personality attributes. This became very unpopular with appraisers, who disliked making such fundamental judgements about their staff. From the 1960s onwards, this approach diminished, though Holdsworth (1991) notes that as late as the 1970s one British retailing organization was asking its managers to appraise staff on 'moral courage'! In its place, organizations settled on rating job-related abilities, such as 'management of staff', 'performance under pressure', 'decision-making'. This kind of approach can still be found, though now what is rated is normally a set of competencies. There are various ways of defining competencies, but in general they can be thought of as observable skills or abilities to complete a managerial task successfully or as behavioural dimensions that affect job performance (Woodruffe, 1996; Sparrow, 1997). The competency labels may not look very different from the job-related abilities mentioned above, but they will usually have been defined in much more detail, with good and poor performance described in behavioural terms; an example of some of the competencies used to describe performance in a customer-facing role in a high street bank is given in box 6.2.

Box 6.2

Example of some of the competencies used by a financial institution to describe effective and ineffective performance in a sales role

The five competencies described below were arrived at by rep grid analysis of the constructs elicited from managers of staff in the role concerned. Each manager was asked to think of examples of six or seven good and poor performers among subordinates in this job. The names of these subordinates were then each written on a separate card, and the manager was presented with three of the cards, two of which had the names of high performers, and the other a low performer. The manager's task was to describe in behavioural terms one way in which two of the three differed from the third. With repetition of this for different triads of cards/names, a series of constructs emerges that define the behavioural differences between good and poor performers. In all, eleven competencies were identified as being of primary importance in this job role.

- **Competency:** *Problem analysis and judgement*
  Effective: Analyses the customer's requirement in a logical fashion. Correctly identifies the combination of products to meet the need. Thinks things through and looks beyond the immediate situation. Displays a capacity for innovation in problem-solving. Makes decisions on a balanced appraisal of the facts.

Continued

Ineffective: Focuses narrowly on the immediate problem without looking at the broader perspective. Offers solutions before analysing the problem sufficiently. Is rigid and unimaginative in matching available products to meet the needs of the customer. Sees things in overly simple, black and white terms. Promises more than can be delivered.

- **Competency:** *Planning and organizing*
  Effective: Organizes the day so that post is dealt with without delay. Plans ahead, looking beyond the immediate situation. Ensures there is cover for absences. Diarizes key dates and events for follow-up. Prioritizes time and effort to maximize opportunities for customer contacts. Does homework on customers and has information that may be required readily accessible. Delegates routine work where possible. Adopts a structured approach to tasks.
  Ineffective: Disorganized and unsystematic in tackling the work. Fails to anticipate problems and does not plan ahead. Misses important dates and events that should have been followed up. Double books self. Gives routine and minor tasks equal priority with more important elements of the job. Not punctual.

- **Competency:** *Motivating others*
  Effective: Sets an example in speed of response, efficiency and dealing with customers. Gives praise where it is due. Provides feedback on results and shares the credit for successes. Involves staff and seeks their views and advice when appropriate. Delegates where possible and encourages initiative. Generates a team spirit and sets targets.
  Ineffective: Gives little or no feedback on the results achieved through leads provided by other staff. Does not encourage staff or demonstrate personal commitment to objectives. Works too independently, not involving others. Claims all the credit personally for what is achieved.

- **Competency:** *Achievement and energy*
  Effective: Energetic and quick in the way work is dealt with. Proactive rather than reactive. Willing to make sacrifices to achieve targets. Takes pride in successes and is not satisfied with attaining the targets set – seeks to exceed them. Responds positively to customers' high expectations. Competitive in a constructive way.
  Ineffective: Lacks drive and vigour in approach. Too willing to settle for the average. Waits for the business to come in instead of going looking for it. Works slowly and does not meet the customers' timescales or standards. Fails to respond to challenges.

- **Competency:** *Tenacity and resilience*
  Effective: Takes disappointments and rejections without being unduly upset by them. Maintains morale in the face of setbacks. Is not deterred by an initially unpromising response from a customer. Does not let rather insensitive behaviour or offhand attitude from customers affect commitment. Displays determination in the face of adversity.
  Ineffective: Is discouraged by rebuffs. Easily hurt by rejection and takes it too personally. Does not press on in the face of an initial lack of positive response from the customer. Easily demotivated and deflected from pursuing objectives. Reacts emotionally when under pressure.

Identifying which job-related attributes or competencies are of chief importance in performing a role or range of roles should result from a systematic process of job or competency analysis. The methods used (questionnaires, critical incidents etc.) are discussed in chapters 2 and 3 and will not be discussed further here. But it is unfortunately the case that the thoroughness and quality of this job analysis varies greatly and is often rather superficial. Turning to *how* these attributes are measured rather than *what* is measured, several different forms of rating scale can be employed. For example, the scale intervals may be simply numerically or alphabetically defined (1–5, a–e), or they may be verbally described (outstanding, very good, good and so on).

Most appraisal forms contain at least one rating – usually of overall performance – and quite often they present a whole series of them relating to different aspects of performance. Rating scales are the vehicle for the quantitative assessment of the individual. Because of this emphasis on the use of ratings in appraisal, much psychological research effort has been expended on trying to find what rating method is the most effective in producing well distributed ratings that differentiate between employees of differing levels of performance in an accurate and reliable way. In other words, what kind of rating method gives us measures of performance that are – to use the frame of reference we associate with psychological testing – psychometrically sound?

Conventional rating scale use has long been recognized as bedeviled with problems (Landy and Farr, 1980); most frequent of these are central tendency (everyone is rated in the middle), halo effect (assessment of one quality of the individual affects the judgement of all his or her other attributes, so all ratings are highly correlated) and positive skew (everyone is rated high – all swans, no geese). For example, Fletcher (1995) examined the appraisal ratings of graduate recruits in a bank over their first three appraisal periods. The appraisal form listed thirteen performance attributes to be assessed. If the appraisal system was yielding valid and accurate measures of these attributes, it would be reasonable to expect that ratings of a specific quality – e.g. written communication skills – would correlate over successive years, and that this correlation would be greater than the intercorrelation of the ratings of different attributes within any one appraisal period (i.e. one should not, on *a priori* grounds, find that an individual's rating on 'numerical skills' should correlate with 'ability to delegate', since these are essentially unrelated attributes). This was not found to be the case, though. The average correlation of individual attributes *across* the first three appraisal periods was 0.42, compared to the average intercorrelation of attribute ratings over the three periods of 0.49 (for the first period 0.43, the second 0.54, the third, 0.49; all significant at the 1 per cent level). Thus, the same phenomenon is observed in appraisal ratings as has often been reported in relation to assessment centres (as we will see below) – the failure to discriminate effectively between dimensions. Not surprisingly, factor analysis showed that, for each appraisal period, only one or sometimes two factors could be extracted from the ratings. Other data from this study suggest that appraisers' ratings across most of the dimensions were influenced by some basic personality attributes of the appraisees; in particular, being active, conscientious and – especially – optimistic (as measured by a personality questionnaire) correlated positively with a whole swathe of ratings. Since there was no direct relationship between these personality characteristics and some of the rating dimensions, e.g. between optimism and 'quality of judgement', the implication is that a halo effect based on a few positive aspects of personality influenced the appraisal ratings.

One response to these problems is the development of behaviourally anchored rating scales, or BARS (Smith and Kendall, 1963). These are carefully and systematically derived scales for assessing performance, and seek to put the person making the assessment into a more objective, observational role, rather than a judgemental one. The process for developing BARS is described in box 6.3.

However, the time and cost it takes to develop BARS discourages many organizations from using them widely; quite apart from anything else, BARS by their nature are rather specific to a single role or group of related roles, and cannot readily be generalized to other jobs. Moreover, the research on how

Box 6.3

Constructing behaviourally anchored rating scales

Although there are a number of variations, the development of BARS usually goes through five stages:

- Examples of behaviours reflecting effective and ineffective job performance are obtained from experts who are knowledgeable about the job to be rated.
- These examples are grouped into a series of separate performance dimensions by the experts.
- Another expert group repeats the second stage, allocating the examples to dimensions. This provides an independent check on the relevance of the behavioural examples to each dimension. Any that are allocated differently by the two groups are probably too ambiguous and should be discarded. As a result of this, the dimensions should be quite independent of each outer.
- Taking each dimension separately, the examples relating to it are rated on a numerical scale by the experts in terms of the degree of effectiveness they represent. Where an example does not get rated similarly by different expert judges, it will be deleted; a high level of agreement on how an example is rated on that dimension is required.
- The resulting dimensions are expressed as scales, the points of which are anchored by the behavioural descriptions arrived at through the preceding development stages. The number of dimensions can vary according to the job; anything from six to nine would be quite typical.

effective they are is not altogether reassuring in demonstrating that they show a significant improvement over more conventional methods (e.g. Jacobs, Kafry and Zedeck, 1980).

BARS represent a pragmatic, methodological solution to the problems with ratings. Another approach is to try to deepen our understanding of the cognitive processes involved in making performance ratings. This is best exemplified in the programme of work carried out by DeNisi (1996). He examines the information acquired by the rater, the cognitive representation of this, how the information is stored and retrieved, and how it is integrated with other factors to come to an assessment decision. This work has produced helpful cognitive models of the rating process, and these have informed some of the various attempts to train people to carry out appraisal ratings. In effect, this is the other major strategy – instead of focusing on the format of the rating scales, one tries to improve the use made of them by the raters themselves. There are various ways of doing this:

- *Rater error training*: teaching raters about the typical errors so they are sensitized to them and, in theory, less likely to make them.
- *Performance dimension training*: training raters in the use of the performance dimensions they are rating people on, and ensuring they can differentiate between them, i.e. they are able correctly to allocate a piece of behavioural 'evidence' to the dimension it should be rated under.
- *Frame of reference training*: seeks to give raters a clear picture of the standards they are rating people against; for example, by giving behavioural examples that would typify performance at each point on the rating scale.
- *Behavioural observation training*: focuses on the initial data collection by giving the raters training in correct observation and recording of behaviour, which should enhance the quality of the ratings they eventually make.

Not surprisingly, the different approaches tend to have different effects and consequences. However, reviews of the relatively few studies on the impact of these training methods (Smith, 1986; Woehr and Huffcutt, 1994) reflect somewhat mixed results; some improvement in rating quality is observed, though it is neither great in scope nor very consistent. The limited progress made by cognitively oriented research on appraisal has led to a move towards a perspective that emphasizes appraisal as a social process, which is addressed in more detail below.

Finally, one other approach to improving the fairness of appraisal should be mentioned, namely the use of more raters. One aspect of this is involving the person appraised more directly in the rating process. Many appraisal schemes, like that described in box 6.1, invite the appraisee to make a self-assessment and then use this as a background to the discussion of the appraiser's ratings. Can people assess themselves accurately? In principle, yes – providing that certain conditions, like having a clear picture of the performance standards of the peers they are comparing themselves with, are met (Mabe and West, 1982). However, they are quite often not met in appraisal, and where rewards are linked to the outcome of the assessment, the objectivity of self-assessment is likely to be an early victim. It seems to work best when individuals are asked to make assessments of their strengths and weaknesses relative to their own overall performance, rather than to compare themselves directly with others on each attribute (Fletcher, 1997a); in other words, when they are asked to say what they are good at and not so good at, without necessarily implying that the latter means they are less effective than their peers in this respect. This is very useful for discussing development needs, but of little value if you are seeking assessments to make comparisons between people.

There is an element of self-assessment in the other main approach to appraisal of performance: measuring performance against results achieved.

Results-oriented appraisal

This approach has become increasingly popular over the past 25 years or so, and originally stems from the concept management by objectives (MBO, or MbyO), which is a rather wider application of the same principles across the whole organization. Results-oriented appraisal focuses on setting objectives (or goals) and reviewing performance against those objectives. The objectives should relate to key aspects of the job, and provide *quantifiable* performance improvement targets for the individual to achieve *within a specified time period*. Manager and subordinate meet annually or more frequently to review progress against last year's objectives and to agree new ones for the year ahead.

The advantages of this approach are held to be that it is:

- more objective, because it rests on quantified measures;
- strongly job-related;
- less likely to engender conflict (because of its greater objectivity, appraiser and appraisee can see what has or has not been achieved).

The disadvantages are:

- it is not as easy to make direct comparisons between people on the basis of achievement against objectives, because the objectives set will vary somewhat from person to person
- it is far from straightforward to express performance in some jobs, or parts of them, in terms of objectives (for example, would it be a good idea simply to set an objective for a surgeon to carry out 25 per cent more operations in a year?)

The most striking thing here is that the research literature strongly supports objective setting. The evidence (e.g. Latham and Lee, 1986) shows that goal setting is effective in raising performance levels – it is claimed that more than 90 per cent of all studies on goal setting show positive effects. Locke et al. (1981) say the median performance improvement level is 16 per cent. Some caution should be expressed here, though, as many of the studies these conclusions are based on have been done in laboratory rather than field settings. The former obviously offer a degree of experimental control that the latter do not, but possibly at the cost of ecological validity; the nature of the task, the attitude of those participating, the rewards offered and many other factors may be very different from what one would find in real-world work situations. Another caveat is that studies on objective setting have been more concerned with quantity of output rather than quality – and quality is often as important, if not more so, than quantity (think back to the issue of objective setting for surgeons mentioned above). In terms of research on the *process* of objective setting, some of the main conclusions (Locke and Latham, 1990a) are:

1   Difficult objectives lead to greater achievement than easy ones.
2   Specific objectives, rather than general exhortations to do well, lead to better achievement.
3   Feedback on performance and achievement is essential.
4   The individual's own level of commitment is also a factor.

So, many appraisal systems today have a strong element of objective setting in them. But, perhaps in recognition of some of the limitations of this approach, they frequently also include some rating scales of competencies or performance dimensions on their appraisal forms.

The Social and Motivational Context of Appraisal

The initial emphasis on ways of assessing performance tended to focus research attention on the technical problems of rating scales etc., and perhaps resulted in less attention being paid to the social and motivational context of appraisal. In time, though, the latter has become the more dominant perspective. This is not surprising, since no matter how good the technical quality of the appraisal methods used, if those who are to be involved in the process – the appraiser and the appraisee – are not committed to the aims of the exercise, then little is likely to be achieved. And commitment to appraisal is often found to be conspicuously lacking. Rowe's (1964) observation, based on examination of appraisals in six UK companies, that 'appraisers are reluctant to appraise' still holds good in many instances today – it is common to find that a high proportion of staff who are supposed to have been appraised have not been. Recent survey evidence suggests that 80 per cent of British organizations express dissatisfaction with their appraisal schemes, chiefly because the schemes are perceived to fail to meet the aims organizations set for them (Fletcher, 1997a). For example, in one survey a key objective of the appraisal systems operated by the organizations contacted was 'motivation', but not one of them assessed their system as being very good in achieving this objective.

What are the problems that give rise to this rather dismal picture? A fundamental one is conflicting aims. The typical appraisal system faces the managers carrying out the appraisals with a potential role conflict: on the one hand, they are communicating an assessment to the appraisees, which may not be in line with how the appraisees see their own performance, while in the same session they are expected to play more of a counselling role, helping staff to improve performance and dealing with problems. It has been suggested that these two roles do not sit well together, because if appraisees become defensive about the assessment made of them, they are less likely to be willing to engage in a constructive search for ways of improving performance. The basic conflict here, then, is between the *assessment* function of appraisal and the *motivational* function of appraisal. This in turn is linked to four other aspects of the situation: the quality of the assessment, the way it is conveyed, the implications for rewards and the personal agenda of the participants.

Quality of assessment

As we have seen, there are difficulties in obtaining accurate and objective measures of ongoing job performance. Staff being appraised may feel that their boss has only a limited view of their performance, or is biased in some way, or is not taking account of other factors beyond their personal control that have impacted on what they have achieved. One particular bias that has been shown to operate in appraisal is attributional bias (Mitchell and Wood, 1980). Social psychological research has demonstrated the pervasive effects of 'fundamental attributional error', which refers to the tendency to interpret the causes of other people's behaviour in terms of their internal dispositions, and to take less account of situational influences than one does in explaining one's own behaviour. Clearly, in the context of performance appraisal, this could lead to serious distortions in judgements of the extent to which an individual's performance has been influenced by external factors. An interesting variation on this was observed by Garland and Price (1977), who found that successful performance by female managers was attributed by prejudiced male managers to luck or the easiness of the task, whereas unprejudiced managers put it down to high ability and good work.

Communicating the assessment

Appraisers are frequently reluctant to convey any critical comments to the appraisee, as they are apprehensive about the defensive reactions they may encounter. When they do make some critical comments, the results are some-times the exact opposite of what they seek to achieve. Meyer, Kay and French (1965), in their seminal work on the General Electric Company of America found that criticism led to lower motivation and little or no behaviour change in those appraised. Another study, by Pearce and Porter (1986), reported a long-term stable drop in organizational commitment as a consequence of staff just being rated as 'satisfactory' – as opposed to more favourably than that – when an appraisal scheme was introduced. In fact, Kluger and DeNisi (1996) concluded from their review of the literature that more than one-third of feed-back interventions (many of which occur in non-appraisal settings) *decreased* performance. While it is possible to convey feedback on performance limita-tions in a way that does not cause counterproductive reactions, the levels of skill and the conditions necessary to achieve this are not found all that often (Fletcher, 1986). For appraisal feedback to be effective, it has to:

- be specific and clear in content;
- be given soon after the event it relates to;
- be balanced in recognizing strengths as well as weaknesses in performance;
- come from a credible source (which in turn reflects the amount and quality of contact between the appraisee and the source, and the expertise of that source);
- be communicated in a sensitive manner (which may need training to achieve).

Links with rewards

An observation that has been made repeatedly (Prince and Lawler, 1986) is that direct links between assessments made in appraisal with rewards, such as pay rises and – to a lesser extent – promotion, cause great difficulty. The reason for this, as has already been noted, is the lack of faith in the accuracy and fair-ness of the assessments made. If an individual is told that she will not be getting as big a pay rise (or none at all) as she hoped because her performance level does not justify it, and she does not feel the assessment of her performance is right anyway, in most cases her reaction is predictably negative.

Personal and political agenda of the participants

Bernardin and Villanova (1986) found that a majority of appraisers and appraisees felt that inaccuracy in performance ratings was more because of deliberate distortion than inadvertent cognitive errors on the part of the raters. Bernardin and Beatty (1984) also suggest that organizational politics affect managers' assessments of staff. Various reasons for this have been suggested

(Dulewicz and Fletcher, 1989; Cleveland and Murphy, 1992), including managers:

- giving more favourable assessments than are warranted to project a positive image of both their unit's and their own performance;
- avoiding confrontation with subordinates and the attendant risk of difficult work relationships thereafter;
- presenting themselves as caring, supportive bosses;
- not giving too high ratings to good performers in case they are promoted out of their team.

From the appraisee's side, personal motives may include wanting to maintain self-esteem, seeking to refute criticism, protecting and enhancing reward and promotion prospects, seeking training opportunities and career development moves (Dulewicz and Flectcher, 1989). Although there is ample evidence that subordinates want feedback on performance, this does not mean that they are going to accept it blindly. In some cases, they want to know what their boss thinks of them so that they can give their own side of the story and correct what they may feel are unwarranted criticisms of their performance. The concept of procedural justice is relevant here, as it deals with perceptions of the fairness of the procedures used for distributing rewards within an organization. Having the opportunity to participate and contribute actively to the appraisal – having a 'voice' in it – and being able to challenge assessments are found to be important factors in determining perceptions of procedural justice (Greenberg and Folger, 1983; Greenberg, 1986).

Tziner, Latham, Price and Haccoun (1996) have produced a questionnaire measure of the extent to which performance appraisals are perceived to be affected by organizational politics, and this aspect of appraisal is likely to see more research attention in the future. The fact is that while organizations have needs that they expect the appraisal system to meet, the people doing the appraisal – and those they are appraising – usually have more personal agendas to follow; these often cause the appraisal process to become less effective in terms of what the organization wanted from it.

Reference was made in this section to the basic conflict of using appraisal as primarily an assessment tool or a way of motivating performance improvement. Organizations traditionally want it to be both, but the problems discussed above demonstrate just how difficult it is to achieve these twin aims – at least, in a single system. The research evidence suggests that accurate assessment is not something that comes readily from appraisal. However, if the assessment element is downplayed, then use of techniques like objective setting does seem to lead to performance improvements. There is, though, another aspect of appraisal that we have hardly mentioned until now, but that has profound implications for whether appraisal is seen as a motivating force; this is its role in *developing* the appraisee.

Appraising and Developing Potential

It is one thing to know how people are performing now, but what about making sure they get the kind of experience and training they are going to need for future roles? And which of them should be promoted to higher levels when the opportunity arises? Appraisal is typically supposed to contribute to answering these questions; the assessment and development of employees' potential are among its aims.

Assessing potential to perform at a higher level is not straightforward. One obvious basis to work from is present performance, as reflected in appraisal and other data. But the reason for having an assessment of potential is precisely because present performance is by no means a completely reliable indicator of future performance, hence the so-called 'Peter principle': people rise to the level of their incompetence, i.e. you keep getting promoted until you reach the position where you cannot do the job well, so you do not get promoted any more. The other problem is that when managers are asked to assess the longer-term potential of their staff, the assessment task they are being faced with is especially difficult. They are being asked to comment on the ability of an individual to do a job at a level that may be above their own, and which they have no direct experience of.

Because of these problems, organizations have increasingly turned to other methods of assessing potential. One of the simplest is to have career review panels made up of senior managers, who periodically review the career progress of more junior managers and decide what promotion or development steps should be taken in each case. However, they now often turn to evidence from either psychometric tests or assessment centres to help them make these judgements.

Using psychometric tests in assessing potential

As tests and their validity are discussed at some length in chapter 4, they are only briefly discussed here. There are a variety of ways in which tests are applied in assessing potential and promotability.

1   They may be given to external candidates as part of a selection procedure, not only to assess suitability for the job vacancy but also to get some idea of the individual's potential beyond that.
2   Internal candidates for a promotion vacancy may be given a battery of tests to assess their suitability for the promotion in question (see box 6.4 for an example).

3   Individuals may go through a testing session as part of a career assessment process that is not related to a specific promotion or job vacancy, but has the assessment of potential as one of its aims.

4   Tests are often included as an element of the assessment centre process (see below).

It is never suggested that tests are sufficient by themselves to assess potential. They should always be employed as an additional input to other sources of information, such as existing performance or career progress to date.

Using assessment centres in assessing potential

The background on assessment centres (ACs) is provided in chapter 2. Essentially, an AC involves the assessment of a group of candidates by a team of assessors, using an integrated series of assessment techniques. Principal among the latter are simulation exercises, such as group decision-making tasks. Although they have become widely used in personnel selection, originally their main roots were in the assessment of the promotability and long-term potential of existing staff (Woodruffe, 1996). In particular, the management

---

Box 6 . 4

An example of the use of tests in a computer company's promotion process

In this large computer manufacturer, middle managers who have been judged to be in the field for promotion are sent to an external consultant psychologist for individual assessment before they attend a promotion board interview. The assessment process includes a battery of cognitive ability tests – numerical, verbal, logical reasoning and imaginative thinking – and one or two personality measures, as well as an in-depth interview with the consultant. The result is a report to the company that covers various aspects of work performance, an analysis of main strengths and limitations and an assessment of suitability for a particular promotion vacancy based on a job description and person specification/competency profile.

The report also offers an opinion on the individual's longer-term potential and makes recommendations for development action needed to improve performance. Before the interview, the senior managers on the promotion board read the report, along with recent appraisal forms completed on the individual, and use this material to guide some of their questioning of the candidate and their assessment of him or her against the job requirements. Shortly afterwards, the candidate attends a feedback session with the assessor, where the content of the report and its career development implications are discussed. In this particular company, the use of tests was a carefully integrated aspect of human resource practice.

progress study carried out by Bray at AT&T (Bray and Grant, 1966) was influential in the adoption of this method. Bray put a group of young managers through a series of assessment procedures which were an AC in everything but name, as part of a research study on management careers. When the data were examined five or more years later, they showed that how the managers performed in the assessment process had predicted rather well the speed with which they would make career progress within the company. Similarly, and even more impressively, Anstey (1977) reported how an AC used to assess 'fast-track' potential among UK civil service entrants yielded a correlation (corrected for selectivity) of 0.66 between AC rating and subsequent career progress – effectively, the number of promotions gained – *over a 30-year period*. To achieve this level of prediction against a measure taken so long afterwards is fairly remarkable. Meta-analysis pulling together a whole range of studies has suggested an average validity of about 0.40 (Gaugler, Rosenthal, Thornton and Bentson, 1987). In general, the level of prediction is much better where the criterion measures are of career advancement (i.e. potential) rather than performance; this is partly because the measures of the former are more objective than measures of the latter (Tziner, Ronen and Hacchen, 1993).

Encouraged by such findings, organizations have turned to using ACs for assessing the potential of:

- junior and middle managers for more senior levels;
- foremen and supervisors for junior/middle management;
- scientific, professional and technical staff for general management or for management within their own specialism.

However, ACs are not without their problems, and have been criticized on various grounds, including the following.

- The dangers of AC outcomes becoming self-fulfilling prophesies. If your are assessed as having potential, development activities are lavished upon you, and not surprisingly you do better in your performance. On the other hand, if you are not assessed as having potential, you are less likely to be put forward for promotion, job moves etc., and you make little progress.
- The fact that the rationale, or construct validity, for ACs is suspect. This revolves around the competencies or dimensions they are assessing, which are supposed to represent behavioural consistencies important in performance. But several studies (e.g. Robertson, Gratton and Sharpley, 1987) have shown that the correlation of ratings within exercises is greater than that across exercises – indicating that what is being assessed is really exercise performance, not competencies. In a sense, this problem is compounded by the fact that ACs have very high face validity for the assessors

and for candidates – they really look like they are assessing what they claim to, and in a very thorough way. Assessors and their organizations may be overconfident about the quality of assessment offered by ACs.

- The impact on candidates of not doing well in an AC, and not being rated as high in potential, has been shown to have lasting detrimental effects on candidates' psychological well-being and motivation (Fletcher, 1991). Perhaps it is the high face validity of ACs that makes 'failing' in them so hard to take. If those assessed see them as being both fair and very thorough, there is little they can do – by rationalization or any other means – to soften the blow of not being identified as having high potential. Understandably, then, attending ACs does seem to generate a degree of anxiety in a fair proportion of candidates (Fletcher, Levatt and Baldry, 1997).

The first point is probably a factor in some of the validity findings, though it has to be said that in the AT&T study (Bray and Grant, 1966) mentioned above the data were not available to the management of the company and were not acted on, so there was no possibility of this kind of contamination affecting the results. The second point remains a persistent problem, though there is some contrary evidence suggesting that dimensions can be used effectively (Lievens, 1998), and especially where the assessors are psychologists rather than line managers (Sagie and Magnezy, 1997). The third issue, about the potential negative impact on candidates of 'pass/fail' type decisions, has been recognized within organizations over a period of years and has resulted in a growing emphasis on the use of a derivation of the AC, the development centre (DC).

The DC is similar in format to the AC, but the focus is much more on the training and development needs of the individual than on coming out with an overall rating of potential. The idea is to capitalize on the learning potential of the AC exercises and to use the information they generate to increase self-awareness of strengths and limitations and to build a development plan for each participant. This largely removes the problem of some people being branded as failures, or, come to that, as crown princes. The assessors may include more personnel, management development and training staff, though senior line managers will often still be involved. Research shows that DCs can lead to better career planning (Jones and Whitmore, 1995).

There are many other methods used to assess and develop employees' potential (see Kidd, 1997; Seegers, 1997), which are outside the range of the present chapter and often operate in ways that are largely independent of the main appraisal and promotion systems. However, there is one method that has become widely adopted in recent years, that started out (in the UK) as a development activity and that is increasingly being drawn into the formal appraisal process. This is multi-level, multi-source feedback, also known as '360 degree feedback'.

360 degree feedback and appraisal

The term 360 degree feedback generally means an individual being rated by subordinates, peers, superiors and – sometimes – clients, as well as doing a self-assessment. These assessments are collected and integrated by either a human resource manager or an external consultant, then fed back to the 'target' manager in the form of a profile of his or her competencies as seen from these differing perspectives. An action plan is then drawn up to tackle any development needs that have been identified.

A few British companies began using 360 feedback systems, sometimes in a more limited form that was essentially upward feedback from subordinates, in the early 1990s, though the method has a longer history in the USA (Redman and Snape, 1992). More recently, though, it has been much more widely adopted in the UK, perhaps because a process that to some extent represents a challenge to normal hierarchical concepts of management has only just now become acceptable. The changes in UK organizations described below have created a new culture and transformed ideas about management, with the result that 360 degree feedback is an idea whose time has come. Some examples of the use of these systems are given in box 6.5.

What do 360 degree feedback systems actually *achieve*? Certainly, many managers receiving this kind of feedback feel it is potent, but in the USA their attitude to it seems to have been broadly positive (McEvoy, 1990). So far, though, there is not a great deal of research evidence about the effectiveness of such systems in bringing about behaviour change in the feedback recipient. A handful of studies report that the ratings managers receive over successive 360 feedback processes show an improvement (Fletcher and Baldry, 1999). But these changes could reflect a variety of extraneous factors, such as increased familiarity with the procedure, or improvements in performance that might take place with greater experience irrespective of receiving feedback. Presumably, much depends on the quality of the 360 degree system and the way it is set up in the first place. We have already noted concerns about the quality of conventional appraisal ratings, and unfortunately many of the same problems may arise with 360 degree feedback. A study of a pilot 360 feedback system in a large oil company (Fletcher, Baldry and Cunningham-Snell, 1997a) found that:

- the 80 individual behavioural ratings did not correspond to the competencies they were meant to;
- these ratings were so intercorrelated that in effect most of them were redundant and all that was being measured was an overall dimension of 'good–bad';
- the ratings did not show any relationship with another criterion measure of performance being used in the company;
- there seemed to be systematic biases that affected specific groups of raters.

B o x   6 . 5

Examples of upward and multi-source feedback

One of the first companies in Britain to introduce upward feedback was the high street retail store, W. H. Smith. Its survey data showed that managers were viewed by staff as being better at decision-making than at motivating subordinates. In the light of this, the company asked staff to rate their managers on 32 attributes. These included such things as:

- communicates relevant information to me;
- plans out work effectively;
- inspires me to do well;
- does not impose unrealistic objectives.

The ratings were done on a questionnaire, which was then mailed back to a consultancy independent from the company for data analysis. A report was compiled for each manager, based on all the responses received. About 300 senior managers were covered by this process. Any who had been in the job for less than three months or who had fewer than three subordinates were excluded (having fewer than three would have made it very hard to maintain anonymity as to which ratings came from which subordinates). The results of this exercise revealed that managers were often weak on interpersonal skills; they scored higher on decision-making and discipline than on motivating, listening and developing staff. The feedback from this upward appraisal was used to plan training and development programmes for the managers concerned. There are four important points to observe about the W. H. Smith scheme:

- the company went to some trouble to pilot it first;
- steps were taken to make it as non-threatening as possible (full briefings, encouraging managers to hand out the questionnaires to their staff themselves etc.);
- the output from it was not linked to pay;
- it was a separate exercise from the normal appraisal process.

An interesting case study of the introduction of a multi-source feedback system is provided by Clifford and Bennett (1997). They describe how initial work on management standards in the Automobile Association was used as a basis for implementing a 360 degree feedback system to bring about a culture change. A 50-item management standards questionnaire, with the response to each question being given on a clearly described six-point effectiveness scale, was used to gather feedback. Each participant sent the questionnaire to his or her boss and first and second level reports subordinates; respondents were encouraged to explore what they valued most and least about the participant. Feedback was handled by internal human resource staff and line managers who had been specially trained for the purpose. The aim was for each participant to emerge with a prioritized development plan. Clifford and Bennett's account gives a picture of a carefully handled process that was being systematically monitored in terms of its operation and impact.

The inescapable conclusion from the research on this scheme is that any development plan arising out of the feedback process could be seriously misguided. If such ratings had been fed into an appraisal process, and possibly been linked to reward decisions, the basis for the assessment and the equity of those reward decisions would be called into question. Given that there is a trend to incorporate 360 degree feedback into the normal appraisal process in some organizations, this is of some concern. However, the 360 degree system in this company was revised on the basis of the research, and in its new form showed vastly improved psychometric qualities (Fletcher et al., 1997a).

This section has looked at the role of performance appraisal in the assessment and development of potential, and has described how this aspect of appraisal has now been at least augmented – and in some organizations completely replaced – by a variety of techniques that fall outside the traditional annual appraisal session. But this reflects part of the wider picture of changes in appraisal practice, and it is this that the chapter concludes with.

Organizational Change and Contemporary Trends in Performance Appraisal

In recent years, performance appraisal systems have begun to take on a very different appearance in some organizations. This is partly owing to the frustration felt with the failure of traditional appraisal methods to deliver what was asked of them, but it also stems from pervasive changes in the nature of organizations themselves. They have delayered (taken out whole management levels), downsized, become more international in their operations and so on. They have also had to operate in an increasingly competitive climate and with greater legal regulation. Those changes in themselves necessitate a different way of operating, and this is signified by the adoption of new systems like total quality management, and an increasing interest in relating individual performance to rewards. All this suggests the need for a new approach to appraisal. For example, if you have fewer management levels, it usually means that individual managers have more subordinates working to them, those subordinates may be geographically spread and the manager may see any one of them fairly infrequently – all of which makes fair and accurate appraisal more difficult. This has fuelled the interest in multi-source, multi-level appraisal.

An increasing recognition that conventional approaches to appraisal do not motivate people, and the need to make the most of the reduced number of employees, has brought about a greater emphasis on development rather than assessment. There is a steady decline of the monolithic appraisal system, which typically involved a universally applied process with an heavy emphasis on the appraisal forms and on using the process primarily for assessment purposes. In its place appraisal seems to be breaking down into three elements:

- A performance planning session that involves reviewing achievement of objectives over the period in question and setting objectives for the period ahead. If performance-related pay comes into the picture, this is often what it is related to.
- A development review, probably based on competencies or skill dimensions, that looks at the training and development needs of the individual. This takes place at a different time of the year from the performance planning session. Where they operate, 360 degree feedback systems may feed into this element of appraisal.
- As we have seen, the assessment of potential is now often supplemented by the use of more objective assessment methods, such as psychometric tests or assessment centres.

These elements are now more often properly integrated into the human resource policies of the organization as whole, in particular performance management systems. These represent a strategy that seeks to create a shared vision of the purpose, aims and values of the organization, and to help each individual employee to understand and recognize his or her part in contributing to them; the overall aim is to enhance individual and organizational performance. Typically, elements of such a strategy will include developing the mission statement and business plan, objective setting and other methods of performance measurement, developing competencies of employees, performance-related pay (sometimes) and various approaches to improving internal communications. Embedding appraisal in a wider approach of this kind turns it into a more effective mechanism, and less of an annual ritual that might otherwise appear to exist in a vacuum. The research evidence is beginning to show that such policies do make an impact on employee attitudes and organizational commitment (Fletcher and Williams, 1996), which in turn can impact on organizational performance (Ostroff, 1992). If this trend continues, performance appraisal may establish itself as a more important contributor to organizational functioning and individual well-being than it has done in the past.

Chapter Summary

Performance appraisal systems vary greatly, but they are found in one form or another in most large organizations. They usually try to achieve many – probably too many – different ends. Much of the emphasis has been on finding ways of assessing people accurately and fairly, but this has proved problematic in the context of today's complex organizations. The perception that appraisal systems have often failed to deliver the increased motivation and improved performance expected of them has led to changes in the orientation of both research and practice in this field, with more attention being paid to employee development. The assessment of potential is now increasingly determined by assessment centres, psychometric tests and the use of multi-source feedback. Organizations have gone through a huge amount of change in recent years, and this has made more traditional approaches to appraisal less relevant. Instead of a single appraisal mechanism, organizations increasingly use a series of linked processes as part of an integrated performance management strategy.

Discussion Points

1   Can line managers accurately and objectively assess the work performance of those under them?

2   How is performance appraisal supposed to motivate people to improve performance?

3   Should pay be linked to performance?

4   What are the best ways of assessing an individual's potential?

5   How have organizational changes affected performance practices?

CHAPTER SEVEN

JOB STRESS AND HEALTH

Pascale Le Blanc, Jan de Jonge
and Wilmar Schaufeli

Contents

Chapter Outline

This chapter focuses on job stress in relation to workers' physical and psychological health. We begin with an outline of job stress as a social problem, followed by a discussion of the main perspectives on (job) stress, resulting in a process model of job stress that will be used as a frame of reference in the remainder of the chapter. In the next section, several leading models on job stress and health are presented and discussed. The role of individual differences as well as workplace social support in the relationship between job stress and health is discussed. Finally, an overview of organizational and individual interventions to reduce job stress is given.

Job Stress as a Social Problem

Job stress is a major concern, not only for the employees involved but also for organizations and society as a whole. Ample evidence suggests that the prevalence of job stress is high. For instance, a survey among nearly 16,000 European workers revealed that 29 per cent considered that their work activity affected their health (Paoli, 1997). The work-related health problems mentioned most frequently were back pain (30 per cent), stress (28 per cent) and overall fatigue (20 per cent). In Britain, a National Survey of Health and Development of almost 1500 young men showed that 38 per cent of the sample were under some or severe 'nervous strain' at work, whereas only 8 per cent were under similar strain at home or in their personal lives (Cherry, 1978).

Prevalence rates of job stress are not only high, but also rising continuously. In Britain, an immense growth of stress-related absenteeism was observed across a 25-year period: from 1955 to 1979 absenteeism due to 'nervousness, debility and headache' increased by 528 per cent (Hingley and Cooper, 1986). In the Netherlands in 1967, when the Disability Security Act was introduced, mental disorders accounted for 11 per cent of workers' disability claims. This rate continued to rise steadily, so that 30 per cent are now assessed as work disabled on mental grounds – the largest single diagnostic group, followed by musculo-skeletal disorders (28 per cent) and cardiovascular disease (8 per cent), respectively (Houtman, 1997).

Needless to say, the expenditures on job stress are huge. It is estimated that the costs of sickness absences for stress and mental disorders exceed £5 billion per year in the UK, which amounts to over 10 per cent of the gross national product (GNP). On average, in the European Union 9.6 per cent of GNP is spent on the consequences of job stress, with the Netherlands in the leading position (13.9 per cent) (Cartwright and Cooper, 1996).

Case Study 7.1

During the past two years, Mr Whyte, a 48-year-old teacher at a vocational training centre, has played a crucial role in the merging of his school with another training centre. It has been a very hectic and busy time because he was one of the advocates of and active agents in that merger. After the merger was concluded Mr Whyte felt very disappointed, since he was not promoted to the newly created job as department coordinator in the new organization. Instead, the job he hoped to receive was offered to a younger colleague who had always been sceptical of the merger. Mr Whyte felt hurt, resentful and unfairly treated; in his opinion he had put much more time and effort into reorganizing the school than his younger colleague – yet he was denied the appropriate reward. Soon after this event, Mr Whyte developed particular symptoms. He had occasionally felt tired before, but now it was different – he felt completely mentally exhausted. It took an extreme effort to take on anything. Previously he had quickly recuperated from his tiredness after a weekend or a couple of days off. Now, he had been on sick leave for over six months and he was still unable to perform his job because he felt extremely tired and anxious. He slept until ten o'clock in the morning, needed an additional couple of hours to wake up properly and felt tired all day long.

These immense costs have prompted action at national level, as well as at European level, with legislation that attempts to reduce job stress. This is particularly true in countries like the UK, Sweden and the Netherlands, and to a somewhat lesser extent in France and Germany (Kompier, De Gier, Smulders & Draaisma, 1994). Modern legislation emphasizes: (a) a broad and positive health concept, i.e. instead of solely combating ill-health, health, safety and well-being at work are promoted; (b) a comprehensive approach, integrating health, safety and well-being at work; (c) active involvement and joint responsibility of employer and employee; (d) self-regulation by providing a supportive environment, e.g. by institutionalizing occupational health and safety services (see also de Gier, 1995).

Thus, job stress is a major and rising concern in industrialized countries and it seems that the level of job stress has increased alarmingly in the past decades. This is illustrated by increasing stress-related absenteeism and work incapacity rates, as well as by rising associated costs.

What Is Job Stress?

The original meaning of the term 'stress' is derived from engineering. By analogy with physical force, it refers to external pressure that is exerted on a person, which in turn results in tension or 'strain' (Kahn and Byosiere, 1992). Within certain limits, people are able to deal with this pressure and adapt to the situation, and to recover when the stressful period is over. This is analogous to the bending and springing back of a metal bar. However, when the

Some time earlier – during that busy period at school – Mr Whyte had given up his hobbies: refurbishing antique furniture and playing bridge. Although he had enough time to pursue these hobbies now, he lacked the energy and didn't fancy them. Instead, he worried a lot and had problems concentrating. For instance, when reading the newspaper, after a few lines he forgot what he read previously. Moreover, he suffered from headaches and neck pain, and felt depressed and restless. Mr Whyte was particularly uncomfortable in interpersonal situations. He felt distressed – his throat was constricted and he was not able to breath normally. As a result he started to avoid social situations and became more and more isolated from colleagues, friends, neighbours and relatives. If things did not work out properly or someone was unkind, Mr Whyte became upset. He was irritable, emotional and easily hurt, which strained his family, especially his two teenaged children. But perhaps most frightening of all, Mr Whyte did not recognize himself any more; he felt powerless and totally out of control. He could not understand what was happening to him.

Source: D. Enzmann (1998) *The Burnout Companion to Research and Practice: a Critical Analysis.* London: Taylor & Francis, p. 20.

pressure is too large, the bar will bend so much that it cannot return to its original position any more. The limiting value to which the system can no longer adapt is dependent upon the quality of the metal and its condition (e.g. temperature). In human beings, an individual's adaptability is determined by personal characteristics, e.g. his or her stress tolerance, and by the environment, e.g. the availability of social support (see below).

However, in everyday language, as well as in the scientific literature, the term 'stress' is used to refer to the cause as well as to the accompanying state of tension, and to the negative consequences of this state. As there is little agreement as to how exactly 'stress' should be defined, there is no general theory of stress. One of the main reasons for this lack of agreement lies in the large number of disciplines with different perspectives involved in stress research, such as biology, psychology, sociology, occupational medicine, and epidemiology (Buunk et al., 1998). Nevertheless, most researchers in the field of stress do agree that three different meanings of the term stress can be distinguished (e.g. Cooper and Payne, 1988; Kasl, 1987; Kahn and Byosiere, 1992; Semmer, 1996): stress as a stimulus, stress as a response and stress as a mediational process between stressor (stimulus) and reaction (response). Each of these perspectives is discussed below, with a focus on *job-related* stress.

Stress as a stimulus: poor work situations

In the field of experimental psychology and ergonomics, stress is primarily regarded as a *stimulus*, i.e. a negative situation or a noxious event that acts on

Table 7.1   Categories of job-related stressors

Category	Stressor
Job content	work over-/underload
	complex work
	monotonous work
	too much responsibility
	dangerous work
	conflicting/ambiguous demands
Working conditions	toxic substances
	poor conditions (noise, vibrations, lighting, radiation, temperature)
	work posture
	physically demanding work
	dangerous situations
	lack of hygiene
	lack of protective devices
Employment conditions	shift work
	low pay
	poor career prospects
	flexible labour contract
	job insecurity
Social relations at work	poor leadership
	low social support
	low participation in decision making
	liberties
	discrimination

the individual and is supposed to have negative effects. This use of the term stress closely resembles its original meaning. In the domain of job stress, stressful stimuli can be categorized under four main categories: job content, working conditions, employment conditions and social relations at work. In table 7.1, major stressors belonging to each of these categories are given.

The amount of stress is defined in terms of the extent of exposure to a noxious stimulus; for example, the higher the working pace, the higher the level of stress. Accordingly, a linear relationship between a stressful stimulus and its (negative) effects is assumed. Until now, most stress research departing from this perspective has focused on job content by studying the stressful effects of certain job characteristics (e.g. Karasek, 1979; Payne, 1979; Karasek and Theorell, 1990).

Stress as a response: job-related strain

In psychophysiology and occupational medicine, stress is viewed as a psychological and/or physiological *response* of the organism to some kind of threat.

This notion of stress is based on Selye's (1978) classical general adaptation syndrome (GAS). According to Selye, exposure to a noxious stimulus triggers a complex of non-specific physiological reactions that are intended to protect the individual against harmful consequences. The GAS consists of three stages: the alarm reaction (mobilization by means of physiological and hormonal changes), the resistance stage (optimal adaptation by activating appropriate systems) and exhaustion (depletion of adaptation energy). Although the GAS may be adaptive initially, negative consequences such as fatigue, tissue damage and high blood pressure may occur if the individual is not able to cope with the stressful stimulus and the stress reactions persist over longer periods of time. As stated above, it is assumed that the same, non-specific, response pattern is triggered by different types of stressful stimuli, and that an individual's thoughts and emotions do not influence the type of response. However, these assumptions have proved to be untenable, as numerous studies have demonstrated that different types of physiological and hormonal reactions may occur, depending on the nature and interpretation of the stimulus and the accompanying emotions. For example, laboratory and field studies by Frankenhaeuser and her colleagues (for an overview see Frankenhaeuser, 1978) have demonstrated that the catecholamines adrenaline and noradrenaline play a main role in mobilizing acute adaptive resources, whereas corticosteroids provide more enduring support in the case of prolonged stress. In a study among sawmill workers, Frankenhaeuser and Gardell (1976) found that stress, as reflected in adrenaline and noradrenaline excretion and in self-reports of irritation, was most severe when the job was highly repetitive, when the worker had to maintain the same posture throughout working hours and when the work pace was controlled by the machine. The build-up of catecholamine arousal during the working day should be regarded as a warning signal, indicating that the organism is forced to mobilize 'reserve capacity', which in the long run is likely to add to its wear and tear. Indeed, interview data showed that an inability to relax after work was a common complaint among high-stress workers. Moreover, the frequency of psychosomatic symptoms, as well as absenteeism, was exceptionally high in this group (Frankenhaeuser, 1978).

Stress as a mediational process

Whereas both the stimulus approach and the response approach to stress emphasize directly measurable factors (characteristics of the environment and measurable stress reactions, respectively), this approach focuses on the *cognitive*, *evaluative* and *motivational processes* that intervene between the stressful stimulus and the reaction (response). According to the mediational approach, stress reactions are a result of the interaction between person and environment. Potentially stressful stimuli may lead to different types of stress reactions in different individuals, depending on their cognitive evaluations (appraisals) of the situation (Lazarus and Folkman, 1984) and the resources they have at their disposal to cope with the stressful situation.

Latack and Havlovic (1992) developed a conceptual framework for coping with job stress. In this framework, a distinction is made between the focus of coping and the method of coping. The focus of coping can be problem-oriented or emotion-oriented. Problem-oriented coping refers to efforts aimed at altering the transaction between person and environment. For instance, it may include behaviours like seeking help or increasing efforts to encounter the threat. Emotion-oriented coping, on the other hand, is defined as efforts aimed at regulating the emotions of a person (e.g. cognitive strategies like avoidance and relaxation techniques). With respect to the method of coping, two dimensions are distinguished. First, coping behaviour can be observable (overt) or not observable (covert). Second, each of these two types of coping behaviour can be aimed at control or at escape. When the focus and/or method of coping do not match the stressor at hand, feelings of stress will be sustained or even intensified. Basically, active ways of coping (e.g. control coping) are to be preferred to passive ones, such as escape coping (e.g. de Rijk, Le Blanc, Schaufeli and De Jonge, 1998), provided that the situation offers possibilities for active intervention.

Although the mediational approach has paved the way for a more theoretical view on the (job) stress process (e.g. the person–environment fit model, discussed below), a main disadvantage is that almost all studies employing this perspective rely exclusively on self-reports of both stressful stimuli and stress reactions. This makes it very difficult to disentangle the occurence of an event, its cognitive evaluation and the individual's reaction to it.

In the preceding paragraphs, a static (stimulus or response) versus a more dynamic perspective (mediational process) on (job) stress was presented. In the remaining part of this chapter, job stress is defined as an experienced incongruence between environmental (job) demands and individual/situational resources that is accompanied by mental, physical or behavioural symptoms. We will refer to stressful stimuli as 'stressors', and to their consequences as 'stress reactions' or 'strains'.

Before we turn to a more detailed description of different types of stress reactions, the distinction between *event* stressors and more continuous or *chronic* stressors should be clarified (Wheaton, 1996). These types of stress define end-points on a continuum standing for variation in how discretely or continuously stressors operate. The defining issue of an event stressor is its discreteness, both in typical time course and in its onset and offset. For example, crossing the road, you notice a fast car dangerously close, which represents a high-priority psychological demand. You rapidly dash out of your path, and are soon back in an unstressed state. However, a second, very different form of stress can be defined that: (a) does not necessarily start as an event, but develops slowly and insidiously as a continuing problematic condition in our social environments and roles; and (b) typically has a longer time course than events, from onset to resolution. This kind of stressors can be referred to as chronic stressors, 'problems and issues that are either so regular in the enactment of daily roles and activities or defined by the nature of daily role enactments or activities that they behave as if they are continuous for the individual' (Wheaton, 1996). Chronic stressors are less self-limiting in nature than a typical event stressor. An event, almost by definition, will end, while chronic stressors are typically open-ended, using up our resources in coping, but not promising resolution. Most generally, chronic job stress arises from one of an array of problems; for instance, excessive task or role demand, excessive complexity, uncertainty, conflict, restriction of choice and under-reward.

An example of a state of chronic job stress is burnout, which can be defined as

> a persistent, negative, work-related state of mind in normal individuals that is primarily characterized by exhaustion, which is accompanied by distress, a sense of reduced effectiveness, decreased motivation, and the development of dysfunctional attitudes and behaviours at work. This psychological condition develops gradually but may remain unnoticed for a long time for the individual involved. It results from a misfit between intentions and reality at work. Often burnout is self-perpetuating because of inadequate coping strategies that are associated with the syndrome. (Schaufeli and Enzmann, 1998, p. 36)

The burnout syndrome is illustrated in more detail by the case of Mr Whyte (case study 7.1).

Stress reactions

Stress reactions (strains) can be expressed in different ways and can be classified in five different clusters: (a) affective, (b) cognitive, (c) physical, (d) behavioural and (e) motivational. In addition, three levels of expression can be distinguished, since stress displays itself not only in the form of individual symptoms, but also in the form of symptoms at the interpersonal and organizational level. In table 7.2, an overview of different types of stress reactions on each of the three different levels is presented.

Of course, stress reactions can differ in their intensity. Sometimes, the negative effects of stressors can easily be overcome by recreation and relaxation. However, in the case of prolonged exposure to stressful stimuli, the individual may not able to reduce his or her (physiological) state of stress, and high activation levels are sustained (Ursin, 1986). This can in turn give rise to chronic physical (e.g. coronary heart disease; Siegrist, 1996) and/or psychological stress complaints (e.g. burnout; Maslach and Jackson, 1986; Schaufeli and Enzmann, 1998).

In the remaining part of this chapter, the process model presented in figure 7.1 is used as a frame of reference. This process model is based upon the insights we gained from several theoretical models and empirical studies concerning job stress and health. The model integrates much of what has been outlined above. According to this process model, different types of job

Table 7.2 Possible stress symptoms at the individual, interpersonal and organizational levels

Type/level	Individual	Interpersonal	Organizational
Affective	anxiety tension anger depressed mood apathy	irritability being oversensitive	job dissatisfaction
Cognitive	helpless-/powerlessness cognitive impairments difficulties in decision making	hostility suspicion projection	cynicism about work role not feeling appreciated distrust in peers, supervisors and management
Physical	physical distress (headache, nausea, etc.) psychosomatic disorders (gastric-intestinal disorders, coronary diseases etc.) impairment of immune system changes in hormone levels		
Behavioural	hyperactivity impulsivity increased consumption of stimulants (caffeine, tobacco) and illicit drugs over- and undereating	violent outbursts aggressive behaviour interpersonal conflicts social isolation/withdrawal aggressive behaviour	poor work performance declined productivity tardiness turnover increased sick leave poor time management
Motivational	loss of zeal loss of enthusiasm disillusionment disappointment boredom demoralisation	loss of interest in others indifference discouragement	loss of work motivation resistance to go to work dampening of work initiative low morale

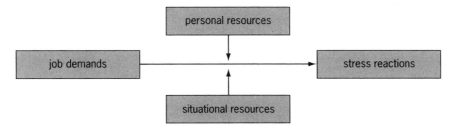

Figure 7.1   A process model of job stress.

demands (stressors) can result in diffent types of stress reactions (strains). Moreover, the relationship between job demands and strains is expected to be moderated by (a) personal resources (e.g. coping styles), and (b) situational resources like workplace social support. The different components of our process model are elaborated in the next section in a discussion of the central themes in current theories on job stress.

Job Stress as a Process

Many different models focusing on job stress have been illuminated in the literature, and most of them are connected with our process model presented in figure 7.1. In this section we discuss several leading models on job stress and health: the Michigan model and the closely related person–environment fit model, the vitamin model, the demand–control–support model and the effort–reward imbalance model. Finally, some attention is given to the role of individual differences and workplace social support in the job stress process.

Early Michigan models and person–environment fit model

The most general job stress models were developed at the Institute for Social Research (ISR) of the University of Michigan (hence the designation 'ISR' or 'Michigan models'). Since the basic model was first devised, several different versions of it have been developed. We confine ourselves to two models here: the basic Michigan model and the elaborated person–environment fit model (see Kahn and Byosiere, 1992). The basic model is a combination of all kinds of conceptual categories rather than the reflection of particular theory. At a later stage attempts have been made to define these factors more precisely and to determine interrelationships.

The Michigan model reflects four main groups of variables, arranged in a causal sequence (see figure 7.2). Organizational characteristics (e.g. company size, hierarchical structure and job description) may lead to psychological stressors, such as role conflict, role ambiguity and role overload. Role conflict arises

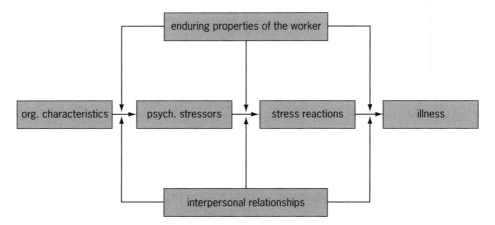

Figure 7.2 The Michigan Model.

when expectations and demands are difficult to meet or mutually incompatible. Role ambiguity occurs when an employee does not have sufficient or adequate information about the nature of the role itself. Finally, role overload is simply having too much to do or perceiving the role as being too difficult (Hingley and Cooper, 1986; Buunk et al., 1998). These stressors, in turn, may lead to stress reactions or strains. Strains are affective, physiological and behavioural responses of the individual (e.g. job dissatisfaction, high blood pressure, high heart rate, absenteeism). Finally, strains may lead to both mental and physical illness, such as depression, cardiovascular disease, cancer and gastric ulcers. The postulated relationships between the four major groups of variables are assumed to be moderated by (a) enduring properties of the individual worker (like type A/B behaviour) and (b) interpersonal relationships (e.g. social support). A type A behaviour pattern is characterized by a sense of time urgency, impatience, restlessness, high work involvement and competitiveness. In contrast, a type B behaviour pattern is characterized by a calmer, more patient and more relaxed way of functioning (Furnham, 1992; Buunk et al., 1998).

Although the all-inclusive Michigan model has a heuristic value and has stimulated a lot of research, several criticisms still remain. The most important criticism is that the model is not based on a theoretical perspective that leads to specific hypotheses. Therefore, it is very difficult to validate the model empirically, which makes refinements greatly needed.

The person–environment (P–E) fit model is an example of such a refinement (e.g. French, Caplan and Harrison, 1982). This model is based on the premise that the interaction between environmental variables and relevant properties of a person determines job-related strains. According to the model, job stress can be defined as either a misfit between the person's opportunities

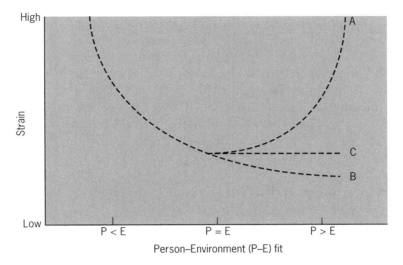

Figure 7.3   Different forms of P–E fit relationships associated with job-related strain.

and environmental supplies or a misfit between the person's abilities and environmental demands. For example, there may be a discrepancy between how fast an assembly line worker can work and the required number of ready-made products. A second element of the P–E fit model is the distinction between objective and subjective misfit. Objective misfit refers to a discrepancy between the actual state or condition a worker is in and the objective characteristics of the work situation. Subjective misfit concerns a discrepancy between a worker's view of himself and his view of the environment. However, usually only the subjective person and subjective environment are assessed, and not their objective counterparts. Additionally, defence mechanisms tend to reduce subjective misfit; for instance, by denial (see French et al., 1982).

A final element concerns the particular types of relationships in the model. For instance, both positive and negative misfit may lead to job stress, assuming curvilinear (U-shaped) relationships (see line A in figure 7.3). Furthermore, the model predicts asymptotic relationships; that is, only a deficit in the person or a surfeit in the environment will lead to strains (line B). Caplan (1983) notes an example where workers with a strong need for self-control may feel threatened by too little opportunity for participation in decision-making. Reducing this deficit will reduce the strain they experience. These workers may experience little further reduction in strain once the opportunity for participation exceeds the minimum they find acceptable. The third relationship reflects a purely linear effect of one P–E fit component relative to the others on job-related strains (line C). In several studies such proposed relationships have indeed been found. For instance, the pioneering study by Caplan et al. (1975) among over 2000 workers found a U-shaped relationship between the misfit of actual and desired complexity of work on the one hand and level of depression on the other. Both too little and too much complexity were related to depression. More recently, Edwards and Harrison (1993) found additional evidence that a perfect fit between what an employee desires and obtains is related to the lowest level of job-related strains.

Despite the plausible idea underlying the model, a few points of criticism must be mentioned (e.g. Buunk et al., 1998). To begin with, the empirical evidence is not very impressive and the model typically receives mixed support. Second, all kinds of strains are lumped together, without distinguishing between direct, short-term reactions (e.g. anxiety) and long-term reactions (e.g. psychosomatic complaints). Finally, as the next models suggest, it may be a mistake to include such a broad array of work conditions under the single umbrella of job stressors.

Vitamin model

Warr (1987) developed in the 1980s his framework of mental health, referred to as the vitamin model (VM). The central idea underlying the VM is that mental health is affected by environmental psychological features, such as job characteristics, in a way that is analogous to the effects that vitamins are supposed to have on our physical health. Warr's framework has three principal parts:

1   Job characteristics are grouped into nine categories that relate differently to mental health outcomes according to the type of 'vitamin' they represent.
2   A three-axial model of affective well-being, a core aspect of mental health, is postulated.
3   It is assumed that persons and situations interact in the prediction of mental health.

Warr (1987) draws an analogy between the way in which vitamins act on the human body and the effects of job characteristics on mental health. Following this line of reasoning, de Jonge and Schaufeli (1998) refer to Warr's vitamins as 'psychological work vitamins'.

Generally, as figure 7.4 shows, the absence of certain job characteristics impairs mental health, whereas their presence initially has a beneficial effect on employee mental health (segment A). Beyond a certain required level, vitamin intake no longer has any positive effects: a plateau has been reached and the level of mental health remains constant (segment B). The next segment shows that a further increase of job characteristics may either produce a 'constant effect' or be harmful and impair mental health (denoted by 'additional decrement'). According to Warr (1987, 1994c), which of the two effects will occur depends on the particular job characteristic.

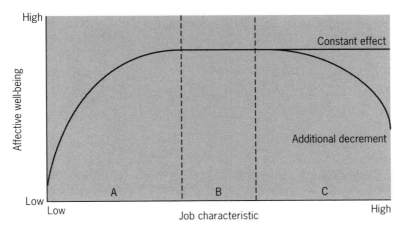

Figure 7.4   The vitamin model.

Table 7.3   The nine job characteristics of the vitamin model

CE job characteristics	AD job characteristics
Availability of money	Opportunity for control
Physical security	Opportunity for skill use
Valued social position	Externally generated goals
	Variety
	Environmental clarity
	Opportunity for interpersonal contact

CE, constant effect; AD, additional decrement.

Warr (1987, 1994c) identified nine job features that may act as determinants of job-related mental health (see table 7.3). Warr assumes that six job characteristics (e.g. opportunities for control and variety) have curvilinear effects (U-shaped). A lack of such features or an excess of such features will affect mental health negatively. For example, the negative impact of excessively high levels of job control has been identified in laboratory as well as occupational studies (e.g. Burger, 1989; de Jonge, Schaufeli and Furda, 1995). The remaining three job characteristics (physical security, availability of money and valued social position) are supposed to follow a linear pattern: the higher such a job characteristic, the higher the level of mental health will be. Warr (1998) noted, however, that it is improbable that the latter associations are purely linear. For instance, it seems plausible that an increase in income will have greater benefits at low income levels than at extremely high income levels. In

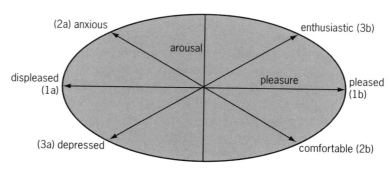

Figure 7.5 Job-related affective well-being.

other words, increased levels are desirable until a certain plateau has been reached.

A principal indicator of *job-related* mental health in psychological research is affective well-being. In order to measure affective well-being empirically, Warr (1998) proposed three dimensions: displeasure to pleasure, anxiety to comfort and depression to enthusiasm (see figure 7.5). Job-related affective well-being has most commonly been studied by measures of job satisfaction, job-related anxiety or tension and occupational burnout and depression.

Finally, in terms of the interaction between persons and situations, the VM is essentially situation-centred, in that it focuses on the association between job characteristics and mental health. However, there are undoubtedly differences between people in the nature of those associations (Warr, 1994c). Therefore, three categories of individual characteristics are viewed as possible moderators of the effects of job characteristics on mental health: *values* (e.g. preferences and motives), *abilities* (like intellectual and psychomotor skills) and *baseline mental health* (i.e. dispositions like negative affectivity).

Moderating effects are expected, especially in the case of a so-called 'matching' individual characteristic (Warr, 1994c). In that respect, individual characteristics which match particular job characteristics will cause a stronger moderating effect than those which lack this matching property. Job autonomy may serve as an example: a matching individual characteristic might be the value 'preference for autonomy'. It is assumed that the preference for autonomy moderates (i.e. changes) the relationship between job autonomy and, for instance, job satisfaction (Warr, 1987). In case of low preference for autonomy, for example, the relationship between autonomy and satisfaction will be zero (or even negative), whereas in case of high preference for autonomy the relationship between the two variables will be positive.

In recent years, a few cross-sectional studies have investigated the patterns proposed by the VM (e.g. Warr, 1990b; Xie and Johns, 1995; de Jonge and Schaufeli, 1998). Most notably, a study by de Jonge and Schaufeli (1998) among 1437 Dutch healthcare workers confirmed several postulated curvilinear relationships by means of a comprehensive empirical test. To summarize all the VM studies briefly, the present results are mixed and inconclusive. Job demands and job control, for instance, seem to be curvilinearly related to some aspects of employee mental health in the way that is predicted by the model, whereas the effect of workplace social support does not follow the model. Furthermore, all studies have failed to take account of the possibly multifaceted ways in which the nine job characteristics may affect job-related well-being. Added to this, longitudinal studies have not been reported yet, which means that causal orders in associations still have to be proved. Finally, there has been no empirical evidence for the interactions between individual and job characteristics as related to employee health *within* the VM.

Demand–control–support model

Since the 1980s, the job demand–control (JD–C) model has dominated the empirical research on job stress and health. The model was introduced by Karasek in 1979 and further developed and tested by Karasek and Theorell (1990; Theorell and Karasek, 1996). In 1988, Johnson and Hall elaborated the JD–C model by adding the dimension of *workplace social support*. This expanded model was called the demand–control–support (DCS) model. In order to understand the principles of both models, we first discuss the JD–C model.

The JD–C model, as depicted in figure 7.6, postulates that the primary sources of stress lie within two basic job characteristics: *psychological job demands* and *job decision latitude*. According to the model, the jobs most likely to show extreme job-related stress reactions (like exhaustion and cardiovascular diseases) are those that combine high demands and low decision latitude. This combination is labelled *high strain* (quadrant 1). There is also an opposite situation termed *low strain*; that is, jobs in which job demands are low and workers' decision latitude is high (quadrant 3). In this situation the model predicts lower than average levels of stress reactions.

The second important assumption of the model is that motivation, learning and personal growth will occur in situations where both job demands and decision latitude are high (*active jobs*; quadrant 2). This assumption is closely related to what might be called 'good stress', since job stressors are translated into direct action (i.e. effective problem-solving), with little strain left to cause job-related stress (Selye, 1956; Karasek et al., 1998). The opposite of this situation is found in *passive jobs*, in which skills and abilities may atrophy (quadrant 4). This situation resembles the 'learned helplessness' phenomenon (Lennerlöf, 1988).

In short, psychological demands and decision latitude affect two psychological mechanisms, reflected by diagonals A and B in figure 7.6. The first mechanism influences the (adverse) health of the employee (diagonal A), while

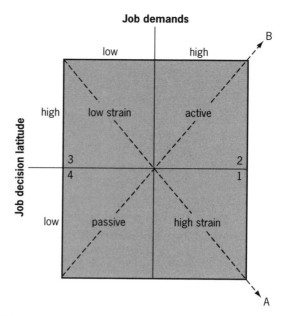

Figure 7.6   The job demand–control model.

the other influences the work motivation and the learning behaviour of the employee (diagonal B).

   The elaborated DCS model (figure 7.7) was developed to examine the joint effects of three instead of two basic characteristics of the work organization, i.e. job demands, job control and workplace social support. In this extended model, both the strain and activity assumptions are split up into *isolated* and *collective* conditions, and the processes are consequently redefined. It is, for instance, assumed that the most unfavourable effects are expected for a combination of high demands, low decision latitude and low social support. This combination is sometimes called *iso-strain* (Johnson and Hall, 1988). Social support is assumed to buffer psychological strain, depending on the degree of social and emotional integration, help and trust between supervisors, colleagues etc. We discuss the (general) function of workplace social support in the job stress process below.

   Two major conclusions can be drawn from the studies using and evaluating the two models (de Jonge and Kompier, 1997). The first conclusion is that large (mostly epidemiological and population-based) studies offer the most support for the model, and for the strain assumption in particular. The second conclusion is that the assumption that the combination of psychological demands, decision latitude and social support involves stronger responses (such as more physical symptoms or more work motivation) is not often sup-

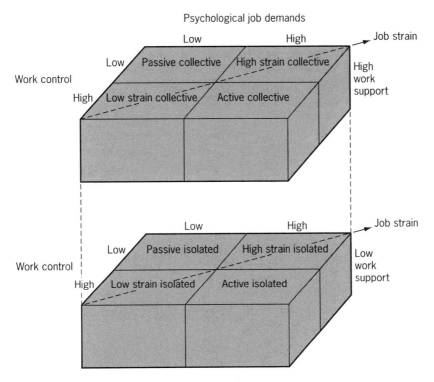

Figure 7.7   The demand–control–support model.

ported. It is more often the case that the three components separately have an impact on the outcome variables than that they reinforce each other in this respect (so-called synergistic effects).

Obviously, the strength of the DCS model lies in its simplicity and practical implications. However, the content and methodology of the model have been commented on in the past few years. Various authors are of the opinion that a number of theoretical and methodological problems remain to be solved (e.g. Jones and Fletcher, 1996; Kasl, 1996; Kristensen, 1996). First, for instance, the conceptualization, operationalization and measurement of the basic dimensions should be elaborated further. Second, since this is a situation-centred model, the issue of objective versus subjective measurement of job characteristics has been neglected thus far. More specifically, the model focuses on characteristics of the work situation, but these are usually determined with the use of self-report questionnaires. Lastly, many studies have failed to take into account individual differences (like locus of control and coping styles), considering only the job factors.

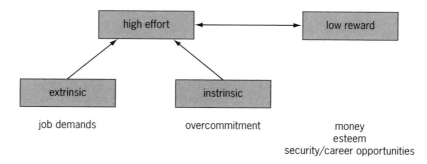

Figure 7.8   The effort–reward imbalance model.

Effort–reward imbalance model

The final model discussed here is the model of effort–reward imbalance at work, developed by Siegrist and his group (e.g. Siegrist, 1996; Peter and Siegrist, 1997). This model has a more sociological focus and shifts from the concept of job control (i.e. control paradigm of job stress) to the reward structure of work (i.e. reward paradigm of job stress).

In the effort–reward imbalance (ERI) model, the work role of an employee is considered a basic tool to link important self-regulatory functions (self-esteem and self-efficacy) with the societal structure of opportunities and rewards (see figure 7.8). Essentially, the model is based upon the principle of reciprocity: high effort spent at work in combination with low reward obtained may cause a state of emotional distress and sympathetic arousal, with an inclination to cardiovascular risks. For example, in the case of Mr Whyte, the effort he invested in reorganizing the school was not rewarded by promoting him to department coordinator. The resulting feelings of unfairness most probably triggered the onset of his stress symptoms.

Effort is evaluated as two components: extrinsic effort or *job demands* (like time pressure, responsibility and physical demands), and intrinsic effort or *overcommitment*. The latter is regarded as a specific personal pattern of coping with job demands and of eliciting rewards that is relatively stable over time, and that may prevent people from accurately assessing cost–gain relations. Overcommitment is assessed by using four dimensions of coping behaviour (need for approval, competitiveness and latent hostility, impatience and disproportionate irritability, and inability to withdraw from work obligations), which are combined to form one latent factor. According to Peter, Geißler and Siegrist (1998), rewards are distributed to employees in three different ways: *money* (i.e. adequate salary), *esteem* (e.g. respect and support) and *security/career opportunities* (e.g. promotion prospects, job security and status consistency).

Published empirical studies with the ERI model are growing rapidly in number, and the combination of high effort and low reward at work has found to be a risk factor for cardiovascular health, sickness absence and self-reported symptoms (e.g. Siegrist, 1996; Peter and Siegrist, 1997; Bosma, Peter, Siegrist and Marmot, 1998; Peter et al., 1998).

Although the ERI model looks very promising in the research domain of job stress and health, several preliminary comments have to be made (see also Kasl, 1996; Siegrist, 1996). First, it seems inconsistent to make a clear distinction between extrinsic and intrinsic efforts, but no clear distinction between extrinsic and intrinsic rewards. Intrinsic rewards, however, seem to be part of the overcommitment construct (i.e. need for approval). Second, one might question the extent to which the overcommitment construct is a stable trait and to what extent it is related to the work environment. For instance, will some employees experience more stress because of their character, or do some job characteristics evoke overcommitment? Third, the term *status inconsistency* is used to describe a misfit between occupation and education in both directions. In the model, both directions reflect low reward or low status control, which is not completely consistent with the work and organization psychology literature. From that point of view, an excess of education over occupational status was seen as a risk factor, and not vice versa. Fourth, because the model encompasses a broad social context, it is remarkable that little attention has been paid so far to the relationship between work and family life as an environmental factor of possible relevance ('work–home interference'). Finally, a last comment concerns the dynamic nature of the ERI model. Longitudinal studies are clearly needed in order to investigate the time-dependent (accumulating) effects on both effort and reward, and on experience of high-cost/low-gain conditions.

Individual differences and job stress

As we mentioned above, individual differences may play an important role in the relationship between job factors and employee health. From a work and organization psychological point of view, researchers are mainly interested in *job-related* individual difference variables (like coping styles or locus of control) and their capacity to explain additional variance in health outcomes. In addition to this, in-depth investigation of the form and nature of individual difference effects (whether or not in combination with job factors) is on the research agenda. The first task, however, is to classify three obvious categories of individual difference variables (Warr, 1987; Payne, 1988; Parkes, 1994):

1 *Genetic characteristics* (e.g. gender, constitution, physique).
2 *Acquired characteristics* (e.g. age, education, social class, skills).
3 *Dispositional characteristics* (e.g. coping styles, preferences and type A/B behaviour).

Space does not allow a complete description of all three categories. In this chapter, we therefore restrict ourselves to the category of individual difference variables that stands out in the literature as being potentially relevant in the job stress process; that is, the dispositional characteristics (e.g. Parkes, 1994; Spector and O'Connell, 1994).

Generally, many job stress studies have shown that the relationship between a certain job stressor and a certain job strain mainly, or even exclusively, occurs in employees with particular dispositional characteristics (e.g. Warr, 1987; Parkes, 1994). For example, a demand–control study by de Rijk and colleagues (1998) involved intensive care unit nurses, and showed a synergistic effect of job demands and decision latitude only if employees dealt with their problems actively. In other words, for nurses who are inclined to use control (i.e. high in active coping), decision latitude acts as a stress buffer, as it attenuates the increase in job strain due to job demands. Although such model-driven findings are obtained more and more, they are not found as consistently as one would expect from a more theoretical point of view (Semmer, 1996). Limitations tend to lie in the design (often cross-sectional surveys) and methodology of the studies reported (moderated or subgroup regression procedures) as well as in the individual difference measures (e.g. Cohen and Edwards, 1989; Parkes, 1994). Furthermore, it remains unclear at what point in time the individual difference variables influence the job stress process. For instance, do they change the objective–subjective stressor relationship, or do they affect the perceptions of job stress as related to affective, cognitive, physical and behavioural outcomes?

To sum up briefly, the results of individual difference studies that were discussed seem to indicate that job stressors have negative effects on the health of all workers, although these may be more severe for some and less severe for others, depending on *specific* dispositional characteristics of the task performers in question.

Workplace social support and job stress

Workplace social support provided by superiors, colleagues and subordinates is generally thought to have an important stress-reducing function. There are numerous definitions and conceptualizations of 'social support'. This concept is used to refer to, for example, the existence of good, pleasant relationships with others, the availability of others in the case of problems and help, understanding and attention provided when one is faced with difficulties. In general, many researchers agreed on a distinction between four conceptualizations of workplace social support that cover most of the definitions (see Buunk, 1990; Peeters, 1994; Sarason and Sarason, 1994):

1   *Social integration:* the number and strength of the connections of the individual worker to others in his or her social network.
2   *Satisfying relationships:* a good organizational climate, and pleasant, close working relationships with superiors, colleagues and subordinates.

3   *Perceived available support:* the appraisal that others can be relied on for direct aid or assistance, information, advice, guidance and empathic understanding.
4   *Actually received support:* once a stressor has come into existence, superiors, colleagues or subordinates may perform supportive acts to reduce job stress.

With regard to the content of workplace social support, a distinction is usually made between four types (House, 1981): *emotional support* (e.g. through empathy, caring, love, trust and concern), *instrumental support* (e.g. direct help provided by others), *informational support* (e.g. advice, information, suggestions or directions) and *appraisal support* (e.g. feedback or social comparison relevant to a person's self-evaluation). It should be emphasized that these four types of support are empirically closely related (Buunk et al., 1998).

The stress-reducing functions of workplace social support are generally referred to as *buffer effects*, which are distinguished from *direct effects* (e.g. Cohen and Wills, 1985). A buffer effect occurs when social support alleviates the impact of job stressors on stress reactions, and has a positive effect when strong job stressors are involved. Direct effects, on the other hand, refer to a positive influence of workplace social support on a person's health, irrespective of whether or not people are under job stress. Empirical research provides evidence for the buffering effects of workplace social support, although the results are not very consistent. In many studies only a few of the investigated buffer effects are found to be significant. With respect to direct effects, a lot of studies have found moderate negative associations between workplace social support and psychological stress reactions (for overviews, see Cohen and Wills, 1985; Buunk et al., 1998).

By clarifying the relationships between different types of job characteristics and health, the above models have given some indications of interventions that can be used to prevent or reduce job stress. In the final section of this chapter, a systematic overview of this type of intervention is presented and discussed.

Interventions to Prevent or Reduce Job Stress

Job stress interventions may focus on three levels:

*   *The organization.* By changing the work situation through organization-based interventions the source of the problem is tackled and the employee's negative reaction is reduced.
*   *The individual–organization interface.* By increasing the employee's resistance to specific job stressors, his or her vulnerability decreases.
*   *The individual.* By learning to cope better with stress in general, the individual prevents negative psychological effects of job stressors.

Table 7.4 Overview of job stress interventions

Focus/purpose	Identification	Primary prevention	Secondary prevention	Treatment	Rehabilitation
Organization	Job stress audit	Improving work content and environment; time scheduling; management development; corporate fitness and wellness programmes; career management	Anticipatory socialization; communication, decision-making and conflict management; organizational development	Institutionalization of occupational health And safety services; employee assistance programmes	Outplacement
Individual/ organization	Personal screening	Time management; interpersonal skills training; promoting a realistic image of the job; balancing work and private life	Peer-support groups; coaching and consultation; career planning	Specialized counselling and psychotherapy	Individual guidance and assistance
Individual	Self-monitoring	Didactic stress management; promoting a healthy lifestyle	Cognitive–behavioural techniques; relaxation		

In addition, job stress interventions may serve five purposes:

- *Identification* (i.e. early detection of job stressors and stress reactions).
- *Primary prevention* (i.e. reduction of job stressors).
- *Secondary prevention* (i.e. altering the ways employees respond to job stressors).
- *Treatment* (i.e. healing those who suffer severely from job stress).
- *Rehabilitation*[1] (i.e. planned return to the previous job).

Levels and purposes of job stress interventions may be combined into a classification table that constitutes a framework for discussing various approaches (see table 7.4; for more elaborate recent reviews see Ivanchevich, Matteson, Freedman and Phillips, 1990; Burke, 1993; Ross and Altmaier, 1994; Murphy, 1996).

Interventions primarily aimed at the organization

Instead of a prime target, reducing job stress is a mere by-product of organization-based interventions. Usually, such interventions are primarily aimed at improving efficiency or effectiveness. Organization-based interventions focus on: (a) surveillance (i.e. job stress audit); (b) removal or reduction of stressors (i.e. improve the job content and the work environment, better time scheduling, improve communication, decision-making and conflict management, and organizational development); (c) improve the fit between the employee and the organization (i.e. career management, anticipatory socialization, management development and outplacement); (d) institutionalization of procedures and services (i.e. corporate fitness and wellness programmes, enrichment of occupational health and safety services and employee assistance programmes).

An employee survey (*job stress audit*) is used to 'take the stress temperature' of the organization by comparing employees across units, locations, occupations or jobs. Typically, screening instruments include several job stressors, ways of coping with stress and mental and physical stress reactions (e.g. the occupational stress indicator: Cooper, Sloan and Williams, 1988).

Improving the job content and the work environment are basically directed towards reducing quantitative and/or qualitative work overload. Broadly speaking, three types of strategies can be followed to reduce workload: (a) job redesign (e.g. job enlargement, by adding duties or responsibilities to the

---

1 Note that, by definition, rehabilitation goes beyond the purely individual level in the sense that it inevitably takes into account the employee's relation with the organization. Therefore, the individual/rehabilitation cell in table 7.4 is empty. Moreover, since we focus on job-related problems, a general discussion of psychotherapy and counselling is beyond the scope of this book. Accordingly, the individual/treatment cell also remains empty.

current job; job enrichment, by restructuring a job so that it is more mean-ingful, challenging and intrinsically rewarding; job rotation, by periodically changing jobs or duties); (b) clarifying the employee's role characteristics (e.g. introduce job descriptions or role clarification to analyse discrepancies in role expectations); (c) improving the physical work environment (e.g. by intro-ducing focus groups, the expertise of the employees can be used to generate ideas and solutions about how to improve stressful working conditions).

Proper time scheduling can reduce the number of working hours (e.g. the introduction of 'mental health days', sabbatical leave, or retreats; the encour-agement of part-time employment and discouragement of excessive overwork).

Management development is primarily implemented through management education and management training. For instance, managers can be given feed-back about their leadership behaviour from regular surveys of their subordi-nates (e.g. as part of a job stress audit).

Career management is the responsibility of the organization, whereas career planning (see below) is the responsibility of the employee. The former con-sists of an institutionalized set of rules and procedures that cover such areas as recruitment, selection, placement, development and promotion.

Corporate fitness and wellness programmes may focus on control of high blood pressure, smoking cessation, weight reduction, physical fitness, reduc-ing lower back pain, health and safety education, reduction of alcohol use or stress management (Schreurs, Winnubst Cooper, 1996).

Anticipatory socialization is the institutionalization of training programmes that promote a more realistic image of the job (see above) or offer potential employees a 'realistic job preview' (i.e. a recruitment procedure that involves exposing applicants to the reality of the workplace before they are eventually hired).

Communication, decision-making and conflict management: formal top-down communication through periodically issued bulletins, the Internet or plenary meetings is increasingly important in today's large-scale, complex and bureaucratic organisations. Ideally, such communication channels should be embedded in a system of participative decision-making so that employees are involved in making important decisions (Jackson, 1983).

Organizational development (OD) is a programme of planned interventions that should improve the internal operations of an organization. OD is both a methodology and a loose guidance system for helping organizations to make healthy changes. As a methodology, OD follows a stepwise approach, includ-ing preparation, data collection, diagnosis and planning, action, evaluation and continuation. As a guidance system, OD includes various techniques, such as survey feedback, training and team development. A central aspect of many OD efforts is participatory action research. This approach involves outside experts (usually researchers) and organization members in a joint process aimed at meeting both research and intervention objectives, such as increasing employ-ees' health and well-being. Typically, this strategy emphasizes participation and collaboration in which researchers and employees are co-learners in an empowering process.

In Europe, the *institutionalization of occupational health and safety services (OHSSs)* has been facilitated by the introduction of new legislation. OHSSs play an indirect role in reducing job stress in at least three ways: (a) by regularly carrying out stress audits and personal screenings; (b) by offering a specialized individual counselling and rehabilitation service for employees with work-related mental problems; (c) by expert consultation in occupational medicine, safety engineering, human factors and occupational psychology.

Employee assistance programmes (EAPs) are worksite-based programmes to assist in the identification and resolution of productivity problems associated with employees impaired by personal concerns, including health, marital, family, financial, alcohol, drug, legal, emotional, stress or other personal concerns which may adversely affect employee job performance (Lee and Gray, 1994). The ultimate concern of EAPs is with prevention, identification and treating personal problems that adversely affect job performance.

Organizations might offer employees *outplacement* services when it is likely that successful rehabilitation can only be achieved in another job outside the organisation. Usually, outplacement is the outcome of a careful self-analysis and opportunity analysis that is carried out as part of a career development process (see below).

Interventions primarily aimed at the individual/ organization interface

This type of intervention seeks to: (a) increase awareness (personal screening); (b) improve individual coping skills (time-management, interpersonal skills training, promoting a realistic image of the job, balancing work and private life); (c) provide emotional and instrumental support at work (peer support groups, coaching and career planning); (d) cure target complaints by intensive treatment (specialized counselling and psychotherapy); (e) rehabilitate employees (individual guidance and assistance).

Personal screening assesses the employee's level of job stress in relation to others in the organization or in the occupation. Basically, similar instruments to those used for a stress audit are employed in personal screening, except that now the focus is on the individual employee.

Time management training teaches the employee to use his or her time efficiently and productively by proper scheduling, planning, prioritizing and delegating duties. It has been successfully included in comprehensive stress management programmes (e.g. Higgins, 1986).

Interpersonal skills training focuses on how to deal with others at work, such as co-workers, customers or clients. Assertiveness (i.e. the ability to respond in a straightforward manner with regard to what one believes, feels and wants) is a key interpersonal skill that is very popular in stress management programmes.

Promoting a realistic image of the job is especially important for avoiding an initial reality shock among novices that might cause early career burnout (Cherniss, 1995). For this purpose, for instance, a mentor system can be used, in which experienced colleagues guide novices.

Balancing work and private life: work and private life can be balanced by setting up clear boundaries between job and home physically as well as psychologically, and by limiting job spillover, pursuing leisure activities that are fun and rewarding and spending time in the company of others.

Peer support groups are groups of co-workers who come together on a more or less regular basis to exchange information, support each other emotionally and try to solve work problems. These groups may vary from loosely organized groups to clearly structured groups that use a specific and systematic approach, such as 'Balint groups' (Rabinowitz, Kusnir and Ribak, 1996).

Coaching and consultation both refer to situations where expert help from a more experienced colleague is offered to employees for (potential) work problems. Consultation pertains to a more or less unique event (e.g. how to deal with a particular customer), whereas coaching designates the process that includes a series of such events (e.g. how to deal with aggressive customers).

Career planning includes two key elements: self-analysis (the assessment of one's strengths, weaknesses, interests and abilities) and opportunity analysis (identification or the range of organizational roles available).

Specialized counselling is offered by professionals such as general practitioners, social workers, counsellors and occupational physicians for employees who are in a temporary crises. *Psychotherapeutic treatment* of job stress is conducted by highly specialized professionals – usually psychiatrists, psychotherapists, or clinical psychologists – who deal with the most complex and severe cases that might include related psychopathology as well (Lowman, 1993).

Guidance and assistance with rehabilitation – the planned return to the previous job after a period of sick leave – should ideally be an integral part of every treatment programme.

Interventions primarily aimed at the individual

Most individual level interventions are well established and have a long and successful history in clinical or health psychology. Principally, individual strategies are aimed towards: (a) increasing the individual's awareness (self-monitoring and didactic stress management); or (b) reducing negative arousal (promoting a healthy lifestyle, cognitive–behavioural techniques and relaxation).

Self-monitoring assumes that by explicitly focusing on the signs and symptoms of distress an individual can increase his or her self-awareness ('know thyself'). A powerful self-monitoring technique is to keep a stress diary, a personal record or log of stress symptoms and related events.

Didactic stress management refers to all kinds of information about job stress that is provided with the intention of increasing awareness and improving self-care. For instance, workbooks are available with tips, tricks and exercises that teach how to deal with job stress (e.g. Fontana, 1989).

Promoting a healthy lifestyle includes the encouragement of regular physical exercise, proper nutrition, weight control, no smoking, enough sleep and periods of rest for relaxation and recharge during the workday and thereafter. Many of these elements are part of corporate fitness and wellness programmes. Of these approaches, physical exercise is perhaps the most powerful antidote to stress (McDonald and Hodgdon, 1991).

Cognitive–behavioural techniques are based on the assumption that cognitions (thoughts) lead to emotions (feelings), which in their turn set in motion specific behaviours (actions). Hence, in order to change emotions or behaviours, cognitions must be altered; for instance, by using cognitive appraisal (putting one's stressful situation into perspective), cognitive rehearsal (learning to tolerate stressors by anticipating) or cognitive restructuring (replacing irrational thoughts and beliefs with more rational cognitions).

Relaxation is considered to be a universal remedy to stress. Therefore, it is the cornerstone of virtually every stress management programme, often in combination with cognitive–behavioural techniques (Murphy, 1996). The goal of relaxation is to teach the aroused individual how to produce voluntarily a positive, alternate physiological response, a state in which he or she deliberately eliminates the undesirable physiological effects of stress.

Chapter Summary

Clearly, job stress is a scientific as well as a social problem. From a scientific point of view it may seem somewhat disappointing that after more than twenty-five years of intensive research a 'grand, unifying theory of job stress' is still not within reach. However, the feasibility of one overarching framework can be seriously questioned, as job demands (stressors) are constantly and rapidly changing owing to social developments. For example, in most industrialized countries there has been a rapid growth of the service sector and a decline of more traditional sectors, such as agriculture and manufacturing. Moreover, new technology has been introduced in both manufacturing and the services, sector, which requires the use of complex cognitive skills such as accuracy and rapid decision-making. As a result of these changes, the nature of job demands (stressors) has shifted from purely physical to mental and emotional demands. This, of course, will have important implications for job stress, and thus for the theoretical models describing it.

Continued

For the time being, each of the four models that has been discussed in this chapter highlights some important aspects of the job stress process. This means that these models are complementary rather than mutually exclusive. So it seems more realistic to pursue an eclectic approach to job stress, in which possible solutions to stress-related problems are derived from one or several models of job stress that best fit the problem at hand.

From a social point of view, reducing job stress is a crucial issue. Unfortunately, the practical applicability of many theoretical models leaves much to be desired. There is still a gap between theoretical knowledge or insight and practical implication. In other words, we do have a lot of tools, but at present we do not have the corresponding operation instructions for real practice. However, despite this shortage, as well as differences in scope, all these models do make it clear that job stress interventions should be targeted primarily on the source of many of the problems, i.e. the stressful working situation. For reasons of 'fine tuning', these work-oriented interventions may be supplemented by measures aimed at the individual worker. As mentioned above, this point of view is also supported by modern labour legislation in many Western countries.

In conclusion, work plays a central part in the lives of many individuals. For that very reason, the serious (human) costs of job stress need to be considered in future decisions on work and employee health.

Discussion Points

1   Which perspective on (job) stress (stimulus, response, mediational process) do you find most attractive, and why?

2   In what different ways may (a) individual differences and (b) workplace social support play a role in the relationship between job stress and health?

3   Which job stress model do you favour, and why?

4   What are the two main hypotheses of Karasek's job demand–control model? What is the reason for its popularity in research on job stress and health?

5   At what levels may job stress interventions occur? Which seems to be most effective?

Key Studies

Karasek, R. A. (1979) Job demands, job decision latitude and mental strain: implications for job redesign. *Administrative Science Quarterly*, 24, 285–308.

Siegrist, J. (1996) Adverse health effects of high-effort/low-reward conditions. *Journal of Occupational Health Psychology*, 1(1), 27–41.

Further Reading

Cooper, C. L. and Payne, R. (eds) (1988) *Causes, Coping and Consequences of Stress at Work*. Chichester: John Wiley & Sons.

Kahn, R. L. and Byosiere, P. (1992) Stress in organizations. In M. D. Dunette and L. M. Hough (eds), *Handbook of Industrial and Organizational Psychology, Volume 3.* (571–650). Palo Alto, CA: Consulting Psychologists Press, pp. 571–650.

House, J. S. (1981) *Work Stress and Social Support*. Reading, MA: Addison-Wesley.

Karasek, R. A. and Theorell, T. (1990) *Healthy Work: Stress, Productivity and the Reconstruction of Working Life*. New York: Basic Books.

Latack, J. C. and Havlovic, S. J. (1992) Coping with job stress: a conceptual evaluation framework for coping measures. *Journal of Organizational Behavior*, 13, 479–508.

Paoli, P. (1997) *Second European Survey on the Work Environment 1995*. Dublin: European Foundation for the Improvement of Living and Working Conditions.

Ross R. R. and Altmaier, E. M. (1994) *Interventions in Occupational Stress*. London: Sage.

Schabracq, M. J., Winnubst, J. A. M. and Cooper, C. L. (eds) *Handbook of Work and Health Psychology*. Chichester: John Wiley & Sons.

Schaufeli, W. B. and Enzmann, D. U. (1998) *The Burnout Companion to Study and Practice: a Critical Analysis*. London: Taylor & Francis.

Theorell, T. and Karasek, R. A. (1996) Current issues relating to psychosocial job strain and cardiovascular disease research. *Journal of Occupational Health Psychology*. 1(1), 9–26.

Warr, P. (1987) *Work, Unemployment, and Mental Health*. Oxford: Clarendon Press.

Warr, P. (1994) A conceptual framework for the study of work and mental health. *Work and Stress*, 8(2), 84–97.

PART III

HUMAN FACTORS
AT WORK

Computer controls. (J. Allan Cash)

CHAPTER EIGHT

WORKLOAD AND TASK ALLOCATION

Andrew J. Tattersall

Contents

Chapter Outline

This chapter first considers the nature of workload and approaches to understanding the relationships between workload, performance and individual well-being. It then reviews the various measures that have been developed to assess workload. Finally, the relationships between work and task design, workload and occupational stress the explored.

What Is Workload?

It is an almost indisputable fact that the vast majority of people are familiar with the term workload and have at least an implicit notion of what constitutes workload. Furthermore, a large number of people complain that they experience problems associated with workload at some time in their working lives. Yet there is not such a clear consensus about what workload actually is.

If one were to ask a group of people to talk about their experience of workload, some might, for example, describe workload as simply being busy or having too many things to do. Others might give a specific example, perhaps meeting a deadline such as completing an essay or preparing a presentation for a meeting. However, such an exercise might involve time pressure, a degree of effort to plan and think about the work, as well as concern to produce good quality work. It might also involve the subjective experience of stress, perhaps reflected in increased anxiety, dissatisfaction or depression, or provoke feelings of lack of control over the situation. The subjective experience is therefore important, but in order to understand the full extent of the implications for people's working lives we also need to consider the underlying cognitive processes and relationships between task demands, resources and effort.

A distinction can readily be made between physical and mental workload, and it should be pointed out at this stage that the main concern in this chapter is with what is termed 'mental workload'. For the assessment of physical workload there are several reliable and established techniques (e.g. Rohmert, 1987), but the quest for valid, reliable and sensitive measures of mental workload has proved to be more elusive. The focus on mental workload reflects the changes in the nature of tasks in many occupations as they have become increasingly cognitively oriented. Consider the tasks of air traffic controllers, pilots, process control operators and medical staff. The primary tasks involve cognitive processes which require memory, attention, perception and communication skills rather than extensive physical demands on personnel. It is less easy to estimate the demands of such tasks and, perhaps more importantly, to predict the consequences of those demands.

Perhaps the primary reason for the difficulty in agreeing an appropriate and all-encompassing definition of mental workload is that it is essentially a multidimensional concept (Gopher and Donchin, 1986; Damos, 1991). The multidimensionality is evident in the measures that have been developed, particularly the subjective measures which attempt to address various dimensions such as mental load, time pressure and stress or frustration.

A simple definition, but one which captures the essence of the problem, is that mental workload can be conceptualized as the costs that human operators incur in performing tasks (Kramer, 1991). Although this definition is rather broad, it emphasizes the negative consequences of workload, leading from demands that are too high or even too low, hence contributing to boredom and inattention to the task. Costs may be observed in terms of performance, well-being, safety and even health. Also important to note is that managing workload may incur costs even under normal operating conditions. What this definition does not address specifically, however, is the transactional nature of workload (e.g. Gopher and Donchin, 1986; Hockey, 1993). If performance on a task is shown to be degraded in some way, or in other words is at poorer levels than those set by either the operator or the managers of the system, then we cannot simply assume that the operator cannot work harder to achieve these goals. This would imply a point at which human processing resources are no longer available to maintain the appropriate level of performance. It is possible that the operator is not motivated to maintain such a high level of effort. This could result from a lack of awareness of the operating goals, inattention to increased demands or, indeed, a strategic process to protect valuable resources for dealing with future predictable or unpredictable events. Suboptimal levels of individual physiological or emotional state caused by illness or environmental conditions may also result in impaired performance.

Why Assess Workload?

The objective behind the development of effective workload assessment methods is to solve practical problems in the workplace. There is certainly evidence to suggest that workload has an effect on performance, well-being, health and safety. An enormous literature on workload assessment has grown over the past two to three decades for which the primary impetus has been the need to design complex task environments that do not place disproportionate demands on the human operator. A large number of applications relate to aviation and process control settings, indicating the relevance to safety critical systems such as air traffic control and aircraft cockpit design. A second application, no less important, is to aid evaluation of the effects of automation or the introduction of new technology and other changes in the nature of work on individual well-being and health. Although less prominent in the literature, a third use for workload measures relates to the assessment of individual operators, perhaps for selection purposes or to identify areas for further training. Workload is therefore a critical problem for both designers and users of work systems.

A distinction that illustrates the two main objectives of research on workload is that between the acute and chronic effects of managing the demands of work (Tattersall, 1994). Their major distinguishing features relate to the timescale over which the effects are manifested and the types of outcome with which they associated. Acute effects can be thought of primarily in terms of direct effects on performance. Poor task and job design may, for example, result in errors, slow response times or situations which promote the neglect of subsidiary tasks. Chronic effects are manifested over a longer timescale. The primary outcomes associated with these effects relate to aspects of individual well-being and health, although these in turn may have indirect effects on performance.

Acute effects of workload

Here, the main focus of interest is on the interference between tasks in dual- or multiple-task situations in which operators have several things to do at once (Damos, 1991; Wickens, 1992). The aim is to design systems in which the tasks are compatible in the sense that they can be carried out concurrently without performance decrements and without operators having to exert undue effort to perform their primary work tasks effectively. Clearly, workload might be a problem in such situations, especially where the demands are varied and irregular. The prototypical example is that of a pilot who may be required to perform a variety of tasks simultaneously: controlling speed, altitude and flight path, communicating with air traffic control and crew members, as well as monitoring state indicators. Other jobs may require short phases of problem-solving, perhaps with longer periods when signals requiring action are infrequent and the task is under control. Nevertheless, the prediction of workload is still an important endeavour both in normal operating conditions and in unusual situations or emergencies.

Many of the approaches in this area are based upon multiple-resource theory (e.g. Wickens, 1984, 1991, 1992), which proposes a number of processing resources, each limited in its capacity. More resources are thought to be demanded by more difficult tasks. However, these resources, characterized as being synonymous with effort or attention, are devoted to different types of information processing. Wickens (1991), for example, contrasted resources relating to the processing of spatial and verbal information (information processing codes), visual and auditory perceptual modalities (modalities) and perceptual-cognitive activity and response processes (processing stages). The extent to which tasks will interfere with each other when carried out concurrently will depend upon the extent to which they compete for common resources.

In the evaluation of multi-task systems, therefore, the prediction of performance will be aided by information about the extent to which the two tasks require the same mode of information presentation (e.g. visual or auditory) or output (e.g. manual or speech), or compete for common central processing resources such as verbal or spatial working memory. An opportunity might arise, following developments in the reliability of speech recognition devices, to change the modality used by operators to perform control actions from manual (pressing keys or typing a command) to speech control. Before implementing the new system it would be wise to evaluate the potential for interference with concurrent tasks. Wickens (1976), for example, found that manual tracking performance was disrupted to a greater extent by a concurrent task that required similar responses than by auditory signal detection, despite the detection task being rated as more difficult by participants.

Norman and Bobrow (1975) introduced the important concepts of resource-limited processes, which are limited by the effort invested in a task and the priority placed upon task performance, and data-limited processes, which are constrained by the quality of information rather than by increases in effort. In work situations, operators may compensate for increases in task demands by increasing the amount of effort invested in the task. Observed performance levels, therefore, may remain constant, but the operator experiences increased workload. Conversely, a reduction in the level of performance may result either because operators cannot maintain the level of effort expenditure required, or because they lower their criteria for adequate performance. Task difficulty alone, therefore, cannot reliably predict the level of observed interference between tasks.

Appropriate workload measures for testing and evaluating systems certainly include primary and secondary task performance measures, and certain subjective and psychophysiological measures. Proper and effective evaluation will ensure that the workload experienced by users of any system is taken account of in system design and development (Wierwille and Eggemeier, 1993).

Chronic effects of workload

A different type of enquiry has focused on the effects of managing the demands of work over relatively lengthy periods of time. The prolonged active management of effort required to meet task demands has implications for short-term well-being and longer-term health, as well as performance. Demands on specific information processing resources are perhaps less critical than the broader job and organizational demands which result in strain (see chapter 7, this volume). The consequences of high levels of workload can be considered as the after-effects of work in which the physiological and emotional state of an individual is affected over a period of time. These changes in state may lead ultimately to subsequent performance decrements at work. For example, individuals may become increasingly fatigued because of the sustained demands in the job that need to be managed effectively, which may result in breakdown of skills over the longer term.

The role of regulatory processes in the transactions between people and working environments is a central feature in the cognitive–energetical framework developed by Hockey (1993, 1997). A model of stress and workload based on observations of individual patterns of response to various demands will enable more accurate prediction to be made of states or situations in which a breakdown in skills might occur. Hockey (1993) distinguished between four different patterns of degradation of performance under stress and high workload. Primary task decrements are the first type, although, in contrast to indirect effects on performance, these tend to be uncommon. Because the primary task is considered to be the high priority task in terms of work-oriented goals, its performance may often be protected by a reallocation of resources or an increase in those devoted to that task. Such regulatory processes should be observable in terms of changes in the performance of secondary (lower priority) tasks or metabolic activity.

The three remaining types refer to patterns of indirect degradation. First, compensatory costs may be observed when performance on the primary task is maintained under high levels of workload. The effort required to deal with the demands as well as the perceived stressfulness of the situation result in reliable hormonal and immunological changes (e.g. Ursin, Baade and Levine, 1978; Frankenhaeuser, 1986). Increased levels of catecholamine excretion accompanied by lower levels of cortisol excretion and anxiety have been shown to be associated with active processing strategies linked with effort investment and increases in subjective perceptions of task control. On the other hand, increased cortisol and noradrenaline excretions are found under conditions associated with lowered control and increased distress (Frankenhaeuser, 1986). Using different measures, Steptoe (1983) observed increased physiological activation, indicated by higher levels of blood pressure and heart rate, when subjects were engaged in effortful problem-solving or activity in a controllable situation.

Second, there may be strategic adjustment towards the use of strategies which involve lower levels of effort and demands on working memory. Air traffic controllers have been found to vary their strategies according to task demand, taking fewer variables into account with increasing traffic load (Sperandio, 1978). Similarly, in a study of process control, Bainbridge (1974) found that individuals under pressure used faster but less accurate methods of finding data values. Chmiel, Totterdell and Folkard (1995) found that following one night's sleep loss and several hours performing an adaptive control task, performance quality could be maintained but the work was carried out more slowly.

Third, the costs of sustained, high levels of workload might be observed as fatigue after-effects. As yet, few systematic analyses of fatigue after-effects have been reported, perhaps due to the requirement for longitudinal, repeated sampling studies. There are, however, indications that these effects might be detectable using work-related tasks carried out at the end of working days. Shingledecker and Holding (1974) found that fatigue was associated with the increased use of low-effort and more risky choices in a fault-finding task. Meijman, Mulder, van Dormelen and Cremer (1992) found that driving examiners invested less effort in performing cognitive probe tasks following working days with higher levels of demand. A study comparing the effects of working and non-working days in city bus drivers reported by Aasman, Wijers, Mulder and Mulder (1988) found less efficient and effective task performance to be associated with increasing workload.

The degree of controllability that operators are able to exert in their interaction with complex systems is clearly an important factor. In general, there is an advantage for active control over passive control, whereby open-loop strategies, involving a greater degree of planning and broader understanding of the system as a whole, are seen to be more skilled and efficient than the closed-loop mode, in which plans to achieve particular sub-goals tend to be short term, small-scale and specific (Umbers, 1979). Umbers found that even experienced operators resort to the closed-loop mode when under high levels of workload or when unfamiliar situations or problems occur. This could be a cause for concern, as remedial action may be applied once critical events have occurred, rather than the more desirable situation in which impending catastrophic events are predicted at a time when something can be done to prevent them occurring.

In summary, there is variation in the way that people approach tasks, and therefore in the effects and consequences of workload. The experience of workload is thus unlikely to depend simply on task load, but on the interaction between task demands, the strategies adopted by an operator to deal with the demands and the level of performance achieved. Assessment techniques might involve the use of performance measures, subjective measures and physiological measures of workload but, additionally, subjective and physiological measures of individual state will be useful to assess the longer-term effects on emotional and physiological well-being and health.

Requirements for Effective Workload Assessment

A range of different measures of workload has been developed, utilizing subjective assessment techniques, performance measures and physiologically based procedures. Unfortunately, they are not all equally effective in all situations, so it is important for researchers and system designers to appreciate the benefits and drawbacks of each in order to choose the most appropriate method for the particular requirements and circumstances. Extensive reviews of these techniques are available, many of which discuss criteria for application (O'Donnell and Eggemeier, 1986; Hancock and Meshkati, 1988; Damos, 1991). Whether a technique is effective and appropriate for a particular situation depends on various factors, including sensitivity to changes in demand, ability to distinguish different kinds of demand and suitability or relevance to that situation.

Sensitivity

The issue of the sensitivity of methods to different levels of primary task load is arguably one of the most critical aspects of workload measurement (Egge-meier, 1988). It relates to whether the technique is actually effective in detecting changes in task demands and identifying conditions of extreme workload. A low level of sensitivity will not allow precise discrimination to be made between different conditions or systems under evaluation. A related concept is temporal sensitivity, which is the rate at which measures respond to variation in the effects of changes in task demands (Wierwille, 1988). Temporal sensitivity may be crucial in particular circumstances in which information is needed rapidly concerning workload changes; for example, to provide support to an operator from the system or from colleagues.

Diagnosticity

Diagnosticity is concerned with the extent to which the technique is able to distinguish between different types of task demands and to identify the particular components within complex tasks that result in difficulty. Diagnosticity is particularly important when one is assessing the introduction of a new piece of equipment or a change in the way that a task is performed. For example, appropriate evaluation might indicate problems with certain task elements. The provision of further training or system support, or the manipulation of the characteristics or timing of the problematic tasks, may alleviate the problems. Secondary task methodology has the potential to be highly diagnostic, whereas primary task measures of performance usually provide a global measure and are not sufficiently sensitive to demands on specific resources. Techniques which provide a general measure of resource allocation or effort, such as some of the subjective and physiological measures, will be less effective, unless specifically related to different task components, systems or functions.

Intrusiveness

Intrusiveness is also a critical property of workload assessment methods. It refers to the extent to which the workload assessment technique disrupts the performance of the primary work task. The more obvious form of intrusion could result from the use of obtrusive equipment or the application of a technique which requires the primary work task to be halted or interrupted while measures are taken. Perhaps less obvious is the potential for certain methods, particularly secondary task methodology, to compete for certain processing resources with the primary work task. If safety is a major concern, as it is in many application domains, such as in air traffic control, space operations and medical intensive care work, then clearly workload assessment techniques that may degrade performance should not be used. The use of physiological measures with which the operators are happy and familiar, post-task interviews and ratings or simulation exercises may provide an alternative to techniques which are suspected to be problematic.

Validity

Validity refers to the extent to which a device measures what it is supposed to, or is claimed to, measure. However, as Moray (1988) has argued, because no clear, precise definition of workload exists it is difficult to establish the validity of different techniques. Perhaps this is why such little attention has been paid to the predictive and construct validity of workload measures. He suggested that the reliability of measures has to be sufficient for practical purposes until such a definition is agreed upon.

Reliability

Reliability is concerned with the accuracy and consistency of measurement. It almost goes without saying that measures should be accurate in their assessment of the load placed on individuals. There should also be a good correlation between the values produced by different techniques if they are used to assess the same dimensions of workload. In practice, however, different workload measures are not always found to be highly correlated (e.g. Yeh and Wickens, 1988). This may be partly owing to the bandwidth of measurement and whether the measures are designed to assess global workload or specific dimensions of workload. Yeh and Wickens (1988) suggested that there may be a dissociation between subjective measures and measures of primary task performance at high levels of task demand which exceed the limits of working memory. Primary task performance measures should then be examined. Under low or underload conditions, on the other hand, subjective measures will provide a more sensitive and reliable measure. It would also be desirable for measures to have a respectable level of test–retest reliability, although as yet few reliability studies on workload measures have been carried out, leading some researchers to question whether some measures have been misused (e.g. Nygren, 1991).

Acceptability, applicability and generality

These criteria relate to the effective practical application of workload measures. Both the ease with which techniques can be applied and the need for special requirements may restrict the application of a technique which might theoretically be very appropriate. Some require specialized, expensive equipment. Some produce results very quickly, whereas others require lengthy data preparation and analytical procedures to be carried out. The extent to which operators are tolerant and accepting of a particular technique, and therefore cooperative, will depend on the time it takes to set up a testing session and their level of comfort during that session. Further, it may be useful to choose a technique that can be used in different situations, facilitating comparisons between different environmental and operating conditions. In all cases, the operational procedures should be standardized as much as possible.

Workload Assessment Techniques

There are three main categories of workload assessment technique: subjective, performance and physiological measures. Many of the techniques satisfy the majority of the above criteria but few possess all the desirable characteristics.

Subjective measures

In comparison to the other techniques, subjective or self-report measures are relatively easy to employ. The notion that we can simply ask operators about what they perceive to be the levels of task demands and the effort that they invest in performing the task is appealing and has face validity. A number of subjective workload assessment techniques have been developed over the years (see, for example, Eggemeier and Wilson, 1991, for a comprehensive review).

The Cooper–Harper scale (Cooper and Harper, 1969), the first of these, was used originally to assess aircraft handling qualities. Ratings from one to ten were derived using a decision tree in which pilots answered yes or not to specific questions about the effort required to perform the task to different standards. Later modifications have been made to the scale to produce a more general workload scale (e.g. Wierwille and Casali, 1983). A rating of one indicates that operator mental effort is minimal and desired performance is attainable, whereas a rating of ten indicates that the task is impossible even with maximum effort.

Among the validated scales that are currently widely used are the NASA task load index (TLX) (Hart and Staveland, 1988) and the subjective workload assessment technique (SWAT) (Reid and Nygren, 1988). They both assess perceived workload on a number of dimensions, usually after the task has been performed. The SWAT was originally based on a system of conjoint measurement in which each of three factors – mental effort, time load and psychological stress – is rated on a three-point scale, giving 27 basic scale points. The NASA TLX assesses workload using six scales: temporal demand, mental demand, mental effort, frustration, physical demand and performance. These six dimensions resulted from an extensive series of laboratory and simulation experiments and psychometric analyses by Hart and colleagues (Hart and

Staveland, 1988). Ratings can be recorded using paper and pencil or a computerized version, and require individual ratings of each of the six dimensions, producing values of 0 to 100 for each dimension. The scales can be combined to give an overall measure of workload using a weighted average of ratings on the six dimensions.

For both the SWAT and the TLX, the rating scale procedure is relatively quick and straightforward. However, the weighting procedure in the case of TLX and the conjoint scaling procedure based on a card sort in the case of the SWAT are much more time consuming. It has recently been suggested that the unweighted scales are as sensitive as the weighted solutions (Nygren, 1991; Moroney, Biers and Eggemeier, 1995), which makes the measures more attractive from a practical viewpoint. Nygren (1991) has suggested that they are both useful, reliable and usually sensitive measures of workload, and that SWAT is sensitive at both individual and group levels. However, he also argued that the psychometric properties of these scales need to be fully understood, in addition to their implications for task performance, before they are applied extensively. As Veltman and Gaillard (1996, p. 324) point out, 'on the basis of rating scales it is not clear whether an operator works hard or thinks that (s)he has to work hard'. This emphasizes the distinction between task demands and operator effort and the issue of construct validity. Despite this problem, for current practical purposes these techniques are relatively well established. Hill, Iavecchia, Byers, Bittner, Zaklad and Christ (1992) compared four subjective workload rating scales for sensitivity, operator acceptance, response requirements and any special procedures they require. All were found acceptable and sensitive to different levels of workload, although depending on the way in which they are used, the diagnosticity of subjective measures may not be great.

There is some concern, however, with the fact that subjective ratings are generally obtained after task completion. Although Moroney et al. (1995) suggest that delays of up to 15 minutes do not tend to have a significant impact on the reliability of ratings, care should be taken when intervening tasks take place or with longer delays. It may be possible to gain more accurate post-task ratings and limit intrusion by using a combination of video recordings of the test session and interviews. Alternatively, subjective techniques which provide ratings of workload during rather than after task performance might be used. Rehmann, Stein and Rosenberg (1983) have argued that concurrent workload evaluation is more accurate than post-task ratings. An example is the instantaneous self-assessment (ISA) technique, which was originally designed for use in air traffic control settings. This technique appears to be a relatively sensitive measure of workload (Tattersall and Foord, 1996), although it provides only a simple estimate of global workload on a five-point scale. The advantage of such a method is that in complex tasks which involve multiple elements or phases, the signals that require a rating to be given can be more satisfactorily related to specific phases and therefore to changing task demands than retrospective ratings. Despite the relatively short time taken to provide ISA ratings, however, Tattersall and Foord (1996) found that there was a degree of interference with the primary task of tracking, whether responses were made by speech or manually.

Other self-report scales may also be valuable in studies of the effects of workload. These include measures of situation awareness, mood and coping. Sarter and Woods (1991) identified situation awareness (SA) as an essential prerequisite for the safe operation of any complex dynamic system, in that it allows operators to interpret and understand a current situation in order to predict future process status and perform effectively. Measures of SA include the situation awareness global assessment technique (SAGAT) (Endsley, 1995a, b) and the situation awareness rating scale (SART) (Taylor, 1989). The SAGAT utilizes a verbal protocol-type technique in which questions relate to operators' perception of the elements in their environment, their understanding of these elements in relation to task goals and the projection of future status of these elements. The SART may be more easily implemented in field settings, but both can be useful if operators' knowledge of current and future system status and dynamics needs to be assessed.

Subjective reports of mood states (e.g. Warr, 1989) can be used as indices of strain as an outcome of the maintenance of work performance under high levels of demand or stress. Measures of behavioural style or coping have been used to identify differences between those individuals who deal with demands by adopting effortful strategies and those with a more passive style in which work demands and problems are put off or suppressed (Hockey and Wiethoff, 1990). They found that fatigue was predicted by level of work demands for junior doctors identified as using an active coping style, whereas there was no such relationship for the 'passive copers'. Significant relationships have been found between subjective states and specific physiological responses, such as between cortisol and subjective distress (Frankenhaeuser, 1986), and effort and heart rate variability (Aasman, Mulder and Mulder, 1987). For many of the relationships between symptoms and work demands to be assessed fully, it will be necessary to carry out repeated measurements over a relatively long period of time using diary methods or multi-measurement techniques (Hockey, 1997).

Performance measures

The two main approaches to performance assessment involve the use of primary task measures and secondary task techniques. The primary task is defined as the task or system function whose workload is to be measured. A secondary task is one that is performed concurrently with a primary task to investigate the workload associated with the latter. If possible, it is always desirable to gain a measure of performance on the task or system which is to be evaluated. In some situations, of course, these measures may be easy to obtain; for example, measuring a pilot's deviation from appropriate levels of speed and flight path during take-off or landing. However, in other situations, such as air traffic control, teaching or nursing, it is difficult to generate a simple measure of a individual's level of performance (e.g. speed, accuracy or errors and slips of action) that would meet the criteria outlined earlier. Owing to the differing characteristics of jobs, primary task measures are also not easily transferable from one situation to another. Another concern is that it is possible to underestimate work demands because operators may apply compensatory effort to cope with the additional demands. Primary task measures may therefore not be immediately sensitive to the effects of changes in task load or working procedures. Thus, only a crude indication of the cumulative effect of sustained and high task demands over a long period may be obtained. The effects of these factors may only be detected by primary task measures once performance suffers or errors are made. From a safety perspective, it might by then be too late to investigate the adequacy of human factors aspects of the system.

Secondary task measures may be more sensitive to changes in demand or working procedures than primary task measures, but unless the allocation of information processing resources to the two tasks is controlled it can be difficult to interpret the observed secondary task performance decrements. Examples of widely used secondary tasks include memory search tasks, choice reaction time tasks, time estimation and simple adding or mental arithmetic tasks. They have, however, to be chosen carefully to avoid intrusion or structural interference with the primary task. That is, the application of the secondary task should not result in primary task decrements simply because the operator is required to make similar manual control actions at the same time or monitor two physically distinct displays at once. Used appropriately they have the potential to be extremely diagnostic. To overcome problems with intrusiveness, it is sometimes possible to use tasks which are already part of the system being evaluated. Such embedded tasks (Shingledecker, 1987) might involve measuring response times to certain communications, signals or events. Some jobs (e.g. medical monitoring) require regular checks to be made of the status of certain parts of the system. In other occupations it is more difficult to incorporate or devise such tasks.

Typically, in investigations using secondary tasks, the operator is instructed to maintain a certain level of performance on the primary task with and without the secondary task. The changes in level of performance of the secondary task are thought to reflect the workload of the primary task (Ogden, Levine and Eisner, 1979). The instructions sometimes emphasize the secondary task, in which case performance on the primary task will indicate the level of difficulty on that task. Tasks that have been used include memory search, time estimation, mental arithmetic or generation of random digits, reaction time and rhythmic tapping (O'Donnell and Eggemeier, 1986; Eggemeier and Wilson, 1991). Casali and Wierwille (1983) concluded that time estimation was the most suitable, in terms of its sensitivity, for primary tasks involving perceptual, communication and motor skills. Using both laboratory and flight simulation settings, Zakay and Shub (1998) found that estimates of particular time periods from the presentation of a beep to the pressing of a button were significantly correlated with subjective ratings of workload and performance measures. This method appears to have potential as a sensitive and relatively non-intrusive measure, although there could be interference problems with primary tasks which involve mental arithmetic or counting.

Physiological measures

Many physiological processes have been proposed to provide indications of effort investment or workload. The underlying assumption behind their use is that as more effort is devoted to the task there will be measurable changes in psychophysiological functioning, reflecting increased central nervous system activity. Measures of cardiac and brain function are the most well researched and frequently used techniques, but other physiological processes have been examined, including respiration, eyeblinks and pupil dilation (see Kramer, 1991; Wilson and Eggemeier, 1991). Other techniques, such as analyses of urine, blood or saliva samples, provide measures of hormonal and immuno-logical changes (e.g. Ursin et al., 1978).

In terms of heart rate, measures of rate and variability of inter-beat intervals have been widely used in workload assessment. A number of studies now suggest that the power in the mid-frequency band of the heart rate variability (HRV) spectrum (0.07–0.14 Hz) is related to the level of mental effort invested in a task by an individual (Mulder, 1980; Aasman et al., 1987; Tattersall and Hockey, 1995). In the assessment of HRV, spectral analysis is used to determine the variations in heart rhythm associated with three physio-logical control mechanisms. The power or energy in the low-frequency band (0.02–0.06 Hz) is related to the regulation of body temperature. The high-frequency band (0.15–0.50 Hz) reflects the influence of respiratory activity, and the mid-frequency band is associated with short-term blood pressure regu-lation. Such variability in the mid-frequency band has been shown to decrease as a function of task difficulty in a number of laboratory tasks and field studies, including actual and simulated flight (Mulder, 1980; Jorna, 1992). Mean heart rate may offer a more sensitive measure of response load, and is certainly influ-enced by physical activity and perhaps anxiety, which may limit its usefulness in relation to workload. Tattersall and Hockey (1995) identified different activities in a simulated flight engineer task, which resulted in different cardio-vascular costs and subjective ratings of effort and concern. Heart rate appeared to be associated with concern, particularly during activities such as landing and take-off, but suppressed HRV and increased subjective ratings of effort were associated with the requirement for problem-solving activity in different activi-ties. There are indications that verbal communication, physical activity and fitness, and even body position and age, may have an effect on HRV, although methods for controlling such effects may be applied (Jorna, 1992). Tattersall and Rowe (1994) observed an effect of physical exercise on HRV, but still found a reliable difference in HRV between periods of exercise with and without a concurrent memory search task.

The electrical state of the brain can be measured using electroencephalography, which involves placing electrodes on the scalp. Of the measures that can be derived from such activity, event-related brain potentials appear to be the most promising in terms of workload assessment. Of a number of indices, the most commonly employed is the P300 component, which is a positive polarity voltage oscillation seen to occur 300 ms following a particular task relevant signal. Kramer, Wickens and Donchin (1983) found that the magnitude of the P300 response decreased with increasing task difficulty and with additional secondary task. Sirevaag, Kramer, Wickens, Reisweber, Strayer and Grenell (1993) used a battery of workload measures to assess the workload and performance of helicopter pilots using digital or verbal communication systems. The P300 component was elicited using an irrelevant probe technique (tones were presented through headphones but did not need a response) rather than probes requiring overt responses to overcome interference problems. Although it did not distinguish clearly between systems it was sensitive to communications load, as were HRV and blink duration. Subjective measures in this case did not discriminate between either systems or load levels. Event-related potentials therefore appear to show some promise in terms of sensitivity, although problems may be encountered in terms of intrusiveness. Perhaps the greatest current challenge, however, is to develop the techniques so that they can be applied effectively outside the laboratory.

The diameter of the pupil has been shown to be significantly related to task demands across a range of tasks, such as problem-solving, reaction time and short-term memory (Beatty, 1982). Although it appears to be sensitive, other factors can have significant effects on the diameter of the pupil, including ambient lighting and emotional changes. In addition, because of the equipment requirements and the need to keep the head relatively still, the method is not easily applicable to field situations and is better used in controlled laboratory settings. Endogenous eyeblinks, those that occur without a specific eliciting stimulus, have been shown to decrease with increased visual attention, often associated with shorter duration blinks. For example, car drivers show lower blink rates when driving in the city compared with motorway driving. However, Wilson and Eggemeier (1991) point out that the measure may not be as effective with tasks that involve the processing of non-visual information. Veltman and Gaillard (1996), for example, using a flight simulator, found that blink duration was sensitive to visual demands but not to a continuous memory task carried out in addition to the flying task.

It is often argued that physiological measures are unobtrusive and objective, in that they can be continuously and independently applied without interfering with the primary task (e.g. Wilson, 1992; Veltman and Gaillard, 1996). Heart rate measures in particular have the potential to be used on a continuous basis and are more likely than other measures to be sensitive to momentary changes in workload over prolonged periods of time. There is an issue over the diagnosticity of physiological measures, in that different techniques are sensitive to different components of human information processing (Kramer, 1991). Care should be taken over the choice of a specific measure to ensure that it is adequate for the particular purpose. A further caution is that physiological processes are sensitive to the effects of physical activity and to emotional factors that may have an effect on physiological functions.

The Application of Workload Assessment Techniques

The choice of an appropriate method for the assessment of workload will depend on the particular task and operating circumstances as well as the aims and scope of the assessment process. A brief summary of the major categories of measure discussed in the preceding section is presented in table 8.1. This provides an indication of the extent to which each measure satisfies certain effectiveness, usefulness and applicability criteria. More detailed, technical information about these measures can be found in O'Donnell and Eggemeier (1986) and Damos (1991).

Studies of workload have involved both laboratory and field experiments. Typically, laboratory studies are characterised by their relatively short-term nature, lower levels of training and expertise on the part of the participants and a lowered risk of failure and subsequent consequences of error. In contrast, field studies are characterized by more realistic demands, in terms of longer-term organizational and personal goals, an extended time period and more serious consequences of errors. The pacing of the tasks also differs in work situations, with tasks often being self-paced but within the context of work schedule and deadline constraints.

Although further laboratory- and field-based studies are necessary to refine workload assessment techniques, it would be desirable to carry out studies in real work settings involving longer-term assessment of individual physiological and affective state in relation to performance. Multi-level measurement techniques will provide the basis for a broad assessment of the impact of different work demands, as well as allowing models of stress and workload management such as that of Hockey (1993, 1997) to be further tested. This should then allow the more accurate prediction of states or situations in which problems in managing workload lead to performance decrements. Such a breakdown in skills is referred to by air traffic controllers as 'losing the picture', when they experience difficulties in attending to, and remembering accurately, relevant information about aircraft under their control. It is precisely this kind of situation that should be avoided in work in which safety is critically dependent upon performance.

A study of the impact of naturally varying workload in air traffic control on a range of measures, including performance, and physiological and affective

Table 8.1 Summary of the capability of different broad categories of workload assessment technique to satisfy different requirements for use

	Intrusiveness	*Sensitivity*	*Diagnosticity*	*Applicability*	*Acceptability*
Subjective measures					
Post-task measures	Generally not intrusive	Good but may depend on length of task	Generally difficult to use diagnostically	Minimal equipment requirements	Very good
Instantaneous measures	Potentially intrusive	Good	Provides only a global measure	Some equipment required, especially if related to specific task elements	Good
Performance measures					
Primary task	Not intrusive	Reasonable but difficulties in interpreting variation	Poor	Depends on task complexity and variability	Should be acceptable to operators
Secondary task	Potential for intrusion	Good	Very good	May require training and extra equipment	Additional demands may be distracting but generally acceptable
Physiological measures					
EEG measures	Not usually a problem	Good	Varies according to specific measure but reasonably good	Extensive equipment and analysis requirements	Some potential problems but not generally found to be problematical
ECG measures	Not intrusive	Good	Not fully established	Extensive equipment and analysis requirements	Not generally found to be problematical

state, provides an example of such an investigation (Farmer, Belyavin, Tattersall, Berry and Hockey, 1991; Tattersall and Farmer, 1995). Controllers were assessed on a range of measures during two different working shifts which differed in the number of planes to be handled. This difference was reflected in subjective ratings of workload, which were higher during the busy, high traffic load shift. Increases in salivary cortisol concentration and noradrenaline excretion during high workload shifts indicated that controllers were actively coping with the demands of high workload shifts. This pattern may have long-term consequences for the health and well-being of controllers if sustained over long periods. The negative consequences of dealing with sustained demands were also apparent in the mood measures which were obtained throughout each day. Anxiety showed a significantly greater increase during high workload days but pre-shift anxiety levels were not affected by workload. In contrast, levels of depression and fatigue were both higher at the start of the day under high workload conditions and elevated during the high workload shift. The sustained demands of the busy summer months in air traffic control appear to result in chronic after-effects of fatigue and depression, whereas anxiety was affected more transiently. It was also found that work demands had a significant effect on visual vigilance sensitivity, the ability to detect signals in noise. Although performance improved during low workload days it did not during high workload days, suggesting that heavy work demands in air traffic control may have a detrimental effect on monitoring performance.

Automation and Task Allocation

Automation has been widely introduced in industrial and other processes with the aims of producing safe, reliable and efficient systems. Probably the single most influential factor in the development of automated systems is the remarkable advancement in computer technology. The sophistication, flexibility, availability and scope for domains of application of computers have increased dramatically in the past two decades. In addition, the cost of computers has markedly reduced. It is perhaps not surprising that system designers have sought increasingly to introduce automation.

Wickens (1992) proposed three further reasons for automation. First, there is no alternative to automation in situations which may be hazardous or dangerous to humans or which humans cannot perform. Some diving operations, for example, may utilize remote or automated systems. The handling of toxic materials in chemical or nuclear plants may require the use of robots or complex control systems. Second, humans may not be able to perform some tasks efficiently because of high levels of workload. The use of autopilots during particular phases of flight provides an extremely useful function. Third, automation may aid or even enhance performance in tasks in which human operators may demonstrate limitations, perhaps in memory or attention. Radar advance warning systems can provide early warning of approaching aircraft or those in the vicinity. In this case, automation assists the operator by providing a better presentation of information for air traffic control.

Although we usually talk of automation as the replacement of human operations by a machine or computer, there are many different types of automation. Sheridan (1980) discussed ten levels that vary in the degree to which the human has a role in task performance and system functioning. In practice, however, although it is relatively easy to automate fully many existing tasks carried out by humans, it has proved to be much more difficult to develop new systems in which some task components are automated within human–machine systems. There is certainly now the opportunity to provide more support for human operators by providing appropriate decision-making facilities and by allowing more flexible 'allocation of control' between human and automated parts of the system. Hockey, Briner, Tattersall and Wiethoff (1989) argued that operator controllability could be enhanced by providing the operator with options relating to the use of automatic systems to aid the execution of work tasks.

A number of dangers of automation have, however, been outlined (e.g. Bainbridge, 1987; Wiener, 1988). Rather thoughtless design may simply require the operator to perform those functions or tasks that have been unable to be automated. Even if this is not the case, there may be difficulties associated with operator control, and skill development and maintenance. First, automation may induce feelings of loss of control and situation awareness when the human is operating 'out of the loop' (e.g. Sarter and Woods, 1992). This may in turn impair performance and increase frustration and anxiety (e.g. Wiener, 1985; Bainbridge, 1987). Second, there is a risk of deskilling of operators in highly automated systems in which they take on the role of a passive monitor rather than having a more active function (Wickens, 1992). A reduction in the use of control skills in general operations may lead to an impairment in performance when such skills are required in critical situations or following system breakdowns. Finally, automation does not always lead to improved performance and levels of operator workload. Within the aviation domain, Danaher (1980) reported that the introduction of automated equipment with the aim of reducing air traffic controller and pilot workload did not always lead to a reduction in errors. Wiener (1985) found that pilots perceived not a decrease, but an increase in mental workload associated with automated systems.

There have been observations of operators overriding automated systems in order to assume control of production or other processes at times when the system is scheduled to be under automatic control. In a report of a study of process control operators in a chemical plant, Hockey and Maule (1995) referred to these as unscheduled manual interventions. Such behaviour suggests a desire for personal control; however, following analyses of interview and observational data, Hockey and Maule (1995) found that motivation to improve the speed and quality of production was the most influential factor in determining the frequency of manual interventions. It is also likely that the degree to which operators trust the automated system to perform the task effectively will influence their interactions with the system (e.g. Lee and Moray, 1992). This issue is likely to become more prominent with the increasing use of automation.

A key element in achieving desirable levels of safety and effectiveness is the selection of the appropriate type and degree of automation. This includes making a decision about which tasks should be allocated to the operator and which to the automated part of the system. The terms 'task allocation' and 'function allocation' are often used interchangeably in the literature and no formal distinction is made here, other than to note that both may be used to refer to allocation of tasks or functions between humans in working groups as well as between humans and machines. In their comprehensive review of task allocation methods, however, Older, Waterson and Clegg (1997) point out that far less attention has been paid to the former than to the latter form of task allocation.

Traditionally, task allocation has been based either on principles such as Fitts' list (Fitts, 1951; Kantowitz and Sorkin, 1987), or simply on the basis of technological or economic constraints. These lists provide features of humans and machines in terms of the strengths and weaknesses of each, suggesting that machines are more effective at performing mathematical and computational operations, integrating information and dealing with predictable events reliably. Human operators are better at making decisions and inductive reasoning. They also tend to be more flexible, particularly when unexpected events occur, and possess experience of previous events. Price (1985) evaluated the potential of such lists for current system design and, although they provide useful suggestions for designers, they do not tend to take into account the expectations and preferences of human operators. Oborne, Branton, Leal, Shipley and Stewart (1993) argued that person-centred design, taking into account such factors, will enable more effective systems to be developed.

Dynamic task allocation

Dynamic control of task allocation (DTA) refers to the flexible allocation of tasks or functions between the operator and the system in human–machine systems. It is sometimes referred to as adaptive control, although this implies some form of adaptation on the part of the system to the individual's level of skill or current state. Such systems differ from fully automated systems and those wholly under the control of a human operator in that some or all of the task elements have the potential to be carried out by either the operator or the system itself. In comparison to more traditional systems, in which tasks are rigidly allocated between the human and the computer, DTA appears to have many benefits (Parasuraman and Mouloua, 1996).

Three main advantages of DTA have been postulated. First, the workload of operators will be maintained at a relatively constant level. Lemoine, Crevits, Debernard and Millet (1995) showed that compared to a no aid condition, both implicit (computer control of task allocation) and explicit (operator control) modes of DTA improved system and human performance on a heavy workload air traffic control task and reduced the global workload experienced by controllers. Second, the resources of the system (both human and computer) will be used more fully. Appropriate DTA should not only improve system performance but also be more accepted by the operator than static automation, which may lead to loss of operator control (Greenstein, Arnaut and Revesman, 1986). Third, while operators will have a relatively flexible role in the system, they will maintain involvement and a coherent view of the system's state and functioning (Rouse, 1981, 1988). This should lead to an enhancement of situation awareness and also prevent decay of manual control and problem-solving skills which may be required in breakdown or emergency situations (Lockhart, Strub, Hawley and Tapia, 1993). If the computer system does break down or make an error, the operator will be familiar with the system and therefore is more likely to be able to make corrective procedures or take over the computer's role. Furthermore, DTA will enhance the operator's ability to diagnose failures and errors made by the computer. It should, however, be noted that these proposals have not yet been extensively tested in empirical studies investigating the effect of adaptive function allocation on performance (Mouloua, Parasuraman and Molloy, 1993).

Control of task allocation

Two types of control of DTA, explicit allocation and implicit allocation, have been distinguished. In the explicit mode the operator allocates tasks to be performed manually or automatically by the system. Explicit task allocation is popular with operators, and also has the advantage of eliminating redundant actions by either the human or the computer. However, a disadvantage is that it may actually increase the operator's overall workload, as he or she has to manage and allocate tasks as well as perform those under manual control. Added to this, the operator may not actually always be aware of performance decrements on certain tasks, and so may not utilize the system's resources fully (Rieger and Greenstein, 1982). Tattersall and Morgan (1997) used the multi-attribute task battery (Comstock and Arnegard, 1992) to assess the effects of explicit and implicit control of DTA in terms of performance, situation awareness and workload. The overall task involved the simultaneous performance of four tasks: tracking, visual monitoring, auditory communications and resource management. The tracking task was a two-dimensional compensatory tracking task. The visual monitoring task required the monitoring and correction of deviations in the level of four gauges and the detection of state changes in two warning lights. The communications task simulated the presentation of auditory air traffic control messages. The task involved the identification of target call signs, followed by appropriate action to change the level of indicated channel frequencies. Resource management required operators to maintain the water level of two main tanks at a specified level by transferring water from four supply tanks. This was achieved by switching any of the eight water pumps linking the tanks on or off. Tattersall and Morgan found beneficial effects of explicit control of two tasks (tracking and resource management) compared with static allocation, in terms of improved performance and situation awareness. However, these effects were only significant at relatively high levels of task demands. In addition, there were indications that the adaptive automation of a single task from the four within this multiple-task environment did not result in such pronounced benefits. Curiously, but perhaps reflecting the need for control, 25 per cent of participants in the explicit allocation group chose never to use the opportunity to automate the tasks.

With the implicit mode of dynamic task allocation, the computer system allocates the tasks to either the human or the computer. Research comparing explicit and implicit modes of DTA indicate that although most system operators prefer explicit task allocation, implicit DTA is superior in terms of overall system performance (Greenstein et al., 1986; Morris, Rouse and Ward, 1988). However, implicit DTA is relatively difficult to implement and it is also difficult to define an allocation criteria for the tasks. In order to allocate tasks effectively, the system needs information on which to base the allocation decisions, and several suggestions of how implicit DTA may be implemented have been proposed. The three main methods are physiologically based adaptation, model-based adaptation and performance-based adaptation.

First, several researchers have discussed the use of biopsychometrics to invoke adaptive automation (Parasuraman, Bahri, Deaton, Morrison and Barnes, 1992; Morrison and Gluckman, 1994). Physiological signals are used which reflect autonomic or brain activity. These in turn are thought to reflect changes in workload and can then be used to trigger shifts in modes of automation (Prinzel, Seerbo, Freeman and Mikulka, 1995). In the few studies to use such methods, only EEG data have been investigated, but it is also possible that ECG or other physiological data would provide suitable information following adequate evaluation studies. One of the problems with the use of EEG signal to implement DTA is that the present state of EEG recording technology offers few application possibilities outside laboratory or clinical environments. Furthermore, additional research is necessary to examine the reliability of this type of adaptive task allocation technique, and the use of other physiological measures to trigger the shift of task allocation.

Second, the model-based adaptation approach proposes that the computer's task allocation strategy is built upon a model of human action strategies. The computer uses the model of human decision-making behaviour to predict the human's actions and perform a task which it predicts the human would not be able to perform effectively. Most studies to compare the effectiveness of explicit and implicit DTA to date have used the model-based mode of implicit DTA (e.g. Greenstein et al., 1986; Morris et al., 1988). The effectiveness of such a method of task allocation is dependent not just on the predictive validity of the model employed but also on the algorithm used to implement information based on the model. Therefore, this method of implementing DTA is problematic as, to date, no reliable model of human action has been developed. However, Greenstein and Revesman (1986) found evidence to suggest that task allocation based on a model of human processing having only a modest predictive validity is capable of enhancing system performance compared to a no aid, control condition. The system in this case was a simulation of a human–computer repair process in which either the computer predicted what the human would do in terms of failure detection and repair (model-based) or the human instructed the computer of the tasks to perform. Greenstein et al. (1986) found that the model-based mode was better than an explicit mode of adaptation in terms of speed of task completion, even though the model produced more redundant actions. This evidence suggests that the development and use of complex all-encompassing models may not perhaps be required for system performance to be improved by implicit dynamic task allocation methods.

Third, the performance-based adaptation method of task allocation is based on data from the continuous tracking of levels of performance of various task variables. In the method discussed by Vanderhaegen, Crevits, Debernard and Millot (1994), constraints relating to previously identified minimum and maximum levels of acceptable workload (in an attempt to avoid both overload and underload) were programmed into the task allocator. Thus, if the level of performance for a particular task variable does not meet a specific criterion, a task or task portion will be reallocated to automated or human control. Kamoun, Debernard and Millot (1989) found that this type of implicit task allocation led to optimal levels of system performance and operator workload. Whether such a method is generalizable to more complex, real-world situations remains to be seen, as it requires the prediction of acceptable levels of demand and performance for each task. Another potential drawback of the use of simple performance criteria to control task allocation is that fluctuations between human and computer control may be induced (Scallen, Hancock and Duley, 1995). This raises a further, general question about the rate of change of adaptation. Despite this reservation, the approach appears to be promising, and some form of performance assessment that feeds into the allocation process is likely to be necessary for any effective method.

All these methods for implementing task allocation dynamically require the development of an appropriate algorithm, which is then utilized by the automated system to transfer control between the human and computer. Unfortunately, this is often problematic, as a poor choice of algorithm may lead to poorer performance than that obtained with static task allocation. From this perspective, therefore, explicit task allocation may be a more practical alternative. It is clear that more research is necessary to investigate and compare the effectiveness of implicit and explicit modes of task allocation, and, further, to investigate the effectiveness of the various forms of implicit task allocation with respect to system performance, mental workload and situation awareness.

A crucial factor for future developments in this area will be to validate on-line methods for assessing workload, situation awareness and control. That is, retrospective measures and methods which require complex post-task analysis are unlikely to be useful if fully dynamic systems are to operate without substantial temporal delay. Task allocation decisions are likely to be highly situation-based, using current measures of system performance and other criteria and, depending on the task allocation logic, a profile of past levels of performance, workload and/or psychophysiological activity (e.g. Hancock and Chignell, 1987).

Feedback to the operator will need to be provided about task allocation changes. This could be done implicitly, with no overt message or change to the displayed information, but it is unlikely that this will be acceptable to operators in most systems, and will probably lead to uncertainty, frustration and loss of control. The alternative is to provide explicit information about the change either through a clear visual or auditory message, or through a change to the interface (e.g. de-emphasizing non-manual tasks by moving them to the periphery of the display or by providing summary information about their progress and status). Whether this should be done prior to the change actually taking place needs to be evaluated.

Clearly, the performance of the overall system and an individual operator's performance on the various sub-tasks is a primary concern for system designers and managers, but the objective and subjective workload experienced by human operators should also be taken into account as levels of perceived workload and task demands may influence performance, and vice versa. An individual's awareness and control of the system is also thought to have an effect on both current and future performance of the system, and may well be affected adversely by different forms of automation.

Chapter Summary

Workload assessment should form a critical part of system design and evaluation of current systems, especially when a change at organizational, individual operator or task level has taken place. This chapter has provided an overview of the concept of mental workload and the practical problems that might be encountered in carrying out workload evaluations in work settings. It has reviewed the different approaches to the assessment of workload and discussed the criteria that should determine the appropriate and effective choice of the type of method and research design for a particular situation. A key distinction was made between workload assessment to examine the short-term and that to examine the long-term consequences of combining various tasks. In the former case, theoretical models of attention allocation should inform studies of interference and the consequences of task demand and task conflict for performance. In the latter case, which has a different temporal orientation, the relationships between work demands and strain are the focus of interest. The effects of individual differences in workload management or effort regulation strategies will determine the extent to which decrements are observed in work performance under difficult conditions. However, high effort control may be associated with costs in terms of changes in affective state and physiological activity, as well as benefits in terms of performance. The consequences of dealing with heavy work demands may therefore only be measurable in the form of trade-offs between performance and other domains of individual activity, and longitudinal sampling of performance as well as subjective and physiological measures may well be required. It is argued that appropriate workplace design should address issues associated with workload, so that potential decrements in individual performance and associated organizational problems are avoided.

Discussion Points

1   What are the different workload assessment techniques?

2   Explain the hazards of automation.

3   Discuss the objectives of workload assessment.

CHAPTER NINE

WORK ENVIRONMENTS AND PERFORMANCE

G. Robert J. Hockey

Contents

Chapter Outline

This chapter examines work performance in the context of normal threats and demands of the environment. It takes a goal theory perspective, in which individuals try to modify their behaviour under stress, in order to maintain an appropriate balance between external work goals and internal or personal goals. It discusses the nature of demands and goals, the control processes that guide behaviour, and the nature of work goals in particular. A general model of demand management is described, based on regulatory control processes, and several alternative adaptive strategies are outlined. The chapter goes on to examine the pattern of decrement observed under stress, and the reasons why such effects are not always obvious. Where work goals are strongly held, serious disruption of central tasks is 'protected' by compensatory control processes. As a consequence, 'latent decrements' may be observed in various secondary aspects of performance, or changes in task strategy. In addition, there are likely to be subjective and physiological costs, which may compromise well-being. Implications for the management of performance at work are discussed, in relation to individual differences and work 'efficiency'.

Introduction

The primary requirement of all work is that employees carry out set tasks. These are determined largely by the goals of the organization, and often embodied as the substantive elements of the job description. The quality of task performance has a major significance not only for productivity, but also for outcomes such as reliability and safety, and, because of its central role in job satisfaction, personal health and well-being. Increasingly, appraisals of personal performance are also used as the main criterion of employees' effectiveness and motivation – and the basis for promotion, pay increases and the like. It therefore becomes important to understand how the achievement of satisfactory performance levels may be compromised by the conditions under which we work. The present chapter considers the different kinds of changes that occur in performance under the threat of environmental factors, and what employees can do to manage such problems.

Work environments vary considerably. Some jobs (nursing, teaching, social work) are recognized as being very demanding, in comparison to the work experiences of most of us. In some organizations, such as large offices and banks, the flow of work is determined largely by managers and supervisors. In others (hospitals, schools and universities) there may be more individual control over what may be done at any one moment, or how tasks are conducted. Some employees work in air-conditioned, noise-attenuated offices. Others have a constant background of loud unpredictable noises, or highly variable levels of heat and cold. Some work in large groups, as in open-plan offices or factory assembly lines; others largely on their own. There are also differences in the scheduling of work. While most people still work a nine to five day, increasing moves towards a '24-hour society' and the desire for 'flexi-time' have meant an inevitable extension of the working day well beyond these traditional boundaries. Many work shifts, including nights, which usually means losing sleep and having severely curtailed lives outside of work.

Work Scenarios

In order to make issues clearer in places, and help to illustrate the way in which generalizations from research might apply in real work situations, I make occasional use of four scenarios, drawn from typical work situations:

- *The PA.* Fiona works as an ambitious PA to a successful marketing executive. She works in an air-conditioned office, with high levels of physical comfort. Her work is demanding, but allows a high level of discretion about how and when tasks may be carried out. However, because of the 'last-minute' nature of many critical activities, she also experiences periods of extreme time pressure, long hours and potential conflicts with her boss.
- *The captain.* Captain French is the experienced master of an oil tanker, sailing regularly between Europe and the Far East. Although much of his work is routine navigation and management, there are also sudden periods of intense load (with potential collisions etc.). Although he does not work shifts (watches), he is called into action whenever there are major problems.
- *The nursing team.* A team of nurses work shifts in an intensive care ward in a children's hospital. In addition to their general clinical responsibilities, they have a high monitoring load (checking instruments and carrying out tests) and a heavy level of emotional demands (concern for the children's welfare).
- *The process control team.* A small team of process operators work in the control room in a semi-automatic plant, producing organic dyes and fertilizers. Their main responsibility is the maintenance of the production process by interaction with a computer system, though they are also required to carry out mechanical maintenance on occasion. They are part of a rotating shift system, with two other teams. The working conditions are noisy, hot and dirty outside the control room, with some degree of physical danger.

While these cannot, in any sense, be considered representative of the working environments encountered across the job spectrum, they allow us to illustrate many of the substantive issues relevant to the discussion.

Environmental Demand

The concept of demand has a central role in current theories of effects of stress on health and performance (e.g. Karasek and Theorell, 1990). The term 'job demands' is often used in work stress, referring specifically to aspects of the work itself (see chapter 7, this volume). In this chapter, however, 'demands' refers to events in both the job and the broader work environment. These include task events, interruptions and distractions, increases in the pace of work, stressors such as noise or heat, interpersonal conflicts and personal (non-work) problems.

Minimally, the management of demands involves *coping* – an appraisal of the event(s) as posing a possible threat to current goals, and the adoption of a suitable plan of action (e.g. Lazarus and Folkman, 1984). For example, our PA, Fiona, has to decide whether an emergent software problem will prevent her completing an urgent task, and – if so – ensure that maintenance is called immediately. If not, she knows that help will be available from a colleague later in the day. The nursing team need to evaluate changing conditions of the children in their care, and determine whether doctors should be called. In cases where a problem has been identified, coping may require the use of increased effort (where the work has become more difficult), or a change of plan (where available resources are no longer adequate for solving the problem). In Captain French's case, an unexpected change of course by another vessel may require him rapidly to compute complex navigational changes for his own vessel. Finally, where the difficulty cannot easily be overcome or circumvented, the goal may have to be modified, or dropped altogether while these conditions remain in place. When there is a major spillage in the process control plant, the team may have to shut down all operations temporarily, rather than only the affected batch.

Three broad kinds of demand may be distinguished (*physical, cognitive* and *emotional*), based on the adaptive bio-cognitive systems that are challenged by work and environmental events (see table 9.1). Some jobs may be demanding because employees have to work hard physically; some because they require employees to carry out complex decision-making and planning tasks; others because they involve a heavy burden of responsibility for the welfare of others. However, all three kinds of demand reflect the essentially *transactional* nature of the human response to stress (Lazarus and Folkman, 1984). This means that dealing with demands involves a recursive process of appraisal, action and reappraisal (Lazarus and Folkman, 1984; Ferguson and Cox, 1997) in which the individual is an active participant.

Physical demands are associated with traditional heavy industry and farming. They are, of course, less common in modern jobs, but not absent, as is sometimes assumed. Most jobs still involve some lifting and carrying, even in offices or control rooms – certainly in nursing and on board ship. The need to move

Table 9.1   Different types of job demands, in terms of impact on human systems

Type of demand	Primary system affected	Nature of demands	Examples of jobs
Physical	Musculo-skeletal	Lifting, carrying, physical stress, constraint	Heavy industry, farming, forestry, construction
Cognitive	Information processing	Mental work, memory, planning, decision-making	Office work, computer work, teaching, finance
Emotional	Emotion	Caring, concern for self and others, interpersonal conflict	Nursing, social work, counselling

around and exercise the musculo-skeletal system may even be fundamental to a generally healthy and effective response to environmental demands. It may therefore be a mistake to remove completely the need for such activity from jobs. Some companies, notably Japanese manufacturing firms, have even introduced exercise programmes as a part of the work structure.

By contrast, *cognitive demands* impinge primarily on the brain processes involved in information processing. They are recognized increasingly as the defining feature of modern jobs – information work of all kinds – and challenge the limitations of the cognitive system for memorizing, comparing, planning, decision-making, concentrating for long periods etc. Because of their prevalence in current work developments, a concern with cognitive demands is also one of the main driving forces in research on work design. Major growth areas focus on human–computer interaction; for example, the increasing use of networks, tele-working, distributed cognition and computer-supported cooperative work (see Chmiel, 1998).

Finally, *emotional demands* are strongly linked to interpersonal events, particularly within the caring professions (nursing, social work etc.), in their emphasis on goals that concern the welfare of others. However, such demands also play a part of most jobs from time to time, whenever conflict, anxiety, concern or caring comes into focus as an issue. Emotional demands may also have an indirect effect on performance in cognitive tasks, because they compete strongly for the control of attention (Oatley and Johnson-Laird, 1987; Taylor, 1991). Current work performance is likely to be compromised by a shift of processing towards other, more personal, goals whenever these are persistent (e.g. worry over an upcoming promotion interview, or your child's exam results). The relevance of emotional demand in this chapter is mainly that such effects may occur as an indirect response to environmental factors which threaten stable performance.

Theoretical Framework

I do not intend to overemphasize the theory aspects of research on environmental stress and human performance. However, an understanding of the general approach adopted is necessary in order to make sense of the way I have approached these issues. It is fair to say that the approach taken here is not a traditional one. As is already implicit in the opening remarks, the emphasis is on active management of demands by workers. It assumes that individuals have choices about how to interpret and deal with environmental factors that threaten their performance (an assumption which, of course, applies equally to non-work activities).

Traditional treatments have usually considered environmental factors one at a time, showing how noise, climatic conditions, sleep deprivation, shift work, time pressure and other factors affect performance (Poulton, 1970; Broadbent, 1971; Hockey, 1983, 1986). Additionally, workers have usually been assumed to be at the mercy of environmental stress, responding passively, and inevitably, to the effects of these undesirable conditions on their system. Effects of noise, for example, were thought to be explicable in terms of their direct effects on arousal (e.g. Wilkinson, 1962). It is now clear that this view is too simple. First, arousal is, itself, a more complex set of processes than previously assumed. Second, the response to arousal effects is dependent on task demands and individual goals (see Hockey, 1986). This is not to say that such effects do not occur at all. For example, Hockey and Hamilton (1983) identified different patterns of baseline effects of a range of environmental stressors, showing that they impose different patterns of strain on underlying cognitive processes. I survey these specific effects of stressors briefly below. Rather, it is now clear that knowledge of the physical or cognitive threat to our bodies and brains is rarely sufficient to allow us to predict what will happen to task performance.

A good example is provided by a study of Lundberg and Frankenhaeuser (1978), showing that noise impaired performance on an arithmetic task on one occasion but not on another. Why should this occur? Fortunately, Lundberg and Frankenhaeuser also measured the physiological and subjective costs associated with having to work on the task under noise. They found that, where arithmetic performance was unimpaired, there was a marked increase in both the level of circulating adrenaline and ratings of subjective effort. However, in the case where performance was impaired by noise, no such changes were observed. As we shall see below, the most satisfactory explanation of this and similar findings is that noise imposes an additional load on our capacity to maintain adequate orientation towards the task. If we can make an additional effort under such circumstances, performance may be protected against disruption, though only at the cost of increased strain in other bodily systems. Alternatively, we may decide not to make such an effort, in which case we are likely to feel less strain, but performance will suffer. Such trade-off options are the routine consequences of having to manage environmental demands in the context of task goals.

Demands and goal management

The central theoretical strand in the theoretical perspective taken here is that effective work requires people to make decisions about how to manage their environment. What are their priorities for task and other goals? How willing (and able) are they to make a sustained effort to maintain required performance standards under difficult circumstances? High levels of workload and difficult work conditions are typically associated with stress. However, this does not appear to be caused by direct activation of the appropriate physiological mechanisms by stressors. Rather, the perception of unwanted environmental conditions and demands gives rise to tension through a disturbance of the relationship between goals and actions, which needs to be resolved by appropriate coping activity (Hockey and Hamilton, 1983; Schönpflug, 1983). From this perspective, performance under stress can only be understood in terms of goal-directed behaviour. The requirement to maintain work goals (or any other cognitive plan) in the face of high workload and environmental stress effectively means having to take on additional emotional demands associated with managing the stress. The treatment of performance in this chapter recognizes the intimate relationship between the required outcomes of work and the adaptive, self-regulatory processes underlying all human–environmental interaction.

Control processes

A central feature of regulatory behaviour is the notion of control processes (e.g. Miller et al., 1960; Carver and Scheier, 1982; Schönpflug, 1983). The use of this kind of model in psychology and biology comes from the application of cybernetics to engineering process control. On this basis, performance is the outcome of a comparison of what is required of the behaviour (the set point to target state in industrial processes) with what is being achieved currently (the controlled variable). Behaviour is then modified until the difference (error signal) is reduced to zero, or some acceptable shortfall. The process through which this occurs is known as 'negative feedback' (since it operates by subtracting the level of the controlled variable from that of the set point). The negative feedback principle is central to all control processes, whether in psychology, biology or engineering, and is one of the most effective ways of ensuring stable levels of behaviour (or any other controlled variable).

There is an important difference, however, between engineering systems and human behaviour. Rather than meet a specific industrial target (however complex), humans are required to satisfy many different goals at different times. This intrinsic flexibility means that switches between goals over the course of the day, or over much smaller time periods, are not only common but necessary features of this need to respond on many motivational fronts. However, effective performance in a given work task requires that such flexibility is resisted, allowing for (a) important goals to be maintained as a target state for the negative feedback process, and (b) behaviour to continue to be adjusted (speeded up, made more accurate) in response to the detected discrepancy. If maintaining goal orientation involves overcoming natural tendencies to switch to other goals, this ought to be reflected in costs of regulatory activity, and this is supported by research on coping and behaviour control (e.g. Schönpflug, 1983; Frankenhaeuser, 1986; Hockey, 1997). Attempts to maintain performance standards under difficult or demanding conditions are effortful, and involve increased activity of bodily systems in stress and response to challenge. Coping with stress at work attracts costs, not only when it fails, but when it succeeds in resolving disruptions in planning and goal-oriented performance.

Environmental Threats to Performance

Although the approach adopted here focuses on the general problems of demand management, environmental stressors may also pose more specific threats for the integrity of performance. Decrements are found more typically in laboratory studies, which, as I discuss below, may be more vulnerable to disruption because of their failure to anchor attention satisfactorily.

Earlier analyses (Hockey, 1979, 1986; Hockey and Hamilton, 1983) emphasized the patterned nature of the specific effects of stressors across different indicators of performance and strategy, based on the use of different kinds of tasks and performance measures. Some stressors appear more likely to impair performance on one group of tasks; others on a different group. For example. loud noise typically impairs performance on tasks that require accuracy or extensive use of short-term memory. Sleep deprivation is likely to cause impairment on tasks involving both accuracy and speed, and a high degree of attentional focusing, as well as having more general effects on memory. Both noise and sleep deprivation have effects which are more pronounced when tasks involve long periods of unbroken attention (Broadbent, 1963). Their effects increase with time spent at work without a break. Working in hot conditions has widespread effects on most aspects of performance, especially tasks which involve more complex decision-making. The effects are related to the exposure time and effective temperature (Ramsay, 1983), but do not appear to increase over time on the job (Broadbent, 1963).

The set of indicators used in the analysis carried out by Hockey and Hamilton (1983) included general alertness, selectivity of attention, processing speed versus accuracy, and short-term memory (STM) capacity. With changes in cognitive theory over the intervening fifteen years or so, and experience of effects in real work tasks, some changes are probably needed to this list. General alertness no longer appears to have strong diagnostic value, as it is likely to be involved in all active regulatory behaviour (see Hockey, 1997). The mechanisms underlying STM have undergone considerable evolution with the development of working memory theory (Baddeley, 1986). In addition, there is a need for a new analysis, which takes into account differential effects of regulatory activity. However, even with these caveats, changes in these indicators can be seen as a profile of the sorts of information processing problems that different conditions may pose. They may be best seen as a guide to how performance might suffer *if no compensatory regulatory activity occurred.*

The most general pattern of decrement is associated with conditions such as noise, danger and subjective states of anxiety. This may be regarded as the modal stress state, involving a subjective state of high activation, high selectivity of attention, a preference for speed over accuracy and reduced STM capacity. Decrements are more common on tasks of long duration, especially where the use of STM is central to maintaining the flow of the work. Selective attention is normally very effective, unless response is required to a number of different events or sub-tasks, in which case only the most important may be maintained. A familiar effect of such stressors is narrowed attention, in which high-priority features of tasks are maintained and secondary aspects neglected. This has been found for noise, threat of shock, danger, and test anxiety (Broadbent, 1971; Baddeley, 1972; Hockey, 1986).

Other stressors are associated with different kinds of changes. For example, STM is not much impaired in hot working conditions, or with extended work periods. In all cases, however, it has become clear that we cannot separate underlying effects on cognitive processes from those relating to changes in performance goals or strategies. An increase in reliance on one kind of process may be the result of a strategic reduction in the use of another. Because of this, patterns of stressor effects cannot be discussed in isolation of an understanding of what someone is trying to do when performing a task, or of the nature of work goals in general.

The Nature of Work Tasks

The emphasis I have placed on self-regulatory control in managing work demands means that human performance needs to be considered as an integral part of the overall adaptive behaviour of the individual. It cannot be regarded as independent of their emotional, biological or motivational needs. Indeed, it could be argued that performance goals are, in some ways, secondary. In relation to our classification of demands, it is likely that this problem applies particularly to cognitive goals.

Vulnerability of cognitive goals

Clearly, the cognitive processes that underlie task activity (reading, under-standing, planning, deciding, checking, remembering and the like) are impor-tant in adaptive behaviour. However, typical work tasks may be considered secondary to those that serve biological goals, such as self-preservation, the provision of adequate food and water, sex and protection of our young (e.g. Frijda, 1986; Tomkins, 1995). Physical and emotional work retains more of these properties, and may be less vulnerable to disruption from environmen-tal factors (though there does not appear to have been a direct test of this hypothesis). Of course, work goals may be established and acted upon effec-tively, but goals relating to emotional states may be more powerful in the long run – even relatively general goals such as the need to feel calm, avoid strain or take rest. The desire for rest or change in the middle of even quite inter-esting work is a particularly powerful regulating process, and may reflect the operation of an active motivational mechanism which is normally experienced as fatigue (Hockey and Meijman, 1998). The problem for performance is that these emotional demands are potentially highly disruptive. They tend to give rise to strong psychophysiological states, which are enduring and not readily subdued (Taylor, 1991; Tomkins, 1995).

Performance goals can be disrupted either by *distraction* from other goals (especially emotional and motivational goals) or simply by *loss of activation* (the difficulty of maintaining orientation towards the task over extended work periods). Consider the problem for Fiona as she works late under time pres-sure, to finish work for a morning meeting. First, she may become increas-ingly aware of small noises in the building, which interrupt her progress. This is the effect of her involuntary response to fear signals. Processing the signals is unavoidable, and interrupts task goals (Oatley and Johnson-Laird, 1987). In overcoming the distraction she has to work harder, while sustaining an uncomfortable state of anxiety. Even in the absence of these external threat signals, however, Fiona will experience increasing difficulties in maintaining concentration the longer she carries on. As we all know, her response should be to take occasional breaks, or to do something else for a few minutes, but the pressure to get the work done makes such a course of action unattractive.

The vulnerability of cognitive goals may, paradoxically, serve an adaptive function. First, as Tomkins (1995) has argued, the potential of emotional states for capturing control of behaviour ensures that motivational priorities in rela-tion to environmental demands will be readily available. However wrapped up we are in our work, it is essential that we shift into emergency mode when-ever circumstances demand. This means that we cannot help but respond not only to obvious biological signals (smelling fire or gas, sensing earth tremors), but to more generalized associations, such as loud or unfamiliar sounds, uncomfortable climatic conditions or signals relevant to hunger, thirst or sex, depending on our current motivational priorities. Interruption of performance goals has further advantages, however. By preventing fixation on short-term or low-level goals, such a mechanism ensures flexibility of behavioural orientation, allowing novel events to be investigated and alternative lines of activity to be pursued. This is not only an essential part of human problem-solving and creativity (Simon, 1967), but a way of ensuring that only strong goals maintain control of action. If Fiona begins to think of her supper, or she finds herself planning a more interesting task due the next day, she will need actively to reinstate the current task goal. This process ensures that only goals that retain their priority over time continue to control our behaviour.

Despite all these problems, human performance can be extraordinarily resistant to disruption – performance appears to be protected from disruption by these strong threats. How is this achieved? Because they are vulnerable, and easily disrupted, I would argue that maintaining cognitive goals requires the services of a specialized regulatory system – selective attention – which can be recruited by goal states in order to overcome distraction and loss of activation. As should be evident from the above, and as Kahneman (1973) has argued, the mechanism of selective attention has considerable consequences for activity in emotional and other bodily systems, because it overrides underlying behavioural and biological predispositions. Before considering the implications of such a mechanism for performance regulation under stress and environmental demand, I want to reconsider the nature of human performance within a broader systems perspective.

A system perspective

Although 'performance' has a variety of meanings in work and everyday life, its technical definition within experimental psychology and human factors has become increasingly specific. Current usage refers to the effectiveness of either general or specific tasks, or the mental operations assumed to underlie task behaviour. Of course, within psychological research, performance tasks are widely used to provide a window on mental activity. However, researchers sometimes fail to appreciate fully the rationale for the use of these methods. From the investigator's point of view, tasks provide an indirect measure of the mechanisms underlying mental processes, or of the functional level of the information processing system or some part of it (how well it can operate at this moment). If a process is operating less effectively (say, under stress or illness, or because of competition from other processes), performance of an appropriate task is assumed to reflect this as a decrement in output or speed or errors. The detection of a decrement is taken as a marker of the additional load or strain placed on the system by the stressor. However, this assumes a rather unusual level of compliance on the part of the 'performer'. The task is an externally imposed goal, requiring employees to manage their actions in such a way that they meet the arbitrary criteria set by someone else. The methodology of performance assumes that the individual internalizes these goals, and maintains them at a very high level of priority for the specified duration. This means constantly refreshing task goals in memory, selectively attending to relevant environmental information, avoiding distraction from competing (more relevant, long-term) goals etc.

Most human performance assessment is thus based on the measurement of a limited range of actions in response to quite specific task goals. This is true both for research under laboratory conditions and for the execution of work tasks. Performance in Fiona's office is judged to be poor when there is a short-fall in meeting output targets (number of customer's bills processed) or an increase in complaints (with errors in billing etc.). Compare this to an assessment of the performance of our chemical processing plant. Typically, this involves a concern with the overall system – not only with the amount of fertilizer, but with the quality control of the product, the level of pollution, accidents and incidents which might compromise safety standards, resources consumed in reaching these production targets (human, financial, energy etc.). A similar concept of system-level *costs* can be used with human performance. Both humans and complex industrial processes, as well as offices, ships, hospitals and all other areas of working life, are *systems*. This means that different components of the overall organization interact in order to achieve goals, with feedback from the behaviour of each acting as an input to the others. This means that increased activity in one part of the system will necessarily have knock-on effects in other areas. When humans carry out work tasks, there is an inevitable spill-over of regulatory activity into other parts of the human bio-cognitive system. These include failures in other (currently less important) activities, emotional and physiological consequences of maintaining orientation towards work goals, the psychological strain from the need to suppress personal and bodily needs, and delayed effects such as the onset of fatigue, which reflects a bias against further exertion of this kind.

Consider the problem faced by Fiona, in trying to meet an urgent deadline to prepare material for her boss's hastily rearranged meeting in Zurich the next morning. After working all day on the task she 'performs' very well. The boss goes off to catch the evening flight, his documents and presentation overheads safely in his briefcase. Yet she has neglected her usual office 'housekeeping' activities, responded hastily (and in an unhelpful manner) to several telephone enquiries and been offhand with office colleagues insisting she take a lunch break with them. On top of all this, she has felt tense all day, and (although she may not be aware of it) her blood pressure and heart rate have remained near the top of their normal ranges. She also has high levels of adrenaline, noradrenaline and cortisol in her blood, consistent with the body making an emergency ('fight or flight') response. These changes remain in the body for some time afterwards (Frankenhaeuser, 1986). When she eventually gets home she will not be able to relax, probably drink more than is good for her and not be able to sleep, wondering whether there will be any comeback from any of the day's little failures.

Effectiveness versus efficiency

The key idea from the use of a broad system perspective is the need to distinguish between *effectiveness* and *efficiency* (Schönpflug, 1983; Hockey, 1996). By far the majority of studies of human performance are concerned only with effectiveness – with how well specific output targets are achieved under different conditions. A concern with efficiency, however, means taking into account the costs to the system as a whole of achieving these outputs. Clearly, despite the difficulties encountered, Fiona's performance is highly effective (in terms of the specific goals set by her boss). There are, however, many costs, and the efficiency of her response is less impressive. This is particularly relevant when comparing conditions in which manifest performance levels do not differ. Increased costs imply that success in maintaining the required standard is achieved at the expense of disruption to other (currently less important) processes. I refer to this as a 'latent decrement', since it reflects a compromised system state which imposes constraints on adaptability in the face of further or changing demands.

Regulatory Control of Demands

One of the most surprising findings of research on human performance under environmental demand is that the effectiveness of primary task actions is typically very high (Kahneman, 1971, 1973; Hockey, 1993, 1996, 1997). This is particularly true of tasks based on classical industrial activities, such as vigilance (monitoring and inspection activities), tracking (manual control of all kinds) and sequential responding (underlying the kind of complex perceptual motor skills found in many office tasks). Where decrements are found, they are usually not serious, have minimal practical implications and are actively managed. In general, the management of performance under stress and high demand may be said to exhibit a 'graceful degradation' (Navon and Gopher, 1979), rather than a catastrophic collapse.

   One intriguing observation is that, where decrements do occur, they are more likely to be in laboratory studies than in real-life work situations. Although the reasons for this have not been formally studied, it is likely to be related to differences in factors such as skill levels and motivation. Laboratory tasks are usually relatively trivial, private, under-learned and transient. Participants are encouraged to work 'flat out' for the duration of the task, without errors. When something goes wrong, or extra burdens are imposed, there is little room for manoeuvre, and errors may occur (though, even here, stability of performance is the norm). By contrast, work tasks are (usually) meaningful and often executed in the public domain. They help to define us individually within the organization. They are also generally well learned and long-lasting. All these factors help to protect them in situations of stress or heavy environmental demand. The real-life context encourages the maintenance of task goals, and the use of sustained levels of effort, if required. Because work tasks are usually carried out well within the capacity of the individual (no one works flat out all the time – if at all), there is usually spare capacity to respond to increased demands. Because tasks are well practised, more strategies are available for meeting new demands, and there are more options about damage limitation (e.g. which subsidiary activities may be neglected).

The compensatory control model

Over the past two decades, with the help of various colleagues (e.g. Hockey and Hamilton, 1983; Hockey, 1986, 1993, 1997; Hockey et al., 1989, 1998), I have developed a compensatory control model to account for these observations of minimal decrement under high demand. The model postulates the operation of a 'performance protection' strategy – an adaptive regulatory process, which helps to maintain output for high-priority task goals within acceptable limits, at the expense of other (low-priority) activities. Overt performance is construed as being driven by the individual's internalization of work goals (how fast to work, how much accuracy is required, the optimal order for actions and so on). As in all control models, performance criteria are assumed to be continually adjusted (through the use of feedback) until they provide an acceptable match to the required reference state. These are set up in response to both long-term and short-term goals, and modified in the light of changes in the perceived costs and benefits of alternative actions.

As I have indicated above, the theoretical framework adopted here also argues that the maintenance of performance goals is an active process under the control of the individual, requiring the mobilization and management of resources. In broad psychological terms, this means making use of planning and mental effort to maintain the priority of work goals, whenever they are threatened by environmental disturbances. A full discussion of the model is inappropriate for the present purposes, though a brief description may be useful. Its main feature (figure 9.1) is the presence of two broad levels of control. Most of human behaviour may be regarded as automatic, requiring little active control. This is managed by a lower-level control loop (A). However, to deal with unexpected or emergency situations, or tasks that are not highly automated, a second, upper-level, mechanism (B) is also included. This supervisory (or executive) process determines the mode of control adopted to resolve discrepancies, based on decisions of goal orientation and effort regulation, and is assumed to be under voluntary control.

A distinction between upper and lower levels appears to be the minimum level of complexity needed to account for the data on the effects of stress and workload on task performance (Broadbent, 1971, 1977; Rasmussen, 1986; Shallice and Burgess, 1993; Chmiel et al., 1995): German action theory

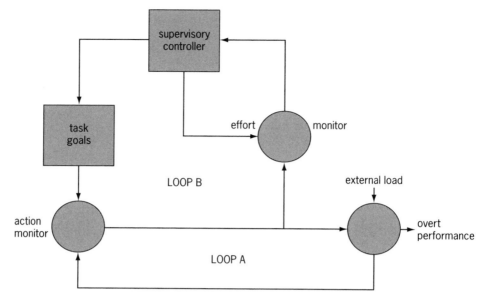

Figure 9.1 Simplified control model of demand regulation. Loop A represents routine regulatory activity, and loop B effort-related control, resulting in either increased effort or a change of task goals. See text for explanation.

typically assumes a multiple-level hierarchy of regulatory control (see Frese and Zapf, 1994). The approach offered here has much in common with that developed by Schönpflug (e.g. 1983, 1986), though it has its origins in the two-level control model of Hamilton et al. (1977) and in Teichner's (1968) hypothesis of compensatory environmental control of stress states. The essential feature of the model is that the regulation of action is assumed to involve cost–benefit decisions about the use of effort in the service of performance goals.

Modes of demand management

A core assumption of the model is that the supervisory system sets an 'effort budget' for a particular task (or work session), based on individuals' current goal priorities, previous experience, anticipated demand and current state (e.g. how energetic they feel). The basis of the model is that effort may be regulated in order to resolve any discrepancy that arises between goals and current performance under the threat of overload. The need for additional resources is signalled by a (metacognitive) effort monitor that senses the regulatory demand in loop A. When this exceeds the set budget the upper-level mechanism is triggered, and either increases effort allocation (the direct control mode) or reduces the level of target goals (indirect control). Both strategies

Table 9.2   Patterns of demand management under stress

Mode	Frankenhaueser categories	Performance level	Psychophysiological state
Engagement	Effort without distress	High	Increased A/NA; reduced C; high alertness
Disengagement	Distress without effort	Unacceptable	Little change, except where criticism or guilt involved (increased C, anxiety, depression)
Strain	Effort with distress	Acceptable	Increased A/NA/C; increased anxiety/fatigue; spill-over after work

A, adrenaline; NA, noradrenaline; C, cortisol.

have the effect of resolving the discrepancy between goals and performance, but with different trade-offs between performance and effort.

In fact, three, rather than two, general modes of demand management may be indentified – labelled *engaged*, *disengaged* and *strain* (table 9.2). These differ in terms of the relationship between the use of direct or indirect control and the current level of demands, and in their implications for the performance/costs trade-off. The three modes map closely on to the patterns of adaptation to work environments identified by Frankenhaeuser (1986), with additional input from our own work.

Engagement

Engagement involves the application of direct coping within the limits of the budget. The executive bias towards increased effort allows performance to be protected under demands from unexpected difficulties, periods of time pressure or additional stress conditions. Such a mode is nevertheless manageable, since it is allows periods of routine activity, and does not exceed the individual's capabilities. It may be considered a standard feature of any complex mental work, especially where employees are actively engaged in their task and 'working well'. It corresponds to Frankenhaeuser's description of 'challenge' situations ('effort without distress'), and is characterized by feelings of enthusiasm and elation – of having had a 'good day'. It also involves increases in catecholamines (adrenaline and noradrenaline), but not cortisol.

A more serious regulatory problem occurs when external demands are greater than expected, so that they exceed the allocated effort budget. There is evidence that subjective limits for maximum effort expenditure are relatively conservative, even for physical tasks (Holding, 1983), so that increases beyond the set 'maximum' are possible. Nevertheless, operating at a very high level for any length of time is likely to be uncomfortable, and to impose considerable strain and give rise to fatigue (Hockey et al., 1989; Hockey and Meijman, 1998). Two control options are available in such circumstances, referred to here as the disengagement and strain patterns.

Disengagement

This mode involves a reduced priority for work goals. It may be achieved by reducing required levels of accuracy or speed, by adopting strategies which make less demands on supervisory control or by neglecting secondary activities. In some cases, individuals may disengage completely from task goals, especially when an attempt at direct coping has little effect (Schultz and Schönpflug, 1982). This would be unusual (though not unheard of) in work contexts, though it is a common adaptive response in less constrained leisure activities. It corresponds to Frankenhaeuser's 'distress without effort' mode of coping, with low levels of catecholamines, but high levels of cortisol and anxiety and depression. While such a strategy helps to combat stress from work overload, it may have unfortunate side-effects. Apart from the reduced performance on the job, there may be a detrimental impact on job-related mental health. Employees may feel depressed or worried that they have not done as much work as they should, or concerned that they may have to make up the shortfall the next day. This is not a problem for the occasional use of such strategies (e.g. to combat sudden fatigue), but may lead to major problems if indirect coping was employed on a regular basis.

Strain

The strain mode is perhaps the most interesting from the point of view of work stress and adaptive behaviour. It is characterized as a striving or struggle to overcome environmental demands in order to maintain task goals. It is assumed that striving effectively increases resources by drawing on the energy mobilization capabilities of the system (Kahneman, 1973). Considered as a voluntary process, striving demonstrates a willingness to sustain an aversive strain state, corresponding to Frankenhaeuser's 'effort with distress'. At the end of a high-strain work day (such as that experienced by Fiona above), employees feel tense and weary, and have increased levels of both catecholamines and cortisol. There are also likely to be spill-over effects in the period following work, affecting the ability to relax or sleep (Frankenhaueser, 1986; Rissler and Jacobson, 1987).

Performance Degradation under Strain

Recognition of the possibility of trade-off between task goals and other (non-task) goals is central to an understanding of performance changes under stress and high workload. Only when work permits employees to operate in an engaged mode are neither performance decrements nor costs likely to be a problem. The adoption of a disengagement strategy protects personal goals, while accepting that primary performance will suffer. In the strain mode, employees maintain primary task goals, but at the expense of secondary aspects of performance and increased personal costs.

Patterns of latent decrement

A concern with at least some of these issues has been well established in research on workload, where primary task decrements are regarded as only one of a number of techniques for detecting differential demands of tasks (see Wickens, 1992; also chapter 8 in this volume). Decrements can also be observed indirectly, through the use of secondary tasks, subjective reports and various physiological measures (see Hockey, 1996). The same kinds of considerations hold for the analysis of performance under the strain mode in response to environmental stress. These are referred to here as *latent* (hidden or dormant) decrements, since their effects on performance are normally masked. However, they imply a reduced capacity for further adaptive response (e.g. to new emergencies), and a smaller safety margin for performance.

Under most environmental circumstances, Primary task goals can be maintained, either by reconfiguration of remaining resources (allowing occasional errors or delays to occur in secondary tasks), or by recruitment of additional resources. As I have stated, this second option is likely to be associated with increased effort, and to lead to further indirect costs (such as increased load on cardiovascular regulation, or sustained levels of stress hormones). It is unclear from what we know at present whether this poses a long-term threat for individual health, but it is possible that a pattern of persistent costs of this kind may underlie the development of stress-related coronary heart disease (Karasek and Theorell, 1990). As I have already pointed out, the protection of primary task performance applies especially to actual work situations (Hockey, 1993). Although degradation of primary task activity is therefore unusual, the operation of such regulatory processes implies that we should be able to observe changes which reflect increased or decreased costs under different conditions. Four more or less distinct forms of latent degradation under the strain mode may be identified (table 9.3).

Secondary task decrements

Secondary task decrements are commonly observed in workload paradigms, and provide an indirect measure of increasing load on primary tasks. Little needs to be said about these, since their general nature is well known (O'Donnell and Eggemeier, 1986; Wickens, 1992; see chapter 8 in this volume). Such effects have been studied less systematically in assessing threats from environmental factors, though they are, in fact, relatively common

Table 9.3 Patterns of latent decrement in performance associated with performance protection under stress and high demand

Decrement type	Characteristics
Secondary decrements	Selective impairment of low-priority task components; neglect of subsidiary activities; attentional narrowing
Strategy changes	Within-task shifts to simpler strategies; reduced demands on working memory; increased control activity
Regulatory costs	Strain of direct coping; increased anxiety, mental effort; sympathetic dominance
After-effects of strain	Post-task preference for low-effort strategies; subjective fatigue; risky decision-making

(Hockey, 1996). One of the best documented forms of secondary task decrement under stress is the narrowing (or funnelling) of attention found in spatially complex tasks. For example, Hockey (1970) found that a central pursuit tracking task was unaffected by noise, while detection of peripheral signals was impaired. Such effects have been found under both laboratory and field conditions, and for a wide range of environmental conditions, e.g. noise, anxiety associated with deep sea diving, threat of shock, fatigue (see Broadbent, 1971; Baddeley, 1972; Hockey, 1979). This type of decrement may also be considered to involve a change of strategy (as below), since the detailed pattern of performance depends on the manipulation of priority differences between task components. In the interpretation of this kind of finding I would argue that what is perceived as primary is protected, and everything else is dealt with only where resources permit.

Strategy changes

By changing the way in which tasks are carried out, the individual may be able to minimize disruption to primary outputs by more effective or simpler management of resources. More time can be allocated to important activities by reducing the time spent on fringe activities (checking effects of interim decisions, or supporting secondary activities). Strategic changes may also involve a shift to less resource-intensive modes of task control, reducing dependency on demanding processes such as working memory. Despite their obvious diagnostic value, such effects have not been well studied, partly because of the complex task environments necessary to analyse strategy changes.

It has been known for some time that, under periods of difficulty or stress, process operators may abandon the open loop control characteristic of skilled performance (in which complex mental models of action sequences are used to guide behaviour) in favour of a simpler closed loop mode (Bainbridge, 1978; Umbers, 1979). This may slow the process or fail to make optimal use of available options, but minimizes the likelihood of serious errors. Similarly, within air traffic control, Sperandio (1978) found that controllers adopted a more 'routinized' work pattern when the number of aircraft contacts increased beyond a 'comfortable' number. They switched from individual 'plane by plane' routing instructions to a fixed procedure for all. By minimizing the planning requirements, this reduces the load on the vulnerable working memory system. Secondary goals such as airport schedules and passenger comfort are sacrificed in the service of the primary goal of safety. In our own research we have found similar kinds of strategy changes.

Strategy changes under stress have been most thoroughly studied by Schönpflug and his colleagues (e.g. Schultz and Schönpflug, 1982; Schönpflug, 1983), in an innovative series of studies making use of simulated work environments, such as clerical work (checking bills, stock-keeping etc.). When students carried out these tasks under time pressure or loud noise, they were observed to make more frequent checks of computerized directories containing information about stock holdings and unit prices. Whereas under normal conditions they typically held the information in memory while making several decisions, under stress they tended to check the lists repeatedly before making each decision. Again, reducing the load on memory helped people to minimize decision errors, though at the expense of increased time costs. As I mentioned above, the attentional narrowing effect may also be interpreted as a strategic change, since it simplifies the way in which the task must be managed.

Two further examples come from studies of effects of sleep deprivation. Chmiel et al. (1995) found no change in decision-making accuracy on an adaptive control task with loss of sleep, but a marked slowing in the rate at which the task was carried out, particularly towards the end of four 1.5-hour work sessions. Finally, in a simulation study of a cabin air pressure/life support system for a spacecraft (Hockey et al., 1998), 'crew members' were required to maintain critical parameters (oxygen, carbon dioxide, pressure) within target limits over a three-hour period. Perhaps surprisingly, operators were able to carry out this complex primary task equally well after a night without sleep. However, performance protection was achieved through a simplification of control strategies. They engaged less in monitoring system parameters, which help in the anticipation of developing problems. Instead, sleep-deprived operators relied more on correcting the system by all-or-none manual interventions, triggered by alarms whenever parameters went slightly out of range.

Psychophysiological costs

Under the effortful compensatory mode, the recruitment of further resources should be revealed as increased activation of physiological systems involved in 'emergency' reactions (e.g. sympathetic and musculo-skeletal responses, neuro-endocrine stress patterns). There are also likely to be effects on mood states, reflecting the affective response to emergency and sustained coping effort. These may be thought of as the unwanted side-effects of the compensatory behaviour that helps to maintain primary performance under threat from environmental conditions. The effect is illustrated in an early study of sleep deprivation (Wilkinson, 1962), in which decrements in arithmetic computation following a night without sleep were smaller for participants who showed increased muscle tension (interpreted as evidence of greater effort to combat sleepiness and maintain orientation towards the task). The performance–cost trade-off is seen more clearly in several studies of noise effects, using more meaningful psychophysiological measures. Lundberg and Frankenhaeuser (1978) observed two different patterns of arithmetic performance and costs under noise in different studies. In one, performance was impaired, but there was no change in levels of adrenaline or in subjective effort. In the other, performance was maintained, but levels of adrenaline and effort were both greater. Noise has also been found to increase heart rate and blood pressure in tasks where no performance decrement occurred (Carter and Beh, 1989; Veldman, 1992).

Unfortunately, there are few studies within real work contexts. This may be because of the difficulty of obtaining psychophysiological measures under such circumstances. However, a recent field study (Rissler and Jacobson, 1987) also found an absence of performance decrements during an intense period of organizational change, again with a compensatory increase in adrenaline and cognitive effort. Such effects illustrate the role of compensatory regulation in the protection of performance, and may be seen as a trade-off between the protection of the primary performance goal and the level of mental effort that has to be invested in the task. They indicate that the regulation of effort is at least partially under the control of the individual, rather than being an automatic feature of task or environmental conditions.

After-effects of strain

A final form of latent degradation may be identified as appearing only after tasks have been completed, in terms of decrements on tasks presented at the end of the work period. These after-effects have also been studied very little, and then normally within a workload/fatigue paradigm (see Broadbent, 1979; Holding, 1983), though they are equally appropriate as a response to working under stressful environmental conditions (Hockey, 1993). Given its long-recognized importance, work fatigue has been studied extensively since the early days of psychology. Nevertheless, the search for a sensitive test of the carry-over effect of sustained mental work on the performance of new tasks has proved elusive. Major research programmes in the intensive post-war period of research on fatigue failed to find any marked effects on post-work tests such as tracking or RT from periods of up to 60 hours' continuous work. Holding (1983) showed that there are methodological difficulties in the analysis of this apparently straightforward problem. Subjects in such experiments appear able to work harder (make more effort) for brief periods to respond to the challenge of the new test, effectively compensating for any reduction in capacity. When tired subjects were provided with alternative ways of carrying out the post-work test, they were more likely to choose one requiring low effort, even though it entailed more risk of error. A similar result was obtained by Meijman et al. (1992) in a study of driving examiners' workload. Participants made less effort (both subjective and physiological) on cognitive tasks after more demanding work days. This approach to fatigue reveals it to be a state in which there is a shift towards preferring activities requiring less effort, or less use of high-level control actions. It may be apparent from what has been said above about compensatory control that, where no options are available (as is usual in such studies), we would expect to see increased costs associated with maintained performance levels.

Work Management Options

An analysis of this sort always appears neater on paper than it is in practice. I have identified four kinds of latent degradation, and we can see how each might, in principle, compromise performance in various work situations. Such effects are neither simple nor inevitable, though they provide a reasonable coverage of what we know about potential decrements associated with environmental factors. What does seem clear, however, is that the patterns of decrement (and costs) observed depend very much on both the particular situation and the individual.

Individual differences

Individuals who generally adopt direct coping strategies as a general way of managing unfavourable environmental conditions will be more likely to protect performance goals. They will tend to appear more effective overall, completing work on time, preventing major problems occurring in work situations and maintaining a high level of quality in their output. On the other hand, they will also be more prone to any of the costs referred to above. We would expect to see more evidence of neglect of minor work activities and cutting corners in such people. We would also expect them to suffer more from the consequences of sustained active coping in terms of physiological and psychological strain. Although not very much is known about the effects of the direct action kind of demand management style, it seems likely that health status will be compromised by overuse of this kind of coping. Problems may manifest themselves in increased incidence of minor symptoms, such as headaches, colds or indigestion, in problems of winding down after work or in reduced well-being. In its extreme form of 'workaholism', such a style may also give rise to more serious longer-term problems, such as chronic heart disease or gastrointestinal disorders (Karasek and Theorell, 1990).

In contrast, people with a generally indirect style of managing demands are less prone to such problems, since they maintain a more relaxed approach to their work: 'If I can't get as much done, it doesn't really matter. The world's not going to end because of it. I'm not going to bust a gut to finish the work tonight.' In many ways, this has to be seen as a healthy, balanced view of work in relation to the broader goals of life. However, as I implied above, it may sometimes lead to psychological problems, particularly those associated with a sense of failure and loss of self-esteem. Failing to complete tasks on time, at least when it happens frequently, will result in conflicts with supervisors and colleagues, and increase the emotional demands of the work environment. As in many cases, it clearly depends on the situation, on factors such as overt competition between employees and on the 'transparency' of individual work outputs. In some ways, indirect coping is more acceptable in teams, as it is recognized that 'everyone can have an off-day' – as long as it is not the same person taking it easy every time.

Efficient work management

Of course, some individuals appear to be able to work effectively under high demand (using direct demand management methods) without any obvious signs of strain. Others suffer strain effects if they make even a minimal effort to maintain work goals under stress. People may differ in various ways, apart from their general predisposition for coping directly or indirectly. These include their overall level of ability, their skill in managing stress, their orientation towards work goals (how strongly they value them), their capacity for effort expenditure and so on. Stress tolerance is frequently cited as a reason why some people work effectively without apparent costs, but, from the control theory perspective, this may itself have at least two components: (a) a greater range of tolerance for the discrepancy between achieved and desired output (not making corrections with every small problem); (b) a more efficient use of regulatory effort when it is used. Such people are efficient in managing environmental stress, in the sense that they know both when and how to change their behaviour, so as to stay on track without excessive effort or unnecessary tweaking. There may also be an additional effect of job skill. Being good at your job means that you can do tasks with less effort anyway, effectively increasing your reserve capacity for coping when problems arise.

Perhaps the main requirement, however, is 'situational flexibility'. Some problems respond well to active engagement – controllable problems, where secondary appraisal (Lazarus and Folkman, 1984) reveals the availability of suitable strategies for dealing with it. Yet we may not wish to use this mode of coping – we may feel hungry or tired from earlier coping, or have a headache. Other situations may not be controllable at all – a nurse sometimes has to accept that babies in her care will die, no matter how hard she tries to prevent it. Process operators sometimes have to reduce production goals, in order to carry out maintenance checks. We all feel a need to operate occasionally as if our lives depended on getting a document finished – in order to get really important things done (both in and out of work). The body and its energetical systems are designed for this – but only when 'emergency reactions' are required. By its very nature, such a mechanism is not designed for regular or normal functioning. If overused it will become less effective and lead to chronic psychological impairment, as in the phenomenon of burnout (see chapter 7, this volume).

A good work management strategy may be to maintain a balance of active and passive coping (and the various shades of involvement in between), preserving the extreme active mode for special occasions. This does not mean that one should cease to be conscientious in one's approach to work. Rather, it means redefining conscientiousness to include concern for oneself and one's health and well-being – the human system. It seems critical, if work is going to become a pleasurable (or at least comfortable) part of our lives in the new millennium, that the hegemony of the protestant ethic approach to work allows us to adopt less urgent responses to problems which really are not emergencies. This will provide the basis of both short-term enjoyment of work and enhanced long-term health for both the individual and the organization.

Chapter Summary

The patterns of performance observed under stress and high demand can be seen to reflect the adaptive response of the broader motivational control system to the ever-changing balance of goal priorities and environmental flux. Maintenance of primary task outputs under difficult conditions can only be achieved by a compensatory process which acts to protect vulnerable cognitive goals from competition from (stronger) emotional and biological goals. While primary performance is often maintained under stress, this compensatory activity normally results in disruption to secondary or auxiliary components of the integrated system performance, and to increases in the involvement of energetic resources (effort). These may represent a source of latent degradation, only revealed as a breakdown in performance under critical conditions, such as sudden, unpredictable surges of load, changes of task priorities, or the requirement to sustain such control over long, unbroken periods. A concern with overall system efficiency, rather than with single task effectiveness, will allow us to understand performance changes in relation to the broader goals and priorities of human behaviour, and the implications of these patterned system changes for the management of both performance and well-being.

D i s c u s s i o n   P o i n t s

1   What kind of considerations would be relevant to deciding whether to adopt the strain or disengagement modes when performance becomes difficult to maintain under stress?

2   A new office system, designed to increase efficiency, is found to increase productivity and the throughput of paperwork. Does this mean that it does what it was supposed to? What criteria of efficiency are relevant (a) in the short term, (b) in the longer term?

3   Think of the kind of work you are involved in (or know something about). Make a list of primary tasks and secondary tasks. What kinds of latent decrements might you expect to see under stress: in the form of (a) secondary task decrements, and (b) strategy short-cuts that might help to maintain performance but that run a greater risk of serious error.

K e y   S t u d i e s

Frankenhaeuser, M. (1986) A psychobiological framework for research on human stress and coping. In M. H. Appley and R. Trumbell (eds), *Dynamics of Stress. Physiological, Psychological and Social Perspectives.* New York: Plenum.

Hockey, G. R. J. (1997) Compensatory control in the regulation of human performance under stress and high workload: a cognitive-energetical framework. *Biological Psychology,* 45, 73–93.

CHAPTER TEN

THE DESIGN AND USE OF WORK TECHNOLOGY

P. E. Waterson

Contents

Chapter Outline

This chapter covers five main areas. The first section deals with the growth of work technologies since the Second World War and provides an outline of the diversity and variety of types of technology in the workplace. The next section deals with the main approaches to the study of work technologies and some of the methods and techniques used to study and inform their design. Following this, three case studies illustrate these approaches, methods and techniques. A final section summarizes the main points from the chapter as well as looking briefly at future areas of study and research. It will become apparent that one of the defining characteristics of the study of new forms of technology and their impact at work and in the home is its multidisciplinary nature. At any one time it is likely that researchers and practitioners from a variety of backgrounds, including *human factors (ergonomics)* and *human–computer interaction (HCI)*, psychology, sociology and computer science, will be involved in a variety of activities aimed at improving the design and use of technological systems. Mainly for this reason, this chapter can only hope to provide some form of 'route map' through the terrain. Much more could have been described and the reader is encouraged to use the further reading to pursue areas not covered here.

This chapter aims to provide an overview of one of the most important developments within the study of work psychology within the past thirty or so years, namely the introduction of new technologies and information systems into the workplace. At the end of the twentieth century the expansion of different types of technology into the home and at work continues with relentless pace. Artefacts such as word processors, spreadsheets and databases are to be found in most office environments, while information systems such as those responsible for process control and manufacturing are in widespread use throughout much of industry. Likewise, the growth of new forms of working have meant that an increasing number of people are making use of electronic mail and the Internet to work from home (Haynes, 1995). Whether in the office, on the shopfloor or at home, the growth of technology during the second half of the twentieth century has been enormous.

Despite the growth of new types of technology and claims that it has the potential to revolutionize how we work, the available evidence suggests a very mixed picture of success combined with widespread failure. Many new technologies prove to be difficult, if not impossible, to use, and in some cases have contributed to disasters and subsequent loss of life. The past few years have seen a number of prominent disasters which have been brought to the attention of the wider public through newspapers and television. These include the failure of systems designed to schedule ambulance call-outs (Page, Williams and Boyd, 1993), advanced technology used to fly aircraft automatically and medical systems which administer dosages of radiation, among others (Collins, 1997; Reason, 1997; Casey, 1998).

Alongside these headline grabbing disasters there is also a growing body of more systematic evidence that technology consistently fails to realize many of the benefits that are claimed for it. Landauer (1995), for example, reviewed economic data relating to the impact of information technology (IT) within the United States over a fifteen-year period and found that productivity decline in the USA broadly coincided with the large-scale deployment and investment of US companies in IT. Strassman (1990) similarly found no consistent relationship between the level of computer spending by US firms and their return on investment. Surveys of managers and IT experts within the UK have revealed a similar picture. Clegg et al. (1996a), for example, found that 80–90 per cent of investments in new technology within the UK fail to meet all of their objectives, while Waterson et al. (1999) show that the performance of computer-based technologies within manufacturing is on the whole disappointing. A key message of this chapter is that technology in all its forms is very much a double-edged sword – it has the potential to enhance, as well as diminish, the lives of its users (Norman, 1998). A major challenge for those involved in the study of work technology is to demonstrate how disasters and poor performance can be avoided; much remains to be done and, as we shall see, research in the area has a long way to go before it meets these objectives.

The Growth of Technology in the Workplace

While there are many important historical events, such as the introduction of machinery and the concept of the division of labour during the industrial revolution (Basalla, 1988; Parker and Wall, 1998, chapter 1), by far the greatest expansion in terms of the use of work-based technologies has occurred during the second half of the present century. The invention of the digital computer shortly after the Second World War led to the rapid deployment of IT into the workplace during the 1950s and continues to the present day. The use of technology within the home took longer to develop and was associated with changes in society, such as the growth of consumerism and the spending power of the individual during the 1960s (Forty, 1986). In the past twenty years perhaps the most significant development in technology has been the invention of the silicon chip and VLSI (very large scale integration) technologies. A major consequence of these new inventions is that they made it possible to build systems which were much faster, smaller and more reliable as compared to earlier technologies. Table 10.1 outlines the main developments in computer-based technology since the 1950s.

As can be seen from table 10.1, the main developments over the course of the past forty or so years have been the shift from large mainframe computers to the desktop variety most of us are familiar with today. A second

Table 10.1   The growth of computer-based technology since the 1950s

Computer type	Approximate growth era	Main users	User issues
Purpose-built research machines	1950s	Mathematicians and scientists	Machine reliability; users must learn programming
Mainframe computers	1960s/1970s	Data processing professionals supplying a service	Users of the output (e.g. managers); system response and flexibility
Minicomputers	1970s	Engineering and other non-computer professionals	Users still do much of the programming; usability starts to be recognized as a problem
Microcomputers	1980s	Almost everyone	Usability most pressing problem
Laptops, notebooks, PDAs (personal digital assistants), the Internet	1990s	Almost everyone	Usability
Information appliances?	2000–	Everyone?	Usability? Security and privacy?

Source: partly adapted from Shackel (1997); see also Nielsen (1993a).

development is the widening of the types of users: in the early days computers were mainly used by specialists, whereas in the 1990s almost everyone uses, or has access to, some form of computer-based technology. Finally, and most importantly, the last column in table 10.1 shows that the major problem from the point of view of the user of computer-based technologies has shifted from issues such as machine reliability and ease of programming to the much wider problem of how to design systems which are easy to use and learn. Assessments of ease of use and learnability, or the usability of work technologies, represent perhaps the major challenge facing researchers in the area of human factors (ergonomics) and HCI in the present day (Carroll, 1997; Norman, 1998). Below I outline the main approaches and methods used by human factors and HCI personnel in attempting to improve the design and general usability of systems. Discussion of the problems likely to face users in the next decade are taken up in the final section of this chapter.

Table 10.2 Examples of manufacturing technologies and their primary domain of application

Type of manufacturing technology	Primary domain of application
Computer-aided design and engineering, e.g. computer-aided design (CAD) and computer-aided software engineering (CASE) tools	Design and production
Electronic data exchange systems (EDI), e.g. on-line computerized links to customer stock levels to enable planning and distribution	Inventory and stock control
Computer-supported collaborative work (CSCW), e.g. the use of computers to aid communication and cooperation between different manufacturing departments	Work organization
Manufacturing resource planning (MRP), e.g. computer-based systems which control the planning and allocation of work among employees	Work organization

Source: Bolden et al. (1997).

The period since the Second World War has also seen an enormous amount of change to the work of people in factories and manufacturing industry in general. Much of the character of blue collar work has shifted from simplified tasks, often on a production line, towards new roles which require higher levels of skill use and knowledge (Wall and Jackson, 1995; Parker et al., 1997). Some of the new demands placed on blue collar workers are a direct result of the use of new technology. Table 10.2 outlines some examples of the kinds of technologies which have been used within manufacturing.

In the next section I consider a number of approaches to the study of work technology. It will become apparent that whatever the location (office or shopfloor) or type of technology (word processor or computer scheduling system), there are a number of generic issues common across the different approaches.

Approaches to the Study of Work Technology

Introduction

As mentioned above, there are a number of different disciplines which share an interest in the design and use of work-related technologies. In what follows it is important to bear in mind that the approaches which I describe are by no means exclusive of one another. In any one study a number of the approaches may be applied, along with different methods. As others have argued (e.g.

Table 10.3   Different types of interfaces with technology and example issues which are studied

Technology interface	Example issues
Human–technology interface	Physical characteristics of the user Workload issues Display design Health and safety
User–technology interface	Job and workspace design User satisfaction Usability Allocation of tasks
Organization–technology interface	Communication and coordination Distribution of power and responsibility Knowledge sharing Participation in design Management of change

Waterson, Clegg and Axtell, 1995, 1997; Carroll, 1997), the study of technology cuts across a number of levels of analysis, including cognitive, organizational and social issues, and to some extent the separation of the approaches has come about through historical accident rather than by design. In the past few years this has been given greater prominence and researchers and practitioners have begun to recognize the importance of viewing the study of technology within what can be labelled an overall systems-based, or 'macroergonomic', framework (Hendricks, 1997).

The systems approach has a number of advantages in terms of understanding the demands technology can place upon the individual and the impact it can have upon social factors involved in work, as well as the influence it may have upon organizational concerns (e.g. power relationships and overall organizational structure). A second advantage is that a systems view allows the researcher to examine the different types of interfaces that should be addressed when considering the impact of a new technology (Hendricks, 1991, 1997; see table 10.3). These interfaces include the user–machine interface (e.g. the study of human and physical characteristics and their application to design), the user–system interface (e.g. the study of how people process and share information within work settings) and the organization–machine interface (e.g. the study of the effect technology can bring to organizational processes, such as communication and the way work is carried out in general).

In addition to viewing the study of technology within a systems-based framework, it is important to bear in mind that the design and use of technology passes through a number of generic phases which are used by the

Table 10.4   Stages and activities in the system development lifecycle

Stage	Activities
Requirements	Where the design problem is initially defined, often in an explicit requirements document
Design	Where the system is shaped and which culminates in the detailed specification of the artefact
Building	Where the system is implemented, constructed or manufactured
Deployment	Where the system is marketed, sold and put into user settings
Maintenance	Where the system is serviced for repairs and enhanced as needed
Redesign (optional)	Where the system is used as the basis of a design effort to produce a new system

Source: Moran and Carroll (1996).

approaches as an organizing framework. Technology typically involves a number of phases during its design, evaluation and implementation (table 10.4).

In general, all the approaches described in this section make reference to the system development lifecycle, and although in reality there is a considerable variation in terms of the timing and content of phases in the lifecycle, it represents an important reference point for researchers and system developers. Each of the phases is associated with a set of activities, and reference is made to these in this section as well as in the case study examples.

Socio-technical systems approaches

The socio-technical systems (STS) approach has a long history, dating back to some of the earliest studies of the use of technology within work settings (e.g. Trist and Bamforth, 1951; Emery, 1959). The approach has a number of distinctive features, the most important of which is the recognition that organizations should consider the joint optimization and parallel design of both social and technical systems when designing new technology. The principle of 'joint optimization' came about as a result of the widespread recognition that great effort is placed upon the technical aspects of the systems, often to the detriment of human and organizational concerns. Such a bias leads to what has been termed a 'technology-led' approach to systems design, and continues to be one of the most prevalent strategies adopted by companies when introducing new technology into the workplace (Blackler and Brown, 1986; Clegg, 1993; Doherty and King, 1998).

Aside from 'joint optimisation', the STS approach provides a number of other principles or guidelines which are designed to be used when introducing technology (Cherns, 1976, 1987). These include:

- methods of working should be minimally specified;
- variances in the work processes (e.g. production breakdowns, changes in product) should be handled at source (i.e. as near as possible to location of breakdown or change-over);
- those who need resources should have access to and authority over them;
- roles should be multifunctional and multiskilled;
- redesign should be continuous, not 'once and for all' change.

Buchanan and Boddy (1983) describe an example of a case study which used the STS approach to evaluate the impact of a new computer system upon the work of biscuit-making operators. They found that different types of application of the new computer technology had very different effects upon the work of operators within the company. The system which controlled dough mixing tasks largely replaced the craft-based skills of doughmen and led to simplified jobs which were less satisfying than those before the introduction of the system. By contrast, the part of the system which controlled weighing tasks largely complemented the work of other operators and led to more interesting and rewarding jobs.

Buchanan and Boddy found that the differential impact of the new technology could largely be explained by the objectives of managers and the way in which the new system was planned and introduced. In the case of mixing tasks, the system largely removed a number of tasks which were viewed as being important in terms of control and decision-making responsibilities among doughmen. These tasks were automated, and managers failed to consider the impact such automation would have upon the quality of life and overall job satisfaction of operators. On the other hand, the new weighing system retained a number of key tasks for operators and removed some tasks which were viewed as being repetitive or tedious to complete. For example, the new weighing system allowed operators to control weighing tasks more effectively and gain rapid feedback on their performance, leading to a more interesting and challenging job as a result. Overall, the case study demonstrated that the implementation of new technology needs to be sensitive to the views of those involved in the change and that the design of the technology should complement, rather than conflict with, existing skills and knowledge levels. Buchanan and Boddy's study also demonstrates that technology can be a 'double-edged sword', as mentioned above.

Application of the STS approach typically involves using a number of methods, including: the use of interviews with those likely to be affected by new technology; questionnaires which are used to evaluate the impact of the technology on psychological aspects of job design (e.g. satisfaction, opportunity for skill usage); and consultation of company documentation and records in order to assess the objectives of the implementation. In addition, techniques such as variance analysis (Davis and Wacker, 1987) and *soft systems analysis* (Checkland, 1981; Clegg and Walsh, 1998) are sometimes used to assess likely areas which may prove problematic when introducing technology (e.g. areas which require high levels of skill and knowledge use in the event of break-downs) and to plan for the introduction of technology by considering specific scenarios of use. The STS approach is also associated with the use of specifi-cally designed tools which support design of both technical and social sub-systems (see case study 1 for an example).

Human factors (ergonomics) and human–computer interaction

The second approach is perhaps the most well known amongst those involved in the study of work technology. Human factors (ergonomics[1]) and HCI differ mainly in terms of breadth of coverage, the former being viewed as encom-passing a wider range of issues (e.g. anatomical and anthropometric charac-teristics of the user) than the latter, which concentrates more upon specific issues such as the design of the user interface and its overall functionality. For the purposes of description the two approaches have been combined in this section.

A particular focus of the HF/HCI approach is upon *cognitive models* of the user and attempts to formalize the types of knowledge that an individual needs to make use of when operating a machine or system (e.g. a word processor or a graphics package). Cognitive models such as TAG (task-action grammar; Payne and Green, 1986) can be used to predict whether one interface will take longer to learn than another. Similarly, the GOMS (goals, operators, methods and selection rules; Card et al., 1983) model has been successfully used in deciding upon alternative interfaces for such applications as workstations for telephone operators (Gray et al., 1993). More recent models have tended to be built within larger cognitive architectures which attempt to simulate aspects of human skill acquisition (e.g. Newell, 1990; Anderson, 1993). In addition, many cognitive models have been built in order to accommodate user inter-action with the external environment and representations such as displays and other interfaces (e.g. Howes and Payne, 1990; Payne, 1991; Zhang, 1997). Olson and Olson (1991) and Howes (1995) provide good reviews of the developments which have taken place in cognitive models during the 1990s.

A second particular focus of the HF/HCI approach is upon *task allocation.*[2] Task allocation generally refers to a systems design problem that concerns assigning system functions to human and machine agents (Sharit, 1997). The

1   The terms 'human factors' and 'ergonomics' are largely synonymous. Human factors is a term which is used more in North America, whereas ergonomics is the preferred term in the UK and Europe (Edholm and Murrell, 1973).
2   Task allocation and function allocation are terms which are sometimes used inter-changeably, and for our purposes we can treat them as synonymous. However, see Cook and Corbridge (1997) and Sharit (1997) for a discussion of the differences between the two.

designers of new computer-based systems are often faced with a number of choices, particularly regarding which tasks should be automated or manually controlled. In addition, developments in technology have meant that tasks can be redistributed between humans and computers, the precise distribution being decided upon by either the computer or the human operator. This recent area is sometimes termed 'dynamic task allocation', and the decision to allocate a task is contingent upon a number of factors, including the workload of the user (e.g. when the operator is overloaded the computer may take charge of the task). In recent years task allocation has been recognized as a critical stage in the design of new systems, partly because it has traditionally been overlooked by designers (Fuld, 1997) and partly because of the development of new methods and tools for task allocation (see Older et al., 1997, for a review, and case study 1; see also chapter 8, this volume).

The final area to be covered in this section is *usability*. As mentioned above, this topic is of central importance to those involved in HF and HCI. Nielsen (1997) draws a distinction between formative and summative evaluation of the usability of a system, the latter taking place after most of the design of the system has been completed, while formative evaluation takes place while design is ongoing and aims to contribute towards it. A number of methods spanning both qualitative (e.g. user questionnaires, interviews and focus groups) and quantitative (e.g. lab-based experiments) approaches have been used to carry out usability testing of an interface or overall system. Some of these methods have been designed to be used to produce fast evaluation results (e.g. *heuristic evaluation*), whereas others are designed to provide conceptual support to designers (May and Barnard, 1995) or integration with the system development process (Lim and Long, 1994). More recently, approaches such as *distributed cognition* and *ethnography* have been used to contribute towards the assessment of wider concerns, such as organizational usability and the overall coordination of work and its relationship to technology. Discussion of these two approaches is taken up in the next section, as they are sometimes seen as providing a bridge between socio-technical systems, HF/HCI and organizational psychology (see Anderson, Heath, Luff and Moran, 1993; Carroll, 1997).

Organizational approaches

Organizational approaches, as one might expect, typically address issues relating to work technology at a higher level of granularity as compared to the other approaches described in this section. The questions that are addressed from an organizational point of view involve a consideration of the social context in which technology is being placed, as well as issues relating to changes to the distribution of power and responsibilities of users which may come about as a result of the technology. A consideration of organizational issues may well extend beyond the normal bounds of system development and

Table   10.5 Organizational   perspectives   and   work technology

Perspective	Central issues
Rationalist	Employment • job loss • levels of hierarchy Centralization/decentralization Formalization
Information Processing	Patterns of communication Social context cues
Motivational	Individual motivations • skill variety • autonomy Interpersonal motivations
Political	Power • vertical distribution • horizontal distribution

Source: based upon Crowston and Malone (1988, p. 1056).

often involves an in-depth understanding of how users incorporate a new system into their work once it has been implemented (Henderson, 1991; Jones, 1995; case study 3).

Crowston and Malone (1988) outline a number of perspectives on work technology using an organizational approach (see table 10.5). Rationalist perspectives concentrate, among other things, upon the impact of technology on employment and job security. For example, a common assumption is that the introduction of technology leads to job losses and decreased employment opportunities; however, as Osterman (1986) has shown, while this may initially be the case, employment typically increases later on as the demands of the technology become evident (e.g. as a result of the need for greater coordination between individuals and groups).

By contrast, the information processing perspective focuses upon issues such as the changes that technology may bring about to communication and coordination patterns among users. Zuboff (1988), for example, has shown that new technologies often reduce the normal patterns of social interaction among IT workers (e.g. face-to-face and informal communication) and hence there is a corresponding need for greater distribution and sharing of knowledge and information in general. Techniques such as cognitive mapping (Daniels, Johnson and de Chernatony, 1995) and the application of new approaches such as activity theory (Blackler, 1995) have been developed in recent years to support the so-called 'informating' abilities of users of new technology.

The growth of *CSCW* systems during the past few years has to some extent led to the development of approaches which cut across cognitive, social and organizational levels of analysis. Hutchins (1995b), for example, outlines the *distributed cognition* approach, which utilizes *ethnography* in order to provide a better understanding of how teams coordinate work among themselves and the artefacts which make up their work environment. Hutchins (1995a) presents an analysis of the distribution of cognitive tasks in an airline cockpit. The analysis shows that airline pilots make use of a number of external cues and aids in the cockpit, including non-verbal cues (e.g. environmental sounds) as well as modifications to designs which are improvised (e.g. empty coffee cups placed on levers signaling they are not currently for use; Norman, 1992, chapter 16).

One of the main strengths of the approach is that it can be used to identify issues which are either taken for granted or not identified by traditional analyses of usability and organizational design. The distributed cognition approach and ethnographic analyses have provided a number of important insights into environments as diverse as ambulance call-out scheduling (McCarthy et al., 1998) and the work of software developers and London Underground operatives (Heath and Luff, 1992; Button and Sharrock, 1994). In addition, the approach has been instrumental in underlining the importance of the idea that technology has an active role to play in changing the cognitive requirements of tasks (see, for example, Hollnagel and Woods, 1983; Woods, 1998).

Case Study Examples

The three case studies have been chosen in order to illustrate the approaches described above. These are: the socio-technical approaches to job redesign (case study 1); HF and HCI (case study 2); and, organizational approaches (case study 3). Case study 1 is an example of a study carried out just prior to implementation of a new computer-based production system. Case study 2 corresponds to the design and evaluation phases in systems development. The final case study is an example of the evaluation stage of system development and took place some time after the system had been introduced within the workplace.

Case study 1: Job redesign in a chemical processing plant

Background   The following study is an example of the use of the socio-technical approach and involves the redesign of a set of jobs and tasks carried out by shopfloor workers within a chemical processing company (Nadin, 1996). At the time the study took place the company was preparing to introduce a new computer controlled production system, which would automate

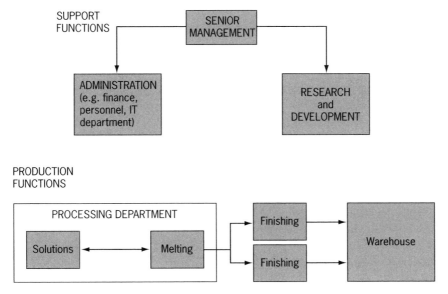

Figure 10.1 Organization of departments within the chemical processing company.
Source: Nadin (1996).

many of the tasks carried out by operatives within the processing department in the chemical plant (figure 10.1).

The jobs that were being redesigned involved two groups of operatives: personnel responsible for preparing chemical solutions (Solutions jobs and tasks) and those responsible for using the chemicals in the department (melting jobs and tasks). One of the main objectives of the study was to redesign these jobs so that they complemented the demands of the new production system, without necessarily conflicting with it.

Methods and findings The study involved two phases. Phase 1 involved gathering information from a selection of those involved in the new implementation of the system. This included carrying out semi-structured interviews with senior managers, supervisors and shopfloor operatives. Another key activity during this phase was the construction of a task analysis which could be used to redesign and reallocate tasks distributed among operatives and the new production system. The method used to derive the task analysis broadly followed the guidelines provided by Stammers and Shepherd (1995).

The second phase of the study involved using a socio-technical tool in a series of three workshops with shopfloor workers and managers within the production department. The tool was based upon previous research which has been carried out within job design and task allocation (Clegg et al., 1996b; Older et al., 1997), and consisted of two stages: the first stage involved

Stage 1

	Scenario 1	Scenario 2	Scenario 3
Scope			
Structure			
Roles			

Stage 2

	Scenario 1	Scenario 2	Scenario 3
Control			
Skill variety			
Work load			
Physical security			
Social contact			
Training			
Efficiency			
Cost			
Quality			
Flexibility			
Communication			
Overall impact			

Figure 10.2   Outline of the two stages in the use of the socio-technical tool.
Source: Nadin (1996).

generating alternative scenarios of existing and new jobs and tasks, the second stage involved evaluating these scenarios using a set of criteria which can be used to assess the suitability of a particular type of job design. Figure 10.2 shows an example of the two stages of the tool.

Table 10.6 shows the resulting designs from the first stage of the tool generated in the workshops. The first scenario in table 10.6 corresponds to the existing allocation of tasks and responsibilities between solutions and melting

Table 10.6 A summary of the scenarios generated using the tool in the workshops (stage 1)

	Scenario 1	*Scenario 2*	*Scenario 3*
Scope	Existing structure	Partial multi-skilling	Complete multi-skilling
Structure	Maintain present boundaries: solutions personnel work upstairs; melting personnel work downstairs	Maintain boundaries but melters share some tasks with solutions personnel (e.g. changing and cleaning lines and vessels)	No boundaries; abandon distinction between solutions and melting personnel; work as one crew and rotate tasks
Roles	Specialized and separated	Overlap of tasks; melters to become partly multi-skilled; solutions to carry out existing tasks	Single role for all crew members combining all tasks

personnel within the department. Scenario 1 involves a high degree of job specialization and separation between the two types of job. At the time of the study, the exact design and impact of the new production system was not known in detail, but it was clear that many changes to individual jobs would take place in the department. One particular change, which was welcomed by all staff in the department, was that solutions and melting operatives would have to share some tasks and work more closely together. The second scenario was therefore generated during the workshops, and represents a partial overlap of tasks and responsibilities which would be shared between the two groups of operatives. Scenario 2 also involves a higher degree of multiskilling and information sharing relative to the existing structure of jobs and tasks within the department (i.e. scenario 1). The third scenario represents a radical alternative to both scenarios 1 and 2 and involves a complete merging of the two types of job and an abandonment of the distinction between the two.

Later in the workshops, participants evaluated the three scenarios using a set of twelve criteria which previous research has shown to be important determinants of psychologically well designed jobs (Warr, 1987). In addition to explicit job design criteria, Nadin (1996) chose to include a set of operational criteria, which included issues related to the cost of a particular job design and its impact upon quality within the department. A selection of the outcomes from this second stage of using the tool is shown in table 10.7.

The chief advantage in using the tool was that it encouraged participants, and in particular managers, to consider a range of human and organizational factors in job design which are rarely addressed in most change initiatives of

Table 10.7 A summary of the evaluation of the scenarios using job design criteria from the workshops (stage 2)

	Scenario 1	Scenario 2	Scenario 3
Control and ownership	Solutions: no change. Melters: manual and some other tasks automated.	Solutions: lose some control and ownership of work area, but gain more freedom as less tied to process. Melters: gain control and shared ownership over some tasks.	Potentially less control for everyone as diffcult to predict proposed human–machine allocations. Potential for less ownership in the department as a whole.
Social contact	Less social contact overall as information on process available on screens.	More contact between solutions and melters	More contact and shared concern with work issues. Scepticism that it would have any impact. Role of supervisor critical.
Work load	Solutions: some scepticism, may lead to more tasks (e.g. supervising process) or no change. Melters: decrease in workload.	Solutions: less potential for overload, especially during peaks. Melters: reduction in workload but potential for increase if tasks have to be done in parallel with others.	Wide range of tasks may cause overload and potential for confusion in roles. New technology may increase workload irrespective of merged roles.
Cost	Costs may potentially increase because of risk of overload. Minimal training costs.	Cost-effective in the long run despite initial training costs.	Expensive: training costs, breakdowns in process due to errors, increased waste.

this kind. For example, use of the tool helped to identify problems with current job designs (i.e. scenario 1, where opportunity for social contact is limited and workload is high for some personnel), and plan for alternative designs. The tool also greatly helped in identifying potential areas of conflict and 'hotspots' in the new job designs. For example, in scenario 2 concern was raised that solutions personnel would lose some control and ownership over their work. Similarly, in scenario 3 there was some concern that the new production system would result in less control for everyone in the department and potentially higher levels of workload owing to difficulties in sorting out the precise allocation of tasks between personnel and the new production system. Although quite a lot of this information was already known about, use of the tool brought concerns and difficulties to the attention of managers and supervisors who were to some extent distanced from the work of shopfloor operatives.

The use of the tool within the workshops was, however, not without a number of problems and difficulties. In many respects these can be seen as typical of the sorts of problems that regularly crop up when new technology is being implemented. For example, the new production system had largely been designed by the time the workshops took place, and involved no previous consultation with potential users. The main consequence of the lack of user involvement in the design of the new system was that some of the time in the workshops was taken up with operators finding out as much as they could about the new system from those responsible for its implementation (e.g. senior managers). This lack of user participation also caused some resentment on the part of some operators; in particular, solutions personnel expressed some anger that they had not been consulted in terms of likely changes which would be brought about in the wake of the new system. Finally, there was widespread concern that the new system would lead to job losses, if not immediately, then at least in the foreseeable future. Both of these problems could to some extent have been alleviated if the company had decided to consult and involve operators earlier in the design of the new system.

Lessons learnt   The following points can be noted.

- The study is in many respects typical of a 'technology-led' implementation. Most of the effort was placed upon technical aspects of system design as compared to a parallel consideration of the role of people-oriented issues, such as job design and the allocation of tasks (Clegg et al., 1996b).
- The tool had a number of advantages which stemmed from its use; for example, it facilitated the consideration of a range of job and work design issues. In addition, the tool provided a permanent record of the decisions made during the workshops which could be used again at a later stage in future design initiatives (see *design rationale*; Moran and Carroll, 1996).
- The study shows that participation in job redesign needs to be sensitive to a number of factors including the different interests of various parties in

the change (e.g. in this case personnel from solutions and melting, as well as managers; Gould, 1988; Axtell et al., 1997; Beyer and Holtzblatt, 1998).

- Although there was little room for improvement as plans for the new system were well under way, in many other cases it may be possible for socio-technical input to be available prior to the design of the technology, and at an earlier phase in a job redesign initiative (Parker et al., 1994; Badham et al., 1996; Blatti, 1996).

Case study 2: The design and evaluation of SuperBook

Background   The second case study is an example of the development of a new product within a large American telecommunications company. The approach taken to the design and evaluation of the new product is largely typical of the kind associated with the work of researchers in the area of HCI, and usability in particular (e.g. Gould, 1988). The product being developed, known as SuperBook, consists of software that allows electronic versions of ordinary printed paper textbooks to be automatically generated (Egan et al., 1989). The on-line versions of SuperBook include a set of information retrieval facilities, such as the use of keywords for searching for information and techniques which allow different parts of a text to be focused in on.

The decision to build SuperBook came about largely as a result of previous studies which had shown some difficulties with electronic books and reading from screen-based material in general. Gould (1981), for example, showed that reading from a computer screen is much slower than from a paper-based version of the same text. One of the main reasons that reading from a computer screen proves difficult for most people is that the size of most computer monitors and their resolution make reading perceptually difficult. Paper-based text has a number of advantages; for example, the reader can keep two or three different pages open at once and can easily refer to other parts of the book, such as a table of contents.

A similar difficulty that people encounter when using electronic books is generating a name with which to search for information in a document. Furnas, Landauer, Gomez and Dumais (1987), for example, have shown that if people are asked to generate a name for something (e.g. a keyword to be used in searching a database), there is only a small probability that any two people will generate the same name. This finding has important implications for the design of search techniques in electronic books; in particular, it underlines the need for such systems to provide a facility whereby a number of alternative labels and commands can be generated by the user when searching documents. Together, the findings that reading from a computer screen is difficult and slow, and that information retrieval needs to be sensitive to the needs of the user, provided the designers of SuperBook with a number of objectives and goals with which to improve the design of electronic books.

Methods and findings   The first version of SuperBook (version 0) incorporated many features which attempted to overcome the problems mentioned above. In order to improve upon the difficulties of reading from a screen, the design included a facility for what are known as 'fisheye views' (Furnas, 1986). The chief advantage of fisheye views is that they allow the reader to focus in upon a specific part of a document, while at the same time being able to view other information in the periphery of the screen. A second feature which was incorporated into the design of early versions of SuperBook was 'unlimited aliasing'; in other words, the reader was not restricted to one term or name for an object in the book, but could use as many terms as he or she liked. Super-Book would make a note of these and automatically update multiple references to the same object.

Aside from the use of psychological research to generate design principles (which is in itself very unusual in practice), one of the main strengths of the approach taken in the development of SuperBook was its orientation to what the original design team called 'formative design-evaluation'. This is defined as: 'designing a system, implementing the design, conducting a behavioural evaluation and observations, and then repeating the design–implementation–evaluation cycle' (Egan et al., 1989, p. 31). Successive versions of Super-Book were evaluated in a series of experiments which compared the electronic version of the book with an equivalent printed version of the text. Figure 10.3 shows a graph of the efficiency of information finding in SuperBook over successive versions of its design (versions 0–2) and compared against a printed version of the text.

In order to test the performance of SuperBook, Egan et al. ran a series of experiments using a commonly available statistics package. Participants in the evaluation experiments were asked to complete a set of problems and searches using electronic and printed versions of the manual for the statistics package. An example of a typical question from these experimental trials was: 'Find the section that describes pie charts and states whether or not they bare a good means for analyzing data.' Aside from taking measures of speed and accuracy in completing these tasks, Egan et al. also asked participants to describe their preferences and general reactions to using SuperBook and the printed version.

As can be seen from figure 10.3, the first version of SuperBook (version 0) proved to be worse than printed text. Information finding efficiency in particular was about 15 per cent lower than with the printed version. A subsequent analysis of the data from the experimental evaluation revealed that one of the main problems with version 0 was that it did not adequately support the use of efficient search and retrieval strategies by users. In particular, version 0 did not provide enough feedback as to the total number of parts of the text that contained the source of the original user query. In addition, the layout of screen items meant that users had to move the screen pointer large distances before an action sequence could be initiated.

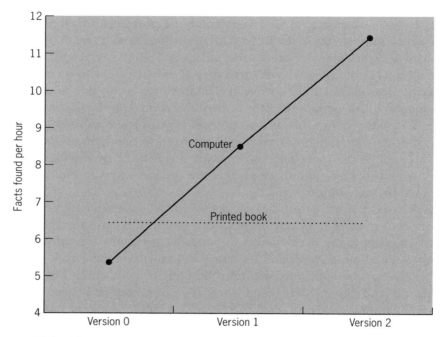

Figure 10.3   Efficiency in finding facts in a technical document with the original printed version and three successive versions of SuperBook.

Source: T. K. Landauer (1995) *The Trouble with Computers.* Cambridge, MA: MIT Press, p. 266. Reproduced with the permission of MIT Press.

The next version of SuperBook improved upon the original design by always providing feedback on search and retrieval and rearranging frequently used screen items so that they were closer together. The outcomes from these changes to the design resulted in the development of later versions, which were once again subjected to experimental evaluation. As a result of these changes, version 2 of SuperBook proved to be more than twice as efficient at supporting information finding compared to version 0 and 67 per cent better than the printed book. In addition to being more efficient to use, later versions of SuperBook were also likely to lead to students answering statistics questions more accurately and gaining better marks overall. Landauer (1995), for example, reports that college students using SuperBook averaged an A− for their essays, as compared to an average of C+ for users of the printed version. One of the main reasons why the electronic book proved to be so successful was that it allowed students to find facts very easily and quickly, while at the same time encouraging them to relate these to other parts of the book using the table of contents. In other words, SuperBook encouraged its users to link together different pieces of information as compared to treating them in isolation, and these factors helped users to relate parts of the book together and as a consequence to learn information in a highly effective manner.

Lessons learnt   Careful attention to aspects of the usability of a new system in tandem with iterative evaluation can greatly enhance and improve upon its overall design. Landauer (1995), in summing up the success of the project, elaborates upon the principles of user-centred system design (UCSD). In particular, he points to three main activities which characterize successful applications of UCSD such as SuperBook:

- *Analysis*: before starting to build a software system, all designers watched and talked to prospective users. They explored what users were trying to accomplish and how a system could get them there.
- *Idea evaluation*: while they were designing, they found some way to try out their ideas that showed how to improve them. They tried possibilities out on people like those who would eventually use them, doing the operations they would do with them.
- *Testing*: when they got something working, they tested to be sure it worked with the prospective users doing the operations they would do with it.

Case study 3: An evaluation of the implementation of groupware

Background   The final case study is an example of the application of the approach broadly taken by organizational psychologists when carrying out research on work technologies, and *CSCW* applications in particular. The study involved the evaluation of an implementation of an application known as Lotus *Notes*,[3] which can be used to support communication and collaboration within groups or between organisations (Orlikowski, 1992). The study took place within a larger American consulting firm, hereafter referred to as Alpha, and involved a total of over ninety interviews with personnel from a variety of positions within the company. Orlikowski also carried out detailed analysis of company documents, as well as extensive periods of observation and attendance at training sessions and meetings.

A particular focus of the study was the changes that were likely to be brought about to work practices and patterns of social interaction within the company as a result of the use of *Notes*. In addition, Orlikowski looked at the impact the technology would have upon people's cognitions, or *mental models*, of their work and its relationship to established policies and norms within the company.

Methods and findings   The *Notes* system had been introduced into Alpha largely on the basis of a recommendation from one of the senior managers within the company. Features such as electronic mail and a shared database were seen as having the potential to 'revolutionize' the work of consultants. The implementation of *Notes* originally followed what might be called a 'big bang' strategy (Eason, 1988), in that the system was introduced rapidly and

3   Lotus *Notes* is a trademark of the Lotus Development Corporation.

with little warning. Orlikowski carried out her research over a five-month period after *Notes* had been in use within the company for a couple of years. Her interviews pointed to two main factors which contributed to the way in which *Notes* was being used within Alpha.

First, she found that cognitive factors played a major role in the adoption, understanding and early use of *Notes*. One of the main conclusions was that the consultants had formed mental models of the technology which were at odds with the model of collaboration and information sharing that *Notes* was designed to support. Instead of viewing *Notes* as a system which allowed users to work over a distributed network, consultants tended to regard the system as like any other 'stand-alone' technology (e.g. word processing, spreadsheet). Part of the reason for this situation could be attributed to the training consultants had been given: this tended to emphasize the idea that *Notes* could increase their personal productivity and underplayed the collaborative features of the technology. In addition, the individual, 'stand-alone' model was reinforced and encouraged by a lack of communication regarding the objectives of the implementation. Most of the consultants only got to hear about the decision to invest in *Notes* through reading about it in the trade press, and had little information about its purpose and potential uses.

A second factor which shaped the use of the system relates to the organizational structure and culture within Alpha. The structural properties of the company that proved to be important covered a number of issues, including reward systems, policies, norms and working practices. For example, the expectation within Alpha was that consultants should charge their work hours directly to clients and that any other time should be accounted for, but not billed. Most of the consultants viewed the use of *Notes* as a non-client-related activity and were therefore disinclined to use the system. Similarly, there was a concern about the policies regarding security and confidentiality of data when using the system. Many consultants felt wary of sharing information and data which could render them individually liable and could also potentially find their way into the wrong hands. Finally, Alpha was similar to many other large consulting companies in that it had a relatively competitive culture. A combination of a pyramid-like hierarchical organization and an 'up or out' career path meant that consultants were reluctant to cooperate or share knowledge with their colleagues and peers.

The study demonstrates that at least in the early adoption of collaborative technologies, cognitive and structural elements will play an important part in influencing how people think about and assess the overall value of the technology (Orlikowski, 1992, p. 203). In the past, researchers have tended to focus upon individual cognitive reactions to technology, often with little attention given to a consideration of organizational factors. More recently, there has been a move towards a position where cognitive, social and organizational factors need to seen in combination and not separately (e.g. Nardi, 1993).

Lessons learnt   Organizations need to adopt a systems-based, or 'macroer-gonomic', approach to the implementation and use of technology, particularly CSCW systems. The systems-based approach draws attention to a number of issues, including:

- communication of objectives and appropriate preparation and training of users;
- the fit between the technology and existing reward systems, policies and work practices, and cultural norms within the organization;
- the importance of viewing technology from a number of different levels of analysis (i.e. cognitive, social and organizational).

Chapter Summary

This chapter began with a discussion of the dissapointing performance of the majority of new technologies, whether on the shopfloor or in the office. While it is likely that the contexts in which technology will be used are likely to expand (e.g. the growth of mobile computing and teleworking), it is even more apparent that the contribution of researchers from all the backgrounds covered here (socio-technical, HF/HCI, organizational) will be essential in the future if these technologies are to realize their benefits. In addition, issues such as security of information and privacy are likely to become important, particularly if the phenomenal growth of the Internet and associated technologies continues at such a rapid pace.

One important area that is likely to develop further is the widening of what we currently term usability to take into account wider social and organizational issues. There is also a corresponding need for theory development which integrates across the various approaches mentioned in this chapter. The present situation is in many respects confusing not only for researchers but also for practitioners working in industry. Alongside new theories which combine accounts of job and work design with interface design, for example, there is a pressing need for practical methods and tools which support task allocation and usability, among others. The use and perceived effectiveness of many current methods and tools is disappointing (Bellotti, 1990; Ainsworth and Kirwan, 1998) and there is considerable room for improvement, but there are also some success stories which provide many reasons for optimism (e.g. Nielsen 1993b; Rudisill et al., 1996; Patterson et al., 1997). Above all, the next few decades need to reverse the trend of failing, or poorly implemented, technologies and see greater involvement and transfer of knowledge between researchers and industry, the ultimate aim being to improve the lives of users both within work settings and outside of them.

Acknowledgements

I would like to thank Jon May and Nik Chmiel for comments on an earlier draft of this chapter. In addition, David Hesse provided some useful input to some of the sections in the chapter.

Key Studies

Carroll, J. M. (1997) Human–computer interaction: psychology as a science of design. *International Journal of Human–Computer Studies*, 46, 501–22.

The Psychologist (1996) Special issue on Engineering Psychology and Cognitive Ergonomics (articles by Stanton, Payne, Long and Dowell, and Shackel), July.

Further Reading

General

Landauer, T. K. (1995) *The Trouble with Computers*. Cambridge, MA: MIT Press.
Preece, J., Rogers, Y., Sharp, H., Benyon, D., Holland, S. and Carey, T. (1994) *Human–Computer Interaction*. Wokingham: Addison-Wesley.
Wilson, J. R. and Corlett, E. N. (eds) (1995) *Evaluation of Human Work*, 2nd edn. London: Taylor and Francis.

Specialized

Monk, A. F. and Gilbert, C. N. (eds) (1995) *Perspectives on HCI: Diverse Approaches*. London: Academic Press.
Norman, D. A. (1998) *The Invisible Computer*. Cambridge, MA: MIT Press.
Parker, S. K. and Wall, T. D. (1998) *Job and Work Design*. London: Sage.

CHAPTER
ELEVEN

SAFETY AT WORK

Contents

- Chapter Outline
- Introduction

CASE STUDY 11.1: *Nuclear power generation at Three Mile Island*

- Individuals and Safety Behaviour
- Human Error
- Accidents, Error and Stress
- Violations of Safety Procedures
- Personality
- Technological Systems, Organizations and Safety: Disasters
- Organizational Safety Practices
- Error Management in Technological Systems
- Chapter Summary
- Discussion points
- Key Studies

C h a p t e r   O u t l i n e

This chapter considers safety when working, and in particular concentrates on the psychological influences apparent in accidents and system breakdowns. There is a high cost to errors and failures, even if there is no personal injury to the worker. At the extreme, errors can cause considerable damage to people and the environment. The chapter first explores individual human error, and then discusses how work and organizational factors contribute to technological systems failures and safety, before outlining a number of ways organizations could consider improving safety.

Introduction

The complexity and efficiency of modern technology in many industries is handled by computerization and automation. Control rooms in nuclear power stations and chemical processing plants in the UK are almost invariably based on computer control and display of the plant processes. In manufacturing, advanced technology utilizing robots and computer control has begun to dominate. Even in jobs where traditional human skills are needed, such as intensive care and antenatal medicine, electronic equipment and displays are used.

The demand placed on human operators by this technology is largely mental rather than physical (McLoughlin and Clark, 1994), and this gives rise to important questions. What do operators understand of the system and technology they control? How does automation affect this understanding, and the cognitive nature of the control task? How much capacity do operators have in dealing with mental workload? What happens when fatigue sets in? Is understanding of routine operations sufficient in an emergency situation? How does stress affect cognitive processing? All these questions are the subject of ongoing research, driven by the need to make hazardous complex systems safe, and technological systems efficient. (See chapter 9, this volume.)

Research has shown that people are limited such that their mental capacities can be overloaded by trying to process too much (see chapter 8 in this volume). Automating part of the technology can help with this, but introduces its own problems, because the task changes from being active to being predominantly passive, where operators monitor equipment rather than control it (Hancock and Scallen, 1996). The change means factors like sustained attention and boredom become important, with consequent lapses of attention likely to produced error. Understanding routine operations may utilize different skills and cognitive processes in contrast to coping with emergency situations, and stress can further alter how the work task is mentally processed (Wickens, 1992).

Individuals and Safety Behaviour

The relationship of individual characteristics to safe behaviour has been investigated from two quite distinct perspectives: on the one hand social psychology, and on the other cognitive psychology. The cognitive psychology tradition focuses on human error performance as a function of mental processing operations, and the social psychology tradition concentrates on personality, attitudes and perceptions. Both traditions have thrown up interesting information on safety at work.

Human Error

Human error, as a field of enquiry, is concerned with why people make mistakes, or forget to do critical parts of their job. The approach concentrates more on the function of cognitive processes in relation to error. It is a growing field of activity. Part of the reason for the interest in human error is that it derives from a tradition that views people as processors of information, and the understanding of how people interact with technology, particularly with computers, has been well served by this approach. Many safety-critical systems can be viewed as providing the people in them with considerable amounts of information which they need to perceive, remember, decide about and take action on. Thus human error has frequently been informed by studies in the nuclear, chemical and aviation industries. However, the principles that have been discovered from such studies apply to many work settings where technology is employed to present information and control activities.

An essential starting point in investigating error is to understand what errors themselves are. Obviously, it would be very difficult to examine each and every error a person made, as if each mistake were somehow unique: a sensible staring point is to ask whether errors fall into a few categories, where each category has distinctive characteristics. That is, we should try to devise a taxonomy of errors. Many proposals for a taxonomy have been put forward which relate the errors observed to underlying mental processes. Freud, for example, proposed that slips of the tongue were a product of the subconscious. Bartlett (1932) suggested that errors in recalling stories were owing to relating new material to old knowledge, structured in schemata. Recall tended to be more regular, meaningful and conventionalized than the original stories.

More modern theorists have put forward a taxonomy which has gained wide acceptance among those considering the impact of technology on safety. Reason (1990) proposes a taxonomy which divides unsafe acts into two broad categories: activities that are unintentional, and those that are intended. Unintended actions are further broken down into slips and lapses, and intended actions into mistakes and violations. Much of Reason's analysis is based on

Case Study 11.1

Nuclear power generation at Three Mile Island

At Three Mile Island, ten miles south of Harrisburg, USA, the flow of water to Unit No. 2's (TM1–2's) nuclear reactor secondary heat removal system was interrupted. The feedwater pumps had shut down as a result of maintenance engineers accidently introducing a small amount of moisture into the plant's instrument air system. The moisture interrupted the air pressure to two valves on the pumps. Emergency feedwater pumps came on automatically, but did not work as planned because water supplying the pumps was blocked by valves left shut in error during maintenance operations a couple of days earlier. This meant that heat was not being removed from the primary coolant around the reactor core, leading to a quick rise in core temperature and pressure. Another automatic safety device then came into operation, stopping the chain reaction. However, the decaying radioactive materials still produced heat, and the temperature and pressure increased further in the core. The pressure was designed to be relieved automatically through a pilot-operated relief valve (PORV), which when open would allow water to pass from the core through a pressurizer vessel into a sump below the reactor. The PORV should have opened, relieved the pressure and then shut automatically. Unfortunately, only 13 seconds into the emergency the PORV stuck open, which meant pressuized radioactive water was pouring out of the core.

The time was 4 a.m. on 28 March 1979. The emergency caused alarm lights to flash, and an auditory alarm to sound in the control room. For the following two hours or so the control room operators tried to get to grips with the cause of the alarm. During the course of this activity the operators actually cut back the injection of water into the reactor coolant, reducing the flow rate from appoximately 1000 to 25 gallons per minute, thus causing serious core damage. The emergency lasted more than 16 hours in total.

As a consequence of the incident there was a serious risk of a 'meltdown', or of hazardous radiation escaping from the plant. Neither of these things happened, although a small amount of radioactive material did escape into the atmosphere, but the incident cost millions of pounds, and the USA halted all further building of nuclear power plants. The report of the analysis of the causes of the incident attributed a number of errors to the control room staff, but highlighted inadequate control room design, procedures and training rather than inadequacies on the part of operators.

Accident investigators observed that the control panel presented operators with too much complex data: 1600 displays and gauges had to be scanned when the alarm sounded to try to establish the source of the problem. At the time there were already 200 flashing displays and gauges, making the diagnosis of the fault difficult. In addition, the control panel did not contain certain critical information, especially the fact that the PORV had not closed, allowing coolant to escape and uncover the reactor core. The panel had an indicator relating to the PORV, but this only showed whether the valve had been commanded shut or not. It did not indicate the actual status of the valve. This could have been discovered by looking at a drain tank water level indicator, but this was positioned behind the main controls.

A further problem was that the backup valves, which, if open, could have allowed water into the secondary heat removal system, were closed. The fact that they were closed was not recognized by the operators because maintenance tags on the control panel partially obscured the lights indicating their status. In addition, the diagnostic system designed to supply information about the plant used a computer printer. During the incident messages were being transmitted to the printer at around 10–15 per second, overloading it. Information was thus not available until later, and just over an hour into the incident the printer jammed, and some data were lost for good. Maintenance crew had introduced moisture into the instrument air system. This same error had occurred on two previous occasions, but the operating company had not taken steps to prevent it happening again.

Operator training consisted mostly of lectures and work in a reactor simulator, and did not provide an adequate basis for coping with real emergencies. Little feedback was given to trainees, and the training programme was not evaluated sufficiently. Training emphasized the dangers of flooding the core, which took no account of a simultaneous loss of core coolant.

There had been an incident prior to TMI-2, at the Davis-Besse plant in 1977, where the PORV had stuck open. The incident was investigated by the plant makers, and by the US Nuclear Regulatory Commission, but the analyses were not collated, and the information regarding appropriate operator action was not communicated widely to the industry. The operators had also interrupted the flow of water to the reactor, but the analyses had been categorized in a publication by the Nuclear Regulatory Commission under 'valve malfunction' rather than 'operator error.'

This illustration shows that any discussion of safety at work needs to consider not just unsafe acts and accidents by and to individuals, but errors and failures at the design and organizational levels which potentially could form the antecedents to industrial calamities such as at Three Mile Island. It is the advent of complex, technological systems, particularly in the nuclear, aviation, chemical and manufacturing industries, which gives impetus to the study of human and systems error, because the consequences of such error can be large scale indeed, as the incident in 1986 at the Chernobyl nuclear power plant in Ukraine so emphatically illustrates.

A psychological perspective on safety at work gives rise to at least two key questions: what is the relationship between individual perceptions, attitudes and cognition, and safety behaviour and technological system failures; and what are the effects of organizational procedures, culture and standards on safety?

diary studies of everyday errors, and case studies of large-scale technological disasters such as that at the Chernobyl nuclear power station in the then USSR. Reason's taxonomy accords closely with that put forward at approximately the same time by Norman (1988), which drew on observations of everyday actions.

An attraction of Reason's conceptualization is that errors are explicitly related to cognitive functioning. Slips and lapses are defined as errors which result from some failure in the execution and/or storage of an action sequence, regardless of whether the plan which guided them was adequate to achieve its objective. Mistakes, on the other hand, are defined as deficiencies or failures in the judgemental and/or inferential processes involved in the selection of an objective, or in how to achieve it, irrespective of whether the actions necessary to realize the objective run according to plan. Violations, in contrast, are not seen as breakdowns in normal cognitive processing, but as deliberate flouting of safety procedures and rules.

Reason terms slips, lapses and mistakes basic error types. There are numerous documented examples of error types from incidents in the nuclear power industry. At the Davis-Besse (1985) plant in the USA, an operator, wanting to start the steam and feedwater rupture control system manually, inadvertently pressed the wrong two buttons on the control panel (a slip). At Chernobyl (1986), a previous operator error had reduced reactor power to well below 10 per cent of maximum. Despite strict safety procedures which prohibited any operation below 20 per cent of maximum power, a team of electrical engineers and operators continued with a planned test programme, contributing to a double explosion within the reactor core (a mistake).

Reason further refined his conceptualization of error types by relating them to a hierarchy of performance levels developed by Rasmussen (1986) over several years. Rasmussen studied, initially, workers engaged in fault-finding in electronic components using a verbal protocol technique. Verbal protocols are obtained by asking the person to explain what he or she is or was doing. Rasmussen's insight was to analyse activity relevant to industrial settings in terms of skill, rule or knowledge-based performance levels. The levels reflect decreasing familiarity with the activity and situation. The skill-based levels is concerned with routine actions in a familiar operating environment. At the other extreme, knowledge-based performance is required in novel situations and circumstances, and is dependent on problem-solving to work out and decide on a course of action. Rule-based performance is where a situation or set of circumstances has been encountered before, and where the action needed is governed by rules of the form *if* (situation) *then* (action). Slips and lapses are, thus, errors at the skill-based level. Mistakes are refined into two types: rule-based and knowledge-based.

Reason views error types as arising out of fundamentally useful mental processes, rather than maladaptive tendencies. Further, his analysis suggests that the basic error types manifest themselves as a result of mental information processing by which 'stored knowledge structures are selected and retrieved in response to current situational demands'. In short, basic errors are tied in to the context present at the time, and result from attentional, memory and inferential failures.

Skill-based errors are associated with inattention or overattention (consciously interrupting automatic activities). Rule-based errors are associated with the misapplication of good rules, or the application of bad rules. Knowledge-based errors are associated with the limitations of human ability to solve problems and reason with new circumstances; for example, the poor ability to reason rationally, or to hold very many bits of information in mind at the same time.

Reason's analysis proposes that mistakes are much harder to detect than slips and lapses, because, he argues, consciousness is tuned to departures from intentions. Mistakes, because they are intended actions, for whatever reason, can go unnoticed for long periods. Such a view is supported by studies on nuclear power operator teams grappling with simulated plant failures (Woods, 1984). In all, nearly two-thirds of errors. went undetected. Half of the execution errors (slips and lapses) were detected by the crews themselves, whereas none of the state identification failures (rule- and knowledge-based mistakes) was.

Reason (1990) does not have much to say about violations. His main concern lies with errors that arise from cognitive processing, rather than deliberate non-compliance with safety procedures. However, violations in themselves have interesting psychological aspects, which have been studied from a more social psychological perspective. Violations are discussed below.

The relationship between errors and accidents at work is by no means clear. The same error may, or may not, lead to an accident, and different errors could produce the same kind of accident. This theme is picked up in the discussion of accident reporting systems below. In a study on the time of day, errors and fatal accidents at work, Williamson and Feyer (1995) show that accidents demonstrated much more variation across 24 hours than did knowledge-, rule- and skill-based errors. In short, there was no direct correspondence between the time when most accidents occurred and errors.

Accidents, Error and Stress

Conceptually, it is sensible to suggest that workplace stress will have an impact on accidents and error. Of course, in order to examine the effect of stress itself, it is necessary to hold a number of other aspects of jobs and tasks constant. However, this is very hard to do. Some jobs are inherently more dangerous than others (deep sea diving compared to office typing, for example), and this could produce more accidents and feelings of stress. There is a large amount of research now on what aspects of workplaces produce feelings of stress (see chapter 7 in this volume), but there are not many studies which relate feeling stressed to accidents.

One tack is to treat conditions at work as stressors and to examine their effects on performance, accidents and errors. The workplace can involve various environmental and social conditions, such as noise and heat, long hours and pressure to complete work to time deadlines. Such environmental conditions can produce changes in the person; for example, we become fatigued after long hours of work, on the same task (Craig and Cooper, 1992), and shiftwork produces a lack of normal sleep, producing a sleep debt which can accumulate over time (Folkard, 1996). It is important to investigate whether these types of factor are involved in accidents and human error; some evidence suggests they are (Folkard, 1997).

Again, it is extremely difficult to research answers to the question of how stressors affect error at work (as opposed to correlating accident frequency with hours of work, say): first, because factors like fatigue are difficult to manipulate; second, because the question demands studying moment-by-moment fluctuations in, say, time pressure, and its effect on error, and this is very hard to do in the workplace. Laboratory studies of environmental stressors on peformance demonstrate that performance is affected by a variety of stressors (see Smith, 1995; Chmiel, 1998, for summaries). Chmiel, Totterdell and Folkard (1995) showed that after loss of a night's sleep, prolonged cognitive adaptive activity was affected. Participants worked more slowly, although maintaining a constant quality of performance. Clearly, if the participants had been under time pressure to produce responses, their quality of performance would be likely to have suffered. There is plenty of evidence for speed–error trade-offs in perceptual-motor tasks (e.g. Rabbitt and Maylor, 1991), and that the trade-off function is sensitive to stressors such as alcohol (Rabbitt, 1986).

An alternative approach, in contrast to measuring cognitive performance directly, is to use questionnaires. Reason and Mycielska (1982) asked 63 university students to keep a diary to record their slips and lapses over a continuous period of seven days. As soon as possible after recording a slip or lapse the students were asked to complete a set of standard ratings, including how well they felt, whether they felt tired and whether they were in familiar surroundings. Reason (1988) summarized the results from this, and other diary studies, as showing a relatively consistent picture associated with everyday cognitive failures. When slips occurred respondents were 'carrying out some highly automatized task in very familiar surroundings', and they were distracted by something in their immediate vicinity, or preoccupied by some inner concern. However, they were not feeling particulary upset, emotional or unwell, and neither did they feel that environmental factors like noise, temperature or poor illumination contributed to cognitive failure. On the other hand, fatigue and time pressure were rated as influential on some occasions, but not on others.

Violations of Safety Procedures

Violations are where workers intentionally break safety procedures and rules. Sabotage is the most extreme reason for violating established rules, but procedures are ignored for many reasons not to do with any desire to wreak havoc. This section does not consider sabotage, but discusses views about why workers do not comply with safety procedures and engage in unsafe behaviour.

Risk perception

A possible influence on why workers do not comply with safety procedures could be that they do not perceive any risk associated with the situation they are in, and/or with other courses of action. In the health field, investigation of subjective beliefs concerning hazards suggests that the likelihood of people engaging in preventative behaviour is a function of their perception of risk involved in an activity, their belief about whether the outcome is serious or not and whether they believe they can do something to prevent the outcome (Rosenstock, 1974). Self-protective behaviour depends in part on a person's subjective estimate of risk.

Risk can be defined in many ways. Two possibilities are 'probability of undesired consequences' and 'weight of undesired consequences (loss) relative to comparable possible desired consequences (gain)'. In a report to the Royal Society, reviewing the research on risk perception since 1983, Pidgeon, Hood, Jones, Turner and Gibson (1992) suggest that risk is appropriately defined as 'threat to people and things they value'.

Pidgeon et al. (1992) argue that it is difficult to separate objective and subjective risk, since all risk assessments involve human judgement, and social, cultural and political influences, and that risk perception is a multidimensional concept because particular hazards mean different things to different social groups. Investigation in the oil and gas industry has shown that different groups of workers perceived the same hazards differently in terms of risk and safety (Mearns and Flin, 1996).

Risk perception involves attention to, and processing of, a diverse range of information relation to hazards. The information can be gained through direct experience of hazards or through sources like the mass media, scientific communications or fellow workers. Goldberg, Dar-El and Rubin (1991) proposed that information about potential threats was assimilated by workers through formal and informal learning both inside and outside the workplace, and through direct and indirect experience of accidents. They found that key factors relating to perception of threat were training and experience specific to the task being performed.

Psychometric studies of attitudes to hazards have shown that people distinguish between risks to individuals and risks to society. Pidgeon et al. (1992)

cite reports that risk perceptions could be measured by two scales: personal safety and threat to society. Slovic, Fischhott and Lichtenstein (1980) asked people to rate 90 hazards (for example, nuclear power, chemical fertilizers, caffeine) with respect to 18 characteristics. Their responses reflected three factors: dread risk (i.e. how uncontrollable and catastrophic the risk was); unknown risk (i.e. how unobservable the risk was); and number of people exposed (including degree of personal exposure). Slovic et al. concluded that perceptions of risk were related to where the risk was in relation to these three factors, and that the most important factor was 'dread risk': the higher a hazard scored on this factor, the more people wanted to see the risk reduced, and controlled through regulation. The hazard scoring highest was nuclear weapons. Subsequent research has shown that the qualitative dimensions that are important for risk perception differ for different hazards. So, for example, Gardner and Gould (1989) found that 'catastrophic potential' was important for nuclear and chemical technologies, but less so for air and car travel.

Researchers have also considered risk perception from the perspective of mental judgements about the probability of events, ignoring for the most part emotional and motivational aspects. The findings from human judgements about uncertain events suggest people are not rational in their judgements, but use cognitive heuristics or 'rules of thumb' to decide whether something is likely to happen or not (Kahneman, Slovic and Tversky, 1982). The heuristics are a type of cognitive bias, useful for the most part, but likely to lead to systemmatic error in some circumstances. Experts are not immune to biases either; for example, they have been shown to be overconfident in their judgements (Svenson, 1989).

Risk perception, or being aware of a hazard, is only one element in the adoption of safe behaviour. Again, drawing on the field of health research, Weinstein (1988) has argued that there are several other aspects to consider. He proposed a 'precaution adoption model' consisting of five stages (the stages shown are for susceptibility. Similar stages were proposed for risk severity and precaution effectiveness):

1   Aware of the existence of the hazard.
2   Aware of the susceptibility of others to the effects of the hazard.
3   Aware of own susceptibility to the hazard.
4   Deciding to act to prevent the hazard causing harm.
5   Acting to prevent the hazard causing harm.

People are defined as being at a particular stage if they accept the central tenet of that stage, which is assumed to encompass accepting the central tenets of any preceding stages (that is, stages form a Guttman scale). Weinstein (1988) has presented evidence that, in terms of beliefs about several risks and their effect on health, the stages can indeed be considered to lie on a continuum described by a Guttman scale.

The Weinstein model is extremely useful for several reasons. First, it provides a framework for characterizing individual differences in terms of beliefs and perceptions about hazards at work. Second, it facilitates discussion about the psychological factors associated with stages of belief. Third, it implies the barriers involved in progressing to different beliefs and perceptions, and in moving towards the voluntary adoption of safety precautions. In particular, it is relatively straightforward to make suggestions about the role of organizational factors, such as communications, in relation to the perceptions of hazards.

However, it is much less clear that a continuum as Weinstein described it would apply in a safety-critical workplace, because such work environments stress the need to act safely. Often there are safety procedures in place which employees are under strong pressure to conform to, whether they believe there is a risk from a hazard or not. This argument leads to the conclusion that at a minimum stage 5 may not be part of the continuum. In short, there are *a priori* grounds for supposing that the characterization of a continuum of stages in the precaution adoption model may not hold in some workplaces. Empirical evidence for this line of reasoning has been found in a safety-critical setting. Soane and Chmiel (1999) asked for risk perceptions from nuclear power workers. The majority of respondents reported acting to take precautions against workplace hazards, while at the same time replying that they did not perceive there was a risk to themselves or others. Soane and Chmiel (1999) have also investigated preferences for informational and emotional safety messages using the Weinstein framework, and found that emotional messages were preferred.

Many theories of risk-taking behaviour assume that people form some judgement of the risk involved, and set that against any benefits. A version of this view is risk homeostasis theory (Wilde, 1982) which proposes that the risk cost is set against the cost of behaving safely, and it is the resultant cost function which is kept within a certain range. Thus, for example, if cars are given extra safety features designed to minimize injury drivers may in fact begin to drive faster. Zero-risk theory (Naatanen and Summala, 1976) proposes that road-users may well judge their own behaviour inaccurately in terms of its riskiness, and think they are driving within safe limits when in fact they are not. The data from Soane and Chmiel showed that some people report adopting safety precautions, whilst not perceiving a risk to themselves and others, and that people in the same study report not adopting precautions and not perceiving risk to themselves or others. The findings suggest strongly that risk perceptions can be separated from acting safely. An analysis of data from accidents at sea is entirely consistent with this observation. Wagenaar (1992) summarizes many accidents from Dutch Shipping Council reports and concludes that a conscious evaluation of risk was absent in almost all of them.

Attitudes to safety

Individual attitudes to safety, and the degree to which they affect safe behaviour in the workplace, have received relatively little attention. Cox and Cox (1991) studied one European company involved in the production and distribution of industrial gases. They found that employee attitudes to safety, collected across five European countries, could be structured along five factors, which included personal scepticism, individual responsibility and personal immunity, as well as attitudes to the safeness of the work environment and perceptions about the effectiveness of arrangements for safety. Personal scepticism involved cynical views on the importance of safety. Individual responsibility referred to the responsibility that people feel they have for working safely, and personal immunity involved the belief that accidents could be avoided by personal expertise and experience.

Attitudes such as those above can be fitted readily into a framework of the categories involved in the causes of accidents proposed by Dejoy (1986) in relation to planning health and safety education strategies. Dejoy outlines three categories: predisposing, enabling and reinforcing. Predisposing factors are personal characteristics, such as beliefs, attitudes, values and perceptions, that affect self-protective behaviour; for example, personal scepticism. Enabling factors are characteristics of the work environment or system that promote or block safe behaviour; for example, training and knowledge. Reinforcing factors refer to actual or expected rewards or punishment as a consequence of the behaviour; for example, management support. Questionnaire studies have shown the usefulness of the framework in understanding the factors that correlate with employees' intentions to comply with safety procedures in work organizations in both the UK and Asia (Smallwood, 1994; Charuwatee, 1996).

Personality

In this context, personality typically refers to a relatively enduring, stable, disposition. Early in the twentieth century a study of accidents in munitions factories in England during the First World War found that the majority of accidents involved relatively few people. Observations like this gave rise to the idea of 'accident-proneness', of certain people having a disposition to accidents (Farmer and Chambers, 1926, cited in Kay, 1987), a concept which has captured the popular imagination. However, subsequent research and analysis has tended not to support the idea that there is a stable personality trait of being accident prone; instead, different people go through periods of being more prone (Reason, 1974). Generally, the highest accident rates are found in young and inexperienced workers. It has been suggested that the reasons behind this observation are that young people are more impulsive and inattentive, and have less family responsibility than older workers. However, use of the term 'proneness' has been criticized because it places too little emphasis on contributory factors outside the person. McKenna (1983) suggests that the term 'differential accident liability' should be used instead.

In terms of differential liability, several questionnaire-based studies have shown that over periods of several months some people are rated, or rate themselves, as more liable to minor 'cognitive failures' (Reason, 1988). Cognitive failures referred to failing to carry out intended actions (i.e. slips and lapses); for example, entering the living room to get a book, and instead finding yourself turning the television on. These kinds of failures tend to be associated with being distracted or preoccupied with something at the time. Although it is tempting to think that some aspect of personality is involved in differential liability, such data much be treated with caution. Statistically speaking, random events which are normally distributed, and sampled over a time period, will show that some events occur more frequently than others (Kay, 1987).

Another aspect of personality which has been studied in the safety context is locus of control. Locus of control (Rotter, 1966) ranges from internal to external. Those who are internal expect their actions to affect what happens to them and others. Externals believe they have little influence on events. Jones and Wuebker (1985) developed a safety locus of control scale and demonstrated that people in lower-risk groups were more internally oriented. Wuebker (1986) further reported that externally oriented employees appeared to have more accidents, although Smallwood (1994) found no relationship.

Technological Systems, Organizations and Safety: Disasters

Several of the major incidents that could have had potentially catastrophic consequences for the world, like the near nuclear meltdown at Three Mile Island in the USA, and the Chernobyl catastrophe in the USSR, have been, at least in part, attributed to human error in operating complex systems. However, in analyses of most of the major disasters in the 1970s and 1980s, Reason (1990) has demonstrated that many features of work organizations contribute to the breakdown of complex technological systems. Understanding safe working with technology therefore involves much more than investigating why individuals engage in unsafe acts. The organizational and system structures and procedures must also be considered.

Reason (1990) divides the contributions people make to system accidents into two broad categories: latent and active errors. Latent errors are present in a system owing to decisions taken by management and regulatory bodies; active errors are unsafe acts taken for a variety of psychological reasons. Large-scale disasters in complex systems are often the result of combinations of active and latent errors, and inadequate safeguards against possible errors. Reason suggests that factors which contribute to fallible management decision-making about safety arise because production goals are balanced against safety goals. Production goals are easily measured and very visible, and when met are rewarded positively. Safety goals, on the other hand, are measured by the absence of accidents, and only highly visible following an accident or near miss.

Organizational Safety Practices

Accident reporting

Industrial sectors differ in the types and severity of accidents incurred in them. The UK Health and Safety Executive reported that, for the period 1987 to 1990, railway staff suffered four times the number of accidental deaths, as a proportion of those at risk, as did the chemical and allied industries. In clothing and footware manufacture, death rates were more than 60 times less than in the manufacture of bricks, pottery, glass, cement etc. One of the highest rates was in the offshore oil and gas sector.

The consequences of accidents at work include injury to workers, lost production, disruption to working patterns, the ruination of machinery and economic and legislative outcomes such as compensation claims. In recent times industrial injury has been at the centre of national policies concerning these issues, and there are various laws governing them. In the UK, the Health and Safety Executive plays a considerable role in monitoring and enforcing safety standards at work, and in the USA a similar function is carried out by the Occupational Safety and Health Administration.

The UK Health and safety Commision produced regulations in 1992 governing the 'management of health and safety at work'. The regulations state that every employer should make a sufficient assessment of the risks to health and safety to employees he or she is responsible for. Risk includes the likelihood that harm will occur, and its severity. How can the causes of fatalities and other injuries at work be understood, and hence the risks assessed?

Brown (1990) proposes that reporting accidents is the only practical way of evaluating system safety under real operating conditions, and of identifying factors which may be contributing to accident causation. He defines an accident as the 'unplanned outcome of inappropriate behaviour'. The important distinction made by this definition is that between antecedent behaviour and the consequences of the behaviour. In other words, workers can be engaged in unsafe actions which may or may not lead to injury, or technological breakdowns. The utility of understanding antecedent behaviour separate from its consequences is clear when you consider that the same action may or may not lead to an accident, and that many different actions could lead to the same kind of accident.

Brown (1990) argues that, to be useful, accident reporting systems at work should: highlight primary safety improvements; capture antecendent behaviour; avoid subjectivity; avoid apportioning blame; detail task and system demands; collect data on all accidents regardless of their consequences; and detail the nature, severity and causes of accidental injury. Many accident reporting systems do not approach these ideals. Often accident reporting is based on retrospective verbal accounts in reaction to an injury or death, rather than near misses and other accidents. Accounts of behaviour leading up to an accident are frequently given after the event, and thus rely on memory (the 'black box' flight recorders fitted to aircraft are notable exceptions). Accident investigations often find someone to blame as an outcome, rather than concentrating on the complexity of the causes.

Reason (1997) gives details of two reporting programmes which do not simply detail accidents, but aim to understand antecedent behaviour. The organizations involved are NASA in the USA and British Airways in the UK. He outlines what these programmes' characteristics are for gaining valuable reports of near accidents (near misses and critical incidents): confidentiality; rapid and useful feedback to those filing reports; ease of making the report; separation of those collecting the report from those involved in disciplinary procedures; indemnity against disciplinary proceedings as far as is practicable.

Safety programmes

The procedures and attitudes of organizations to work safety influence the degree of hazard at work. It is no accident that industries with a very good record on safety are those like aviation and chemicals, where safety is seen as of paramount importance, and where there are many safety-orientated regulations governing work practices. Safety programmes are designed to increase safety at work, and to overcome reasons for unsafe behaviour in workers.

Booth (1986) has estimated that approximately three-quarters of machinery accidents could have been prevented if proper precautions had been taken. The precautions encompass using goggles to protect the eyes, following proper start-up and shut-down procedures and utilizing safety guards. Workers may not follow safety procedures because they are not aware of them, or they are inconvenient, or they are not part of the workgroup climate.

Safety programmes have tended to concentrate on worker training in safe procedures. Thus employees learn about the procedures and the way to carry them out. However, simply knowing a procedure does not mean a worker will comply with it; thus, organizational means to increase safety are also important. One technique which has been demonstrated to be effective uses behaviour modification principles. Haynes, Pine and Fitch (1982) reduced accident rates in bus drivers working in urban transport by 25 per cent using a safety behaviour modification programme. First, safety performance feedback was made public by posting drivers' safety records in the lunchroom. Second, drivers were put into teams that competed against each other's safety record. This meant that the reward related to the group rather than an individual. Finally, winning drivers and teams were given cash and prizes for outstanding safety records. Thus safe behaviour was rewarded. The reward need not be so obvious. Merely posting safety records and publicly recognizing good safety performance has produced increases in safety.

Safety climate

A close link has been observed between the success of safety programmes and safety climate (Zohar, 1980). Other research has shown that groups with a 'safety climate' had safer work areas. Work groups with experienced and orga- nized leaders were related to fewer accidents (Butler and Jones, 1979). Safety climate can be determined by examining structural properties of organisations such as system complexity and leadership style (James and Jones, 1974), but is often measured by eliciting worker perceptions about organizational com- mittment to safety, such as the perceived importance of safety training, man- agement's attitudes to safety and so on.

Zohar (1980) found several organizational characteristics that distinguished production companies with high and low accident rates. A consistent factor in low accident companies was management committment to safety, manifested, for example, by the personal involvement of top management in routine safety activities, and by safety being given a high priority in company meetings and production scheduling. A second factor was the importance given to safety training. A third factor was the existence of open communication and frequent contact between workers and management. A fourth characteristic of low acci- dent companies was 'good house-keeping', namely orderly plant operations and high usage of safety devices. Companies with good safety records also had distinctive ways of promoting safety. These included: guidance and counselling rather than admonition and enforcement; praise and recognition for safe job performance; and enlisting workers' families in safety promotions.

Through examination of the organizational characteristics, Zohar (1980) developed eight dimensions of safety climate in a questionnaire. These were: the importance of safety training programmes; management attitudes to safety; effects of safe conduct on promotion; the level of risk in the workplace; the pace of work demands related to safety; the status of the safety officer; the effects of safe conduct on social status; and the status of the safety commit- tee. Zohar then validated his measure of safety climate on production workers in 20 large (over 500 workers) factories from four industrial sectors: metal fabrication, food processing, chemicals and textiles. Safety inspectors rank- ordered the factories according to their safety practices and accident preven- tion programmes, and good agreement was found between the ranks and the safety climate scores.

Zohar (1980) then extracted the smallest number of climate dimensions that discriminated between different factories. These were the perceived importance of safety training programmes, the perceived effects of required work pace on safety, the perceived status of the safety committee and the perceived status of the safety officer. Subsequent investigators have boiled down the measurement of safety climate to just two factors: workers' perceptions of management committment to safety, and workers' involvement in safety, albeit in a different industrial sector, construction (Dedobbeleer and Beland, 1991).

Error Management in Technological Systems

Naturally enough, many companies are motivated or regulated to produce safe working conditions and systems. In safety-critical hazardous environments, such as nuclear power, chemical processing and aviation, a strong emphasis has been placed on safety. Two distinct approaches to making technological work systems safer can be distinguished. The first attempts to assess how reliable workers are at what they do, and to design the system accordingly. The second approach accepts that people vary in their performance, and that inevitably they will make errors. Therefore, the system itself should take the human factor into account, and be designed with human fallibility in mind.

Human reliability studies

The flavour of this approach can be gained by considering one of the techniques involved. THERP stands for technique for human error rate prediction (Miller and Swain, 1987). The approach taken is to treat the person in the same way as equipment, a valve, for example, and to assess how likely it is that the person will fail given a particular operating condition. The human error probability (HEP) is expressed as a ratio of the number of errors made on a task to the number of opportunities for errors. Preferably, the HEP assessment is based on actual performance. However, performance data are often lacking, and the assessment is made through an analyst's judgement, or from simulator studies. Once HEPs are obtained for various tasks or procedures they can be combined systematically. The objective of THERP is to relate the probability of human error to system failures, either including or excluding other factors, such as equipment functioning, that influence system behaviour. Although the human reliability approach is attractive, the various techniques have several shortcomings (Wickens, 1992). First, they ignore human cognitive functioning. Second, assessments rely heavily on expert opinion rather than performance data. Third, treating people in the same way as equipment ignores the fact that people often correct their own errors, whereas when machines fail they are repaired or replaced by others. Fourth, when people make an error, that in itself may affect the likelihood of a subsequent error. The view summarized by Reason (1990) is that human reliability analysis has some way to go before it can be considered a reliable and valid approach.

Error tolerant systems

Perrow (1984, 1994) argues that system accidents are 'normal' in the sense that however hard the attempts to avoid them are, serious accidents are inevitable. However, Perrow identifies particular types of system where 'normal' accidents will happen. The systems are complex, and tightly coupled. Complexity refers to a system having many different parts, where the parts interconnect with each other in non-straightforward ways. In contrast, systems could be linear, like an assembly line, and/or simple. Tight coupling implies that the system has only one method of achieving its goals, has invariant sequences and has little slack in it in terms of supplies, equipment or personnel, and delays in processing are not possible. Systems which fall into this category are aircraft, nuclear plants and chemical plants according to Perrow's analysis.

It follows from Perrow's analysis that making a system error-tolerant means making it less complex and/or making it less tightly coupled.

Error reduction

A key reason for studying error is to try to reduce it. Considerable effort has gone into equipment design, system design and safety procedures. From the psychological perspective reviewed in this chapter several ways to reduce error suggest themselves. The key premise behind the suggestions is that errors arise because of a mismatch between the properties of a system as a whole and the characteristics of human information processing.

Norman (1988) proposes, *inter alia*, that a good conceptual model of the system be promoted on the part of its users, and that the structure of tasks be simplified to minimize the load on vulnerable cognitive processes, such as planning and problem solving. He also suggests that constraints on what system users can do should be designed with safety in mind, and that the system should be designed to make error recovery possible.

Frese (1987) suggests that training should allow people to make mistakes so that they can learn from them. Training should encourage and support an active, exploratory approach to the system. Training in a simulator could try to create emergency scenarios as well as normal operations to give operators experience they could draw on in a real emergency. Unfortunately, it is very difficult to foresee, and hence simulate, what real emergencies contain. Others have suggested that external aids, like memory prompts, be part of the system support.

Chapter Summary

This chapter has sought to outline the main psychological approaches to safety in work settings, with an emphasis on technological work systems. Accidents were distinguished in terms of antecedent behaviours and consequences. Psychological approaches to safety at work have been informed by cognitive and social psychology. Human error was discussed in terms of its relationship to cognitive processing of information. Errors were divided into those that were the result of unintended or intended actions. Unintended actions are slips and lapses, and were related to attention and memory failures. Intended actions are rule- or knowledge-based mistakes, and related to inferential processes. Violations of safety procedures were discussed in relation to perceptions of and attitudes to hazards and safety from a social psychology perspective. Organizational and systems approaches to safety discuss how organizational culture influences safety behaviour, and how error analyses could explain technological systems disasters. Finally, various influences on how work organizations and systems could be made safer were outlined.

Discussion Points

1 In what ways do individual and organizational factors interact to produce unsafe working conditions?

2 How is risk related to safety at work?

3 What are the benefits of viewing human error as a consequence of normal cognitive functioning?

4 Can technological systems be made safer through organizational interventions?

Key Studies

Pidgeon, N., Hood, C., Jones, D., Turner, B. and Gibson, R. (1992) *Risk: Analysis, Perception and Management*. London: The Royal Society.

Reason, J. T. (1990) *Human Error*. Cambridge: Cambridge University Press.

PART IV

ORGANIZATIONS AT WORK

Teamwork. (Ace Photo Library)

CHAPTER TWELVE

LEADERSHIP AND MANAGEMENT

Viv Shackleton and Peter Wale

Contents

Some of the many questions which arise when one is considering leadership in any type of organization are those which relate to what leadership is, what it is that leaders do and what makes them different from followers or subordinates. When people consider some of the well known leaders in history, such as Churchill, Hitler and Napoleon, or more recently leaders such as John F. Kennedy, Chairman Mao or Margaret Thatcher, it prompts the question as to what made them different from others and enabled them to become leaders. Of course, leaders exist in all walks of life and all types of organization, and especially in business organizations. It is towards this latter group that we turn our attention in this chapter, and try to answer these and other questions.

The chapter starts by looking at the definition of leadership and at the distinction between leaders and managers. We then turn to some of the major approaches to leadership, including the trait approach, the early Ohio State and Michigan Universities studies, contingency theories, a normative model, attribution theories and transactional and transformational theories. Next, we turn to the slippery and illusive topic of charisma and leadership, followed by the contentious question of whether leaders are necessary at all in certain work situations. Finally, we conclude the chapter with a discussion of why leaders sometimes 'derail' and are forced to end their period of leadership.

What Is Leadership?

There are many different definitions of leadership, but all involve the three important components of *group*, *influence* and *goal*. Leadership is usually examined in the context of a *group*, and particularly work groups. Leaders are people who *influence* the behaviour of the others in the group. Research on leadership stresses that there must be a group *goal* to be accomplished. So leadership is the process in which an individual influences group members towards the attainment of group or organizational goals.

The influence that a leader has on a group can be exercised in a number of ways. It can be by a direct approach, where the leader commands and controls everything that happens, as in the case of the captain of a ship, or it can be more subtle, where he or she guides and facilitates the group's behaviour so that the goal of the group is accomplished. The influencing, however, is often two-way. Leaders may influence followers, but equally followers, by virtue of their own characteristics or expertise, often influence leaders to lead in one way rather than in another. The leadership style, for example, of a consultant working in a hospital alongside qualified but junior doctors may be vastly different from that of a leader or supervisor in the police or armed services.

Table 12.1 The major ways in which management and leadership differ

Management	Leadership
Planning and budgeting Making detailed steps and timetables for achieving results	*Establishing direction* Developing a vision for the future and plans for achieving the vision
Organizing and staffing The allocation of tasks and staffing to carry them out; also delegating responsibility	*Aligning people* Communicating the vision so that others understand it and agree with it
Controlling and problem-solving Monitoring the results of a plan, identifying problems and solving them	*Motivating and inspiring* Energizing people towards the vision so that they overcome barriers to change
Outcomes: order and predictability Produces predictability so that others can rely on consistent results	*Outcomes: change* Produces definite changes such as new products, or new directions

Source: Adapted from Kotter (1990).

The difference between leaders and managers

Although there is a current tendency to describe leaders and managers as one and the same thing, many researchers suggest a clear distinction between the two. Bennis and Nanus (1985), for example, suggest that leadership is *path finding*, while management is *path following*; that leadership is about *doing the right things*, while management is about *doing things right*. They believe that management is concerned with carrying out others' plans and strategies for the organization, while leadership is about having a vision for the future. Obviously, some managers do carry out both functions and can be described as leaders, but clearly others do not.

The distinction between leaders and managers is supported by Kotter (1990), who believes that management is concerned with activities which are implemented to bring *consistency and order* to the organization, while leadership is concerned more with *constructive or adaptive change*. Kotter suggests that there are four major ways that management and leadership differ (see table 12.1). From the distinctions made by Bennis and Nanus and also Kotter, we can see that managers are concerned more with running their part of the organization and ensuring that tasks such as preparing accounts, or meeting deadlines, or sending out invoices, are done when necessary. Leadership, on the other hand, involves having a view of what is important for the future success of the organization and how to implement change.

The possible traits and characteristics of leaders and the choices open to them on how to influence the group comprise one of main areas investigated by leadership researchers. Considerable work has been done examining the traits of leaders, styles of leadership and whether one style is more effective than another.

The great man/great woman approach

In the past, leadership was conceptualized as being due to the characteristics of a person. Leadership research prior to the 1950s was very much concerned with the *trait approach*, which sought to identify and define the traits and characteristics that distinguished leaders from non-leaders. Although some early research into the trait approach suggested that leaders were generally taller and more intelligent than followers (Stodgill, 1974), it failed at that time to reveal any consistent findings that leaders possessed any particular personality traits which set them apart from others. The recent acceptance that leaders can be leaders on some occasions and in some circumstances, and followers on others, lends some weight to this. If any particular personality traits identified leaders from subordinates, then it would follow that they would be leaders on all occasions and in all situations. Much in fact depends on the nature of the task and the characteristics of the others in the group as to who emerges as leader.

Despite earlier misgivings, more recent work, and particularly meta-analysis of work published prior to the 1950s, suggests that leaders may well possess some traits after all which distinguish them from followers. Meta-analysis is a method of pooling together the results of a large number of separate research studies in order to determine the effect of variables based on sample sizes of thousands of subjects, not just the small number typically associated with individual studies. From these studies, it is now generally accepted that a small number of traits may be possessed by leaders, but that it is the capacity to create a vision and implement it that is important in being an effective leader.

House and Baetz (1979) maintain that the very nature of leadership means that the traits of sociability, need for power and need for achievement must be important for leaders. Empirical research by Lord et al. (1986) concludes that leaders tend to be more dominant, extrovert, intelligent, masculine, conservative and better adjusted than non-leaders. Kirkpatrick and Locke (1991) suggest that leaders can be distinguished by the traits of self-confidence, honesty and integrity, drive and persistence, cognitive ability, leadership motivation and knowledge of the business of the group or organization.

Although in recent years the trait approach has made something of a comeback, research has so far only identified a comparatively small number of traits which distinguish leaders from followers. A clear distinction between effective and non-effective leaders has not been established. However, clearly traits do matter after all and research is beginning to show which ones are important.

Leadership Style

While the trait approach implied that leaders would have comparatively consistent characteristics, the style approach is more concerned with identifying and describing the behaviour of leaders; that is, what they did, rather than what they were. The style approach suggests that leaders can learn how to be effective leaders. Research at two American universities, Ohio State and Michigan, carried out independently of each other in the 1960s, attempted to identify and describe the important behaviours involved.

Research at Michigan University concentrated on looking at the differences in behaviour between effective and ineffective leaders. This revealed that effective leaders tended to be *employee-centred* – that is, concerned about their subordinates – whereas ineffective ones tended to be *job-centred*; that is only concerned with the tasks carried out. The two styles of behaviour were believed to be at the opposite ends of a continuum, suggesting that a leader could exhibit either job-centred or employee-centred behaviour, but not both.

Simultaneous influential research at Ohio State University looked at understanding the principles of leadership by asking subordinates to describe their boss's style. This was conducted mainly in relation to military leaders by asking subordinates, in questionnaires, how often their leader engaged in certain kinds of behaviour, such as helping with personal problems or criticizing poor work and behaviour. By means of factor analysis, nine types of behaviour were reduced to four main factors.

1   *Consideration:* the extent to which leaders and their subordinates have consideration of feelings and warmth between each other and relationships built on reciprocal liking and trust.
2   *Initiating structure:* the extent to which the leader provides clear-cut definitions of role responsibility and structures work towards the achievement of a goal.
3   *Production emphasis:* the extent to which the leader is influenced by production targets.
4   *Sensitivity:* the extent to which the leader is sensitive to the needs of the followers.

The two dimensions of consideration and initiating structure have since been identified in many other, more recent, studies, in which they are variously described as relationship-orientated or employee-centred and task-orientated or production-centred. There are many other similar descriptions. However, the results from the Ohio and Michigan studies raise the question of whether effective leaders are concerned only with people or with both tasks and people. The Ohio study in particular suggested that considerate leaders were more concerned with a pleasant atmosphere and high morale but were viewed by superiors as less effective because they were reluctant to reprimand or establish standards. Production often suffered as a consequence. Structuring leaders, on the other hand, were concerned less with employee satisfaction but were seen by superiors to be more effective. This of course raises the question of whether concern for both people and the task is possible in an effective leader.

To answer this question, Blake and Mouton, in 1964, developed a managerial grid on which a leader can plot his or her own style on the dimensions of concern for people and concern for tasks, with a scale ranging from 1 (low) to 9 (high) for each. This has helped to show that leaders can in fact be high on both dimensions yet still be effective. There have been many other similar versions of this. In the latest version, known as the 'leadership grid' and developed by Blake and McCanse (1991), there are various combinations of concern for people and concern for task, which describe five major leadership styles:

1   Team management, or 9.9 style (the first figure refers to concern for task, the second to concern for people), relies on interdependence through having a common stake in the group's purpose. This leads to mutual trust and respect between the leaders and followers.
2   Middle of the road management, or 5.5 style, is about balancing the need to get the work done and keeping morale at a satisfactory level. The objective is adequate performance.
3   Impoverished or *laissez-faire* management, or a 1.1 style, is typified by the execution of the least possible effort to get the work done and keep the group together.
4   Country club management, or a 1.9 style, involves having a thoughtful approach to the needs of people in the group in order to maintain a friendly atmosphere.
5   Task management (also known as authority/obedience management), or a 9.1 style, stresses the importance of arranging work in such a way that human elements can affect it only to a minimum.

The managerial grid makes the assumption that there is one best style of leadership, this being the 9.9 style, or 'high-high', as it is also known. The assumption is that the most effective leader is one who combines concern for people with concern for tasks. However, the evidence for this is not convincing, as it ignores the great variation in human behaviour in different situations and the fact that different leadership styles or behaviour might be appropriate in different circumstances.

Studies by other researchers into the style approach have identified other types of leadership behaviour, which can be classified as 'directive autocrat', 'permissive autocrat', 'directive democrat' and 'permissive democrat'. The two opposite dimensions of *autocratic–democratic* relate to the extent to which leaders allow subordinates to get involved in decision-making, while *permis-*

sive–directive is concerned with the extent to which leaders direct activities. The question of whether or not one style is superior to another depends largely on how skilled or experienced the subordinate is.

There are a number of criticisms of the style approach. First is the problem of *causality* relating to the variables of leader style and work output. The fact that the two are correlated does not necessarily mean that one causes the other. While we would expect that leadership style can cause high output, a study by Greene (1975) suggests quite the opposite: that output in fact influences the style of leadership. The problem in describing the behaviour of the leader also ignores the fact that a leader may behave very differently towards one individual compared to another. Another problem concerns the fact that there may be *informal leadership* in the group; that is, someone in the group who exerts influence while not being the designated leader. Research may thus be focusing on the wrong person. Finally, the *absence of situational variables* concerns the failure of the style approach to allow for other variables which may have an effect on the relationship between behaviour and outcome.

While research studies into the style approach have shown that one style may be better than another in some cases, no one single style has so far been shown to be appropriate, or the most effective, in all circumstances. It is this gap in information which led to the next major development in leadership research – the contingency approach.

Contingency Theories of Leadership

The contingency approach to leadership attempts to establish and describe how the *situation* in which the leader and group find themselves has an effect on the leadership behaviour used. The question posed by this research is: when is one type of leadership behaviour more appropriate than another? The answer is that the style or behaviour adopted by the leader is contingent (or dependent) upon the context and circumstances of the situation he or she is in. Contingency theories set out and describe how the leader's behaviour and the situation interact.

One such contingency model, the situational leadership theory developed by Hersey and Blanchard (1988), follows on from the Ohio State and Michigan studies, in that it takes as its starting point the fact that there are two dimensions of leader behaviour, task behaviours and relationship behaviours. Hersey and Blanchard describe four typical leadership styles: encouraging, coaching, delegating and structuring. A particular leader behaviour is considered to be more appropriate in one situation than it would be in another. By 'situation', Hersey and Blanchard refer to the *willingness* and *ability* of people to do their work as well as the *nature* of the work and the *climate* of the organization.

A key variable in Hersey and Blanchard's theory, is the factor of follower (or worker) *maturity*. This refers to the subordinate's understanding of the job and commitment to it. Maturity is made up of both job maturity, refer-ring to aspects such as experience, ability and knowledge, and psychological maturity, which is measured in terms of persistence, independence, willingness and attitude to work. When a subordinate has low levels of maturity, a high task and low relationship combination of leader behaviour would be most suit-able. This is a *structuring style*. At the highest levels of maturity, a subordinate may require very little task or relationship behaviour from the leader. This would then be a *delegating style*.

Although situational leadership theory has much appeal and is liked by both management trainers and working managers, it is not supported by much empirical evidence. While research by Vecchio (1987) found some support for the theory, it also revealed that it might be most applicable and effective for only those subordinates with low levels of maturity.

Fiedler's contingency model

One of the first true contingency theories of the leadership process was devel-oped by Fiedler (1967). The theory states that leader performance is depen-dent upon both the leader's personal characteristics and the degree to which the leader controls the situation. The key variable in the theory is the *least pre-ferred co-worker* (LPC) and how positively the leader views him or her. Leaders are asked to rate the person they have least liked to work with the LPC on a set of 18 eight-point scales. An example of one of these scales is: Friendly 8-7-6-5-4-3-2-1 Unfriendly. A low LPC score indicates that the leader describes the worker he or she doesn't like in very negative terms, while a high LPC indicates a more positive attitude on the part of the leader. High LPC leaders are described as relationship-orientated in view of the fact that they feel positive even about people they don't like, while low LPC leaders are described as task-orientated.

In addition to the LPC, Fiedler's theory is also dependent upon three contingency variables that determine the extent to which the situation is favourable to the leader by providing control over subordinates. *Group atmos-phere* describes how accepted the leader is by the group, and thereby how com-mitted the group is likely to be to the task and objectives. *Task structure* refers to the extent to which the roles of the subordinates and the tasks and goals of the group are clearly defined. Different leader behaviours would obviously be required for routine tasks from those needed for non-routine tasks. *Posi-tion power* refers to the extent to which the leader controls and can adminis-ter rewards and punishments.

How favourable the situation is for the leader is determined by dividing each aspect of the situation into high or low, good or poor, strong or weak, and then combining these aspects to give a combined rating (see figure 12.1). According to this model, the situation is most favourable for the leader when relations with subordinates are good, the leader has strong position power and

Most favourable situation for leader						Least favourable situation for leader	
1	2	3	4	5	6	7	8
Group atmosphere							
Good	Good	Good	Good	Poor	Poor	Poor	Poor
Task structure							
High	High	Low	Low	High	High	Low	Low
Leader position power							
Strong	Weak	Strong	Weak	Strong	Weak	Strong	Weak
Desirable leader							
Low LPC	Low LPC	Low LPC	High LPC	High LPC	High LPC	High LPC	Low LPC

Figure 12.1   Fiedler's contingency theory.
Source: Fiedler (1967).

the task is highly structured. According to the model, when the situation is either very favourable or very unfavourable to the leader (as in column 1 and column 8 in figure 12.1), low LPC (that is, task-orientated) leaders will be more effective than high LPC (relationship orientated) leaders. When the situation is a mixture or is indeterminate in favourability (as in columns 4 and 5), then a high LPC leader will be most effective.

There are many problems with, and criticisms of, Fiedler's contingency theory. Not least of these is that it does not explain how leader LPC rating affects group performance; or why low LPC leaders are more effective in extreme situations, be they favourable or unfavourable. Despite this, several studies, including those by Strube and Garcia (1981) and Peters et al. (1985), concluded that the research does tend to support the model, although not for every situation and not as strongly in practice as in laboratory studies.

Vroom–Yetton–Jago normative model

Another contingency model of leader behaviour is that by Vroom and Yetton (1973), which was updated and extended by Vroom and Jago (1988). This model concentrates particularly on leadership decision-making and how much leaders should involve subordinates in the decision-making process. Vroom and Yetton suggest that leaders usually adopt one of five distinct methods for reaching decisions. These are:

Al   *Decide alone* from personal knowledge without discussing with anyone.
All   *Seek information from one or more subordinates* but then decide alone.
Cl   *Consult with selected individuals* and seek information but not solutions, and then still decide alone.

C11   *Consult with the whole group together*, using them as consultants, but retain the final decision themselves.

G11   *Share the problems* with the whole group and mutually decide what to do.

Although the theory addressed the question of how a leader should choose one decision-making style rather than another, it does not suggest one best style. Instead it points to questions that leaders should ask themselves before deciding whether to involve others or not. These questions relate to such factors as the time available, the decision quality, subordinates' commitment and satisfaction and the likely acceptance by them of the decision. Although there are problems with the theory, there is also evidence (e.g. Margerison and Glube, 1979; Field, 1982) to suggest that managers using the five methods in the model are seen as more effective and have workers who are more satisfied.

Path-goal theory

The final contingency approach mentioned here is path-goal theory, developed by House (House and Mitchell, 1974). This concerns itself with the issue of what motivates workers in a given circumstance, subject to a calculation of what lies in it for them. This is dependant upon the *expectancy, instrumentality* and *valence* in the situation. *Expectancy* relates to the belief that effort will result in performance. *Instrumentality* is the belief that the individual's performance will be rewarded, and *valence* is how much the reward or outcome is valued. The motivation to act, to work or to achieve goals can be calculated by multiplying the three factors.

   The basic principle or belief underlying path-goal theory is that subordinates will react favourably to a leader to the extent that they believe the leader can help them to achieve and attain their goals. The theory states that there are four types of leader behaviour which can affect subordinate motivation. These are *directive, supportive, participative* and *achievement-orientated* leadership. The four behaviours are defined as:

- *Directive leadership:* being clear about what subordinates are expected to do; giving guidance; scheduling and coordinating the work.
- *Supportive leadership:* considering the needs of subordinates; showing concern for their welfare; creating a friendly work climate.
- *Participative leadership:* consulting subordinates and taking into account their suggestions and opinions.
- *Achievement-orientated leadership:* setting challenging goals; seeking improvements in performance; expressing confidence that subordinates will achieve high standards.

House suggests that one feature of an effective leader is being flexible enough to be able to use any of the four styles depending on the circumstances.

Reviews of empirical research aimed at testing path-goal theory have shown mixed results (Indvik, 1986). For example, directive leader behaviours do seem to increase subordinate satisfaction for unstructured tasks but not for structured tasks, as suggested by the theory. But many key hypotheses, such as that effective leaders use many styles dependent on the situation, have not been tested or have yielded equivocal results. All one can say at the present time is that the theory has not been fully tested.

All the contingency approaches to leader behaviour attempt to answer the question of when one style or type of leadership is more appropriate than another. Different models stress different factors as being important, and the effectiveness of the leader's behaviour depends on the context it is in. It is perhaps hard to say that one model stands out as preferable to another. All are useful, and the question of which is preferable really depends on the situation the group and leader find themselves in.

Attribution Theory

Attribution theory can be defined as the manner in which people try to discover cause and effect relationships in the events that occur all around them. It relies on the principle that any event can have a variety of causes. The theory suggests that we all observe the behaviour of others and then attribute causes to that behaviour. This idea can equally be applied to leadership and the events which take place in leader–follower interactions. As we shall see, although attributions can be, and often are, made accurately, the attributions of leaders and subordinates can also be at odds and affected by many variables.

First put forward by Heider (1958), attribution theory focuses on the inferences that are used to determine someone else's disposition from observations of his or her behaviour. Central to the theory is the proposal that people see behaviour as caused either by the individuals themselves, i.e. *dispositional* (an internal attribution), or by the environment, i.e. *situational* (an external attribution). To illustrate this, let us imagine a police officer shouting and appearing agitated while trying to arrest a seemingly innocent motorist in front of a crowd of people. The crowd may decide that the officer was hard, aggressive and unreasonable, and many may decide to complain about his actions. Some may even go as far as to try to help the motorist to escape. Research shows that people do have a strong tendency to attribute the actions of others to internal, dispositional, factors when evidence to the contrary is lacking.

There could of course be other explanations for the incident described. The crowd could conclude that the car was stolen and the arrest was taking place at the end of a long chase. In that case they would be making an external or situational attribution, and might regard the officer as brave and even assist, instead of condemning, him. So the conclusions reached in coming to either an internal or external attribution can often have dramatic and far-reaching effects.

Kelley's (1967) theory of causal attribution extends the work of Heider and attempts to describe and explain exactly how we come to decisions about internal or external causes. Kelley believes that, in making an attribution, we should consider *consensus*, that is, the extent to which others also behave in the same manner. Then we should consider *consistency*. This is the extent to which this person acts the same at other times in the same situation. Finally, we should consider *distinctiveness*, this being the extent to which this person behaves the same in other situations. The combined analysis of the three factors forms the basis for making decisions about the causes of a person's behaviour.

There is quite a lot of empirical support for the theory (e.g. Jones and Nisbett, 1971; Ross, 1977; Nisbett and Ross, 1985). However, there are two caveats. First, people only tend to engage in the elaborate thought processes of attributing internal or external causes when they notice unexpected actions by others which they cannot easily explain. Second, people are inclined to explain others' actions in terms more of internal causes ('it's because she is lazy' or 'he is mean', for example) than of external ones (the traffic or the weather, for example). This is probably because it is easier to label someone with a trait (lazy or mean) than to think through varieties of possible external reasons. So prevalent is this tendency that it has been called the *fundamental attribution error*.

Attribution theory of leadership

As we have pointed out, attribution theory can be applied to leadership. The attribution theory of leadership suggests that a leader's judgement about an employee's actions is influenced by the leader's attribution of the causes of the employee's performance. The attribution the leader makes for the causes determines how the leader responds, just as much as does the actual performance itself. For example, if a leader attributes employee poor performance to something temporary, like domestic problems at home, the leader is less likely to reprimand than if he or she thought it was due to laziness or lack of interest.

An attributional model of leadership developed by Mitchell and Wood (1979) (see figure 12.2) attempts to link leaders' actions to employees' poor performance. Research by Green and Mitchell (1979) showed that leaders do analyse employees' performance in relation to consensus, consistency and distinctiveness. Mitchell and Wood (1980) conducted a classic study concerning nurses. They gave accounts of errors committed by nurses to nursing supervisors. These accounts suggested that there were either external causes (such as pressure of work or poor equipment) or internal causes (such as lack of skill or effort on the part of the nurse). Supervisors were asked what actions they

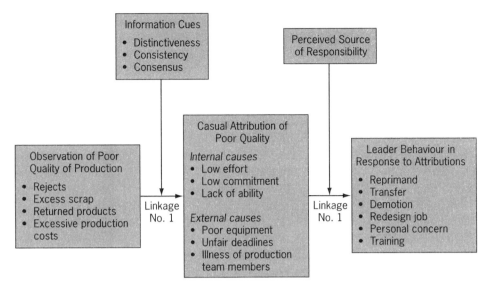

Figure 12.2 An attributional leadership model.
Source: adapted from Mitchell and Wood (1979).

proposed to put the situation right. Where they perceived the causes as external, they directed action towards the environment, suggesting changes to work loads or equipment, for example. Where they perceived the errors as internally caused, they directed action towards the nurses, such as recommending training in the use of the equipment. So the theory was supported. The leader's behaviour did reflect his or her attributions concerning the causes of a problem.

Employee likeability and other variables

While much of the evidence supports the theory, some research suggests that other factors can have an influence on the type of attributions made. Turban et al. (1990) found that a supervisor's liking for a subordinate positively influences the evaluation of performance and the type of action taken against the subordinate. Dobbins and Russell (1986a) found that liking or not liking has an effect on the type of action taken after poor performance, and that this can lead to negative reactions from employees (see figure 12.3). Ilgen et al. (1981) found that if the leader's own rewards are affected by the subordinate's poor performance, then the leader is likely to rate the employee more highly and respond more favourably. The response can also be affected by previous work history and whether an apology is offered.

Further research by Dobbins and Russell (1986b) reveals that leaders do not always get everything their own way. Subordinates also attribute causes to

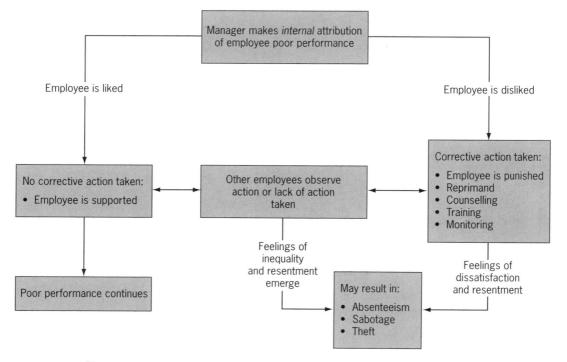

Figure 12.3 The effects of a manager's corrective action based on liking a subordinate.
Source: based on Dobbins and Russell (1986).

their leaders' behaviour and develop either positive or negative attitudes towards them. While leaders often attribute low group performance to subordinates, the subordinates themselves attribute it to the leader. It appears that each blames the other, whatever the real causes of the poor group performance may be. Clearly, attributions are important for all concerned. Effective leadership, it seems, lies just as much in recognizing and understanding the causes of performance as it does in dealing with the actual performance itself.

Transactional and Transformational Leadership

Most of the early approaches to leadership can be defined as *transactional*. A leader attempts to motivate followers by transactions; that is, appealing to their self-interest and exchanging valued rewards, such as pay or status, in return for effort. Transactional leaders clarify the role of subordinates, initiate structure, reward and punish them, show them consideration and attempt to meet their social needs.

Transformational leadership is a process in which leaders and followers transform each other: that is raise each other to higher levels of effort by engagement and by appealing to higher levels of morality or values. Transformational leaders attempt to arouse in subordinates an awareness of the key issues and priorities for the group or for the organization. They try to enthuse them, engage the whole person and seek to concern them with their own achievement, aspirations and personal development and fulfilment.

Bass (1985), who coined the term transformational, views transactional and transformational leadership as processes that are distinct but not mutually exclusive. An effective leader can use one or the other, but most often will use both. In fact, leaders should use both transactional and transformational behaviours in certain situations to be effective.

Transactional leadership

Transactional leadership, according to the Bass model, has two components. These are management-by-exception and contingent reward.

Management-by-exception   This is leadership by spotting and correcting mistakes. When a follower makes an error, or fails to do something he or she has agreed to do, the leader applies corrective action, such as a reprimand. If all is going well, the leader takes no action. There are two types of management-by-exception (MBE). With *passive MBE* the leader only corrects when there are problems, and does so reluctantly. With *active MBE* the leader actively monitors the situation and searches for, or is alert for, errors. Followers with MBE leaders try to avoid mistakes by maintaining the status quo and being reluctant to make changes or take risks. Needless to say, this is not a very desirable stance in most organizations.

Contingent reward   Here a leader attempts to exchange rewards for effort or performance. A leader specifies what tasks should be accomplished and offers to provide rewards only when the task has been performed to the required standard. Sales departments often very publicly reward top performers with bonuses, holidays, trophies and so on, to signal to everyone the rewards that can be obtained by exceptional performance.

Transformational leadership

Bass's model of transformational leadership has four components.

Individualized consideration   Here leaders show interest in the personal and professional development of followers. They make themselves aware of followers' needs and provide challenges and opportunities to learn, often by delegating stretching tasks, to raise the skill and confidence levels of subordinates. In this way, it is hoped that followers will increasingly develop competence and be prepared to take the initiative.

Intellectual stimulation   Here the leader stimulates followers to think, to use their imagination, to challenge assumptions and the accepted 'tried and trusted' methods of doing things. The leader has to be able to create a broad, imaginative picture and to be willing to accept bizarre and unusual ideas.

Inspirational motivation   This is leadership that inspires others by envisaging the future. A leader paints a picture of the future that is both optimistic and realistic, and encourages followers to raise their expectations and effort towards this attainable goal.

Idealized influence   Here the leader is a role model and can be described as charismatic. The leader demonstrates supreme confidence in the vision. He or she is persistent and determined in pursuing objectives and takes full responsibility for his or her actions. Followers are likely to have an emotional attraction to the leader, to describe the leader as charismatic and show great trust in that person.

Laissez-faire leadership

The final component of Bass's model is *laissez-faire* leadership. In effect, this is not leadership at all. It describes leaders who are not involved with followers' work and avoid taking a stand. They shelve problems rather than resolving them. The leader lets followers do as they please, and is absent, disorganized and indifferent.

The evidence

Bass'a model has been influential in stimulating a large number of studies, both by his own research team and by others. These studies have examined the relationship between transactional and transformational leadership on the one hand and variables such as leadership effectiveness and follower satisfaction on the other. The work has been helped by a questionnaire called the Multifactor Leadership Questionnaire (MLQ) (Bass and Avolio, 1997) based on the Bass model, which allows subordinates to rate leaders on the seven components described above. A summary of the evidence is provided by Bryman (1992). He shows that:

1 *Laissez-faire* leadership is highly undesirable.
2 Idealized influence and inspirational motivation are the two factors most likely to be associated with desirable outcomes, such as satisfaction, effectiveness and extra effort.
3 Individualized consideration and intellectual stimulation are the next most important factors. Individualized consideration is usually more important than intellectual stimulation except where extra effort is the outcome.

4   Contingent reward is fairly importantly associated with follower satisfaction and extra effort, and leader effectiveness.
5   Results for management-by-exception are inconsistent. Active management-by-exception seems more effective than its passive form.

While research on the Bass model has produced a good number of consistent findings, there is a problem with most of the studies. This is because most published work uses a correlational design and a correlation between two factors does not imply that one causes the other. So it could be that transformational leadership causes effectiveness and satisfaction, or the other way round, or that they are both caused by a third factor. All we can safely say is that the two factors are associated together.

One reason why they are associated together could be the *common method variance* problem. When perceptual measures of leader effectiveness and of leader behaviour are taken at the same time, from the same people, the correlations between these two variables could be increased artificially by respondents trying to answer questions consistently. That this potential for artificially increasing the correlation does happen in practice is evident from the findings of studies that have used *independent measures of effectiveness*. Yammarino and Bass (1990), for example, found that there was a correlation of 0.97 with the common method variance problem (i.e. followers provided perceptions of both transformational leadership and performance), but only 0.34 when there were independent performance measures. So the strength of the relationship is in the same direction, but considerably smaller. However, the bulk of the evidence shows that transformational leaders are seen as more effective than merely transactional leaders.

Charismatic Leadership

Whenever one thinks of leadership, the concept of charisma is not far behind. This is particularly so if one thinks of political leaders such as John F. Kennedy, Martin Luther King, Winston Churchill or Alexander the Great. Charismatic leadership can be defined as the ability to 'make ordinary people do extraordinary things in the face of adversity' (Conger, 1991), and the word charisma comes from the Greek for 'divinely inspired gift'. Does the study of charisma have a place in business leadership? Many people think it does. While only a small minority of leaders and managers in organizations would be described by their followers as charismatic, those that are can indeed motivate, lead, inspire and enthuse those around them to great achievements. So it is worth exploring how it is that some leaders come to be labelled as charismatic.

Charisma is best seen not as the possession of certain traits, or as the result of special situations, but as an interaction between these two factors, which leads to a special relationship between a leader and his or her followers. The 'special relationship' between Hitler and the German people before and during the Second World War, to take a 'dark side' example, can be seen as a result of his oratory and vision to capture the mood of the moment at a time of depression and humiliation after the First World War.

House's theory

House's (1977) theory of charismatic leadership is a good example of the interactionist approach, considering, as it does, leader traits, behaviours and conditions. According to House, the *traits* of charismatic leaders include high self-confidence, strong beliefs in their own views and a need for power. The *behaviours* include setting an example, setting high expectations, providing an attractive vision of the future, arousing motivation and impression management. This last behaviour means creating the impression that the leader is highly competent by displaying confidence, talking about past successes and brushing off setbacks. The leader arouses motivation through rousing speeches and appealing to followers' emotions. *Conditions* or the context have to be right for charismatic leadership to flourish. House says that conditions that are stressful or reaching crisis point are those that are most likely to bring forth charismatic leaders.

The empirical evidence is generally supportive of House's theory. Howell and Higgins (1990) showed that executives who had spearheaded innovations in their organization, called 'product champions', were more likely to behave in ways that communicated ideological goals and demonstrated confidence in themselves and in followers. These behaviours are three of those listed by House as charismatic. A study by Podsakoff et al. (1990) asked followers to complete a questionnaire describing their superior. Managers who articulated a vision, modelled desired behaviours and expected a lot of their followers (all behaviours characteristic of charismatic leaders, according to House) had subordinates who took on extra work or responsibility, trusted their superior more and were more loyal.

Conger and Kanungo's attribution theory

Conger and Kanungo (1987) take a slightly different view of charisma. They view it as an attribution process, meaning that people attribute charisma to leaders in organizations in specific situations. Certain behaviours, which can be learned or adopted by leaders, make it more likely that charisma will be attributed to them. Many of these behaviours are similar to those listed by House in his theory. Leaders who articulate a vision which paints a very different picture from the existing state of affairs, who are unconventional in their methods of attaining the vision and who show self-confidence and enthusiasm about the vision are more likely to be viewed as charismatic. They also use persuasive appeals to the emotions of followers. The use of personal power (through force of personality) rather than position power (through use of hierarchical position), and a demonstrated concern for others, rather than oneself, are also important behaviours.

Are Leaders Really Necessary?

So far we have discussed leaders and managers as if no group or organization could possibly function or survive without them. But is this necessarily the case? Most of us can no doubt think of groups we have known which appear to have managed quite well without a leader, or of groups where the nominated leader has been totally ineffective. This prompts the question of whether leaders really are necessary after all. Meindl and Ehrlich (1987) suggest that people do have a strong tendency to romanticize leadership and see it as more important than it really is. They believe that the significance and value attributed to leadership as the cause of good or bad group performance tends to enhance or detract from the perceived performance, making it seem better, or worse, than it really is.

In order to test the romaticization view of leadership, Meindl and Ehrlich gave information about an imaginary firm to four groups of business students. Included in the data were descriptions of the firm's strengths. This information was varied so that different groups received different reasons for the firm's strengths. These were its top management team, *or* the quality of the employees, *or* consumer preferences, *or* national regulatory policies. When asked to rate the performance of the firm, students rated the firm more favourably when its success was attributed to the top management team than when it was attributed to any of the other factors. The investigators concluded that people have a tendency to romanticize or overemphasize the importance of leadership and its effect on organizational outcomes such as profitability.

Meindl (1992) argues the case for a reinvention of leadership by suggesting that researchers should examine leadership in terms not so much of who and what the *leader* is, but more who and what the *followers* are. He suggests that the emergence of leadership depends heavily on the follower's state of mind and as an experience which he or she undergoes. As might be expected, there are criticisms of both this idea and the romanticization of leadership. Both Yukl (1989) and Bass (1990b) believe that it trivializes leadership and relegates it to a very minor role in the dynamics of groups and organizations.

Kerr and Jermier (1978) have developed a model which proposes that a number of factors can *substitute* for, or *neutralize*, leadership, resulting in leaders having a limited effect on outcomes. Leaders may be unnecessary because of subordinate, task or organization characteristics. Subordinate characteristics include a high level of knowledge, experience or commitment. Task characteristics include highly structured, routine tasks or those that are intrinsically satisfying. Organizational characteristics include a cohesive work group, or formal plans, goals and areas of responsibility. Each or all of these characteristics may make the presence of a leader unnecessary.

Evidence for the model is limited, but a study by Podsakoff et al. (1993) lends it some support. A broad selection of employees from different organizations were asked to give their perceptions of various leadership behaviours and substitutes for leadership that were evident in their jobs. The investigators found support for the model. Job performance and attitudes were more strongly associated with the various substitutes for leadership in the jobs than they were with the various leaders' behaviours.

Derailment

So far in this chapter, we have looked implicitly or explicitly at what makes a leader or manager successful, and the circumstances that are conducive to good performance. But there is another side to the 'success' coin. This is the question: what are the factors which contribute to individuals failing to continue to be successful once they have become leaders? Researchers have called this term *derailment*. Researchers at the Center for Creative Leadership in Greensboro, North Carolina, USA, first investigated the derailment question and coined the term. A study by McCall and Lombardo (1983) looked at 80 top executives in large organizations. They asked:

1   Why were derailed executives successful in the first place?
2   What were the 'fatal flaws' that led to derailment?
3   What events made those flaws surface?
4   How did those who derailed differ from those who made it to the top?

A person who had derailed was defined as someone who had achieved a very high level but had not gone as high as the organization had expected. He or she may have been demoted or fired, accepted early retirement, reached a plateau or had responsibilities reduced. Those who had 'made it to the top' were defined as having reached one of the top twenty positions in the organization or as having lived up to their full potential, as the organization saw it.

In many ways, the successful individuals and the derailers were remarkably similar. Both were very bright, with strong professional or technical skills, were ambitious, worked hard and were prepared to make sacrifices in order to get on. Persons in both groups had been identified as having high potential by the corporation and had excellent track records. So why was it that one group reached a plateau or derailed, and the other group continued on to further promotion and responsibilities? There were a number of reasons.

1   Over-managing. This is the inability to delegate work to others, a failure to build responsibility and authority in others (i.e. to empower them) and a constant monitoring, meddling or controlling of the work of subordinates.
2   Ambition is one thing, but derailers tended to be over-ambitious. They left a trail of bruised and bitter people behind them. Eventually, the over-ambitious had their come-uppance.
3   The inability to be strategic. Up to a certain level in an organization, there is no real need to be strategic. You get on by doing, by being concerned with the 'how', with tactics and being operational. But more senior positions increasingly call for the person to be strategic, to be concerned with the 'what' rather more than the 'how'.

But the single most important factor that distinguished the derailers from the more successful was poor interpersonal skills. Derailers were much more often described as abrasive, cold, aloof, arrogant, intimidating or insensitive. Those who continued to be successful were more diplomatic, avoided confrontations and were generally skilled in dealing with others. This failure to get on with others was particularly noticeable in male derailers. Later work by the Greensboro team (Lombardo and Eichinger, 1989) added to the picture of poor interpersonal skills by showing that derailers were more likely to have poor relationships with senior managers. They were less able to persuade or influence them; or they were unable to adapt to a new boss with a different style; or they had been over-dependent on one boss and then this 'shelter' had moved on, exposing the derailer's weak spot; or they had disagreements about strategy.

Research in Britain on derailment has run parallel to the American research, based on the trait approach. Work at Cranfield School of Management by Tyson et al. (1986) gave the 16PF (a well known 16 factor personality questionnaire) to over 200 redundant executives attending outplacement counselling designed to help them back into work. Just as in the Center for Creative Learning work, both groups were intelligent, independent, emotionally adjusted and had good leadership potential. Compared to a similar group of still employed executives, the redundant ones were less shrewd and self-critical, and more imaginative, bold, forthright, uninhibited and unconventional. A similar British study by Brindle (1992), also using the 16PF, along with another questionnaire, the Occupational Personality Questionnaire, with redundant managers, showed that derailers were less warm, emotional and traditional and more conceptual, innovative and independent.

Putting together the conclusions from the derailment studies gives a fairly consistent picture. First, conceptual intelligence helps you reach a certain level of success, but it doesn't protect you from being derailed. Practical street-wise intelligence does. You need both. If you are aware of the politics and realities of organizational life and can act on that awareness to play the organizational

Finserve

People often think that accountancy is dull and boring. Whether or not you agree is a matter of personal choice. But no one could reasonably accuse the professional accountancy firms in Britain in the past 10–15 years of leading a dull life. The changes in their structure, composition and client base and their frequent mergers and acquisitions have given those involved with the leadership and strategy of these firms much to occupy their thoughts.

One such firm we will call Finserve. The case is based on a real firm, but with a change of name to spare its blushes. In the 1980s it appointed a new managing partner, Henry, as the leader and chief executive of the firm. Although an accountant by profession, Henry was a far cry from the conservative, careful, meticulous and staid individual who conforms to the popular stereotype of the boring accountant.

Finserve was a medium-sized firm. It had offices in most major cities in the UK with around six partners in each office and a head office in the City of London. To Henry, this medium size presented a problem for the firm. It was not of sufficient size to appeal to the large international companies, such as BP, Ford or Marks and Spencer, who placed their business with one of the five or so large international accountancy firms. But nor was it small enough to survive with low costs, just a few partners in one or two offices, and a local, loyal clientele.

Another problem for Henry was his colleagues, the partners who, like himself, owned the firm. They had been used to being traditional accountants with clients they had known for years. They were not accustomed to promoting the business, selling other services or even looking at the profit from each piece of business. Despite being accountants, they were surprisingly unconcerned with business, even down to invoicing clients sometimes years after the work had been done. They liked what they did and, for most of them, making money for the firm was secondary. All this had to change.

Henry's role, as he saw it, was to transform Finserve. It was a 'do or die' mission for the firm. If it didn't 'reinvent' itself, it would either be swallowed up by one of the big boys or go bust. There was no place any longer for medium-sized firms with the costs and attitudes of Finserve.

Henry set about tackling the problem on a number of fronts. He tirelessly promoted the idea of change at partner meetings, annual get-togethers and every time he met a partner. He

game, then you have a better chance of keeping on climbing up the greasy organizational pole, or of keeping your job when bad times arrive. Sadly, it is the imaginative, unconventional and independent-minded managers who are less likely to stay the course. Second, you need self-awareness and interpersonal skills. Bluntness, abrasiveness, an intimidating style and a failure to get on with others are all associated with derailment. It is particularly important to have good relationships with superiors and the sensitivity and skill to manage disagreements. Finally, you need to be adaptable to different cultures, was messianic in his fervour. He explained the need to:

- become more entrepreneurial;
- consider costs and profits;
- rationalize the client base;
- become more specialized (a niche player);
- become more sophisticated at marketing.

This set the scene and the strategy.

He then commissioned a consultancy to set up a series of assessment for development workshops for all partners. These are similar to assessment centres (see chapter 2) but are aimed at assessing strengths, weaknesses and development needs (e.g. training) of participants. This allowed the partners to assess what they themselves were good at, and what they needed to change about themselves to fit in with the new strategy (e.g. to be more proactive with clients). For some partners, it allowed them to decide not to stay with the 'new' Finserve. The partnership also made many other changes to the way it worked, including relocating its head office away from London, moving more into the growth area of consultancy and recruiting specialist partners in the niches it aimed to occupy.

No one should underestimate the difficulties of moving a traditional firm of accountants like Finserve into a different market and with a different 'mindset' towards business. Henry was certainly a transformational leader, with a strong vision for the future of the firm. His style, though, alienated some partners. He had a brusque, no-nonsense, highly assertive way with people. Some accused him of being autocratic. His brilliant mind, his belief in himself and his cause, his eccentric personality, his preference for strong, emotive language and his workaholic tendencies all encouraged others to see him as charismatic. He was certainly the right leader at the right time for Finserve.

Within a few years Finserve was profitable and growing. It exists today as a successful, independent, medium-sized firm. Once the transformation was complete, the partners voted Henry out of the position of managing partner and replaced him with a more transactional and consultative leader. Henry remains with Finserve to this day but is something of an outsider within the firm, having many outside contacts and a reputation among his clients for innovation and radical thinking.

business cycles and, above all, changes of senior management. Of course, the politically astute spot the changes before others do, and the interpersonally skilled manage the changed relationships well. Applying your intelligence in socially acceptable ways is the key to continuing to be successful.

So the picture from the British studies is of a derailer as someone who is rather artless, and who doesn't possess 'nous', cool realism and political sensitivity. Bright, imaginative and creative, certainly, but less able to be self-aware and to get the message across to senior managers in an acceptable form.

Chapter Summary

Questions about leadership have exercised people's minds since written history began. In the past fifty years or so, some answers to questions such as what leadership is, what makes leaders successful and what situations help or hinder the exercise of leadership have begun to emerge. But we are still a long way from knowing even a part of what there is to know about business leadership. Moreover, organizations are dynamic. Many organizations are becoming more global, faster paced, less hierarchical, more innovative, more responsive and more diverse. But that is only for now. The only certainty is change. So the qualities, behaviours and approaches adopted by leaders in the 1980s or 1990s may be very different from those required in the 2000s. But you can be sure that researchers will be there to observe, categorize, monitor and theorize about the changing phenomenon of leadership.

Discussion Points

1   Is there a difference between leadership and management? If so, what is it?

2   Can you think of charismatic leaders? How are they different from non-charismatic leaders? Are such leaders always a positive and helpful influence for an organization and its members?

3   How far do you agree that much of leadership theory comes down to reinterpreting the discovery of the early Ohio State and Michigan studies, namely that the two key components of leadership and management are people orientation and task orientation?

4   If you were a practising manager, which of the many theories of leadership would you find most instructive and useful?

5   Do leaders really make a difference to organizational effectiveness?

Key Studies

Meindl, J. R. (1992) Reinventing leadership: a radical, social psychological approach. In K. Murnigham (ed.), *Social Psychology in Organizations: Advances in Theory and Research.* Englewood Cliffs, NJ: Prentice Hall.

Yammarino, F. J. and Bass, B. M. (1990) Transformational leadership and multiple levels of analysis. *Human Relations*, 43, 975–95.

Further Reading

Bryman, A. (1992) *Charisma and Leadership in Organizations*. London: Sage.

Grint, K. (1997) *Leadership: Classical, Contemporary and Critical Approaches*. Oxford: Oxford University Press.

Hooper, A. and Potter, J. (1997) *The Business of Leadership: Adding Lasting Value to Your Organization*. Aldershot: Ashgate Press.

Hughes, R. and Ginnett, R. (1998) *Leadership: Enhancing the Lessons of Experience*, 3rd edn. New York: McGraw-Hill.

Leavy, B. and Wilson, D. (1994) *Strategy and Leadership*. London: Routledge.

Shackleton, V. J. (1995) *Business Leadership*. London: Routledge.

Wright, P. (1996) *Managerial Leadership*. London: Routledge.

Yukl, G. (1994) *Leadership in Organization*, 3rd edn. Englewood Cliffs, NJ: Prentice Hall.

CHAPTER THIRTEEN

MOTIVATION IN THE WORKPLACE

Jeremy J. Foster

Contents

This chapter summarizes the main theories of work motivation, which can be divided into two major groups, depending on whether they are addressing the question 'why do people work?' or the question 'what factors change people's willingness or persistence at work?' When you have finished reading this chapter you should be able to:

- summarize the major tenets of the theories;
- group the theories into types;
- evaluate the theories in terms of empirical support and practical relevance;
- discuss the relationhsip between work motivation and job satisfaction.

Case Study 13.1

Sarah is aged 23 and left school when she was 16. She works in the clerical department of a firm which manufactures clothes for a chain of high street department stores. In her department there are six other people on the same grading as Sarah, two people on the grade above and the office manager, Chris.

Each year, all the members of the department have staff appraisals, where they discuss their performance over the previous year and plans are laid for the coming years. At the last appraisal meeting, Sarah was told that her supervisors were concerned about her level of motivation, as at times her performance had been below the level expected of her and she

did not seem to be as interested in the job as they would have liked.

Sarah had said that she had been doing the job for six years, and that she frequently found it 'boring'. She also said that she had been disappointed not to have been promoted to the higher grade in the round of promotions the previous years, and that she felt that the night school qualifications she had earned since leaving school meant she was now overqualified for the job she was doing.

As you read this chapter, try to think what each of the process theories of work motivation suggests could be done to alter Sarah's level of motivation. Some brief comments are given at the end of the chapter.

Introduction

Motivation is a fundamental issue in psychology, since it seeks to answer the question 'Why do people do x?' It is often seen to include three features, which Arnold, Robertson and Cooper (1995) identify as direction, effort and persistence.

The general aims of studying motivation in the workplace can be seen from contrasting perspectives. Traditionally, work in this area (and in organizational psychology generally) has been funded by and intended to fulfil the aims of management. So the goal was to understand what motivates people at work so that their motivation could be increased; it was assumed that in its turn this would lead to them working harder and increase the profitability of the organization. Even if we disregard for the moment the validity of the assumption that 'more motivated workers are harder workers', this view is contentious and seems to rest on outdated attitudes about the nature of work, the workers and the relationship between workforce and management. So modern writers are likely to claim that the aim of studying worker motivation is to promote humanitarian aims of increasing the workforce's feelings of fulfilment, personal satisfaction and achievement.

Before I describe the formal theories of work motivation, it is worth noting that, according to McGregor's (1960) distinction, managers hold one of two alternative ideologies about worker motivation. These are known as Theory X and Theory Y, but you should note that they are not theories, just a set of assumptions. Theory X assumes that workers are inherently lazy, dislike work and have to be forced and controlled by a combination of rewards and penalties. Theory Y assumes that workers have a psychological need to work, they want to achieve and have responsibility. These two approaches or ideologies are also seen in the various theories of work motivation that have been put forward by organizational psychologists.

A number of theories of work motivation have been proposed, and it is helpful to divide them into categories. Muchinsky (1993) suggests that they can be divided into three types: those which presume people are motivated by internal factors (need theories), those which presume people are rational (expectancy theory and goal-setting theory), those which presume people are motivated by external factors (equity theory).

An alternative way of categorizing them is to distinguish between 'content' and 'process' theories. Content theories are concerned mainly with the general question 'Why do people work?' On subset of this group, which includes the theories of Maslow and McClelland, seeks to derive an account of work motivation from a more general account of human motivation. Another subset, which general account of human motivation. Another subset, which includes Jahoda's theory, derives its concepts from a consideration of unemployed people and a third subset bases an account of work motivation on the study of employees.

Process theories concentrate on the question 'What factors affect people's willingness or persistence at work?' Some of them (such as goal-setting theory) emphasize motivation while others (such as equity theory) emphasize job satisfaction. As you read the descriptions of the various theories in this chapter, you might find it helpful to complete the diagram shown in figure 13.1, which is intended to help you to understand this categorisation system. A completed version is given as figure 13.6, so you can compare your responses with mine.

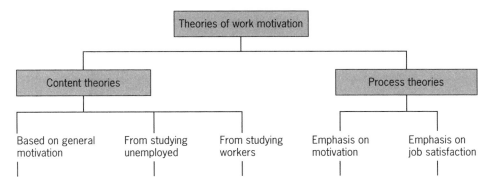

Figure 13.1 Types of theory of work motivation.

Content Theories Linked to Accounts of General Motivation

Maslow

Maslow (1954) put forward the notion of a hierarchy of needs, summarized in figure 13.2. Physiological needs are at the bottom of the hierarchy and self-actualization is at the top. The hierarchy means that higher needs are only attended to when the lower needs have been satisfied.

To a psychologist trained in the traditional scientific methodology, one of the surprising features of organizational psychology is its willingness to accept ideas which are based on a flimsy empirical foundation. The lack of its accept-ability to academic commentators is shown by comments such as these:

> These motivational conceptions, although intuitively appealing, do not easily lend themselves to empirical test. (Vroom, 1964, p. 38)

> Acceptance of the theory is . . . largely an act of faith since very little research has been done to verify it. (Murrell, 1976, p. 71)

> Maslow's theory . . . is far more philosophical than empirical. (Muchinsky, 1993, p. 329)

Such comments indicate dissatisfaction that the theory is not testable in the usual sense of scientific theories. Among the points that the critics make are: it is unclear how the variables can be measured; it is unclear which needs lead to which behaviours or which behaviours are determined by which need; it is unclear how the theory could be used to guide managers on how to increase workers' motivation; it is unclear how to fit some motives which do affect worker behaviour into Maslow's scheme (Argyle, 1989, gives the example of money).

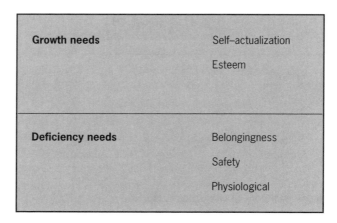

Figure 13.2   Maslow's hierarchy.

Attempts to translate the theory into empirical terms have been made, but the success of this enterprise is very doubtful according to the review of Wahba and Bridwell (1976), who concluded that the theory has received little clear support. Furnham (1997) asserts that the theory has some useful ideas: people have different needs which relate to work behaviour, and organizations as a whole may be classified in terms of the needs they satisfy. One could say that the first of these statements is so obvious that it hardly needs Maslow to say it, and that the second is by no means obvious and probably is not true: roles or jobs might be classified according to the needs they satisfy, not organizations. On a more positive note, Rollinson, Breadfield and Edwards (1998) argue that the popularity of the theory among managers means that it may prompt them to consider subordinates' needs and whether the organization is likely to meet them.

McClelland and need for achievement (nAch)

McClelland (1967) devised a theory based on the list of needs propounded by Murray in the 1930s, such as the need for achievement (known as nAch) which is the need to accomplish something difficult, the need for affiliation (nAff) which means the need to cooperate with other people, and a more recent construct, the need for power (nPow), a need to control the activities of other people.

The theory has been used to consider whether people in different types of occupation have particular patterns of needs: for example, do entrepreneurs have a notable higher nAch? Do successful managers have a special profile, such as being high on nPow and low on nAff?

The continuing popularity of the concept is shown by the development of questionnaires for measuring nAch (Cassidy and Lynn, 1989), and by their use in studies intended to answer questions such as those given above (e.g. Langan-Fox and Roth, 1995). The underlying assumptions are: (a) that people differ in terms of their standing on certain key constructs; and (b) that these key constructs are nAch, nAff etc. It is the second of these assumptions which is the more debatable, since there are many other candidates, such as Protestant work ethic (Furnham, 1997, pp. 59–60, 219–20) and employment commitment (Banks and Henry, 1993). It is worth remembering that such constructs as nAch or the Protestant work ethic may be more relevant to some people than others and may not apply to workers at all levels, of both sexes, in all cultures. I return to this question of individual difference below.

The status of need for achievement theory is questionable. Locke and Henne (1986, p. 13) wrote that 'Achievement theory at this point can only be described as in a state of chaos', since measures of the construct do not correlate with each other and it is unclear how the motive is translated into goals. Rollinson et al. (1998) point out that McClelland's claim that people can be trained to have a higher nAch is inconsistent with the assumption that needs are acquired in early childhood. They also observe that need theories ignore the effects of cultural factors, as they assume a universality which may well not be valid, and – as an example of this cultural limitation – 'convey the impression that work is the most important way in which humans can satisfy their needs' (p. 164), which may be less true in Europe than in the United States, where the theories originated.

Content Theories Derived from Studies of Unemployed Workers

Jahoda

An alternative way of deducing the motivation underlying work is to study those who have lost their work and examine the consequences of being unemployed. There is now a huge literature on the psychological effects of unemployment, but the precursor was the 1931 study by Jahoda of the unemployed in the Austrian village of Marienthal. A description of the research will be found in Fryer (1992), but the important point for theories of work motivation is Jahoda's distinction between latent and manifest needs. She argued that work not only provides the means of earning a living, the manifest need, but also fulfils latent needs such as those for social contact, status in the community, purposefulness and time structure. The loss of the opportunity to fulfil these latent needs is one of the major costs of unemployment for the individual.

There is no doubt that Jahoda's account had a major impact on the study of unemployment and continues to exert great influence. But the negative consequences she found do not always occur: some people find unemployment liberating rather than damaging. However, this does seem to require that the latent needs she identified are fulfilled. This might be achieved, for example, by the individual taking on voluntary work.

Content Theories Derived from Studies of Worker Behaviour

Money

Perhaps the most obvious answer to the question 'Why do people work?' is 'For the money'. This idea has a long history. Within organizational psychology it can be seen as a major assumption underlying Taylor's 'scientific management', described in chapter 1. But the fact that people do unpaid, voluntary work demonstrates that money is not necessarily the reason for working. So the question 'Why work?' needs to be rephrased: 'Why do people work at their paid job?' In this form, the answer 'for the money' may seem more acceptable; but there are good reasons for denying that this is the complete answer. These 'good reasons' come from four lines of evidence. One concerns how people say they would behave if they did not need the money, the so-called lottery question. Harpaz (1989) found that the percentages of respondents who claimed they would continue to work varied for men from 66 per cent in Britain to 95 per cent in Japan. (In most countries the percentages for women were slightly lower than those for men.) The second line of evidence comes from Mayo's work, including the Hawthorne studies and the human relations school which developed from it, which is summarized below. This work can be seen as denying the adequacy of the narrowly financial doctrine of work motivation, arguing that people do not necessarily try to maximize their own financial rewards but have other motives. The third line of evidence comes from the distinction between instrumental and intrinsic orientations to work. The basic point of this distinction is that those with an intrinsic orientation do not see the pay as the main gain they obtain from working. The fourth line of evidence that work is not motivated exclusively by money comes from studies into the nature of job satisfaction, where it has been found that pay is only one component. The concept of job satisfaction is discussed below.

Elton Mayo

Mayo (1993) developed his theory from the outcome of studies of worker behaviour, the famous Hawthorne studies. These began as an investigation to discover the optimal level of illumination for assembling electrical equipment. It was found that almost regardless of the environmental changes introduced the output of the workers increased, and this led to the notion of the 'Hawthorne effect', the idea that the subjects in an investigation respond to the fact that they are being studied.

Subsequent studies of how workers behaved in work groups which were created specially for the purpose were taken to demonstrate that workers' behaviour is influenced by their informal groups: the group will develop norms about the 'proper' amount of work to do, and workers will keep to these norms rather than maximize their own level of income. This in turn suggests that workers place rewards such as social integration above financial ones. This was taken as demonstrating the importance of social needs in motivating workers, which was the essential doctrine of what is known as the human relations movement.

Muchinsky (1993, p. 17) comments that the Hawthorne studies 'opened up new vistas for industrial psychology . . . while not considered "perfect" examples of field research, [they] are regarded as the greatest single episode in the formation of industrial psychology'. To say that the studies are not considered a perfect example of field research is rather understating the situation. Murrell (1976) devoted 12 pages of a 144-page book to the Hawthorne studies, describing them in detail and providing a fine example of an academic in full cry. The tone of his remarks is shown by these quotations: 'a bit of bad experimentation, written so that important facts are obscured and some false conclusions drawn' (p. 56); 'the experimenters' ideas became so completely fossilized that everything else they did seems to have been done with the object of proving that they were right. . . . The consequence was that even when they were staring them in the face, results which contradicted their preconceived ideas were ignored' (pp. 67–8).

Despite such criticisms, it is hard to disagree with Furnham's judgement that 'there have been few subsequent studies, of whatever scientific quality, that have had such an influence' (p. 82). They set the tone of theorizing about work motivation for a generation, and were the foundation for the view that the financial motive is not the sole or even the most important one.

Warr's vitamin model

A further example of deducing an account of motivation from an examination of work behaviour and unemployment is Warr's vitamin model (Warr, 1987). This suggests that a work environment provides nine features which affect mental health, and which are shown in the left-hand column of table 13.1. Each of the features except the need for money is seen as related to a human need, so the model implies that there are eight needs or motives underlying work behaviour.

The reason why it is called the vitamin model is that the nine features are divided into two types, as shown in the central column of table 13.1: AD (standing for additional decrement) and CE (standing for constant effect). The physical body reacts against excessive levels of vitamin A or D, but high intakes of vitamins C or E do not cause negative effects. Similarly, high levels of type AD environmental features, such as 'opportunity for control', produce a negative effect on mental health, whereas high levels of type CE features, such as money, do not. This relationship is illustrated in figure 13.3.

Table 13.1　Warr's vitamin model: the nine environmental features and their matching personal characteristics

Environmental feature	Type	Matching personal characteristic
1　Opportunity for control	AD	High GNS,[a] high ability
2　Opportunity for skill use	AD	High GNS, relevant unused skills
3　Externally generated goals	AD	High GNS high nAch
4　Variety	AD	High GNS
5　Environmental clarity	AD	High GNS, external control beliefs
6　Availability of money	CE	High desire for money
7　Physical security	CE	High desire for physical security
8　Opportunity for interpersonal contact	AD	High sociability
9　Valued social position	CE	High desire for social esteem

[a] Growth need strength.

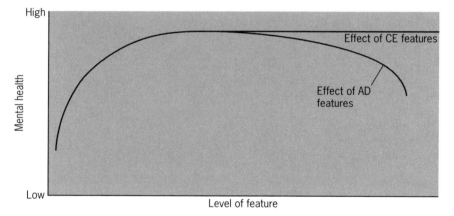

Figure 13.3　Warr's vitamin model: the effect of increasing strength of environmental features on mental health.

Warr suggests that people vary in the extent to which their personal characteristics match the environmental variables, and some of the matching personal characteristics are shown in the right-hand column of table 13.1. For example, people who are highly sociable are well matched with an environment which provides a high opportunity for social contact. According to the model, if someone's personal characteristics do not match the environmental feature, he or she will be more contented when the environmental feature is low. For example, a person who does not have high sociability will be happier in an environment which has low opportunity for interpersonal contact. The personality determinants of well-being are emphasized in later expositions of the model; Warr (1996, p. 235) comments that 'people's feelings about their work are thus a function both of that work itself and also of their own personality'.

The vitamin model provides a system for describing all job environments, and also non-job environments, by seeing how far they possess the nine environmental features. Jobs can be psychologically 'good' or 'bad', and those which are 'bad' can be shifted towards the 'good' end of the dimension by redesigning them: 'the vitamin model can provide a useful basis for determining the goals of intervention at the level of both the job and the organization' (Warr, 1987, p. 298).

Process Theories

The theories mentioned so far have dealt with the question 'Why do people work?' The second group of theories deal with the question 'What factors influence how hard people work?' One obvious answer is to say that people will work harder if they believe that working hard will provide the rewards they want. This is the basis of expectancy of VIE theory.

Expectancy (VIE) theory

It is the use of the three concepts of valence, instrumentality and expectancy that leads to the theory being known as VIE theory. The basic idea of the theory, described by Vroom (1964), is that people are motivated to behave so that they obtain the outcomes which they believe will provide the results they desire. Put in this form, it may seem common sense, but let us first explain the main concepts.

The theory assumes that for an individual any outcome has a valence, an emotional response which can be positive (if the alternative is attractive), negative (if it is unattractive) or zero (if the person is indifferent). Outcomes can be first-level, the direct result of the behaviour such as being paid for doing a task, or second-level, such as gaining promotion because you have consistently done the task well.

Achieving a first-level outcome may make it more likely that a second-level outcome will also be achieved. For example, doing your job and getting paid (achieving the first-level outcome) may make it more likely that you will be promoted (achieve the second-level outcome). But, on the other hand, it may not: it could be that obtaining promotion is not dependent on doing the job, but is determined by other factors, such as the length of time you have worked for the employer, or how well you get on with your boss. The degree to which the person believes that gaining the second-level outcome is the result of achieving the first-level one is referred to as instrumentality. It is a perceived relationship which can vary between +1 and −1.

Expectancy, which he describes as an action–outcome association, is defined by Vroom (1964, p. 17) as 'a momentary belief concerning the likelihood that a particular act will be followed by a particular outcome'. In more recent statements of the theory, expectancy has been defined more specifically as 'the perceived relationship between effort and performance' (Muchinsky, 1993, p. 337). Van Eerde and Thierry (1996) note that this redefinition confounds expectancy with instrumentality.

One of the key aims of the theory is to explain the force which leads someone to act in a particular way. It is suggested that in deciding to behave in a certain way, we look at the expectancies, what we think will be the outcomes of acting in that way, and the valence of each outcome. Each expectancy is multiplied by its valence, so that unattractive outcomes (which have a negative valence) have a negative overall value, while attractive outcomes (which have a positive valence) have a positive overall value. The overall values for all the outcomes are added together, so that the force on the person (F_i) to act is defined as:

$$F_i = f_i\left[\sum(V_j E_{ij})\right]$$

Furnham (1997, p. 272) expresses the major tenet of the theory with commendable brevity: 'it has been shown that the stronger the attractiveness of a certain outcome, and the more people believe that their jobs are instrumental in achieving the outcome, the stronger the person will be motivated to the work'.

How can the theory be tested? One way is to correlate scores on a measure of force with some criterion of effort. There have been difficulties raised, however. There have been arguments about how to measure V, I and E; whether the multiplications in the formulae are necessary, whether one should use between- or within-subjects designs. Although many studies have used between-subjects designs to see whether people with a high VIE score also score higher on a criterion measure, this is not how the theory was originally stated. It was intended to predict how one person acted when presented with alternative behaviours. In their meta-analysis, Van Eerde and Thierry (1996) report that VIE correlates with performance +0.19, with effort +0.29, with intention +0.42 and with preference +0.74. But they observe that 'Vroom's models do not yield higher effect sizes than the components of the models' (p. 581), i.e. the predictions using VIE combined are no better than using valence, instrumentality or expectancy alone. Nevertheless, the theory has been used to explain people's job preferences (e.g. Herriot and Ecob, 1979) and in studying the behaviour of the unemployed (e.g. Feather, 1992).

Muchinsky (1993, p. 339) asserts that expectancy theory 'provides a rich rational basis for understanding motivation in a given job'. He notes that the theory implies that there must be desired outcomes for an employee (although the theory does not consider just what the desired outcomes are), the person must believe that there is some relationship between work performance and attainment of outcomes, and people should see a relationship between how hard they try and how well they perform.

A number of writers have noted that one would expect personality attributes to be a significant factor in expectancy theory. The expectancy that a particular action will be followed by a certain outcome relies on people accepting that their own effort influences their level of performance. One of the popular concepts of recent years is locus of control, defined by Spector (1988, p. 335) as 'a generalized expectancy that rewards, reinforcements or outcomes in life are controlled wither by one's own actions (internality) or by other forces (externality)'. So people with an external orientation will be less likely to be motivated, as they will have lower expectations that their efforts will be instrumental in achieving their outcomes.

Self-efficacy is another feature related to expectancy: the fact that you expect that a certain action will be followed by a desirable outcome dwell not mean much if you also believe that you are unable to perform the action. Bandura (1989, p. 416) observed that 'The predictiveness of expectancy-value theory can be enhanced by including the self-efficacy determinant.'

VIE theory has been commended on its practical applicability. Furnham (1997), for example, suggests that it implies that people should have it made clear to them that their effort will lead to performance, that rewards should be clearly linked to performance, that rewards should have positive valence for employees. (So a company might use a cafeteria-style reward system, in which employees choose between alternative rewards, such as an increase in pay or a longer holiday entitlement.)

Goal-setting theory

This theory was put forward by Locke (1968) and there is a large literature to support its basic tenets, which are:

- difficult goals lead to higher performance than easy goals;
- specific goals lead to higher performance than general ones;
- feedback on performance is necessary if difficult specific goals are to show their benefits.

There are some qualifications to make to the bald statements listed above. First, the goals need to be accepted by the employee; there has been some debate about whether this means that the employees should participate in setting their goals, but the general conclusion is that this is not necessary (Tubbs, 1986). Second, the difficult goals cannot be too difficult: if they are, they will not be accepted (you can almost hear the reaction, 'That's impossible!') and will not be motivating.

Arnold et al. (1995, p. 221) describe goal-setting theory as 'probably the most consistently supported theory in work psychology', and also praise it

for being 'magnificently clear about how managers can enhance the performance of their employees'. Extensive reviews such as those of Tubbs (1986)
and Weldon and Weingart (1993) suggest that the theory has obtained
widespread support when applied to both individuals and groups of employees. The success of the theory is not always so clear-cut when it is applied in
real organizational settings: Yearta, Maitlis and Priner (1995), for example,
found a negative relationship between goal difficulty and performance and
suggest that the theory may not apply when there are multiple goals which are
remote in time.

An interesting application of goal-setting theory in an actual situation is
described in Cooper, Phillips, Sutherland and Makin (1994). They report how
they obtained baseline measures of safe and unsafe behaviours in nine departments of a manufacturing company. Groups of employees in each department
agreed on a safety goal that was difficult but achievable, and measures of goal
commitment were obtained. The departments were observed for 16 weeks,
with both safety behaviour and accident rates being recorded and feedback
provided in the form of charts being posted up within each department. The
results showed that 'levels of safe behaviour improved in most departments,
with the majority attaining the goal some of the time' (p. 229), and that there
was a 21 per cent decrease in the plant's overall accident rate, leading Cooper
et al. to assert that 'the utilization of goal setting and feedback to improve
industrial safety performance in the UK can be very effective' (p. 233).

One of the emphases in goal-setting theory concerns the extent to which
the person accepts the goal, which is part of the internal psychology of the
person. This interest in the effects of internal psychological conditions is also
prominent in the job characteristics model.

Job characteristics model

The job characteristics model (Hackman and Oldham, 1976) goes beyond
merely establishing correlations between attributes of the job or workers and
job satisfaction or job performance, and emphasizes the need to establish the
intervening psychological variables. The model is shown in figure 13.4. You
will see that there are five job characteristics, and these are linked to psychological states. It is the person's standing on these states which influences the
personal and work outcomes, not the job characteristics themselves.

Of the five core job dimensions, skill variety, autonomy and feedback are
self-explanatory. Task identity is 'the degree to which the job requires completion of a "whole" and identifiable piece of work', while task significance is
'the degree to which the job has a substantial impact on the lives or work of
other people' (Hackman and Oldham, 1976, p. 257). (It is not obvious why
impact on one's own life is not included in task significance.)

According to the model, any job has a potential motivating score (MPS),
which is calculated by taking the mean of the job's score on skill variety, task

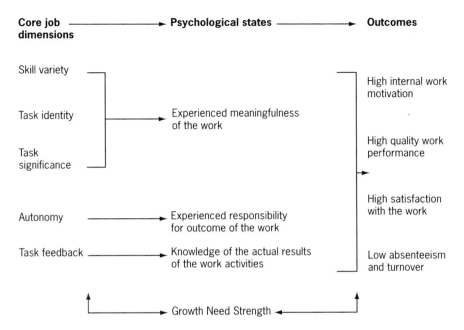

Figure 13.4   The job characteristics model of Hackman and Oldham (1976).

identity and task significance and multiplying that mean by its autonomy and by its feedback scores:

$$\text{MPS} = \frac{(\text{skill variety} + \text{task identity} + \text{task significance})}{3} \times \text{autonomy} \times \text{feedback}$$

Observe that this formula implies that if either autonomy or feedback has a value of zero, then MPS will be zero.

The final component of the model is employee growth need strength (GNS): individuals differ in terms of how far they wish to 'grow', or fulfil higher-order needs. People high on GNS 'will respond more positively to a job high in motivating potential' (Hackman and Oldham, 1976, p. 258). This construct allows the model to explain why some people react negatively to attempts to increase motivation by increasing autonomy, skill variety etc.: if you have low GNS, you do not want more autonomy.

Hackman and Oldham (1976, p. 276) observed that the model deals with aspects of jobs 'that can be altered to create positive motivational incentives for the job incumbent'. One of the main implications of the job characteristics model is that the motivating potential of a job can be increased if its standing on the core job dimensions is increased, and this was interpreted as enriching jobs, so that the worker had more autonomy and responsibility.

Reviewing the model, Locke and Henne (1986) state that the theory shows consistent validity with respect to job satisfaction: perceptions of the five core characteristics do correlate with measures of satisfaction. They note that support for the moderating effect of GNS is not as strong, and that the theory is much less successful in its predictions concerning job performance.

You will have noticed that the job characteristics model is concerned with job performance and job satisfaction. Job satisfaction has been one of the most heavily researched topics in organizational psychology, with interest in its components, its measurement, its causes and its consequences. The definition and measurement of job satisfaction have spawned a vast literature of their own. The two are closely related, since the definition will determine how it is to be measured; if you define it as single entity, the measuring instrument will differ from what is needed if you define job satisfaction in terms of a set of components. Cook, Hepworth, Wall and Warr (1981) surveyed a large number of measures, and Warr (1990a, 1996) devised scales to assess the wider constructs of job-related anxiety–contentment and depression–enthusiasm which are seen as aspects of mental well-being.

The close link between work motivation and job satisfaction arises because it is assumed that a high level of motivation will have both psychological and behaviour consequences. The psychological consequences will include job satisfaction and organizational commitment, and the behavioural effects will be that a 'satisfied' worker will, compared with a 'dissatisfied' colleague, demonstrate desirable work-related behaviour such as higher output, low absenteeism and lower likelihood of leaving the job.

Whether these behavioural effects actually do occur is an empirical question. There have been numerous investigations into the correlates of job satisfaction, particularly the relationship with worker output. Meta-analyses suggest that when the results of many studies are aggregated, the correlation with labour turnover is about −0.40 (Muchinsky and Tuttle, 1979) and with absenteeism assessed as total time lost is about −0.24 (Farrell and Stamm, 1988). But the correlation between job satisfaction and output is disappointingly low: Iaffaldano and Muchinsky (1985) give a figure of +0.17. Remember that correlation does not establish causation: it could be that high job performance produces high job satisfaction rather than the other way round. Nevertheless, the low correlation has prompted researchers to consider what variables might be affecting the link between the two. For example, Petty, McGee and Cavender (1984) reported that the correlation is higher, at +0.31, for people in managerial jobs. You could go on looking for moderating variables, but what is needed is some underlying theory to provide some structure to the search. The job characteristics model did this by suggesting the internal psychological constructs which lie between job characteristics and consequences such as job satisfaction and performance.

One of the most widely known theories of job satisfaction is that associated with Herzberg. It gained its fame partly because it contradicted the common assumption about the relationship between satisfaction and dissatisfaction.

Herzberg's two-factor theory of job satisfaction

The two-factor theory was the outcome of a study on the sources of job satisfaction and job dissatisfaction. The initial study (Herzberg, Mausner and Snyderman, 1959) used what is known as the critical incident technique: accountants and engineers from Pittsburgh were interviewed and asked to describe the circumstances which led them to feel particularly good or particularly bad about their job. Herzberg concluded that those factors leading to satisfaction, which he referred to as motivators, were qualitatively different from those which lead to dissatisfaction, which he called hygiene factors. Motivators included such events as receiving recognition and being given responsibility, while hygiene factors included relations with superiors, working conditions and pay.

The practical implications of the theory may not be immediately apparent but are in fact enormous. The conventional view of job satisfaction and dissatisfaction was that they formed a single dimension, so satisfaction could be promoted by removing dissatisfaction: if a worker was located toward the dissatisfied end of the scale, removing the source of dissatisfaction would move him or her towards the satisfied end. The two-factor theory asserts that this is not what happens. Removing sources of dissatisfaction will make the person non-dissatisfied, but not positively satisfied. To bring about actual satisfaction, the relevant factors (motivators) must be manipulated, and these are not the same type of factors (hygiene factors) that influence dissatisfaction. The practical implication of the theory was that to increase job satisfaction one needs to examine the motivators, and this led to the use of job enrichment, which I describe below.

Herzberg's theory has not fared well when subjected to critical academic evaluation. King (1970) argued that the theory as stated is ambiguous and imprecise, and Murrell (1976, p. 74), observing that it seems to apply (if at all) to white-collar workers, commented 'Since it is on the shop floor that most of the action is, the idea that you can ignore the so-called "hygiene" factors could be quite dangerous.' There have been numerous attempts to test it using different methods and types of respondent, and it has been found that the original results do not reappear when different ways of gathering data are used or different types of employee are studied (King, 1970). Contemporary writers tend to dismiss it.

Met expectations theory

The topic of job dissatisfaction among newly recruited employees is one that has prompted particular interest, since recruitment is an expensive process and the costs are lost if the new employee does not stay very long. One approach has been to consider the expectations that new employees have about the job, and how far these are met.

An implication of expectancy (VIE) theory is that people will work to achieve the outcomes they expect to follow successful performance. One would presume that if these expected outcomes did not follow, the person would be disillusioned and this would affect his or her subsequent behaviour. This is the essential idea underlying the met expectations theory of job satisfaction proposed by Porter and Steers (1973): workers become dissatisfied if their expectations about their job are not met. Reviews of the theory suggest that the correlation between job satisfaction and met expectations is around +0.39 (Wanous, Poland, Premack and Davis, 1992).

It would seem to follow from the met expectations hypothesis that one way of reducing potential dissatisfaction among the workforce is to bring their expectations into line with reality. This implication underlies the use of realistic job previews (RJPs), which have spawned a considerable literature in their own right: McEvoy and Cascio (1985) provide a review in which they compare the effects of RJPs and job enrichment for reducing labour turnover, and conclude that job enrichment is about twice as effective as RJPs.

The notion of met expectations argues that job dissatisfaction depends on processes within the individual: do I feel my expectations are being met? One criticism of this idea is to point out that it ignores the social context of the individual: perhaps our views of our job are influenced by our beliefs about the situation of those around us. This is the basis of equity theory.

Equity theory

The basic idea of equity theory comes from the work of Adams (e.g. 1963), and asserts that people estimate the inputs they put into their job and the outputs they receive and form a ratio between them; they also do this for significant others, so people have two ratios, one for themselves and one for the significant other. They then compare the two, and decide whether their own ratio is greater than, less than or equal to that of the significant other. If their own ratio is more favourable than that of the other, they feel overpaid (and guilty); if the ratio is less favourable, they feel underpaid (and angry); if the ratios are equal, they experience equity and feel satisfied. Feelings of inequity are assumed to be motivating: the person will try to reduce such feelings by bringing the two ratios into balance.

The ratios can be brought into balance by the person changing her own ratio: if she feels overpaid, she might increase her input by working longer hours; if she feels underpaid, she might reduce her input by working less hard or she might increase her output by stealing from the workplace. These are behavioural methods of changing the ratio. An alternative is to alter the judgements that underlie the estimate of the ratio. So the underpaid might decide that their outputs are greater than they had previously thought because, for example, they have flexible hours and they had not put that into the equation when estimating their outputs. They might also change their estimates of the outputs or inputs for the significant other.

You might have noted that in summarizing the theory I have already indicated one of its drawbacks: it is imprecise. Because there are alternative ways of dealing with feelings of inequity, just how a person will act so as to bring the ratios into balance is not specified. Furthermore, you may have asked: 'Who is the significant other? With which other person do we choose to compare our own input/output?' One possible way of reducing perceived inequity would be to change the significant other: if you find that comparing your ratio to that of another person suggests that you are overpaid, why not compare your ratio with that of a different person? The question of who is chosen to be the comparison other has been one of the major areas of investigation for those using the concepts of equity theory (e.g. Law and Wong, 1998).

These issues have been highlighted in recent years in the United Kingdom following the privatization of what had been public utilities, such as water or electricity companies. The directors of these new companies have obtained increases in pay, and become known as 'fat cats'. This should, according to equity theory, make them feel guilty. They could reduce this guilt by arguing that people in similar jobs in other countries, such as the USA, are even higher paid – an example of changing the significant other to reduce feelings of inequity.

Equity theory was initially based on laboratory studies, and when applied to real situations it has been found that the overpaid situation is not as motivating as the underpaid one: people are more willing to accept too much money than too little. Nevertheless, Furnham (1997) suggests that the theory tells managers that employees need to feel that they are fairly dealt with.

Landy's opponent-process model of job satisfaction

There is a temptation to think that introducing some change to the job which increases worker satisfaction will solve the problem, and that any increase in satisfaction will be maintained. But psychology has found in many areas that constant input does not lead to constant output: the process of adaptation means that a constant input will have a diminishing output. This idea was applied to the notion of job satisfaction in the opponent-process theory propounded by Landy (1978). The implications of this are that a continuing constant input will produce a declining level of positive feeling, but its termination will produce a marked negative feeling. Landy applies this notion to goal-setting theory, arguing that 'early in a goal-setting career, individuals will actively resist goal setting . . . as experience with goal setting and goal attainment increases, resistance should decrease . . . and derived pleasure from goal attainment should increase' (p. 543). The general implication of this approach is that one should not expect interventions intended to increase job satisfaction to be immediately popular, and neither should one expect them to retain for ever the popularity level they eventually reach.

Job Enlargement and Enrichment

One approach to increasing work motivation has been to examine the design of jobs so as to increase people's responsibility, autonomy and amount of feedback. Such a programme follows from the theories of Herzberg, Warr, Hackman and Oldham, from expectancy and goal-setting theories. It is worth noting that, despite their different constructs and content, the theories converge when it comes to suggesting what managers should do to increase worker motivation.

Job enlargement is usually thought of as adding other jobs of a similar level to a particular job, whereas job enrichment is adding tasks of a higher level: for example, an assembler may have the job 'enriched' by being asked to inspect the quality of the assembling as well as doing the assembling itself. Attempts to decide whether job enlargement and/or enrichment fulfil the hopes placed in them tend to suffer because it is impossible to run true experiments in real-world situations, so there are many variables fluctuating together; consequently, it is not possible to specify exactly what factors are producing any changes in worker attitude or behaviour that are seen. So it is not surprising that academic reviewers of job enlargement tend to be less enthusiastic than practitioners: Muchinsky (1993, p. 442), for example, asks what can be concluded about the effectiveness of job redesign and gives a rather cautious answer: 'the results vary depending on the criterion . . . most studies report mixed findings . . . it is difficult to generalize findings across diverse situations'. Loher, Noe, Moeller and Fitzgerald (1985), surveying research on the relation between job characteristics and job satisfaction, concluded that there was support for efforts to increase job satisfaction through the use of job enrichment. But they also emphasize that there is no guarantee: 'the results . . . warn that simply enriching jobs will not necessarily hold the same amount of benefit for everyone' (p. 287). Nevertheless, there seems little doubt that job enrichment can be successful, even if the precise causes of the effects are unclear. I have already referred to the meta-analysis of McEvoy and Cascio (1985), which indicated that job enrichment is superior to realistic job previews in reducing labour turnover.

Integrating the Theories

You will have noticed that this chapter has strayed from work motivation to job satisfaction. Various authorities have attempted to integrate the two topics. One example is that of Locke and Latham (1990b), who assert that the motivation to work is best explained by integrating elements of three theories: goal setting, expectancy and social-cognitive (self-efficacy) theory.

They point out that there is a counterintuitive relationship between valence and goal level. You might suppose that people are more satisfied at attaining higher goals, and this is indeed so. But if people are asked to rate their expected satisfaction with each of a number of performance levels, the ratings are lower for people with high goals: valence and goal level are negatively related. Locke and Latham give the example of students' grades. If you have the goal of getting 75 per cent, you will be dissatisfied at a mark of 65 per cent and even more dissatisfied with a mark of 55 per cent. But if your goal was 55 per cent, you will be satisfied at getting that, more pleased if you get 65 per cent and 'over the moon' if you get 75 per cent. This is because higher goals mean higher standards for achieving self-satisfaction: someone with higher goals has to achieve more to feel the satisfaction of a goal achieved. High goals and high self-efficacy lead people to persist longer at tasks than low goals or low self-efficacy.

To account for affective reactions to rewards and punishments, Locke and Latham use goal theory, equity theory, attribution theory and job character-istics theory. Performance that is successful in relation to a given standard is appraised positively and leads to self-satisfaction. They also note that attribu-tion theory suggests that success is likely to be attributed to the self, and failure is likely to be attributed to others. Locke and Latham argue that job satisfac-tion is likely when employees (a) feel successful in relation to goals at work that possesses the five core attributes of job characteristics theory, (b) are rewarded equitably for high performance and (c) receive equitable noncon-tingent rewards (such as basic pay, job security, congenial co-workers).

They note that job satisfaction has no simple relationship with performance; the behaviour that is most strongly associated with job satisfaction is staying/quitting the job, and the attitude that is most strongly associated with job sat-isfaction is organizational commitment. They describe a model known as the 'high performance cycle', shown in figure 13.5, which acknowledges that the effect of satisfaction on performance is indirect. Only if satisfaction leads to commitment and its goals and only if those goals are challenging and accom-panied by high self-efficacy will high performance result.

Individual Differences

The importance of considering individual differences has been acknowledged by the various theories, and many of them emphasize constructs such as growth need strength, self-efficacy and locus of control. But one feature which has received less interest than one might expect is culture. Many writers seem to assume that what has been found in developed Western cultures (especially the USA) is likely to be true for any other culture. This may be true for other

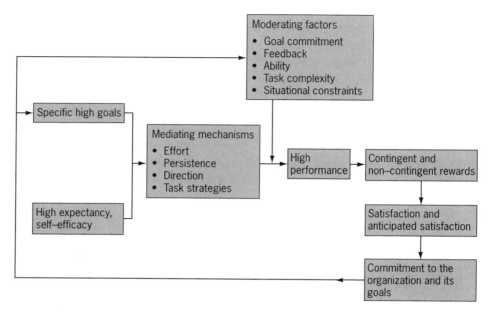

Figure 13.5   The high performance cycle of Locke and Latham (1990).

developed cultures such as those in Western Europe, Australia and Israel. But whether it is also true for Asian or African societies is more questionable.

Bond and Smith (1996) reviewed cross-cultural work in organizational psychology, and a quotation may give the flavour of their discussion: 'achievement motivation, at least in East Asian collectivist cultures, is more socially oriented . . . the Western pattern of compulsive working with attendant health risks appears here to be attenuated by the centrality of family within Chinese culture' (p. 224). An example of the implications of cultural differences is provided by Pearson and Chong (1997), who studied job satisfaction among Malaysian nurses. They concluded that 'the relative importance of a relationship-orientated job design for the job satisfaction of the Malaysian nurses was clearly demonstrated' (p. 370). Pearson and Chong note that their conclusion disagrees with Western literature, which has suggested that the social dimension of job satisfaction is insignificant and they express the importance of cultural differences with some force: 'the designers of training programmes, and job redesign in particular, for Malaysian health care workers would be advised to consider the realities of the local cultural conditions, rather than blindly applying the strategies and techniques that have been formulated in Western developed countries' (p. 370).

Even within a developed Western economy, it is important to consider how far subcultural differences, such as those between white- and blue-collar workers, may limit the applicability of the theories of work motivation. The variable of employment commitment has already been mentioned; it was measured (Banks and Henry, 1993) using items such as 'having almost any job is better than being unemployed', and found to vary according to the career trajectory of the school-leavers studied. Thomas and Wetherell (1974), in a study of male school-leavers, distinguished between what they referred to as an instrumental orientation and a white-collar orientation to work, and found evidence that it is transmitted from generation to generation. One might expect those with very low employment commitment or a strong instrumental orientation to be much less amenable to any attempt to increase their job motivation using the enrichment style approach recommended by contemporary theories. Whether these constructs can all be subsumed under the heading of growth need strength has yet to be established.

General Overview

You have probably felt overloaded with theories of work motivation and are asking whether it matters which theory one uses. Evaluation of the theories can be approached in different ways. The academic route is to look at the empirical support for the theory. Does it offer testable hypotheses? Are the hypotheses supported by the evidence? The practical approach is to ask whether the theory offers suggestions about how it can be used in the real world, whether it advises an employer how to increase worker motivation. Most of the theories are able to offer such advice, and have been praised for so doing.

The way one seeks to alter motivation will depend on the model one adopts. If you are using Herzberg's theory, you will try to increase job satisfaction by considering how the motivators can be manipulated. If you are using goal-setting theory, you will consider the precision, difficulty and personal involvement of a person's goals. A common feature of modern theories is that they see worker motivation as depending on a clear set of goals and a clear reward structure.

Muchinsky quotes Katzell and Thompson (1990) as having identified seven practices that can raise motivation of workers:

- ensure workers' motives and values are appropriate for their jobs;
- make jobs attractive and consistent with workers' motives and values;
- define work goals that are clear, challenging, attractive, attainable;
- provide workers with resources that facilitate their effectiveness;
- create supportive social environments;
- reinforce performance;
- harmonize these elements into a consistent socio-technical system.

Some of these ideas may seem rather self-evident, but there is a notable contrast with the 'common-sense' theory of work motivation which was prevalent a century ago. The contemporary theories emphasize the need for the employer or manager to be more than a source of financial rewards and to understand the needs of the workforce, consider the issue of job design and enhance the well-being of those below him or her.

Sarah's Case

Expectancy theory

The theory suggests that you should identify Sarah's goals, the outcomes with a positive valence, and then make clear how these goals can be obtained: the link between performance and attainment. If attaining the goals requires a certain level of performance, it is important that Sarah feels she can reach that level (self-efficacy).

Goal-setting theory

This theory suggests that it is necessary to identify challenging but specific goals for Sarah, which she accepts, and to provide regular feedback on how far she is meeting them through her performance.

Job characteristics model

This approach suggests that one should identify Sarah's growth need strength, as this will influence the way the situation should be manipulated. To increase her motivation, increase felt meaningfulness, responsibility and knowledge of results. This might involve enriching the job, giving more autonomy and more feedback.

Herzberg's theory

To increase motivation, examine the motivators. Arrange the situation so that Sarah is rewarded for good performance by receiving recognition and greater autonomy.

Met expectations

The key notion here is that Sarah should have realistic expectations about the rewards she can attain. This might involve probing her current expectations, and discussing with her whether they are realistic. If they are not, they need to be altered. Once realistic expectations are identified, the situation needs to be set up so that they can be met.

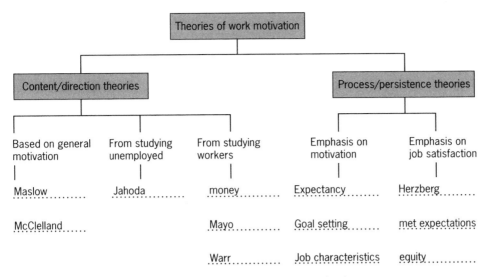

Figure 13.6 One way of categorizing theories of work motivation.

Equity theory

This emphasizes the need to ensure that Sarah feels fairly dealt with relative to her colleagues. You might look at why others were promoted and she was not, whether her night school qualifications are being recognized. (These represent an increase in her 'inputs'; but have they been followed by an increase in her 'outputs'? If not, her ratio of inputs to outputs has altered while she might feel that the ratios of her colleagues have not.)

Do not forget the main lesson from Landy's model: you must not expect that any effect brought about by any changes to the situation will be permanent. The adaptation process means that it is necessary to monitor the situation regularly and expect the positive consequences of any change to tail off over time.

As a further point, suppose that Sarah's company is in Malaysia: how does this effect the ways you might try to change Sarah's motivation?

Chapter Summary

Theories of work motivation can be divided into 'content' and 'process' theories. 'Content' theories based on accounts of general motivation (Maslow, McClelland) are not well regarded, because they do not yield readily testable predictions.

Continued

Four lines of evidence were mentioned to support the view that the need for money is not an adequate account of work motivation. Jahoda made the distinction between latent and manifest needs, while Mayo emphasized social needs. Warr's vitamin model has a wider scope than most theories since it also applies to non-job environments. 'Process' theories emphasize either motivation or job satisfaction. Expectancy theory proposes that behaviour depends on three constructs (V, I, E), but seems better at predicting preferences rather than behaviour. Goal-setting theory, which suggests that people work better when they have difficult, specific and accepted goals, is well regarded. The job characteristics model indicates the psychological dimensions which determine motivation and incorporates the notion of growth need strength. Among the theories emphasizing job satisfaction, Herzberg's two-factor theory of job satisfaction distinguished hygiene factors from motivators but has been heavily criticized, while met expectations theory led to the notion of realistic job previews. Equity theory suggests that judgements of our job satisfaction depend on a social comparison process. Landy's opponent-process theory points out that if the job environment is stable, job satisfaction will not be. One example of an attempt to integrate a number of theories is Locke and Latham's high performance cycle. The theories have been developed in Western developed economies, and may need to be modified if they are to be applied in other cultures.

Discussion Points

1 Which of the theories is best suited to including cultural differences in work motivation?

2 Taking any two of the theories, consider whether they are relevant to people who are not working, such as retired people. Should they be relevant to non-workers?

3 What are the main criteria one should use in judging the theories, and what is the most important single criterion?

4 Would the theories be different if they had been constructed by the workforce rather than for management?

5 Do the theories help us to understand the work/home interface, and people's needs to balance the demands of work and home?

C H A P T E R
F O U R T E E N

TEAMS: THE CHALLENGES
OF COOPERATIVE WORK

Kerrie L. Unsworth and
Michael A. West

Contents

Chapter Outline

Teamworking is seen by many organizations as an effective strategy for organizing work. Eighty-two per cent of companies with 100 employees or more reported that they used teams (Gordon, 1992). Of the top flight Fortune 1000 companies, 28 per cent used self-managing teams in 1987; this figure rose to 68 per cent in 1993. What makes teamworking effective? How can people work most successfully in teams? In this chapter we examine research evidence which suggests ways to maximize team effectiveness.

To illustrate the issues surrounding teamworking, we use primary health care teams as an example. Primary health care teams usually consist of one or more family doctors or general practitioners (GPs), nurses, health visitors (such as midwives or psychotherapists) and receptionists. Primary health care teams are the first point of call for many of us when we feel sick or need assistance in the prevention of illness.

What Are Teams and Why Are They Important?

What is a 'team'? Definitions of a 'team' generally suggest a number of conditions which must be satisfied before a group of people can be called a team. First, members of the group have *shared goals* in relation to their work. They *interact with each other* in order to achieve those shared objectives. Team members also have *well defined and interdependent roles*, and they have an *organizational identity as a team*, with a defined organizational function. Take the example of a primary health care team. They have shared objectives, in that all members are interested in maintaining and improving health in the local population (West and Slater, 1996). They interact in order to achieve this goal, such that doctors rely on nurses to perform health check-ups, and everyone relies on the receptionists to make the process of patient appointments manageable. They have well defined roles based on skills, knowledge and background, such as GPs (e.g. diagnosis and treatment), health visitors (e.g. children's developmental assessments), receptionists (e.g. responding to calls from patients and booking appointments) and practice nurses (e.g. minor dressings and routine treatments). Finally, they have a concept of themselves, more or less, as a whole unit: a primary health care team.

So why do people work in teams? In general, teams can achieve an aim or a goal that could not be accomplished easily by an individual working alone. Midwives and health visitors have specialist skills which general practitioners do not. Indeed, in most organizations, a mix of skills is required to provide complex services or produce sophisticated products. Mohrman, Cohen and Mohrman (1995) offer these reasons for implementing team-based working in organizations:

- teams enable organizations to speedily develop and deliver products and services cost effectively, while retaining high quality;
- teams enable organizations to learn (and retain learning) more effectively;
- time is saved if activities, formally performed sequentially by individuals, can be performed concurrently by people working in teams;
- innovation is promoted because of cross-fertilization of ideas;
- teams can integrate and link information in ways that an individual cannot.

Moreover, teamworking can help to improve productivity. Macy and Izumi (1993) conducted a meta-analysis of 131 field studies of organizational change and found that team development interventions and the creation of autonomous teams (that is, teams which have substantial responsibility for their own work) had a large influence upon financial measures of organizational performance. Applebaum and Batt (1994) reviewed 12 large-scale surveys and 185 case studies of managerial practices and concluded that team-based working led to improvements in organizational performance on measures of both efficiency and quality. However, there are also difficulties associated with working in teams. Steiner (1972) argued that, for the most part, actual team productivity is less than its potential productivity because of 'process losses'. These process losses can be grouped into two categories: coordination problems and motivational problems (Stroebe and Frey, 1982).

Coordination problems are those encountered owing to the problems of arranging and integrating other people. Obviously, the larger the team, the more problems there will be with coordination. Arranging times for meetings, coordinating tasks, integrating and passing on information are all activities which have the potential to limit the effectiveness of the team.

On the other hand, motivational process losses occur when individuals use less effort in performing a task in a group than when performing the same task by themselves. For example, Latané, Williams and Harkins (1979) measured the sound of people's clapping and found that they clapped louder when they were measured individually than when they clapped in a group. They named this phenomenon 'social loafing'. It occurs because people appear to reduce their efforts unconsciously when they are in a context where their efforts are masked by the collective effort of others. Although many researchers have found social loafing in laboratory groups, Erez and Somech (1996) found less of an effect when examining social loafing effects in real work teams. They compared teams in kibbutzim (where the group is more valued than the individual) and urban settings (where the individual is more valued than the group), as well as comparing different goal-setting approaches, communication and rewards. Erez and Somech found that the social loafing effect only occurred with the urban respondents who were given a 'do-your-best' goal for the team task. Therefore, despite the potential process loss, it appears that

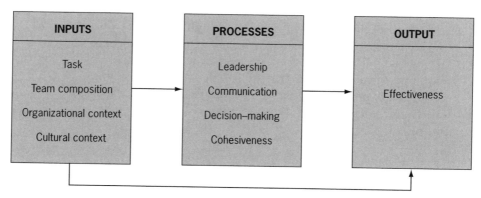

Figure 14.1   The input–process–output model.

social loafing can be diminished by the use of specific goals, intragroup communication and incentives for teamworking.

A useful framework for examining teams is the input–process–output model. Figure 14.1 illustrates the model. In essence, it suggests that inputs (such as team composition and task) affect the effectiveness of the team both directly and indirectly via team processes (such as cohesion and leadership). We discuss these inputs and processes in turn.

First, what exactly is team effectiveness? There is no easy answer to this question. Following Guzzo and Dickson (1996, p. 309), however, we define team effectiveness in broad terms. Thus, effectiveness is indicated by: (a) team produced outputs (e.g. number of patients treated, reduction in waiting time, reduction in patient complaints); (b) the consequences a team has for its members; or (c) the enhancement of a team's capability to perform effectively in the future.

Inputs into the Team

The inputs into the team include the task the team must perform, the team members and the organizational and national/cultural context within which the team performs. A team works towards specific outcomes, e.g. a primary health care team has the task of maintaining and improving a community's health. Teams also consist of diverse individuals, and team composition will clearly influence team effectiveness. The team works for and within an organization, and so will be affected by the interaction with the surrounding organizational context. Finally, the team exists within a wider society, which will affect the team's fundamental beliefs and value systems, i.e. the cultural context. We consider each of these factors in turn.

Input 1: the task

Team performance depends upon the task which has to be performed; in fact, much of the variance in performance can be explained by the task (Kent and McGrath, 1969), be it winning a football match, making a television programme, placing people with disabilities in employment, managing the development of a new product or providing health and care for a local community.

How do tasks affect team performance? Kent and McGrath (1969) found that differences in the cognitions required for different tasks led to different outcomes. For example, their production tasks (e.g. describe a house in the country) led to teams performing high on originality but low on issue involvement, while the discussion tasks (e.g. should abortion be legalized) led to high issue involvement but very low originality. When teams performed the problem-solving task (e.g. how can you safely cross a motorway at night), they were most likely to perform highly on action orientation. Therefore, the task that the team completed had an effect on the team's performance on the various indicators.

However, there are ways to classify tasks other than by their cognitive requirements. Probably the most widely cited task classification system is that developed by Hackman and colleagues (Hackman, 1990; Hackman and Lawler, 1971; Hackman and Oldham, 1975): the job characteristics scale. This system identifies five characteristics of motivating tasks and argues that team effectiveness will be increased when these characteristics are strong (all other things being equal). They include:

- *Autonomy*: the amount of responsibility the team has over work and workload.
- *Task variety*: the extent of variety present in the tasks assigned to the team.
- *Task significance*: the degree to which the task is important to the team, the organization and wider society.
- *Task identity*: the degree to which the task represents a clear and whole piece of work.
- *Task feedback*: the amount of feedback available from completing the task itself.

Research suggests that this model successfully predicts team effectiveness in, for example, administrative support roles (Campion, Medsker and Higgs, 1993), professional jobs (Campion, Papper and Medsker, 1996) and technical, customer service, clerical and management teams (Cohen, Ledford and Spreitzer, 1994).

Using Hackman's model, how would a primary health care team classify the task of improving health and preventing illness? Their autonomy is high: they largely decide among themselves how to do their work. Task variety is relatively high, as many different patients present a range of problems and challenges to the team. Task significance is, of course, very high: the health of a community literally affects that community's survival. Task identity is high in certain cases where an individual's illness is treated solely within the health centre, but can be low when patients must be referred to specialists. More-over, task feedback is extremely low. Thus, a primary health care team has relatively highly motivating tasks, yet members are hampered in their overall effectiveness by low task identity and low task feedback.

Input 2: team composition

The mix of people with different occupations in a team clearly affects the team's performance: if a primary health care team had only GPs, without any nurses, health visitors or receptionists, it would not be very effective. Similarly, a team can have a mix of personalities, backgrounds and characteristics. But what is the ideal mix?

Team diversity, whether in relation to education, professional background, ethnicity or gender, offers both opportunities and challenges in the quest for effectiveness. However, the impact of this diversity, whether it be positive or negative, is dependent upon the self-categorization of team members. Self-categorization occurs because people habitually classify things, attitudes and people into groups for ease of understanding and efficient cognition. If people consider themselves as members of a particular group (whether it be based on gender, ethnicity, work role etc.), that group is their *ingroup*. Those who do not belong in that ingroup are termed *outgroup* members. Social identity theory (Tajfel, 1978; Tajfel and Turner, 1979; Hogg and Abrams, 1988) pro-poses that ingroup members evaluate their ingroup on dimensions that not only differentiate them maximally from the outgroup, but also show the ingroup in a more positive fashion – hence discrimination occurs.

What are the implications for teams? Consider the case when the team itself is the most salient categorizing characteristic: the whole team becomes the ingroup and there will be no outgroup discrimination within the team. For example, if a female nurse identifies with the health care team as a whole, she will see every other team member as a part of her 'ingroup', regardless of sex or professional background. Because there are no outgroups within the team, the team's diversity will not be as salient and may not influence its effective-ness. If, on the other hand, she identifies only with the other women within the team, then gender diversity will produce an ingroup/outgroup differenti-ation based upon gender, and thus a more pronounced influence of diversity on the effectiveness of the team.

So, assuming that diversity is a salient issue within the team, does it enhance or detract from team effectiveness? This depends upon the type of diversity under question. Diversity of task-relevant skills and knowledge is good: het-erogeneity of task-related characteristics implies that each team member will have relevant and distinct skills that he or she can contribute to the accomplishment of the task at hand. Much research supports this proposition. For example, Wiersema and Bantel (1992) examined the diversity of top management teams of 100 of the largest manufacturing companies in the USA. They found that diversity of educational specializations among the top management team was related to a more adaptive organization and more effective strategic change. Similarly, Bantel (1993) reported that the management teams of banks which were heterogeneous with respect to education and functional background developed clearer corporate strategies. These findings suggest that task-related diversity can lead to greater team effectiveness.

However, teams which are diverse in task-related attributes are often diverse in relation to attributes inherent in the individual, such as age, gender and ethnicity. These relations-oriented characteristics can cause differentiation between ingroups and outgroups, and thus trigger stereotypes and prejudices (Tajfel, 1978; Tajfel and Turner, 1979; Hogg and Abrams, 1988), which can inhibit team effectiveness.

Various studies have shown that turnover rates are higher in teams that are heterogeneous with respect to age (e.g. Wagner, Pfeffer and O'Reilly, 1984; Jackson, Brett, Sessa, Cooper, Julin and Peyronnin, 1991). Jackson et al. (1991) also suggest that age diversity can have its greatest effects when the differences between the ages reflect differences in values, attitudes and perspectives. For example, both risk-taking propensity and problem-solving processes are related to age; if age heterogeneity is present within the team, conflict may arise over the degree of risk that should be taken for a particular problem.

What of gender and ethnic diversity? We noted above that social identity theory implies that if team members perceive each other as outgroup members, there may be negative repercussions due to discrimination and prejudice. But is there any evidence to support this claim? One experimental study examined the effects of ethnic diversity over time and showed that effects diminish as group members gain experience with each other (Watson, Kumar and Michaelsen, 1993). These researchers grouped students into either culturally homogeneous work groups (i.e. all members of the same nationality and ethnic background), or culturally heterogeneous work groups. They then observed, rated and evaluated the groups over a 17-week period. Their results showed that group interaction and performance was more effective in the homogeneous than the heterogeneous teams until the last point of measurement, where homogeneous and heterogeneous teams were rated equally. Thus it appears as though team members' identities changed – from an ethnic ingroup to a team ingroup.

Researchers examining gender diversity, however, have not produced such clear-cut results. Some studies have shown that mixed-sex teams perform better than same-sex teams (e.g. Hoffman, 1959; Hoffman and Maier, 1961). However, other studies have shown quite the opposite (e.g. Kent and McGrath, 1969; Clement and Schiereck, 1973; Mabry, 1985). To solve the puzzle, many researchers have concentrated upon gender and ethnicity effects on communication within the team.

Communication requires common understandings, meanings and language conventions. However, people from different backgrounds, by they gender or ethnic backgrounds, will have differing linguistic traditions and norms. Therefore, it is especially easy for misunderstandings and misperceptions to occur (Brick, 1991). Additionally, women's contributions to team discussions may be ignored, dismissed or seen as offensive due to a violation of sex-role stereotypes (Unsworth, 1994); while the contribution of team members of ethnic minorities may be downgraded because of their accents (Gallois and Callan, 1981; Callan, Gallois and Forbes, 1983; Giles and Street, 1985).

Thus, we find that diversity is a double-edged sword: it is needed for innovation and creative solutions, yet it can cause conflict, turnover and an imbalance in team contributions.

Input 3: organizational context

The organization within which a team functions influences team effectiveness in a variety of powerful ways. Researchers, such as Hackman (1990) and Tannenbaum, Beard and Salas (1992), have proposed many contextual factors that may impact upon the team's effectiveness. We concentrate on the following:

- how people are rewarded in the team and organization;
- the technical assistance available to support the team in its work;
- whether the organizational climate is supportive both of people and of teamworking;
- the extent of competition and political intrigue within the organization;
- the level of environmental uncertainty (in relation to the task, customers, suppliers, market share etc.).

Motivational theories (e.g. Vroom, 1964), have long emphasized the importance of rewards for improving the performance of individuals. Behaviour theorists describe how rewards strengthen behaviour, especially when the reward is explicitly contingent upon that behaviour. Desired rewards increase a team's performance by reinforcing high performance behaviour and good teamwork. However, team performance is most effective when rewards are administered to the team as a whole and not to individuals, and when they provide incentives for collaborative rather than individualized work.

The climate of the organization – how it is perceived and experienced by those who work within it – will also influence the effectiveness of teams (Allen, 1996). Organizational climate is usually defined as a set of perceptions that reflect how the employee views and appraises the work environment and organizational attributes (e.g. James and Jones, 1974; James, Joyce and Slocum, 1988). Where the climate is characterized by high control, low autonomy for employees, lack of concern for employee welfare and limited commitment to training, it is unlikely teamworking will thrive (Markiewicz and West, 1997). The extra commitment and effort demanded in team-based organizations requires organizational commitment to the skill development, well-being and support of employees (Mohrman et al., 1995).

Similarly, competition and intrigue will undermine team-based working. Teamwork depends on shared objectives, participative safety, constructive controversy and support (West, 1990; West and Anderson, 1996), which cannot exist in a competitive and untrusting environment. In a comprehensive study of team-based organizations involving both questionnaire and case study methods, Mohrman et al. (1995) have demonstrated that inter-team competition is a major threat for team-based working. Teams which compete may develop greater commitment to the team's success than to the organization's success. Thus, the primary health care team may focus on increasing the financial benefits to the team at the expense of the wider National Health Service. Teams competing against, rather than supporting, each other may withhold vital information or fail to offer valuable support in the process of trying to achieve team goals, without reference to wider goals of the organization. Thus, primary health care teams may fail to pass on information about former patients to other teams, focusing their efforts on their own team's immediate demands.

When people work in uncertain environments, teamworking can enhance their performance. There is also evidence that performance benefits of teamworking which accrue in relatively uncertain environments are greater than those which are gained in relatively predictable environments. In an ingenious field study, Cordery, Mueller and Smith (1991) examined the creation of teams in two water processing settings in Australia. In one setting, the environment was such that the level of natural phosphates and pollutants was unpredictable and difficult to manage (uncertain environment); in the other these factors were relatively constant. The introduction of teamworking led to significant improvements in performance – but only in the uncertain environment.

Overall, evidence is mounting that the organizational context within which teams operate is a powerful determinant of team effectiveness (Hackman, 1990; Mohrman et al., 1995; Guzzo, 1996). Yet consultants and practitioners often remain fixed on intra-team processes, at the expense of contextual factors, in their efforts to improve team effectiveness. Another important influence that is often ignored is the cultural context within which the team is located.

Input 4: cultural context

Interest in the cultural context of teams and organizations is manifested most clearly in Geert Hofstede's work in the late 1960s and early 1970s. He surveyed over 117,000 IBM employees in 40 countries. From these data, he was able to classify the countries along four dimensions: individualism–collectivism, power distance, uncertainty avoidance and masculinity–femininity (Hofstede,

1980). Individualism–collectivism is the degree to which people define themselves as individuals or as group members. Power distance is the degree of formality with superiors, e.g. employees in low power distance countries may call their boss by his or her first name, whereas employees in high power distance countries may use a title. Uncertainty avoidance is the degree of ambiguity about the future that can be tolerated. Finally, the masculinity–femininity dimension is concerned with whether achievements (masculine) or interpersonal relationships (feminine) are valued in the workplace. Hofstede showed that, for example, the UK is a relatively low power distant, low uncertainty avoidant, highly individualistic, masculine culture. Spain, in contrast, exhibits a culture of high power distance and uncertainty avoidance and a more collectivist, feminine culture; the Netherlands has a culture with a more masculine perspective, low power distance, high uncertainty avoidance and high individualism.

Such differences in value systems will influence team processes and performance. Indeed, the very definition of a 'team' may change across cultures. In cultures such as the UK, the USA and Australia, which score highly on individualism (i.e. they emphasize individuals in the workplace), teams are seen more as a set of distinctive persons, each having a unique contribution to a specific part of the task. However, in more collectivist cultures, such as Hong Kong and India, teams are viewed as having shared responsibility for all aspects of the task. Consequently, teamworking is likely to be much easier to implement in collectivistic cultures (Smith and Noakes, 1996).

Other effects of the cultural context can be related to team processes. In the West, researchers have discounted trait theories of leadership, in favour of more situational-based theories. However, consistently effective leadership characteristics have been identified in other cultures (e.g. Misumi, 1985; Bond and Hwang, 1986). The social loafing effect identified in Western societies is apparently non-existent and sometimes reversed in China and Israel (Earley, 1987, 1993). Similarly, current Western thinking is that group participation is useful in enhancing performance (e.g. Cummings and Worley, 1993). However, cultures that emphasize formal, distant relationships with superiors have reported negative effects of participation (Marrow, 1964).

Finally, the implications of cultural context spread far wider than is immediately implied by Hofstede's dimensions. For example, attitudes towards time can have a substantial impact upon teamworking. Smith and Noakes (1996) describe how latecomers to a team meeting were perceived negatively in the USA, but positively in Brazil.

Processes

In the previous section, we examined how teams are formed and the context in which they operate. Now, we examine the way in which teams work. In order to accomplish a task, teams must be led, communicate, make decisions and work together cohesively. They will also generate a team climate which denotes the general atmosphere that the team works in. It is these processes that we concentrate upon here.

Process 1: leadership

What is the influence of leadership in teams? Eden (1990) found that Israeli defence force platoons which trained under leaders with high expectations of them performed better on physical and cognitive tests. George and Betten-hausen (1990) studied groups of sales associates reporting to a store manager and found that the better the leader's moods, the fewer employees quit. Obvi-ously, the leader has an important impact upon the team. Currently, the most influential approach to team leadership suggests two types of leaders: transac-tional and transformational (Bass, 1990a).

Transactional leaders focus on transactions, exchanges and contingent rewards and punishments to change team members' behaviours. Transactional leadership styles focus more upon task-oriented behaviours, and interventions to reward required behaviour and draw attention to, or even punish, gaps in perfomance. Transactional leadership has the following components:

1   Contingent reward and punishment.
2   Active management by exception – following team members' performance and taking action when mistakes occur.
3   Passive management by exception – waiting until mistakes become serious problems before taking action.

Transformational leadership involves influencing team members through charisma and visioning. These leadership styles encourage team members to think not only of their individual performance and completing their task in order to accomplish an individual objective (as with goal-setting and reward systems used by transactional leaders), but also of completing the task in order to help the team as a whole. Transformational leaders inspire their team; team members work effectively because of the vision and influence of the leader. There are four related, but distinct, components within transformational lead-ership: charisma, inspirational motivation, intellectual stimulation and individ-ualized consideration. Charismatic characteristics include displaying conviction and trust and emphasizing commitment, purpose and loyalty. Transforma-tional leaders motivate by visioning an appealing future, challenging standards, encouraging their team and promoting enthusiasm. The third component is intellectual stimulation: questioning assumptions and beliefs, stimulating new perspectives and encouraging the expression of ideas. Finally, individualized consideration means that transformational leaders deal with team members at an individual level, by developing, coaching, listening and teaching each person.

Autonomous work groups (sometimes called self-managed teams) are teams where there is no formal leader; they are increasingly popular in today's organizations. In these teams, leaders are emergent rather than selected – leadership is often highly dependent upon the task or challenge facing the team at any particular moment. Such self-managed teams have been effective in contexts such as nursing (Weisman, Gordon and Cassard, 1993), mineral processing plants (Cordery et al., 1991) and other manufacturing and service industries (Macy and Izumi, 1993; Cordery, 1996; Guzzo, 1996). Cordery (1996) outlines five reasons for improved team performance using self-managed teams.

1   Autonomous work teams make decisions more rapidly in response to changing and uncertain environments.
2   Decisions which are made in trusting and open climates, such as those found in autonomous work teams, are more likely to be creative and innovative.
3   Being a part of an autonomous work group creates opportunities for new learning, which aids performance, both because employees are able to see 'the big picture' owing to greater responsibility, and because their skills are more fully utilized.
4   Self-managed teams increase the self-efficacy of team members. Williams and Lillibridge (1992) showed that people who felt they had control over their environments (i.e. similar to those in autonomous working groups) perceived themselves to be more competent at their jobs.
5   Finally, the job characteristics of those in self-managed teams, including autonomy, feedback, task significance, task identity and skill variety (Hackman and Lawler, 1971; Hackman and Oldham, 1975), are related to job satisfaction, intrinsic motivation, lower absenteeism and better work performance.

The influences of leadership processes, be they vested in one person or distributed throughout teams, are therefore manifold and potent.

Process 2: communication

Communication is the glue that holds the team together. Without communicating a team cannot survive. But what factors of communication affect team effectiveness? We will concentrate on two aspects: the need for a facilitator in group situations; and the impact of information technology on team communication.

When talking to another person, we have a natural reliance upon eye contact and body language when talking to others in order to signal various cues, such as *It's your turn to talk now*, and *I agree (or disagree) with what you are saying*. In a group situation, these cues are more difficult to interpret correctly because of the number of people participating in interactions.

It is often necessary, therefore, for teams to have a facilitator directing the discussions at meetings. Carletta, Fraser, Krauss and Garrod (1996) compared team meetings in manufacturing companies which were facilitated by the team leader or by a junior team member, or shared among the team. They found that when a team leader facilitated a meeting he or she overcame the difficulties of group discussion; however, it was accomplished only by exercising strong control. However, when the facilitation was shared among the team, or performed by a junior member, meetings were more participative. Discussion was also more active, while still maintaining order and consensus.

In this age of increasing technology, computer-mediated communication is becoming more and more prevalent. But what is the influence of computer-mediated technology on communication in teams at work? This technology includes such things as voice messaging and teleconferencing. Rice and Shook (1990) examined the use of voice mail (a computer-assisted telephone system which allows users to store and forward spoken messages) in organizations. The results were positive: voice messaging overcame some communication restraints, such as the requirement to write message slips to others, as well as the constraint of both employees needing to be available at the same time. Rice and Shook conclude that voice mail is valuable for coordinated, collaborative tasks (such as teamworking) and has considerable potential. One communication technology which does not realise its full potential, however, is teleconferencing. Teleconferencing (or the use of telephone and/or video systems to create a meeting between people who are physically separated) intuitively appears a very valuable technology. It allows teams to work across large physical distances yet communicate as a group. However, Egido (1990) concluded that although expectations for its success were high, teleconferencing does not adequately substitute for face-to-face meetings.

Process 3: decision-making

Team decision-making includes four elements: describing the problem; identifying possible solutions; evaluating and choosing the best solution; and implementing the solution. We discuss each of these steps below.

Problem definition must necessarily begin with problem recognition. Scanning the environment increases the chances of discovering a problem before it becomes unmanageable (Cowan, 1986). However, in some teams, problems are regarded as threats and identification of problems by team members is discouraged (Miceli and Near, 1985). Nevertheless, groups that do not engage in extensive scanning and discussion of problems may prevent appropriate planning and action.

A team that is 'problem-minded' – that is, one that focuses upon the problem rather than just the solutions – will be more effective (Maier and Solem, 1962; Maier, 1970). Maier and colleagues also found that defining the problem through breakdown and analysis of its components improved team decision-making. Similarly, problems which are defined from a number of different perspectives are likely to produce a wider variety of solutions.

Producing this variety of solutions in the second stage of decision-making is thought to increase the chances of obtaining a high-quality, innovative decision. Brainstorming is one technique used to generate many solutions. Osborn (1963) described brainstorming as a process with four basic principles: (a) criticisms of others' suggestions is prohibited; (b) free thinking and wild, obscure solutions are welcomed; (c) quantity not quality of solutions is the primary aim; and (d) combination or modification of the ideas will be required. A common experience of brainstorming is that of 'piggy-backing', where voicing an idea may lead others to have related, but complementary, suggestions. However, although brainstorming is recognized as useful for generating ideas, physical and psychological barriers may impede the process. For example, production blocking may occur, whereby team members are unable to contribute ideas because another team member is talking. Perhaps the best method of obtaining solutions is a modified version of brainstorming: team members individually record their solutions before sharing them all with other group members (see Diehl and Stroebe, 1987).

Evaluation of solutions must be based upon task-related criteria. For example, Janis (1982, 1989) identified the dangers of non-evaluation in a phenomenon called 'groupthink'. This occurs when team members are more interested in maintaining harmony within the group than in reaching a high-quality decision. A famous example of groupthink is the 'Bay of Pigs' invasion in 1961. A team of expert advisors, together with US President John Kennedy, decided to support an invasion of Cuba using a small group of ill-trained exiles and the US Air Force. The expert group were highly cohesive, isolated from alternative sources of information and led by a man who clearly favoured attack. Within days the invasion failed and Kennedy and his team subsequently acknowledged the incorrectness of their decision. They had evaluated and chosen a decision which was not based upon information or reality; it was driven by consensus-seeking.

Implementing the chosen decision and successfully maintaining it depends upon participation levels within the team. Employees who participate in decision-making have greater satisfaction with, commitment to and ownership of decisions than those who do not (Coch and French, 1948; Whyte, 1955). Thus, as Landy and Trumbo (1976) suggest, participators in the decision-making process will be less likely to allow the implementation to fail.

Finally, another influence on team decision-making is a minority within the team disagreeing with the other team members. Such minority dissent (Moscovici, Mugny and Avermaet, 1982; Nemeth, 1986; Nemeth and Owens, 1996) can bring about enduring change in attitudes through sustained task-related conflict. A numerical or power minority (such as two doctors in a team of eight) can influence decision-making, as a result of the cognitive or social conflict generated by the minority's consistent and coherent disagreement with the dominant view. Because of this conflict, other team members examine team problems and issues more thoroughly, and think more creatively and widely around the topic. Therefore, if the two doctors argue that greater nurse involvement in diagnosis and treatment would make the team more effective, their persistent and coherent arguments are likely to bring about an enduring change (not always or necessarily in the direction of the doctors' arguments) in the other team members' views (Nemeth and Owens, 1996). Thus, minority dissent and conflict arising from that dissent adds to the effectiveness of decision making.

Process 4: cohesiveness

Cohesiveness refers to the degree of attraction and liking among team members and their liking for the team as a whole. Cohesiveness can influence team effectiveness by increasing team members' helping behaviours, as well as increasing motivation (see Isen and Baron, 1991). There is some evidence suggesting that members of socially integrated groups experience higher morale and satisfaction (Shaw, 1981), and Shaw and Shaw (1962) found that highly cohesive groups devoted more time to planning and problem-solving than teams low in cohesion. Similarly, Ouchi (1980) found that highly cohesive teams had lower communication and coordination costs and could thus apply greater attention to problems under time pressure. Mullen and Copper (1994) found that the relationship from team performance to cohesion was stronger than that from cohesion to team performance. This finding suggests that it is effective performance which increases team cohesion (i.e. when the team does well, members like each other more), more than cohesion affecting performance.

Process 5: team climate

Team climate, similar to organisational climate, is the atmosphere within the team, or 'the way things are around here'. Reichers and Schneider (1990) define climate as shared perceptions of both formal and informal policies, procedures and practices. These underlying values and beliefs can influence performance, productivity and innovation (e.g. Burke and Litwin, 1992).

In a study of over 40 primary health care teams, Peiró, Gonzalez and Ramos (1992) examined the effect of team climate on team members' stress and job satisfaction. The dimensions of climate they used were support, respect for rules, goal-oriented information and innovation. They found that these dimensions of team climate were significantly related to the level of role conflict, ambiguity, job tension and overall job satisfaction felt by the team members. Thus, a good team climate is related to happy, unstressed, satisfied team members.

West (1990) focused in upon one of the dimensions used by Peiró et al. (1992) – a climate for innovation. He proposes four factors for an innovative climate: vision, participative safety, support for innovation and task orientation.

- *Vision:* a clear, shared, negotiated, attainable and evolving ideal of a valued outcome which gives the team focus and direction.
- *Participative safety:* reduces resistance to change, encourages commitment and empowerment and allows all team members' opinions to be heard in a safe environment.
- *Support for innovation:* helps to reduce threat, which is often present when forwarding new and original ideas to the team.
- *Task orientation:* commitment to excellence and high-quality innovations.

West and Anderson (1996) investigated innovation in top management teams and found these four facets of team climate to be influential predictors. Support for innovation was the principal predictor of innovation, while participation predicted the number of innovations introduced by top management teams, and task orientation predicted the administrative effectiveness of the introduced innovations.

Developing Teams

The previous sections outlined the different influences of inputs and processes on team effectiveness. How can we now build upon these ideas to promote team effectiveness? Tannenbaum, Salas and Cannon-Bowers (1996) detailed five areas of interventions that help to actualize team potential.

The first of these domains relates to team composition. Systematic methods of recruiting and selecting new team members will help to ensure smooth and effective running of the team. This happens via three avenues: greater possibility of identifying skillful individuals; greater control over task-related skill heterogeneity of the team; and increased likelihood of selecting individuals who are able to work in a team environment. Stevens and Campion (1994) divide the prescribed knowledge, skills and abilities (KSAs) of teamworking into two main categories: interpersonal and self-management KSAs. The need for interpersonal skills is increased in teamworking, they argue, because the amount of interpersonal interaction increases. Thus, each team member must be able to deal with and manage interpersonal situations and group problem-solving competently. Team members must be able to resolve conflict, both constructive and destructive, identify and implement collaborative problem-solving techniques, and communicate openly, supportively and non-evaluatively. The trend towards autonomous work groups in organizations suggests the need for the self-management KSAs. Each individual needs to possess certain abilities of goal-setting and planning for a team in order for it to be effective; this requirement is needed to an even greater extent in self-managing teams. For example, a team member must be able to help to establish, monitor and evaluate team goals, coordinate activities and help to establish expectations and workloads.

Diversity is another element of team composition and team development which requires careful consideration. With the rise of multinational corporations, managing diversity has become a pressing concern. Generally, research suggests that awareness of cultural differences is the key to managing diversity (e.g. Bartz, Hillman, Lehrer and Mayhugh, 1990; Girndt, 1997). But how do we make people aware of the differences between cultures in their team? And once team members are aware, how should they then react? One method, outlined by Girndt (1997), is to train team members to become aware of, and recognize, misunderstandings in interactions. She suggests that the most important signals of a misunderstanding are time delays in responding to communication, non-verbal signs of offence, withdrawal from the interaction or verbal signs of anger. The hardest component in managing diversity, however, is understanding why the negative response occurred and making the reasons for the misunderstanding explicit. Girndt proposes two approaches: directly explaining one's own beliefs and behaviours and then asking for the other team member's beliefs; or indirectly, by comparing that individual's behaviours with others from the same cultural group. Once an understanding has been reached about the differences in cultures, the team can negotiate common methods and beliefs. This can be a compromise between the different cultures, a choice of one over the others or the generation of a completely different set of rules. Either way, the value systems and methods of working of different team members are brought 'into the open', and this prevents misinterpretations and prejudices from escalating.

The second area of team development described by Tannenbaum and colleagues (1996) is team building – in other words, developing team processes. The processes that the interventions target can differ widely depending upon the particular exercise, but most interventions will improve team norms, attitudes, climate and cohesiveness. One intervention widely regarded as important in team building is clarification of both team and individual goals (e.g. West, 1990; Tannenbaum et al., 1996; Markiewicz and West, 1997; West and Unsworth, 1997). West and Unsworth (1997) outline ten steps to developing a clear and motivating team vision (see box 14.1).

Associated with team building is the notion of team training. Tannenbaum and colleagues (1996) describe a training method which causes team members to share mental models. Mental models are maps that each team member has in his or her mind regarding the team and its objectives, methods for achieving objectives, procedures, norms etc. Having such similar conceptualizations of the team and its components promotes coordination among members, even when there are no explicit instructions regarding the activity. A method of cross-training whereby team members 'swap' tasks and perform other members' duties for a period of time enhances this shared mental model. By allowing each team member to experience the tasks and needs of team-mates, a more consensual understanding of the team will develop.

Leadership development is the fourth approach to team development. A number of different strategies have been proposed to improve leader behaviour, including leadership training, coaching and 360° feedback. Markiewicz and West (1997) suggest three main functions in which team leaders must be trained and competent:

B o x   1 4 . 1

Developing a team vision

Step 1. Organize a team meeting that everyone can attend. The process of developing a team vision is often most effective when organized as an 'away day' for team members and a facilitator. However, no matter where the process takes place, it is imperative that each team member attends. It is also important that each team member is focused upon the issues and understands the importance of developing a team vision.

Step 2. Ask each team member to note down his or her views on each element of team vision, i.e. the degree of overlap with the organizational vision, customer emphasis, quality emphasis, value to the wider society, team climate relationships, growth and well-being of team members and relationships with other teams within and outside the organization.

Step 3. Pair team members together and ask them to compare their views. Ask them to note down similarities of values, and also to take special notice of areas on which their views differ. Encourage discussion and debate about the reasons for their beliefs.

Step 4. Bring the discussion back to the whole team. Starting with the first element of team vision, ask each pair to give their opinion on where the team stands. Once all views have been heard for each particular element and have been noted on a central board, begin a discussion around the ideas presented. For elements in which there is discrepancy among team members, ask each member for the reasons behind his or her opinions. Bring about consensus through discussion, debate and full participation from all team members.

Step 5. Once the elements of the team vision have been clarified, express these values in a short, concise, motivating mission statement. Once again, each team member must participate in the discussion around the articulation of the statement and agree upon its final form.

Step 6. From the phrases of the mission statement, develop a list of goals that describe the team's overall aims. Again, participation, sharedness and clarity are extemely important.

Step 7. Objectives must then be derived from each of the team's goals. These should be shared, attainable, clear and measurable.

Step 8. From each objective, develop action plans which specify a clear route to reaching the goal destination. Again, these action plans need to be shared, attainable and clear.

Step 9. Finally, a document needs to be prepared which sets out the mission statement, the goals of the team, the objectives which relate to each goal and the action plans which relate to each objective. Each team member should read this document and make any disagreements or worries known to other members of the team.

Step 10. Repeat this process regularly to ensure that changes to the team or the team's environment are incorporated in the team's vision.

---

1 *Managing the team:* setting clear objectives, clarifying the roles of team members, developing individual tasks, evaluating individual contributions, providing feedback on team performance and reviewing team processes, strategies and objectives.

2   *Coaching individuals:* listening, recognizing and revealing feelings, giving feedback and agreeing goals.
3   *Leading the team:* creating favourable performance conditions for the team, building and maintaining the team as a performing unit and coaching and supporting the team.

Finally, the last group of interventions for team development are those concerning work redesign. This involves modifying the task and its characteristics (e.g. autonomy, skill variety, task significance, task identity, task feedback). One method of improving the motivating potential of these characteristics, already outlined in this chapter, is the notion of self-managing teams. Similarly, having fluid teams that permeate across project boundaries can help to improve task organization.

Promoting team development in each of these five domains (team selection, team building, team training, leadership development and work redesign) leads to improved team performance, as well as enhanced satisfaction and well-being of team members (Sonnentag, 1996; Tannenbaum et al., 1996).

Chapter Summary

What are the messages that the student of organizational psychology can take from research on teamworking in organizations? The development of teamwork in modern organizations has made the topic one of the most frequently discussed and addressed among researchers, consultants and practitioners. The burgeoning of prescriptive and theoretical accounts of effective teamworking is testament to this. However, for all the practitioner and academic attention paid to the topic, it is clear that we have gleaned few axiomatic principles about effective teamwork. This is largely because teamworking in organizational settings is a complex phenomenon. Much depends on the nature of the task, the composition of the team, the organizational context and, indeed, the cultural context within which teamworking occurs.

All of this implies that we are in the early stages of research on understanding how groups of people can work together effectively within organizations in the form that has come to be known as teams. But rather than this being seen as an overwhelming challenge, the limited progress which has been made to date by researchers who have met the challenge of studying teamworking in context suggests that we can make important and exciting progress. The task for organizational psychologists is to continue this work and address the fundamentally important question of how groups of people can most effectively work together to achieve their shared goals, with outcomes that would not be possible if they simply worked separately and non-collaboratively.

D i s c u s s i o n   P o i n t s

1 Describe a team you have once been in. Discuss the advantages and disadvantages you found in being in that team.

2 'Diversity is a double-edged sword'. Explain this statement.

3 What is groupthink? Is the concept applicable to the family as well as the organization?

4 What are the advantages and disadvantages of the computer-mediated communication technology: voice mail and teleconferencing?

5 Discuss the five areas of team development and explain how each can improve team effectiveness.

K e y   S t u d i e s

Macy, B. A. and Izumi, H. (1993) Organizational change, design and work innovation: a meta-analysis of 131 North American field studies – 1961–1991. In *Research in Organizational Change and Design, Volume 7.* Greenwich, CT: JAI Press.

Campion, M. A., Medsker, G. J. and Higgs, A. C. (1993) Relations between work group characteristics and effectiveness: implications for designing effective work groups. *Personnel Psychology*, 46, 823–50.

F u r t h e r   R e a d i n g

Guzzo, R. A. and Dickson, M. W. (1996) Teams in organizations: recent research on performance and effectiveness. *Annual Review of Psychology*, 46, 307–38.

Hackman, J. R. (1990). *Groups that Work (and Those that Don't): Creating Conditions for Effective Teamwork.* San Francisco: Jossey Bass.

Smith, K. G., Smith, K. A., Olian, J. D., Sims, H. P. Jr, O'Bannon, D. P. and Scully, J. A. (1994) Top management team demography and process: the role of social integration and communication. *Administrative Science Quarterly*, 39, 412–38.

Sundstrom, E., De Meuse, K. P. and Futrell, D. (1990) Work teams: applications and effectiveness. *American Psychologist*, 45, 120–33.

West, M. A., Borrill, C. S. and Unsworth, K. L. (1998) Team effectiveness in organizations. In C. L. Cooper and I. T. Robertson (eds), *International Review of Industrial and Organizational Psychology, Volume 13.* Chichester: John Wiley & Sons.

CHAPTER FIFTEEN

ORGANIZATIONAL CHANGE AND DEVELOPMENT

Barbara Senior

Contents

Chapter Outline

In order to survive and prosper in increasingly turbulent environments, organizations need, constantly, to develop and change. However, the concept of *change* is not a homogeneous one, and organizational change can take many forms. Designing and implementing change is not straightforward. Consequently, a number of important issues need to be considered. This chapter begins the discussion with a description of different types of change. This is followed by an exploration of organizational strategy, structure and culture, as important issues in working with change. Finally, the process of organizational development is addressed as an all-encompassing approach to change which uses the behavioural sciences for its foundation.

The Nature of Change

Varieties of change

On the basis of an examination of numerous organizational studies and case histories, Tushman, Newman and Romanelli (1988, p. 707) propose a model of organizational life which consists of 'periods of incremental change, or convergence, punctuated by discontinuous changes'. They suggest there are two types of converging change – fine-tuning and incremental adaptations – both of which have the common aim of maintaining the fit between an organization's strategy, structure and processes. However, while fine-tuning is aimed at doing better what is already done well, incremental adaptation involves small-scale changes in response to minor shifts in the environment – what the authors popularly call the '10 per cent change'. Converging change allows an organization to perform what it does more effectively, optimizing the consistencies between strategy, structure, people and processes. However, converging change, which drives organizations towards stability, can also be a major source of resistance when, for whatever reason, an organization's strategy must change and discontinuous or 'frame-breaking' change is required; that is, 'revolutionary' change which reshapes the entire nature of the organization. An example of this can be found in the privatization of British Rail, resulting in the splitting of the management of the rail infrastructure (the track, stations, timetabling, signalling etc.) from the running of the trains.

A similar typology is put forward by Australian academics Dunphy and Stace (1993), who use the same terms (fine-tuning and incremental adjustment) as Tushman et al. for what they call 'scale type 1' and 'scale type 2' change. Where Dunphy and Stace go beyond Tushman et al. is in, apparently, splitting what Tushman et al. termed frame-breaking change into two categories: 'modular transformation', which implies frame-breaking change at sub-organizational

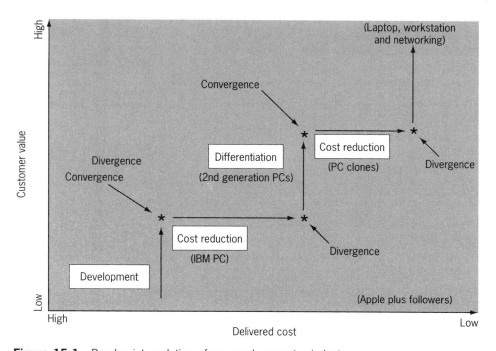

Figure 15.1 Breakpoint evolution of personal computer industry.

Source: Paul Strebel (1996) *Mastering Management.* London: Financial Times Pitman Publishing, p. 546.

level, and 'corporate transformation', which implies frame-breaking change throughout the organization. This is a useful development in detailing more clearly the different levels at which frame-breaking change can take place.

More recently, Strebel (1997) echoes these divisions with his concepts of convergent and divergent 'breakpoints' to describe the behaviour of organizations at an industry level. His argument rests on the idea of a 'cycle of competitive behaviour' which involves two main phases. One is the innovation phase, when someone discovers a new business opportunity. This triggers a breakpoint, which causes a *divergence* in competitors' behaviour as they attempt to exploit the new offerings. This is followed by the second phase of *convergence*: a phase of consolidation and cost-cutting which continues until the least efficient organisations leave the scene and the returns from cost reduction decline sufficiently to force a search for new business opportunities, which bring about a new divergent breakpoint, with the cycle starting all over again. Figure 15.1 illustrates this cycle with an example from the computer industry. From this, it can be seen that the first Apple computer, the arrival of the Macintosh and, most recently, the new chips and software have all triggered divergent breakpoints. In between these times, organizations' offerings begin to *converge* as they imitate each other, and changes are made mainly for improvement and cost-reduction. However, as growth rates decline and customers

Case Study 15.1

A case of radical, paradigm challenging change: all change at Selfridges

Selfridges, the large London department store, took a deliberate decision to reorient its market focus to attract younger, newer customers as well as the ones whose mothers and grand-mothers had traditionally shopped at the store. In doing this they made changes to the product lines, eliminating some entirely and bringing a new image to others. They carried out a massive refurbishment of the store and introduced team-based working on the shop floor. A new chief executive led the strategy change, with some newly appointed senior staff managing the changed structure. Large-scale training and development of staff was used to support the change in attitudes and working practices required for the new strategy to be a success.

become restless, conditions arise to trigger the next divergent breakpoint, with new offerings of products/services.

The predictability of change

The models discussed above are built on a similar theme – convergent type change is contrasted with more radical, paradigm challenging change (see case study 15.1). Each type of change occurs in response to different environmental scenarios. Thus, convergent change is more likely when organizations operate in environments which Ansoff and McDonnell (1990) describe as 'predictable and forecastable by extrapolation' or 'partially predictable threats and oppor-tunities', and which Stacey (1996, pp. 23–4) calls 'closed' or 'contained' change situations. Radical, frame-breaking or divergent change is a more likely response to what Ansoff and McDonnell term 'unpredictable surprises', and what Stacey describes as 'open-ended' change situations. It is not easy, how-ever, to predict the types of change situation faced by organizations at specific times.

On the one hand, if, as some writers maintain (e.g. Kast and Rosenzweig, 1970; von Bertanlanfy, 1971; Checkland, 1972; McAleer, 1982), organiza-tions are striving, continuously, for a state of equilibrium where the forces for change coming from the environment are balanced by the forces for stability, there is, apparently, no necessity for frame-breaking, discontinuous change. On the other hand, the world is not ideal and, as Grint (1997) forcefully argues, defining the precise state of the economic, technological, social and political environment in which organizations operate is by no means easy, if it can be done with confidence at all. This makes it difficult for managers to carry out the adjustments which might be necessary to maintain a 'fit' between organizational strategy, structure and processes. In addition, writers such as Tushman et al. (1988) and Johnson (1987, 1988) describe a phenomenon whereby managers and other organizational personnel become so comfortable with 'how we work here' and 'what we hold important here' that they also become impervious to warning signs of impending difficulties from the environment – whether this is from competitors, a change in interest rates, the advent of some new technological innovation or changes in people's living and working habits. This, in turn, results in what Johnson (1988, p. 44) terms 'strategic drift'; that is, a process whereby an organization's strategy becomes less and less in tune with the environment in which it exists. This widening gap between an organization's strategy and the demands of customers, competitors, technology and other forces eventually necessitates organizational change of a more radical nature, which, although it might be planned, is by no means easy to achieve (Grint, 1997). Consequently, many issues must be addressed when organisational change is being designed. Not least among these is recognizing the type of change situation facing an organization at any particular time.

Diagnosing change situations

A number of writers (e.g. Open University, 1985a,b; Flood and Jackson, 1991; McCalman and Paton, 1992) have devised ways of categorizing change situations in order to suggest what kind of approach to change should be taken.

Two main approaches emerge, which, according to McCalman and Paton and the Open University, form two opposite ends of a change continuum. Thus, situations of change can be positioned on a continuum ranging from 'hard' situations at one end to 'soft' situations at the other (or in respective Open University terms, 'difficulties' and 'messes'):

Hard situations or difficulties
- tend to be smaller scale;
- originate internally;
- are less serious in their implications;
- can be considered in relative isolation from their organizational context;
- have clear priorities as to what might need to be done;
- generally have quantifiable objectives and performance indicators;
- have a systems/technical orientation;
- generally, involve relatively few people;
- have facts which are known and which can contribute to the solution;
- have agreement by the people involved on what constitutes the problem;
- tend to have solutions of which the type at least is known;
- have known timescales;

- are 'bounded' in that they can be considered separately from the wider organizational context and have minimal interactions with the environment.

Soft situations or messes
- tend to be larger scale;
- originate externally;
- have serious and worrying implications for all concerned;
- are an interrelated complex of problems which cannot be separated from their context;
- have many people of different persuasions and attitudes involved in the problem;
- have subjective and at best semi-quantifiable objectives;
- not everything is known and it is not clear what need to be known;
- have little agreement on what constitutes the problem let alone what might me possible solutions;
- have usually been around for some time and will not be solved quickly, if at all, bringing about an improvement may be all that can be hoped for;
- fuzzy timescales;
- are 'unbounded' in that they spread throughout the organisation and, sometimes, beyond.

According to McCalman and Paton, increasing complexity of a task does not necessarily imply problems which are more of a mess than a difficulty. Problems become messes when issues associated with the *people* in the situation increase, *as well as* those associated with the task. For instance, although playing chess at a high standard demands high-level skills and intellect and there are an unbelievably high number of possible moves that can be made, the problem of winning can still be thought of as a difficulty, in that all the possible moves and combinations of moves could be defined and remembered even if, in practice, this is unlikely. By contrast, increasing competition for an organization's products, causing the introduction of new working practices, is an example of a messy problem. This is because not everyone will agree there is a problem and a need for new working practices. Some will interpret this action as a wish to reduce the numbers of staff. Others may see it as an attempt to split up possibly troublesome groups. Yet others may even view it optimistically in terms of getting extra experience and, perhaps, new responsibilities. Management is likely to think of it as a 'good thing', while any trade union will want to know what is in it for the other employees. What is more, if the changes have implications for pay and status, the possible 'losers' will see the world very differently from the possible 'winners'.

Accounts of how to deal with hard change situations or difficulties can be found in Senior (1997). These are termed 'hard systems' models of change. They imply that clear quantifiable measurable change objectives can be set for which a number of agreed options for change can be worked out. With an emphasis on being able to set measurable criteria against which to measure the success of the change, applying hard systems models of change is relatively straightforward given the type of change required. Of particular interest here, however, is the process of organizational development (OD) as a philosophy and approach to change that is all-encompassing in its claim to address small- and large-scale change and to build what might be termed 'change capable' organizations. As a prelude to describing this approach, three important issues associated with change management are addressed. These are concerned with the strategy, structure and culture of organizations – all three of which are inevitably involved in any large-scale, transformational change.

Organizational Strategy, Structure and Change

Johnson and Scholes (1997, p. 10) define strategy as follows:

> Strategy is the *direction* and *scope* of an organisation over the *long term*: ideally, which matches its *resources* to its changing *environment*, and in particular its *markets, customers* or *clients* so as to meet *stakeholder* expectations.

The term stakeholders is taken to represent anyone with an interest in, and affected by, the policies and practices of the organization. This includes customers, suppliers, shareholders, financiers – that is, interested parties outside the organization – but also the employees, a group of people of the utmost importance in that it is they who will have to implement any change. What is more, the achievement of an organization's strategy, and the goals and objectives which it implies, requires that tasks are allocated among employees according to 'the formal pattern of interactions and coordination designed by management to link the tasks of individuals and groups in achieving organizational goals' (Bartol and Martin, 1994, p. 283) – that is, the organizational structure.

The strategy–structure 'fit'

Frame-breaking, transformational change, by definition, implies a change in an organization's strategy, which in turn implies an examination of its structure and ways of operating. This assumption rests on the notion of the strategy–structure 'fit' (Miles and Snow, 1984). Consequently, as table 15.1 shows, particular product/market strategies are assumed to require particular organizational structures.

This in turn implies that organizations can identify and plan for a particular type of strategy and, equally well, design a structure to go with it. However, although prescriptions for how to carry out strategic planning abound (as any

Table 15.1 Evolution of organization forms

	Product/market strategy	Organization structure	Core activating and control mechanisms
1800	Single product or service. Local/regional markets	Agency	Personal direction and control
1850	Limited, standardized product or service line. Regional/national markets	Functional	Central plan and budgets
1900	Diversified, changing product or service line. National/international markets.	Divisional	Corporate policies and division profit centres
1950	Standard and innovative products or services. Stable and changing markets.	Matrix	Temporary teams and lateral resource allocation devices such as internal markets, joint planning systems etc.
2000	Product or service design. Global, changing markets.	Dynamic network	Broker-assembled temporary structures with shared information systems as basis for trust and coordination

Source: based on Miles and Snow (1984), copyright © 1984, by The Regents of the University of California.

book on strategic management will show), writers such as Mintzberg, Quinn and James (1988) question, seriously, the idea that strategy formulation is simply the result of rational-logical thinking and planning. They argue that strategy is just as likely to *emerge* as the result of social and political processes, implying a more changeable view of strategy than many writers would subscribe to. This in turn makes matching structure to strategy that much more difficult. In addition, concentrating on a strategy–structure fit tends to ignore other factors which influence structure, such as size, technology used and the need for some parts of an organization to be structured differently from others.

Structures for change

In contrast to the strategy-structure fit thesis – or, indeed theories, which link size and structure (see Pugh, 1973; Child, 1988) or technology and structure (see Woodward, 1965; Perrow, 1967; Thompson, 1967; Butler, 1991) – Burns and Stalker, as long ago as 1961, suggested that 'organically' structured organizations were inherently more able to cope with change, whatever their strat-

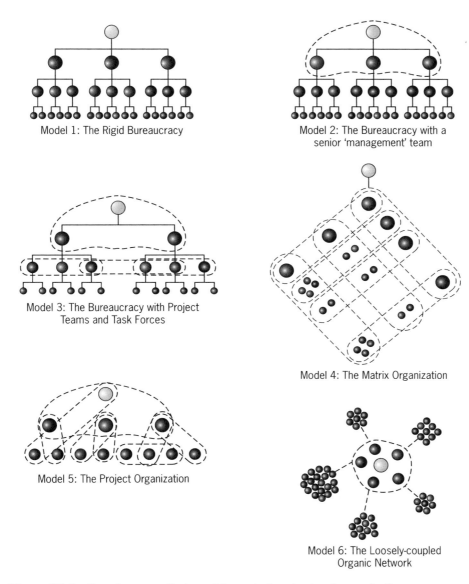

Figure 15.2 From bureaucratic to matrix, project and network organizations.
Source: Gareth Morgan (1989) *Creative Organization Theory.* London: Sage, p. 66.

egy, than organizations structured on 'mechanistic' lines. More recently, compared to more bureaucratic forms of organization (see figure 15.2), Morgan (1989) describes the virtues of 'project' organizations and 'loosely coupled organic networks' in the context of turbulent, dynamic environments. In these more loosely structured organizations, a small number of permanent staff set the strategic direction and provide the necessary operational support to sustain

Case Study 15.2   TFW Images

TFW Images was formed in 1989 by two ex-employees of IBM, who became the managing director and creative director of the company. They were very soon joined by a sales director with experience from a range of companies, mainly manufacturing. The main business of TFW Images is communications in its widest sense. Examples of its activities are: designing corporate brochures which might include annual reports as well as advertising material; designing and organizing conferences and all the material to goes with them; and creating company logos and other symbols of corporate identity.

TFW Images' main client was, and still is, IBM. In fact, the rise of the company coincided with the large-scale changes which IBM went through as it refocused its efforts away from the mainframe computer market towards that of the personal computer market. As technology began to replace people, TFW Images was able to take advantage of the willingness of companies like IBM to outsource some of their design requirements.

From a high point of employing, directly, seventeen people (two of whom were in Paris), TFW Images now has seven direct employees. Of the original three directors, one remains, the creative director, although he does not currently carry a particular title.

In a volatile market – there are other competitors and the fortunes of IBM are less certain nowadays – one reason for the company's success is its ability to maintain a

the network. A larger number of groupings and other organizations enter into permanent or temporary partnerships as the changing nature of the market dictates.

Finally, the 'virtual organization' is proposed by Davidow and Malone (1992) (and commented on by Chesborough and Teese, 1996). Put simply, 'the virtual organization is a temporary network of companies that come together quickly to exploit fast-changing opportunities. Different from traditional mergers and acquisitions, the partners in the virtual organization share costs, skills, and access to international markets. Each partner contributes to the virtual organization what it is best at' (Luthans, 1995, p. 487). Case study 15.2 gives an example of an organization which unarguably operates as a 'loose-coupled network' and is arguably a virtual organization.

Contingency or 'one best way'

The discussion above suggests that organizational structure can be designed to 'match' the strategy or be designed in flexible mode, assuming all organizations are involved in change. The former implies a contingency approach to matching strategy and structure, while the latter implies there is one 'best way' of structuring given the turbulent times in which organizations live. Both these views, however, assume that organizations are prey to whatever environments throw at them. This is not strictly true. Organizations are able, to some extent, flexible structure which can be tailored to the demands of the market. Essentially, TFW Images is an organization which 'brokers' services from other organizations to bring its products to the market. Thus, rather than employing printers, photographers, illustrators, market researchers and additional writers and designers directly, it closely associates with other companies and independent consultants who offer these services. The use of sophisticated computer systems facilitates the transfer of the part-finished products from one part of the network to another, wherever it might be in the world.

Most recently, TFW Images has joined in partnership with Omni-Graphics, a well established design company operating mainly in the publishing and arts spheres of activity. Examples of Omni-Graphics' activities are: the design of calenders, brochures for and the layout of art galleries and the design of news magazines.

Given the equality of skills and size of the two organizations, the benefits of the partnership will come from their complementary activities (TWF Images is business-oriented, while Omni-Graphics is arts-oriented) and the financial advantages which will flow from this. The management of the two partner organizations will remain separate and they will keep their own names. Thus, to any client, nothing will have changed. Yet, conceptually and financially, a new overarching organization has been 'virtually' created.

to manipulate their environments. For instance, political decisions can be influenced through lobbying, customers influenced by advertising and people's expectations of employment influenced by the way groups of organizations design jobs. Monopoly or oligopoly conditions clearly help organizations to modify their environments. This, in turn, allows managers to exercise what Child (1972) terms 'strategic choice'. Indeed, managers frequently choose not to pursue strategies and design structures which would reduce their power base, and others will resist change which erodes their position or status. In addition, the pervasiveness of organizational cultures plays a significant, and maybe dominant, role if anything more than incremental change is to happen.

Organizational Culture and Change

The definitions of organisational strategy and structure above refer to the *formal* elements of what can be thought of as organizational life. French and Bell (1990) refer to these (which also include organizational systems and procedures, products and services, financial resources and management) as the visible part of the 'organisational iceberg'. However, equally important to organizational life and to this discussion is the invisible part of the iceberg: the *informal* organization (or in Stacey's, 1996, terminology, the *shadow* organization). This consists of elements such as employees' values, attitudes and beliefs, which form part of the organizational culture and which, to a large extent, influence the power 'games' and emergent norms of behaviour unique to any organization. The metaphor of the organizational iceberg implies that, just as a ship only knows the extent of the hidden part of an iceberg when it collides with it, so an organization's culture is difficult to discern until some norm or unwritten rule is transgressed. Consequently, changing an organization's culture is mostly about changing something that cannot be directly experienced or seen.

The meaning of culture

There are a multitude of definitions of organizational culture (e.g. Kroeber and Kluckholn, 1952; Hofstede, 1981; Brown, 1995). Schein encapsulates the meaning of most when he says it is 'The deeper level of basic assumptions and beliefs that are shared by members of an organization, that operate unconsciously and define in a basic "taken for granted" fashion an organization's view of its self and its environment' (Schein, 1992, p. 6). Describing a particular organization's culture in these terms, however, is difficult. What might be looked for, therefore, are manifestations of the culture, such as the style of language used and behaviour patterns in the form of rites, rituals, stories, myths and legends (Brown, 1995); the style of leadership, degree of tolerance of conflict, type of reward systems and tolerance of risk (Robbins, 1993). Alternatively, writers such as Deal and Kennedy (1982) and Handy (1993) propose a typology of cultures. Deal and Kennedy name four culture types as tough-guy macho culture, work hard/play hard culture, bet-your-company culture and process culture, all of which are related to the way organizations act towards the market environment. By contrast, Handy speaks of power, role, task and person cultures, which are closely allied to different organizational structure types. For instance, the first of these mirrors the 'one-boss', all-powerful structure, resembling a spider in the middle of a web. The second is typical of a hierarchical, bureaucratic structure, and the third related closely to a matrix structure. The person culture is reminiscent of organizations such as law and medical practices, where professionals are usually self-employed but share a common strategic focus and marketing and office facilities.

The pervasiveness of culture

The notion that culture encompasses almost everything that happens in an organization is put forward by Pacanowsky and O'Donnell-Trujillo (1982) and Morgan (1997) and is embodied in Johnson and Scholes's (1997) concept of a 'cultural web' (see figure 15.3). Central to the web is the 'organizational paradigm'; in more ordinary language, 'the way we do things around here'. Making up the paradigm are not only the stories, symbols, rituals and routines mentioned above, but also the more formal parts of the organizational iceberg;

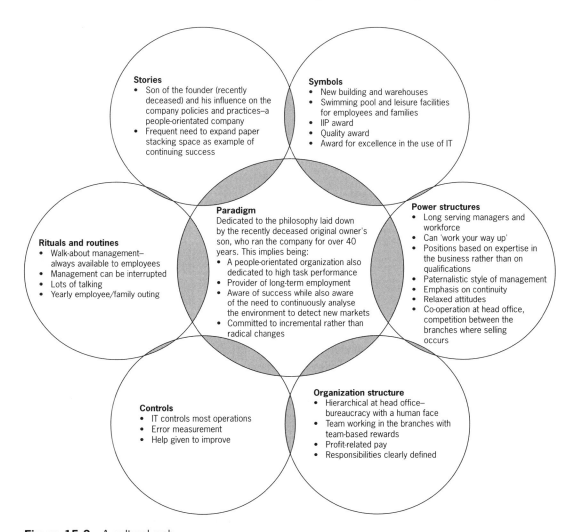

Figure 15.3   A cultural web.

Source: Barbara Senior (1997) *Organisational Change.* London: Financial Times Pitman Publishing, p. 286.

that is, the control systems, power structures and organizational structures. Figure 15.3 shows how the cultural web can be used to describe an organization's unique culture.

Constructing a cultural web takes time and much effort. Each one is unique and has to be started from 'scratch'. What is more, questioning different people in different functions or places might result in several different cultural webs. The effort is, however, well worth while. Organisations such as Hay Management Consultants (see Heracleous, 1995) have assembled cultural webs to depict current and future (desired) cultures, in order to plan changes and move from the one to the other.

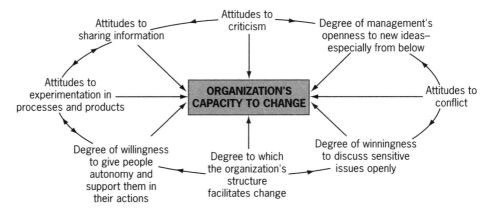

Figure 15.4 Organizational culture and change.

Source: Barbara Senior (1997) *Organisational Change*. London: Financial Times Pitman Publishing, p. 133.

Cultures for change

There are a number of different views on the relationship between culture and change. Figure 15.4 depicts various elements of organizational culture as they might influence organizations' capacity to change. Descriptions of these influences surface in Kanter's (1983, p. 101) depiction of 'segmentalist' and 'integrative' cultures (mirrored by the Open University's concepts of defensive and supportive cultures):

Segmentalist cultures
- compartmentalize actions, events and problems;
- see problems as narrowly as possible;
- have segmented structures with large numbers of departments walled off from one another;
- assume problems can be solved by carving them up into pieces, which are then assigned to specialists who work in isolation;
- divide resources up among the many departments;
- avoid experimentation;
- avoid conflict and confrontation;
- have weak coordinating mechanisms;
- stress precedent and procedures.

Integrative cultures
- are willing to move beyond received wisdom;
- combine ideas from unconnected sources;
- see problems as wholes, related to larger wholes;
- challenge established practices;

- operate at the edge of competencies;
- measure themselves by looking to visions of the future rather than by referring to the standards of the past;
- create mechanisms for exchange of information and new ideas;
- recognize and even encourage differences, but then be prepared to cooperate;
- are outward looking;
- look for novel solutions to problems.

What is clear from both Kanter's and the Open University's writings is that segmentalist or defensive cultures will militate against organizational change, particularly frame-breaking or transformational change. Consequently, the question arises as to how far an organization's culture can be changed in line with changes such as those mentioned above.

Changing organizational culture to bring about organizational change

From the discussion above, it is difficult to deny the importance of culture as a dominant influence on the whole of organizational life. Therefore, in order to bring about any kind of significant organizational change, the organization's culture must be managed accordingly. This is evident in the arguments which recommend organizations to take on the characteristics of a supportive (integrative) culture (see Kanter, 1983) linked to an organic structure (Burns and Stalker, 1961), or those which will bring excellence in performance (see Peters and Waterman, 1982). From these points of view, permanent organizational change will only be brought about by first changing people's attitudes and values.

However, changing an organization's culture is not easy, as Morgan (1989, p. 158) points out when he writes: 'Changing corporate culture is not like changing a suit of clothes. One can change surface appearances, e.g. by giving the corporation a new image . . . and espousing new philosophies and beliefs. But to have a significant and lasting impact, basic values also have to change.' Difficulties in changing cultures are illustrated by Schwartz and Davis's (1981) account of AT&T, which, in the late 1970s undertook a large-scale corporate and organizational reorientation. Schwartz and Davis (1981, p. 31) write: 'Despite the major changes in structure, in human resources, and in support systems, there is a general consensus both inside and outside AT&T that its greatest task in making its strategy succeed will be its ability to transform the AT&T culture. *It will probably be a decade before direct judgements should be made as to its success*' (italics added).

A study by a group of MBA students of a medium-sized American company manufacturing a range of sources and food dressings showed how it had recently embarked on a three-phase programme of culture change which was estimated to take up to six years. An evaluation after the first phase – which mainly involved senior and supervisory managers – indicated some improvement in communications between vertical levels of staff, but less so across departments; improvements in team working but with more yet to be done; and improvements in devolving decision-making and increasing organizational commitment. At less than the half-way point in the programme, support and production staff had yet to become involved in this process.

These two organizations, presumably, considered culture change to be possible. However, Schwartz and Davis quote a case where the president of an engineering company resigned after six years of trying to change the company's culture from being production-oriented to being market-oriented. At this point he reckoned he had managed to dent but not change the culture. It seems desirable, therefore, before embarking on culture change, to carry out an assessment of 'cultural risk'; that is, an assessment of the degree to which the prevailing culture of an organization will support or inhibit changes in organizational functions as they relate to the implementation of the corporate strategy.

Assessing cultural risk

Essential to an assessment of cultural risk is the ability to measure organizational culture. There are many ways of doing this, and Furnham and Gunter (1993) give a list of such measures. However, measuring organizational culture, of itself, is only a means to an end. The end, in this context, is to determine how culture should be managed as part of the process of organizational change.

It was in pursuit of this end that Schwartz and Davis devised a framework for assessing culture in terms of descriptions of the way management tasks are typically handled in companywide, boss-subordinate, peer and interdepartment relationships, so as to assess the degree of cultural compatibility with any proposed strategic change. Table 15.2 is an example of Schwartz and Davis's corporate culture matrix, which they designed to carry out the first part of this process. It has been completed for the UK-based division of a company in the computer services industry.

The results of an analysis such as the one shown in table 15.2 can be used to assess the compatibility of an organization's culture to any proposed changes in its approach to its strategy, structure and operations. The framework for this comparison is shown in figure 15.5 as a matrix which allows elements of the proposed strategy changes to be plotted against their importance to that strategy, and the degree to which they are compatible with the culture. From this matrix, it can be seen that, if a proposed change is positioned in the top right hand corner, the chance of it being acceptable to the prevailing culture is low. For instance, consider the case where managers of an organization have assessed the organizational culture (say through the use of Schwartz and Davis's matrix) to be reminiscent of Handy's 'role-oriented'

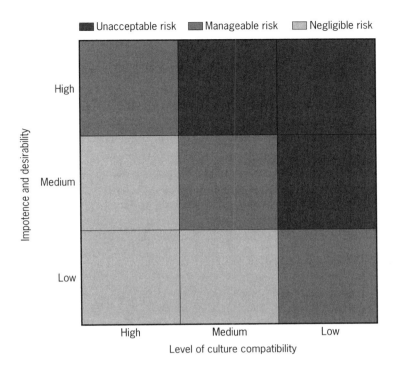

Figure 15.5 Assessing cultural risk.

Source: based on H. Schwartz and S. M. Davis (1981) Matching corporate strategy and business strategy. *Organizational Dynamics*, Summer, 41.

culture or Deal and Kennedy's 'process' culture. At the same time, top management has formulated a new corporate strategy, which suggests that a move to a matrix structure *is highly desirable* for the successful implementation of this strategy. Consequently, the *importance* of the need for a change in the structure from a bureaucratic, hierarchical one to a matrix-based one would position the change at the top of the vertical axis in figure 15.5. On the other hand, it is clear that the prevailing culture is not compatible with that which the proposed new strategy appears to require. The level of compatibility between the change and the culture is, therefore, low – positioning it at the right hand end of the horizontal axis in figure 15.5. The overall effect is to position the suggested change in the top right cell of the matrix – a position that implies an important, very desirable change but a culture which is most unlikely to support it.

The key to the shading of the cells in figure 15.5 shows that this is one of the most risky change situations. By contrast, if the prevailing culture was more like the one depicted in table 15.2 – a less rule-bound, more participative and innovation-oriented culture – then the level of culture compatibility with the proposed structural change would be high. The consequence of this would be to position the change in the top left cell of the matrix, resulting in a situa-

Table 15.2 Corporate culture matrix

Task	Relationships				Summary of culture in relation to tasks
	Company-wide	Boss–subordinate	Peer	Inter-department	
Innovating	Innovation if part of the mission	Bosses open to suggestions	Teamwork	Teamwork	Encourage creativity and innovation
Decision-making	Has to fit in with strategy	Input from subordinates encouraged – boss has final word	Collective decisions	Work together to produce an integrated package	Collaborative decision-making but boss has the final word; corporate strategy rules
Communicating	Easy, use of e-mail and phone	Friendly	Face-to-face and open	Easy, use of e-mail and phone	Easy, informal and friendly communications
Organizing	Market focus	Democratic	Professional relationships	Collaborative	Organized on the basis of skills and professional relationships
Monitoring	Shareholder-led organization	Meet short-term profit targets and deadlines	Project management	Project management	Need to meet short-term profit goals
Appraising and rewarding	Encourage performers	Hard work = good rewards	Results important	Results important	Meritocracy
Summary of culture in relationship to relationships	Allow freedom to managers as long as they operate within the strategy and meet profit targets, output-oriented	Friendly, rely on each other for success	Highly skilled professionals who help each other out	Work together to support sales	Overall performance and profit matter in a culture which welcomes dynamic and performance related individuals

Source: matrix adapted from Schwartz and Davis (1981, p. 36), example from the author's own experience.

tion which is risky, but manageable. Other elements of the proposed change might be low in level of culture compatibility but of low importance in the overall change strategy. They would, therefore, be positioned towards the lower right-hand part of the matrix.

Assessing cultural risk in this way helps to pinpoint areas of likely resistance to change because of an incompatibility between an organization's culture and the culture required for the changes being proposed. In addition, it allows choices to be made with regard to: (a) ignoring the culture; (b) managing around the culture; (c) trying to change the culture to fit the strategy; and (d) changing the strategy to fit the culture, perhaps by reducing performance expectations.

Ignoring the culture The first of these options is not recommended unless the organization has sufficient resources to draw on to weather the likely resistance and the possibility of an initial down-turn business.

Managing around the culture The second option – managing around the culture – is a real possibility given that there are, in most cases, more ways than one of achieving desired goals. Table 15.3 reproduces Schwartz and Davis's example of how to manage around an organization's culture. This outlines four typical strategies that companies might pursue, and what Schwartz and Davis call the 'right' organizational approaches to implement them. The final two columns set out the cultural barriers to these 'right' approaches and the alternative approaches which could, therefore, be used.

Changing the culture The third option of changing the culture to fit the desired strategic changes is also a possibility but, as much of the literature cautions, this can be an extremely difficult and lengthy process, particularly if the culture is a strong one (Scholz, 1987; Furnham and Gunter, 1993). Furthermore, there are strong arguments (e.g. Hope and Hendry, 1995) against cultural change as a concept for organizations of the 2000s, given what Hope and Hendry (p. 62) describe as the move away from the large-scale hierarchies characteristic of the multinationals of the previous decades, towards much leaner and more focused units, or even the virtual organizational structures discussed above. According to Hope and Hendry, this move has been accompanied by an increase in the employment of what Drucker (1992) calls 'professional knowledge workers', but also by an erosion of security of employment and predictable career paths, with consequent difficulties of employee control. Two problems are said to arise from this. The first is that the 'knowledge workers' who are likely to flourish in these new types of organization are least likely to be open to cultural manipulation. Second, any new managerial practice must allow for a degree of cynicism in the context of the downsizing which has removed several layers of middle management and therefore removed the opportunity for steady advancement, once assumed as almost everyone's right.

Table 15.3   How to manage around company culture

	Strategy	'Right' approach	Cultural barriers	Alternative approaches
Company A	Diversify product and market.	Divisionalize.	Centralized power. One-man rule. Functional focus. Hierarchical structure.	Use business teams. Use explicit strategic planning. Change business measures.
Company B	Focus marketing on most profitable segments.	Fine-tune reward system. Adjust management-information system.	Diffused power. Highly individualized operations.	Dedicate full-time personnel to each key market.
Company C	Extend technology to new markets.	Set up matrix organization.	Multiple power centres. Functional focus.	Use programme coordinators. Set up planning committees. Get top management more involved.
Company D	Withdraw gradually from declining market and maximize cash throw-offs.	Focus organization specifically. Fine-tune rewards. Ensure top management visibility.	New-business driven. Innovators rewarded. State-of-the-art operation.	Sell out.

Source: Schwartz and Davis (1981, p. 44).

As a consequence of all this, 'employees in general may be less receptive to evangelical calls for shared cultural values' (Hope and Hendry, 1995, p. 62).

Even when culture change is desired, the literature does not help in deciding whether cultural change is possible or whether managers requiring organizational change should work around the culture. Some methods of bringing about culture change depend upon education and persuasion, or, in some cases, coercion, to help to bring about changes in attitudes (Anthony, 1994). Others rely more on changing recruitment, selection, promotion, reward and redundancy policies to alter the composition of the workforce and so retain those who have the desired beliefs, values and attitudes associated with the desired culture (Dobson, 1988). It seems that a combination of approaches would be most effective unless the organizational changes proposed can be, themselves, changed to be more compatible with the existing culture.

Changing the strategy to match the culture   Schwartz and Davis give the merging of two organizations as an example of changing the strategy to be more compatible with the existing cultures. This choice for an organization is similar to that of managing around the culture, and further emphasizes the possibilities inherent in the idea put forward by Child (1972) that organizations are able to choose the means by which they achieve their ends. Consequently, some accommodation between changing the culture and adapting the strategy is more likely to be accepted.

Overall, compromise between these different approaches to managing organizational culture within a context of organizational change is counselled. Using a process which combines education and persuasion (to bring about attitude and value change) with changes in structures and systems (to bring about changes in behaviour) will help to modify organizational culture, as it is linked to organizational change on a broader scale. This chapter concludes with a discussion of organizational development as an approach to designing and implementing change, based on the assumption that people matter.

Organizational Development: an Approach to Lasting Change

According to French and Bell (1990, p. 17), in their book entitled *Organization Development: Behavioral Science Interventions for Organizational Improvement*, organization development (OD) is:

> A top-management-supported, long-range effort to improve an organization's problem-solving and renewal processes, particularly through a more effective and collaborative diagnosis and management of organization culture – with special emphasis on formal work team, temporary team, and inter-group culture – with the assistance of a consultant-facilitator and the use of the theory and technology of applied behavioral science, including action research.

Cummings and Worley (1993, p. 1) in their book entitled *Organization Development and Change*, write that OD is:

> a process by which behavioral knowledge and practices are used to help organizations achieve greater effectiveness, including improved quality of life, increased productivity, and improved product and service quality . . . the focus is on improving the organization's ability to assess and to solve its own problems. Moreover, OD is oriented to improving the total system – the organization and its parts in the context of the larger environment that impacts upon them.

An examination of these definitions confirms some distinguishing characteristics of the OD approach to change. These are:

1 It emphasizes goals and processes but with a particular emphasis on processes. The notion of organizational learning (Argyris and Schon, 1978) as a means of improving an organization's capacity to change is implicit in OD approaches.

2   It deals with change over the medium to long term; that is, change which needs to be sustained over a significant period of time.

3   It involves the organization as a whole as well as its parts.

4   It is participative, drawing on the theory and practices of the behavioural sciences.

5   It has top management support and involvement.

6   It involves a facilitator who takes on the role of a change agent (Buchanan and Boddy, 1992).

7   It concentrates on planned change, but as a process that can adapt to a changing situation rather than as a rigid blueprint of how change should be done.

The OD approach to change is, above all, an approach which cares about people and believes that people at all levels of an organization are, individually and collectively, both the drivers and the engines of change.

OD: an action research based model of change

According to McCalman and Paton (1992, p. 135), 'change is a continuous process of confrontation, identification, evaluation and action'. They go on to write that the key to this is what OD proponents refer to as an action research model. French and Bell (1990) identify action research as a collaborative effort of data gathering, data discussion, action planning and action between the leaders and facilitators of any change and those who have to enact it. Therefore, action research is, as its name suggests, a combination of research and action. This means collecting data relevant to the situation of interest, feeding back the results to those who must take action and collaboratively discussing the data to formulate an action plan, followed by taking the necessary action.

A number of things distinguish this approach from the hard systems model of change mentioned above. First, it is not a 'one-off' event which ends when a change has been completed. In their article describing the application of OD in an American electricity utility, Alpander and Lee (1995) illustrate this: 'Organizations which are successful in maintaining their competitiveness have learned to view change not as a one-time event, but an ongoing process necessary to remain on the cutting edge in meeting customer needs.' Second, it is an iterative or cyclical process which is continuous and which, if OD is taken as part of an organization's philosophy of action, continues as part of everyday organizational life. Third, each of the components of the model (diagnosis, data gathering, feedback to the client group, data discussion and work by the client group, action planning and action) may be used to form each of the phases that make up a typical OD process. On the other hand, these components may, collectively, form cycles of activity *within* each stage of the OD process. Finally, the OD approach to change is firmly embedded in the assumption that all who are or might be involved in any change should be part of the decision-making process to decide what that change might be

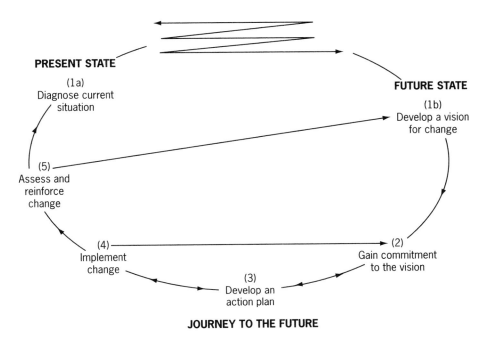

Figure 15.6 The OD model for change.

Source: Barbara Senior (1997) *Organisational Change*. London: Financial Times Pitman Publishing, p. 266.

and to bring it about. It is not, as some other models of change suggest, a project planned and implemented by senior managers or some designated project manager with the assumption that other workers in the organization will automatically go along with it.

Building on the concept of action research, figure 15.6 shows the stages of the OD model. Of note here is the emphasis on the role of the change agent, as evidenced by positioning this person or group in the centre of the diagram. The role of the facilitator or change agent is discussed below. What follows first is a summary of the stages which make up the OD model itself.

Stages 1a and 1b: The present and the future

The stages of diagnosing the current situation and developing a vision for change are probably the most important stages of the OD process. The zigzag lines and labelling of 1a and 1b in figure 15.6 indicate the symbiotic relationship between the two. Stage 1a involves gathering data not only about the organizational environment but also on matters internal to organizations, such as:

* individuals' motivation and commitment to their work and organization;
* recruitment practices, career paths and opportunities;
* prevailing leadership styles;

The Body Shop's charter and mission statement

The Body Shop's Trading Charter

We aim to achieve commercial success by meeting our customers' needs through the provision of high quality, good value products with exceptional service and relevant information which enables customers to make informed and responsible choices.

Our trading relationships of every kind – with customers, franchisees and suppliers – will be commercially viable, mutually beneficial and based on trust and respect.

The Body Shop's Mission Statement – our reason for being

to dedicate our business to the pursuit of social and environmental change

To CREATIVELY balance the financial and human NEEDS of our stakeholders: employees, customers, franchisees, suppliers and shareholders.

To COURAGEOUSLY ensure that OUR business is ecologically sustainable, meeting the needs of the *present* without compromising the *future*.

- employee training and development provision;
- intra- and inter-group relationships;
- organizational structure and culture.

Data gathering, therefore, is done at the individual, group and organizational levels and should include those things which form barriers to organizational performance as well as those which contribute to organizational success.

Stage 1b involves creative thinking in the sense of looking for 'something new'. This might imply a different strategy in terms of products, services or markets. It might also imply a change in structure and culture including the way people are managed and led. Burnside (1991, p. 193) writes: 'A vision can be described as a living picture of a future, desirable state. It is living because it exists in the thoughts and actions of people, not just in a written document. It is a picture because it is composed not of abstractions but of images.' Pat Snelson (1996) of RS Components (see figure 15.3) writes that a vision must:

- drive the business forward;
- inspire;
- yield sustainable advantage.

The development of the Body Shop charter and mission statements (see case study 15.3) was achieved through groups of employees from all levels of the organization meeting off-site at intervals of many months.

Case study 15.3 shows how visions can be quite broad in focus, a view which is supported by Johnson and Scholes, who point out that mission statements

To MEANINGFULLY contribute to local, national and international communities in which we trade, by adopting a code of conduct which ensures *care, honesty, fairness and respect*. To PASSIONATELY campaign for the protection of the environment and human and civil rights, and *against animal testing* within the cosmetics and toiletries industry.

To TIRELESSLY work to narrow the gap between principle and practice, while making fun, *passion* and *care* part of our daily lives.

Source: The Body Shop case study (1995), *Kellogg School of Management*, Northwestern University, Evanston, IL, USA; and The Body Shop International plc, Brighton, UK.

should be visionary in their representation of the desired future state of an organization. Moreover, it is from these statements, and the operating objectives which flow from them, that the gap between an organization's current situation and what is desired can be identified.

Stage 2: Gain commitment to the vision and the need for change

It is at this stage of the process that feedback from the results of stages 1a and 1b is most important. Unless those individuals and groups concerned and involved with the change have been consulted and have participated in the process to this point, there will be little incentive for them to 'buy into' the new vision and the change process that will follow it. It is not, however, sufficient merely to inform people of the vision and the necessity for change. This is because visions for change are rarely so clearly structured that information from all levels of the organization can be ignored. As Smith (1995, p. 19), writing on the realities of involvement in managing change, states, 'no top manager can know at the outset (of any change) exactly what needs doing, what information is needed, or where it is located'.

Jones (1994, p. 49) a colleague of Smith, writes of 'listening to the organisation'. Reporting research with top management on the reasons why large-scale programmes of change often fail, Smith writes that nearly all the managers interviewed reported on how much they had underestimated the importance of communication. However, as Jones writes, this is not simply a question of senior management shouting louder from the top. This will not identify and bring to the surface the doubts that people have and their fears of what change might mean for them. Neither will it surface any problems with implementing the vision which top managers may not be able to see for themselves.

Far from shouting from the top, the action research cycle of collecting and analysing data, and feeding back the results, should be maintained here, because 'Vision statements only work when the needs of those at the bottom of the organisation are integrated upwards with the needs of the market' (Lloyd and Feigen, 1997, p. 37).

Stage 3: Develop an action plan

The development of an action plan can be thought of as beginning the phase of managing the transition from an organization's current state to its desired future state as shown by the 'journey to the future' label in figure 15.6. However, it also continues the process of gaining commitment to the vision but with a somewhat changed emphasis on *how* that vision can come about. A number of issues are important in this stage of the OD process. One is the issue of *who* is to guide the planning and, later, the implementation of the change. Another is the issue of precisely *what* needs to change to achieve the vision, while a third is *where* any intervention should take place.

The role of a change agent   The success of using an OD approach to facilitating change rests on the qualities and capabilities of those who act as the facilitators of change. Moving organizations from current to future changed states is not easy, and requires knowledge and skills which some managers do not possess. In addition, many managers are so close to the day-to-day issues and problems of managing that they are unable to stand back from the current situation to take a long look at how things might be different. For these and other reasons, such as a need for managers to learn themselves how to manage change, the use of a change agent is usually deemed desirable in most OD approaches to change. However, the change agent as facilitator of change does not necessarily have to be from outside the organization – he or she might very well come from a part of the organization other than that which is the focus of the change. Indeed, some large organizations have departments or divisions which are specifically set up to act as OD consultants to the rest of the organization. For instance, Selfridges, the large London and Manchester based department store, has a director of strategic change.

Buchanan and Boddy (1992, pp. 92–3) devote a complete book to the subject of the change agent. In it they give a helpful list of the competencies of effective change agents. These are:

Goals

1   Sensitivity to changes in key personnel, top management perceptions and market conditions, and to the way in which these impact on the goals of the project in hand.

2 Clarity in specifying goals, in defining the achievable.
3 Flexibility in responding to changes outside the control of the project manager, perhaps requiring major shifts in project goals and management style, and risk taking.

Roles
4 Team building abilities, to bring together key stakeholders and establish effective working groups, and clearly to define and delegate respective responsibilities.
5 Networking skills in establishing and maintaining appropriate contacts within and outside the organization.
6 Tolerance of ambiguity, to be able to function comfortably, patiently and effectively in an uncertain environment.

Communication
7 Communication skills to transmit effectively to colleagues and subordinates the need for changes in project goals and in individual tasks and responsibilities.
8 Interpersonal skills, across the range, including selection, listening, collecting appropriate information, identifying the concerns of others and managing meetings.
9 Personal enthusiasm, in expressing plans and ideas.
10 Stimulating motivation and commitment in others involved.

Negotiation
11 Selling plans and ideas to others, by creating a desirable and challenging vision of the future.
12 Negotiating with key players for resources, or for changes in procedures, and to resolve conflict.

Managing up
13 Political awareness, in identifying potential coalitions, and in balancing conflicting goals and perceptions.
14 Influencing skills, to gain commitment to project plans and ideas from potential sceptics and resisters.
15 Helicopter perspective, to stand back from the immediate project and take a broader view of priorities.

Buchanan and Boddy's list is reminiscent of the characteristics of 'transformational' leaders discussed by Tichy and Ulrich (1984). According to McCalman and Paton (1992, p. 147), the roles taken on by effective change agents are:

1 To help the organization to define the problem by asking for a definition of what it is.

2   To help the organization to examine what causes the problem and diagnose how this can be overcome.
3   To assist in getting the organization to offer alternative solutions.
4   To provide direction in the implementation of alternative solutions.
5   To transmit the learning process that allows the client to deal with change on an ongoing basis by itself in the future.

In contrast to the concept of a change agent, Kotter (1996) uses the concept of a 'guiding coalition' and suggests the four key characteristics of position power, expertise, credibility and leadership as being essential for it to be effective. What is clear, however, is that individual change agents and guiding coalitions cannot, by themselves, cause widespread change to happen. What they can do is set targets for change which, collectively, will move the organization and its members much closer to realizing the vision which was developed in stage 1b and further refined in stage 2. Having done this, the issue becomes: 'Who is to do what, with what kind of involvement by others?'

Responsibility charting   Beckhard and Harris (1987, pp. 104–8) have developed a technique called 'responsibility charting', which assesses the alternative behaviours for each person or persons involved in a series of actions designed to bring about change. They describe the making of a responsibility chart (see figure 15.7) as follows:

> Responsibility charting clarifies behaviour that is required to implement important change tasks, actions or decisions. It helps reduce ambiguity, wasted energy, and adverse emotional reactions between individuals or groups whose interrelationship is affected by change. The basic process is as follows:
>   Two or more people whose roles interrelate or who manage interdependent groups formulate a list of actions, decisions, or activities that affect their relationship (such as developing budgets, allocating resources, and deciding on the use of capital) and record the list on the vertical axis of a responsibility chart. They then identify the people involved in each action or decision and list these 'actors' on the horizontal axis of the form.

The actors identified can include: R, the person who has the *responsibility* to initiate the action and who is charged with ensuring it is carried out; A, those whose *approval* is required or who have the power to *veto* the decision (this could be the responsible person's superiors); S, those who can provide *support* and resources to help the action to take place; I, those who merely need to be *informed* or consulted but who cannot veto the action. French and Bell advise certain ground rules when making a responsibility chart. These include assigning responsibility to only one person and avoiding having too many people with an approval–veto function on an item. They also advise that the support function is critical to the success of any change.

R = Responsibility (not necessarily authority)
A = Approval (right to veto)
S = Support (put resources towards)
I = Inform (to be consulted before action but with no right of veto)

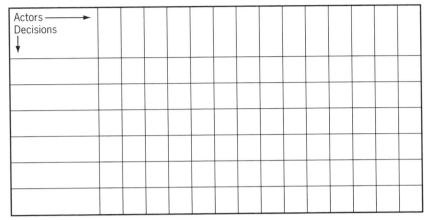

Figure 15.7 Example of a responsibility chart.

The what and where of change Pugh (1986) has devised a matrix of possible change initiatives based on the different issues which can hamper change and the level at which they occur. Table 15.4 shows what has become known as the 'Pugh OD matrix'. This matrix can be used to help with action planning (as represented by the initiatives listed in italics) about (a) the type of intervention required to facilitate change in line with the organization's vision (represented by the columns), and (b) the level at which it should take place (represented by the rows). For instance, at the level of the individual, problems may be occurring because there are few opportunities for promotion from the job of factory floor supervisor to higher levels of management, sales people see no reason to change given their current bonus plan and many middle managers have made their jobs to suit their own needs rather than those of the organization. Problems at the inter-group level might include marketing and production arguing about the feasibility of setting up a new production line to satisfy what the marketing staff consider to be a market opportunity. Intervention is frequently required at the organizational level when an organization's structure prevents the emergence of, let alone action upon, initiatives which could be beneficial to the organization as a whole.

Beckhard and Harris (1987, p. 73) suggest the following organizational subsystems, any of which can be considered as a starting point for change:

- *Top management:* the top of the system.
- *Management-ready systems:* those groups or organizations known to be ready for change.

Table 15.4 The Pugh OD matrix

	Behaviour (What is happening now?)	Structure (What is the required system?)	Context (What is the setting?)
Organizational level	General climate of poor morale, pressure, anxiety, suspicion, lack of awareness of, or response to, environmental changes Survey feedback, organizational mirroring	Systems goals poorly defined or inappropriate and misunderstood; organization structure inappropriate, centralization, divisionalization or standardization; inadequacy of environmental monitoring mechanisms Change the structure	Geographical setting, market pressures, labour market, physical condition, basic technology Change strategy, location, physical condition, basic technology
Intergroup level	Lack of effective cooperation between sub-units, conflict, excessive competition, limited war, failure to confront differences in priorities, unresolved feelings Intergroup confrontation (with third party consultant), role negotiaton	Lack of integrated task perspective; sub-unit optimization, required interaction difficult to achieve Redefine responsibilities, change reporting relationships, improve coordination and liaison mechanisms	Different sub-unit values, lifestyle; physical distance Reduce psychological and physical distance; exchange role, attachments, cross-functional groups

Group level	Inappropriate working relationships, atmosphere, participation, poor understanding and acceptance of goals, avoidance, inappropriate leadership style, leader not trusted, respected; leader in conflict with peers and superiors Process consultation, team building	Task requirements poorly defined; role relationships unclear or inappropriate; leader's role overloaded, inappropriate reporting procedures. Redesign work relationships (socio-technical systems), self-directed working groups	Insufficient resources, poor group composition for cohesion, inadequate physical set-up, personality clashes. Change technology, layout, group composition
Individual level	Failure to fulfil individuals' needs; frustration responses; unwillingness to consider change, little chance for learning and development Counselling, role analysis, career planning	Poor job definition, task too easy or too difficult Job restructuring/modification, redesign, enrichment, agree on key competencies	Poor match of individual with job, poor selection or promotion, inadequate preparation and training, recognition and remuneration at variance with objectives. Personnel changes, improved selection and promotion procedures, improved training and eduction, bring recognition and remuneration in line with objectives.

Source: Pugh (1986).

- *'Hurting' systems*: a special class of ready systems in which current conditions have created acute discomfort.
- *New teams or systems*: units without a history and whose tasks require a departure from old ways of operating.
- *Staffs*: subsystems that will be required to assist in the implementation of later interventions.
- *Temporary project systems*: *ad hoc* systems whose existence and tenure are specifically defined by the change plan.

In addition to the issue of where change interventions might take place, the planning of OD interventions must take account of the degree of change needed; that is, the scope of the change activities. In terms of the Pugh OD matrix, this means considering whether (a) people's *behaviour* needs to change, and/or (b) the *organization's structure and systems* need to change, and/or (c) the *context or setting* needs to change. As action moves from the left-hand column through to the right-hand column, a greater degree of intervention and commitment is required. A useful starting point, therefore, is the left column of the matrix. Subsequent moves towards the right-hand column should only be taken as it becomes necessary because of the dictates of the problem.

One of the axioms of action research is that the process of developing an action plan for change should be done through consultation and collaboration with those who will implement the change, thus reinforcing commitment to change. Beckhard and Harris's (1987, p. 72) concept of the action plan being a 'road map' for the change effort is a useful one. In addition, they write that an effective action plan should have the following characteristics:

- *Relevance*: activities are clearly linked to the change goals and priorities.
- *Specificity*: activities are clearly identified rather than broadly generalized.
- *Integration*: the parts are closely connected.
- *Chronology*: there is a logical sequence of events.
- *Adaptability*: there are contingency plans for adjusting to unexpected forces.

The last of these characteristics is particularly important. As anyone knows, it is all well and good setting out on a journey with the route well defined beforehand. However, because of the many things which exist to thwart the best laid plans (for instance, in the case of the road map and journey, traffic, passenger sickness, road works, accidents and so on). The plan must be flexible enough to adapt to the changing circumstances of not only *what* needs to change, but also possible changes in the transition process itself. Consequently, as figure 15.6 shows, the development of an action plan must always be linked closely to its subsequent implementation.

Stage 4: Implement the change

Any text dealing specifically with organization development as a change methodology contains details of different techniques and methods for initiating and implementing change (see, for instance, French and Bell, 1990; Cummings and Worley, 1993). In addition, the discussions in previous chapters of the book can be used to inform the implementation of change at the individual and group levels. The discussion of changing strategy, structures and cultures in this chapter can be drawn upon for advice on how to implement change at the organizational level.

The role of short-term wins

Implementing change which will ultimately transform an organisation is a *long-haul* process and it is understandable if commitment to the vision becomes somewhat weakened on the way (hence the the feedback arrows to stages 2 and 3 shown in figure 15.6). Consequently, the achievement of 'short-term wins' (Kotter, 1996) is important, both as a motivating factor and as a mechanism for tracking progress towards the longer-term goals. Kotter (p. 123) identifies six ways in which short-term wins can help organizational transformations. There are:

- provide evidence that sacrifices are worth it;
- reward change agents with a pat on the back;
- help to fine-tune vision and strategies;
- undermine cynics and self-serving resisters;
- keep bosses on board;
- build momentum.

Short-term wins do not, however, happen automatically as part of the change process. They have to be planned *deliberately* so that they become much more probabilities than possibilities. According to Kotter (pp. 121–2), a short-term win has three characteristics: (a) it is visible, so large numbers of people can see for themselves whether the result is real or just hype; (b) it is unambiguous, so there can be little argument over the call; (c) it is clearly related to the change effort.

An example of a short-term win is when a company reduces delivery time on one of its ten main products by a predetermined percentage in a predetermined time; or when the number of customer complaints reduces by (say) 50 per cent during the first half of the year; or when a group of employees' jobs become easier to do because they are getting more relevant information in a more timely way. Short-term wins are not 'We expect to increase our sales in the next couple of months'; nor the fact that two previously sworn enemies are now talking pleasantly to each other, unless the outcome is some further improvement in morale and organizational performance.

The setting and assessment of short-term wins links the implementation stage of the OD process to the more all-embracing assessment of the organization's progress towards its vision and the continuing reinforcement of the change process itself.

Stage 5: Assess and reinforce the change

Assessing change   For change situations located at the 'hard' end of the change spectrum, it is relatively easy to assess the extent to which change has been achieved. The setting of 'hard' objectives and quantifiable performance measures makes this a more straightforward process. However, in the softer, more 'messy' situations where OD type change methodologies tend to be used, change is an evolving process concerned not only with changes in quantifiable performance objectives, but more frequently with changes in attitudes, behaviours and cultural norms, where measurement is bound to be less precise. Even so, measurement of these things is possible. It is also desirable in terms of its role in providing positive feedback that the change process is 'working', and in testing how far the organization has moved towards achievement of its vision.

A number of ways are available for measuring the softer issues associated with change:

1   *A regular survey or cultural audit,* which can potentially cover all staff and whose results can be quantified and quickly disseminated. The Nationwide Building Society is an example of an organization which uses such a system as part of its commitment to continuous improvement.
2   *Interviews with individuals or focus groups,* which allow the collection of more qualitative, in-depth information. The Body Shop called this 'gazing into the mirror'.
3   *An examination of turnover and absenteeism rates* as an indication of general morale and well-being (see Parker, Chmiel and Wall, 1997).
4   *An analysis (through observation or questionnaire) of group performance* in terms of task achievement, but also in terms of the quality of meetings (including number of meetings and length) and leader performance.
5   *'Picturing the organization';* that is, asking staff to present their perception of the organisation in graphical or image terms rather than in words (see Flood and Jackson, 1991; Morgan, 1997). Alternatively, it might be in the form of a 'rich picture' (Checkland, 1981); that is, a collage of images represented by drawings and symbols connected by other symbols depicting the relationships between them. Figure 15.8 is an example of a rich picture depicting changes in the organization of services for people with learning difficulties, from hospital-based provision to 'care in the community' provision.

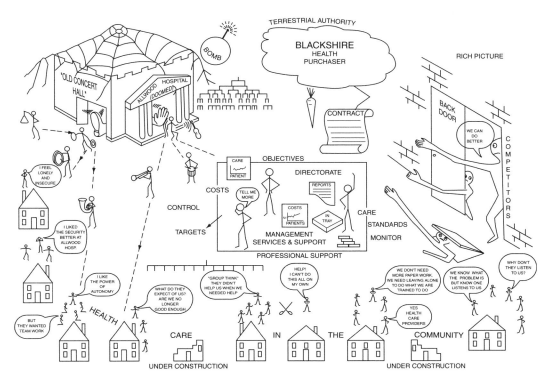

Figure 15.8 Rich picture of changes in the organization of services for people with learning difficulties.

Source: Barbara Senior (1997) *Organisational Change.* London: Financial Times Pitman Publishing, p. 286.

When the rich pictures about an organization start to resemble images closely related to the vision, management can have some confidence that the change has been successful in respect of how employees feel about it.

Reinforcing and consolidating change Farquhar, Evans and Tawadey (1989, p. 49) write: 'A real danger in the process of organisational change is the failure to carry it through sufficiently far. Companies may be tempted to relax when the immediate crisis recedes while they still have not addressed the deeper organisational problems which generated the crisis.' The lesson from this is that the new order resulting from any change needs to be institutionalized. This is well put by Mabey and Pugh (1995, p. 50): 'Individuals need to be held personally accountable for prescribed initiatives; new working relationships and boundaries between different working groups need to be negotiated; ways of recognising and rewarding desirable behaviours and attitudes need to be devised to demonstrate that the organisation is serious about the change strategies that have been set.'

It is pointless expecting people's behaviour to change if this is not reinforced by concomitant changes in personnel policies and practices, including appraisal, career development and reward systems. In addition, staff training and development needs to reorient itself to the needs of the new vision and the changes which help to guide its attainment. According to Farquhar et al., this is particularly important with regard to middle managers. While change can happen fast at the top (often through bringing in new people) and be accepted at the lower levels of organization (particularly if the rewards for change are clear), middle managers as the bridging function between the two may be slower to accept new cultures, policies and practices. Yet it is middle management which must make change work. They must, therefore, be given the new skills they will need – particularly when structures and cultures are expected to change.

More generally, the action research model of data collection, data analysis and feedback for action is just as important at this stage of OD as at any other. Any change programme is stressful, but if employees continue to own any changes this stress will become not negative stress, but positive pressure to accept that change can be the norm with the adoption of innovative, change-oriented behaviour.

Chapter Summary

The subject of organizational change and development is large. Almost all organizational and human resources issues are relevant to change management. Consequently, only some issues have been chosen for discussion here. The fact that change is a multidimensional concept has been emphasized. Major issues of changing strategies, structures and cultures have been discussed. Finally, as befits a text written from a psychological perspective, OD, as a people-focused approach to change and organizational development, has been described. The hope is that this chapter will have given readers a greater appreciation of change, as a phenomenon which influences almost all of organizational life.

Discussion Points

1   Discuss the proposition that 'All change can be categorized as *either* incremental *or* frame-breaking'. Use examples from your own experience of the nature of change in organizations.

2   How useful are the concepts of 'hard' and 'soft' change situations for determining an appropriate approach to designing and implementing organizational change?

3   Explain what is meant by 'assessing cultural risk'.

4   Discuss the advantages and disadvantages of using an OD approach to design and implement organizational change.

PART V

ISSUES FOR WORK AND ORGANIZATIONAL PSYCHOLOGY

Open workplace. (Ace Photo Library)

C H A P T E R
S I X T E E N

AGAINST ALL ODDS:
MANAGING DIVERSITY

Rebecca Lawthom

Contents

Chapter Outline

In this chapter the focus is on *difference* within the context of the workplace, namely those differences between individuals that are important in terms of the way we judge others. Initially, workplace approaches to equality flourished in the 1970s and 1980s under the slogan of 'equal opportunities'. The debate was then framed in terms of equal access to jobs and rights, regardless of social group membership, providing abilities were equal. More recently, the approach, which deals with individual differences in occupational terms, has been termed 'managing diversity'. This more inclusive term deals with the visible and less visible ways in which exclusion and discrimination are used in the workplace and is therefore a potentially more inclusive set of practices than earlier attempts at equality. I examine the nature of managing diversity; the ways in which organizations can and do adopt this approach; and evaluate its effectiveness as a way of conceptualizing and dealing with difference.

Difference in the Workplace

Labour markets in the twentieth century have undergone tremendous change in terms of employee diversity. In the late twentieth century, changing demographics (particularly in 'developing countries') indicate a workforce which is increasingly heterogeneous (Johnson and Packer, 1987). In the USA, Johnson and Packer suggest, by the year 2000, 85 per cent of growth within the workforce will be among black men and women (an inclusive term encompassing non-white races). Other US estimates suggest that by 2020 whites will be in the minority. Women, who are entering the workforce at increasing rates, are also transforming employment participation. Despite affirmative action schemes in the USA (which legally positively discriminate for minority groupings in the workplace), women and non-white members remain in the lower ranks of organizations (e.g. Braham, 1989). Similar trends, though less dramatic, are predicted in UK settings (Rajan, 1990).

In the past two decades, enormous changes have taken place in the composition of the UK workforce. Broadly, there are more women (e.g. Ellison, 1994), ethnic minorities (e.g. Sly, 1994), older workers and people with caring responsibilities (e.g. Berry-Lound, 1993). These demographic estimates suggest that organizations will increasingly need to recruit, select, train and retain workers who are 'different' from the traditional white organizational man.

Responses to Difference in the Workplace

Current legislation in UK settings consists of anti-discrimination legislation on grounds of sex (Equal Pay Act 1984 and Sex Discrimination Act 1986), race

(Race Relations Act 1976) and disability (Disability Discrimination Act 1996). These laws do not permit unfair discrimination towards individuals on the basis of sex, race and disability, but the onus is placed on the individual (who may feel discriminated against) to take legislative action. Moreover, current UK legislation does not extend to gay or lesbian workers. Research has clearly indicated that even when groups are 'protected' by legislation, this does not necessarily remove barriers or harassment in the workplace. Unlike the in USA, where quotas or targets enable companies to practice affirmative action, the UK legislation provides only a framework to be adhered to. Employees who feel discriminated against have to take employers to court, often at great financial and personal expense. Companies can comply with and interpret legislation very loosely. The basic premise of equal opportunities is that talent and ability are spread equally through all groups, including men and women, able bodied and disabled people, and all ethnic groupings.

While many employees claim to be equal opportunity employers, groups of employers can still experience discrimination (Aitkenhead and Liff, 1991). Collinson, Knights and Collinson (1990) showed that companies that had clear statements of equal opportunity policy still operated in a discriminatory fashion in the recruitment process.

Honey, Meager and Williams (1993) surveyed employment practices of disabled workers in the UK. Only one in twenty organizations approached the legal quota (of disabled employees), and over 50 per cent expressed stereotypical views of disabled people and their ability to do the job. However, three-quarters of companies who had employed disabled workers experienced no difficulties and half incurred no extra cost. This study demonstrates the way in which prejudice and stereotyping might effect disabled people's chances of obtaining employment (given the number of disabled workers within organizations), despite evidence to the contrary once inside the organization (regarding difficulties and costs). Gay and lesbian workers similarly report discrimination when applying for jobs (22 per cent) and in promotion (24 per cent), and almost half experienced harassment due to their sexuality (Stonewall, 1993).

Melamed (1995) examined the gender gap in the career success of men and women. She compared the importance of sex discrimination to alternative explanations: personality characteristics, human capital attributes, demographics, career choices, labour market forces and structural organizational features. Results revealed that while many of these factors explained a large amount of the variance in career success, over 55 per cent of the gender gap was attributed to sex discrimination. The 'glass ceiling' effect is well documented in the literature (e.g. Burke and McKeen, 1992). The progress of women in organizations is obstructed by the presence of an invisible 'glass' barrier which is explained in a variety of ways (Melamed, 1995). Recent research suggests a second, higher, ceiling for women in executive positions (Lyness and Thompson, 1997). Women's internal attributes are often presumed to explain career variation: women have lower salary expectations (Stevens, Bavetta and Gist, 1993) and managers attribute performance less to ability than in male counterparts (Greenhaus and Parasuraman, 1993). Moreover, structural factors and social norms place career and commitment in conflict for both women and employers. For example, women who choose to have children and return to work are in an individious position – seen as less committed than their child-free counterparts (within organizations) and expected by society to be perfect mothers (in the absence of quality state childcare).

Even in organizations where discrimination is addressed in the form of affirmative action, there is still potential for discrimination. In 1991, the UK government launched a programme named Opportunity 2000, aimed to increase the number of women in organizations. However, Heilman (1994) showed that women who were recruited and promoted within this initiative carried a 'stigma of incompetence' and experienced lower self-confidence and backlash from other organizational members. This supports Cockburn's work (1990), which showed that men (in companies where equal opportunities were practised) felt resentment and competition from women.

The differential treatment of men and women has been well researched (e.g. Dipboye, 1987), but understandings of race (e.g. Cox and Nkomo, 1986; Nkomo, 1992) and disability (McHugh, 1991) are less well developed. There are a few studies, however, which examine the attributions of managers regarding race in organizational settings. Braich (1992) examined the attributions and management styles of 24 black and white managers in six organizations. Using repertory grid techniques to elicit management styles, she found differences based on race and whether managers were equal opportunity managers or not. A scenario-based task which required managers to rate ability found black managers more generously rating both black and white employees and placing more emphasis on relationship and interaction issues. Moreover, black people and women were not attributed the same amount of credit (in identical situations) as white people and men (respectively) when being considered by managers.

The finding of differential treatment features repeatedly in studies of race and gender. Gordon, DiTomaso and Farri (1991) interviewed managers and workers in areas such as managerial, peer and subordinate expectations, communication, conflict and cooperation, career plans, work coordination and cultural and subcultural styles of interaction. Black employees reported that their competence was frequently questioned, despite comprehensive job selection and relevant job credentials. This resulted in unchallenging assignments, poor visibility and poor advancement opportunities. Women similarly felt the effect of this 'invisibility' syndrome, where commitment levels and childcare responsibilities were positioned in conflict by managers. Braich's and Gordon et al.'s studies and many others (e.g. Deaux and Emswiller, 1974; Falkenberg, 1990) suggest that managers, when assessing competence, fall back on stereotypes to form judgements. White males are assumed competent unless proven otherwise, while other groups are presumed to be less competent until they have proven themselves (e.g. Braham, 1989).

B o x   1 6 . 1

To examine bias inherent in the way we think about different groups in society, spend a few minutes thinking about the colours *black* and *white*. What associations and phrases come to mind?

Phrases that you may have thought of include the following. White is usually associated with cleanliness, purity or virginity. Phrases include white as the driven snow; whitewash; whiter than white; show the white feather. Black words or phrases have rather different associations: black sheep of the family; black looks; blackmail; blacklist; black as the ace of spades; Black Death; black market, black magic; black art; black humour. At a conscious level we use these words in everyday situations, but upon examination our language has colour within it. These words are not simply descriptions but carry with them a set of values and expectations, at an unconscious level.

The exercise in box 16.1 demonstrates (in a very simplistic way) the way in which our language and thinking is itself biased. If this example is extrapolated to stereotypes, our thinking is often rooted in exaggerated, unfounded assumptions about the way a group is or behaves. Given that research (of which only a flavour is presented here) suggests that people who are 'different' are treated unfairly, there is a clear case for action.

The Theoretical Components of Managing Diversity

Thomas (1992) terms the individuals who comprise the organization and take part in its activities the 'multidimensional mixture'. The 1990s phenomenon of managing diversity rests on the assumption that difference, heterogeneity and diversity between people can in some way be managed or harnessed for the benefit of all. Moreover, this perspective appears to place a more positive value on diversity. However, what do we mean by diversity? The definition of diversity advocated by Triandis, Kurowski and Gelfand (1993, p. 772) is: 'any attribute that humans are likely to use to tell themselves "that person is different from me"'. Given the inclusive nature of this definition, Triandis et al. (1993) see workplace diversity as a 'virgin field, lacking theoretical frameworks'. However, a definition proposed by Kandola and Fullerton (1994, p. 19) provides a useful starting point:

> The basic concept of managing diversity accepts that the workforce consists of a diverse population of people. The diversity consists of visible and non-visible differences, which will include factors such as sex, age, background, race, disability, and personality and work style. It is founded on the premise that harnessing these differences will create a productive environment in which

When we come into contact with people we make some judgements about where they come from, what type of personality they have and how similar or dissimilar they appear to be to ourselves. Psychologists have proposed a variety of theories to account for this: social comparison, attribution; social identity; person perception theory. Think of an organization or institution you have some knowledge of, e.g. a workplace or university. What factors do you use in order to judge people (particularly when you first encounter them)? Can these easily be distinguished as visible and non-visible?

everybody feels valued, where their talents are being fully utilised and in which organizational goals are met.

It would therefore appear that diversity management is not about what the majority population does to the minority group and, unlike some of the equal opportunities literature, does not operate on a 'difference as deficit' principle (Fine, Johnson and Ryan, 1990). Employees are not expected to assimilate into the dominant culture in order to fit in. This is an approach that works with difference, acknowledging diversity as an intrinsic piece of the organization.

Seeking to examine the impact of diversity on the organization's internal environment, Cox (1991, 1993) writes of the diversity climate within an organization having three levels. At the individual level, prejudice is experienced as bias towards outgroups. At the group level, the tendency is to view collectivities of people as being 'ingroups' or 'outgroups'. Here, majority and minority cultures retain individual identities but intergroup conflict may be a feature. At the organizational level, the focus is on the structural integration of diversity in the hierarchy and formal structure. In addition, informal social networks and management systems are important sources of potential bias, which generate obstacles to participation from minority cultures.

Some of the visible factors you might come up with in the activity in box 16.2 include 'race', age, gender, national origin, social class, disability, attractiveness, height/weight distribution, organizational position or status, physical abilities and intellectual abilities. The inferred sources of difference might include marital status, education, economic class, religion, sexual orientation, personality, political affiliation, geographic origins and state of health (e.g. AIDS). However, your list of visible and non-visible sources of diversity is probably very different from the one generated above in terms of visible versus inferred and the features which seem important to you. This clearly reflects your social upbringing and preconceptions about what constitutes difference and the importance you place upon it.

A body of research that has examined cultural difference supports this. Hofstede's work on organizational cultures (1980) examined organizations in thirty different countries, with workers of various cultural identities, and found diverse nationalities stressing and valuing different human characteristics. Hofstede (1980) defined culture as a 'mental programme' which controls behaviour. Human nature often prevents appreciation of the good points of other cultures, and we can become 'ethnocentric'. Broadly, this is the exaggerated tendency to believe that the characteristics of one's own group or race are superior to those of other groups or races. If each individual at work is operating along similar ethnocentric lines (using one's own culture as the standard), then heterogeneity in the workplace and the wider ramifications need to be addressed. How might our biases affect work allocation, recruitment, selection or promotion? In organizational settings, not only do individuals have their own preconceptions that can cause misunderstandings, but these misunderstandings create and maintain an organizational culture, affecting values and behaviours. Loden and Rosener (1991) list six assumptions which are embedded in contemporary organizational culture: 'otherness' is a deficiency; diversity poses a threat to efficient functioning; expressing discomfort with dominant values shows oversensitivity; those who are different wish to assimilate into the dominant group; equal treatment means the same treatment; managing diversity requires changing people not the culture. These shared norms can be implicit ways of controlling and managing attitudes and behaviour towards otherness. The implicit nature of these norms suggests that organizations need, first, to be aware and, second, to change potentially harmful practices.

The way in which discrimination is handled within organizations is clearly different depending on whether it originates from an equality or a diversity perspective. Whereas workplace equality measures involve a disregard of difference (as managers are assumed to make decisions on the basis of equal treatment), managing diversity perspectives suggests that managers should be actively trying to value and manage diversity.

The Benefits of Managing Diversity

The legislation concerning equality, actual statistics on employment participation and research findings provide good reasons for action in terms of more inclusive employment practices. However, organizations, if they are to embrace diversity initiatives, require strong reasons with evidence for changing their orientations to equality. The law has encouraged employers to create a fair and equal working environment but, in practice, relies on the ethics of those in positions of power, i.e. managers. There is evidence to suggest that homogeneity is often perpetuated in the workforce through managers recruiting in their own image (e.g. Alimo-Metcalfe, 1994). While, ethically, managing diversity has often become part of the moral agenda of corporate leadership, it is unlikely that change will occur unless there are clear gains promised. This tension between equality as morality and equality as profit has led certain commentators to argue that the moral issue is being sold as a business issue (e.g. Biswas and Cassell, 1996). The business case argues that employing and developing those with diverse talents and skills, those who might traditionally have been excluded as different, results in enhanced performance and competitive advantage.

A body of research that examines diversity is inconclusive in terms of positive outcomes. Work on the impact of diversity on work team composition (Jackson, 1991) suggests both advantages and disadvantages for effective functioning. Positive benefits might be increased innovation (Bantel and Jackson, 1989) and potential productivity (Jackson, 1991), and the reduction of 'groupthink' (given greater employee heterogeneity). On the downside, evidence relates diversity to stress, turnover, communication and interpersonal attraction (Adler, 1990; Storey, 1991). Riordan and Shore (1997) examined the effects of individual similarity to workgroup demography, in relation to individual attitudes. They found that race similarity affected attitudes towards the work group and views on promotional possibilities. Gender and tenure similarity was not significant in influencing attitudes. Research on organizational demography has suggested that gender and race differences between members is associated with reduced levels of organizational attachment and social integration for individuals who are different at work (in terms of race and gender), even if in a majority in society, i.e. white and male (Tsui, Egan and O'Reilly, 1992). Organizational heterogeneity impacts on individuals' work experiences, in addition to the impact at more macro levels. Cox and Blake (1991) review findings which suggest that companies that manage diversity gain multiple benefits. Proactive businesses can expect to:

- reduce costs of high turnover and absenteeism among new entrants, who will experience a more comfortable context at work, and more traditional employees who may feel threatened by new diversity;
- ease the burden of recruiting scarce labour;
- enhance their position in terms of image with minority groupings that are clients, customers or service recipients;
- reduce conflict between groups at work, transforming negative energy into innovation and enhanced performance;
- lower communication barriers, impacting on problem-solving.

This formidable catalogue of competitive advantages suggests that doing diversity is of great cost benefit. While the business case for diversity may be a convenient selling feature, evidence which firmly relates diversity to effectiveness is needed if managers are to be persuaded to change.

Implementation of Diversity Approaches

What does managing diversity entail? What initiatives have been proposed and adopted in organizational settings? In an ideal world, where difference is valued, interventions, which deal with diversity, operate at many levels. Triandis et al. (1993) propose four interventions:

- societal change, through government policy, tax incentives and large-scale educational programmes;
- organizational change in terms of operating procedures – affirmative action and educational programmes;
- interpersonal relationship change in terms of understanding the views of other members;
- attitudinal change in terms of interpersonal processes (those which reside within the individual).

Psychologists have mainly focused on the last two levels in terms of actual interventions. Kandola and Fullerton (1994) examined the use of 40 possible diversity initiatives from the literature. From a sample of 2000 UK companies, 285 organizations returned the survey. Findings suggested ten frequently implemented initiatives: equal opportunities (EO) policies; EO monitoring; EO strategy; physically changing the work environment; eliminating age criteria from selection procedures; harassment policy; flexible working arrangements; time off beyond legal requirements for carers; fair selection training for recruiters; and having ongoing contact with local/national specialist groups (e.g. disability). Those least implemented include assistance on career breaks, target setting, childcare assistance and surveying opinion on equal opportunities. A clear pattern emerged of policies and monitoring being introduced or in place, while more controversial issues, such as affirmative action or childcare, were largely neglected. In terms of the success of initiatives, the introduction of equal rights and benefits for part-time workers and allowing time off for caring responsibilities were judged to be of universal benefit (defined as actions relating to equalizing treatment between staff). The least successful involved setting targets, using positive action and initiatives which tended to focus on particular groups (which conflicts with the ethos of managing diversity and is not of universal benefit).

Kandola and Fullerton (1994) found that many organizations implemented policies with little understanding of how they fitted in with overall objectives, and little or no evaluation of whether these actions were successful. Given the many choices facing managers in organizations, research confirms that, in practice, they choose easier options rather than more strategic responses.

To examine the way in which an organization might approach managing diversity, let us look at case study 16.1 (cited in Totta and Burke, 1995).

A bank in North America took the decision in 1989 to manage diversity. A new management team that swept in made a commitment to workplace diversity as a central business objective. Examining representation of different groups within the organizations, general underrepresentation and senior management underrepresentation were features of the workforce. While 75 per cent of the workforce were female, only 6 per cent of executives and 13 per cent of senior managers were female. The communities in which the bank served were diverse, and a workforce who more closely matched the indigenous populations would enhance customer service. The new corporate strategic plan set out the bank's intention to be a fair and equitable employer. In articulating this commitment more precisely, the following points were drawn up:

- We will create a diverse workforce, which represents and reflects, at all levels and in all groups, the wider community of the bank's customers.
- We will ensure that the workplace is equitable and all employees will have an equal opportunity of career progression.
- We will create a supportive work environment in which equality and diversity goals inform and influence all other business goals.

While many companies publish or talk about equality and opportunity, what characterizes this organization is the determined nature and commitment to follow through. Aware of the huge cultural change this initiative will bring, the bank needed to integrate diversity fully as an assumption within each business decision. The bank set up task forces comprised of employees. Their goals were to identify barriers to diversity and devise structures and programmes which would enable the bank to reach its goals.

Activity

What measures do you think might be useful in overcoming diversity? Which would you prioritize?

The first task force examined the advancement of women. Within a year the task force had published a report with 26 action plans to overcome the problem. By the end of the second year, two task forces proposed 54 action plans: one on the employment of aboriginal people and the other on the employment of disabled people. Another task force was set up to meet the needs of people who came from visible minorities (i.e. non-white). The task forces were carefully structured to ensure maximum impact. The philosophy was underpinned by five elements:

- *Executive sponsorship*: senior executives sponsored each task force, ensuring executive level interest and underlining the importance of the diversity message.
- *Employee participation*: different regions, levels and groups were mixed together, ensuring grassroots input and involvement in decisions. In this way people who faced barriers became part of the solution rather than the problem group.
- *Getting the facts out*: task forces examined and debunked myths and false assumptions of why groups were underrepresented. To ensure inclusion, they sent each member of the organization a personally addressed copy of the report, emphasizing employee representation.
- *Inclusive approach*: while each task force examined barriers faced by a particular group, the central aim was the removal of obstacles for all. Managers were targeted with programmes to enable them to understand their new roles in a diverse workplace.
- *Accountability and integration*: detailed action plans and deadlines ensured integration and managerial accountability. This signalled to all the importance of the issue in terms of centrality and time.

Given these changes, what do you think the outcomes were?

While *women* had traditionally made up 75 per cent of the workforce, they formed only 6 per cent of executives and 13 per cent of senior managers. The assumptions, such as women being too old, too young, too committed to childcare, less educated, not skilled enough, and the response that time would sort things out, were challenged and demolished. Task forces, interviews and surveys were carried out. A workshop aiming to raise gender awareness was developed, and action plans recommended 50 per cent participation in management development programmes. Other action plans were put into place and focused on opportunity for all; for example, an on-line career network accessible to all and an executive advisor programme which pairs those seeking career development and mentors. To balance work and family life, new policies were implemented. Flexitime, flexible workweek and job sharing are available to all employees. These arrangements have led to equivalent productivity and satisfaction. Rather than defining these as women's issues or family programmes, work life programmes allow flexibility for all employees in the form of extended leave and people care days (paid time off to tend to personal matters which are scheduled in work time, e.g. taking an elder parent to the doctor).

Employees who were *minorities* were subject to a range of myths and false assumptions. The task force on disabled people found that cost was a factor in meeting the needs of disabled employees. The task force clarified the minimal costs of the equipment and found they could be offset by government funds. The importance of managing diversity was crystallized by a new appointment, a vice president for workplace equality. Changing individuals takes a long time and many people found it hard to see how their own assumptions unconsciously affected job behaviour and decision-making. In order to ensure that the job of valuing diversity is not the sole responsibility of the vice president, a network of people form a core team, equality coordinators and advisory councils. Weaving diversity and equality issues into the fabric of the bank's culture, the following are indicative of policies and procedures.

- *Business planning*: managers must set goals for recruitment and selection of underrepresented groupings.
- *Performance review*: managers are assessed in terms of meeting this target, and creating a climate which values diversity. The manager is also accountable for the performance of the work team, thus preventing hiring becoming a numbers game.
- *Staffing*: recruitment and selection procedures include outreach work and competency-based interviewing to remove some of the bias associated with interviewing.
- *Corporate values:* induction and codes of conduct emphasize that discrimination against people is prohibited. Sponsorship money funds the education and career development of underrepresented groups.
- *Learning:* workshops on gender and diversity awareness reinforce diversity.
- *Communication:* senior management messages, handbooks, news magazines and videos (whether news or training) all reiterate the message of commitment to diversity.
- *Public relations:* publicity about goals and task forces is released to the media. Marketing and recruitment campaigns emphasize diversity.

This bank clearly not only espouses diversity but also has implemented diversity as a core value in the company. Cultural change is continuing, with constant re-examination of bias and apathy. The bank is not satisfied with surface change and recognizes that culture is multifaceted and less amenable to change.

Case study 16.1 informs our understanding of diversity. The mission statement, which values diversity, is followed through with sponsorship, participation, accountability and inclusion at all levels. Both attitudinal change (e.g. workshops) and change in policy and practice occurs (e.g. recruitment, selection etc.). What form does a managing diversity initiative typically take? Copeland (1988) notes measures that are included in a valuing diversity programme. These are: community initiatives and publicity to target people typically underrepresented; mentoring support and developments to counteract the 'glass ceiling' effect; managerial training to educate regarding stereotypes and cultural barriers; access to career development track jobs and providing benefits which include all. One company in the USA, heralded as a family friendly organization, was keen to embrace diversity. One of its initiatives was to retain and attract talented working mothers through job sharing. Part-timers received 80 per cent of full-time benefits, clearly a strategy for retention (cited in Adams, 1995). These features are similar to good human resource management practices (Liff and Wacjman, 1996), characterized as 'new industrial relations' (Guest, 1987; Legge, 1989; Storey, 1995), with the emphasis on the role of the individual in career development and the enhancement of involvement and commitment in organizations.

How is managing or embracing diversity different from equal opportunity legislation? Many models of diversity have originated primarily from the USA, where demographic predictions are making more immediate impact. Bartz, Hillman, Lehrer and Mayhugh (1990) propose a model which strives towards cultural heterogeneity. The model considers five areas:

1   Organizational acceptance and commitment: where the concept of managing diversity is embraced by top management and communicated to all.
2   Understanding the concept of diversity and attributes of major subpopulations: organization-wide awareness training, which examines differences in race, culture, disability and gender.
3   Work styles and motivation: individualized performance management models would be used to identify work style preferences.
4   Developmental needs and career aspirations: development and acquisition should be stressed rather than training (a short-term fix).
5   Personal needs: flexitime, childcare facilities, employee assistance programmes are ways in which organizations can cater for diverse personal needs.

Other models show similar features (e.g. Rosen and Lovelace, 1991), but there is a lack of empirical work which tests impact in real-life organizational settings. Kandola and Fullerton (1994) propose an image of diversity as MOSAIC. The powerful image of mosaic sees difference as constructing a pattern, a whole organization, and the whole being comprised of individuality. Six features are present in this model:

- *Mission and values*: managing diversity needs to be dovetailed into business objectives, mission statements and vision. This avoids diversity becoming seen as important to some employees.
- *Objective and fair processes*: key processes and systems should be monitored to ensure fairness. Recruitment techniques, selection, induction and appraisal systems are all potential areas of bias.
- *Skilled workforce*: aware and fair. The workforce should be aware of diversity and developed and managed appropriately.
- *Active flexibility*: working patterns, policies and practices should be flexible, addressing work/life needs of all individuals. For example, employees could choose from a cafeteria of benefits rather than employees with families being targeted for certain policies and incentives.
- *Individual focus*: individuals are managed, not groups.
- *Culture that empowers*: a culture should be consistent with the principle of managing diversity. Features here include devolved decision-making, participation and consultation.

Copeland's (1988) review of managing diversity initiatives indicates a plethora of measures which are compatible with good human resource practice. Is there a distinction between human resource management practices and managing diversity initiatives? Dass and Parker (1996) review approaches to the management of diversity, classifying them along two dimensions: a programmatic approach which involves developing separate but ongoing programmes for each diversity concern, and a non-programmatic approach, which involves creating an integrated process which deals with diversity. Adapting DeLuca and McDowell's (1992) programmed versus non-programmed model of initiatives, Dass and Parker (1996) and a third: the episodic approach. This approach represents an isolated attempt to manage diversity, because it does not link with ongoing organizational activities. For example, a manager may investigate a complaint of sexual harassment and a report may be produced, but nothing substantive changes. The incident or reporting of it begins a process which is accommodating and reactive, not proactive. The programmatic approach involves setting up a stable and ongoing programme of initiatives. This may focus on disability, work family needs etc., and new programmes arise in line with issues. Here, the approach can be flexible but the existence of many different programmes can make implementation quite difficult. The process or non-programmatic approach embodies simplicity and structural integration. Rather than setting up individually tailored programmes, the organization delegates responsibility to line managers. For example, an appraisal system might include diversity goals for managers.

Kandola and Fullerton (1994) found that a number of organizational interventions were positively related to the successful strategic implementation of managing diversity. These were clear vision, senior management support, auditing needs, the setting of objectives, clear communication, establishing accountability and the coordination and evaluation of actions. Hammond and Holton (1991) noted that organizations that were better at managing strategic change were also better at managing diversity initiatives. Diversity is more than a quick fix for organizations, and this has implications for evaluation of programmes.

One of the problems of valuing or managing diversity, in a practical sense, is the clear lack of empirical research which evaluates initiatives effectively. Many of the theoretical approaches are useful in clarifying the terms of the debate but lack rigorous testing in actual organizational settings. Ellis and Sonnenfeld (1994) claim that diversity programmes are justified purely on the basis of generic statistics and strategic mission statements. Programmes and initiatives range from fast track programmes, targeted training, monitoring and multicultural workshops to corporate communications. The success of these programmes in terms of better sensitivity and enhanced productivity is largely unaddressed. Moreover, many programmes which are evaluated are short term in nature, e.g. a day. These workshops make the assumption that contact (in a structured format) with other organizational members will clear up any misperceptions and facilitate better working. However, Thompson and DiTomaso (1988) warn of 'band-aid' programmes, which ensure that participants 'plug in' for a day without cultural change. Hewstone and Brown (1986), in their work on groups, similarly point out that short-term fixes are dangerous in terms of stereotype change. Differences need to be carefully handled over time, addressing both individual and organizational cultural change.

Models of managing diversity and the fact that difference is actively addressed demonstrate the shift away from their equal opportunities predecessor. Anti-discrimination legislation aims to give individuals the same rights to pay, conditions etc. Equal opportunities policies within organizations are widespread, contributing to what Jewson and Mason (1986) term a 'liberal' approach to equal opportunities. The equal opportunities framework positions women, disabled people and minority groups as 'other' (presuming there is a norm), focusing largely on issues of discrimination. It is traditionally a personnel or human resource management function, which relies on remedial and/or positive action. In contrast, diversity originates from the organizational literature, which acknowledges that 'normal' behaviour is defined as the behaviour of employees who are white, male, able bodied heterosexuals from mainstream ethnic groups (Nkomo, 1992). Thus, managing diversity aims to be broader in focus, with all individuals being diverse or different and awareness and change being the responsibility of all personnel throughout the organization. It embraces differences among *all* employees and takes into account culture and strategy. The notion of workplace diversity is not merely 'old wine in new bottles'; it is fundamentally different from equal opportunities in both assumption and practice.

Who Manages Diversity?

Despite the inclusive coverage of the diversity principle, managers will continue to play a major role in both strategic decisions about managing diversity and the implementation of such initiatives. Given the overlap between good human resource initiatives and valuing diversity, are managerial skills different when managing diversity?

Research addressed above suggests the existence of gender stereotypes and racial stereotypes in workplace settings. Given the inflexible and resistant nature of stereotypes, are there specific competencies or skills related to diversity? At an individual level, self-knowledge and reflection on biases and filters can help to evaluate people differently (e.g. Kennedy and Everest, 1991; Carr-Ruffino, 1996). McEnrue (1993) suggests that certain qualities are necessary for effective cross-cultural communication, such as the capacity to be non-judgmental, to demonstrate empathy, to be flexible and to acknowledge ignorance. While many of these skills are relevant to diversity, they share many of the features of good leadership skills.

Organizational Processes to Manage Diversity

Valuing diversity and incorporating difference are concepts which are beyond the scope of one individual. A manager may show a propensity to manage difference, but can he or she achieve substantive change? Case study 16.1 demonstrated the way in which managing diversity as a value system permeated the whole organization, even to the appointment of a new vice president. In this section I examine the processes within organizations which might facilitate diversity.

Alimo-Metcalfe (1994) likens the progress of women into organizational hierarchies as akin to waiting for fish to grow feet. Her research indicates that processes of assessment, used in selection, promotion, spotting for fast track development and appraisals, are mechanisms which operate against women's development. Processes such as recruitment, selection, induction and appraisals, which appear benign, are value laden, explicitly devaluing or failing to recognize women's competencies (or those of any minority group).

Recruitment is the process the organization uses to attract applicants. Organizations often complain that certain sectors of the population do not apply for work. How can diversity be addressed here? Kandola and Fullerton's research (1994) indicated that organizations which tried to target under-represented groups by advertising (e.g. in ethnic media) were not entirely successful. Rather than examining the problem, a solution was found which did not address the problem. Recruitment needs to be examined with reference to a wider context.

Selection techniques are procedures used by the organization to discriminate between employees. While unfair discrimination refers to wrongful discrimination, a fair selection procedure should discriminate between a group of employees. A large body of research in this area suggests that selection procedures need to be both valid (effective) and fair. Schmitt (1989) concludes that assessment centres and work sample tests are both valid and fair selection procedures. Even techniques which are valid and fair may impact differentially on certain groups. Processes such as job analysis, diverse pilot samples, trained selection personnel and monitoring of the process should continually inform the selection process.

Induction is the process by which the individual becomes socialized into the organization. Those in a minority group will inevitably take longer owing to the lack of role models and/or support mechanisms (e.g. Kanter, 1977). Bauer and Green (1994) found that initial impressions lasted for months, and newcomers who were more involved in work-related activities felt more integrated. Induction and socialization are clearly central to diversity, as newcomers who fail to feel integrated may soon exit the organization. Kandola and Fullerton (1994) recommend the following: clearly state what the organization values, assign mentors to newcomers, design a flexible induction programme and ensure induction personnel are fully trained.

Appraisals take many forms in organizations. Broadly, they review and evaluate past performance and future training needs. To make this process fair, criteria need to be linked to specific behavioural competencies rather than personality. Objectives can be jointly set and the process of meeting them open to negotiation. Appraisal training and openness about the process make the system visible and accountable.

These processes, if enacted, should ensure that people are recruited, selected, inducted and developed using fair criteria. Using objective job criteria and systematic procedures should allow employers to ensure diversity is valued, and new candidates are not clones of the organization, or 'yes men'. Being systematic and rigorous should allow inclusion, as fair procedures minimize the effect of stereotyping and ethnocentrism.

Evaluation of Managing Diversity

In this chapter, we have touched on the notion of affirmative action, different legislative frameworks and the morality of valuing diversity. Positive action frameworks benefit specifically the targeted group (race or gender), but how does this affect others? Managing diversity approaches seem to conceptualize the notion of difference in a variety of ways. Liff (1996) writes of approaches being classified as accommodating, valuing, dissolving and utilizing differences. Policies which accommodate differences may make positions genuinely open to men and women, or recruit underrepresented groups and support them by mentoring. The valuing difference approach acknowledges difference, and organizations may provide training in awareness to perpetuate knowledge. Policies here may be based upon differentiation as a way of securing equality. Dissolving differences involves treating people as individuals, and thus not using equality to guide decision-making. For example, training needs may be addressed regardless of race or gender, and the aim is to create an environment where everyone is valued. The last approach (not really claimed by managing diversity proponents) would be utilizing difference. Here, differentiating between groups is an important precursor to policy-making, e.g. parallel career tracks for 'career' women and family women, the 'mommy track' (Shwartz, 1992).

Managing diversity is often portrayed as a fair solution to handling difference. However, fairness can be viewed from diverse perspectives. Prasad and Mills (1997) see the upsurge of interest shown in managing diversity in the management and organizational literature as a journey from 'showcase to shadow'. They argue that diversity has received largely positive publicity (showcasing) both in terms of long-term economic benefits and in terms of application (the idea that organizations can implement diversity initiatives). This happy face of managing diversity implies success, often at a superficial level. The shadows in the showcase are a 'host of gender conflicts, race tensions and cultural frictions' (p. 12).

Prasad and Mills (1997) see major shortcomings in the diversity showcase. First, diversity has multiple meanings, which may conflict: these range from proportional representation of different groups, to overcoming prejudice or changing the fabric of work practices in keeping with cultural influences of various groups. Second, the contributions of diversity programmes are questioned as being no more than training interludes, which do not impact upon discrimination. Examining discrimination at a societal level, the authors note that the growth of the new right in many democratic countries suggests that dominant groups do not always welcome multiculturalism. Indeed, diversity initiatives occur within organizations, while books are published which 'claim' scientific proof that certain races have superior intelligence (Murray and Hernstein, 1994). It would appear that managing diversity might have to deal with this backlash.

Third, organizations share a number of norms, values and cultural preferences (Schein, 1985) which result in organizational monoculturalism. The homogeneity of organizational culture and subsequent similarities in codes of dress, demeanour, performance and commitment expectations make it almost impossible to accommodate, under one organizational roof, the variety of multicultural preferences, such as home/work boundaries or the place of work in society (e.g. Martin, 1992). So while individual members may quickly acculturate, organizations will structurally position difference as otherness – going against the norm. Martin (1992) makes the point that motherhood is a barely tolerated form of career deviance. Critiquing the assumptions of managing diversity in this way frames diversity as a buzzword, a product to be consumed. In this context, Prasad and Mills (1997) warn of the danger of visibly consuming diversity (e.g. sensitive celebration of different cultural festivals) while leaving the dominant culture of organizations and workplaces undisturbed (Jacoby, 1994). Cassell (1996) similarly sees the managing diversity paradigm as having goals in business success and competitive advantage, rather than social justice. These critiques suggest that inequality as conceptualized within managing diversity is neutralized and reframed in a socially acceptable language. This calls for diversity to be examined in a social, political, cultural and historical context.

The Future of Diversity at Work

Managing diversity is a complex issue for individuals, organizations and institutions, which Moorhead and Griffen (1995) term a 'tossed salad'. In this chapter, I have outlined what constitutes diversity and provided a rationale that justifies diversity approaches in terms of perceived benefits, demography and morality. Different approaches to diversity were then examined in the form of models and an actual case study used. The implications of diversity were outlined in terms of actual organizational processes, such as recruitment and development. Conceptually, the framing of difference and resolution was reviewed in both equal opportunity and managing diversity frameworks. Having outlined the nature of the managing diversity debate, is diversity 'old wine in new bottles' or a radically new approach, which deals with difference? The challenges presented within a multicultural workforce are complex and invisible and resistance to change is found at both individual and institutional levels. The complexity of diversity and the understanding that difference itself (colour, gender and disability) is socially constructed make the possibility of change more difficult. Managing diversity approaches can have a constructive role to play in securing equality for all in workplace settings. However, the essential difficulty of defining what constitutes managing diversity and how this might differ from equal opportunities is a thorny issue. To provide novel resolutions to the concept of difference, initiatives need to be inclusive, but organizations do not exist within a vacuum. They are mini reproductions of the society in which they are embedded. Kandola and Fullerton (1994) discuss the overlap between the diversity-oriented organization and the learning organization, since both share the aim of realization of the potential of *all* employees. The basis for this is the idea that 'organizing is the repeated occurrence of the knowledge process' (Herriot and Pemberton, 1995), irrespective of whether this is undertaken under managing diversity or learning organization banners.

The language and terminology of the managing diversity school assumes that difference can be managed or valued differently, and this is questionable if we apply psychological theory to complex human relationships (e.g. the literature on culture change). The assumption that heterogeneity is best will be difficult to emphasize in organizations. Organizations have traditionally had human resource systems based on models of homogeneity which promote similarity. Jackson (1992) shows how traditional human resource models foster homogenization, recruiting practices emphasize hiring people from sources that have been historically reliable, selection procedures stress choosing candidates similar to those who have been successful, training programmes foster uniform ways of thinking and policies are designed to limit supervisor latitude in addressing employees' unique needs. This type of approach has been coined 'homosocial reproduction' by Kanter (1977), referring to the tendency of selection and promotion systems to allow to pass through only employees who fit with the characteristics of the dominant coalition.

In order to address and challenge 'otherness' within organizations (and society), we need to examine the social, political, cultural and historical context in which diversity has evolved. If occupational/organizational psychology is to make a difference, practitioners and theorists need to see the wood and the trees, the shadows and the showcase of the managing diversity debate.

Discussion Points

1 Consider the economic/business and moral case for managing diversity. How does it differ from traditional equal opportunity approaches?

2 Identify the primary stakeholders in implementing a managing diversity programme in an organization. How would you communicate the benefits to the different stakeholders?

3 Explore the links between managing diversity approaches and other kinds of organizational initiatives, e.g. the learning organization?

Key Studies

The literature for managing diversity is a mix of practitioner texts (case study and anecdotal evidence) and theoretical papers (with limited empirical work). For a good overall review of the managing diversity paradigm, read: Triandis, H. C., Kurowski, L. L. and Gelfand, M. J. (1993) Workplace diversity. In H. C. Triandis, M. D. Dunnette and L. M. Hough (eds) *Handbook of Industrial and Organizational Psychology, Volume 3.* Palo Alto, CA: Consulting Psychologists Press.

A good practitioner text, which blends theory and practice well, is: Kandola, R. and Fullerton, J. (1994) *Managing the Mosaic: Diversity in Action*. London: IPD.

For critical insight and awareness of the wider issues try: Prasad, P. and Mills, A. J. (1997) From showcase to shadow: understanding the dilemmas of workplace diversity. In P. Prasad, A. J. Mills, M. Elmes and A. Prasad (eds), *Managing the Organizational Melting Pot, Dilemmas of Workplace Diversity*. Newbury Park, CA: Sage.

CHAPTER SEVENTEEN

JOB PERFORMANCE AND THE AGEING WORKFORCE

Peter Warr

Contents

Chapter Outline

This chapter examines the relationship between age and performance of several kinds, and explores possible explanations of the findings reported. It reviews the nature and consequences of experience and expertise, and looks specifically at the acquisition of new skills and knowledge at different ages. A general model of the factors likely to influence job effectiveness is outlined, covering information-processing ability, expertise, personality and motivation.

Introduction

Many developed countries face a growing imbalance in the age distribution of their working populations. Associated with a temporary increase in the birth rate in the 1940s and 1950s and a later decline in family size, the proportion of older workers will increase and that of younger ones decline. For example, in 1996 some 46 per cent of the labour force of the European Union were aged over 40; by 2020, it is projected that this value will have increased to 54 per cent (European Commission, 1997). Within the United Kingdom, projected labour force changes between 1996 and 2006 are as follows: ages 16 to 34 (excluding students), a decline of 13 per cent; ages 35 to 54, an increase of 12 per cent; ages 55 to 64, an increase of 30 per cent (Ellison, Tinsley and Houston, 1997). A similar pattern will be found in the USA, Australia and other countries (World Health Organization, 1993; Warr, 1994a). One implication is that employers will be less able to attract and retain younger staff, especially those who have high educational qualifications and are in demand from many organizations; older employees will have to fill the gaps.

Furthermore, the nature of paid work has changed considerably in recent years, so that many older staff are likely to experience task demands that are different from those with which they have been familiar. All developed countries have seen a shift away from agriculture and manufacturing industry to the services sector, which in many cases now accounts for more than two-thirds of all jobs. Hard manual labour is less common in developed countries than it once was, and most older as well as younger workers are likely to require cognitive and interpersonal skills rather than physical strength. Many jobs now depend on information technology, with associated mental demands on operators. Furthermore, the pace of change has been increased by greater international competition and multinational ownership. A major question in many countries at present is how far older workers are able to meet the challenges which will increasingly face them. We need to learn more about their strengths and weaknesses relative to younger employees.

The dividing line between workers who are 'younger' and 'older' is of course not a fixed one. Many commentators consider the age of 50 as a threshold, but some view employees as becoming 'older' at 45 or even 40. Attitudes to older people and older workers tend to be somewhat negative (Kite and Johnson, 1988). Pessimistic age stereotypes are widespread, and are associated with many older people's experiences of age discrimination in recruitment, selection and promotion (Walker, 1997). Older workers who lose their jobs are likely to remain unemployed for longer periods than younger people, and as many as 80 per cent of British personnel managers report that age discrimination is a problem in their area of work (Warr and Pennington, 1993).

Are Older Workers Less Effective than Younger Ones?

Linked to the widespread prejudice against older people in the labour market is a common belief that they tend to be less good at their jobs than younger people. However, research findings point clearly to the contrary: across jobs as a whole there is no significant difference between the job performance of older and younger workers. The average correlation coefficient between age and job performance from more than 100 investigations is about +0.06 (McEvoy and Cascio, 1989).

Sometimes older workers are found to be less effective than younger ones, and sometimes they are definitely better; correlations in different settings range from −0.44 to +0.66. Three recent illustrations are as follows. Among operatives aged between 19 and 62 in a meat-packing plant, the correlation between age and rated performance was almost zero (+0.07) (Schwoerer and May, 1996). For sales representatives aged between 21 and 62 that value was +0.34: older people were much better (Liden, Stilwell and Ferris, 1996). For hospital nurses between 21 and 61 years, the correlation of age with supervisors' ratings of overall performance was −0.22: older nurses were considered to be less good (Ferris, Yates, Gilmore and Rowland, 1985).

There is some evidence for age differences in specific job-related attributes, but the wide between-person variation at all ages means that any given individual may be an exception to the general pattern. There is undoubtedly an increase in knowledge with age, although that is not necessarily linear. Older employees are considered by personnel managers to be more reliable, careful, loyal and interpersonally skilled, but they are viewed as less willing to change than are their younger colleagues (Warr and Pennington, 1993). A scale of self-reported work-role flexibility was correlated −0.30 with age in a study by Birdi, Allan and Warr (1997).

More generally, it is clear that different job demands are likely to give rise to different correlations between age and performance. However, the presence of either positive or negative associations with age in specific studies cannot be linked to different kinds of work, because most research reports lack sufficient information about the tasks involved. A conceptual, rather than empirical, approach appears to be necessary, and an overall framework is suggested below.

Although absence because of sickness is often found to be greater at older ages, the opposite is the case for 'voluntary' absence, when people take time off work without medical or organizational approval (Martocchio, 1989; Hackett, 1990). The overall age pattern of absenteeism thus depends on the mix of those two effects in a particular organization, and in many cases either there is no overall age difference or younger employees are absent more often than older ones. Accidents at work are more common at younger ages, especially among inexperienced staff, although older peoples' fewer accidents may be more serious (Dillingham, 1981; Laflamme and Menckel, 1995). In respect of staff turnover, older people are less likely to leave their employer voluntarily (e.g. Doering, Rhodes and Schuster, 1983), partly because they are less able to obtain new jobs.

Some studies have examined a range of job behaviours in conjunction with financial indicators, to determine the overall outcome of employing older staff. For example, an American hotel group was unable to recruit enough younger people to handle reservation enquiries by telephone, and decided to appoint above the ages which previously had been usual. Productivity comparisons were subsequently made between reservations agents aged below 50 and those aged 50 and above. Older staff were found to be slower (with telephone conversations being somewhat longer) but equally likely to arrange a reservation. They were substantially less likely to leave the company, with considerable savings in recruitment and initial training costs. In terms of wage, health and pension expenditure, the typical older worker was found to require annually about 9 per cent less than the average younger one, principally because of lower turnover rates and resulting savings on the recruitment and training of new staff. It was concluded that 'hiring older workers was a success' (McNaught and Barth, 1992, p. 60).

Why Might One Expect Older Workers to Be Less Effective?

Although older employees are on average no better or worse than younger ones, hundreds of laboratory and psychometric studies have demonstrated that they perform less well in certain forms of information-processing. A general indicator is in terms of measures of 'fluid' intelligence, covering abilities such as seeing relationships among unfamiliar patterns, drawing inferences from relationships and understanding implications between different elements. It has long been established that older people in the working population (and of course beyond that) perform less well on tests of fluid intelligence than do their younger counterparts (e.g. Salthouse, 1991a). The effects are not great on average, and their implication for job performance is not fully clear, but they are consistently found.

Particular problems are faced by older people in mental processing which involves 'working memory': carrying out operations on one set of material while other information is held in temporary storage (one's working memory) before being brought back into active processing. For instance, in a laboratory investigation people might be presented with a list of words to keep in mind, then asked to carry out a task of logical reasoning about different material, before recalling the initial list of words. Older individuals tend to be less effective in working memory tasks than younger people (Craik and Jennings, 1992); for instance, the average correlation with age was −0.36 in the meta-analysis by Verhaeghen and Salthouse (1997).

Working memory is widely involved in complex mental processes, as different elements are mentally manipulated and held in store before a conclusion is reached. It appears that the age decrement in this activity can account for many other processing differences between older and younger people. For example, Salthouse (1991a) studied performance on several reasoning tasks as a function of age (between 20 and 84 years). Measures were also taken of each person's working memory effectiveness, and those indicators were found to account substantially for the age decrement in reasoning itself. It appears that age decrements in reasoning ability derive largely from decrements in working memory.

Older people's poorer information-processing of many kinds is also associated with a general cognitive slowing (Welford, 1985; Myerson, Hale, Wagstaff, Poon and Smith, 1990); the average correlation between age and processing speed was −0.52 in the meta-analysis by Verhaeghen and Salthouse (1997). Slower reactions may sometimes be problematic in their own right, but they can also have a more general effect, degrading mental activities which superficially do not seem to demand rapid processing. Since processing capacity is limited, there is a need to pass information through the system rapidly before it is lost or overtaken by other material. Slower processing will lead to greater information loss as one mental activity follows another, especially in complex, sequential operations; even small failures early in such a sequence necessarily lead to deficits in later performance.

Several researchers have examined whether older people's slower mental processing underlies their poorer working memory as well as their lower cognitive effectiveness of other kinds. Perhaps cognitive performance declines somewhat at older ages because operations cannot be executed within the necessary time and because the products of earlier activity are no longer available (having been lost because of a previous too-slow operation). Salthouse (1991b, 1993a, 1996) has demonstrated that this is often the case. Across a wide range of mental tasks, slower information-processing at older ages was found to contribute to poorer performance at older ages.

How early do these cognitive decrements become apparent? Many investigations into ageing have examined people in their seventies and eighties, and it might be thought that a pattern observed across those later years will not be present within the working population. In fact, cross-sectional decrements are often found in samples below 65 years, although they are not as great as those present across later decades (Salthouse, 1985; Verhaegen and Salthouse, 1997).

It is important to emphasize that the poorer and slower mental processing observed at older ages is only found when tasks are complex, placing considerable demands upon a person. It has frequently been found that age differences are more apparent when psychological resources are more strongly challenged. Greater task difficulty arises from substantial speed demands and/or from the need to progress through many successive mental operations, drawing repeatedly upon working memory. Extremely complicated tasks, requiring a large number of processing steps, are particularly likely to be affected by cognitive slowing (Myerson et al., 1990). In the very many other cases where cognitive processes are not greatly challenged, age differences are not found at all or are substantially smaller than in the published accounts of age deterioration; those typically examine performance only in highly demanding tasks (Craik and Jennings, 1992; Craik and Jacoby, 1996).

Age decrements are also smaller when difficult cognitive processes can be supported by environmental cues. Although much mental activity is conducted entirely through *internal* manipulation and reorganization, some processes can receive assistance from the environment. For example, recognizing something from a list of alternatives requires less mental initiation than recalling it through internally generated searches of all relevant elements in one's memory. Associated with that difference, recognition shows a smaller cross-sectional age decrement than recall (Craik and Jennings, 1992; Kausler, 1994). When environmental cues are available (as in menus on a computer screen or elsewhere, recall suggestions at appropriate locations or personal lists of reminders), age differences are less likely than when all processing has to be carried out 'in the head'. More generally, age differences are greatest 'when processes must be self-initiated in a consciously controlled manner and when a different attentional set from that induced by habit, or by a specific environment, must be established' (Craik and Jacoby, 1996, p. 113).

Does Not Experience Help Older Workers?

Despite the fact that older people are sometimes less effective than younger ones in processing information, it seems likely that they have often gained advantages over the years. We should thus consider possible effects of *experience* (practising a task over a period of time) and its outcome *expertise* (declarative or procedural knowledge, sometimes viewed as 'wisdom').

Previous relevant experience is known to be significantly associated with effective job performance. A meta-analysis of earlier studies by McDaniel,

Schmidt and Hunter (1988) yielded an average estimated population correlation of +0.21 between relevant prior experience and work performance. Given that older employees typically have greater experience, it is likely that, when positive associations are found between age and job performance, these will be mediated by amount of experience. That was found to be the case by Schwab and Heneman (1977) and Giniger, Dispenzieri and Eisenberg (1983): positive age performance correlations (median = +0.29) became non-significant (median = +0.02) after statistical control for years of experience.

Maher (1955) found that older sales staff were rated more positively than younger ones in almost every respect. In terms of product knowledge (in a company with more than 1000 items in its catalogue), the correlation with age was as high as +0.59; increased time-in-the-job is clearly very helpful in the acquisition and consolidation of relevant knowledge. The value of experience in enhancing social knowledge and interpersonal skills was particularly emphasized by Perlmutter, Kaplan and Nyquist (1990). In their study of food service employees between 20 and 69, age was found to be correlated +0.36 with performance effectiveness.

One form of expertise (an outcome from experience) is seen through tests of 'crystallized' intelligence, a person's knowledge of vocabulary and his or her ability to understand and manipulate verbal expressions. Crystallized intelligence is typically found to be greater in older samples. For example, Stankov (1988) reported a correlation of crystallized intelligence with age of +0.27 between the ages of 20 and 70 (compared to a value of −0.31 for fluid intelligence, above).

Although psychometric tests of crystallized intelligence typically focus upon verbal activity, expertise is of course acquired much more widely than merely in terms of vocabulary. Several investigators have devised measures of practical knowledge about issues in daily life, showing that older individuals typically score more highly than younger ones (e.g. Denney, 1989). Baltes (1990) has developed this point into a general model of 'wisdom', emphasizing that wisdom (highly developed declarative and procedural knowledge and judgement) is acquired through experience across many years.

Specifically job-related expertise has been studied through tests of job knowledge by Hunter (1986) and Borman, White, Pulakes and Oppler (1991). In both cases, this form of job expertise was significantly associated with supervisory ratings of performance. From a meta-analysis of previous studies, Dye, Reck and McDaniel (1993) obtained an average correlation of +0.22 between job knowledge test score and job performance (for success in training the value was +0.27), but age patterns were not examined in that research.

Expertise includes greater 'automatization' of behaviour, as people move from controlled, effortful cognition to execute fast strings of action, which are not under direct conscious control once initiated but which free mental resources and permit simultaneous processing of information. In addition, experts perceive and recall large meaningful patterns in their domain, made possible by their superior and more organized knowledge base (Charness and Bosman, 1990), and can more rapidly process new material within their established knowledge structures (Hess, 1994).

However, research has emphasized that expertise is very much domain-specific; an expert in one area may be ineffective elsewhere. This fact has led to the development of models of 'selective optimisation with compensation' (e.g. Baltes, 1990), primarily applicable to ages beyond the workforce but also relevant to younger people. 'Selective' refers to older people's restriction of activity to fewer domains; 'optimization' covers behaviours which can maintain and improve expertise; and 'compensation' involves procedures to counteract the declines which might occur in processing activities.

Possible compensation at older ages was illustrated in a study by Salthouse (1984) of typists aged between 19 and 72. Although older typists were clearly slower in laboratory measurements of response speed, they were able to type as fast as younger ones. It turned out that older typists achieved this by means of looking in advance further ahead along the line to be typed, so that they were processing at any one time longer chunks of material than were younger typists. That greater anticipation permitted older people to compensate for declining perceptual-motor speed by beginning keystroke preparation earlier.

However, despite the greater average experience of older people relative to younger ones, there are some activities and knowledge domains in which *younger* individuals tend to be more experienced and expert. This occurs in relation to technological developments to which younger cohorts have been more exposed than older ones. For example, at the present time younger employees in general have had more experience of computer-related activity (during their education and spare time) than have older ones; the correlation between age and years of computer experience was −0.46 in the study by Czaja and Sharit (1993).

Under What Conditions Are Young–Old Similarities or Differences Expected?

Given the multiple influences of processing effectiveness and relevant expertise, it is desirable to create an overall framework which can identify possible relationships between age and performance: positive, negative or neutral. One suggestion is given in table 17.1, which builds upon themes introduced earlier. Eight main types of activity (in a job or elsewhere) are proposed, although in reality the variation is of course continuous rather than in discrete categories as set out here.

The framework is based upon a distinction between those information-processing activities in which older people (OP in the table) are less effective

Table 17.1 Age, information-processing effectiveness and expertise: eight types of activity

Pattern of information-processing effectiveness	Can expertise help?	Pattern of relevant expertise	Expected age pattern	Type of activity
Complex mental activities, perhaps with no environmental support				
1 OP < YP	No	n.a.	OP < YP	Age-impaired
2 OP < YP	Yes	OP > YP	OP = YP	Age-counteracted
3 OP < YP	Yes	OP = YP	OP < YP	Age-impaired
4 OP < YP	Yes	OP < YP	OP << YP	Greatly age-impaired
Less complex mental activities, perhaps with environmental support				
5 OP = YP	No	n.a.	OP = YP	Age-neutral
6 OP = YP	Yes	OP < YP	OP > YP	Age-enhanced
7 OP = YP	Yes	OP = YP	OP = YP	Age-neutral
8 OP = YP	Yes	OP < YP	OP < YP	Age-impaired

OP, older people; YP, younger people; n.a., not applicable.

than younger ones (YP) (OP < YP) and those in which there is no difference between the age groups (OP = YP). As outlined above, age decrements in working memory and processing speed are associated with widespread cognitive performance decrements at older ages. Those decrements are more pronounced in complex, effortful mental work and when no environmental support is available. These cases, where OP < YP in terms of information-processing effectiveness, are shown in the first half of table 17.1.

Other cases, of less rapid or less complex mental activity, where OP = YP in terms of information-processing effectiveness, are presented in the second half of the table. (No cases of OP > YP are included, since more effective average basic processing is not found at older ages.) The second column of table 17.1 asks whether expertise can help performance in a particular circumstance; as illustrated above, knowledge-based expertise can be widely useful. Third, we need to ask whether older or younger individuals are more likely to have expertise which is relevant and useful, identified in the table as OP > YP, OP = YP or OP < YP. On these bases, activities may be defined as age-impaired, age-counteracted, age-neutral or age-enhanced.

Type 1 tasks involve mental activities in which knowledge-based expertise cannot be useful in information-processing; for instance, in tasks involving only working memory or speeded reactions. As summarized above, activities of those kinds are to varying extents age-impaired. In type 2 and type 3 activities, older people are again less effective in terms of basic information-processing, but they differ in the balance of their relevant expertise. In cases where OP > YP in expertise, older people's greater knowledge and more sophisticated perspectives in the domain permit some compensation for their limitations; but when OP = YP in terms of relevant expertise, age impairment in task performance is again expected. In settings where younger people are both more effective at information-processing and more expert (type 4), a substantial age decrement is expected. This is likely to occur during initial work in many computer-based jobs at the present time, since between-cohort differences in education have led to marked age differences in relevant expertise. More generally, such a pattern is expected in many activities whose technical content is changing rapidly, so that older employees' knowledge may become outdated at the same time as young people's education provides them with an initial greater expertise.

The other types of activity in table 17.1 mirror the first four, but basic information-processing is here equally effective at all ages. That is widely the case in many jobs, where discussions with clients or colleagues are at a relaxed pace, errors can be rectified without difficulty, established routines are followed, individual tasks are quite simple and work activities are well within the resources of an employee. As a result of the different condition in the first column (OP = YP, rather than OP < YP), the expected outcomes are more favourable to older people. Activity types 5, 6 and 7 are identified as either age-neutral or age-enhanced, and only in the final case (with greater expertise at younger ages) is age impairment expected.

The eight-part framework in table 17.1 draws attention to the fact that older people are expected to be worse than younger ones in only four conditions: types 1, 3, 4 and 8. Of those, types 4 and 8 are unusual cases, where younger individuals in general are more expert than older ones; age imbalance undoubtedly occurs, but it is not common. Types 1, 3 and 4 represent conditions where older people suffer from impaired information-processing effectiveness of the kinds illustrated above. In some jobs such processing is sufficiently important to suggest than an overall age decrement in job performance will be found, but in many other cases demands do not approach the limits of a person's information-processing capacity, so that age differences in performance are not expected. And across all jobs there are wide differences between the capabilities of different employees irrespective of their age.

The framework presented here leaves unresolved the location within table 17.1 of specific jobs examined in the research literature; published reports typically lack information which would make possible their allocation to one of the eight categories. Furthermore, the relative prevalence of each of the types of activity is unknown; which are more common and which are less common? That presumably varies between different sectors, professions and job levels. There is now a need to obtain information about the operation of the two main features (information-processing effectiveness and relevant expertise) in particular employment settings.

Are There Age Differences in Learning?

Given the central importance of expertise in the relative performance of younger and older workers (in six of the eight categories of table 17.1), it is clearly essential to examine how expertise may be increased through learning by older members of the workforce. Three issues need to be examined: whether older and younger people are likely to engage in different amounts of learning activity, whether they are differentially successful in the learning which they undertake and whether they transfer in different degrees their learning from a training setting into work activities.

In respect of participation in learning at different ages, findings are clear: older people are relatively inactive as learners (e.g. Green, 1993; Warr, 1994b). For example, in Britain as a whole fewer than half as many employees in their fifties are trained in a given period relative to those in their twenties (Department of Employment, 1994), and a similar ratio has been observed for voluntary own-time learning in a large British company (Warr and Birdi, 1998).

The age difference in participation arises from a number of sources. For example, older employees tend to have lower educational qualifications (as standards have increased for later cohorts), so they may lack both underpinning knowledge (often important for new learning) and recent learning experience which enhances their confidence. Lower educational qualification is strongly associated with lower confidence about one's ability to acquire new skills and knowledge ($r = +0.40$ in the study by Warr and Birdi, 1998), and there is evidence that recent experience may make people's orientation to training more positive (Nordhaug, 1989).

Associated with age-related differences in educational qualifications and learning confidence, older workers are generally less motivated to take part in training (Warr, 1994b; Warr and Birdi, 1998). Many older employees see substantial learning as difficult, unrewarding and not part of their typical lifestyle. Age-related norms and differential social pressures at different ages also influence employees' motivation for training. In many settings it is likely that the support for training provided by a company's policies and by individual managers (Noe and Wilk, 1993; Maurer and Tarulli, 1994) will be greater for younger than for older employees. Aspects of an organization's culture may thus combine with individual differences in education, confidence and motivation in ways that reduce training and learning activity by older workers.

A second issue is whether older and younger individuals are equally successful in the learning which they undertake. This has been studied both in occupational training settings and in laboratory research. Kubeck, Delp, Haslett and McDaniel (1996) examined previous research into training, deriving the overall conclusion that older individuals, relative to younger ones, showed less mastery (in post-tests) of training material and took longer to complete the training. The average correlation between employees' training attainment and age was found to be −0.21; for time to complete training, the correlation was +0.40. In a meta-analysis of results from laboratory studies, Verhaegen and Salthouse (1997) reported an average correlation of −0.33 between age and memory for previously presented material. Many specific studies illustrating this age decrement have been summarized by Kausler (1994).

It follows from the slower learning of older people that, if maximum training time is restricted to that appropriate for younger ones, learning attainment will be somewhat poorer at older ages. This can occur even in relatively young samples if training time is short and the task is difficult. For example, success in air traffic control training was related on average (across four samples) −0.26 to age, in samples with a median age of 27 (Trites and Cobb, 1964). In other cases – for example, in open learning where individuals can adjust the time allocated to different elements – age may not be linked to poorer outcomes, but older learners may experience greater learning difficulty, having to adapt to a perceived greater workload by investing greater effort; this was reported by Warr and Bunce (1995).

The third aspect of age and learning raised earlier concerned the transfer of what is learned into work settings. Transfer is typically viewed as having two aspects: the retention of learned material in its original (or an identical) context, and its generalization to new but related settings.

The retention of learned material is strongly affected by the degree of initial learning, such that material which is more practised or 'over-learned' is better retained (e.g. Patrick, 1992; Swezey and Llaneras, 1997). Older people are expected to retain less material than younger ones because of a probable difference in the degree of initial learning. As indicated earlier, older learners acquire new material more slowly than younger ones, so that after any given period of time they have on average learned less than younger people. Although everyone may have reached an acceptable level of learning in a training course, it will regularly be the case that younger individuals have consolidated material to a greater degree. Given older learners' poorer acquisition and consolidation on average, a tendency for them to retain less is expected.

Research into forgetting at different ages has been of two main kinds, examining recall for events in real life or for material learned in the laboratory. Studies of the recall of previous life events suffer from the difficulty that one cannot control or measure the degree to which information was initially encoded and consolidated, or the frequency with which it has been recalled (and thus further consolidated) in intervening years. Control of initial learning is more possible in laboratory investigations, from which it appears that, when people of different ages reach equivalent levels of initial learning, their rate of forgetting is very similar. However, when the different groups receive merely the same number of learning trials (and thus older people's learning is less advanced), retention is significantly better at younger ages (Kaulser, 1994).

In respect of the second component of transfer (generalization of learned material to new but related situations), age differences are again expected, although research evidence is lacking. Among factors influencing amount of transfer are the opportunities available to use learned material and the support provided by an organization for the application of new learning. It seems likely that on average those factors will be more favourable to younger employees, so that transfer of training occurs less among older people.

An age difference may also be expected in relation to wider organizational support for transfer. When supervisors and colleagues encourage and reward the application of taught material (providing a positive 'transfer climate'), motivation to transfer is greater and training is more likely to yield positive outcomes in the work setting (Ford, Quiñones, Sego and Sorro, 1992; Tracey, Tannenbaum and Kavanagh, 1995; Warr, Allan and Birdi, 1999). Consistent with the fact that younger workers are asked more frequently to undertake training and with the negative attitudes widely held about older people, it seems likely that encouragement to apply new learning is more often given to younger employees.

How Can Older Workers' Learning and Transfer Be Increased?

As outlined above, older employees can certainly learn, retain and transfer new material, but they are in general somewhat less successful in those respects than younger ones. Given the widespread need for increased learning among the workforce in a period when that workforce is ageing, it is important to develop and test procedures to remedy the relative problems of older individuals identified here.

A consistent theme is the need to increase older employees' learning motivation (e.g. Belbin, 1965; Belbin and Belbin, 1972; Sterns and Doverspike, 1988; Plett and Lester, 1991; Warr and Pennington, 1993; Warr, 1994a,b; Warr and Birdi, 1998). Possible actions include: public recognition of learning achievements through awards, symbols etc.; encouragement from older role models, who report favourably on their training activities; publicity and specific guidance geared to older staff as well as younger ones; and possibly making promotion or transfer contingent upon specific learning achievements.

Older people's learning confidence also often needs to be boosted. In some cases, this might involve a graded sequence from simple to more difficult training experiences, to ensure that confidence is built up in a preliminary learning activities before exposure to complex learning tasks. In other cases, pre-training as part of a current programme is desirable. Pre-training may aim to increase the content expertise of some older employees. If a person lacks necessary underpinning knowledge (declarative or procedural), he or she will soon fall behind in any training activity requiring that knowledge. For example, some older individuals with limited education (many years previously) may need assistance with basic skills of literacy or numeracy. The general need is to bring everyone to an acceptable level of content expertise before principal training activities commence.

A second form of pre-training is in terms of learning strategies and associated study skills which might assist in a given setting, helping unpractised older individuals to 'learn how to learn'. For example, advice might be useful about cognitive learning strategies such as mental organization or about behavioural learning strategies to gain assistance from fellow trainees, as might suggestions about self-monitoring and procedures to reduce anxiety when progress is felt to be poor (Warr and Allan, 1998). Procedures for time management and the personal scheduling of learning activities might also be discussed as part of this pre-training.

Training procedures need to be based upon older individuals' limitations, as well as their expertise. For example, since most adult learning in everyday life takes the form of active problem-solving, 'guided discovery learning' may be particularly effective (Belbin, 1965, 1969). Learning situations should be created through which a person finds out himself or herself the principles and relationships which are important in the area. Discovery tasks should be set for individuals or small groups, who should be encouraged to ask themselves questions (which they seek to answer) about the material being studied. For example, Czaja (1996) reported that 'goal-oriented training' reduced time and errors by requiring learners to work out the answers to defined questions with help from a specially designed manual.

Asssociated with several suggestions in this area, there is an overriding need to alter negative stereotypes about older employees. Older adults as a group can learn as much as younger ones, provided that some steps of the kind illustrated here are taken. However, the more that special procedures to assist older people are substantial and time-consuming, the more likely is it that negative attitudes will be reinforced, since older employees' problems will become more visible and (in the short term) more costly. It may be wise to argue for interventions of the kind illustrated here on the grounds that *everyone's* learning will be improved, rather than arguing specifically the case for older learners. That theme can be linked to the development of a 'continuous learning culture', which encompasses employees of all ages but recognizes the needs of older ones specifically because of their growing numbers in the labour market.

Non-cognitive as well as Cognitive Features

In seeking to understand the job and learning performance of older people relative to younger ones, most authors have concentrated on the cognitive features examined here: information-processing effectiveness and relevant expertise. However, it is clear that job performance is also determined by non-cognitive processes of motivation, interests and personal syles. These have been almost entirely absent from the literature on age and employment, and urgently need to be investigated. Four components likely to influence job effectiveness are as follows.

1   *Information-processing ability*, sometimes referred to as 'cognitive ability' (Hunter, 1986; Borman et al., 1991), 'fluid intelligence' (Cattell, 1963), 'mechanics of the mind' (Baltes, 1990) or 'intelligence-as-process' (Ackerman, 1996). This cognitive attribute has often been shown to predict job performance (Hunter and Hunter, 1984) and training success (Ackerman, Kanfer and Goff, 1995; Ree and Carretta, 1998) in studies which do not examine age differences.

2   *Expertise*, sometimes referred to as 'wisdom' (Baltes, 1990), 'pragmatic knowledge' (Baltes, 1990), 'crystallized intelligence' (Cattell, 1963), 'practical intellingence' (Sternberg and Wagner, 1986) or 'intelligence-as-knowledge' (Ackerman, 1996). As described above, job-related expertise has been shown to predict overall job effectiveness. Job knowledge is also significantly associated with success in training, over and above the impact of cognitive ability (Ree, Carretta and Teachout, 1995).

Several studies have examined job performance as a function of information-processing ability in combination with relevant expertise (measured in terms of job knowledge). It appears that greater processing ability leads to greater expertise, which in turn yields better job performance (Borman et al., 1991; Schmidt and Hunter, 1992; Ree et al., 1995). Given that expertise can be retained over long periods, especially with continuing practice, the slightly lower information-processing scores sometimes observed at older ages may have little impact in job settings: job-related expertise is a major predictor of performance.

3   *Personality*, which may be construed in terms of relatively broad concepts (e.g. the 'big five' traits) or through a larger number of more specific features. The big five are usually identified as neuroticism (or emotional stability), extraversion (or surgency), agreeableness, conscientiousness and openness to experience (or intellect) (e.g. Goldberg, 1990). A larger number of characteristics are covered in, for example, the Occupational Personality Questionnaire (Saville and Holdsworth, 1993), which contains scales of 30 more focused attributes, such as being persuasive, independent, practical, innovative, worrying and decisive. There is growing evidence that personality attributes significantly predict job performance (e.g. Tett, Jackson and Rothstein, 1991). Borman, White and Dorsey (1995) have expanded the predictors of job performance beyond information-processing ability and job expertise, to show that aspects of personality (in terms of conscientiousness) make additional contributions to performance over and above cognitive factors.

4   *Motivation and interests*, covering a wide range of affective (emotional) factors which can influence behaviour at work and elsewhere. Under this heading we might consider specifically vocational interests such as those described by Holland (1973): realistic, artistic, investigative, social, enterpris-

ing and conventional. In addition, people vary in their more specific interests; for example, relative to particular activities in their job. Interests tend to be linked to broader motivations, which both energize and direct activity.

Motivational characteristics overlap with the preceding three categories. For example, an interest in scientific and engineering jobs tends to be associated with greater mathematical ability (Ackerman and Heggestad, 1997). Motivation and information-processing ability work together to determine the areas in which expertise will be acquired, as well as the depth of that expertise; people who are both highly motivated and highly able will acquire greater expertise than others in the areas which interest them.

What is known about age differences in these four determinants of behaviour? Most research (illustrated in this chapter) has focused on information-processing, consistently showing that older people tend to be less effective in several ways when task demands are substantial. Research attention needs now to switch from the first element of this framework to examine the other components. It is clear that relevant expertise affects job performance, but research is lacking into age patterns and determinants. Furthermore, almost nothing is known about the other two elements (personality, and motivation and interests) in relation to age and work performance. In each case we need to know a great deal more about the nature of age differences, the factors giving rise to any difference and the impact of an age difference on job performance.

Cross-sectional age patterns in big five personality attributes have been summarized by McRae and Costa (1990). Evidence suggests that older adults are less extraverted and have higher scores on agreeableness, but that no overall age differences exist for neuroticism, conscientiousness or openness to experience. These broad characteristics may also be divided into smaller attributes. In a large sample of British adults, cross-sectional age decrements were found in respect of persuasiveness, outgoingness, affiliativeness, being democratic, change-oriented, conceptual, innovative, competitive, achievement-oriented and decisive; conversely, older people were more modest, traditional, detail-conscious and conscientious; for other scales, age differences were small (Saville and Holdsworth, 1993).

Such differences are extremely likely to be reflected in the work behaviour of employees of different ages. In seeking to understand age patterns at work, it is essential to consider personality patterns as well as cognitive factors. That is also the case with the fourth determinant of behaviour, motivation. In respect of personal values which are context-free (not restricted to the workplace), studies have suggested that older adults tend to have less concern for personal achievement and skills and have greater interest in more interpersonal goals (Hess, 1994). It is not known how far those differences are reflected in variations in *job-related* motivation. However, older workers are likely to have different job concerns from younger ones, associated with their changed family position and perceptions of themselves at different stages in the life course. Warr (1997) has drawn together the limited empirical evidence about preferences at different ages for key job features, suggesting that across the years overall decreases are likely in the importance of high job demands, job variety and feedback; increases with age seem possible in employees' concern for job security and physical security; and an interest in skill utilization and in a high wage is likely to increase and then decrease across the years of employment.

Almost no systematic research has addressed these issues. One possibility is that, whatever the *average* pattern, inter-individual differences in motivation and interest become greater at older ages. The importance of giving specific consideration to the actual characteristics of individuals at any age, rather than making general assumptions based on group membership, is very clear.

Although findings about information-processing ability and expertise have advanced our understanding about age differences in job settings, we are still far away from a complete grasp of the issues affecting older and younger people's work behaviour. The prime need at present is the adoption of a broader perspective, looking not only at processing ability and relevant expertise, but also at age patterns in personality traits and in motivation and interests.

Chapter Summary

Many countries' populations are becoming older, and there is a need to learn more about the relative strengths and weaknesses of older and younger workers. Considerable prejudice operates against older people, but on average their work performance is equal to that of younger individuals. Psychologists' studies have concentrated on age-decrements in information-processing in laboratory tasks, but expertise deriving from experience often benefits older individuals. The acquisition of new knowledge and skills is particularly important in a time of rapid job changes, and procedures are needed to assist older employees to be more active learners. Research attention should shift from cognitive issues to examine age patterns in motivation and personality.

Discussion Points

1   What is the likely effect on organizational effectiveness of the removal of older employees through enforced redundancy or early retirement?

2   How can older staff experience job satisfaction if promotion is no longer possible in flat organizations?

3   What is the relationship between laboratory studies of information-processing and behaviour in job settings?

CHAPTER EIGHTEEN

THE CHANGING NATURE OF WORK

Michael Frese

Contents

Chapter Outline

This chapter covers plausible developments in the way jobs and work will be done in the future. In addition, the chapter addresses the question of what interesting research and practical issues for work and organizational psychology will appear in the future.

Introduction

Students in university today will work in the organizations and companies of the future. Thus, the question of changes in the nature of work is of paramount interest to students. There is no doubt that the world of work is changing. If a worker from the late nineteenth century was catapulted into a modern workplace, he or she would have difficulties understanding it: its speed, the emphasis on timeliness of production and service, the technology used, the cleanliness and safety, the emphasis on customer satisfaction and quality, the modularity of the products, the non-military nature of the organization, the courtesy and at the same time distance in social relations at work (including relations between men and women, and between different ethnic groups), the speed with which product lines are changed, the international nature of production and of the workforce, and relations with foreign companies (this can be seen from the writings of Taylor, 1911; Ford, 1922; Marx, 1967; Licht, 1983).

In short, work life has undergone tremendous changes within the past 100 years. This chapter asks the question: what kind of research is required if work and organizational psychology is to be able to deal with future problems? Thus, we want to know what changes the next 50–100 years will bring about. Only two things are certain: first, it is very likely that we will make erroneous forecasts; second, some of the changes will take place much more slowly than we expect. As evidence for the first statement, just think of the fact that, at the time of writing, people had just become accustomed to the fact that the East Asian tigers (Thailand, South Korea, Hong Kong etc.) were the inevitable leaders of future markets when the crisis in these countries led to a serious economic depression there. All the forecasters who thought of these markets as the most important ones for the future turned out to be wrong (at least for a certain period).

As evidence for the second statement, think of the fact that at the beginning of the computer revolution (starting in earnest in the late 1970s, with the advent of personal computing), it was estimated that human intelligence would soon be replaced by computer technology (e.g. Feigenbaum and McCorduck, 1984) and that a paperless office would develop. Neither of these two predictions has come true. However, there are developments in that direction. In rule-governed areas computer-supported decision-making has become more commonplace (e.g. stock exchange, medicine, technical supplies, logistics) and in specialized non-work related areas (e.g. chess) computer intelligence has made tremendous gains. Similarly, there has been more and more use of electronic databanks, although this has not led to or even approached the paperless office.

Future Prediction: Methods and Perspectives

Most frequently, people tend to extrapolate from current trends. For example, in the 1960s, there were numerous futurists who extrapolated energy use into the future and predicted that all fossil energy would be depleted in the early part of the twenty-first century. In the meantime, new technology and the energy conservation movement have helped us to conserve energy to a large extent; in addition, new energy technologies have been developed. Thus, while we all have to use extrapolations to make predictions for the future, we should be cautious, and also describe the counter-forces to these extrapolations.

Catastrophe and chaos theory and system perspectives (Buckley, 1968) have emphasized two issues. The first is that small developments can have enormous effects, even in other places. The fact that Hitler was rejected as a student in an art school may have led him to become a politician, with enormous consequences. Small causes may have large effects that are difficult to foresee. Second, there are counter-movements by systems, which work against certain trends that appear obvious. A good example is the effect of the computer revolution in the office. In contrast to strong cost savings projected by the computer industry, there were essentially no savings. However, quality standards for written and oral presentations increased: just think of the fancy multi-coloured overheads or the near professional printing quality of reports common today, which were out of reach for most office workers twenty years ago. Thus, the system (in this case office work) did not lead to cost savings, as anticipated, but to higher quality reports.

In addition, there are two limiting conditions for changes that are inherent in every system. First, organizations are conservative (Katz and Kahn, 1978). New technology research has shown that the potential of new technology is usually not realized at once. At any one time, the organization uses an evolutionary approach (Pomfrett et al., 1985) and changes the work situation only a little. Therefore, the changes are usually much smaller than one would expect (Kling, 1980; Agervold, 1987; Frese and Zapf, 1987). Another system characteristic that leads to inherent conservatism is human nature (Nicholson, 1998). As Nicholson shows, any attempt to reduce hierarchies in organizations may produce counter-tendencies, by which hierarchies develop even when 'non-hierarchical structures' are advocated. Human nature may tend to reintroduce hierarchies even if they are counterproductive.

A further approach to the attempt to understand the future of work is to research jobs at the cutting edge of new technology and new organization empirically. The best model for such jobs is software design because software designers work with very new technology and most new and interesting organizational approaches have been attempted there. Some findings on this profession are reported in this chapter.

The scenario approach has also been used to forecast the future. It asks the question: which alternative scenarios are plausible and how are alternative trajectories of developments developed based on these scenarios. For example, what will happen to future workplaces in Europe if the influence of the labour unions collapses across Europe in the same way as it did in the United Kingdom? Or what will happen to workplaces in Western Europe when Eastern Europe is integrated into the European Union? This is a plausible approach that helps to make the prerequisites of our predictions more explicit.

These introductory statements are intended to make us sufficiently humble with regard to predictions of the future. Having said this, I shall now venture into looking at potential trends at the workplace, potential counter-forces and potential consequences. One reason for looking into the future is to ask the question: which issues should be studied by work and organizational psychology to help to solve new problems when they appear.

Trends that Describe the Job of the Future and Consequences for Work and Organizational Psychology

The following points constitute a summary of the trends discussed in the literature (Storey, 1994; Bridges, 1995; Howard, 1995; Rifkin, 1995):

- dissolution of the unity of work in space and time;
- faster rate of innovation;
- increased complexity of work;
- global competition;
- development of larger and smaller units;
- changing job and career concepts;
- more team work;
- reduced supervision;
- increased cultural diversity.

These trends are discussed below.

Dissolution of the unity of work in time and space

With the advent of the Internet and computer-based work, it has been possible to overcome restrictions imposed by time and space. For example, I have written a paper with two American colleagues whom I had never met before; we communicated only via e-mail. Some car designers already work on a 24-hour schedule: when the designers in Tokyo stop working, the European designers take over. When they stop their shift in the evening, their American colleagues continue where the Europeans have left off. At the consulting firm

Anderson in Paris, people do not have individual offices any longer, but are assigned an office whenever they need one. Within minutes, their individual filing cabinet is rolled into this office and their own telephone number and e-mail connection is installed. A final example of a virtual office can be found at Pacific Bell Directory, which had a special contract with a hotel chain, built up its own offices there and asked its salespeople to work from hotel rooms (using a modem and phones as tools to connect to the main office) (Goves, 1995; Wigand et al., 1997). In the USA telecommuting is used more frequently than in Europe, with 11 million workers using this mode of distributed work at least part of their time (Cascio, 1998). Obviously, telecommunication is a broad concept that includes the use of e-mail and sophisticated groupware with concurrent video-conferencing.

There is enormous potential in the fact that one does not need to be at one's office to be able to work with other people. People using telecommuting seem to like it and prefer it to working in an office; they even argue that they have fewer distractions and work more productively (Chapman et al., 1995; Cascio, 1998). Productivity was found to be enhanced by 2–40 per cent through teleworking (Chapman et al., 1995). However, these positive effects have been recorded up to now only in situations where people volunteer for telework (Chapman et al., 1995). The position may change when people who do not want to participate in telework are forced into it.

There are many counterforces to the widespread use of telework. Some forms of work carry legal requirements that make it difficult to use telework. For example, many bank and insurance jobs cannot legally be done from home, because privacy cannot be ensured in the homes of the teleworker (this is certainly more important in Europe, with its strict privacy laws, than in other parts of the world). Similarly, many managers and business owners want to *see* their employees at work with their own eyes. Many organizations do not want to invest in an uncertain technology and assume that it will be difficult to keep up organizational commitment. On the other band, certain political decisions have made it necessary to invest in telework; for example, the decision by Germany to distribute the capital across two cities (Bonn and Berlin) has led to a need for information technology to deal with decision-making across these two cities (Schmidt and Wolf, 1997). In all, there is little doubt that telework has been growing, that it has been profitable where used and that it will continue to grow in the future.

Obviously there are important implications for work and organizational psychology that derive from the 'dissolution of the unity of time and space at work' that accompanies telework.

- There are problems of coordination. How can the organization make sure that everyone knows his or her tasks? Tasks that require fine-grained communication are better done face to face than in computer-mediated groups (Straus and McGrath, 1994).

- How do organizations overcome the problem of reduced organizational commitment? Telework reduces the chances of feeling that one belongs to the organization (Chapman et al., 1995). Of particular difficulty is developing a common culture in virtual organizations.
- Communication patterns change when the computer is used (at least to a certain extent). There is a large literature in this area, which I will not summarize here. There is some evidence that communication becomes more democratic because status differences cannot be conveyed as vividly via the computer as in face to face communication (Kiesler et al., 1984).
- How can a culture of telecommunication be developed and furthered? At the moment, there is evidence that people use rougher and less sophisticated language when typing something into the computer.
- There is an overabundance of information in today's telecommunication systems. Obviously, a large amount of what one receives is not really important. How can these systems help to differentiate uninformative garbage from information that is needed?
- In what phase of work do projects get better or worse support through computer-based groupwork?

Faster rate of innovation

There will be more pressure to innovate (Kanter, 1984) because of pressures from the global market and because the time available to create new products from new knowledge is reduced. Hamel and Prahalad (1994) have argued that competition between firms will be more and more on 'opportunity shares' (shares in future markets with products that may not exist yet). This is of particular importance for European countries, which have fallen behind the USA and Japan in terms of innovativeness and patents.

There are various implications for work and organizational psychology. First, we need good models of individual and group innovation to support innovatory behaviour. There tend to be two types of models. One is related to the creative element of innovation. A good model for group innovation (West and Anderson, 1996; West et al., 1997) showed the importance of group reflexivity and support for innovation. For individuals, this perspective was developed by, for example, Oldham and Cummings (1996). Another approach relates innovation to personal initiative: to achieve innovation, one has to have a good idea; but in addition it is necessary to implement the idea, which requires personal initiative (Frese, 1997).

Second, it makes sense to differentiate between process (how to produce) and product innovation; different psychological processes may apply to these two types of innovation. Third, work and organizational psychology can contribute to helping people to learn faster. We will have to change how we carry out training. The traditional training literature has rightfully argued that it is necessary to do a task analysis first. However, the change of work perspective in this chapter implies that tasks will change so quickly that it will be difficult to train for specific tasks; instead, people need meta-skills. This poses a dilemma: we know that it is very difficult to train general skills because transfer to new areas is difficult (Baldwin and Ford, 1988). We need to learn much more about how to develop transferable skills. The most probable starting point is to train for self-regulation (Karoly, 1993). If, for example, we have to boost our motivation to approach a new situation with curiosity when we really do not want to, self-regulatory processes apply. Another starting point is to teach people to train themselves (or at least to feel responsible for their own training needs). A learning approach may be triggered by the occurrence of errors and problems (Frese, 1995a). However, it is likely that people will learn from an error only if they do not feel anxious about making errors and do not feel the need to cover up errors (Rybowiak et al., 1999).

This leads us to a point of organizational learning. The organizational culture itself must support learning. New strands of research are required here; one important issue is the error culture, which determines whether people feel at ease discussing errors, and, thereby, learn from them. It has been shown that companies with a mastery-oriented error culture are more profitable than those with a timid error culture (Van Dyck et al., 1998). A learning organization needs to support curiosity, there needs to be safety to explore (West et al., 1977) and general uncertainty avoidance needs to be low. Uncertainty avoidance (Hofstede, 1991) may be of particular importance for learning. Under high uncertainty avoidance (such as exists in Germany), there is probably a high drive to learn from mistakes so as to not repeat them. On the other hand, there is little room for exploration because people want to be sure that they can do something well immediately. Thus, learning from an error is restricted to an anxious avoidance of the error, and errors are not really used as a trigger to learn something new about a system. On the other hand, in cultures with low uncertainty avoidance (e.g. Ireland), there are many chances to learn, but motivation to get it right after one has made a mistake may be a little lower. At present, we know very little about these processes.

Organizations can succeed as learning organizations only if they encourage and support curiosity among their members. Everything that increases curiosity will also increase innovation. This means, of course, that companies like 3M, which forces its employees to spend a certain amount of time dreaming up new products or ideas, will in the last analysis do the right thing. On the other hand, companies tend to reduce time pockets that can be used for such a pursuit of ideas with better (and tighter) organization. Thus, at some point in time, innovation may be hindered by the very effectiveness of the organization.

Increased complexity of work

While there is little effect of new technology *per se* (Kern and Schumann, 1984; Frese and Zapf, 1987), changes in work organization interacting with new technology will make work intellectually more demanding. Moreover, since the rate of change is increasing, this implies that new knowledge has to be acquired constantly.

The factors that contribute to an increase in work complexity are production for small niches, customization and customer orientation. Most car companies already work on a principle of demand, with each car being specified individually and separately. Complexity of work also increases because of increasing environmental turbulence and ever faster developing fashions and global changes. The most important implications for work and organizational psychology are in the following areas:

First, what can be done for less intelligent people? Complex work presupposes a high degree of intelligence (Ree and Caretta, 1998). Thus, jobs for less intelligent people will become scarcer and scarcer. Worldwide competition will increase and modern technology makes it possible that work will move from the industrialized world to the underdeveloped world. This produces serious problems in the industrialized world; for example, a continuously unemployed lower class, with a welfare mentality, high crime rates, social unrest and widespread dissatisfaction. We do not yet have a solution but work and organizational psychologists need to develop one. This may mean searching for job characteristics that do not need a high degree of cognitive ability and it may mean that those jobs will have to be economically subsidized in some way. It may also be useful to develop improved and fine-tuned concepts of training for this group of people.

Politically, there have been two approaches to this problem. Neo-liberalism attempts to reduce the wages for this group to a large extent (making them comparable to the Third World and, thus, competitive again). Social democracy attempts to keep up the wages for this group; however, to induce companies to employ them, jobs have to be subsidized. Moreover, there has been a trend to force people into work (e.g. in Denmark).

Second, a similar problem appears for people who are not very socially competent. The increase in customer orientation makes it necessary to employ people with good social skills. While social skills can be more easily learnt than cognitive abilities, the problem persists of what to do with people who have difficulties in learning appropriate customer-oriented skills.

Third, in general self-esteem and self-efficacy become much more important because they help motivation, even with complex tasks. Fourth, intellectual work becomes more dominant. At the moment, most of our job analysis or appraisal methods are geared towards non-intellectual work. This makes it important to concentrate more on intellectual regulation of work (Frese and Zapf, 1994).

Global competition

There is no doubt that there is now more global competition than in the past, and it is highly likely that this trend will increase. In the 1960s, 7 per cent of the US economy was exposed to international competition; in the 1980s, this climbed to above 70 per cent (Gwynne, 1992). Global competition will reign not only on the company level but also more and more on the individual level. With better communication devices, software developers in India compete for work with software developers in the Netherlands or Switzerland. The strongest competitors with German construction workers are British, Portuguese and Polish workers who work as small-scale entrepreneurs in Germany, selling their labour power. In order for more highly developed countries to be able to hold their own in this competition, their highly paid workers have to improve their skills, be more active, show more initiative, be more reliable and be more up-to-date than their competitors (who will usually earn less).

There are important implications for work and organizational psychology.

- Since people's ideas and attitudes become more important for increasing productivity, the development of work and organizational psychology itself becomes a factor that will determine whether or not a society will be able to compete globally.
- Companies have to become more imaginative in stimulating self-reliance and initiative (Frese, 1997). Without active cooperation and individual self-starting and long-term involvement in the company, the company will not be able to compete well.
- A high degree of employee initiative is particularly important when companies have to deal with turbulence and changes. Since globalization increases the amount of turbulence in companies' environment, companies have to learn to react flexibly to it.
- International cooperation will become more important. The most obvious issue for work and organizational psychology is that there will be a higher need for cross-cultural management. Managers will need to have skills in negotiating, leading, organizing and planning across cultures. There will be more international project work (particularly across European countries) and there will be more internationally assigned managers who have to deal with living in cultures other than their own. The expertise of work and organizational psychology will be needed in all these areas.
- It is much more difficult for smaller companies to make use of globalization. Partly, this is a function of the thought patterns of small-scale entrepreneurs, who may not even think about international activity. Work and organizational psychologists might help to overcome thought barriers here.
- Globalization leads to a reduction of the power of the labour unions. While labour unions may have contributed to a certain degree of inflexibility, they have also helped to increase the degree of procedural and distributive justice in companies. Thus, other groups will have to take care of justice issues in the organizations. The stability of employer–employee relations may be negatively affected by the lack of a clear and historically powerful representation of employees.

Development of larger and smaller units

There is a curious polarization appearing in the world of organizations. On the one hand, organizations are becoming bigger and bigger, forever increasing in size through mergers and acquisitions. This is done despite the fact that most mergers and acquisitions do not lead to the expected positive effects and often have even negative ones (Hogan and Overmyer-Day, 1994). On the other hand, large units are consistently decreasing in size (Kozlowski et al., 1993) and more and more small start-up firms are appearing. Moreover, there is evidence that smaller units employing from 10 to 150 people are more flexible, work better with each other and show a higher degree of innovative potential (Simon, 1996; Nicholson, 1998). Organizations develop networks with each other instead of employing more and more people in their ranks. Of course, some companies attempt to be big and at the same time attempt to mimic the 'small is beautiful' strategy of small-scale enterprises, e.g. the Swiss-Swedish firm of Avery Brown Bovery (ABB), which governs its total company with sales of US$28 billion produced by 220,000 employees worldwide with only 140 people in its headquarters (International Herald Tribune, 1992).

More research on the issue of the size of companies would be interesting. It is most likely that a contingency theory will be needed. For example, companies that rely on innovation, cohesion of the employees and a good working climate may be better being small. In contrast, companies that thrive particularly on economies of scale in supplies and supporting demands will tend to do better when they are large.

Another important issue is the development of small-scale entrepreneurs. Large companies often leave important niches open, and it is small-scale entrepreneurs who can occupy them. Organizational psychologists have been too much oriented towards big business. More emphasis should be placed on the psychology of small-scale entrepreneurs and the organizational issues of small-scale businesses (Frese, 1998).

Changing job and career concepts

Some authors have argued that the notion of jobs as we know them will evaporate (Bridges, 1995; Rifkin, 1995). First, there is a clear reduction of jobs in the traditional production and service industries. With every re-engineering attempt, the number of blue and white collar workers is reduced tremendously. Louisville Capital Holding reduced its back office staff from 1900 to 1100, while increasing business by 25 per cent after re-engineering (Bridges, 1995). Second, technological innovation leads to a reduction of personnel. For example, cashier jobs (the third largest clerical group in the USA) will be cut by 10–15 per cent by new scanning equipment (Rifkin, 1995); in Britain, there are already some supermarkets where people scan their own shopping. This trend will probably be increased by electronic shopping. Third, temporary and project work is increasing. A symbol of this is that temporary employment agencies have had the highest increase in sales and number of employees (Bridges, 1995). More and more companies are outsourcing, employing people only on a project basis, or they are even reducing the company to a virtual company, consisting of a network of small-scale entrepreneurs. Fourth, modern companies are changing the job concept. For example, Phillips introduced the idea of an umbrella contract. People are now frequently assigned to projects and not to jobs. For example, Microsoft has no regular working hours, and people are accountable to their project team, which is itself accountable to the larger project. When a project ends, employees move on to another project (Bridges, 1995). 'The dejobbed system lacks the normal kind of "edges" that tell workers when they have done a normal, satisfactory job. Since they are expected to do *anything necessary* to accomplish the expected results, they are no longer protected by the boundaries of a job' (Bridges, 1995, p. 42).

All this makes the concept of employability attractive (van Dam, 1998). Every employee has to be interested in developing his or her skills. Employees will be less dependent upon one company. Projects will be selected by different characteristics. For example, people will attempt to participate in projects that allow them to develop their skills and that make it possible to work with new technology or new procedures. Continuous development of professionalism will become more important.

From a work and organizational psychology perspective, this has positive consequences. Traditional jobs have been designed with a Tayloristic perspective. Tayloristic jobs have tended to take away authority from workers; it was given to the supervisor, the bureaucracy, the assembly line etc. In contrast, these newer jobs for professionals will make it necessary for them to develop their skills to a higher degree and will decrease the division of labour typical of Taylorism.

On the other hand, there will be periods of unemployment much more regularly than in traditional jobs, in which people stayed with one company and continued to work in one job, or made their careers within one company. Moreover, loss of jobs in large companies and the emphasis on project work and networks make it necessary to develop a more entrepreneurial spirit. This is particularly important in Europe, which has fewer entrepreneurs than other areas of the world (such as North America or developing countries).

Obviously, employees cannot keep up a high degree of commitment to and identification with one company if they know that they will work in different projects in different companies in a few years. Thus, commitment will be largely with the content of the project and the project group. It is likely that commitment to the professional group will also grow (e.g. being a civil engineer or a psychologist), because the (continuous) development of professionalism is important. Employability implies a certain degree of professionalism.

Since people compete both inside the company and in the external market for new projects and contracts, they have to behave much more entrepreneurially (even if they are employed). They have to decide which strategies to use, which markets they want to target (e.g. which market niches within the company), how they want to market themselves etc. For example, it will be much more important to ask the question of whether a student of work and organizational psychology has chosen a research programme that has obvious practical and scientific relevance in the future. Obviously, these are difficult tasks that need to be tackled as part of professional life and increase the requirements on cognitive and social skills.

Individuals will have to think of market issues even when they have a stable employer. They will have to make strategic decisions, e.g. whether or not they want to participate in a certain project or whether they want to orient themselves towards a certain market segment (a certain area of expertise). They also have to market themselves within their profession, within their company and across relevant segments across companies (and even across countries to a certain extent). Individuals will have to network to a larger extent than is typical today. Complex decisions have to be made that are risky. Thus, good feedback has to be proactively sought and flexible adjustments of one's orientations and skills will be much more necessary. These are all topics that need to be supported by more knowledge from work and organizational psychology.

Since these decisions need to be made by individuals themselves and cannot be delegated to the company any longer, the individual has to show more personal initiative (Frese, 1997, 1998); this includes decisions to participate in some form of training. Much training will be in the form of self-training, because the company will not be responsible in the same way for continuing education.

One additional problem is that one needs to get good career advice not only at the start of one's career but throughout one's lifetime. Career changes may occur more frequently than today. The integration of one's career with one's private life may be enhanced under those circumstances. The traditional division between work and leisure may become less strong than it is today. Given that project work is more dominant, that there are more transitional periods between projects and that people work more from home, there may be a development to combine work and leisure to a higher degree again (the division between work and leisure did not exist in farming a few hundred years ago).

More team work

Womack et al. (1990) showed that in Japan 69 per cent of all car workers were working in groups, while the figures were 17 per cent in the USA and less than 1 per cent in Europe, and the introduction of group work has since been seen as important for improving productivity. Group work that is being introduced, particularly in Europe (Germany and Holland), is often related to tradition and to experiences with semi-autonomous groups (Antoni, 1994).

Group work will be more common in the future. First, if production responsibilities are given back to the shopfloor (as is found in all new production concepts), single individuals will not be able to make decisions by themselves. Since there are dependencies among shopfloor workers, team decisions have to made. This implies that group participants should know something about each other's work (therefore, there is a need for job rotation). Second, new production methods (like lean production) are geared towards reducing coordination costs by reducing the number of supervisors. Coordination is then carried out within production units (teams). Third, increasing complexity will increase the need for coordinated efforts. Since highly complex decisions require input from different disciplines, there will be a greater need for interdisciplinary team work. Interdisciplinary work is difficult because people have to be able to talk about their own discipline in ways that other people understand, have to learn to understand the basics of another discipline quickly and have to learn to appreciate the different approaches taken by various disciplines (which is as difficult as cross-cultural learning at times; Baron, 1993). Often there will be only one person from each discipline in the group, so that reliance on this person's expertise is quite high. Finally, teams will have to react to environmental turbulence, and local shopfloor teams are better regulators of such turbulence (see the sociotechnical system approach of Emery and Trist, 1969).

One implication of a higher degree of team work is the higher need for good social and communication skills. One reason why the concept of emotional intelligence (Goleman, 1995) has proved attractive to so many people may be that it is required in team work. It is interesting that the automobile companies that invested in Eastern Germany have selected even blue collar workers using assessment centres in order to gauge explicitly the social skills of their newly employed blue collar workers, who are working in lean, team-based production systems. Team training and team development measures may become much more important (the teams are often assembled from scratch for each new project). Thus, from the employee's point of view, it is important to integrate into the team quickly. From the employer's point of view, team development is needed to make the team function well within a shorter period of time.

Teams are not necessarily more efficient than individuals working separately. There is ample evidence that, for creative tasks, this is not the case (Diehl and Stroebe, 1987). While certain tasks (e.g. interdisciplinary ones) require teams despite the loss of productivity, these results suggest that the tendency to do team work may be reduced by counter-tendencies to increase individual work again.

Reduced supervision

Lean production (Womack et al., 1990) and other organizational techniques of restructuring have decreased the number of managers. Thus, a higher degree of responsibility for production and service is given to the shopfloor again. Moreover, telework reduces the amount of direct supervision possible. Therefore, supervisors' functions change; they should not intervene directly in day-to-day affairs but should be mentors of the groups they supervise (Emery and Trist, 1969). Reduced supervision also reduces the outside structure of the job and makes shop floor initiative necessary. The theory of leadership substitution (Kerr and Jermier, 1978; de Vries, 1997) can help to explain how one can deal with this situation. Standardization, a high degree of professionalism, intrinsically satisfying tasks and formalization reduce the need for leadership.

Major problems remain. How can companies make sure that ethical behavior is upheld throughout the company when there is very little direct influence? Supervisors have often been the carriers of organizational knowledge – a function that is much more difficult to develop if there is little knowledge of the concrete work done by employees. Errors and negative error consequences may increase if there is little supervision. Impetus for change is sometimes carried forward by supervisors (and organizational changes are made possible because first-line supervisors smooth the transition in various ways). The upkeep of organizational culture, holding up the symbols and values of the organization, and organizational socialization (Morrison, 1993) are other issues. All these functions of supervisors need to be developed within future organizations with a leaner structure.

Increased cultural diversity

Cultural diversity will increase. The European Union itself makes it necessary for different nationalities to work together in teams across the different European countries. In the USA, more than 50 per cent of workers will be members of ethnic minorities (e.g. blacks, Hispanics) and women soon. While there is more and more knowledge about dealing with cultural diversity, intercultural work means that people from cultures that are deeply suspicious of each other, for historical reasons (e.g. the Dutch and Germans or French and English) or cultural reasons (e.g. Muslims and Christians), will have to work together. This goes beyond understanding another culture and implies dealing with prejudices and animosities.

An added factor is language, when, for example, Europeans have to work together. This goes beyond the issue of which language is used in meetings. Some approaches are language dependent; concepts are used in a certain common cultural framework of understanding and their importance is often historically and culturally based. I have been to international meetings in Europe which were supposed to increase understanding of each other's approaches; however, people went away with even more problems in understanding what people from the other language group actually wanted to say, and prejudices were enhanced rather than reduced.

Software Development as an Example of a Cutting-edge Job

Jobs at the cutting edge of modern technology that can be empirically researched are a good indicator of future trends in the workplace. Software design is such a job. A study of the work situation of this profession comes to the conclusion that the following aspects are of primary importance (Brodbeck and Frese, 1994; Frese and Hesse, 1993):

- a high degree of learning by oneself (new techniques and methods etc.);
- a high degree of working in groups;
- a high degree of communication with co-workers;
- a high degree of interdisciplinary work (e.g. with customers who are experts in another area);
- a high degree to which people determine for themselves how they are solving problems.

These empirical observations reinforce the above mentioned trends and again point at the importance of self-reliance.

Conclusion

Most of the above-mentioned trends increase the importance of self-reliance and initiative. Self-reliance implies that one is able to rely on one's knowledge, skills and motivation; it enables people to stay in the race. Personal initiative implies that a self-starting and proactive approach is taken. The paradigmatic work using self-reliance and initiative is self-employment. More and more professions will increase the level of self-employment, largely because networks of self-employed people will work together, larger units will mimic self-employment for their constituents (e.g. in profit centres), internal entrepreneurs (intrapreneurs) will be encouraged within companies and people will have to participate in an internal market for their skills (mimicking the outside market and, thus, becoming similar to a small-scale entrepreneur). Changes in qualification requirements and in training needs are immense. However, anxiety and insecurity will increase correspondingly. As happens frequently in radical change situations, there are losers and winners. For this reason, work and organizational psychology has to find ways of making it possible for potential losers to participate in these change processes and to deal with the requirements. Some work and organizational psychology is already prepared for these issues, but much more research has to be done and practical approaches have to be tried out and evaluated. It is most likely that psychological processes will be generally perceived to be more important than so far. Thus, work and organizational psychology has to take up the challenge of changing workplaces. Obviously, as pointed out in the introductory comments, none of the changes will develop without provoking counter-movements. For example, there will be attempts to reduce the pressures of globalization and to enhance job security. There will be attempts to keep Tayloristic workplaces intact. I do not argue that there is a mechanistic movement towards higher complexity, a need for self-reliance and entrepreneurship. It is possible to hold back the tide, at least for some time. However, effort and energy will have to be expended that would be better used to develop methods of dealing with the changes that are ahead of us in the world of work.

Chapter Summary

This chapter has suggested that the following trends describe the future of jobs and work: the dissolution of the unity of work in space and time; a fast rate of innovation; increased complexity of work; global competition; the development of larger *and* smaller units; changing job and career concepts; more teamwork; reduced supervision; and increased cultural diversity. What each development means for work and organizational psychology has been described, together with the kind of research and practice that we will have to do in the future.

Discussion Points

1   Think of a job that you know well and develop several scenarios for how this job will have changed in 20 and 30 years from now. Produce optimistic and pessimistic scenarios. Produce a scenario in which the organizations are very conservative or in which they make many changes.

2   What issues will become important for managers of a firm in 30 years and for labour union officials? What kind of projects would they want work and organizational psychologists to have researched so that they can help them in making decisions?

3   Think of losers and winners of the development of work. How can psychology help the losers and the winners.

adverse impact: the extent to which the selection process unfairly discriminates between minority groups.

affirmative action: an approach to difference which positively discriminates for minority groups. The process may involve setting quotas or targets and actively recruiting and developing certain sections of the population.

ASCO: the Australian Standard Classification of Occupations is a system for categorizing jobs and occupations on the basis of skills and specialization.

assess: produce a comprehensive description of an individual or of a situation by reviewing and integrating information from a range of sources. Such sources could be observation, interview, the results of tests, laboratory investigation or other methods of systematically gathering information.

assessment centre: *not* primarily a location, but a special, complex process of various tests given to small groups of applicants, tasks (individual and group) presented to them and interviews with them, so that the results are integrated as a basis for selection decisions in appointments to managerial or similar complex posts, or for admission to some form of advanced training course.

attribution theories: theories which are concerned with the cognitive processes by which people explain their own, and others people's, behaviour and outcomes of behaviour.

automatic learned behaviour: that which is not under direct conscious control once initiated.

autonomous work groups: teams where there is no formal leader; leaders are emergent rather than selected, depending on the situation at hand.

autonomy: independence, freedom from external control or influence, personal liberty and availability of choice.

brainstorming: a technique used to generate many solutions whereby the team generates as many solutions as possible while deferring judgement on the ideas until later.

change agent: someone given responsibility for facilitating organizational change; can be a member of the organization but is frequently an external consultant.

charismatic leaders: leaders who are able to make ordinary people do extraordinary things in the face of adversity. Well known examples include Martin Luther King, Winston Churchill and Alexander the Great.

cognitive ergonomics: 'the interaction between tools and the user, with special emphasis on the cognitive processes of understanding, reasoning, and the use of knowledge' (Green and Hoc, 1991).

cognitive models: 'Understanding the psychology of users involves predicting user performance at the computer interface. A cognitive model is a mechanism for making such predictions' (Howes, 1995).

competency: job-related performance, or an underlying characteristic of a person that results in effective and/or superior performance in a job.

computer-based training: some or all of the training programme involves a computer, rather than a trainer, presenting training materials or tutorials to the trainee.

Complexity of work: complexity is defined by the number of elements at work, and the relationships among these elements.

concurrent validity: an approach to the examination of criterion-related validity whereby selection and criterion ratings are obtained from an existing group of job incumbents already working for the organization.

constructivist perspective: a more recent approach to selection which focuses on the involvement of both the applicant and the organization in a bilateral decision-making process.

contingency table: a cross-tabulation between

individuals' selection ratings and evaluations of job performance.

contingency theories: the approach to leadership which states that a leader's style or behaviour is, or should be, contingent (dependent) on the context or situation she or he is in.

convergent validity: this is a requirement for assessment centre construct validity andz-would be apparent if the correlations of the same dimension across exercises were high.

correlation coefficient: a statistical measure which assesses the association between two variables, e.g. selection performance and job performance.

costs: the hidden and unwanted consequences of actions which achieve some primary goal. They may be subjective, physiological or performance-related: see *latent degradation*.

criterion contamination: various errors which may bias ratings of the criterion, e.g. personal liking bias, similar-to-me effect.

criterion/criteria: either (a) performance criteria, dimensions of job performance which can be measured or rated with acceptable reliability; or (b) screening criteria, verifying information on candidate biographical details, knowledge, skills, abilities and other factors (KSAOs) or personality factors which can be used to screen-in or screen-out applicants.

criterion-related validity: the extent to which the future performance of the job incumbent is predicted accurately.

critical incident technique: a job analysis technique in which SMEs provide many spcific behavioural descriptions of incidents resulting in effective or ineffective performance.

CSCW (computer-supported collaborative working, or groupware): 'the sharing of software and hardware among groups of people working together so as to optimize the shared technology for maximum benefit to all who use or are affected by it' (Preece et al., 1994).

cultural dimensions: dimensions along which societies can be located, including individualism–collectivism (the degree to which people define themselves as individuals or as group members), power distance (the degree of formality with superiors), uncertainty avoidance (the degree of ambiguity about the future that can be tolerated) and masculinity–femininity (whether achievements or interpersonal relationships are valued).

demands: the level of situational change which impinges upon current task goals. These may be task-related (workload – cognitive, emotional or physical) or environmental (noise, social influences, interruptions etc.).

derailment: the term used by researchers at the Center for Creative Leadership to describe the process by which some leaders and managers fail to continue to be successful. They reach a plateau, get fired, get demoted or fail to live up to their earlier promise; they become derailed.

descriptors: a brief description of a distinct sample of behaviour used as part of an assessment process. To be useful in assessment it would have to be one of a set of selected descriptors, all referring to a particular kind of behaviour which could be observed, and each of which had been assigned to a specific grade on a scale from some such high point as 'highly commended' to a low point of 'not acceptable as effective/suitable'.

design rationale: 'Design rationale is the notion that design goes beyond merely accurate descriptions of artefacts, such as specifications, and articulates and represents the reasons and the reasoning processes behind the design and specification of artefacts' (Moran and Carroll, 1996).

diagnosticity: the extent to which a workload measure is able to distinguish between demands imposed by separate information processing components of a primary task.

difficulties: a term used by the Open University, which means essentially the same as hard situations.

dimension (in personality measurement): a term used instead of 'characteristic'. A well developed and standardized personality questionnaire will produce scores, for a person responding to the questions, on a number of characteristics. Since each score will be on a particular scale, and since a conceptual model of personality, as assessed by the questionnaire, can be thought of as describable in some form of multidimensional space, the term 'dimension' comes to be used instead of 'characteristic' when the strength or degree of presence of the characteristic is being invoked.

direct discrimination: when a conscious decision is made to reject certain applicants on the basis of irrelevant criteria, such as race or sex.

discontinuous, divergent or frame-breaking change: revolutionary change; frequently change of strategy, structure and systems.

discriminant validity: this is a requirement for assessment centre construct validity and would be apparent if the correlations between different dimensions within the same exercise were small.

discrimination: the process of excluding people on the basis of visible or inferred characteristics.

distributed cognition: 'A theoretical framework that explains cognitive activities as embodied and situated within the context in which they occur. It accounts for the socially and cognitively distributed work activities of a group of people and their interactional use of artefacts' (Preece et al., 1994).

distributive justice: the extent to which the candidate perceives the *outcome* of the selection process to be fair.

diversity climate: the way in which diversity initiatives are experienced in the organization's internal environment.

diversity: differences are part of individuality and thus any attribute which distinguishes one individual from another (e.g. race, sexuality, gender, age) contributes to diversity.

electrocardiogram (ECG): recording of the electrical activity of the heart using electrodes placed across the chest.

electroencephalogram (EEG): recording of the electrical activity of the brain using electrodes placed on the scalp.

electro-oculogram (EOG): eye blink and eye movement data are derived from this electrical measure of eye activity.

emotion-oriented coping: efforts aimed at regulating the emotions of a person (e.g. cognitive strategies like avoidance or relaxation techniques).

employee-centred (or relationship-orientated) leaders: leaders who are concerned about, and place emphasis on, their relationships with their subordinates.

enabler/facilitator: a person who *intervenes* on a basis of respect for the autonomy of a client or group. Information, comment and advice will be offered in such a way that the recipients retain control of their management of a situation and of themselves. An enabler/facilitator will ease the process of individual thinking by offering comments, asking questions and offering feedback about events and processes observed.

equal opportunities: a system of managing employee difference by providing equal opportunities for recruitment, selection and promotion. This school of thought is based on the premise that equal treatment for all will eradicate inequality.

ergonomics: an interdisciplinary science based on the anatomy, physiology and psychology of work and on the design of equipment. Ergonomics is concerned to devise systems which will take account of human factors in the work situation by devising support for limitations on human functioning and enabling the optimum use of human capabilities.

ethnocentrism: the tendency of individuals to believe that the characteristics associated with one's own race are superior to those of other races.

ethnography: 'involves the ethnographic participating, overtly or covertly, in people's daily lives for an extended period of time, watching what happens, listening to what is said, asking questions – in fact, collecting whatever data are available to throw light on the issues that are the focus of the research' (Hammersley and Atkinson, 1995).

evaluation: assessment of the effectiveness and value of training in terms of how much is learned, trainees' reactions and financial costs/saving.

event-related brain potential: voltage oscillations in the brain that can be recorded in response to a specific event.

exercise effect: the term used to refer to the typical finding in assessment centre research, which indicates that the correlations of different dimensions within exercises are higher than the correlations of the same dimension across exercises. This finding indicates that assessment centre construct validity is weak, since it is designed to measure the job-relevant dimensions.

expertise: declarative or procedural knowledge acquired as a result of experience.

feedback: information available to a trainee through his or her sense organs concerning the nature and results of his or her performance. A distinction is made between 'intrinsic' feedback that is *normally* available during task performance and 'extrinsic' feedback that is added to facilitate learning in the training situation, e.g. a trainer's comments concerning how performance can be improved.

fishbowl: a technique in which one group of people sit in a circle, surrounded by an outer circle of another group. The inner group discuss a topic, situation or even the members of the other group, while the outer group maintain silence and listen. It is a *group dynamics* technique.

five factor model (FFM): the big five model of personality has received substantial cross-national research support. The big five personality factors are: neuroticism, extroversion, openness to experience, agreeableness and conscientiousness.

glass ceiling: an invisible barrier, which prevents certain groups of people from reaching the more senior positions in organizations.

group dynamics: a body of knowledge, concepts and practices, primarily concerned with the way people behave in and experience being in groups where all members know each other or can come together. It was a dominant topic in the 1950s and grew out of the work of one of the founding fathers of social psychology, Kurt Lewin. From an interest in leadership and the responses of individuals in a social context to different styles of leadership, it developed into the study of people in groups, particularly in all forms of face-to-face groups. It was one of the foundation areas from which the field of organizational psychology developed.

groupthink: a decision-making process that leads to low-quality decisions, occurring when team members are more interested in maintaining harmony within the group than with reaching a high-quality decision.

hard change situations: situations where the technical and people issues are straightforward.

heterogeneity: variety, mixture, difference.

heuristic evaluation: 'a way of finding usability problems in a design by contrasting it with a list of established usability principles' (Nielsen, 1997).

hierarchical task analysis: a type of task analysis, developed by Annett and Duncan (1967), that progressively breaks a task or area of work into a hierarchical array of sub-tasks (or subgoals), with their associated plans that describe the conditions under which each is performed.

homosocial reproduction: the tendency of selection and promotion systems to filter out employees who do not comply with characteristics of the dominant coalition (i.e. senior management).

human factors (ergonomics): the 'study of human abilities and characteristics which affect the design of equipment, systems and jobs…and its aims are to improve efficiency, safety and well-being' (Clark and Corlett, 1984).

human–computer interaction: 'the discipline

concerned with the design, evaluation, and implementation of interactive computing systems for human use and with the study of the major phenomena surrounding them' (ACM SIGCHI, 1992).

incremental or converging change: changes within the organizational paradigm.

incremental validity: assesses the extent to which one selection method (e.g. personality tests) adds additional predictive validity above and beyond other selection methods (e.g. assessment centre).

indirect discrimination: arises when a selection method turns out (unintentionally) to be favourable to one particular group of applicants, despite similar treatment for all groups.

individual-oriented interventions: interventions primarily aimed at the individual (e.g. didactic stress management).

innovation: changes in product and processes that are new to the organization.

instruction: a synonym for training, sometimes used more frequently in educational than in occupational contexts.

instructional systems development (ISD) models: these models view training development as a system that can be broken down into the different functions or tasks that have to be performed by the person(s) responsible for training development. In a sense, each model is itself a task analysis of the task of developing, implementing and evaluating a training programme.

intervene/intervention: whatever a psychologist does to promote some immediate or ultimate response from a person or a group. As defined in the Shorter Oxford English Dictionary, 1993, 'intervention' is a 'coming between, an interfering, especially so as to modify or prevent a result or outcome'. Usage of the word by psychologists would rephrase that as: '. . . so as to modify, prevent *or promote* a result or an outcome'. Forms of intervention are cathartic, catalytic, supportive confronting, informative, prescriptive.

intrusiveness: the extent to which a workload assessment disrupts primary task performance.

job analysis: the systematic collection of data describing the tasks that comprise a job and the knowledge, skills, abilities and other characteristics that enable a person to carry out those tasks.

job characteristics model: a theory of work performance in which outcomes such as work motivation, job satisfaction and work effectiveness depend on the core job characteristics of skill variety, task identity, task significance, autonomy and feedback.

job diagnostic survey: a questionnaire developed on the basis of the job characteristics model and used for analysing the design of jobs.

job stress: an experienced incongruence between environmental (job) demands and individual/situational resources that is accompanied by mental, physical or behavioural symptoms.

job: all the tasks performed by a person in order to fulfil the duties of his or her occupation.

job-centred (or task-orientated) leaders: leaders who are primarily concerned with tasks carried out, and getting the job done, rather than with the feelings or views of subordinates.

job concept: the way we perceive the nature of a job is a historical artefact that developed during the industrial revolution; researchers argue that this kind of concept is dissolving, in favour of project work.

job-free measures: frequency and importance ratings for job analysis that are useful for between-job comparisons. Job-free measures of importance quantify consequences in terms that apply across jobs, e.g. extent of injury in the case of possible accidents, or value of loss in terms of monetary value, or labour hours of reworking in the case of quality defects or errors. Job-free measures of frequency quantify in terms of hourly, daily etc., rather than relative to the frequency of other events in the job, such as the highest or lowest frequency of occurrence.

job-oriented: any job analysis method that collects information about the tasks and duties carried out on the job, in terms of descriptions of the outcomes accomplished by the tasks.

job-relative measures: frequency and importance ratings for job analysis that are 'ipsative', which is relative in magnitude to other ratings for the same job, e.g. most frequent, but not comparable across jobs.

***laissez-faire* leaders:** these are hardly leaders at all. They are leaders who are not involved with followers' work, avoid taking a stand, let followers do as they please and are absent, disorganized and/or inefficient.

latent degradation: hidden decrements in performance associated with protection of primary task goals – secondary decrements, strategy changes, psychophysiological costs and strain after-effects: see *costs*.

leadership: the process in which an individual influences group members towards the attainment of group or organizational goals.

managerial grid: a grid, developed by Blake and Mouton (1964), on which a manager or leader can plot his or her style of leadership along the dimensions of concern for people and concern for tasks.

mental models: 'a mental representation that people use to organize their experience about themselves, others, the environment, and the things with which they interact. The functional role of mental models is to provide predictive and explanatory power for understanding these phenomena' (Preece et al., 1994).

mental workload: the costs that human operators incur in performing tasks (Kramer, 1991).

messes: an alternative term to 'soft change' situations.

meta-analysis: a statistical technique to pool together the results of a large number of separate research studies in order to determine the effect of variables based on sample sizes of thousands of subjects, rather than the small samples typically associated with individual studies.

minority dissent: a decision-making process occuring when a numerical minority within a team disagrees with the majority, which can result in an enduring change in attitudes.

modes of demand management: the general strategy used to regulate performance, particularly under high demands. The three modes – engaged, disengaged and strain – differ with respect to level of management resources available and the priority for performance or personal goals.

multiculturalism: embracing and accepting diverse cultural traditions and customs.

multitrait-multimethod matrix: the correlation matrix between measures of traits (or dimensions, such as leadership, communication) in various methods (or exercises, such as group discussions, interviews). This is used to investigate assessment centre construct validity.

organization development (OD): when an organization is structured and has a culture able to build a process of continuous problem-solving and renewal.

organizational climate: a set of perceptions that reflect how the employee views and appraises the work environment and organizational attributes.

organizational iceberg: a metaphor to denote the formal aspects of organizational functioning as the visible smaller part of an iceberg, with the informal aspects as the invisible larger part of the iceberg.

organizational monoculturalism: the way in which a dominant cultural system pervades an organization.

organizational-level interventions: interventions primarily aimed at the organization (e.g. employee assistance programmes).

PAQ: the position analysis questionnaire is an off-the-shelf job analysis instrument for which a trained job analyst rates the job on items concerning information input, mental processes, work output, relationships with other persons, job context and other job characteristics.

person–job fit: the degree to which an individual's KSAOs permit the person to perform the job effectively.

person–organization fit: the degree of congruence between an individual employee's values, beliefs and attributes on the one side, and the organization's culture on the other.

person–team fit: the degree of fit between an individual and his or her proximal day-to-day work group or team.

predictive validity: an approach to the examination of criterion-related validity whereby job performance ratings are obtained after a period of employment with an organization and then compared with measures of selection performance.

predictivist perspective: the traditional approach to selection, which focuses on the organization's perspective.

predictor(s): methods of candidate assessment which are used to predict future job performance by an organization.

primary task: a task whose workload is to be measured.

problem-oriented coping: efforts aimed at altering the transaction between person and environment (e.g. seeking help).

procedural justice: the extent to which the candidate perceives the selection *process* as fair.

rating: the term for a subjective assessment made on an established scale. It enables rough information to be obtained about the degree to which characteristics exist. The information is 'rough' because the procedure rests on a number of assumptions. The more these are specified and taken into account the more reliable (less 'rough') the information becomes.

recruitment: attracting applicants through advertising, word-of-mouth or other methods. It can be used to include the pre-screening phase of selection.

regulatory control: the mechanism by which dynamic systems (such as humans) maintain stable patterns of behaviour towards goals. It operates by comparing required behaviour with feedback from the results of actions, and modifying actions accordingly.

reliability: the extent to which an assessment technique measures with consistency.

responsibility charting: assesses the alternative behaviours for each person involved in a series of actions to bring about change.

restriction of range: artefactual limitation of the distribution of ratings either in predictor measures or in criterion measures (e.g. in a predictive validity study, criterion ratings for successful candidates only will be available).

scenario: a holistic picture of how a change in one or several parameters changes the way we work, the way we live etc.

secondary task: a task performed concurrently with a primary task to assess the workload of the primary task. It is assumed that levels of secondary task performance will reflect the resource demands of the primary task.

selection: employment decisions made by responsible members of an organization, usually choosing between multiple candidates, and using one or more methods of candidate assessment. It can include the decision of the candidate whether to accept or reject an offer of employment made by an organization.

sensitivity: the extent to which a workload assessment technique is able to discriminate between different levels of workload.

social loafing: a reduction of task-related effort by individuals when performing in a group compared to performing individually.

socialization impact: the impact of selection methods upon candidates' expectations, preferences, attitudes and beliefs about the job role and organization as an employer.

sociotechnical systems theory: a theory of work design based on jointly optimizing the social and technical systems of the organization.

socio-technical theory: 'the theory is concerned with the analysis and design of work organisations and proposes the need for joint optimisation and parallel design of its social and technical subsystems' (Clegg, 1995).

soft change situations: situations where both the technical and peoples issues are complex and interdependent.

soft systems analysis: 'primarily a method for investigating problems located within a system. The method is used to plan and implement change, although it can be also used to design new systems. Typically, the focus of the method is on rather complex systems involving human activity' (Clegg and Walsh, 1998).

strain: a reaction to a stressor that can be affective (e.g. anxiety), cognitive (e.g. helplessness), physical (e.g. headache), behavioural (e.g. overactivity) or motivational (e.g. disillusionment).

strategic drift: occurs when an organization's strategy becomes less and less in tune with its environment.

strategy–structure fit: the degree to which an organization's structure aligns itself with its strategy.

stressor: a negative situation or a noxious event that acts on the individual and is supposed to have negative effects (e.g. work overload).

subject matter experts: SMEs are people whose experience in relation to the job makes them a good source of information about the job. They may be people such as past and present job incumbents, supervisors, customers and training instructors.

task analysis: 'A systematic analysis of the *behaviour* required to carry out a *task* with a view to identifying areas of difficulty and the appropriate training techniques and learning aids necessary for successful instruction' (Department of Employment, 1971).

task feedback: the amount of feedback available from completing the task itself.

task identity: the degree to which the task represents a clear and whole piece of work.

task inventory: a comprehensive list of tasks that may be performed in a number of closely related jobs. The list can be used as a ques-

tionnaire to obtain frequency and importance ratings from incumbents, so that the task profile of a job can be constructed.

task significance: the degree to which the task is important to the team, the organization and wider society.

task variety: the extent of variety present in the tasks assigned to the team.

task: an important element of a job which can be identified as achieving a specific result.

team climate: the atmosphere within the team, or 'the way things are around here'.

team effectiveness: performance criteria indicated by team-produced outputs, effect on team members' well-being and satisfaction and the enhancement of their future performance.

team: a group of people with well defined and interdependent roles, who interact with each other in order to achieve shared goals.

training development: completion of all the tasks involved in identifying training needs and training content, designing training, implementing training and evaluating and revising the training programmes as necessary.

training objectives: equivalent to behavioural objectives. As suggested by Mager (1962), each objective should specify clearly the activity that the trainee should be able to do after training, the conditions under which this activity should be performed and the level of performance required in terms of speed, accuracy etc.

training programme: a systematic sequence of units of instruction, each of which is specified in terms of its duration, its method of delivery (e.g. lecture, training book, computer-based training) and who is responsible for administering it.

training: 'The systematic development of the *attitude/knowledge/skill behaviour pattern* required by an individual in order to perform adequately a given *task* or *job*' (Department of Employment, 1971).

trait approach: the approach to leadership research which seeks to identify and define the individual traits and characteristics of leaders which distinguish them from non-leaders. Also called the great man/great woman approach.

transactional leaders: leaders who motivate followers by appealing to their self-interest and exchanging valued rewards, such as pay or status, for their effort.

transactional leadership: leadership style focused on transactions, task-oriented behaviors, exchanges and contingent rewards and punishments to change team members' behaviours.

transfer of learning: application of learned behaviour in new (usually job) situations.

transformational leaders: leaders who raise followers to higher levels of effort by engaging their emotions and by appealing to their morality or values.

transformational leadership: leadership style involving charisma, inspirational motivation, intellectual stimulation and individualized consideration.

unfair discrimination: selection of candidates upon factors which are deemed in employment law to be unacceptable (e.g. sex, ethnic origin, disabilities which can be reasonably accommodated for, marital status, trade union membership). Precisely what constituted discriminatory behaviour in selection therefore varies between countries and changes over time in line with newly enacted legislation.

usability: 'A measure of the ease with which a system can be learned or used, its safety, effectiveness and efficiency, and the attitude of its users towards it' (Preece et al., 1994).

utility analysis: an estimate of the cost-effectiveness of selection.

validation feedback loops: when information on the accuracy of selection is used to modify and improve the process.

validity generalization: the extent to which the findings of one validation study can be generalized to another selection situation.

validity: the extent to which a technique measures what it purports to measure.

virtual organization: a temporary network of companies and groups which come together to exploit fast-changing opportunities, usually in situations of high risk.

worker-oriented: any job analysis method that collects information in the form of descriptions of behaviours required and the actions carried out, rather than the outcomes of execution of the task components.

working memory: carrying out mental operations on one set of material, while holding other information in temporary storage.

workplace social support: the existence of good, pleasant relationships with others, the availability of others in the case of problems, and help, understanding and attention provided when one is faced with difficulties.

BIBLIOGRAPHY

Aasman, J., Mulder, C. and Mulder, L. J. M. (1987) Operator effort and the measurement of heart-rate variability. *Human Factors*, 29, 161–70.

Aasman, J., Wijers, A. A., Mulder, G. and Mulder, L. J. M. (1988) Measuring mental fatigue in normal daily working routines. In P. A. Hancock and N. Meshkati (eds), *Human Mental Workload*. Amsterdam: North-Holland.

Ackerman, P. L. (1996) A theory of adult intellectual development: process, personality, interests, and knowledge. *Intelligence*, 22, 227–57.

Ackerman, P. L. and Heggestad, E. D. (1997) Intelligence, personality, and interests: evidence for overlapping traits. *Psychological Bulletin*, 121, 219–45.

Ackerman, P. L., Kanfer, R. and Goff, M. (1995) Cognitive and noncognitive determinants and consequences of complex skill acquisition. *Journal of Experimental Psychology: Applied*, 1, 270–304.

ACM Special Interest Group on Computer–Human Interaction (1992) *Curriculum Development Group Technical Report*. New York: ACM Press.

Adams, J. S. (1963) Towards an understanding of inequity. *Journal of Abnormal and Social Psychology*, 67, 422–36.

Adams, S. M. (1995) Part-time work: models that work. *Women in Management Review*, 19(7), 21–31.

Adler, N. J. (1990) *International Dimensions of Organizational Behavior*, 2nd edn. Boston: Kent.

Agervold, M. (1987) New technology in the office: attitudes and consequences. *Work and Stress*, 1, 143–53.

Ainsworth, L. and Marshall, F. (1998) Issues of quality and practicality in task analysis: preliminary results from two surveys. *Ergonomics*, 41(11), 1607–17.

Aitkenhead, M. and Liff, S. (1991) The effectiveness of equal opportunities policies. In J. Firth-Cozens and M. A. West (eds), *Women at Work: Psychological and Organizational Perspectives*. Milton Keynes: Open University Press.

Alimo-Metcalfe, B. (1994) Waiting for fish to grow feet! Removing organizational barriers to women's entry into leadership positions. In M. Tanton (ed.), *Women in Management: a Developing Presence*. London: Routledge.

Allen, N. J. (1996) Affective reactions to the group and organization. In M. A. West (ed.), *Handbook of Work Group Psychology*. Chichester: Wiley.

Alpander, G. G. and Lee, C. R. (1995) Culture, strategy and teamwork, the keys to organizational change. *Journal of Management Development*, 14(8), 4–18.

Anderson, J. R. (1987) Skill acquisition: compilation of weak-method problem solutions. *Psychological Review*, 94, 192–210.

Anderson, J. R. (1993) *Rules of the Mind*. Hillsdale, NJ: Lawrence Erlbaum.

Anderson, N. R. (1992) Eight decades of employment interview research: a retrospective meta-review and prospective commentary. *European Work and Organizational Psychology*, 2, 1–32.

Anderson, N. (1997) The validity and adverse impact of selection interviews: a rejoinder to Wood. *Selection and Development Review*, 13(5), 13–17.

Anderson, N. and Herriot, P. (eds) (1997) *International Handbook of Selection and Assessment*. Chichester: Wiley.

Anderson, N. and Ostroff, C. (1997) Selection as socialisation. In N. Anderson and P. Herriot (eds), *International Handbook of Selection and Assessment*. Chichester: Wiley.

Anderson, N. R. and Shackleton, V. J. (1993) *Successful Selection Interviewing*. Oxford: Blackwell.

Anderson, R., Heath, C., Luff, P. and Moran, T. P. (1993) The cognitive and the social in human–computer interaction. *International Journal of Man–Machine Studies*, 38, 999–1016.

Andrews, D. H. and Goodson, L. A. (1980) A comparative analysis of models of instructional design. *Journal of Instructional Development*, 3, 2–16.

Annett, J. and Duncan, K. D. (1967) Task analysis and training design. *Occupational Psychology*, 41, 211–21.

Annett, J., Duncan, K. D., Stammers, R. B. and Gray, M. J. (1971) *Task Analysis*. Training Information No. 6. London: HMSO.

Ansoff, I. H. and McDonnell, E. J. (1990) *Implanting Strategic Management*. Englewood Cliffs, NJ: Prentice Hall.

Anstey, E. (1977) A 30-year follow-up of the CSSB procedure, with lessons for the future. *Journal of Occupational Psychology*, 50, 149–59.

Anthony, P. (1994) *Managing Culture*. Buckingham: Open University Press.

Antoni, C. (1996) *Teilautonome Arbeitsgruppen*. Weinheim: Psychologie Verlags Union.

Applebaum, E. and Batt, R. (1994) *The New American Workplace*. Ithaca, NY: IER Press.

Argyle, M. (1939) *The Social Psychology of Work*, 2nd edn. London: Penguin.

Argyris, C. and Schon, D. (1978) *Organizational Learning*. Reading, MA: Addison-Wesley.

Arnold, J., Cooper, C. L. and Robertson, I. T. (1995) *Work Psychology*, 2nd edn. London: Pitman.

Arvey, R. D. (1992) Fairness and ethical considerations in employee selection. In *New Approaches to Employee Management: Fairness in Employee Selection, volume 1*. Greenwich, CT: JAI Press, pp. 1–19.

Arvey, R. D. and Sackett, P. R. (1993) Fairness in selection: current developments and perspectives. In N. Schmitt and W. Borman (eds), *Personnel Selection in Organizations*. San Francisco: Jossey-Bass.

Australian Bureau of Statistics (1997) *Australian Standard Classification of Occupations*, 2nd edn. Canberra, ACT: Australian Bureau of Statistics.

Ausubel, D. P. (1960) The use of advance organisers in the learning and retention of meaningful verbal material. *Journal of Educational Psychology*, 51, 267–72.

Axtell, C. M., Waterson, P. E. and Clegg, C. W. (1997) Problems integrating user participation into software development. *International Journal of Human Computer Studies*, 47, 323–45.

Baddeley, A. D. (1972) Selective attention and performance in dangerous environments. *British Journal of Psychology*, 63, 537–46.

Baddeley, A. D. (1986) *Working Memory*. Oxford: Oxford University Press.

Baddeley, A. D. and Longman, D. J. A. (1978) The influence of length and frequency of training session on the rate of learning to type. *Ergonomics*, 21, 627–35.

Badham, R., Couchman, P. and Selden, D. (1996). Winning the socio-technical wager: change roles and the implementation of self managing work cells. In R. J. Koubek and W. Karwowski (eds), *Manufacturing Agility and Hybrid Automation: volume 1*. Louisville, KY: IEA Press.

Bainbridge, L. (1974) Analysis of verbal protocols from a process control task. In E. Edwards and F. P. Lees (eds), *The Human Operator in Process Control*. London: Taylor and Francis.

Bainbridge, L. (1978) The process controller. In W. T. Singleton (ed.), *Analysis of Practical Skills. Volume I. The Study of Real Skills*. Baltimore: University Park Press.

Bainbridge, L. (1987) Ironies of automation. In J. Rasmussen, K. D. Duncan and J. Leplat (eds), *New Technology and Human Error*. Chichester: Wiley.

Baldwin, T. T. (1992) Effects of alternative modelling strategies on outcomes of interpersonal-skills training. *Journal of Applied Psychology*, 77(2), 147–54.

Baldwin, T. T. and Ford, J. K. (1988) Transfer of training: a review and directions for future research. *Personnel Psychology*, 41, 63–105.

Baltes, P. K. (1990) Psychological perspectives on human aging: the model of selective optimization with compensation. In P. B. Baltes and M. M. Baltes (eds), *Successful Aging*. Cambridge: Cambridge University Press.

Bandura, A. (1989) Perceived self-efficacy in the exercise of personal agency. *The Psychologist: Bulletin of the British Psychological Society*, 10, 411–24.

Banks, M. H. and Henry, P. (1993) Change and stability in employment commitment. *Journal of Occupational and Organizational Psychology*, 66, 177–84.

Bantel, K. A. (1993) Strategic clarity in banking: role of top management team demography. *Psychological Reports*, 73, 1187–201.

Bantel, K. A. and Jackson, S. E. (1989) Top management and innovation in banking: does the composition of the top team make a difference? *Strategic Management Journal*, 10, 107–24.

Baron, J. (1993) Why teach thinking? An essay. *Applied Psychology: an International Review*, 42, 191–213.

Bartlett, F. (1932) *Remembering*. Cambridge: Cambridge University Press.

Bartol, K. M. and Martin, D. C. (1994) *Management*, 2nd edn. Maidenhead: McGraw-Hill International.

Bartram, D., Anderson, N., Kellet, D., Lindley, P. and Robertson, I. (1995) *Review of Assessment Instruments (Level B) for Use in Occupational Settings*. Leicester: BPS Books.

Bartram, D., Burke, E., Kandola, R., Lindley, P., Marshall, L. and Rasch, P. (1997) *Review of Ability and Aptitude Tests (Level A) for Use in Occupational Settings*. Leicester: BPS Books.

Bartz, D. E., Hillman, L. W., Lehrer, S. and Mayhugh, G. M. (1990) A model for managing workforce diversity. *Management Education and Development*, 21(5), 321–6.

Basalla, G. (1988) *The Evolution of Technology*. Cambridge: Cambridge University Press.

Bass, B. M. (1985) Leadership: good, better, best. *Organizational Dynamics*, Winter, 26–40.

Bass, B. M. (1990a) *Bass and Stodgill's Handbook of Leadership*. New York: Free Press.

Bass, B. M. (1990b) Editorial: towards a meeting of minds. *Leadership Quarterly*, 1, 1–3.

Bass, B. M. and Avolio, B. J. (1995) *Multifactor Leadership Questionnaire*. Redwood City, CA: Mind Garden Inc.

Bassi, L. J., Cheney, S. and Van Buren, M. (1997) Training industry trends 1997. *Training and Development*, November, 46–59.

Bauer, T. N. and Green, S. G. (1994) Effect of newcomer involvement in work-related activities: a longitudinal study of socialization. *Journal of Applied Psychology*, 79(2), 211–23.

Beatty, J. (1982) Task-evoked pupillary responses, processing load and the structure of processing resources. *Psychological Bulletin*, 91, 276–92.

Beckhard, R. and Hanis, R. T. (1987) *Organizational Transitions, Managing Complex Change*, 2nd edn. Reading, MA: Addison-Wesley.

Belbin, E. and Belbin, K. M. (1972) *Problems in Adult Retraining*. London: Heinemann.

Belbin, K. M. (1965) *Training Methods for Older Workers*. Paris: OECD.

Belbin, K. M. (1969) *The Discovery Method in Training*. London: HMSO.

Bellotti, V. M. E. (1990) A framework for assessing the applicability of HCI techniques. In D. Diaper, D. J. Gilmore, G. Cockton and B. Shackel (eds), *Human–Computer Interaction – INTERACT '90*. Amsterdam: Elsevier.

Bennis, W. G. and Nanus, B. (1985) *Leaders: the Strategies for Taking Charge*. New York: Harper and Row.

Bernardin, H. J. and Beatty, R. W. (1984) *Performance Appraisal: Assessing Human Behavior at Work*. Boston: Kent.

Bernardin, H. J. and Villanova, P. (1986) Performance appraisal. In E. Locke (ed.), *Generalizing from Laboratory to Field Settings*. Lexington, MA: Lexington Books.

Berry-Lound, D. J. (1993) *A Carer's Guide to Eldercare*. Horsham: The Host Consultancy.

Beyer, H. and Holtzblatt, K. (1998) *Contextual Design: Defining Customer-centered Systems*. San Francisco: Morgan Kaufmann.

Birdi, K., Allan, C. and Warr, P. B. (1997) Correlates and perceived outcomes of four types of employee development activity. *Journal of Applied Psychology*, 82, 845–57.

Biswas, R. and Cassell, C. (1996) Strategic HRM and the gendered division of labour in the hotel industry: a case study. *Personnel Review*, 25(2), 19–34.

Blackler, F. (1995) Activity theory, CSCW and organisations. In A. F. Monk and G. N. Gilbert (eds), *Perspectives on HCI: Diverse Approaches*. London: Academic Press.

Blackler, F. and Brown, C. (1986) Alternative models to guide the design and introduction of new technologies into work organisations. *Journal of Occupational Psychology*, 41, 211–21.

Blake, R. R. and McCanse, A. A. (1991) *Leadership Dilemmas: Grid Solutions.* Houston: Gulf Publishing.

Blake, R. and Mouton, J. (1964) *The Managerial Grid.* Houston: Gulf Publishing.

Blake, R. and Mouton, J. (1972) *The Diagnosis and Development Matrix.* Houston: Scientific Methods.

Blatti, S. (1996) Participative methods to support technical and organisational change for improved competitiveness. In R. J. Koubek and W. Karwowski (eds), *Manufacturing Agility and Hybrid Automation: volume 1.* Louisville, KY: IEA Press.

Body Shop Case Study (1995) *Kellogg School of Management.* Evanston, IL: Northwestern University/Brighton: The Body Shop International plc.

Bolden, R., Waterson, P. E., Warr, P. B., Clegg, C. W. and Wall, T. D. (1997) A new taxonomy of modern manufacturing practices. *International Journal of Operations and Production Management*, 17(11), 1112–30.

Bond, M. H. and Hwang, K. K. (1986) The social psychology of Chinese people. In M. H. Bond (ed.), *The Psychology of the Chinese People.* Hong Kong: Oxford University Press.

Bond, M. H. and Smith, P. B. (1996) Cross-cultural social and organizational psychology. *Annual Review of Psychology*, 47, 203–35.

Borman, W. C., Hanson, M. A. and Hedge, J. W. (1997) Personnel selection. *Annual Review of Psychology*, 48, 299–337.

Borman, W. C., White, L. A. and Dorsey, D. W. (1995) Effects of ratee task performance and interpersonal factors on supervisor and peer performance ratings. *Journal of Applied Psychology*, 80, 168–77.

Borman, W. C., White, L. A., Pulakos, E. D. and Oppler, S. H. (1991) Models of supervisory performance ratings. *Journal of Applied Psychology*, 76, 863–72.

Bosma, H., Peter, R., Siegrist, J. and Marmot, M. (1998) Two alternative job stress models and the risk of coronary heart disease. *American Journal of Public Health*, 88(1), 68–74.

Bowers, C. A., Baker, D. P. and Salas, E. (1994) Measuring the importance of teamwork: the reliability and validity of job/task analysis indices for team-training design. *Military Psychology*, 6, 205–14.

Bownas, D. A. and Bernardin, H. J. (1988) Critical incident technique. In S. Gael (ed.), *The Job Analysis Handbook for Business, Industry, and Government, volume 2.* New York: Wiley, pp. 1120–37.

Boyatzis, R. E. (1982) *The Competent Manager: a Model for Effective Performance.* New York: Wiley.

Braham, J. (1989) No, you don't manage everyone the same. *Industry Week*, 238, 28–35.

Braich, R. (1992) Fear of a black planet: a study of managing diversity. Unpublished MSc thesis, Institute of Work Psychology, University of Sheffield.

Branson, R. K., Rayner, G. T., Cox, L., Furman, J. P., King, F. J. and Hannum, W. H. (1975) *Interservice Procedures for Instructional Systems Development: Executive Summary and Model.* Talahassee, FL: Center for Educational Technology, Florida State University.

Bray, D. and Grant, D. L. (1966) The assessment centre in the measurement of potential for business management. *Psychological Monographs*, 80(17), whole issue.

Brick, J. (1991) *China: a Handbook in Intercultural Communication*. Sydney: Macquarie University.

Bridges, W. (1995) *Jobshift*. London: Allen and Unwin.

Briggs, L. I. and Wager, W. W. (1981) *Handbook of Procedures for the Design of Instruction*, 2nd edn. Englewood Cliffs, NJ: Educational Technology Publications.

Brindle, L. (1992) Winners and losers in the career stakes. *Human Resources*, Spring, 95–8.

Broadbent, D. E. (1963) Differences and interactions between stresses. *Quarterly Journal of Experimental Psychology*, 15, 205–11.

Broadbent, D. E. (1971) *Decision and Stress*. London: Academic Press.

Broadbent, D. E. (1977) Levels, hierarchies and the locus of control. *Quarterly Journal of Experimental Psychology*, 29, 181–201.

Broadbent, D. E. (1979) Is a fatigue test now possible? *Ergonomics*, 22, 1277–90.

Brock, A. (1998) Pedagogy and research. *The Psychologist*, 11, 169–71.

Brodbeck, F. C. and Frese, M. (eds) (1994) *Produktivitaet und Qualitaet in Software Projekten* (*Productivity and Quality of Software Projects*). Munich: Oldenbourg.

Brown, A. (1995) *Organisational Culture*. London: Pitman.

Brown, I. (1990) Accident reporting and analysis. In J. Wilson and N. Corlett (eds), *Evaluation of Human Work*. London: Taylor and Francis.

Browning, R. C. (1968) Validity of reference ratings from previous employers. *Personnel Psychology*, 21, 389–393.

Bryman, A. (1992) *Charisma and Leadership in Organizations*. London: Sage.

Buchanan, D. A. and Boddy, D. (1983) Advanced technology and the quality of working life: the effects of computerized controls on biscuit-making operators. *Journal of Occupational Psychology*, 56, 109–19.

Buchanan, D. and Boddy, D. (1992) *The Expertise of the Change Agent: Public Performance and Backstage Activity*. Hemel Hempstead: Prentice Hall.

Buckley, W. (ed.) (1968) *Modern Systems Research for the Behavioral Scientist*. Chicago: Aldine.

Bunderson, C. V. (1977) Analysis of needs and goals for author training and production management systems. Technical Report 1, MDA-903-76-C-0216. San Diego, CA: Courseware.

Burger, J. M. (1989) Negative reactions to increases in perceived personal control. *Journal of Personality and Social Psychology*, 56, 246–56.

Burke, R. J. (1993) Organizational-level interventions to reduce occupational stressors. *Work and Stress*, 7, 77–8.

Burke, R. J. and McKeen, C. A. (1992) Women in management. In C. L. Cooper and I. T. Robertson (eds), *International Review of Industrial and Organizational Psychology*. New York: Wiley.

Burke, W. W. and Litwin, G. H. (1992) A causal model of organizational performance and change. *Journal of Management*, 18(3), 523–45.

Burns, T. and Stalker, G. M. (1961) *The Management of Innovation*. London: Tavistock.

Burnside, R. M. (1991) Visioning: building pictures for the future. In J. Henry and D. Walker (eds), *Managing Innovation*. London: Sage.

Butler, M. C. and Jones, A. P. (1979) Perceived leader behavior, individual characteristics, and injury occurrence in hazardous work environments. *Journal of Applied Psychology*, 64, 299–304.

Butler, R. (1991) *Designing Organizations: a Decision Making Perspective*. London: Routledge.

Button, G. and Sharrock, W. (1994) Occasioned practices in the work of software engineers. In M. Jirotka and J. Goguen (eds), *Requirements Engineering: Social and Technical Issues*. London: Academic Press.

Buunk, B. P. (1990) Affiliation and helping interactions within organizations: a critical analysis of the role of social support with regard to occupational stress. In W. Stroebe and M. Hewstone (eds), *European Review of Social Psychology, volume 5*. Chichester: Wiley.

Buunk, B. P., de Jonge, J., Ybema, J. F. and de Wolff, Ch. J. (1998) Psychosocial aspects of occupational stress. In P. J. D. Drenth, H. Thierry and Ch. J. de Wolff (eds), *Handbook of Work and Organizational Psychology, volume 2: Work Psychology*, 2nd edn. Hove: Psychology Press.

Bycio, P., Alvares, K. M. and Hahn, J. (1987) Situational specificity in assessment center ratings: a confirmatory factor analysis. *Journal of Applied Psychology*, 72, 463–74.

Byham, W. C. (1971) The assessment centre as an aid in managerial development. *Training and Development Journal*, 25, 10–22.

Callan, V. J., Gallois, C. and Forbes, P. A. (1983) Evaluative reactions to accented English: ethnicity, sex role and context. *Journal of Cross-Cultural Psychology*, 14(4), 407–26.

Campbell, D. T. and Fiske, D. W. (1959) Convergent and discriminant validation by the multitrait–multimethod matrix. *Psychological Bulletin*, 56, 81–105.

Campbell, D. T. and Stanley, J. C. (1966) *Experimental and Quasi-experimental Designs for Research*. Chicago: Rand McNally.

Campbell, J. P. and Pritchard, R. D. (1976) Motivation theory in industrial and organisational psychology. In M. D. Dunnette (ed.), *Handbook of Industrial and Organizational Psychology*. Chicago: Rand McNally.

Campion, M. A. (1988) Interdisciplinary approaches to job design: a constructive replication with extensions. *Journal of Applied Psychology*, 73, 467–81.

Campion, M. A. (1989) Ability requirement implications of job design: an interdisciplinary perspective. *Personnel Psychology*, 42, 1–24.

Campion, M. A. (1994) Job analysis for the future. In M. G. Rumsey, C. B. Walker and J. H. Harris (eds), *Personnel Selection and Classification*. Hillsdale, NJ: Lawrence Erlbaum, pp. 1–12.

Campion, M. A. and McClelland, C. L. (1991) Interdisciplinary examination of the costs and benefits of enlarged jobs: a job design quasi-experiment. *Journal of Applied Psychology*, 76, 186–98.

Campion, M. A. and McClelland, C. L. (1993) Follow-up and extension of the interdisciplinary costs and benefits of enlarged jobs. *Journal of Applied Psychology*, 78, 339–51.

Campion, M. A., Medsker, G. J. and Higgs, A. C. (1993) Relations between work group characteristics and effectiveness: implications for designing effective work groups. *Personnel Psychology*, 46, 823–50.

Campion, M. A., Papper, E. M. and Medsker, G. J. (1996) Relations between work team characteristics and effectiveness: a replication and extension. *Personnel Psychology*, 49, 429–689.

Campion, M. A. and Thayer, P. W. (1985) Development and field evaluation of an interdisciplinary measure of job design. *Journal of Applied Psychology*, 70, 29–43.

Caplan, R. D. (1983) Person–environment fit: past, present, and future. In C. L. Cooper (ed.), *Stress Research*. Chichester: Wiley.

Caplan, R. D., Cobb, S., French, J. R. P. Jr, Harrison, R. V. and Pinneau, S. R. Jr (1975) *Job Demands and Worker Health: Main Effects and Occupational Differences*. Washington, DC: US Government Printing Office.

Card, S. K., Moran, T. P. and Newell, A. (1983) *The Psychology of Human–Computer Interaction*. Hillsdale, NJ: Erlbaum.

Carletta, J., Fraser-Krauss, H. and Garrod, S. (1996) Speaking turns in face-to-face workplace groups: the role of the communication mediator. Unpublished manuscript, Human Communication Research Centre, Universities of Edinburgh and Glasgow.

Carroll, J. M. (1997) Human–computer interaction: psychology as a science of design. *International Journal of Human–Computer Studies*, 46, 501–22.

Carr-Ruffino, N. (1996) *Managing Diversity*. San Francisco: Thompson International.

Carter, N. L. and Beh, H. C. (1989) The effect of intermittent noise on cardiovascular functioning during vigilance performance. *Psychophysiology*, 26, 548–59.

Cartwright, S. and Cooper, C. L. (1996) Public policy and occupational health psychology in Europe. *Journal of Occupational Health Psychology*, 1, 349–61.

Carver, C. S. and Scheier, M. F. (1982) Control theory: a useful conceptual framework of personality-social, clinical and health psychology. *Psychological Bulletin*, 92, 111–35.

Casali, J. C. and Wierwille, W. W. (1983) A comparison of rating scale, secondary task, physiological and primary task workload estimation techniques in a simulated flight task emphasizing communications load. *Human Factors*, 25, 623–42.

Cascio, W. F. (1995) Whither industrial and organizational psychology in a changing world of work? *American Psychologist*, 50(11), 928–39.

Cascio, W. F. (1998) The virtual workplace: a reality now. *Industrial Organizational Psychologist*, 35, 32–6.

Casey, S. (1998) *Set Phasers on Stun and Other True Tales of Design, Technology, and Human Error*, 2nd edn. Santa Barbara, CA: Aegean Publishing Company.

Cassell, C. M. (1996) A fatal attraction? Strategic FIRM and the business case for women's progression at work. *Personnel Review*, 25(5), 51–66.

Cassidy, T. and Lynn, R. (1989) A multifactorial approach to achievement motivation: the development of a comprehensive measure. *Journal of Occupational Psychology*, 62, 301–12.

Cattell, K. B. (1963) Theory of fluid and crystallized intelligence. *Journal of Educational Psychology*, 54, 1–22.

Cellar, D. F., Miller, M. L., Doverspike, D. D. and Klawsky, J. D. (1996) Comparisons of factor structure and criterion-related validity coefficients for two measures of personality based on the five factor model. *Journal of Applied Psychology*, 81, 694–704.

Chan, D., Schmitt, N., DeShon, P., Clause, C. S. and Delbridge, K. (1997) Reactions to cognitive ability tests: the relationships between race, test performance, face validity perceptions, and test-taking motivation. *Journal of Applied Psychology*, 82(2), 300–10.

Chapman, A. J., Sheehy, N. P., Heywood, S., Dooley, B. and Collins, S. C. (1995) The organizational implications of teleworking. In C. L. Cooper and I. T.

Robertson (eds), *International Review of Industrial and Organizational Psychology*. Chichester: Wiley.

Charness, N. and Bosman, E. A. (1990) Expertise and aging. In T. M. Hess (ed.), *Aging and Cognition: Knowledge, Organization, and Utilization*. Amsterdam: Elsevier.

Charuwatee, P. (1996) An investigation of perceived organizational safety climate: employees' intentions to behave safely and their predictors. Unpublished MSc thesis, University of Sheffield.

Checkland, P. B. (1972) Towards a systems based methodology for real world problem solving. *Journal of Systems Engineering*, 3(2).

Checkland, P. B. (1981) *Systems Thinking, Systems Practice*. Chichester: Wiley.

Cherniss, C. (1995) *Beyond Burnout: Helping Teachers, Nurses, Therapists and Lawyers Recover from Stress and Disillusionment*. New York: Routledge.

Cherns, A. B. (1976) The principles of socio-technical design. *Human Relations*, 29, 783–92.

Cherns, A. B. (1987) The principles of socio-technical design revisited. *Human Relations*, 40, 153–62.

Cherry, N. (1978) Stress, anxiety and work: a longitudinal study. *Journal of Occupational Psychology*, 51, 259–67.

Chesborough, H. W. and Teese, D. J. (1996) When is virtuous virtuous? *Harvard Business Review*, January/February, 65–73.

Child, J. (1972) Organization structure, environment and performance: the role of strategic choice. *Sociology*, January, 1–22.

Child, J. (1988) *Organizations: a Guide to Problems and Practice*, 2nd edn. London: Paul Chapman.

Chmiel, N. (1998) *Jobs, Technology and People*. London: Routledge.

Chmiel, N., Totterdell, P. and Folkard, S. (1995) On adaptive control, sleep loss and fatigue. *Applied Cognitive Psychology*, 9, S39–S53.

Christal, R. E. and Weissmuller, J. J. (1988) Job-task inventory analysis. In S. Gael (ed.), *The Job Analysis Handbook for Business, Industry, and Government, volume 2*. New York: Wiley, pp. 1036–50.

Clark, T. S. and Corlett, E. N. (1984) *The Ergonomics of Workspaces and Machines: a Design Manual*. London: Taylor and Francis.

Clarke, L. (1994) *The Essence of Change*. Hemel Hempstead: Prentice Hall.

Clegg, C. W. (1993) Social systems that marginalise the psychological and organisational aspects of information technology. *Behaviour and Information Technology*, 12, 261–6.

Clegg, C. W. (1995) Sociotechnical theory. In N. Nicholson (ed.), *The Blackwell Encyclopedic Dictionary of Organizational Behavior*. Oxford: Blackwell.

Clegg, C. W., Axtell, C., Damodaran, L., Farbey, B., Hull, R., Lloyd-Jones, R., Nicholls, J., Sell, R. and Tomlinson, C. (1996a) Information technology: a study of performance and the role of human and organizational factors. *Ergonomics*, 40(9), 851–71.

Clegg, C. W., Coleman, P., Hornby, P., Maclaren, R., Robson, J., Carey, N. and Symon, G. (1996b) Tools to incorporate some psychological and organizational issues during the development of computer-based tasks. *Ergonomics*, 39(3), 482–511.

Clegg, C. W. and Walsh, S. (1998) Soft systems analysis. In G. Symon and C. Cassell (eds), *Qualitative Methods and Analysis in Organizational Research*. London: Sage Publications.

Clement, D. E. and Schiereck, J. J. (1973) Sex composition and group performance in a visual signal detection task. *Memory and Cognition*, 1(3), 251–5.

Cleveland, J. N. and Murphy, K. R. (1992) Analyzing performance appraisal as goal-directed behavior. *Research in Personnel and Human Resources Management*, 10, 121–85.

Clifford, L. and Bennett, H. (1997) Best practice in 360 degree feedback. *Selection and Development Review*, 13(2), 6–9.

Closs, S. J. (1993) *JIIG-CAL Reference Manual*. London: Hodder and Stoughton.

Coch, L. and French, J. R. (1948) Overcoming resistance to change. *Human Relations*, 1, 512–32.

Cockburn, C. (1990) Men's power in organizations: 'equal opportunities interviews'. In J. Hearn and D. Morgan (eds), *Men, Masculinities and Social Theory*. London: Unwin Hyman.

Cohen, S. and Edwards, J. R. (1989) Personality characteristics as moderators of the relationship between stress and disorder. In R. W. J. Neufeld (ed.), *Advances in the Investigation of Psychological Stress*. New York: Wiley.

Cohen, S. G., Ledford, G. E. and Spreitzer, G. M. (1994) *A Predictive Model of Self-managing Work Team Effectiveness* (CEO Publication No. T94-28(271)). Los Angeles: University of Southern California.

Cohen, S. and Wills, T. A. (1985) Stress, social support and the buffering hypothesis. *Psychological Bulletin*, 98(2), 310–57.

Collins, A. (1997) *Crash – Ten Easy Ways to Avoid a Computer Disaster*. London: Simon and Schuster.

Collinson, D. L., Knights, D. and Collinson, M. (1990) *Managing to Discriminate*. London: Routledge.

Comstock, J. R. and Arnegard, R. J. (1992) *The Multi-Attribute Task Battery for Human Operator Workload and Strategic Behavior Research*. Hampton, VA: NASA Langley Research Center.

Conger, J. A. (1991) Inspiring others: the language of leadership. *Academy of Management Executive*, 5, 31–45.

Conger, J. A. and Kanungo, R. (1987) Toward a behavioral theory of charismatic leadership in organizational settings. *Academy of Management Review*, 12, 637–47.

Conway, J. M., Jako, R. A. and Goodman, D. E. (1995) A meta-analysis of interrater and internal consistency reliability of employment interviews. *Journal of Applied Psychology*, 80, 565–79.

Cook, C. and Corbridge, C. (1997) Tasks of functions: what are we allocating? In E. F. Fallon, M. Hogan, L. Bannon and J. McCarthy (eds), *Proceedings of the First International Conference on Allocation of Functions*. Louisville, KY: IEA Press.

Cook, J. D., Hepworth, S. J., Wall, T. D. and Warr, P. (1981) *The Experience of Work*. London: Academic Press.

Cook, M. (1993) *Personnel Selection and Productivity*, 2nd edn. Chichester: Wiley.

Cooper, C. L. and Payne, R. (eds) (1988) *Causes, Coping and Consequences of Stress at Work*. Chichester: Wiley.

Cooper, C. L., Sloan, S. J. and Williams, S. (1988) *Occupational Stress Indicator Management Guide*. Windsor: NFER-Nelson.

Cooper, G. E. and Harper, R. P. (1969) The Use of Pilot Rating in the Evaluation of Aircraft Handling Qualities. Moffett Field, CA: NASA-Ames Research Center. Report No. NASA TN-D-5153.

Cooper, M. D., Phillips, R. A., Sutherland, V. J. and Makin, P. J. (1994) Reducing accidents using goal setting theory and feedback: a field study. *Journal of Occupational and Organizational Psychology*, 67, 219–40.

Copeland, L. (1988) Learning to manage a multicultural workforce. *Training*, May, 48–56.

Cordery, J. L. (1996) Autonomous work groups. In M. A. West (ed.), *The Handbook of Work Group Psychology*. Chichester: Wiley.

Cordery, J. L., Mueller, W. S. and Smith, L. M. (1991) Attitudinal and behavioural outcomes of autonomous group working: a longitudinal field study. *Academy of Management Journal*, 34, 464–76.

Cowan, D. A. (1986) Developing a process model of problem recognition. *Academy of Management Review*, 11, 763–76.

Cox, S. and Cox, T. (1991) The structure of employees attitudes to safety: a european example. *Work and Stress*, 5, 93–106.

Cox, T. H. (1991) The multicultural organization. *Academy of Management Executive*, 5(2), 34–47.

Cox, T. H. (1993) *Cultural Diversity in Organizations: Theory, Research and Practice*. San Francisco: Berrett-Koehler.

Cox, T. H. and Blake, S. (1991) Managing cultural diversity: implications for organizational competitiveness. *The Executive*, 5, 45–56.

Cox, T. H. and Nkomo, S. (1986) Differential appraisal criteria based on race of the ratee. *Group and Organizational Studies*, 11, 109–19.

Craig, A. and Cooper, K. (1992) Symptoms of acute and chronic fatigue. In A. P. Smith and D. Jones (eds), *Handbook of Human Performances, volume 3*. New York: Academic Press.

Craik, F. I. M. and Jacoby, L. L. (1996) Aging and memory: Implications for skilled performance. In W. A. Rogers, A. D. Fisk and N. Walker (eds), *Aging and Skilled Performance*. Mahwah, NJ: Erlbaum.

Craik, F. I. M. and Jennings, J. M. (1992) Human memory. In F. I. M. Craik and T. A. Salthouse (eds), *The Handbook of Aging and Cognition*. Hillsdale, NJ: Erlbaum.

Cronbach, L. J. (1970) *Essentials of Psychological Testing*. New York: Harper and Row.

Cronbach, L. J. and Gleser, G. C. (1965) *Psychological Tests and Personnel Decisions*, 2nd edn. Urbana: University of Illinois Press.

Cronbach, L. J. and Snow, R. E. (1977) Individual differences in learning ability as a function of instructional variables. Unpublished report, School of Education, Stanford University.

Crowston, K. and Malone, T. W. (1988) Information technology and work organisation. In M. Helander (ed.), *Handbook of Human–Computer Interaction*. Amsterdam: Elsevier Science Publishers.

Cummings, T. G. and Worley, C. G. (1993) *Organization Development and Change*, 5th edn. St Paul, MN: West.

Cunningham-Snell, N., Fletcher, C., Anderson, N. and Gibb, A. (1997) Candidates' perceptions of procedural fairness: a longitudinal study on the impact of unmet expectation. Paper presented at the British Psychological Society London Conference, London.

Czaja, S. J. (1996) Aging and the acquisition of computer skills. In W. A. Rogers, A. D. Fisk and N. Walker (eds), *Aging and Skilled Performance*. Mahwah, NJ: Erlbaum.

Czaja, S. J. and Sharit, J. (1993) Age differences in the performance of computer-based work. *Psychology and Aging*, 8, 59–67.

Dachler, M. P. (1994) A social-relational perspective of selection. Paper presented at the 23rd International Congress of Applied Psychology, Madrid, July.

Damos, D. L. (ed.) (1991) *Multiple-Task Performance*. London: Taylor and Francis.

Danaher, J. W. (1980) Human error in ATC system operations. *Human Factors*, 22, 535–45.

Daniels, K., de Chernatony, L. and Johnson, G. (1995) Validating a method for mapping managers mental models of competitive industry structures. *Human Relations*, 47, 975–91.

Dass, P. and Parker, B. (1996) Diversity: a strategic issue. In E. E. Kossek and S. A. Lobel (eds), *Managing Diversity: Human Resource Strategies for Tramforming the Workplace*. Cambridge, MA: Blackwell.

Davidow, W. H. and Malone, M. S. (1992) *The Virtual Corporation*. New York: Harper Business.

Davis, L. E. and Wacker, G. J. (1987) Job design. In G. Salvendy (ed.), *Handbook of Human Factors*. New York: John Wiley.

Deal, T. E. and Kennedy, A. A. (1982) *Corporate Cultures: the Rites and Rituals of Corporate Life*. Reading, MA: Addison-Wesley.

Dean, R. A. and Wanous, J. P. (1984) Effects of realistic job previews on hiring bank tellers. *Journal of Applied Psychology*, 69, 61–8.

Deaux, K. and Emswiller, T. (1974) Explanations of successful performance on sex linked tasks: what is skill for the male is luck for the female. *Journal of Personality and Social Psychology*, 29, 80–5.

Dedobbeleer, N. and Beland, F. (1991) A safety climate measure for construction sites. *Journal of Safety Research*, 22, 97–103.

de Gier, E. (1995) Occupational welfare in the European Community: past, present, and future. In L. R. Murphy, J. J. Hurrell, S. L. Sauter and G. P. Keita (eds), *Job Stress Interventions*. Washington, DC: American Psychological Association.

de Jonge, J. and Kompier, M. A. J. (1997) A critical examination of the Demand-Control-Support Model from a work psychological perspective. *International Journal of Stress Management*, 4(4), 235–58.

de Jonge, J. and Schaufeli, W. B. (1998) Job characteristics and employee well-being: a test of Warr's Vitamin Model in health care workers using structural equation modelling. *Journal of Organizational Behavior*, 19(4), 387–407.

de Jonge, J., Schaufeli, W. B. and Furda, J. (1995) Job characteristics: psychological work vitamins? Paper presented at the IV ENOP Conference, Munich.

Dejoy, D. (1986) A behavioural-diagnostic model for self-protective behaviour in the workplace. *Professional Safety*, 31, 26–30.

DeLuca, J. M. and McDowell, R. N. (1992) Managing diversity: a strategic 'grass roots' approach. In S. F. Jackson and Associates (eds), *Diversity in the Workplace – Human Resource Initiatives*. New York: Guildford Press.

Dempster, F. N. (1996) Distributing and managing the condition of encoding and practice. In E. L. Bjork and R. A. Bjork (eds), *Memory. Handbook of Perception and Cognition*, 2nd edn. San Diego, CA: Academic Press.

DeNisi, A. S. (1996) *Cognitive Approach to Performance Appraisal: a Programme of Research*. London: Routledge.

Denney, N. W. (1989) Everyday problem solving: methodological issues, research findings, and a model. In L. W. Poon, D. C. Rubin and B. A. Wilson (eds), *Everyday Cognition in Adulthood and Late Life*. Cambridge: Cambridge University Press.

Department of Employment (1971) *Glossary of Training Terms*, 2nd edn. London: HMSO.

Department of Employment (1994) *Training Statistics*. London: HMSO.

de Rijk, A. E., Le Blanc, P. M., Schaufeli, W. B. and de Jonge, J. (1998) Active coping and need for control as moderators of the Job Demand-Control Model: effects on burnout. *Journal of Occupational and Organizational Psychology*, 71, 1–18.

De Vries, R. E. (1997) Need for leadership. Doctoral dissertation, Tilburg.

Diehl, M. and Stroebe, W. (1987) Productivity loss in brainstorming groups: towards the solution of a riddle. *Journal of Personality and Social Psychology*, 53, 447–509.

Dillingham, A. E. (1981) Age and workplace injuries. *Aging and Work*, 4, 1–10.

Dipboye, R. L. (1987) Problems and progress of women in management. In K. S. Koziara, M. Moscow and L. Tanner (eds), *Working Women: Past, Present and Future*. Washington, DC: Bureau of National Affairs.

Dipboye, R. L. (1997a) Organizational bafflers to implementing a rational model of training. In M. A. Quiñones and A. Ehrenstein (eds), *Training for a Rapidly Changing Workplace: Applications of Psychological Research*. Washington, DC: American Psychological Association.

Dipboye, R. L. (1997b) Structured selection interviews: why do they work? Why are they underutilized? In N. Anderson and P. Herriot (eds), *International Handbook of Selection and Assessment*. Chichester: Wiley.

Dobbins, G. H. and Russell, J. M. (1986a) The biasing effects of subordinate likeableness on leaders' responses to poor performers: a laboratory and field study. *Personnel Psychology*, 39(4), 759–77.

Dobbins, G. H. and Russell, J. M. (1986b) Self-serving biases in leadership: a laboratory experiment. *Journal of Management*, 12(4), 475–83.

Dobson, P. (1988) Changing culture. *Employment Gazette*, December, 647–50.

Doering, M., Rhodes, S. K. and Schuster, M. (1983) *The Aging Worker: Research and Recommendations*. Beverly Hills, CA: Sage.

Doherty, N. F. and King, M. (1998) The consideration of organisational issues during the systems development process: an empirical analysis. *Behaviour and Information Technology*, 17, 41–51.

Donald, D. G. and Hodgdon, J. A. (1991) *Psychological Effect of Aerobic Fitness Training: Research and Theory*. New York: Springer.

Drucker, P. (1992) The new society of organizations. *Harvard Business Review*, September/October, 95–104.

Dulewicz, S. V. and Fletcher, C. (1989) The context and dynamics of performance appraisal. In P. Herriot (ed.), *Assessment and Selection in Organizations*. London: Wiley.

Dunphy, D. and Stace, D. (1993) The strategic management of corporate change. *Human Relations*, 46(8), 905–20.

Dye, D. A., Reck, M. and McDaniel, M. A. (1993) The validity of job knowledge measures. *International Review of Selection and Development*, 1, 153–7.

Earley, P. C. (1987) Intercultural training for managers: a comparison of documentary and interpersonal methods. *Academy of Management Journal*, 30, 685–98.

Earley, P. C. (1993) East meets West meets Mid-East: further explorations of collectivistic and individualistic work groups. *Academy of Management Journal*, 36, 319–48.

Eason, K. D. (1988) *Information Technology and Organisational Change*. London: Taylor and Francis.

Eden, D. (1990) Pygmalion without interpersonal contrast effects: whole groups gain from raising manager expectations. *Journal of Applied Psychology*, 75, 394–8.

Edholm, O. G. and Murrell, K. F. H. (1973) *The Ergonomics Research Society: a History 1949–1970*. London: Taylor and Francis.

Edwards, J. R. and Harrison, J. V. (1993) Job demands and worker health: three-dimensional reexamination of the relationship between person–environment fit and strain. *Journal of Applied Psychology*, 78, 628–48.

Egan, D. E., Remde, J. R., Gomez, L. M., Landauer, T. K., Eberhardt, J. and Lochbaum, C. C. (1989) Formative design-evaluation of SuperBook. *ACM Transactions on Information Systems*, 7(1), 30–57.

Eggemeier, F. T. (1988) Properties of workload assessment techniques. In P. A. Hancock and N. Meshkati (eds), *Human Mental Workload*. Amsterdam: North-Holland.

Eggemeier, F. T. and Wilson, C. F. (1991) Performance-based and subjective assessment of workload in multi-task environments. In D. L. Damos (ed.), *Multiple-Task Performance*. London: Taylor and Francis.

Egido, C. (1990) Teleconferencing as a technology to support cooperative work: its possibilities and limitations. In J. Galegher, R. E. Kraut and C. Egido (eds), *Intellectual Teamwork: Social and Technological Foundations of Cooperative Work*. Hillsdale, NJ: Lawrence Erlbaum Associates.

Ellis, C. and Sonnenfeld, J. A. (1994) Diverse approaches to managing diversity. *Human Resource Management*, 35(1), 79–109.

Ellison, K., Tinsley, K. and Houston, N. (1997) British labour force projections: 1997–2006. *Labour Market Trends*, 105(2), 51–67.

Ellison, R. (1994) British labour force projections: 1994 to 2006. *Employment Gazette*, April, 111–22.

Emery, F. E. (1959) *Characteristics of Socio-technical Systems* (Document No. 527). London: Tavistock Institute of Human Relations.

Emery, F. E. and Trist, E. L. (1969) Socio-technical systems. In F. E. Emery (ed.), *Systems Thinking*. London: Penguin.

Endsley, M. R. (1995a) Toward a theory of situation awareness in dynamic systems. *Human Factors*, 37, 32–64.

Endsley, M. R. (1995b) Measurement of situation awareness in dynamic systems. *Human Factors*, 37, 65–84.

Erez, M. and Somech, A. (1996) Is group productivity loss the rule or the exception? Effects of culture and group-based motivation. *Academy of Management Journal*, 39(6), 1513–37.

European Commission (1997) *Employment in Europe 1997.* Luxembourg: Office for Official Publications of the European Commission.

Falkenberg, L. (1990) Improving the accuracy of stereotypes within the workplace. *Journal of Management,* 16, 107–18.

Farmer, B. and Chambers, E. G. (1926) *A Psychological Study of Individual Differences in Accident Rate.* London: Industrial Health Research Board.

Farmer, E. W., Belyavin, A. J., Tattersall, A. J., Berry A. and Hockey, G. R. J. (1991) *Stress in Air Traffic Control II: Effects of Increased Workload.* RAF Institute of Aviation Medicine Report No. 701.

Farquar, A., Evans, P. and Tawadey, K. (1989) Lessons from practice in managing organizational change. In P. Evans, E. Doz and A. Laurent (eds), *Human Resource Management in International Firms: Change, Globalization, Innovation.* London: Macmillan.

Farrell, D. and Stamm, C. L. (1988) Meta-analysis of the correlates of employee absence. *Human Relations,* 41, 211–27.

Feather, N. T. (1992) Expectancy-value theory and unemployment effects. *Journal of Occupational and Organizational Psychology,* 65, 315–30.

Feigenbaum, E. A. and McCorduck, P. (1984) *The Fifth Generation.* New York: Signet.

Feltham, R. T. (1991) Assessment centres. In P. Herriot (ed.), *Assessment and Selection in Organizations.* Chechester: John Wiley and Sons.

Ferguson E. and Cox, T. (1997) The functional dimensions of coping scale: theory, reliability and validity. *British Journal of Health Psychology,* 2, 109–29.

Ferlie, E. and Bennett, C. (1993) Patterns of strategic change in health care: district health authorities respond to AIDS. In J. Hendry, G. Johnson and J. Newton (eds), *Strategic Thinking, Leadership and the Management of Change.* Chichester: Wiley.

Ferris, G. K., Yates, V. L., Gilmore, D. C. and Rowland, K. M. (1985) The influence of subordinate age on performance ratings and causal attributions. *Personnel Psychology,* 38, 545–57.

Fiedler, F. E. (1967) *A Theory of Leadership.* New York: McGraw-Hill.

Field, R. H. G. (1982) A test of the Vroom–Yetton normative model of leadership. *Journal of Applied Psychology,* 67, 532–7.

Fills, P. M. (1962) Factors in complex skill training. In R. Glaser (ed.), *Training, Research and Education.* New York: Wiley.

Fine, M. G., Johnson, F. L. and Ryan, M. S. (1990) Cultural diversity in the workplace. *Public Personnel Management,* 19(3), 305–19.

Fine, S. A. (1988) Functional job analysis. In S. Gael (ed.), *The Job Analysis Handbook for Business, Industry, and Government, volume 2.* New York: Wiley, pp. 1019–35.

Fine, S. A. and Getkate, M. (1995) *Benchmark Tasks for Job Analysis: a Guide for Functional Job Analysis (FJA) Scales.* Mahwah, NJ: Lawrence Erlbaum Associates.

Fitts, P. M. (1951) *Human Engineering for an Effective Air Navigation and Traffic Control System.* Washington, DC: National Research Council.

Flanagan, J. C. (1954) The critical incident technique. *Psychological Bulletin,* 51, 327–58.

Fleishman, E. A. and Quaintance, M. F. (1984) *Taxonomies of Human Performance.* Orlando, FL: Academic Press.

Fletcher, C. (1986) The effects of performance review in appraisal: evidence and implications. *Journal of Management Development*, 5, 3–12.

Fletcher, C. (1991) Candidates' reactions to assessment centres and their outcomes: a longitudinal study. *Journal of Occupational Psychology*, 64, 117–27.

Fletcher, C. (1995) New directions for performance appraisal; some findings and observations. *International Journal of Selection and Assessment*, 3, 191–6.

Fletcher, C. (1997a) *Appraisal: Routes to Improved Performance*, 2nd edn. London: Institute of Personnel and Development.

Fletcher, C. (1997b) Performance appraisal in context: organizational changes and their impact on practice. In N. Anderson and P. Herriot (eds), *International Handbook of Selection and Assessment*. Chichester: Wiley.

Fletcher, C. (1997c) Self-awareness – a neglected attribute in selection and assessment. *International Journal of Selection and Assessment*, 5(3), 183–7.

Fletcher, C. and Baldry, C. (1999) Multi-source feedback systems: a research perspective. In C. L. Cooper and I. T. Robertson (eds), *International Review of Industrial and Organizational Psychology, volume 14*. New York/London: Wiley.

Fletcher, C., Baldry, C. and Cunningham-Snell, N. (1997) The psychometric properties of 360 degree feedback: an empirical study and a cautionary tale. *International Journal of Selection and Assessment*, 6, 19–34.

Fletcher, C. and Kerslake, C. (1992) The impact of assessment centres and their outcomes on participants' self-assessments. *Human Relations*, 45, 73–81.

Fletcher, C., Lovatt, K. and Baldry, C. (1997) A study of state, trait and test anxiety, and their relationship to assessment centre performance. *Journal of Social Behavior and Personality*, 12, 205–14.

Fletcher, C. and Williams, R. (1996) Performance management, job satisfaction and organisational commitment. *British Journal of Management*, 7, 169–79.

Flood, R. L. and Jackson, M. C. (1991) *Creative Problem Solving: Total Systems Intervention*. Chichester: Wiley.

Folkard, S. (1996) Body rhythms and shiftwork. In P. Warr (ed.), *Psychology at Work*. London: Penguin.

Folkard, S. (1997) Black times: temporal determinants of transport safety. *Accident Analysis and Prevention*, 29, 417–30.

Fontana, D. (1989) *Managing Stress*. London: Routledge.

Ford, H. (1922) *My Life and Work*. Garden City, NY: Doubleday, Page and Co.

Ford, J. K., Quiñones, M. A., Sego, D. J. and Sorra, J. S. (1992) Factors affecting the opportunity to perform trained tasks on the job. *Personnel Psychology*, 45, 511–27.

Forty, A. (1986) *Objects of Desire: Design and Society since 1750*. London: Thames and Hudson.

Frankenhaeuser, M. (1978) Psychoneuroendocrine approaches to the study of emotion as related to stress and coping. In H. E. Howe and R. A. Dienstbier (eds), *Nebraska Symposium on Motivation 1978*. Lincoln: University of Nebraska Press.

Frankenhaeuser, M. (1986) A psychobiological framework for research on human stress and coping. In M. H. Appley and R. Trumbell (eds), *Dynamics of Stress. Physiological, Psychological and Social Perspectives*. New York: Plenum.

Frankenhaeuser, M. and Gardell, B. (1976) Underload and overload in working life: outline of a multidisciplinary approach. *Journal of Human Stress*, 2, 35–46.

Fredericksen, T. R. and White, B. Y. (1989) An approach to training based upon principled task decomposition. *Acta Psychologica*, 71, 89–146.

French, J. R. P. Jr, Caplan, R. D. and Harrison, R. V. (1982) *The Mechanisms of Job Stress and Strain*. Chichester: Wiley.

French, W. L. and Bell, C. H. Jr (1990) *Organization Development – Behavioral Science Interventions for Organization Improvement*. Englewood Cliffs, NJ: Prentice Hall International.

Frese, M. (1987) Human–computer interaction in the office. In C. Cooper and I Robertson (eds), *International Review of Industrial and Organizational Psychology*. London: Wiley.

Frese, M. (1995a) Error management in training: conceptual and empirical results. In C. Zucchermaglio, S. Bagnara and S. U. Stucky (eds), *Organizational Learning and Technological Change*. Berlin: Springer.

Frese, M. (1995b) Entrepreneurship in East Europe: a general model and empirical findings. In C. L. Cooper and D. M. Rousseau (eds), *Trends in Organizational Behavior*. Chichester: Wiley.

Frese, M. (1997) Dynamic self-reliance: an important concept for work. In C. L. Cooper and S. E. Jackson (eds), *Creating Tomorrow's Organizations*. Chichester: Wiley.

Frese, M. (ed.) (1998) *Erfolgreiche Unternehmensgründer* (*Successful Business Founders*). Göttingen: Verlag für Angewandte Psychologie.

Frese, M. and Hesse, W. (1993) The work situation in software-development – results of an empirical study. *Software Engineering Notes*, 18(3), A65–A72.

Frese, M. and Zapf, D. (1987) Die Einführung von neuen Techniken am Arbeitsplatz verändert Qualifikationsanforderungen, Handlungsspielraum und Stressoren kaum: Ergebnisse einer Längsschnittuntersuchung. *Zeitschrift für Arbeitswissenschaft*, 41, 7–14.

Frese, M. and Zapf, D. (1994) Action as the core of work psychology; a German approach. In H. C. Triandis, M. D. Dunnette and L. Hough (eds), *Handbook of Industrial and Organizational Psychology*. Palo Alto, CA: Consulting Psychologists Press.

Frijda, N. (1986) *The Emotions*. Cambridge: Cambridge University Press.

Fryer, D. (1992) Editorial: introduction to Marienthal and beyond. *Journal of Occupational and Organizational Psychology*, 65, 257–68.

Fuld, R. B. (1997) The fiction of function allocation revisited. In E. F. Fallon, M. Hogan, L. Bannon and J. McCarthy (eds), *Proceedings of the First International Conference on Allocation of Functions*. Louisville, KY: IEA Press.

Furnas, G. W. (1986) Generalized fisheye views. In *Proceedings of CHI '86*. New York: Association of Computing Machinery.

Furnas, G. W., Landauer, T. K., Gomez, L. M. and Dumais, S. T. (1987) The vocabulary problem in human–system communication. *Communications of the ACM*, 30, 9964–71.

Furnham, A. (1992) *Personality at Work: the Role of Individual Differences in the Workplace*. London: Routledge.

Furnham, A. (1997) *The Psychology of Behaviour at Work*. Hove: Psychology Press.

Furnham, A. (1998) *The Psychology of Behaviour at Work. The Individual in the Organization*. Hove: Psychology Press.

Furnham, A. and Gunter, B. (1993) Corporate culture: diagnosis and change. In C. L. Cooper (ed.), *International Review of Industrial and Organizational Psychology*. Chichester: Wiley.

Gael, S. (ed.) (1988) *The Job Analysis Handbook for Business. Industry, and Goverment, volumes 1 and 2*. New York: Wiley.

Gagné, R. M. (1985) *The Conditions of Learning and Theory of Instruction*. New York: CBS College Publishing.

Gagné, R. M., Briggs, L. J. and Wager, W. W. (1992) *Principles of Instruction Design*, 4th edn. New York: Harcourt Brace Jovanich.

Gallois, C. and Callan, V. J. (1981) Personality impressions elicited by accented English speech. *Journal of Cross-Cultural Psychology*, 12(3), 347–59.

Gardner, G. T. and Gould, L. C. (1989) Public perceptions of the risks and benefits of technology. *Risk Analysis*, 9, 225–42.

Garland, H. and Price, K. H. (1977) Attitudes towards women in management, and attributions of their success and failure in managerial positions. *Journal of Applied Psychology*, 62, 29–33.

Gatewood, R. D. and Feild, H. S. (1994) *Human Resource Selection*, 3rd edn. Orlando, FL: The Dryden Press.

Gaugler, B. B., Rosenthal, D. B., Thornton, G. C. and Bentson, C. (1987) Meta-analysis of assessment centre validity. *Journal of Applied Psychology*, 72, 493–511.

George, J. M. and Bettenhausen, K. (1990) Understanding prosocial behaviour, sales performance and turnover: a group-level analysis in a service context. *Journal of Applied Psychology*, 75, 698–709.

Gick, M. L. and Hollyoak, K. J. (1987) The cognitive basis of knowledge transfer. In S. M. Cormier and H. D. Hagman (eds), *Transfer of Learning: Contemporary Research and Applications*. New York: Academic Press.

Giles, H. and Street, R. L. Jr (1985) Communicator characteristics and behaviour. In M. L. Knapp and G. R. Miller (eds), *Handbook of Interpersonal Communication*. Newbury Park, CA: Sage Publications.

Gilliland, S. W. (1993) The perceived fairness of selection systems: an organizational justice perspective. *Academy of Management Review*, 18, 696–734.

Gilliland, S. W. (1994) Effects of procedural and distributive justice on reactions to a selection system. *Journal of Applied Psychology*, 79, 691–701.

Gilliland, S. W. and Honig, H. (1994) The perceived fairness of employee selection systems as a predictor of attitudes and self-concept. In S. W. Gilliland (Chair), *Selection from the Applicant's Perspective: Justice and Employee Selection Procedures*. Symposium presented at the ninth annual conference of the Society for Industrial and Organizational Psychology, Nashville, TN, April.

Giniger, S., Dispenzieri, A. and Eisenberg, J. (1983) Age, experience, and performance on speed and skill jobs in an applied setting. *Journal of Applied Psychology*, 68, 469–75.

Girndt, T. (1997) An intervention strategy to managing diversity: discerning conventions. *European Journal of Work and Organizational Psychology*, 6(2), 227–40.

Glaser, R. (ed.) (1962) Psychology and instructional technology. In R. Glaser (ed.), *Training, Research and Education*. New York: Wiley.

Goettl, B. P. and Shute, V. J. (1996) Analysis of part-task training using the backward transfer technique. *Journal of Experimental Psychology: Applied*, 2(3), 227–49.

Goettl, B. P., Yadrick, R. M., Connolly-Gomez, C., Regian, W. and Shebilske, W. L. (1996) Alternating task modules in isochronal distributed training of complex tasks. *Human Factors*, 38, 330–46.

Goffin, R. D., Rothstem, M. G. and Johnston, N. G. (1996) Personality testing and the assessment center: incremental validity for managerial selection. *Journal of Applied Psychology*, 81, 746–56.

Goldberg, A., Dar-El, R. and Rubin, A. (1991) Threat perception and the readiness to participate in safety programs. *Journal of Organizational Behaviour*, 12, 109–22.

Goldberg, L. R. (1990) An alternative 'description of personality': the big five factor structure. *Journal of Personality and Social Psychology*, 59, 1216–29.

Goldberg, L. R. (1993) The structure of phenotypic personality traits. *American Psychologist*, 48, 26–34.

Goldstein, I. L. (1993) *Training in Organizations: Needs Assessment, Development and Evaluation*, 3rd edn. Monterey, CA: Brooks Cole.

Goleman, D. (1995) *Emotional Intelligence*. New York: Bantam.

Gopher, D. and Donchin, E. (1986) Workload – an examination of the concept. In K. R. Boff, L. Kaufman and J. P. Thomas (eds), *Handbook of Perception and Human Performance. Volume II: Cognitive Processes and Performance*. New York: Wiley.

Gordon, G. G., DiTomaso, N., Fams, G. F. (1991) Managing diversity on research and development groups. *Research Technology Management*, 34, 18–23.

Gordon, J. (1992) Work teams: how far have they come? *Training*, October, 59–65.

Gould, J. D. (1981) Composing letters with computer-based text editors. *Human Factors*, 23, 593–606.

Gould, J. D. (1988) How to design usable systems. In M. Helander (ed.), *Handbook of Human–Computer Interaction*. Amsterdam: North-Holland.

Goves, M. (1995) Welcome to the 'virtual' office. *Jerusalem Post Money Magazine*, 5 April, 10.

Gray, W. D., John, B. E. and Atwood, M. E. (1993) Project Ernestine: validating a GOMS analysis for predicting and explaining real-world task performance. *Human–Computer Interaction*, 8, 237–309.

Green, F. (1993) The determinants of training of male and female employees in Britain. *Oxford Bulletin of Economics and Statistics*, 55, 103–22.

Green, S. and Mitchell, T. R. (1979) Attributional processes of leaders in leader–member interactions. *Organizational Behaviour and Human Performance*, 23, 429–58.

Green, T. R. G. and Hoc, J.-M. (1991) What is cognitive ergonomics? *Le Travail Human*, 54(4), 291–304.

Greenberg, J. (1986) Determinants of perceived fairness of performance evaluation. *Journal of Applied Psychology*, 71, 340–2.

Greenberg, J. and Folger, R. G. (1983) Procedural justice, participation, and fair process effect in groups and organizations. In P. B. Paulus (ed.), *Basic Group Processes*. New York: Springer-Verlag.

Greene, C. N. (1975) The reciprocal nature of influence between leader and subordinate. *Academy of Management Journal*, 20, 32–46.

Greenhaus, J. H. and Parasuraman, S. (1993) Job performance and career advancement prospects: an examination of gender and race effects. *Organizational Behavior and Human Decision Processes*, 55, 273–97.

Greenstein, J. S., Arnaut, L. Y. and Revesman, M. E. (1986) An empirical comparison of model-based and explicit communication for dynamic human–computer task allocation. *International Journal of Man–Machine Studies*, 24, 355–63.

Greenstein, J. S. and Revesman, M. E. (1986) Two simulation studies investigating means of human–computer communication for dynamic task allocation. *IEEE Transactions on Systems, Man and Cybernetics*, SMC-16, 726–30.

Grint, K. (1997) *Fuzzy Management: Contemporary Ideas and Practices at Work*. New York: Oxford University Press.

Guest, D. (1987) Human resource management and industrial relations. *Journal of Management Studies*, 24(5), 503–22.

Guion, R. M. (1997) *Assessment, Measurement, and Prediction for Personnel Decisions*. London: Lawrence Erlbaum Associates.

Guzzo, R. A. (1996) Fundamental considerations about work groups. In M. A. West (ed.), *Handbook of Work Group Psychology*. Chichester: Wiley.

Guzzo, R. A. and Dickson, M. W. (1996) Teams in organizations: recent research on performance and effectiveness. *Annual Review of Psychology*, 42, 307–38.

Gwynne, S. C. (1992) The long haul. *Time*, 28 September, 34–8.

Hackett, K. D. (1990) Age, tenure, and employee absenteeism. *Human Relations*, 43, 601–19.

Hackman, J. R. (ed.) (1990) *Groups that Work (and Those that Don't): Creating Conditions for Effective Teamwork*. San Francisco: Jossey-Bass.

Hackman, J. R. and Lawler, E. E. (1971) Employee reactions to job characteristics. *Journal of Applied Psychology*, 55(3), 259–86.

Hackman, J. R. and Oldham, G. R. (1975) Development of the job diagnostic survey. *Journal of Applied Psychology*, 60, 159–70.

Hackman, J. R. and Oldham, G. R. (1976) Motivation through the design of work: test of a new theory. *Organizational Behavior and Human Performance*, 16, 250–79.

Halliday, F. E. (1995) *England: a Concise History*. London: Thames & Hudson.

Hamel, G. and Prahalad, C. K. (1994) Competing for the future. Boston: Harvard Business Review Press.

Hamilton, P., Hockey, G. R. J. and Reijman, M. (1977) The place of the concept of activation in human information processing theory: an integrative approach. In S. Dornic (ed.), *Attention and Performance VI*. New York: Academic Press.

Hammersley, M. and Atkinson, P. (1995) *Ethnography: Principles in Practice*, 2nd edn. London: Routledge.

Hancock, P. A. and Chignell, M. H. (1987) Adaptive control in human–machine systems. In P. A. Hancock (ed.), *Human Factors Psychology*. Amsterdam: North-Holland.

Hancock, P. A. and Meshkati, N. (eds) (1988) *Human Mental Workload*. Amsterdam: North-Holland.

Hancock, P. and Scallen, S. (1996) Allocating functions in human–machine systems. In R. Hoffman (ed.), *Psychology beyond the Threshold: a Festschrift for William N. Dember*. Hillsdale, NJ: Lawrence Erlbaum.

Handy, C. (1993) *Understanding Organizations*. London: Penguin.

Harpaz, I. (1989) Non-financial employment commitment: a cross-national comparison. *Journal of Occupational Psychology*, 62, 147–50.

Hart, S. G. and Staveland, L. E. (1988) Development of a NASA TLX (Task Load Index): results of empirical and theoretical research. In P. Hancock and N. Meshkati (eds), *Human Mental Workload*. Amsterdam: Elsevier.

Hartley, J. and Davies, I. K. (1976) Preinstructional strategies: the role of pretexts, behavioural objectives, overviews and advance organisers. *Review of Educational Research*, 46(2), 239–65.

Harvey, R. J. (1991) Job analysis. In M. D. Dunnette and L. M. Hough (eds), *Handbook of Industrial and Organizational Psychology, volume 2*, 2nd edn. Palo Alto, CA: Consulting Psychologists Press, pp. 71–163.

Haynes, C. (1995) *How to Succeed in Cyberspace*. London: ASLIB.

Haynes, K. S., Pine, R. C. and Fitch, H. G. (1982) Reducing accident rates with organizational behavior modification. *Academy of Management Journal*, 25, 407–16.

Hays, R. T. (1992) Systems concepts for training systems development. *IEEE Transactions on Systems, Man and Cybernetics*, 22(2), 258–66.

Heath, C. and Luff, P. (1992) Collaboration and control: crisis management and multimedia technology in London Underground line control rooms. *CSCW Journal*, 1, 69–94.

Heider, F. (1958) *The Psychology of Interpersonal Relations*. New York: John Wiley.

Heilman, M. E. (1994) Affirmative action: some unintended consequences for working women. *Research in Organizational Behaviour*, 16, 125–69.

Henderson, A. (1991) A developmental perspective on interface, design and theory. In J. M. Carroll (ed.), *Designing Interaction: Psychology at the Human–Computer Interface*. Cambridge: Cambridge University Press.

Hendricks, H. W. (1991) Human factors in organisational design and management. *Ergonomics*, 34, 743–56.

Hendricks, H. W. (1997) Organizational design and macroergonomics. In G. Salvendy (ed.), *Handbook of Human Factors and Ergonomics*. London: Wiley.

Heracleous, L. (1995) Spinning a brand new cultural web. *People Management*, 2 November.

Heron, J. (1989) *The Facilitator's Handbook*. London: Kogan Page.

Heron, J. (1990) *Helping the Client*. London: Sage.

Herriot, P. (1989) Selection as a social process. In M. Smith and I. T. Robertson (eds), *Advances in Staff Selection*. Chichester: Wiley.

Herriot, P. and Anderson, N. (1997) Selecting for change: how will personnel and selection psychology survive? In N. Anderson and P. Herriot (eds), *International Handbook of Selection and Assessment*. Chichester: Wiley.

Herriot, P. and Ecob, R. (1979) Occupational choice and expectancy-value theory: testing some modifications. *Journal of Occupational Psychology*, 52, 311–24.

Herriot, P. and Pemberton, C. (1995) *Competitive Advantage through Diversity*. London: Sage.

Hersey, P. and Blanchard, K. H. (1988) *Management of Organizational Behavior*, 5th edn. Englewood Cliffs, NJ: Prentice Hall.

Herzberg, F., Mausner, B. and Snyderman, B. (1959) *The Motivation to Work*. London: Granada.

Hesketh, B. (1997) Dilemmas in training for transfer and retention. *Applied Psychology: an International Review*, 46(4), 317–86.

Hess, T. M. (1994) Social cognition in adulthood: aging-related changes in knowledge and processing mechanisms. *Developmental Review*, 14, 373–412.

Hewstone, M. and Brown, R. (eds) (1986) *Contact and Conflict in Intergroup Encounters*. Oxford: Blackwell.

Higgins, N. C. (1986) Occupational stress and working women: the effectiveness of two stress reduction programs. *Journal of Vocational Behavior*, 29(1), 66–78.

Hill, S. G., Iavecchia, H. P., Byers, J. C., Bittner, A. C., Zaclad, A. L. and Christ, R. E. (1992) Comparison of four subjective workload rating scales. *Human Factors*, 4, 429–39.

Hingley, P. and Cooper, C. L. (1986) *Stress and the Nurse Manager*. London: Wiley.

Hockey, G. R. J. (1970) The effect of loud noise on attentional selectivity. *Quarterly Journal of Experimental Psychology*, 22, 28–36.

Hockey, G. R. J. (1979) Stress and the cognitive components of skilled performance. In V. Hamilton and D. M. Warburton (eds), *Human Stress and Cognition*. Chichester: Wiley.

Hockey, G. R. J. (ed.) (1983) *Stress and Fatigue in Human Performance*. Chichester: Wiley.

Hockey, G. R. J. (1986) Changes in operator efficiency as a function of environmental stress, fatigue and circadian rhythms. In K. R. Boff, L. Kauffman, and J. Thomas (eds), *Handbook of Perception and Human Performance, volume 2*. Chichester: Wiley.

Hockey, G. R. J. (1993) Cognitive-energetical control mechanisms in the management of work demands and psychological health. In A. D. Baddeley and L. Weiskrantz (eds), *Attention, Selection, Awareness and Control. A Tribute to Donald Broadbent*. Oxford: Oxford University Press.

Hockey, G. R. J. (1996) Skill and workload. In P. B. Warr (ed.), *Psychology at Work*, 4th edn. Harmondsworth: Penguin.

Hockey, G. R. J. (1997) Compensatory control in the regulation of human performance under stress and high workload: a cognitive-energetical framework. *Biological Psychology*, 45, 73–93.

Hockey, G. R. J., Briner, R. B., Tattersall, A. J. and Wiethoff, M. (1989) Assessing the impact of computer workload on operator stress: the role of system controllability. *Ergonomics*, 32, 1401–18.

Hockey, G. R. J. and Hamilton, P. (1983) The cognitive patterning of stress states. In G. R. J. Hockey (ed.), *Stress and Fatigue in Human Performance*. Chichester: Wiley.

Hockey, G. R. J. and Maule, A. J. (1995) Unscheduled manual interventions in automated process control. *Ergonomics*, 38, 2504–24.

Hockey, G. R. J. and Meijman, T. F. (1998) The construct of psychological fatigue: a theoretical and methodological analysis. In Proceedings of the Third International Conference on Fatigue and Transportation, Coping with the 24-hour Society, Fremantle, Australia.

Hockey, G. R. J., Payne, R. L., and Rick, J. T. (1995) Intra-individual patterns of hormonal and affective adaptation to work demands: an n = 2 study of junior doctors. *Biological Psychology*, 42, 393–411.

Hockey, G. R. J., Wastell, D. G. and Sauer, J. (1998) Effects of sleep deprivation and user-interface on complex performance: a multilevel analysis of compensatory control. *Human Factors*, 40, 233–53.

Hockey, G. R. J. and Wiethoff, M. (1990) Assessing patterns of adjustment to the demands of work. In S. Puglisi-Allegra and A. Oliviero (eds), *Psychobiology of Stress.* Dordrecht: Kluwer.

Hoffman, L. R. (1959) Homogeneity of member personality and its effect on group problem-solving. *Journal of Abnormal and Social Psychology*, 58, 27–32.

Hoffman, L. R. and Maier, N. R. F. (1961) Sex differences, sex composition, and group problem-solving. *Journal of Abnormal and Social Psychology*, 63, 453–6.

Hofstede, G. (1980) *Culture's Consequences: International Differences in Work-related Values.* Beverly Hills, CA: Sage.

Hofstede, G. (1981) Culture and organisations. *International Studies of Management and Organizations*, 10(4), 15–41.

Hofstede, G. (1991) *Cultures and Organizations.* London: McGraw-Hill.

Hogan, E. A. and Overmyer-Day, L. (1994) The psychology of mergers and acquisitions. In C. L. Cooper and I. T. Robertson (eds), *International Review of Industrial and Organizational Psychology 1994.* Chichester: Wiley.

Hogan, J. and Brinkmeyer, K. (1997) Bridging the gap between overt and personality-based integrity tests. *Personnel Psychology*, 50, 587–600.

Hogg, M. and Abrams, D. (1988) *Social Identifications: a Social Psychology of Intergroup Relations and Group Processes.* London: Routledge.

Holding, D. H. (1983) Fatigue. In G. R. J. Hockey (ed.), *Stress and Fatigue in Human Performance.* Chichester: Wiley.

Holdsworth, R. (1991) Appraisal. In F. Neale (ed.), *The Handbook of Performance Management.* London: Institute of Personnel Management.

Holland, J. L. (1973) *Making Vocational Choices: a Theory of Careers.* Englewood Cliffs, NJ: Prentice Hall.

Hollnagel, E. and Woods, D. D. (1983) Cognitive systems engineering: new wine in new bottles. *International Journal of Man–Machine Studies*, 18, 583–600.

Hollway, W. (1991) *Work Psychology and Organisational Behaviour.* London: Sage.

Honey, S., Meager, N. and Williams, M. (1993) *Employers' Attitudes towards People with Disabilities.* Dorset: BEPC.

Hooghiemstra, T. (1992) Integrated management of human resources. In A. Mitrani, M. Dalziel and D. Fitt (eds), *Competency Based Human Resource Management: Value-driven Strategies for Recruitment, Development, and Reward.* London: Kogan Page, pp. 17–45.

Hope, V. and Hendry, J. (1995) Corporate cultural change – is it relevant for the organisations of the 1990s? *Human Resource Management Journal*, 5(4), 61–73.

Hough, L. M. (1992) The 'Big Five' personality variables – construct confusion: description versus prediction. *Human Performance*, 5, 139–55.

House, J. S. (1981) *Work Stress and Social Support.* Reading, MA: Addison-Wesley.

House, R. J. (1977) A 1976 theory of charismatic leadership. In J. G. Hunt and L. L. Larson (eds), *Leadership: the Cutting Edge.* Carbondale: Southern Illinois University Press.

House, R. J. and Baetz, M. L. (1979) Leadership: some empirical generalizations and new research directions. In B. M. Straw (ed.), *Research in Organizational Behaviour, volume 1.* Greenwich, CT: JAI Press.

House, R. J. and Mitchell, T. R. (1974) Path–goal theory of leadership. *Journal of Contemporary Business*, 3, 81–97.

Houtman, I. L. D. (ed.) (1997) *Trends in en rondom arbeid en gezondheid* (*Trends in Work and Health*). Amsterdam: NIA'TNO.

Howard, A. (ed.) (1995) *The Changing Nature of Work*. San Francisco: Jossey-Bass.

Howell, J. M. and Higgins, C. A. (1990) Leadership behaviors, influence tactics, and career experiences of champions of technological innovation. *Leadership Quarterly*, 1, 249–64.

Howes, A. (1995) An introduction to cognitive modelling in human–computer interaction. In A. F. Monk and G. N. Gilbert (eds), *Perspectives on HCI: Diverse Approaches*. London: Academic Press.

Howes, A. and Payne, S. J. (1990) Display-based competence: towards user models for menu-driven interfaces. *International Journal of Man–Machine Studies*, 33(6), 637–55.

Huffcutt, A. T. and Arthur, W. Jr (1994) Hunter and Hunter (1984) revisited: interview validity for entry-level jobs. *Journal of Applied Psychology*, 22, 184–90.

Human Resource Business Consultants Ltd and Industrial Relations Services (1993) *Competency and the Link to HR Practice*. London: Human Resource Business Consultants Ltd and Industrial Relations Services.

Hunter, J. E. (1986) Cognitive ability, cognitive aptitudes, job knowledge, and job performance. *Journal of Vocational Behavior*, 29, 340–62.

Hunter, J. E. and Hunter, R. F. (1984) Validity and utility of alternative predictors of job performance. *Psychological Bulletin*, 96, 72–98.

Hutchins, E. (1995a) How a cockpit remembers its speeds. *Cognitive Science*, 19, 126–289.

Hutchins, E. (1995b) *Cognition in the Wild*. Cambridge, MA: MIT Press.

Idaszak, J. R. and Dragow, F. (1987) A revision of the Job Diagnostic Survey: elimination of a measurement artifact. *Journal of Applied Psychology*, 72, 69–74.

Iles, P. A. and Robertson, I. T. (1997) The impact of personnel selection procedures on candidates. In N. Anderson and P. Herriot (eds), *International Handbook of Selection and Assessment*. Chichester: Wiley.

Ilgen, D. R., Mitchell, T. R. and Frederickson, J. W. (1981) Poor performers: supervisors' and subordinates' responses. *Organizational Behaviour and Human Performance*, 27, 386–410.

Indvik, J. (1986) Path–goal theory of leadership: a meta-analysis. Paper presented at the Academy of Management Conference, Chicago.

International Herald Tribune (1992) A giant that helps IBM think small. *International Herald Tribune*, 3 March, 10.

Invancevich, J. M., Matteson, M. T., Freedman, S. M. and Phillips, J. S. (1990) Worksite stress management interventions. *American Psychologist*, 45, 252–61.

Isen, A. M. and Baron, R. A. (1991) Positive affect as a factor in organizational behavior. In L. L. Cummings and B. M. Staw (eds), *Research in Organizational Behavior, volume 13*. Greenwich, CT: JAI Press.

Jackson, P. R. and Wall, T. D. (1991) How does operator control enhance performance of advanced manufacturing technology? *Ergonomics*, 34, 1301–11.

Jackson, P. R., Wall, T. D., Martin, R. and Davids, K. (1993) New measures of job control, cognitive demand, and production responsibility. *Journal of Applied Psychology*, 78, 753–62.

Jackson, S. (1992) Stepping into the future: guidelines for action. In S. Jackson and Associates (eds), *Diversity in the Workplace: Human Resource Initiatives*. New York: Guildford Press.

Jackson, S. E. (1983) Participation in decision making as a strategy for reducing job-related strain. *Journal of Applied Psychology*, 68, 3–19.

Jackson, S. E. (1991) Team composition in organizational settings: Issues in managing an increasingly diverse workforce. In S. Worchel, W. Wood and J. Simpson (eds), *Group Process and Productivity*. Newbury Park, CA: Sage.

Jackson, S. E., Brett, J. F., Sessa, V. I., Cooper, D. M., Julin, J. A. and Peyronnin, K. (1991) Some differences make a difference: individual dissimilarity and group heterogeneity as correlates of recruitment, promotions and turnover. *Journal of Applied Psychology*, 76, 675–89.

Jacobs, R., Kafry, D. and Zedeck, S. (1980) Expectations of Behaviourally Anchored Rating Scales. *Personnel Psychology*, 33, 595–640.

Jacoby, R. (1994) The myth of multiculturalism. *New Left Review*, 208, 121–6.

James, L. R. and Jones, A. P. (1974) Organizational climate: a review of theory and research. *Psychological Bulletin*, 81, 1096–112.

James, L. R., Joyce, W. F. and Slocum, J. W. Jr (1988) Comment: organizations do not cognize. *Academy of Management Review*, 13(1), 129–32.

Janis, I. L. (1982) *Groupthink: a Study of Foreign Policy Decisions and Fiascos*, 2nd edn. Boston: Houghton Mifflin.

Janis, I. L. (1989) *Crucial Decisions*. New York: The Free Press.

Jewson, N. and Mason, D. (1986) The theory and practice of equal opportuntities: liberal and radical approaches. *Sociological Review*, 34(2), 307–34.

Johnson, G. (1987) *Strategic Change and the Management Process*. Oxford: Blackwell.

Johnson, G. (1988) Processes of managing strategic change. *Management Research News*, 11(4/5), 43–6.

Johnson, G. and Scholes, K. (1997) *Exploring Corporate Strategy: Texts and Cases*. Hemel Hempstead: Prentice Hall.

Johnson, J. V. and Hall, E. M. (1988) Job strain, work place social support, and cardiovascular disease: a cross-sectional study of a random sample of the Swedish working population. *American Journal of Public Health*, 78(10), 1336–42.

Johnson, P. (1992) *Human–Computer Interaction: Psychology, Task Analysis and Software Engineering*. Maidenhead: McGraw-Hill.

Johnson, W. B. and Packer A. (1987) *Workforce 2000. Work and Workers in the 21st Century*. Indianapolis: Hudson Institute.

Jones, E. E. and Nisbett, R. E. (1971) *The Actor and the Observer: Divergent Perceptions of the Causes of Behavior*. Morristown, NJ: General Learning Press.

Jones, F. and Fletcher, B. C. (1996) Job control and health. In M. J. Schabracq, J. A. M. Winnubst and C. L. Cooper (eds), *Handbook of Work and Health Psychology*. Chichester: Wiley.

Jones, J. and Wuehker, L. (1985) Development and validation of the safety locus of control scale. *Perceptual and Motor Skills*, 61, 151–61.

Jones, M. (1995) Organizational analysis and HCJ. In A. F. Monk and G. N. Gilbert (eds), *Perspectives on HCI: Diverse Approaches*. London: Academic Press.

Jones, P. (1994) Which lever do I pull now? The role of 'emergent planning' in managing change. *Organisations and People*, 1(1), 46–49.

Jones, R. G. and Whitmore, M. D. (1995) Evaluating developmental assessment centres as interventions. *Personnel Psychology*, 48, 377–88.

Jorna, P. G. A. M. (1992) Spectral analysis of heart rate and psychological state: a review of its validity as a workload index. *Biological Psychology*, 34, 237–58.

Kahn, R. L. and Boysiere, P. (1992) Stress in organizations. In M. D. Dunette and L. M. Hough (eds), *Handbook of Industrial and Organizational Psychology, volume 3*. Palo Alto, CA: Consulting Psychologists Press.

Kahneman, D. (1971) Remarks on attentional control. In A. F. Sanders (ed.), *Attention and Performance III*. Amsterdam: North-Holland.

Kahneman, D. (1973) *Attention and Effort*. Englewood Cliffs, NJ: Prentice Hall.

Kahneman, D., Slovic, P. and Tversky, A. (eds) (1982) *Judgement under Uncertainty: Heuristics and Biases*. Cambridge: Cambridge University Press.

Kamoun, A., Debernard, S. and Millot, P. (1989) Comparison between two dynamic task allocations. In Proceedings of the Second European Meeting on Cognitive Science Approaches to Process Control, Siena, Italy.

Kandola, R. and Fullerton, J. (1994) *Managing the Mosaic: Diversity in Action*. London: IPD.

Kanter, R. M. (1977) *Men and Women of the Corporation*. New York: Basic Books.

Kanter, R. M. (1983) *The Change Masters*. London: Routledge.

Kantowitz, B. and Sorkin, R. (1987) Allocation of functions. In C. Salvendy (ed.), *Handbook of Human Factors*. New York: Wiley.

Karasek, R. A. (1979) Job demands, job decision latitude and mental strain: Implications for job redesign. *Administrative Science Quarterly*, 24, 285–308.

Karasek, R., Brison, C., Kawakami, N., Houtman, I., Bongers, P. and Amick, B. (1998) The Job Content Questionnaire (JCQ): an instrument for internationally comparative assessments of psychosocial job characteristics. *Journal of Occupational Health Psychology*, 3(4), 322–55.

Karasek, R. A. and Theorell, T. (1990) *Healthy Work: Stress, Productivity and the Reconstruction of Working Life*. New York: Basic Books.

Karlsson, T. and Chase, P. N. (1996) A comparison of three prompting methods for training software use. *Journal of Organizational Behaviour Management*, 16, 27–44.

Karoly, P. (1993) Mechanisms of self-regulation: a systems view. *Annual Review of Psychology*, 44, 23–52.

Kasl, S. V. (1987) Methodologies in stress and health: Past difficulties, present dilemma's future directions. In S. V. Kasl and C. L. Cooper (eds), *Job Control and Worker Health*. Chichester: Wiley.

Kasl, S. V. (1996) The influence of the work environment on cardiovascular health: a historical, conceptual, and methodological perspective. *Journal of Occupational Health Psychology*, 1(1), 42–56.

Kast, F. E. and Rosenzweig, J. E. (1970) *Organization and Management: a Systems Approach*. New York: McGraw-Hill.

Katz, D. and Kahn, R. L. (1978) *Social Psychology of Organizations*, 2nd edn. New York: Wiley.

Katzell, R. A. and Austin, J. T. (1992) From then to now: the development of industrial–organizational psychology in the United States. *Journal of Applied Psychology*, 77, 803–35.

Katzell, R. A. and Thompson, D. E. (1990) Work motivation: theory and practice. *American Psychologist*, 45, 144–53.

Kausler, D. H. (1994) *Learning and Memory in Normal Aging*. San Diego: Academic Press.

Kay, H. (1987) Accident proneness. In R. L. Gregory (ed.), *The Oxford Companion to the Mind*. Oxford: Oxford University Press.

Keenan, T. (1995) Graduate recruitment in Britain: a survey of selection methods used by organizations. *Journal of Organizational Behavior*, 16, 303–17.

Keenan, T. (1997) Selecting for potential: the case of graduate recruitment. In N. Anderson and P. Herriot (eds), *International Handbook of Selection and Assessment*. Chichester: Wiley.

Keller, J. M. (1983) Motivational design of instruction. In C. M. Reigeluth (ed.), *Instructional Design Theories and Models. An Overview of Their Current Status*. Hillsdale, NJ: Lawrence Erlbaum.

Keller, J. M. and Kopp, T. W. (1987) An application of the ARCS model of motivational design. In C. M. Reigeluth (ed.), *Instructional Design Theories and Models. An Overview of Their Current Status*. Hillsdale, NJ: Lawrence Erlbaum.

Kelley, H. H. (1967) Attribution theory in social psychology. In D. Levine (ed.), *Nebraska Symposium on Motivation, volume 15*. Lincoln: University of Nebraska Press.

Kennedy, J. and Everest, A. (1991) Putting diversity into context. *Personnel Journal*, September, 50–4.

Kent, R. N. and McGrath, J. E. (1969) Task and group characteristics as factors influencing group performance. *Journal of Experimental Social Psychology*, 5, 429–40.

Kern, H. and Schumann, M. (1984) *Das Ende der Arbeitsteilung*. Munich: Beck.

Kerr, S. and Jermier, J. M. (1978) Substitutes for leadership: their meaning and measurement. *Organizational Behavior and Human Performance*, 22, 375–403.

Kerr, W. A. (1950) Accident proneness of factory departments. *Journal of Applied Psychology*, 34, 167–70.

Kidd, J. M. (1997) Assessment for self-managed career development. In N. Anderson and P. Herriot (eds), *International Handbook of Selection and Assessment*. Chichester: Wiley.

Kiesler, S., Siegel, J. and McGuire, T. W. (1984) Social psychological aspects of computer-mediated communication. *American Psychologist*, 39, 1123–34.

King, N. (1970) Clarification and evaluation of the two-factor theory of job satisfaction. *Psychological Bulletin*, 74, 18–31.

Kirkpatrick, D. L. (1959) Techniques for evaluating training programmes. *Journal of the American Society of Training Directors*, 13, 3–9, 21–6.

Kirkpatrick, D. L. (1960) Techniques for evaluating training programmes, II. *Journal of the American Society of Training Directors*, 14, 13–18, 28–32.

Kirkpatrick, S. A. and Locke, E. A. (1991) Leadership: do traits matter? *The Executive*, 5(2), 48–60.

Kirwan, B. and Ainsworth, L. K. (1992) *A Guide to Task Analysis*. London: Taylor and Francis.

Kite, M. E. and Johnson, B. T. (1988) Attitudes toward older and younger adults: a meta-analysis. *Psychology and Aging*, 3, 233–44.

Kling, R. (1980) Social analyses of computing: theoretical perspectives in recent empirical research. *Computing Surveys*, 12, 61–110.

Kluger, A. N. and DeNisi, A. (1996) The effects of feedback interventions on performance: a historical review, a meta-analysis, and a preliminary feedback intervention theory. *Psychological Bulletin*, 119, 254–84.

Knights, D. and Raffo, C. (1990) Milk round professionalism in personnel recruitment: myth or reality? *Personnel Review*, 19, 28–37.

Kompier, M., de Gier, E., Smulders, P. and Draaisma, D. K. (1994) Regulations, policies and practices concerning work stress in five European countries. *Work and Stress*, 8, 296–318.

Konovsky, M. A. and Cropanzano, R. (1991) Perceived fairness of employee drug testing as a predictor of employee attitudes and job performance. *Journal of Applied Psychology*, 76, 698–707.

Kotter, J. P. (1973) The psychological contract: managing the joining-up process. *Californian Management Review*, 15(3), 91–9.

Kotter, J. P. (1990) *A Force for Change: How Leadership Differs from Management*. New York: Free Press.

Kotter, J. P. (1996) *Leading Change*. Boston: FIBS Press.

Kozlowski, S. W., Chao, G. T., Smith, E. M. and Hedlund, J. (1993) Organizational downsizing: strategies, interventions and research implications. In C. L. Cooper and I. T. Robertson (eds), *International Review of Industrial and Organizational Psychology 1993*. Chichester: Wiley.

Kraemer, K. L. and Pinsonneault, A. (1990) Technology and groups: assessments of the empirical research. In J. Galegher, R. E. Kraut and C. Egido (eds), *Intellectual Teamwork: Social and Technological Foundations of Cooperative Work*. Hillsdale, NJ: Lawrence Erlbaum Associates.

Kraiger, K. and Cannon-Bowers, J. A. (1995) Measuring knowledge organisation as a method for assessing learning during training. *Human Factors*, 37, 804–16.

Kram, K. E. (1985) *Mentoring at Work*. Glenview, IL: Scott Foreman.

Kramer, A. F. (1991) Physiological metrics of mental workload: a review of recent progress. In D. L. Damos (ed.), *Multiple-Task Performance*. London: Taylor and Francis.

Kramer, A. F., Wickens, C. D. and Donchin, E. (1983) An analysis of the processing demands of a complex perceptual-motor task. *Human Factors*, 25, 597–621.

Kristensen, T. S. (1996) Job stress and cardiovascular disease: a theoretic critical review. *Journal of Occupational Health Psychology*, 1(3), 246–60.

Kroeber, A. L. and Kluckholn, F. (1952) *Culture: a Critical Review of Concepts and Definitions*. New York: Vintage Books.

Kubeck, J. E., Delp, N. D., Haslett, T. K. and McDaniel, M. A. (1996) Does job-related training performance decline with age? *Psychology and Aging*, 11, 92–107.

Kuhn, T. (1962) *The Structure of Scientific Revolutions*. Chicago: University of Chicago Press.

Kulik, C. T. and Oldham, G. R. (1988) Job diagnostic survey. In S. Gael (ed.), *The Job Analysis Handbook for Business, Industry, and Government, volume 2*. New York: Wiley, pp. 936–59.

Kulik, C. T., Oldham, G. R. and Langner, P. H. (1988) Measurement of job characteristics: comparison of the original and revised Job Diagnostic Survey. *Journal of Applied Psychology*, 73, 462–6.

Laflamme, L. and Menckel, E. (1995) Aging and occupational accidents: a review of the literature of the last three decades. *Safety Science*, 21, 145–61.

Landauer, T. K. (1995) *The Trouble with Computers*. Cambridge, MA: MIT Press.

Landy, F. J. (1978) An opponent process theory of job satisfaction. *Journal of Applied Psychology*, 63, 533–47.

Landy, F. J. (1989) *Psychology of Work Behavior*, 4th edn. Pacific Grove, CA: Brooks/Cole.

Landy, F. J. (1993) Job analysis and job evaluation: the respondent's perspective. In H. Schuler, J. L. Farr and M. Smith (eds), *Personnel Selection and Assessment: Individual and Organizational Perspectives*. Hillsdale, NJ: Lawrence Erlbaum Associates, pp. 75–90.

Landy, F. J. (1997) Early influences on the development of industrial and organizational psychology. *Journal of Applied Psychology*, 82, 467–77.

Landy, F. J. and Farr, J. L. (1980) Performance rating. *Psychological Bulletin*, 87, 72–107.

Landy, F. J., Shankster, L. and Kohler, S. S. (1994) Personnel selection and placement. *Annual Review of Psychology*, 46, 261–96.

Landy, F. J. and Trumbo, D. A. (1976) *Psychology of Work Behavior*. Homewood, IL: Irwin.

Landy, F. J. and Vasey, J. (1991) Job analysis: the composition of SME samples. *Personnel Psychology*, 44, 27–50.

Langan-Fox, J. and Roth, S. (1995) Achievement motivation and female entrepreneurs. *Journal of Occupational and Organizational Psychology*, 68, 209–18.

Latack, J. C. and Havlovic, S. J. (1992) Coping with job stress: a conceptual evaluation framework for coping measures. *Journal of Organizational Behavior*, 13, 479–508.

Latané, B., Williams, K. and Harkins, S. (1979) Many hands make light the work: the causes and consequences of social loafing. *Journal of Personality and Social Psychology*, 37, 822–32.

Latham, G. P. and Lee, T. W. (1986) Goal setting. In E. Locke (ed.), *Generalizing from Laboratory to Field Settings*. Lexington, MA: Lexington Books.

Law, K. S. and Wong, C. (1998) Relative importance of referents in pay satisfaction: a review and test of a new policy-capturing approach. *Journal of Occupational and Organizational Psychology*, 71, 47–60.

Lazarus, R. S. and Folkman, S. (1984) *Stress, Appraisal and Coping*. New York: Springer-Verlag.

Lee, C. and Gray, J. A. (1994) The role of employee assistance programmes. In C. L. Cooper and S. Williams (eds), *Greating Healthy Work Organizations*. Chichester: Wiley.

Lee, J. D. and Moray, N. (1992) Trust, control strategies and allocation of function in human machine systems. *Ergonomics*, 35, 1243–70.

Legge, K. (1989) Human resource management: a critical analysis. In J. Storey (ed.), *New Perspectives on Human Resource Management*. London: Routledge.

Lemoine, M. P., Crevits, I., Debernard, S. and Millot, P. (1995) Men–Machines Cooperation: toward an experimentation of a multi-level co-operative organisation in air traffic control. International Workshop on the Design of Co-operative Systems, Antibes, France.

Lennerlof, L. (1988) Learned helplessness at work. *International Journal of Health Services*, 18(2), 207–22.

Levine, E. L., Spector, P. E., Menon, P. E., Narayanon, L. and Cannon-Bowers, J. (1996) Validity generalization for cognitive, psychomotor, and perceptual test for craft jobs in the utility industry. *Human Performance*, 9, 1–22.

Licht, W. (1983) *Working for the Railroad*. Princeton, NJ: Princeton University Press.

Liden, K. C., Stilwell, D. and Ferris, G. K. (1996) The effect of supervisor and subordinate age on objective performance and subjective performance ratings. *Human Relations*, 49, 327–47.

Lievens, F. (1998) Factors which improve the construct validity of assessment centres: a review. *International Journal of Selection and Assessment*, 6, 141–52.

Liff, S. (1996) *Managing Diversity: New Opportunities for Women?* Warwick Papers in Industrial Relations, 57. Industrial Relations Research Unit, Warwick University.

Liff, S. and Wajcman, J. (1996) 'Sameness' and 'difference' revisited: which way forward for equal opportunity initiatives? *Journal of Management Studies*, 33(1), 79–94.

Lim, K. Y. and Long, J. B. (1994) *The MUSE Method for Usability Engineering*. Cambridge: Cambridge University Press.

Lloyd, B. and Feigen, M. (1997) Real change leaders: the key challenge to management today. *Leadership and Organization Development Journal*, 18(1), 37–40.

Locke, E. A. (1968) Toward a theory of task motivation and incentives. *Organizational Behavior and Human Performance*, 3, 157–89.

Locke, E. A. and Henne, D. (1986) Work motivation theories In C. L. Cooper and I. T. Robertson (eds), *International Review of Industrial and Organizational Psychology 1986*. Chichester: Wiley.

Locke, E. A. and Latham, G. P. (1990a) *A Theory of Goal-setting and Task Performance*. Englewood Cliffs, NJ: Prentice Hall.

Locke, E. A. and Latham, G. P. (1990b) Work motivation and satisfaction: Light at the end of the tunnel. *Psychological Science*, 1, 240–6.

Locke, E. A., Shaw, K. N., Saari, L. M. and Latham, G. P. (1981) Goal setting and task performance: 1969–1980. *Psychological Bulletin*, 90, 125–52.

Lockhart, J. M., Strub, M. H., Hawley, J. K. and Tapia, L. A. (1993) Automation and supervisory control: a perspective on human performance, training and performance aiding. In Proceedings of the Human Factors and Ergonomics Society 37th Annual Meeting.

Loden, M. and Rosener, J. B. (1991) *Workforce America! Managing Employee Diversity as a Vital Resource*. Homewood, IL: Business One Irwin.

Loher, B. T., Noe, R. A., Moeller, N. L. and Fitzgerald, M. P. (1985) A meta-analysis of the relation of job characteristics to job satisfaction. *Journal of Applied Psychology*, 70, 280–9.

Lombardo, M. M. and Eichinger, R. W. (1989) *Preventing Derailment: What to Do before It's too Late*. Greensboro, NC: Center for Creative Leadership.

Lord, R. G., DeVader, C. L. and Alliger, G. M. (1986) A meta-analysis of the relation between personality traits and leadership perceptions: an application of validity generalization procedures. *Journal of Applied Psychology*, 71, 402–10.

Lowman, R. L. (1993) *Counseling and Psychotherapy of Work Dysfunctions*. Washington, DC: American Psychological Association.

Lundberg, U. and Frankenhaueser, M. (1978) Psychophysiological reactions to noise as modified by personal control over noise intensity. *Biological Psychology*, 6, 55–9.

Luthans, F. (1995) *Organizational Behavior*, 7th edn. New York: McGraw-Hill.

Lyness, K. S. and Thompson, D. E. (1997) Above the glass ceiling? A comparison of matched samples of female and male executives. *Journal of Applied Psychology*, 82(3), 359–75.

Mabe, P. A. and West, S. G. (1982) Validity of self-evaluation of ability: a review and meta-analysis. *Journal of Applied Psychology*, 67, 280–96.

Mabey, C. and Pugh, D. (1995) Unit 10, Strategies for managing complex change. Course B751, *Managing Development and Change*. Milton Keynes: Open University.

Mabry, E. A. (1985) The effects of gender composition and task structures on small group interaction. *Small Group Behavior*, 16(1), 75–98.

McAleer, W. E. (1982) Systems: a concept for business and management. *Journal of Applied Systems Analysis*, 9, 99–129.

McCall, M. W. and Lombardo, M. M. (1983) *Off the Track: Why and How Successful Executives Get Derailed*. Greensboro, NC: Center for Creative Leadership.

McCalman, J. and Paton, R. A. (1992) *Change Management: a Guide to Effective Implementation*. London: Paul Chapman.

McCarthy, J. C., Healey, P. G. T., Wright, P. C. and Harrison, M. D. (1998) Accountability of work activity in high-consequence work systems: human error in context. *International Journal of Human Computer Studies*, 47(6), 735–66.

McClelland, D. C. (1967) *The Achieving Society*. New York: Free Press.

McClelland, D. C. (1973) Testing for competence rather than for intelligence. *American Psychologist*, 28, 1–14.

McCormick, E. J. (1976) Job and task analysis. In M. D. Dunnette (ed.), *Handbook of Industrial and Organizational Psychology*. Chicago: Rand McNally, pp. 651–96.

McCormick, E. J., Mecham, R. C. and Jeanneret, P. R. (1989) *Technical Manual for the Position Analysis Questionnaire (PAQ)*. Logan, UT: PAQ Services (revised 1997).

McDaniel, M. A., Schmidt, F. L. and Hunter, J. E. (1988) Job experience correlates of job performance. *Journal of Applied Psychology*, 73, 327–30.

McDaniel, M. A., Whetzel, D. L., Schmidt, F. L. and Maurer, S. (1994) The validity of employment interviews: a comprehensive review and meta-analysis. *Journal of Applied Psychology*, 79, 599–616.

McDonald, D. G. and Hodgdon, J. A. (1991) *Psychological Effect of Aerobic Fitness Training: Research and Theory*. New York: Springer.

McEnrue, M. P. (1993) Managing diversity: Los Angeles before and after the riots. *Organizational Dyamics*, 21(3), 18–29.

McEvoy, G. M. (1990) Public sector managers' reactions to appraisal by subordinates. *Public Personnel Management*, 19, 201–12.

McEvoy, G. M. and Cascio, W. F. (1985) Strategies for reducing employee turnover: a meta-analysis. *Journal of Applied Psychology*, 70, 342–53.

McEvoy, G. M. and Cascio, W. F. (1989) Cumulative evidence of the relationship between employee age and job performance. *Journal of Applied Psychology*, 74, 11–17.

McGregor, D. (1960) *The Human Side of Enterprise*. New York: Mcgraw-Hill.

McHenry, J. J., Hough, L. M., Toquam, J. L., Hanson, M. A. and Ashworth, S. (1990) Project A validity results: the relationship between predictor and criterion domains. *Personnel Psychology*, 43(2), 335–54.

McHugh, M. (1991) Disabled workers: psychosocial issues. In M. Davidson and J. Earnshaw (eds), *Vulnerable Workers: Psychosocial and Legal Issues*. Chichester: Wiley.

McLoughlin, I. and Clark, J. (1994) *Technological Change at Work*, 2nd edn. Buckingham: Open University Press.

McNaught, W. and Barth, M. C. (1992) Are older workers 'good buys'? A case study of Days Inn of America. *Sloan Management Review*, 33, 53–63.

McRae, K. K. and Costa, P. T. (1990) *Personality in Adulthood*. New York: *Guilford Press*.

Macy, B. A. and Izumi, H. (1993) Organizational change, design and work innovation: a meta-analysis of 131 North American field studies – 1961–1991. *Research in Organizational Change and Design, volume 7*. Greenwich, CT: JAI Press.

Mager, R. F. (1962) *Preparing Instructional Objectives*. Palo Alto, CA: Fearon Publishers.

Maher, H. (1955) Age and performance of two work groups. *Journal of Gerontology*, 10, 448–51.

Maier, N. R. F. (1963) *Problem-solving Discussions and Conferences: Leadership Methods and Skills*. New York: McGraw-Hill.

Maier, N. R. F. (1970) *Problem Solving and Creativity in Individuals and Groups*. Monterey, CA: Brooks Cole.

Maier, N. R. F. and Solem, A. R. (1962) Improving solutions by turning choice situations into problems. *Personnel Psychology*, 15(2), 151–7.

Margerison, C. and Glube, R. (1979) Leadership decison-making: an empirical test of the Vroom and Yetton model. *Journal of Management Studies*, 16, 45–55.

Markiewicz, L. and West, M. A. (1997) *Team-based Organization*. Aberdeen: Grampian/ECITB.

Marrow, A. J. (1964) Risks and uncertainties in action research. *Journal of Social Issues*, 20, 5–20.

Martin, J. (1992) *Cultures in Organizations: Three Perspecitves*. New York: Oxford University Press.

Martocchio, J. J. (1989) Age-related differences in employee absenteeism: a meta-analysis. *Psychology and Aging*, 4, 409–14.

Marx, K. (1967) *Capital*. Penguin: Harmondsworth.

Maslach, C. and Jackson, S. E. (1986) *Maslach Burnout Inventory*. Palo Alto, CA: Consulting Psychologists Press.

Maslow, A. (1954) *Motivation and Personality*. New York: Harper and Row.

Matthieu, J. E., Tannenbaum, S. I. and Salas, E. (1992) Influences of individual and situational characteristics on measures of training effectiveness. *Academy of Management Journal*, 35(4), 828–47.

Maurer, T. J. and Taruli, B. A. (1994) Investigation of perceived environment, perceived outcome, and person variables in relationship to voluntary development activity by trainees. *Journal of Applied Psychology*, 79, 3–14.

May, J. and Barnard, P. (1995) The case for supportive evaluation during design. *Interacting with Computers*, 7(2), 115–43.

Mayer, R. E. (1979) Twenty years of research on advance organisers: assimilation theory is still the best predictor of results. *Instructional Science*, 8, 133–67.

Mayo, E. (1933) *The Human Problems of Industrial Civilization*. New York: Macmillan.

Mearns, K. and Flin, R. (1996) Risk perception in hazardous industries. *The Psychologist*, 9, 401–4.

Medawar, P. B. (1969) *Induction and Intuition in Scientific Thought*. London: Methuen.

Meijman, T. F., Mulder, G., van Dormelen, M. and Cremer, R. (1992) Workload of driving examiners: a psychophysiological field study. In H. Kragt (ed.), *Enhancing Industrial Performance*. London: Taylor and Francis.

Meindl, J. R. (1992) Reinventing leadership: a radical, social psychological approach. In Keith Murnigham (ed.), *Social Psychology in Organizations: Advances in Theory and Research*. Englewood Cliffs, NJ: Prentice Hall.

Meindl, J. R. and Ehrlich, S. B. (1987) The romance of leadership and the evaluation of organizational performance. *Academy of Management Journal*, 30(1), 91–109.

Melamed, T. (1995) Barriers to women's career success: human capital, career choices, structural determinants, or simply sex discrimination. *Applied Psychology: an International Review*, 44(4), 295–314.

Merrill, M. D. (1983) Component display theory. In C. M. Reigeluth (ed.), *Instructional Design Theories and Models. An Overview of Their Current Status*. Hillsdale, NJ: Lawrence Erlbaum.

Merrill, M. D., Reigeluth, C. M. and Faust, G. W. (1979) The instructional quality profile: a curriculum evaluation and design tool. In H. F. O'Neil (ed.), *Procedures for Instructional Systems Development*. New York: Academic Press.

Messinger, G. S. (1985) *Manchester in the Victorian Age*. Manchester: Manchester University Press.

Meyer, H. H., Kay, E. and French, J. R. P. (1965) Split roles in performance appraisal. *Harvard Business Review*, 43, 123–9.

Miceli, M. P. and Near, J. P. (1985) Characteristics of organizational climate and perceived wrong-doing associated with whistle-blowing decisions. *Personnel Psychology*, 38, 525–44.

Miles, R. E. and Snow, C. C. (1984) Fit, failure and the hall of fame. *California Management Review*, 26(3), 10–28.

Miller, G. A., Galanter, E. and Pribram, K. H. (eds) (1960) *Plans and the Structure of Behavior*. New York: Holt, Rinehart and Winston.

Mintzberg, H., Quinn, J. B. and James, R. M. (1988) *The Strategy Process: Concepts, Contexts and Cases*. London: Prentice Hall.

Misumi, J. (1985) *The Behavioral Science of Leadership: an Interdisciplinary Japanese Research Program*. Ann Arbor, MI: University of Michigan Press.

Mitchell, T. R. and Wood, R. E. (1979) An empirical test of an attributional model of leaders' responses to poor performance. In Richard C. Huseman (ed.), *Academy of Management Proceedings*. Starkville, MS: Academy of Management.

Mitchell, T. R. and Wood, R. E. (1980) Supervisors' responses to subordinate poor performance: a test of an attributional model. *Organizational Behaviour and Human Performance*, 25, 123–38.

Mohrman, S. A., Cohen, S. G. and Mohrman, A. M. Jr (1995) *Designing Team-based Organizations*. San Francisco: Jossey-Bess.

Moorhead, G. and Griffen, R. W. (1995) *Organizational Behavior: Managing People and Organizations*. Boston: Houghton Mifflin.

Moran, T. P. and Carroll, J. M. (1996) Overview of design rationale. In T. P. Moran and J. M. Carroll (eds), *Design Rationale: Concepts, Techniques and Use*. Hillsdale, NJ: LEA.

Moray, N. (1988) Mental workload since 1979. In D. J. Oborne (ed.), *International Reviews of Ergonomics, volume 2*. London: Taylor and Francis.

Morgan, G. (1989) *Creative Organization Theory: a Resource Book*. London: Sage.

Morgan, G. (1997) *Images of Organization*. London: Sage.

Morgeson, F. P. and Campion, M. A. (1997) Social and cognitive sources of potential inaccuracy in job analysis. *Journal of Applied Psychology*, 82, 627–55.

Moroney, W. F., Biers, D. W. and Eggemeier, F. T. (1995) Some methodological considerations in the application of subjective workload measurement techniques. *Interational Journal of Aviation Psychology*, 5, 87–106.

Morris, N. M., Rouse, W. B. and Ward, S. L. (1988) Studies of dynamic task allocation in an aerial search environment. *IEEE Transactions on Systems, Man and Cybernetics*, 18, 376–89.

Morrison, E. W. (1993) Longitudinal study of the effects of information seeking on newcomer socialization. *Journal of Applied Psychology*, 78, 173–83.

Morrison, J. G. and Gluckman, J. P. (1994) Definitions and prospective guidelines for the application of adaptive automation. In M. Mouloua and R. Parasuraman (eds), *Human Performance in Automated Systems: Current Research and Trends*. Hillsdale, NJ: Lawrence Erlbaum Associates.

Moscovici, S., Mugny, G. and van Avermaet, E. (eds) (1985) *Perspectives on Minority Influence*. Cambridge: Cambridge University Press.

Mouloua, M., Parasuraman, R. and Molloy, R. (1993) Monitoring automation failures: effects of single and multi-adaptive function allocation. In Proceedings of the Human Factors and Ergonomics Society 37th Annual Meeting.

Muchinsky, P. M. (1993) *Psychology Applied to Work*. Pacific Grove, CA: Brooks/Cole.

Muchinsky, P. M. and Tuttle, M. L. (1979) Employee turnover: an empirical and methodological assessment. *Journal of Vocational Behavior*, 14, 43–77.

Mulder, G. (1980) *The Heart of Mental Effort*. Groningen: University of Groningen.

Mullen, B. and Copper, C. (1994) The relation between group cohesiveness and performance: an integration. *Psychological Bulletin*, 115, 210–27.

Murphy, K. R. (1986) When your top choice turns you down: effects of rejected offers on the utility of selection tests. *Psychological Bulletin*, 99, 133–8.

Murphy, K. R. (1997) Meta-analysis and validity generalization. In N. Anderson and P. Herriot (eds), *International Handbook of Selection and Assessment*. Chichester: Wiley.

Murphy, L. R. (1996) Stress management techniques: secondary prevention of stress. In M. J. Schabracq, J. A. M. Winnubst and C. L. Cooper (eds), *Handbook of Work and Health Psychology*. Chichester: Wiley.

Murray, C. and Hemstein, R. (1994) *The Bell Curve: Intelligence and Class Structure in American Life*. New York: Free Press.

Murrell, H. (1976) *Motivation at Work*. London: Methuen.

Myerson, J., Hale, S., Wagstaff, D., Poon, L. W. and Smith, G. A. (1990) The information-loss model: a mathematical theory of age-related slowing. *Psychological Review*, 97, 475–86.

Naatanen, R., and Summala, H. (1976). *Road User Behaviour and Traffic Accidents*. Amsterdam: North-Holland.

Nadin, S. (1996) Participative tools to facilitate job design: further development of the scenarios tool and a consideration of issues associated with participation. MSc Occupational Psychology thesis, Institute of Work Psychology, University of Sheffield.

Nardi, B. (1993) *A Small Matter of Programming: Perspectives on End User Computing*. Cambridge, MA: MIT Press.

Navon, D. and Gopher, D. (1979) On the economy of the human information processing system. *Psychological Review*, 86, 214–55.

Nemeth, C. (1986) Differential contributions of majority and minority influence. *Psychological Review*, 93, 23–32.

Nemeth, C. and Owens, J. (1996) Value of minority dissent. In M. A. West (ed.), *Handbook of Work Group Psychology*. Chichester: Wiley.

Newell, A. (1990) *Unified Theories of Cognition*. Cambridge, MA: Harvard University Press.

Nicholson, N. (1998) How hardwired is human behavior? *Harvard Business Review*, July/August, 135–47.

Nielsen, J. (1993a) Noncommand user interfaces. *Communications of the ACM*, 36(4), 83–99.

Nielsen, J. (1993b) *Usability Engineering*. Boston: Academic Press Professional.

Nielsen, J. (1997) Usability testing. In G. Salvendy (ed.), *Handbook of Human Factors and Ergonomics*. London: Wiley.

Nisbett, R. E. and Ross, L. (1985) *Human Inference: Strategies and Shortcomings of Social Judgement*. Englewood Cliffs, NJ: Prentice Hall.

Nkomo, S. M. (1992) The emperor has no clothes: rewriting 'race' in organizations. *Academy of Management Review*, 17(3), 487–513.

Noe, R. A. (1986) Trainees' attributes and attitudes: neglected influences on training effectiveness. *Academy of Management Review*, 11(4), 736–49.

Noe, R. A. and Schmitt, N. (1986) The influence of trainee attitudes on training effectiveness: test of a model. *Personnel Psychology*, 39, 497–523.

Noe, R. A. and Wilk, S. L. (1993) Investigation of the factors that influence employees' participation in development activities. *Journal of Applied Psychology*, 78, 291–302.

Nordhaug, O. (1989) Reward functions of personnel training. *Human Relations*, 42, 373–88.

Norman, D. (1988) *The Psychology of Everyday Things*. New York: Basic Books.

Norman, D. A. (1992) Coffee cups in the cockpit. In *Turn Signals are the Facial Expressions of Automobiles*. New York: Addison-Wesley.

Norman, D. A. (1998) *The Invisible Computer*. Cambridge, MA: MIT Press.

Norman, D. A. and Bobrow, D. G. (1975) On data-limited and resource-limited processes. *Cognitive Psychology*, 7, 44–64.

Nygren, T. E. (1991) Psychometric properties of subjective workload measurement techniques: implications for their use in the assessment of perceived mental workload. *Human Factors*, 33, 17–33.

O'Donnell, R. D. and Eggemeier, F. T. (1986) Workload assessment methodology. In K. R. Boff, L. Kaufman and J. P. Thomas (eds), *Handbook of Perception and Human Performance. Volume II: Cognitive Processes and Performance*. New York: Wiley.

Oatley, K. and Johnson-Laird, P. L. (1987) Towards a cognitive theory of emotions. *Cognition and Emotion*, 1, 29–50.

Oborne, D. J., Branton, R., Leal, F., Shipley, P. and Stewart, T. (1993) *Person-centred Ergonomics: a Brantonian View of Human Factors*. London: Taylor and Francis.

Ogden, C. D., Levine, J. M. and Eisner, E. J. (1979) Measurement of workload by secondary tasks. *Human Factors*, 21, 529–48.

Older, M. T., Waterson, P. E. and Clegg, C. W. (1997) A critical assessment of task allocation methods and their applicability. *Ergonomics*, 40, 151–71.

Oldham, G. R. (1996) Job design. In C. L. Cooper and I. T. Robertson (eds), *International Review of Industrial and Organizational Behavior*. Chichester: Wiley, pp. 33–60.

Oldham, G. R. and Cummings, A. (1996) Employee creativity: personal and contextual factors at work. *Journal of Applied Psychology*, 39, 607–34.

Olson, J. S. and Olson, G. M. (1991) The growth of cognitive modelling since GOMS. *Human–Computer Interaction*, 5, 221–66.

Ones, D. S., Viswesvaran, C. and Schmidt, F. L. (1993) Comprehensive meta-analysis of integrity test validities: findings and implications for personnel selection and theories of job performance. *Journal of Applied Psychology*, 78, 679–703.

Open University (1985a) Managing and messy problems. In Block I: Problems in Organizations, *Course T244, Managing in Organizations*. Milton Keynes: Open University.

Open University (1985b) Block III, Course T244, *Managing in Organizations*. Milton Keynes: Open University.

Orlikowski, W. J. (1992) Learning from *Notes*: organizational issues in groupware implementation. In *Proceedings of Computer-Supported Collaborative Work' 92*. New York: ACM Press.

Osborn, A. F. (1963) *Applied Imagination*. New York: Scribner.

Osterman, P. (1986) The impact of computers on the employment of clerks and managers. *Industrial and Labor Relations Review*, 39, 175–86.

Ostroff, C. (1992) The relationship between satisfaction, attitudes and performance: an organizational level analysis. *Journal of Applied Psychology*, 77, 963–74.

Ostroff, C. and Rothausen, T. J. (1996) Selection and job matching. In D. Lewin, D. Mitchell and M. Zaidi (eds), *Handbook of Human Resources*. Greenwich, CT: JAI Press.

Ouchi, W. G. (1980) Markets, bureaucracies and clans. *Administrative Science Quarterly*, 14, 21–37.

Owens, W. A. (1976) Background data. In M. D. Dunnette (ed.), *Handbook of Industrial and Organizational Psychology*. Chicago: Rand McNally.

Pacanowsky, M. E. and O'Donnell-Trujillo, N. (1982) Communication and organizational culture. *Western Journal of Speech Communication*, 46, Spring, 115–30.

Page, D., Williams, P. and Boyd, D. (1993) *Report of the Inquiry into the London Ambulance Service*. London: South West Thames Regional Health Authority.

Paoli, P. (1997) *Second European Survey on the Work Environment 1995*. Dublin: European Foundation for the Improvement of Living and Working Conditions.

PAQ Services (1997) *User's Manual for the Position Analysis Questionnaire (PAQ)*. Logan, UT: PAQ Services, Inc.

Parasuraman, R., Bahri, T., Deaton, J. E., Morrison, J. C. and Barnes, M. (1992) *Theory and Design of Adative Automation in Aviation Systems*. Progress Report No. NAW-CADWAR-92033-60. Warminster, PA: Naval Air Warfare Center, Aircraft Division.

Parasuraman, R. and Mouloua, M. (eds) (1996) *Automation and Human Performance*. Hillsdale, NJ: Erlbaum.

Parker, S. K., Chmiel, N. and Wall, T. (1997) Work characteristics and employee well-being within a context of strategic downsizing. *Journal of Occupational Health Psychology*, 2(4), 289–303.

Parker, S. K., Mullarkey, S. and Jackson, P. R. (1994) Dimensions of performance effectiveness in high-involvement work organizations. *Human Resource Management Journal*, 4, 1–21.

Parker, S. K. and Wall, T. D. (1998) *Job and Work Design: Organizing Work to Promote Well-being and Effectiveness*. Thousand Oaks, CA: Sage.

Parker, S. K., Wall, T. D. and Jackson, P. R. (1997) 'That's not my job': developing flexible employee work orientations. *Academy of Management Journal*, 40, 899–929.

Parkes, K. R. (1989) Personal control in an occupational context. In A. Steptoe and A. Appels (eds), *Stress, Personal Control and Health*. Chichester: Wiley.

Parkes, K. R. (1994) Personality and coping as moderators of work stress processes: models, methods and measures. *Work and Stress*, 8(2), 110–29.

Pasmore, W. A. (1988) *Designing Effective Organizations: the Sociotechnical Systems Perspective*. New York: Wiley.

Patrick, J. (1991) Types of analysis for training. In J. E. Morrison (ed.), *Training for Performance. Principles of Applied Human Learning*. Chichester: Wiley.

Patrick, J. (1992) *Training: Research and Practice*. London: Academic Press.

Patrick, J., Gregov, A. and Halliday, P. (1999) Analysing and training task analysis. *Instructional Science*.

Patrick, J., James, N. and Friend, C. (1996) A field study of training fault-finding. *Le Travail Humain*, 59, 23–44.

Patrick, J., Michael, I. and Moore, A. (1986) *Designing for Learning – Some Guidelines*. Birmingham: Occupational Services Ltd.

Patterson, M. G., West, M. A., Lawthom, R. and Nickell, S. (1997) *Impact of People Management Practices on Business Performance*. London: Institute of Personnel and Development.

Payne, R. L. (1979) Demands, supports, constraints and psychological health. In C. Mackay and T. Cox (eds), *Response to Stress: Occupational Aspects*. London: IPC.

Payne, R. (1988) Individual differences in the study of occupational stress. In C. L. Cooper and R. Payne (eds), *Causes, Coping and Consequences of Stress at Work*. Chichester: Wiley.

Payne, S. J. (1991) Display-based action at the user-interface. *International Journal of Man–Machine Studies*, 35, 275–89.

Payne, S. J. and Green, T. R. G. (1986) Task-action grammars: a model of the mental representation of task languages. *Human–Computer Interaction*, 2, 93–133.

Pearce, J. L. and Porter, L. W. (1986) Employee responses to formal appraisal feedback. *Journal of Applied Psychology*, 71, 211–18.

Pearn, M. (1993) Fairness in selection and assessment: a European Perspective. In H. Schuler, C. J. L. Farr and M. Smith (eds), *Personnel Selection and Assessment: Individual and Organizational Perspectives*. Mahwah, NJ: Lawrence Erlbaum.

Peeters, M. C. W. (1994) *Supportive Interactions and Stressful Events at Work: an Event-recording Approach*. Nijmegen: Quickprint.

Peiró, J. M., Gonzalez, V. and Ramos, J. (1992) The influence of work team climate on role stress, tension, satisfaction and leadership perceptions. *European Review of Applied Psychology*, 42(1), 49–58.

Perlinutter, M., Kaplan, M. and Nyquist, L. (1990) Development of adaptive competence in adulthood. *Human Development*, 33, 185–97.

Perrow, C. (1967) *Organizational Analysis: a Sociological View*. London, Tavistock.

Perrow, C. (1984) *Normal Accidents: Living with High Risk Systems*. New York: Basic Books.

Perrow, C. (1994) Accidents in high-risk systems. *Technology Studies Offprint*, 1, 1–20.

Peter, R., Geißler, H. and Siegrist, J. (1998) Associations of effort–reward imbalance at work and reported symptoms in different groups of male and female public transport workers. *Stress Medicine*, 14, 175–82.

Peter, R. and Siegrist, J. (1997) Chronic work stress, sickness absence, and hypertension in middle managers: general or specific sociological explanations? *Social Science and Medicine*, 45(7), 1111–20.

Peters, L. H., Hartke, D. D. and Pohlmann, J. T. (1985) Fiedler's contingency theory of leadership: an application of the meta-analysis procedures of Schmidt and Hunter. *Psychological Bulletin*, 97, 224–85.

Peters, T. J. and Waterman, R. H. (1982) *In Search of Excellence*. New York: Harper and Row.

Pettigrew, T. F. and Martin, J. (1987) Shaping the organizational context for Black American inclusion. *Journal of Social Issues*, 43(1), 41–78.

Petty, M. M., McGee, G. W. and Cavender, J. W. (1984) A meta-analysis of the relationships between individual job satisfaction and individual performance. *Academy of Management Review*, 9, 712–21.

Pidgeon, N., Hood, C., Jones, D., Turner, B. and Gibson, R. (1992) *Risk: Analysis, Perception and Management*. London: The Royal Society.

Plett, P. C. and Lester, B. T. (1991) *Training for Older People*. Geneva: International Labour Office.

Podsakoff, P. M., MacKenzie, S. B., Morrman, R. H. and Fetter, K. (1990) Transformational leader behaviors and their effects on follower's trust in leader, satisfaction, and organizational citizenship behaviors. *Leadership Quarterly*, 1, 107–142.

Podsakoff, P. M., Niehoff, B. P., MacKenzie, S. B. and Williams, M. L. (1993) Do substitutes for leadership really substitute for leadership? An empirical examination of Kerr and Jermier's situational leadership model. *Organizational Behavior and Human Decision Processes*, 54, 1–44.

Pomfrett, S. M., Olphert, C. W. and Eason, K. D. (1985) Work organisation implications of word processing. In B. Shackel (ed.), *Human–Computer Interaction*. Amsterdam: Elsevier.

Popper, K. (1963) *Conjectures and Refutations*. London: Routledge and Kegan Paul.

Popper, K. (1991) *The Poverty of Historicism*. London: Routledge (first published in 1957).

Porter, L. W. and Steers, R. M. (1973) Organizational, work, and personal factors in employee turnover and obsenteeism. *Psychological Bulletin*, 80, 151–76.

Postmes, T. (1997) Social influence in computer-mediated groups. PhD thesis, University of Amsterdam.

Poulton, E. C. (1970) *Environment and Human Efficiency*. Springfield, IL: Thomas.

Prasad, P. and Mills, A. J. (1997) From showcase to shadow: understanding the dilemmas of workplace diversity. In P. Prasad, A. J. Mills, M. Elmes and A. Prasad (eds), *Managing the Organizational Melting Pot: Dilemmas of Workplace Diversity*. Newbury Park, CA: Sage.

Preece, J., Rogers, Y., Sharp, H., Benyon, D., Holland, S. and Carey, T. (1994) *Human–Computer Interaction*. Wokingham: Addison-Wesley.

Premack, S. Z. and Wanous, J. P. (1985) A meta-analysis of realistic job preview experiments. *Journal of Applied Psychology*, 70, 706–19.

Price, H. E. (1985) The allocation of functions in systems. *Human Factors*, 27, 33–45.

Primoff, E. S. and Eyde, L. D. (1988) Job element analysis. In S. Gael (ed.), *The Job Analysis Handbook for Business, Industry, and Government, volume 2*. New York: Wiley, pp. 807–24.

Prince, J. B. and Lawler, E. E. (1986) Does salary discussion hurt the developmental performance appraisal? *Organizational Behavior and Human Decision Processes*, 37, 357–75.

Prinzel, L. J., Scerbo, M. W., Freeman, F. G. and Mikulka, P. J. (1995) A bio-cybernetic system for adaptive automation. In Proceedings of the Human Factors and Ergonomics Society 39th Annual Meeting.

Pugh, D. S. (1973) The measurement of organisation structures: does context determine form? *Organisational Dynamics*, Spring, 19–34.

Pugh, D. (1986) Organizational development. In Block IV, *Planning and Managing Change*. Milton Keynes: Open University.

Pugh, D. (1993) Understanding and managing change. In C. Maybey and B. Mayon-White (eds), *Managing Change*, 2nd edn. London: Paul Chapman.

Quiñones, M. A. (1995) Pretraining context effects: training assignment as feedback. *Journal of Applied Psychology*, 80(2), 226–38.

Rabbitt, P. (1986) Models and paradigms in the study of stress effects. In C. R. J. Hockey, A. W. K. Gaillard and M. G. H. Coles (eds), *Energetics and Human Information Processing*. Dordrecht: Martinus Nijhoff.

Rabbitt, P. and Maylor, E. (1991) Investigating models of human performance. *British Journal of Psychology*, 82, 259–90.

Rabinowitz, S., Kusnir, T. and Ribak, J. (1996) Preventing burnout: Increasing professional self-efficacy in primary care nurses in a Balint group. *American Association of Occupational Health Nurses*, 44, 28–32.

Rajan, A. (1990) *1992: a Zero Sum Game: Business, Know How and Training Challenges in an Integrated Europe*. London: Industrial Society.

Ramsay, J. D. (1983) Heat and Cold. In G. R. J. Hockey (ed.), *Stress and Fatigue in Human Performance*. Chichester: Wiley.

Rasmussen, J. (1986) *Human Information Processing and Human Machine Interaction*. Amsterdam: North-Holland.

Rauch, A. and Frese, M. (2000) Psychological approaches to entrepreneurship. *International Review of Industrial and Organizational Psychology*, forthcoming.

Reason, J. T. (1974) *Man in Motion*. London: Weidenfeld.

Reason, J. T. (1988) Stress and cognitive failure. In S. Fisher and J. Reason (eds), *Handbook of Life Stress, Cognition and Health*. Chichester: Wiley.

Reason, J. T. (1990) *Human Error.* Cambridge: Cambridge University Press.

Reason, J. T. (1997) *Managing the Risks of Organizational Accidents.* Aldershot: Ashgate.

Reason, J. T. and Mycielska, K. (1982) *Absent-minded? The Psychology of Mental Lapses and Everday Errors.* Englewood Cliffs, NJ: Prentice Hall.

Redman, T. and Snape, E. (1992) Upward and onward: can staff appraise their managers? *Personnel Review,* 21, 32–46.

Ree, M. J. and Carretta, T. R. (1998) General cognitive ability and occupational performance. In C. L. Cooper and I. T. Robertson (eds), *International Review of Industrial and Organizational Psychology, volume 13.* Chichester: Wiley.

Ree, M. J., Carretta, T. K. and Teachout, M. S. (1995) Role of ability and prior job knowledge in complex training performance. *Journal of Applied Psychology,* 80, 721–30.

Rehmann, J. T., Stein, E. S. and Rosenberg, B. L. (1983) Subjective pilot workload assessment. *Human Factors,* 25, 297–307.

Reichers, A. E. and Schneider, B. (1990) Climate and culture: an evolution of constructs. In B. Schneider (ed.), *Organizational Climate and Culture.* Oxford: Jossey Bass.

Reid, G. B. and Nygren, T. E. (1988) The subjective workload assessment technique: a scaling procedure for measuring mental workload. In P. A. Hancock and N. Meshkati (eds), *Human Mental Workload.* Amsterdam: North-Holland.

Reigeluth, C. M. (ed.) (1983) *Instructional Design Theories and Models. An Overview of Their Current Status.* Hillsdale, NJ: Lawrence Erlbaum.

Reigeluth, C. M. and Stein, F. S. (1983) The elaboration theory of instruction. In C. M. Reigeluth (ed.), *Instructional Design Theories and Models. An Overview of Their Current Status.* Hillsdale, NJ: Lawrence Erlbaum.

Reilly, R. R. and Chao, C. T. (1982) Validity and fairness of some alternative employee selection procedures. *Personnel Psychology,* 35, 1–62.

Rennie, S. (1993) Equal opportunities as an ethical issue. *Equal Opportunities Review,* 51.

Rice, R. E. and Shook, D. E. (1990) Voice messaging, coordination and communication. In J. Galegher, R. E. Kraut and C. Egido (eds), *Intellectual Teamwork: Social and Technological Foundations of Cooperative Work.* Hillsdale, NJ: Lawrence Erlbaum Associates.

Rieger, C. A. and Greenstein, J. S. (1982) The allocation of tasks between the human and computer in automated systems. In Proceedings of the IEEE 1982 International Conference on Cybernetics and Society, Seattle, WA.

Rifkin, J. (1995) *The End of Work.* New York: Jeremy Tarcher/Putnam.

Riordan, C. M. and Shore, L. M. (1997) Demographic diversity and employee attitudes: an empirical examination of releational demography within work units. *Journal of Applied Psychology,* 82(3), 342–58.

Risher, H. (1997) The end of jobs: planning and managing rewards in the new work paradigm. *Compensation and Benefits Review,* 29, 13–17.

Rissler, A. and Jacobson, L. (1987) Cognitive efficiency during high workload in final system testing of a large computer system. In H. J. Bullinger and B. Shackel (eds), *Human Computer Interaction (Interact '87).* Amsterdam: Elsevier-North Holland.

Robbins, S. P. (1993) *Organizational Behavior: Concepts, Controversies, Applications*, 6th edn. Englewood Cliffs, NJ: Prentice Hall.

Robertson, I. T. (1993) Personality assessment and personnel selection. *European Review of Applied Psychology*, 43, 187–94.

Robertson, I. T., Gratton, L. and Sharpley, D. (1987) The psychometric properties and design of managerial assessment centres: dimensions into exercises won't go. *Journal of Occupational Psychology*, 55, 171–83.

Robertson, I. T., Iles, P. A., Gratton, L. and Sharpley, D. (1991) The impact of personnel selection and assessment methods on candidates. *Human Relations*, 44, 693–982.

Robertson, I. T. and Kandola, R. S. (1982) Work sample tests: validity, adverse impact and applicant reaction. *Journal of Occupational Psychology*, 55, 171–82.

Robertson, I. T. and Kinder, A. (1993) Personality and job competencies: the criterion-related validity of some personality variables. *Journal of Occupational and Organizational Psychology*, 66, 225–44.

Robertson, I. T. and Smith, J. M. (1989) Personnel selection. In J. M. Smith and I. T. Robertson (eds), *Advances in Selection and Assessment*. Chichester: John Wiley.

Robson, C. (1993) *Real World Research*. Oxford: Blackwell.

Rohmert, W. (1987) Physiological and psychological work load measurement and analysis. In G. Salvendy (ed.), *Handbook of Human Factors*. New York: John Wiley.

Rollinson, D., Broadfield, A. and Edwards, D. J. (1998) *Organizational Behaviour and Analysis*. Harlow: Addison-Wesley.

Rose, M. (1975) *Industrial Behaviour*. London: Allen Lane.

Rosen, B. and Lovelace, K. (1991) Piecing together the diversity puzzles. *Human Resource Magazine*, 36, 78–84.

Rosenstock, I. (1974) The health belief model and preventative health behaviour. *Health Education Monologue*, 2, 356–86.

Ross, L. (1977) The intuitive psychologist and his shortcomings: distortion in the attribution process. In L. Berkowitz (ed.), *Advances in Experimental Social Psychology, volume 10*. New York: Academic Press.

Ross, R. R. and Altmaier, E. M. (1994) *Interventions in Occupational Stress*. London: Sage.

Rotter, J. (1966) Generalised expectancies for internal versus external locus of control. *Psychological Monographs*, 80, whole no. 609.

Rouse, W. B. (1981) Human–computer interaction in the control of dynamic systems. ACM Computing Surveys, 13, 71–99.

Rouse, W. B. (1988) Adaptive aiding for human – computer control. *Human Factors*, 30, 431–43.

Rowe, K. H. (1964) An appraisal of appraisals. *Journal of Management Studies*, 1, 1–25.

Rudisill, M., Lewis, C. H., PoIson, P. B. and McKay, T. D. (eds) (1996) *Human–Computer Interface Design: Success Stories. Emerging Methods and Real-world Context*. San Francisco: Morgan Kaufmann.

Rutherford, P. D. (1995) *Competency Based Assessment: a Guide to Implementation*. Melbourne: Pitman Publishing.

Ryan, A. M. and Sackett, P. R. (1987) Pre-employment honesty testing: fakability, reactions of test takers, and company image. *Journal of Business and Psychology*, 1, 248–56.

Rybowiak, V., Garst, H., Frese, M. and Batinic, B. (1999) Error Orientation Questionnaire (EOQ): reliability, validity and different language equivalence. *Journal of Organizational Behavior*, in the press.

Rynes, S. (1993) Who's selecting whom? Effects of selection practices on applicant attitudes and behavior. In N. Schmitt and W. Borman (eds), *Personnel Selection in Organizations*. San Francisco: Jossey-Bass.

Rynes, S. L. and Connerly, M. L. (1993) Applicant reactions to alternative selection procedures. *Journal of Business and Psychology*, 2(3), 261–77.

Sackett, P. R., Burns, L. R. and Callahan, C. (1989) Integrity testing for personnel selection: an update. *Personnel Psychology*, 42, 491–529.

Sackett, P. R. and Dreher, G. F. (1982) Constructs and assessment centre dimensions: some troubling empirical findings. *Journal of Applied Psychology*, 67, 401–10.

Sackett, P. R. and Wanek, J. E. (1996) New developments in the use of measures of honesty, integrity, conscientiousness, dependability, trustworthiness, and reliability for personnel selection. *Personnel Psychology*, 49, 787–830.

Sagie, A. and Magnezy, R. (1997) Assessor type, number of distinguishable categories and assessment centre construct validity. *Journal of Occupational and Organizational Psychology*, 70, 103–8.

Saks, A. M. (1995) Longitudinal field investigation of the moderating and mediating effects of self-efficacy on the relationship between training and newcomer adjustment. *Journal of Applied Psychology*, 80(2), 211–25.

Salgado, J. F. (1997) The five factor model of personality and job performance in the European community. *Journal of Applied Psychology*, 82(1), 30–43.

Salthouse, T. A. (1984) Effects of age and skill in typing. *Journal of Experimental Psychology: General*, 113, 345–71.

Salthouse, T. A. (1985) Speed of behavior and its implications for cognition. In J. E. Birren and K. W. Schaie (eds), *Handbook of the Psychology of Aging*, 2nd edn. New York: Van Nostrand Reinhold.

Salthouse, T. A. (1991a) *Theoretical Perspectives on Cognitive Aging*. Hillsdale, NJ: Erlbaum.

Salthouse, T. A. (1991b) Mediation of adult age differences in cognition by reductions in working memory and speed of processing. *Psychological Science*, 2, 179–83.

Salthouse, T. A. (1993a) Speed mediation of adult age differences in cognition. *Developmental Psychology*, 29, 722–38.

Salthouse, T. A. (1993b) Speed and knowledge as determinants of adult age differences in verbal tasks. *Journal of Gerontology: Psychological Sciences*, 48, P29–P36.

Salthouse, T. A. (1996) The processing-speed theory of adult age differences in cognition. *Psychological Review*, 103, 403–28.

Sanchez, J. I., Zamora, A. and Viswesvaran, C. (1997) Moderators of agreement between incumbent and non-incumbent ratings of job characteristics. *Journal of Occupational and Organizational Psychology*, 70, 209–18.

Sarason, B. R. and Sarason, I. G. (1994) Assessment of social support. In S. A. Shumaker and S. M. Czajkowski (eds), *Social Support and Cardiovascular Disease*. New York: Plenum Press.

Sarter, N. B. and Woods, D. D. (1991) Situation awareness: a critical but ill-defined phenomenon. *International Journal of Aviation Psychology*, 1, 45–57.

Sarter, N. B. and Woods, D. D. (1992) Pilot interaction with cockpit automation: operational experiences with the Flight Management System. *International Journal of Aviation Psychology*, 2, 303–22.

Saville and Holdsworth Ltd (1993) *OPQ Concept Model Manual and User's Guide*. Thames Ditton: Saville and Holdsworth Ltd.

Scallen, S. F., Hancock, P. A. and Duley, J. A. (1995) Pilot performance and preference for short cycles of automation in adaptive function allocation. *Applied Ergonomics*, 26, 397–403.

Schaufeli, W. B. and Enzmann, D. U. (1998) *The Burnout Companion to Study and Practice: a Critical Analysis*. London: Taylor and Francis.

Schein, E. (1985) *Organizational Culture and Leadership*. San Francisco: Jossey-Bass.

Schein, E. (1987) *Process Consultation. Volume II: Lessons for Managers and Consultants*. Reading, MA: Addison-Wesley.

Schein, E. (1992) *Organizational Culture and Leadership*, 2nd edn. San Francisco: Jossey-Bass.

Schmidt, F. L. and Hunter, J. E. (1992) Development of a causal model of processes determining job performance. *Current Directions in Psychological Science*, 1, 89–92.

Schmidt, F. L. and Hunter, J. E. (1998) The validity and utility of selection methods in personnel psychology: practical and theoretical implications of 85 years of research findings. *Psychological Bulletin*, 124, 262–74.

Schmidt, F. L., Hunter, J. E. and Pearlman, K. (1982) Assessing the economic impact of personnel programs on workforce productivity. *Personnel Psychology*, 35, 333–47.

Schmidt, R. and Wolf, G. (eds) (1997) *Polikom Konferenz*. Berlin: Projekttraeger Informationstechnik des BMBF bei der DLR.

Schmitt, N. (1976) Social and situational determinants of interview decisions: implications for the employment interview. *Personnel Psychology*, 29, 79–101.

Schmitt, N. (1989) Fairness in employment selection. In M. Smith and I. T. Robertson (eds), *Advances in Selection and Assessment*. Chichester: John Wiley

Schmitt, N. and Cohen, S. A. (1989) Internal analyses of task ratings by job incumbents. *Journal of Applied Psychology*, 74, 96–104.

Schmitt, N., Ford, J. K. and Stults, D. M. (1986) Changes in self-perceived ability as a function of performance in an assessment centre. *Journal of Occupational Psychology*, 59, 327–35.

Schmitt, N., Gooding, R. Z., Noc, R. A. and Kirsch, M. (1984) Meta-analysis of validity studies published between 1964 and 1982 and the investigation of study characteristics. *Personnel Psychology*, 37, 407–22.

Schneider, B. and Konz, A. M. (1989) Strategic job analysis. *Human Resource Management*, 28, 51–63.

Schneider, B., Kristof-Brown, A. L., Goldstein, H. W. and Smith, D. B. (1997) What is this thing called fit? In N. Anderson and P. Herriot (eds), *International Handbook of Selection and Assessment*. Chichester: Wiley.

Schneider, B. and Schmitt, N. (1986) *Staffing Organizations*, 2nd edn. Prospect Heights, IL: Waveland Press.

Schneider, J. R. and Schmitt, N. (1992) An exercise design approach to understanding assessment centre dimension and exercise constructs. *Journal of Applied Psychology*, 77, 32–41.

Scholz, C. (1987) Corporate culture and strategy – the problem of strategic fit. *Long Range Planning*, 20(4), 78–87.

Schönpflug, W. (1983) Coping efficiency and situational demands. In G. R. J. Hockey (ed.), *Stress and Fatigue in Human Performance*. Chichester: Wiley.

Schönpflug, W. (1986) Behaviour economics as an approach to stress theory. In M. H. Appley and R. Trumbell (eds), *Dynamics of Stress*. New York: Plenum.

Schreurs, P. J. G., Winnubst, J. A. M. and Cooper, C. L. (1996) Workplace health programmes. In M. J. Schabracq, J. A. M. Winnubst and C. L. Cooper (eds), *Handbook of Work and Health Psychology*. Chichester: Wiley.

Schuler, H. (1993) Social validity of selection situations: a concept and some empirical results. In H. Schuler, C. J. L. Farr and M. Smith (eds), *Personnel Selection and Assessment: Individual and Organizational Perspectives*. Mahwah, NJ: Lawrence Erlbaum.

Schultz, P. and Schonpflug, W. (1982) Regulatory activity during states of stress. In W. Krohne and L. Laux (eds), *Achievement, Stress and Anxiety*. Washington, DC: Hemisphere.

Schwab, D. P. and Heneman, H. G. (1977) Effects of age and experience on productivity. *Industrial Gerontology*, 4, 113–17.

Schwartz, F. N. (1992) Women as a business imperative. *Harvard Business Review*, March/April, 104–14.

Schwartz, H. and Davis, S. M. (1981) Matching corporate strategy and business strategy. *Organizational Dynamics*, Summer, 30–48.

Schwoerer, C. E. and May, D. K. (1996) Age and work outcomes: the moderating effects of self-efficacy and tool design effectiveness. *Journal of Organizational Behavior*, 17, 469–87.

Scriven, M. (1967) The methodology of evaluation. In R. Tyler, R. M. Gagné and M. Scriven (eds), *Perspectives of Curriculum Evaluation*. AERA Monograph Series on Curriculum Evaluation, No. 1. Chicago: Rand McNally.

Seegers, J. J. J. L. (1997) Assessing development needs. In N. Anderson and P. Herriot (eds), *International Handbook of Selection and Assessment*. Chichester: Wiley.

Selye, H. (1956) *The Stress of Life*. New York: McGraw-Hill.

Selye, H. (1978) *Stress*. Utrecht: Het Spectrum.

Semmer, N. (1996) Individual differences, work stress and health. In M. J. Schabracq, J. A. M. Winnubst and C. L. Cooper (eds), *Handbook of Work and Health Psychology*. Chichester: Wiley.

Senior, B. (1997) *Organisational Change*. London: Financial Times and Pitman Publishing.

Shackel, B. (1997) Human–computer interaction – whence and whither? *Journal of the American Society for Information Science*, 48(11), 970–86.

Shackleton, V. J. and Newell, S. (1991) Management selection: a comparative survey of methods used in top British and French companies. *Journal of Occupational Psychology*, 64(1), 23–36.

Shackleton, V. J. and Newell, S. (1997) International selection and assessment. In N. Anderson and P. Herriot (eds), *International Handbook of Selection and Assessment*. Chichester: Wiley.

Shallice, T. and Burgess, P. (1993) Supervisory control of action and thought selection. In A. D. Baddeley and L. Weiskrantz (eds), *Attention, Selection, Awareness and Control: a Tribute to Donald Broadbent*. Oxford: Oxford University Press.

Sharit, J. (1997) Allocation of functions. In G. Salvendy (ed.), *Handbook of Human Factors*, 2nd edn. New York: Wiley.

Shaw, M. E. (1981) *Group Dynamics: the Psychology of Small Group Behavior*. New York: McGraw-Hill.

Shaw, M. E. and Shaw, L. M. (1962) Some effects of sociometric grouping upon learning in a second grade classroom. *Journal of Social Psychology*, 57, 453–8.

Shepherd, A. (1985) Hierarchical task analysis and training decisions. *Programmed Learning and Educational Technology*, 22(3), 162–76.

Shepherd, A. (1993) An approach to information requirements specification for process control tasks. *Ergonomics*, 36, 805–17.

Shepherd, A. and Duncan, K. D. (1980) Analysing a complex planning task. In K. D. Duncan, M. M. Gruneberg and D. Wallis (eds), *Changes in Working Life*. Chichester: Wiley.

Sheridan, T. (1980) Computer control and human alienation. *Technology Review*, 10, 61–73.

Shimmin, S. and Wallis, D. (1994) *Fifty Years of Occupational Psychology in Britain*. Leicester: Division and Section of Occupational Psychology, British Psychological Society.

Shingledecker, C. A. (1987) In-flight workload assessment using embedded secondary radio communications tasks. In A. H. Roscoe (ed.), *The Practical Assessment of Pilot Workload*. Neuilly sur Seine: AGARD.

Shingledecker, C. A. and Holding, D. H. (1974) Risk and effort measures of fatigue. *Journal of Motor Behavior*, 6, 17–25.

Siegrist, J. (1996) Adverse health effects of high-effort/low-reward conditions. *Journal of Occupational Health Psychology*, 1(1), 27–41.

Simon, H. A. (1967) Motivational and emotional controls of cognition. *Psychological Review*, 74, 29–39.

Simon, H. (1996) *Die heimlichen Gewinner*. Frankfurt: Campus.

Sirevaag, E. J., Kramer, A. F., Wickens, C. D., Reisweber, M., Strayer, D. L. and Grenell, J. F. (1993) Assessment of performance and mental workload in rotary wing aircraft. *Ergonomics*, 36, 1121–40.

Slovic, P., Fischhoff, B. and Lichtenstein, S. (1980) Facts and fears: understanding perceived risk. In R. C. Schwing and W. A. Albers (eds), *Societal Risk Assessment: How Safe Is Safe Enough?* New York: Plenum Press.

Sly, F. (1994) Ethnic groups and the labour market. *Employment Gazette*, May, 147–60.

Smallwood, J. (1994) Informal knowledge in the safety context. Unpublished MSc thesis, University of Sheffield.

Smith, A. (1995) Detenninants of human performance in organizational settings. In C. Cooper and I Robertson (eds), *International Review of Industrial and Organizational Psychology*. London: Wiley.

Smith, B. (1995) Not in front of the children: the realities of 'involvement' in managing change. *Organisations and People*, 2(2), 17–20.

Smith, D. E. (1986) Training programs for performance appraisal. *Academy of Management Review*, 11, 22–40.

Smith, M. and Robertson, I. T. (1993) *The Theory and Practice of Systematic Personnel Selection*, 2nd edn. London: Macmillan.

Smith, P. B. and Noakes, J. (1996) Cultural differences in group processes. In M. A. West (ed.), *Handbook of Work Group Psychology*. Chichester: Wiley.

Smith, P. C. and Kendall, L. M. (1963) Retranslation of expectations. *Journal of Applied Psychology*, 47, 149–55.

Smither, J. W., Reilly, R. R., Millsap, R. E., Pearlman, K. and Stoffey, R. W. (1993) Applicant reactions to selection procedures. *Personnel Psychology*, 46, 49–76.

Snelson, P. (1996) How to 'deep six' strategic planning. Nene College of Higher Education/University of Leicester MBA Speakers' Day.

Soane, E. and Chmiel, N. (1999) Emotional risk communication and safety precautions in the workplace. Paper presented at the British Psychological Society Annual Conference, Belfast, April.

Sonnentag, S. (1996) Individual well-being. In M. A. West (ed.), *Handbook of Work Group Psychology*. Chichester: Wiley.

Sorcher, M. and Goldstein, A. P. (1972) A behavioural modelling approach in training. *Personnel Administration*, 35, 35–41.

Sparrow, P. (1997) Organizational competencies: creating a strategic behavioural framework for selection and assessment. In N. Anderson and P. Herriot (eds), *International Handbook of Selection and Assessment*. Chichester: Wiley.

Spector, P. E. (1988) Development of the work locus of control scale. *Journal of Occupational Psychology*, 61, 335–40.

Spector, P. E. and O'Connell, B. J. (1994) The contribution of personality traits, negative affectivity, locus of control and Type A to the subsequent reports of job stressors and job strain. *Journal of Occupational and Organizational Psychology*, 67, 1–11.

Spencer, L. M. (1983) *Soft Skill Competencies*. Edinburgh: Scottish Council for Research in Education.

Sperandio, A. (1978) The regulation of working methods as a function of workload among air traffic controllers. *Ergonomics*, 21, 367–90.

Stacey, R. (1996) *Strategic Management and Organisational Dynamics*. London: Pitman.

Stammers, R. B. and Shepherd, A. (1995) Task analysis. In J. R. Wilson and E. N. Corlett (eds), *Evaluation of Human Work*, 2nd edn. London: Taylor and Francis.

Stankov, L. (1988) Aging, attention, and intelligence. *Psychology and Aging*, 3, 59–74.

Steiner, D. D. and Gilliland, S. W. (1996) Fairness reactions to personnel selection techniques in France and the United States. *Journal of Applied Psychology*, 81, 134–41.

Steiner, I. D. (1972) *Group Process and Productivity*. New York: Academic Press.

Steptoe, A. (1983) Stress, helplessness and control: the implications of laboratory studies. *Journal of Psychosomatic Research*, 27, 361–7.

Sternberg, K. J. and Wagner, K. K. (eds) (1986) *Practical Intelligence: Nature and Origins of Competence in the Everyday World*. Cambridge: Cambridge University Press.

Sterns, H. L. and Doverspike, D. (1988) Training and developing the older worker: implications for human resource management. In H. Dennis (ed.), *Fourteen Steps in Managing an Aging Workforce*. Lexington, MA: Lexington Books.

Stevens, C. K., Bavetta, A. G. and Gist, M. E. (1993) Gender differences in the acquisition of negotiation skills: the role of goals, self efficacy and perceived control. *Journal of Applied Psychology*, 78(5), 723–35.

Stevens, M. J. and Campion, M. A. (1994) The knowledge, skill, and ability requirements for teamwork: implications for human resource management. *Journal of Management*, 20(2), 503–30.

Stodgill, R. (1974) *Handbook of Leadership*. New York: Free Press.

Stokes, G. S., Hogan, J. B. and Snell, A. F. (1993) Comparability of incumbent and applicant samples for the development of biodata keys: the influence of social desirability. *Personnel Psychology*, 46, 739–62.

Stone, D. L. and Jones, G. E. (1997) Perceived fairness of biodata as a function of the purpose of the request for information and gender of the applicant. *Journal of Business and Psychology*, 11(3), 313–23.

Stonewall (1993) *Less Equal than Others. A Survey of Lesbians and Gay Men at Work*. London: Stonewall.

Storey, B. (1991) History and homogeneity: effects of perceptions of membership groups on interpersonal communication. *Communication Research*, 18(2), 199–221.

Storey, J. (ed.) (1994) *New Wave Manufacturing Strategies*. London: Paul Chapman.

Storey, J. (1995) *Human Resource Management: a Critical Text*. London: Routledge.

Strassman, P. A. (1990) *The Business Value of Computers: an Executive's Guide*. New Canaan, CT: Information Economics Press.

Straus, S. G. and McGrath, J. E. (1994) Does the medium matter? The interaction of task type and technology on group performance and member reactions. *Journal of Applied Psychology*, 79, 87–97.

Strebel, P. (1997) *Breakpoint: How to Stay in the Game. Mastering Management, part 17*. London: Financial Times.

Stroebe, W. and Frey, B. S. (1982) Self-interest and collective action: the economics and psychology of public goods. *British Journal of Social Psychology*, 21(2), 121–37.

Strube, M. J. and Garcia, J. E. (1981) A meta-analytic investigation of Fiedler's contingency model of leadership effectiveness. *Psychological Bulletin*, 90, 307–21.

Svenson, O. (1989) On expert judgement in safety analyses in the process industries. *Reliability Engineering and System Safety*, 25, 219–56.

Swezey, R. W. and Llaneras, K. E. (1997) Models in training and instruction. In G. Salvendy (ed.), *Handbook of Human Factors and Ergonomics*, 2nd edn. New York: Wiley.

Taffaldano, M. T. and Muchinsky, P. M. (1985) Job satisfaction and job performance: a meta-analysis. *Psychological Bulletin*, 97, 251–73.

Tajfel, H. (1978) *Differentiation between Social Groups: Studies in the Social Psychology of Intergroup Relations* (European Monographs in Social Psychology, No. 14). London: Academic Press.

Tajfel, H. and Turner, J. C. (1979) An integrative theory of intergroup conflict. In W. G. Austin and S. Worchel (eds), *The Social Psychology of Intergroup Relations*. Monterey, CA: Brooks/Cole.

Tannenbaum, S. I., Beard, R. L. and Salas, E. (1992) Team building and its influence on team effectiveness: an examination of conceptual and empirical developments. In

K. Kelley (ed.), *Issues, Theory and Research in Industrial/Organizational Psychology*. London: North-Holland.

Tannenbaum, S. I., Matthieu, J. E., Salas, E. and Cannon-Bowers, J. A. (1991) Meeting trainees' expectations: the influence of training fulfilment on the development of commitment, self-efficacy, and motivation. *Journal of Applied Psychology*, 76, 759–69.

Tannenbaum, S. I., Salas, E. and Cannon-Bowers, J. A. (1996) Promoting team effectiveness. In M. A. West (ed.), *Handbook of Work Group Psychology*. Chichester: Wiley.

Tannenbaum, S. I. and Yukl, G. (1992) Training and development in work organisations. *Annual Review of Psychology*, 43, 399–441.

Tattersall, A. J. (1994) Practical guidelines for the assessment of workload. In J. Wise, D. J. Garland and V. D. Hopkin (eds), *Human Factors Certification of Advanced Aviation Systems*. Orlando, FL: Embry-Riddle Publications.

Tattersall, A. J. and Farmer, E. W. (1995) The regulation of work demands and strain. In S. L. Sauter and L. R. Murphy (eds), *Organizational Risk Factors for Job Stress*. Washington, DC: American Psychological Association.

Tattersall, A. J. and Foord, P. S. (1996) An experimental evaluation of instantaneous self-assessment as a measure of workload. *Ergonomics*, 39, 740–8.

Tattersall, A. J. and Hockey, G. R. J. (1995) Level of operator control and changes in heart rate variability during simulated flight maintenance. *Human Factors*, 37, 682–98.

Tattersall, A. J. and Morgan, C. A. (1997) The function and effectiveness of dynamic task allocation. In D. Harris (ed.), *Engineering Psychology and Cognitive Ergonomics: Integration of Theory and Application*. Aldershot: Avebury.

Tattersall, A. J., Morgan, C. A. and Newman, M. D. (1997) Investigations of operator and system control of dynamic task allocation. In D. Fallon, M. Hogan, L. Bannon and J. McCarthy (eds), *Revisiting the Allocation of Functions Issue, volume 1*. Louisville, KY: IEA Press.

Tattersall, A. J. and Rowe, S. J. (1994) Exercise, effort and cognitive performance. *Contemporary Ergonomics*. London: Taylor and Francis.

Taylor, F. W. (1911) *Scientific Management*. New York: Harper and Row.

Taylor, R. M. (1989) Situational awareness rating technique (SART): the development of a tool for aircrew systems design. In Proceedings of the AGARD AMP Symposium on Situational Awareness in Aerospace Operations, CP478. Seuilly sur Seine: NATO AGARD.

Taylor, S. E. (1991) Asymmetrical effects of positive and negative events: The mobilization–minimization hypothesis. *Psychological Bulletin*, 110, 67–85.

Teichner, W. H. (1968) Interaction of behavioral and physiological stress reactions. *Psychological Review*, 75, 51–80.

Tennyson, R. D., Schott, F., Seel, N. M. and Dijkstra, S. (eds) (1997) *Instructional Design: International Perspectives. Volume 1: Theory, Research and Models*. Mahwah, NJ: Lawrence Erlbaum.

Tett, R. P., Jackson, D. N. and Rothstein, M. (1991) Personality measures as predictors of job performance: a meta-analytic review. *Personnel Psychology*, 44, 703–42.

Thayer, P. W. (1997) A rapidly changing world: some implications for training systems in the year 2001 and beyond. In M. A. Quiñones and A. Ehrenstein (eds), *Train-

ing for a Rapidly Changing Workplace: Applications of Psychological Research. Washington, DC: American Psychological Association.

Theorell, T. and Karasek, R. A. (1996) Current issues relating to psychosocial job strain and cardiovascular disease research. *Journal of Occupational Health Psychology*, 1(1), 9–26.

Thomas, F. and Wetherell, D. (1974) *Looking Forward to Work.* London: HMSO.

Thomas, R. R. (1990) From affirmative action to affirming diversity. *Harvard Business Review*, Spring, 107–17.

Thomas, R. R. (1992) Managing diversity: a conceptual framework. In S. E. Jackson and Associates (eds), *Diversity in the Workplace: Human Resource Initiatives.* New York: Guildford Press.

Thompson, D. E. and DiTomaso, N. (1988) *Ensuring Minority Success in Corporate Management.* New York: Plenum Press.

Thompson, J. D. (1967) *Organizations in Action.* New York: McGraw-Hill.

Thorndike, E. L. and Woodworth, R. S. (1901) The influence of improvement in one mental function upon the efficiency of the other functions. *Psychological Review*, 8, 247–61, 384–95, 553–64.

Tichy, N. M. and Ulrich, D. O. (1984) The leadership challenge – a call for the transformational leader. *Sloan Management Review*, Fall, 59–68.

Tomkins, S. S. (1995) *Exploring Affect. The Selected Writings of Sylvan S. Tomkins* (ed. E. V. Domos). New York: Cambridge University Press.

Toplis, J., Dulewicz, V. and Fletcher, C. (1997) *Psychological Testing: a Manager's Guide*, 3rd edn. London: Institute of Personnel and Development.

Totta, J. M. and Burke, R. J. (1995) Integrating diversity and equality into the fabric of the organization. *Women in Management Review*, 10(7), 32–9.

Tracey, J. B., Tannenbaum, S. I. and Kavanagh, M. J. (1995) Applying trained skills on the job: the importance of the work environment. *Journal of Applied Psychology*, 80, 239–52.

Triandis, H. C., Kurowski, L. L. and Gelfand, M. J. (1993) Workplace diversity. In H. C. Triandis, M. D. Dunnette and L. M. Hough (eds), *Handbook of Industrial and Organizational Psychology, volume 3.* Palo Alto, CA: Consulting Psychologists Press.

Trist, E. L. and Bamforth, K. W. (1951) Some social and psychological consequences of the long-wall method of coal-getting. *Human Relations*, 4, 3–38.

Trites, D. K. and Cobb, B. B. (1964) Problems in air traffic management III: implications of training-entry age for training and job performance of air traffic control specialists. *Aerospace Medicine*, 35, 336–40.

Tsui, A. S., Egan, T. D. and O'Reilly, C. A. (1992) Being different: relational demography and organizational attachment. *Administrative Science Quarterly*, 37, 549–79.

Tubbs, M. E. (1986) Goal-setting: a meta-analytic examination of the empirical evidence. *Journal of Applied Psychology*, 71, 474–83.

Tupes, E. C. and Christal, R. E. (1992) Recurrent personality factors based on trait ratings. *Journal of Personality*, 60, 225–51.

Turban, D. B., Jones, A. P. and Rozelle, R. M. (1990) Influences of supervisor liking of a subordinate and the reward context on the treatment and evaluation of that subordinate. *Motivation and Emotion*, 14(3), 215–33.

Tushman, M. L., Newman, W. H. and Romanelli, E. (1988) Convergence and upheaval: managing the unsteady pace of organizational evolution. In M. L.

Tushman and W. L. Moore (eds), *Readings in the Management of Innovation*. New York: Ballinger.

Tyson, S., Barclay, C. and Handyside, J. (1986) *The 'N' Factor in Executive Survival*. Cranfield: Cranfield Press.

Tziner, A., Latham, G., Price, B. and Haccoun, R. (1996) Development and validation of a questionnaire for measuring perceived political considerations in performance appraisal. *Journal of Organizational Behaviour*, 17, 179–90.

Tziner, A., Ronen, S. and Hacohen, D. (1993) A four-year validation study of an assessment center in a financial corporation. *Journal of Occupational Behavior*, 14, 225–37.

Umbers, I. G. (1979) Models of the process operator. *International Journal of Man–Machine Studies*, 11, 263–84.

Uniform Guidelines on Employee Selection Procedures (1978) 43 *Federal Register*, 38295 (25 August). Available on the World Wide Web: http://dol.gov/dol/esa/public/regs/cfr/41cfr/toc_Chapt60/60_3_toc.htm.

Unsworth, K. L. (1994) Perceptions of assertion in the workplace: the impact of ethnicity, sex and organizational status. Unpublished manuscript, University of Queensland, Australia.

Ursin, H. (1986) Energetics and the self regulation of activation. In G. R. J. Hockey, A. W. K. Gaillard and M. G. H. Coles (eds), *Energetics and Human Information Processing*. Dordrecht: Marinus Nijhoff.

Ursin, H., Baade, E. and Levine, S. (1978) *Psychobiology of Stress*. New York: Academic Press.

Van Dam, K. (1998) The concept of employability. Manuscript, Tilburg University.

Vanderhaegen, F., Crevits, I., Debernard, S. and Millot, P. (1994) Men–machines cooperation: toward an activity regulation assistance for different air traffic control levels. *International Journal of Human–Computer Interaction*, 6, 1–43.

Van der Veer, G. C., Lenting, B. F. and Bergevoet, B. A. J. (1996) GTA: groupware task analysis – modelling complexity. *Acta Psychologica*, 91, 297–322.

Van De Water, T. J. (1997) Psychology's entrepreneurs and the marketing of industrial psychology. *Journal of Applied Psychology*, 82, 486–99.

Van Dyck, C., Frese, M. and Sonnentag, S. (1998) Organizational error management climate: on enhanced error handling and organizational performance. Manuscript, Department of Psychology, University of Amsterdam.

Van Eerde, W. and Thierry, H. (1996) Vroom's expectancy models and work-related criteria: a meta-analysis. *Journal of Applied Psychology*, 81, 575–86.

Vecchio, R. P. (1987) Situational leadership theory: an examination of a prescriptive theory. *Journal of Applied Psychology*, 72, 444–51.

Veldman, H. (1992) Hidden effects of noise as revealed by cardiovascular analysis. PhD Thesis, University of Groningen, The Netherlands.

Veltman, J. A. and Gaillard, A. W. K. (1996) Physiological indices of workload in a simulated flight task. *Biological Psychology*, 42, 323–42.

Verhaegen, P., Marcoen, A. and Goossens, L. (1993) Facts and fiction about memory aging: a quantitative integration of research findings. *Journal of Gerontology: Psychological Sciences*, 48, P157–P171.

Verhaegen, P. and Salthouse, T. (1997) Meta-analyses of age-cognition relations in adulthood: estimates of linear and non-linear age effects and structural models. *Psychological Bulletin*, 122, 231–49.

von Bertanlanfy, L. (1971) *General Systems Theory.* Harmondsworth: Penguin.

Vroom, V. H. (1964) *Work and Motivation.* New York: Wiley.

Vroom, V. H. and Jago, A. G. (1988) *The New Leadership: Managing Participation in Organizations.* Englewood Cliffs, NJ: Prentice Hall.

Vroom, V. H. and Yetton, P. W. (1973) *Leadership and Decision-making.* Pittsburgh: University of Pittsburgh Press.

Wagenaar, W. A. (1992). Risk taking and accident causation. In J. F. Yates (ed.), *Risk-Taking Behaviour.* Chichester: John Wiley & Sons.

Wagner, W. G., Pfeffer, J. and O'Reilly, C. A. (1984) Organizational demography and turnover in top management groups. *Administrative Science Quarterly,* 29, 74–92.

Wahba, M. A. and Bridwell, L. T. (1976) Maslow reconsidered: a review of research on the need hierarchy theory. *Organizational Behavior and Human Performance,* 15, 212–40.

Walker, A. (1997) *Combating Age Barriers in Employment.* Dublin: European Foundation for the Improvement of Living and Working Conditions.

Wall, T. D. and Jackson, P. R. (1995) New manufacturing initiatives and shopfloor work design. In A. Howard (ed.), *The Changing Nature of Work.* San Francisco: Jossey-Bass.

Wall, T. D., Jackson, P. R. and Mullarkey, S. (1995) Further evidence on some new measures of job control, cognitive demand and production responsibility. *Journal of Organizational Behavior,* 16, 431–55.

Wanous, J. P., Poland, T. D., Premack, S. L. and Davies, K. S. (1992) The effects of met expectations on newcomer attitudes and behaviours: a review and meta-analysis. *Journal of Applied Psychology,* 77, 288–97.

Warr, P. B. (1987) *Work: Unemployment and Mental Health.* Oxford: Oxford University Press.

Warr, P. B. (1990a) The measurement of well-being and other aspects of mental health. *Journal of Occupational Psychology,* 63, 193–210.

Warr, P. B. (1990b) Decision latitude, job demands, and employee well-being. *Work and Stress,* 4(4), 285–94.

Warr, P. B. (1994a) Age and employment. In H. C. Triandis, M. D. Duimette and L. M. Hough (eds), *Handbook of Industrial and Organizational Psychology, volume 4,* 2nd edn. Palo Alto, CA: Consulting Psychologists Press.

Warr, P. B. (1994b) Training for older managers. *Human Resource Management Journal,* 4, 22–37.

Warr, P. B. (1994c) A conceptual framework for the study of work and mental health. *Work and Stress,* 8(2), 84–97.

Warr, P. B. (1996) Employee well-being. In P. Warr (ed.), *Psychology at Work,* 4th edn. London: Penguin.

Warr, P. B. (1997) Age, work, and mental health. In K. W. Schaie and C. Schooler (eds), *The Impact of Work on Older Adults.* New York: Springer.

Warr, P. B. and Allan, C. (1998) Learning strategies and occupational training. In C. L. Cooper and I. T. Robertson (eds), *International Review of Industrial and Organizational Psychology, volume 13.* London: Wiley.

Warr, P. B., Allan, C. and Birdi, K. (1999) Predicting three levels of training outcome. *Journal of Occupational and Organizational Psychology,* in the press.

Warr, P. B. and Birdi, K. (1998) Employee age and development activity. *International Journal of Training and Development,* 2, 190–214.

Warr, P. B. and Bunce, D. (1995) Trainee characteristics and the outcomes of open learning. *Personnel Psychology*, 48, 347–75.

Warr, P. B. and Pennington, J. (1993) Views about age discrimination and older workers. In Institute of Personnel Management (eds), *Age and Employment: Policies. Attitudes and Practices*. London: Institute of Personnel Management.

Waterson, P. E., Axtell, C. M. and Clegg, C. W. (1995) The interplay between cognitive and organisational factors in software development. In Proceedings of Human–Computer Interaction (INTERACT 95), Lillehammer, Norway.

Waterson, P. E., Clegg, C. W. and Axtell, C. M. (1997) The dynamics of work organization, knowledge and technology during software development. *International Journal of Human–Computer Studies*, 46, 79–101.

Waterson, P. E., Clegg, C. W., Bolden, R., Pepper, K., Warr, P. B. and Wall, T. D. (1999) The use and effectiveness of modern manufacturing practices: a survey of UK industry. *International Journal of Production Research*, 37(10), 2271–92.

Watson, W. E., Kumar, K. and Michaelsen, L. K. (1993) Cultural diversity's impact on interaction process and performance: comparing homogeneous and diverse task groups. *Academy of Management Journal*, 36, 590–602.

Weinstein, N. D. (1988) The precaution adoption process. *Health Psychology*, 7, 355–86.

Weisman, C. S., Gordon, D. L. and Cassard, S. D. (1993) the effects of unit self-management on hospital nurses' work process, work satisfaction and retention. *Medical Care*, 31(5), 381–93.

Weldon, E. and Weingart, L. R. (1993) Group goals and group performance. *British Journal of Social Psychology*, 32, 307–34.

Welford, A. T. (1985) Changes of performance with age: an overview. In N. Charness (ed.), *Aging and Human Performance*. Chichester: Wiley.

West, M. A. (1990) The social psychology of innovation in groups. In M. A. West and J. L. Farr (eds), *Innovation and Creativity at Work*. Chichester: Wiley.

West, M. A. and Anderson, N. R. (1996) Innovation in top management teams. *Journal of Applied Psychology*, 81, 680–93.

West, M. A., Garrod, S. and Carletta, J. (1997) Group decision-making and effectiveness: unexplored boundaries. In C. L. Cooper and S. E. Jackson (eds), *Creating Tomorrow's Organizations*. Chichester: Wiley.

West, M. A. and Pillinger, T. (1995) Innovation in UK manufacturing. Research report, Institute of Work Psychology, University of Sheffield.

West, M. A. and Slater, J. (1996) *Teamworking in Primary Health Care: a Review of Its Effectiveness*. London: Health Education Authority.

West, M. A. and Unsworth, K. L. (1997) Developing a team vision. In Parker, G. (ed.), *Handbook of Best Practices for Teams, volume 2*. Hillsdale, NJ: HRD Press.

Wheaton, B. (1996) The domains and boundaries of stress concepts. In H. B. Kaplan (ed.), *Psychosocial Stress: Perspectives on Structure, Theory, Life-course and Methods*. San Diego, CA: Academic Press.

Whyte, W. F. (1956) Problems of industrial society. *Social Problems*, 4, 148–60.

Wickens, C. D. (1976) The effects of divided attention on information processing in tracking. *Journal of Experimental Psychology: Human Perception and Performance*, 2, 1–13.

Wickens, C. D. (1984) Processing resources in attention. In R. Parasuraman and R. Davies (eds), *Varieties of Attention*. New York: Academic Press.

Wickens, C. D. (1991) Processing resources and attention. In D. L. Damos (ed.), *Multiple-task Performance*. London: Taylor and Francis.

Wickens, C. D. (1992) *Engineering Psychology and Human Performance*, 2nd edn. New York: HarperCollins.

Wiener, E. L. (1985) Beyond the sterile cockpit. *Human Factors*, 27, 75–90.

Wiener, E. L. (1988) Cockpit automation. In E. L. Wiener and D. C. Nagel (eds), *Human Factors in Aviation*. San Diego, CA: Academic Press.

Wiersema, M. F. and Bantel, K. A. (1992) Top management team demography and corporate strategic change. *Academy of Management Journal*, 35, 91–121.

Wierwille, W. W. (1988) Important remaining issues in mental workload estimation. In P. Hancock and N. Meshkati (eds), *Human Mental Workload*. Amsterdam: Elsevier.

Wierwille, W. W. and Casali, J. G. (1983) A validated scale for global mental workload measurement applications. In Proceedings of the 27th Meeting of the Human Factors Society, Santa Monica, CA. Wierwille, W. W. and Eggemeier, F. T. (1993) Recommendations for mental workload measurement in a test and evaluation environment. *Human Factors*, 35, 263–81.

Wiethoff, M. and Hockey, G. R. J. (1996) Intra-individual analysis of the demand–strain relationship: a multi-level field study of the impact of natural variations in the workload of junior doctors. *Applied Psychology: an International Review*.

Wigand, R., Picot, A. and Reichwald, R. (1997) *Information, Organization and Management*. Chichester: Wiley.

Wilde, G. J. S. (1982). The theory of risk homeostasis: implications for safety and health. *Risk Analysis*, 2, 209–25.

Wilkinson, R. T. (1962) Muscle tension during mental work under sleep deprivation. *Journal of Experimental Psychology*, 64, 565–71.

Williams, K. J. and Lillibridge, J. R. (1992) Perceived self-competence and organizational behavior. In K. Kelley (ed.), *Issues, Theory and Research in Industrial/ Organizational Psychology*. Amsterdam: North-Holland.

Williamson, A. and Feyer, A.-M. (1995) Causes of accidents and time of day. *Work and Stress*, 9, 158–64.

Wilson, D. C. (1992) *A Strategy of Change*. New York: Routledge.

Wilson, G. F. (1992) Applied use of cardiac and respiratory measures: practical considerations. *Biological Psychology*, 34, 163–78.

Wilson, G. F. and Eggemeier, F. T. (1991) Psychophysiological assessment of workload in multi-task environments. In D. L. Damos (ed.), *Multiple-task Performance*. London: Taylor and Francis.

Wingrove, J., Glendinning, R. and Herriot, P. (1984) Graduate pre-selection: a research note. *Journal of Occupational Psychology*, 57, 169–72.

Woehr, D. J. and Huffcutt, A. I. (1994) Rater training for performance appraisal: a quantitative review. *Journal of Occupational and Organizational Psychology*, 67, 189–206.

Womack, J. P., Jones, D. T. and Roos, D. (1990) *The Machine that Changed the World*. New York: Rawson.

Woodruffe, C. (1996) *Assessment Centres: Identifying and Developing Competence*, 2nd edn. London: Institute of Personnel and Development.

Woodruffe, C. (1997) *Assessment Centres: Identifying and Developing Competence*. London: Institute of Personnel Management.

Woods, D. (1984) Some results on operator performance in emergency events. *Institute of Chemical Engineers Symposium Series*, 90, 21–31.

Woods, D. D. (1998) Designs are hypotheses about how artifacts shape cognition and collaboration. *Ergonomics*, 41(2), 168–73.

Woodward, J. (1965) *Industrial Organization: Theory and Practice*. London: Oxford University Press.

Woodworth, R. S. and Schlosberg, H. (1954) *Experimental Psychology*. London: Methuen.

World Health Organization (1993) *Aging and Working Capacity*. Geneva: World Health Organization.

Wuebker, L. (1986) Safety locus of control as a predictor of industrial accident and injuries. *Journal of Business and Psychology*, 1, 19–30.

Xie, J. L. and Johns, G. (1995) Job scope and stress: can job scope be too high? *Academy of Management Journal*, 38(5), 1288–309.

Yammarino, F. J. and Bass, B. M. (1990) Transformational leadership and multiple levels of analysis. *Human Relations*, 43, 975–95.

Yearta, S. K., Maitlis, S. and Briner R. B. (1995) An explanatory study of goal setting in theory and practice: a motivational technique that works? *Journal of Occupational and Organizational Psychology*, 68, 237–52.

Yeh, Y. Y. and Wickens, C. D. (1988) Dissociation of performance and subjective measures of workload. *Human Factors*, 30, 111–20.

Yukl, G. A. (1989) *Leadership in Organizations*, 2nd edn. Englewood Cliffs, NJ: Prentice Hall.

Zakay, D. and Shub, J. (1998) Concurrent duration production as a workload measure. *Ergonomics*, 41, 1115–28.

Zhang, J. (1997) The nature of external representations in problem solving. *Cognitive Science*, 21(2), 179–217.

Zohar, D. (1980) Safety climate in industrial organizations: theoretical and applied implications. *Journal of Applied Psychology*, 65, 96–102.

Zuboff, Z. (1988) *In the Age of the Smart Machine: the Future of Work and Power*. New York: Basic Books.

INDEX